Violent Londo

Violent London

2000 Years of Riots, Rebels and Revolts

Clive Bloom
Emeritus Professor, Middlesex University, UK
www.clivebloom.com

palgrave
macmillan

First published 2003 by Sidgwick & Jackson and 2004 by Pan Books.
This revised paperback edition published 2010
by PALGRAVE MACMILLAN

Palgrave Macmillan in the UK is an imprint of Macmillan Publishers Limited, registered in England, company number 785998, of Houndmills, Basingstoke, Hampshire RG21 6XS.

Palgrave Macmillan in the US is a division of St Martin's Press LLC, 175 Fifth Avenue, New York, NY 10010.

Palgrave Macmillan is the global academic imprint of the above companies and has companies and representatives throughout the world.

Palgrave® and Macmillan® are registered trademarks in the United States, the United Kingdom, Europe and other countries.

ISBN 978–0–230–27559–1   paperback

This book is printed on paper suitable for recycling and made from fully managed and sustained forest sources. Logging, pulping and manufacturing processes are expected to conform to the environmental regulations of the country of origin.

A catalogue record for this book is available from the British Library.

Library of Congress Cataloging-in-Publication Data

Bloom, Clive.
    Violent London : 2000 years of riots, rebels, and revolts / Clive Bloom. — Rev. pbk. ed.
        p. cm.
    Includes bibliographical references and index.
    ISBN 978–0–230–27559–1 (pbk.)
    1. London (England)—History.   2. Riots—England—London—History.   3. Violence—England—London—History.   4. Insurgency—England—London—History.   5. Revolutions—England—London—History.   6. Political violence—England—London—History.
7. Government, Resistance to—England—London—History.   I. Title.
    DA677.B65 2010
    942.1—dc22

                                                                    2010027487

10   9   8   7   6   5   4   3   2   1
19 18 17 16 15 14 13 12 11 10

Printed and bound in Great Britain by
CPI Antony Rowe, Chippenham and Eastbourne

FOR JOE

who had his glasses broken at Cable Street
and then got a clip from his father

1923–2001

Contents

Acknowledgements

Special thanks are due to Monty Kolsky and Michael Whine at the Board of Deputies of British Jews; to Richard Bartlett of Harlow Town Museum; to Francis Grew of the Museum of London; Chris Myant of the Commission for Racial Equality; Graham Dalling of the Palmers Green Local History Unit; Howard Bloch, formerly at the Local Studies Department at Lewisham; Captain David Horn of the Guards Museum; the archivists of the Public Records Office; British Library; Royal Archives; London Metropolitan Archives; Imperial War Museum; Archives of the House of Lords; Archives of the House of Commons; National Army Museum; London Transport Museum; Westminster Reference Library; Westminster Archives; Bruce Castle Archives; local study units of Waltham Forest, Edmonton, Sutton, Redbridge, Croydon, Brixton, Camden and Islington. Thanks must also go to S. I. Martin, Gerry Gable, Jonathan Krego, John Nicholson, Jerry White, Sherrie Ralton, Frances Kacher, Sasha Denton, James Bloom, John Davis and Graham Macklin. Thanks are also due to colleagues at Middlesex University, Vivien Miller, Alan Fountain and Miriam Rivett for being so supportive. This work could not have been completed without the skill of my copy editor, Nicholas Blake, the devotion and care of my wife, Lesley, and the encouragement and patience of my editors Gordon Scott-Wise and Ingrid Connell.

In reconciling primary sources and archival documents with the scholarly investigations of previous historians a number of anomalies in the records have come to light. Rather than offer the reader long explanations, I have tried to clarify the evidence and provide the most likely scenario. When this is not clear I have indicated so that readers can decide for themselves.

Acknowledgements to the Palgrave Edition

Since publishing the first edition, I have had the good fortune to meet a number of people mentioned in the book or associated with the events or politics described. These include John Nicholson, Yasmin Alibhai Brown, Peter Tatchell and Ian Bone. Their comments and advice have been invaluable.

I owe a debt to the archivists at Greenwich Local History Museum; Nancy Langfeldt and the librarians at the Bishopsgate Institute; Jo Parker, Tim Foster and Gary Heals at the Vestry House Museum, Walthamstow; Robert Thwaite and Renata Pillay at the Bruce Castle Museum, Haringey; my gratitude must also be extended to the people at Housmans bookshop and Resonance FM, including Malcolm Hopkins, William Hudson and Nick Hamilton as well as Latvian expert Philip Ruff, East End specialist Clive Bettington and doyen of revolutionary flag iconography, David B. Lawrence. A special thank you goes to a reader, Mark Take who took it upon himself to go through the book with a fine tooth comb in order to weed out my errors. I have made corrections and incorporated some of his suggestions. It goes without saying that I owe a debt to my editor Michael Strang. I would also like to thank Debbie Cole and Mary Payne for their work on this edition.

Riot is a tumultuous disturbance of the peace by three or more persons assembled together with an intent mutually to assist one another by force, if necessary, against anyone who opposes them in the execution of a common purpose, and who execute or begin to execute that purpose in a violent manner so as to alarm at least one person of reasonable firmness and courage.

Lord Scarman, *The Brixton Disorders:*
Report of an Inquiry (1994)

And so I sat in the centre of this old city that I loved, which itself sat at the bottom of a tiny island. I was surrounded by people I loved, and I felt happy and miserable at the same time. I thought of what a mess everything had been, but that it wouldn't always be that way.

Hanif Kureishi, *The Buddha of Suburbia* (1990)

The essence of national security is . . . the protection of the country against attack by foreign military forces. The term is broader than this, but not so broad as to encompass all of the national interest. Its focus is the protection of the country and in particular its government.

Whitfield Diffie and Susan Landau,
Privacy on the Line (1998)

Permissions

The author wishes to acknowledge the following: Her Majesty Queen Elizabeth II for permission to reproduce items RAVIC/L14/141 and RAPS/GV1/PS from the Royal Archives; the Board of Deputies of British Jews for permission to reproduce various extracts from letters and reports; the *Daily Mail* for kind permission to reprint an article in the edition of 6 June 1936; *Class War* and Movement Against the Monarchy for permission to reproduce extracts from their various Web pages.

List of Illustrations

List of Plates

The aftermath of Boudicca's attack on London: three skulls found in the Walbrook Stream bed. (Courtesy of The Museum of London)

Wat Tyler is killed by Sir William Walworth in the presence of Richard II. (Engraving by Harris from *Froissart's Chronicles*, courtesy of Mary Evans Picture Library)

The racking of Protestant martyr Cut[h]bert Simson in Queen Mary's reign. (A woodcut from Foxe, *Acts and Monuments*, II, 1576. Author's collection)

The conspirators in the infamous Gunpowder Plot. (Author's collection)

The House of Commons as it was in 1624. (Contemporary engraving)

John Lilburne in 1641. (From an engraving by George Glover. Author's collection)

The Golden Boy memorial, now on Cock Street. (Courtesy of Debra Kacher)

Titus Oates. (Contemporary engraving)

Judge Jeffreys, Lord Chief Justice. (Engraved from a portrait by Sir Godfrey Kneller. Author's collection)

A contemporary illustration of the murder of Sir Edmund Berry Godfrey and the assault on John Arnold. (Contemporary cut in *Ussher's Protestant School*)

Egan the thieftaker is pilloried at Smithfield, and stoned to death. (From the *Newgate Calendar*. Author's collection)

An eighteenth-century hanging at Tyburn, from a contemporary print entitled *The Execution of Thomas Idle*. (Author's collection)

The burning and plundering of Newgate during the Gordon Riots, 7 June 1780. (Unnamed artist, published by Fielding and Walker 1 July 1780, courtesy of Mary Evans Picture Library)

A contemporary caricature of the eighteenth-century politician John Wilkes. (Author's collection)

Charles James Fox. (An engraving from a picture by Sir Joshua Reynolds. Author's collection)

Arthur Thistlewood, leader of the Cato Street conspirators, at his trial. (Author's collection)

'Black Monday' – the break up of the Social Democratic Federation meeting in Trafalgar Square, 1886. (From the *Illustrated London News*, 13 February 1886. Author's collection)

Henry Hyndman, founder of the SDF. (From the *Illustrated London News*, 13 February 1886. Author's collection)

John Burns, founder of the Battersea branch of the SDF. (From the *Illustrated London News*, 13 February 1886. Author's collection)

The police observation post in Trafalgar Square, built in the late nineteenth century. (Courtesy of Debra Kacher)

Anarchist meeting as imagined by *Illustrated News* in the nineteenth century. (Author's collection)

'X' marks the spot: cottage in Chingford where 'Jacob Lepidus' died during the events of the Tottenham Outrage in 1909. (Courtesy of Vestry House Museum, Walthamstow)

Winston Churchill attends the Sidney Street siege in 1911. (Courtesy of Hulton Getty)

Mrs Pankhurst is arrested outside Buckingham Palace, 21 May 1914. (Courtesy of Mary Evans Picture Library)

An anti-German mob attacks a shop in the East End in 1915. (Courtesy of Hulton Getty)

The Indian MP Shapurji Saklatvala, from *Punch*. (*Punch*, 14 June 1926. Author's collection)

Anti-Jewish propaganda published by Arnold Leese. (Author's collection)

A pre-war Mosley rally – the black shirts had been banned by this time. (Courtesy of *Searchlight*)

William Joyce, 13 March 1940. (Courtesy of *Searchlight*)

Geoffrey Hamm leaving court after being arrested for rioting. (Courtesy of *Searchlight*)

Arnold Leese of the Imperial Fascist League. (Courtesy of *Searchlight*)

The Growth of London

0   miles   10

Enfield

Barnet

Harrow

Haringey

Waltham Forest

Redbridge

Havering

Hillingdon

Brent

Camden

Islington

Hackney

Barking & Dagenham

Ealing

Westminster

Kensington & Chelsea

Hammersmith

City

Tower Hamlets

Newham

Southwark

Hounslow

Lambeth

Greenwich

Bexley

Richmond

Wandsworth

Lewisham

Kingston

Merton

Croydon

Bromley

Sutton

1914–1939	1850	—·— Greater London Council, 1965–1986
1850–1914	Roman London	Place names refer to post-1965 London Boroughs

xvii

Preface to the Palgrave Edition

This is a completely revised, corrected and expanded edition of *Violent London* which was originally published in 2003 and updated for the first paperback edition in 2004. Since the book's original publication things have changed in the manner of protest and in law enforcement. London too has changed. The building of the Olympic stadium and its infrastructure will bring its own security needs and the changes to East London will bring pressures and concerns as yet unknown.

Violent London was intended as a synoptic record of the history of political protest, riot and disorder, two thousand years of London's street politics and, to some extent, moral health. As such it was the first attempt to bring together a host of ephemeral and distinct activities that might otherwise have been forgotten. It was certainly not the first book to record London's radical temperature, but it was the first time that this history had been taken out of the hands of academics or local specialists whose detailed analyses too often focused either on very specialized historical periods or tried to make wider claims for a continuous history of radical outrage which was predominantly biased toward a Marxist political framework. It was clear that such analysis was in need of revision and a broader stroke which eliminated some of the concerns of theory and elevated the specific experiential nature of protest. As such, this book deals as much with the anecdotal as with the general and as much with personal experience and memory as with theory.

The publication of this edition has been expanded to cover the latest legal changes to governmental policy in dealing with public order and the consequences for policing as well as looking at the changing tactics of protesters. It takes us from the where the old edition left off and follows the protests of a number of new groups as well as the terror attacks on 7 July 2005, the emergence of a powerful new right-wing politics and the death of Ian Tomlinson at the G20 protests. Thus I have added two new chapters to cover these major and traumatic events. At the same time I have included sections to previous chapters in which an expansion is called for or where further information has come to light since publication. This is especially true in those sections dealing with Tudor London and the seventeenth-century Fifth Monarchists in the capital and the action of the Green Ribboners. I have also added more information as to the early history of London, the rise of parliament in the

medieval period and the origins of 10 Downing Street. With specific regard to the rise of terrorism, I have added more information
on the Tottenham Outrage of 1909, the Houndsditch murders of
1910 and the Siege of Sidney Street of 1911 all of which have caused
researchers to rethink aspects of the cases and look more closely at
various anomalies.

Has protest changed in London since the publication of the last
edition? Not perhaps in quantity nor in violence although violence
has increased and that mostly from the authorities. What has come
to prominence since the last edition is a moral agenda defining but
outside the political sphere proper. When voters feel impotent or
when protestors are ignored by parliament, moral anger and frustration replace political debate with calls for natural justice and
rightness – a moral agenda replaces political talk as people spill
into the street. The Iraq war, climate change, fox hunting legislation, the greed of world bankers and their bonuses and politicians
who are seen to be working the system whilst others are laid-off
infuriate and frustrate the public who feel ignored by their representatives and who feel they are treated with contempt by those
who seem above the law and outside legal redress. More importantly the servants of the general public, the police, have more
and more been perceived as the instruments of the rulers, so much
so that they themselves were forced to address the issue of public
confidence in a report produced by Her Majesty's Inspectorate of
Constabulary in July 2009 called, *Adapting to Change* which followed the G20 and other difficult protests that year. The essential message of the report was that policing of public order events
must be lawful, consensual and legal, not provocative and aggressive. The contents and implications of this report are discussed in
Chapter 28.

Perhaps the most unusual, entertaining and inventive demonstrations were those between October 2003 and September 2004
when 'Fathers 4 Justice', a group formed to fight governmental
restrictions on parental access, decided to climb various buildings including the High Courts, Tower Bridge and Buckingham
Palace dressed as the Super Hero characters Batman and Robin and
Spiderman. The Fathers 4 Justice campaign reached the House of
Commons itself on May 19, 2004 when Guy Harrison and Ron
Davis, threw two condoms filled with purple flour, one of which
hit Tony Blair, the prime minister. Soon dubbed the 'Fun Powder
Plot', the incident was, as BBC correspondent Andrew Marr commented, 'a serious joke', one of a number of such slapstick theatrics
by various protest groups. These (mostly) one-man affairs effectively breached maximum security, disrupted traffic and caused
huge official embarrassment whilst bringing the point of the

demonstration to the attention of a greater audience, previously unaware that a problem had existed.*

The biggest causes don't always have the biggest impact. Perhaps the lease effective demonstrations have been those associated with climate change in the capital in the years between 2004 and 2010. This is at first quite surprising as climate change has been high on politician's tick lists, but the crucial point is that main-stream parties have outmanoeuvred both activists and Green parties by absorbing key issues or by simply ignoring or undermining other concerns. Nevertheless, climate change protestors too often mix their demands with other causes thus diluting the message, or travel to other countries to riot ineffectively before the closed doors of the rich and powerful. So called climate camps have also proved to be of little effect.

The secret locations flashed from mobile phone to mobile phone in order to keep the police guessing have resulted in camps set up in places like Blackheath which is neither a central nor significant location and thereafter creates little more than a temporary and illegal equivalent of a rock festival. The 1,000 or so participants of the Blackheath climate change camp in August 2009 were effectively hived off and quarantined by their own action. The threatened follow-up climate camp planned to coincide with the run up to the world talks at Copenhagen in 2009 which was to have disrupted either Kensington and Chelsea, Lambeth, Westminster or the City and was to have culminated in 'the Wave' (5 December 2009), the biggest climate change protest yet to be held outside parliament was simply a damp squib.

The right way to live has become the right lifestyle to have: not a single-issue argument as in the old days, but a whole package of values, some anarchist, some libertarian, but more often old-fashioned Trotskyist socialism in which anti-Americanism, anti-capitalism, anti-Heathrow expansionism and anti-fat cat-ism mix: a higgledy-piggledy composition of the positive virtues of environmental concern, support for Palestine and a new world based on citizenship of 'Planet Earth'. There is no one cause any more, there are only a plurality of causes. It is this pluralism that will unite groups as disparate as Class War, Green Peace and the International Union of Sex Workers. To some extent, it is the old revolt of youth against age, of the powerless

---

*Street demonstrations by individuals continued into 2010. On 19 May a naked woman draped herself on a London cab in protest over the war in Afghanistan whilst a day later two Greenpeace environmentalists, Ben Stewart and Jens Loewe entered the head office of British Petroleum and hoisted a flag in protest against the pollution following the Deepwater Horizon disaster. The flag depicted the logo of BP covered in oil.

against those in power, of radicalism and alternative lifestyle against the innate conservatism of those who rule. For the most part all the usual suspects will turn up, the same folks who turn up for any anti-authority gig whatever the actual cause. They number between five and eight thousand young people and students or those who were young in the days of the squatting movement of the 1970s. The new counterculture is small and self defining, keeping in contact through current media: the internet, web sites, twitter. They are secretive and defensive, breaking banker's windows or trouncing McDonalds as acts of petty defiance in the cause of the revolution.

Where climate change demonstrators have been more effective is on single-issue problems such as the protests against Heathrow's proposed expansion, protests that have been embraced by locals whose villages would have been demolished and by a large section of concerned well-wishers, including Conservative leader David Cameron and many middle-class people whose consciences see such actions as economically questionable and morally distasteful. For the most part, climate change and general environmental issues have been embraced by the general public through the massive information and propaganda machines of the government and NGOs. All this would not have been at all effective without the untiring work of two generations of climate change activists, but, perhaps the message is getting stale and becoming clichéd and is not proving effective against the right's recent vociferous denial of the human element in climate change. Ultimately climate change protest is part of a 'moral' revolution against parliamentary politics, a moral disgust with the corruption of politics and politicians; climate change policy has however, to be formulated by politicians. The moral ambivalence of participating in the political process whilst being contemptuous of it has effectively weakened opposition in London (rather than in other parts of the country) since the heyday of direct action and bicycle protest.

The combination of conservatism, traditionalism, middle-England values and single-issue 'moral' politics is quite another matter and likely to end up succeeding where other causes fail.* Especially

---

*This is especially true if there is sense of injustice. The affection attached to the fighting skills, tradition, honour and even loyalty of the gurkhas meant that the campaign to allow them to settle in Britain after fighting in a number of British conflicts seemed right and proper despite the general concern with immigrants during 2009. The essentially patriotic and conservative campaign led by Joanna Lumley was hugely popular especially when Lumley hectored and lectured an unresponsive government. A strong sense of British fair play, so derided as 'Blimpish', meant that the protest gained rapid and effective support, not the least of which was from the armed services.

when such values are ignored or ridiculed by the intellectual elite, Parliament and 'hippy do gooders'. Thus the emergence of the Countryside Alliance, which came together around a combination of issues that were felt by supporters to have been ignored by the metropolitan elite, was cause for thought. Their rally on 22 September 2002 was a force with potential to change laws by the very strength of the numbers of protesters who were law-abiding citizens and conscientious voters. The importance of this rally compared to the later and much bigger 'Not in My Name' rally which mobilized similar people against Tony Blair's policy in Iraq was simply that the Countryside Alliance were fighting against legislation and attitudes that directly affected their incomes and way of life, something far more potent than a march, however large, based upon moral values and legalistic principles alone.

Thus the march on parliament to disrupt the debate on the anti-hunting bill was a direct consequence of that attack on rural values the Countryside Alliance had been warning against. The *Daily Mail* characterized the demonstrators as those people who 'are the silent majority who pay their taxes and uphold the law' (16 September 2004). A rally of about 20,000 people came to Westminster on 15 September 2004 with celebrity support from actor Jeremy Irons and explorer Ranulph Fiennes. Model Chloe Bailey had walked for three days dressed as a fox which she saucily stripped off to reveal the slogan, 'For fox sake, don't ban hunting'. It was an angry and determined march, but not without humour and irony. Some of the demonstrators were determined to go a little further for the cause and planned to get inside the chamber and confront MPs. Police were out in force and in riot gear even though the march of 2002 had been wholly peaceful. Whilst various accounts exist of the trouble outside parliament as to whether there was shoving by the crowd or the throwing of smoke bombs or fireworks, the police decided to act. Unfortunately, the police response soon got out of hand and their actions were filmed live on television. Blooded hunt supporters, many dressed in rugby shirts were seen by viewers not as anarchist thugs, but as the sort of upright 'chaps' who were being brutalized by the police who seemed to be using wholly disproportionate force against non-resisters. A large number of people needed medical attention, many for head wounds from police batons.

As the bloody battle continued outside the chamber some of the demonstrators in a co-ordinated and audacious plan had breached security and invaded the House. Otis Ferry, son of Bryan Ferry of the group Roxy Music, was able to gain the dispatch box to harangue the relatively few MPs who actually attended the debate (the prime minister did not attend). Frock-coated attendants with ceremonial silver swords bundled the attackers away. It had appeared that a number of men dressed as building workers had entered Westminster with passes, moved swiftly into the Committee corridor and then entered an area of the press gallery where the security cameras were not working.

The protesters got into the Palace of Westminster dressed in suits and got beyond security clearance and into the central lobby. They then went up to the Upper Committee Room, where they changed into white t-shirts, broke down a door to the Commons' Chamber and entered as described above. One protester got in via the Members' Lobby, but entrance was so easy, it appeared, that either builders had left a door unsecured or there was inside help, perhaps by a researcher. Apparently, they had tried the route the previous day dressed as builders with letters that allowed entry. Either way, the attack was notified to the BBC before it took place. Once inside they stripped off their clothing to reveal their protest t-shirts and descended more stairs behind the Speaker's chair. Now they burst in, first one then four more hunt supporters. Approximately a minute and a half later they were tackled by the Serjeant at Arms and his staff and arrested by police. It was not the breach of security that hurt MI5 or Special Branch so much as the embarrassment of the whole fiasco. This was clearly a well-plotted and ingenious plan by upper-class activists with insider help planned, not in some anarchist squat, but in the well-healed drawing rooms of Kensington. The suspect list reads like a role call of Britain's elite and their retainers: Otis Ferry; Luke Tomlinson, rugby player and friend of Princes William and Harry; John Holliday, a hunt servant; David Redvers, a race horse owner; Andrew Elliott an auctioneer and huntsman from Ledbury, Herefordshire.

The newspapers had a field day with their headlines on the following day (16 September 2004): 'Tally Ho!' laughed the *Daily Express*, 'For Fox Sake' was the *Sun*'s response and the *Daily Mirror* had 'Toff with their Heads'. The *Daily Mail* had the greatest coverage preferring to see the day's events as 'Civil War', a theme that Simon Heffer later developed in the paper the next day when he claimed that 'the United Kingdom [was] no longer a democracy' (17 September 2004), ironically a theme taken up more broadly by those who felt ignored after the 'Not in My Name' marches, but whose allegiance to the right-wing stance of Simon Heffer would have been unlikely. The pro-Hunting rally was the first symptom of a serious breach of confidence in parliament and its leaders, made worse by being televised live (even if the BBC allegedly doctored their coverage to minimize police violence) and was itself a moral protest against those who were perceived to threaten a way of life. Whatever the pros and cons of hunting, the bill passed into law by 356 to 166 votes, the ban enforced from 2006. The police were vilified as 'thugs' and the policing on the day named as a 'police riot', perhaps the first true instance of that public loss of confidence in the ability of the police to keep law and order impartially, with discipline and without undue force which was to finally come to a head with the deaths of Jean Charles de Menezes (after 7/7) and Ian Tomlinson (G20). With the election of 2010 returning a minority Conservative government a 'free' vote is promised on fox hunting – the Countryside Alliance will march and this time the odds are on having the Act abolished.

To deal with the changing landscape of protest which seemed, with breaches of security and rioting on the doorstep, to be getting rapidly out of hand as well as being wary of terrorist attacks and of violent anti-war protests the government proposed within its new serious crime legislation a clause that would exclude problematic disturbance around Westminster, effectively removing the right to petition parliament which had existed for hundreds of years as a right of the 'people' and allowing the government to deal with the problem of Brian Haw who was ruining the lawns of Parliament Square with his one-man tented vigil against the Iraq war and Tony Blair personally. Haw was becoming the outward symptom of the moral outrage of the middle classes.

Brian Haw's vigil against a war he considers immoral could claim a precedent in the one-man campaign for liberty waged by John Lilburne in the seventeenth century and which has been recently renewed in the campaign of Barking activist Billy Bragg who has refused to his pay taxes whilst big bonuses are handed to the bosses of the Royal Bank of Scotland. Such protests are focused reminders of the difference between what is perceived as natural justice and parliamentary law, too often seen nowadays as in opposition. Brian Haw was finally arrested on 25 May 2010 after nine years of 'illegal' squatting on Parliament Square. He was arrested under Section 5 of the Public Order Act at 8 a.m. for obstructing officers from searching his tent during the security sweep of the area prior to the Queen's speech setting out the Coalition government's commitment to 'the principles of freedom, fairness and responsibility'. He was taken into custody with another protester Barbara Tucker who attempted to aid him. At the same time Boris Johnson was seeking a High Court order to move the 'democracy village' from the same area. Although the camp was effectively trespassing on GLA land, Christopher Knight, the professor sacked by East London University for his comments before the G20 protests, suggested that the removal would result in violence.[1] Protesters were removed by bailiffs on 16 July 2010 without violence.

Part 4 of the Serious Organized Crime and Police Act 2005, was a reaction to a symptom of growing fear of disorder and dissent and was passed in an atmosphere of panic. Whilst public demonstration and march law are covered in Part 2 of the Criminal, Justice and Public Order Act, 1994 changing circumstances meant that additional laws were designed to silence serious extra-parliamentary opposition which took place near parliament itself. The legislation dealt with authorization of demonstrations and the notice needed for them, what constituted a 'designated area', possible offences, trespass and the use of loudspeakers. The law formed part of larger legislation regarding harassment and anti-social behaviour (ASBOs).*

The significant part of the new law was its political control of 'designated areas' which meant that the Secretary of State could create areas that were banned from public meetings and protests, however small. Apart from land belonging to the Crown and land belonging to the Royal family (effectively private property) the Home Secretary could arbitrarily designate an area as barred from public access by claiming the decision was in the interests of 'national security'.[3] The main area to be quietly cordoned off was parliament itself with a huge area, including the other side of the river, ruled out of bounds. Thus 'no point in the area so specified may be more than one kilometre in a straight line from the point nearest to it in Parliament Square'.[4]

Anyone trespassing on a designated area was now breaking the law and would be liable to imprisonment of fifty-one weeks, a policeman 'in uniform' being entitled to arrest such a trespasser on reasonable suspicion of a breach. This effectively gave the police powers to stop and search people taking suspicious photographs or on suspicion that their presence was politically motivated. Such police rights were apparently reinforced with the new terror legislation and have gained notoriety with tourists being stopped on the South Bank and an outside broadcast of a BBC children's programme being stopped on suspicion of terroristic intent. Demonstrations that would be allowed would only be legal if written notice was sent to the 'Commissioner of Police of the Metropolis' at least six days prior to the event.[5] A series of complex conditions and requirements follow, one of which effectively banned the use of loudspeakers, a feature of demonstrations since the 1930s.

The legislation, if administered would have effectively censored the exhibition of art by Brian Haw's supporters provocatively held at Tate Britain in 2007, the gallery being within the one kilometre designated area. It was obvious to all that this legislation was less to do with security and more to do with closing down dissent, which, of course rose. More to the point the clause has proved impossible to apply. One of the first to test the new laws was Maya Evans who alongside Milan Rai stood at the Cenotaph in Whitehall and read

---

*The political activist and comedian Mark Thomas was actually arrested for being 'overconfident' at a rally in Docklands during 2007 when he was protesting against the arms trade. In 2010, he was awarded £1,200 in compensation for wrongful arrest and the police apologized for their own behaviour.[2]

out the names of the ninety-seven British soldiers who had then died in Iraq. Ms Evans, a member of 'The Justice not Vengeance' group was the first person found guilty of breaching the new provisions under the Act on 7 December 2005.[6] She was fined £100 and given a 12 month conditional discharge at Bow Street Magistrate's Court by district judge Caroline Tubbs. On 8 October 2007, the Stop the War Coalition decided to challenge the ban on marches being held within one kilometre of Westminster. A banning order having been lifted, about 2,000 to 3,000 protesters led by Brian Haw and Tony Benn proceeded down Whitehall. The most interesting and successful attempt to circumvent the restrictions about holding demonstrations in the exclusion zone around parliament came on the night of 6 April 2009, when Tamils living in Britain held a 'spontaneous' demonstration on Westminster Bridge in protest at the increasingly brutal endgame the Sri Lankan armed forces were playing to crush the Liberation Tigers of Tamil Eelam (known as the 'Tamil Tigers').

An estimated 3,500 Tamils had been contacted by mobile phone to form a 'flash mob' which had descended with such speed that police had been caught off guard. It was a potentially new threat from a hitherto unrecognized quarter, organized by the newest technology and techniques. As it was known that the Tamil Tigers pioneered suicide bombing, the panic may have had a basis. This realized itself in the threat of mass drownings in the Thames and at least two men had to be rescued from the cold waters of the river by the RNLI. In the morning sensing a situation that was deteriorating police in riot gear turned up.

By dawn of 7 April, between 500 and 900 demonstrators, including children, and all waving Tamil Tiger flags (banned in the United Kingdom), had effectively taken over Parliament Square and were camped in front of Portcullis House demanding to see the prime minister, Gordon Brown. By midday, around 500 remained vowing to camp indefinitely on Parliament Green, something they continued for 73 days. The police, unable to move people on decided to take a 'sensitive approach',[7] which effectively moved people on to neutral ground where 'they would not disrupt the local community', but demonstrators seemed to have a different impression as people were manhandled away, one old lady allegedly with a 'boot mark imprinted on her arm'.[8] A march on 11 April attracted some 60,000 people by police estimates.

As expected the demonstration fizzled out alongside Tamil hopes in their homeland. The cost to police was £7.1 million. Caught off guard and looking slightly foolish, police put out an apparent piece of deliberate misinformation to blacken the demonstration's aims and discredit its leaders. Seven months after the events, police claimed that Parameswaram Subramaniyan, a hunger striker, who had starved for 24 days as part of the protest, was actually eating smuggled fast food as he supposedly lay on his death bed. This the police claimed had come to light after special monitoring equipment had been deployed despite the fact that Subramaniyan had been attended by parmedics and a consultant from Queen Mary's hospital in Sidcup, Dr Josephine Francis had found nothing suspicious.*

Without doubt the greatest threat to London has been posed most recently by Islamic terrorists who learned many of their bombing techniques from the Tamil Tigers. The events and aftermath of the 7 July attacks which are dealt with in detail in Chapter 27 nevertheless occurred amidst growing concerns over immigration, asylum seekers and perceived benefit fraud by foreigners. This in turn has been driven by the *moral agenda* descibed above whereby ordinary (often 'working-class') people feel cheated by the liberal 'establishment', 'the chattering classes' and by those 'bleeding heart' liberal 'intellectuals' who supposedly run the media. This in turn has led to a revival of low-level racism and religious intolerance and an upturn in the political fortunes of the British National Party and the greater radicalization and self-imposed ghettoization of Islamicists, many of whom have been and are being radicalized at university.

Institutions such as the School for Oriental and African Studies (SOAS) for instance, which is part of the University of London in Bloomsbury, are considered so problematic by the security services, that Special Branch has asked lecturers to monitor student attitudes, a request considered insulting by most who uphold freedom of speech, but which may be necessary in terms of national security. Indeed, the need to monitor such institutions, regardless of the ethics of free speech, is evident in invitations by the Islamic Society of SOAS, which in 2009, invited Azzam Tamin of the 'Institute of Islamic Thought', to give a talk in which he advocated 'martyrdom'. Controversial preachers were still being invited to talk at universities in 2010, even though they breached university rules regarding homophobia and anti-semitism. Thus Sheik Abdullah Hakim Quick was invited by the Islamic Society of King's College in the Strand to talk on 'environmentalism' during its Green Week on 25 February, 2010 (and the University of East London the weekend after) even though he had allegedly advocated killing homosexuals and thought Jews were 'filth'. Such abuses of free speech have been reproduced on other campuses.

Ethnic division has broadly taken two opposing but worryingly complementary directions. On the one hand there has been a rise in

---

*In March 2010, Subramanyam announced that he would take action against the *Sun* and the *Daily Mail* for false claims of eating secretly in his tent.

low-level racism and religious intolerance. This has been on both sides of the divide, but low-level Islamic anti-semitism has grown around conspiracy myths surrounding the destruction of the Twin Towers, by the intractability of the Palestine question and by Israel's 'Operation Cast Lead' against Hizbollah in 2009. Latent anti-semitism, however, may erupt in the most unlikely quarters. On Holocaust Day 2009, a dedication ceremony in Ilford, East London, was interrupted by jeering boy scouts. On the whole, anti-semitism has only grown through immigration from Eastern Europe and poor education amongst some sections of the Moslem community. Joined to this sense of grievance brought on by ideas of Western duplicity and the idea of a worldwide Jewish conspiracy is the growing concern amongst British Moslems that Britain's involvement in wars in Iraq and Afghanistan are wars against Islam generally and this in turn has led to greater radicalization of some politically minded Islamists. Iraq and Afghanistan were far from the cause of British Islamic radicalization which was going on before 2001, but these wars certainly remain a continuing form of grievance.

To aggravate the situation Islamic groups use inflammatory websites such as 'Islam4UK' to demand Sharia Law for Britain and provoke media interest by the suggestion of mass rallies in Trafalgar Square, a tactic that attracted universal headlines in October 2009. The preacher, British born Anjem Choudary (whose organization is now proscribed), had already called for all British women to be forced to wear the burkha and was now 'making it clear in the heart of London the need for Shari'ah law'. His press release continued that 'on [the day of the march] we will call for a complete upheaval of the British ruling system . . . and demand the full implementation of Shari'ah in Britain.' There was, of course no intention of marching, the demands merely being a provocation that the organizers knew would grab the headlines of right-centre newspapers such as the *Daily Express* whose headline screamed 'Now Moslems demand: Give Us Full Sharia Law' (15 October 2009). The headline was accompanied by Nelson's Column topped by a minaret sporting a black flag. The march was never really intended to go ahead, but it was a publicity coup for a relatively unknown group with little means at their disposal. The trick was again used to maximum effect when the same group threatened to march against the British war effort through Wootton Bassett (known for its respectful lining of its roads when the dead of the Afghan War are flown back to Britain). The march, which, of course was quietly dropped some time later provoked over a quarter of a million angry responses. Such threats are effective and very inexpensive.

Such threats, although provocative are of no real consequence and yet they reinforce the belief in large sections of the population that 'immigrants' are too numerous, find it too easy to enter the country and abuse our benefits and that there is overcompensation by government towards certain minorities whose 'real' interests and allegiances lie outside the United Kingdom. Accompanying this there has been the collapse of confidence in parliament and the feeling that MPs and their 'masters' in the European Union (with their insistence on Human Rights) have sold out on core British values, so that many working-class populations and many others besides feel ghettoized in their own country.

This is very important outside London where a number of councils which have acute housing and other problems already boast councillors from the far-right British National Party (BNP), whose resurgence as a political force is due as much to frustration with the mainstream parties and apparent corruption as with a rise in racism per se, and whose leader Nick Griffin (though hardly respectable – party rules banned Black members until 2009) sat in the European Parliament but lost in the contest for the seat of Labour MP Margaret Hodge in Barking in the May Elections of 2010.

Griffin, then a respectable MEP, was invited onto the BBC's premier political talk show, *Question Time* on 22 October 2009 amid waves of protest, a massive police cordon and demonstrations outside the broadcast in Wood Lane, Shepherd's Bush. Griffin had been pelted with eggs by anti-fascists in the previous June and there was certainly the possibility that protesters might have relished 'chucking a chapatti' at their enemy, a suggestion made soon after by opponents of the BNP. This rather gentle and playful form of admonishment means to humiliate by irony!

The respectability that the British National Party has gained has however not stopped the more vociferous of its followers going on the attack to 'defend' the British way of life against perceived Moslem extremists by joining splinter groups of their own. Thus the English Defence League (EDL) staged a demonstration at Marble Arch on Sunday 13 September 2009 against the annual Al-Quds march on behalf of the oppressed of Palestine. The group appears to be led by Stephen Gash, whose Colonel Blimp looks seem to emphasize his belligerent English patriotism, being both the co-ordinator of the website 'The English Claim of Right' which campaigns for an independent English nation and parliament and the more vociferous Stop the Islamification of Europe (SIOE) which is aligned to other extreme European nationalist parties. Gash was born in Cumbria and he has stood for parliament as a member of the English Democrat party against Tony Blair in his constituency of Sedgefield in July 2007. He gained 177 votes or 0.6 per cent of the vote. About the same time Gash met Anders Gravers, the founder of Stop the Islamification of Denmark and between them they have formed further alliances across Europe.

The organization had first come to the attention of the authorities when militant Moslems demonstrated as the Royal Anglian Regiment paraded through Luton. The counter-demonstration by the 'United People of Luton' led to clashes and arrests as did the protest by the Moslem extremists. Football supporters from North London, Bristol, Portsmouth, Southampton, Derby, Cardiff and the West Midlands then created the EDL.[9] The organization is a strange mixture of unpleasant thuggishness, the football 'firms' of the 1980s and patriotic idealism found in the right-wing groups of the past as well as in Protestant Unionism. The group turns up to oppose all Moslem rallies or marches.

The emergence of the EDL has been one symptom of the growing number of new threats posed by Islamic terrorists, environmental protesters and right-wing organizations to internal security and the various services dedicated to fighting these threats have had to adjust to areas of significance that are no longer focused on the Soviet Union or Irish nationalism, which is not to say that the threat from both is not real, simply that it is diminishing. After the murder in London of Alexander Litvinenko in November 2006, the deterioration of relationships between Russia and Britain was so 'serious' that a large part of the secret services budget had to be redirected to Cold War-style counter-intelligence, there being 'no decrease in the numbers of undeclared Russian intelligence officers in the UK . . . conducting covert activity' and there were still lingering concerns regarding the potential activities of the Real IRA, the Continuity IRA and Northern Irish loyalists.[10]

The acceleration of terrorist activity remained the top concern of the *Intelligence and Security Committee's Annual Report* for 2007–8. In it was highlighted the continuing concerns generated by the various investigations and reports on the attack of 7 July 2005. The 'severe threat' which had not diminished 'since July 2005' from 'al-Qaeda and related terrorist groups', *'was on a scale not previously encountered'* (emphasis in original).[11] In the attempt to diminish the risk posed, recruitment of specialists has increased, surveillance has widened, new detention laws have been enacted and raids and arrests have multiplied, there being forty-six convicted terrorists who had participated in fifteen major conspiracies or major incidents by the time the report was published.[12] At the same time, preventative activity such as investigating the role of cyberspace and targeting centres of subversive thought in mosques or universities has been approved in order to 'stop people drifting towards the radical edge of faith . . . and potentially out into terrorism'.[13]

The intelligence services increased the proportion of their budget targeted at Islamic terrorists from 23 per cent in 2001/2 to 56 per cent directly after the July 7 bombings, whilst in MI6 (SIS) and GCHQ the proportion 'rose significantly' although the figures were not released.[14] In all, since 2005, the security agencies have hugely increased their budgets because it is not only Islamic terrorists that pose a threat. There is still the fear over ecological and industrial sabotage. GCHQ monitors telephone and internet communication routinely as such communication may relate to 'terrorism; weapons of mass destruction; global instability; civil emergencies and state-led threats' and there have been controversial calls from Jim Gamble a former senior police officer and now Chief Executive of the Child Exploitation and Online Protection Agency and Keir Sturmer, Head of the Criminal Prosecution service that all internet communication by everyone in the United Kingdom be stored for a certain period in order to enable the authorities to get a clear picture of crime and social unrest.[15]

It is in the arena of personal security and privacy that some of the hardest battles were to be fought after the attacks on the Twin Towers. Indeed it may be said that this event alone stimulated the considerable increase in budgets, law reform and surveillance that came to a type of crisis in 2007 to 2008, in which government and the prime ministers Blair and Brown in particular seem to have lost patience with the 'will of the people'. It is during this time that an increasingly authoritarian government brought forward its plans for longer 'house' detention of un-convicted suspects, brought forward their plans for *non-voluntary* identification cards (suggested as voluntary in the 2005 Labour manifesto) and began looking into more sophisticated surveillance techniques based on the monitoring of school children and DNA and car number-plate data bases.

Not only adults were being fingerprinted during these years, schoolchildren were routinely fingerprinted without consent and for no good reason. On 4 March 2007, *The Times* 'reported on leaked government plans to fingerprint children between the ages of eleven and sixteen and to hold the information on a secret database, with the intention of processing around half a million children annually by 2014'.[16] This was a breach of both the Human Rights Act and the Data Protection Act but it was also a subtle way to soften later attitudes in adulthood to identity cards (ID cards), biometrics and DNA testing for government data bases.

Perhaps most controversially the government pushed ahead with the idea of ID cards using the spurious idea that such identification would protect the ordinary citizen against identity fraud, terrorism and crime. They further proposed that the European Union followed suit with Europe-wide surveillance and control. More worryingly, such cards were possibly to have secreted within them sophisticated recognition and tracking chips or Radio Frequency Identification (RFID), a form of monitoring device developed for retailing but applicable to human labelling.

So far-reaching are the implications of RFID tagging in consumer products, that a coalition of more than 40 consumer, privacy and civil liberties groups from at least nine countries, including the American Civil Liberties Union, Liberty UK, the Electronic Privacy Information Centre, Electronic Frontier Finland, and British think-tank The Foundation for Information Policy Research, have issued a joint call for a voluntary moratorium on RFID tagging 'until a formal technology assessment process involving all stakeholders, including consumers, can take place'. . . .

If personal identity were to be linked with unique RFID tag numbers, individuals could be profiled and tracked without their knowledge or consent. For example, a tag embedded in a shoe could serve as a de facto identifier for the person wearing it. Even if item-level information remains generic, identifying items people wear or carry could associate them with, for example, particular events like political rallies.[17]

Suspecting the language of RFID was deeply disturbing to the public, the government rebranded the device as 'contactless' or 'proximity' chips. The further possibility that such chips might be implanted in humans as VeriChips was not so far-fetched as experiments on willing guinea pigs were already underway, however medical tests seemed to prove a relationship between such implants and cancerous growth and stopped further overt testing of such products. Needless to say, ID registration was (and indeed remained until the 2010 election of the Coalition) intended to become compulsory with draconian fines and imprisonment for those refusing to comply. Immigrants already have to register, whilst a slow introduction may soften the current sense of distrust for those already here.*

At the same time as these debates are occurring the police have perfected Automatic Number Plate Recognition (ANPR) in order, so it is claimed, to prevent illegal immigration, gangsterism and 'anarchist vehicles', the police using roadside cameras to aid stop and search methods and data surveillance. The aim is to register sixteen million number plates a day and hold the data for two years. It is quite clear

---

*An example of what happens when you own an ID card, and it is defaced, is apparent in the case of 11-year-old Elliz McKenzie of East Dulwich who inadvertently had a scratched photograph on her Oyster card. The card which allows free travel on London Transport must remain unblemished. The scratched card meant that it was confiscated by an inspector and reported as breaching the 'behaviour code' which could result in Elliz being criminalized and sentenced to community service.[18] School children had their fingerprints forceably taken at Capital City Academy in Brent, North West London in order to 'buy' school lunches. Around 3,500 schools use such personal data already. City Academy were forced to apologize and wipe the data.[19]

that such potential restriction on movement has serious implications for protests and the movement of protesters in the future, much of whose time may have to be used to fight the very techniques now used by the security and police forces. 'Dataveillance' or the accumulation and synthesis of personal information will mean that the government and organizations it favours will be able to have a complete political, biological, social and political profile of everyone in the United Kingdom. This will effectively abolish both the idea of the person and of the private. What al-Qaeda's attack on the Twin Towers heralded was the age of governmental paranoia, a paranoia that had been born in the atmosphere of Thatcherite fears regarding 'the enemy within', but perfected in New Labour's own missionary zeal.

This is all reminiscent of the thinking of George Orwell and it is a sobering thought that in 1984 Margaret Thatcher had to stand up in parliament to refute his ideas whilst in 2010 surveillance cameras are trusted by the population (some even give you orders against anti-social behaviour in Middlesbrough) and *Big Brother* is now a popular series worldwide. This combination of spying or snooping and game shows was further developed in 2009 by the company 'Internet Eyes' who wished to install closed circuit television cameras (CCTV) into ordinary people's houses but trained on street activity. The idea which was trialed in Stratford upon Avon, was intended to have viewers look for criminal activity and be rewarded with money if an arrest was made.

The scheme was to supplement the 4.2 million public cameras many of which were not watched. The scheme reported in *The Times* on 6 October was roundly condemned by civil rights groups. It is ironic, in view of what has been said, that the ubiquity of closed circuit television cameras (CCTV), which take our picture 300 times daily and proliferate at the rate of one to every fourteen people, and that are not television but *spy* cameras, were precisely the surveillance technology that might have indicted the police who brought about the death of Ian Tomlinson.

It is certainly not the case that only left-wing, anarchist or Islamic organizations pose a significant threat to public order. Such groups as the EDL were one of a number of right-wing associations which have come to public attention. Another is Casuals United whose counter-demonstration on 10 August 2009 against an anti-fascist rally in Birmingham was staged in the middle of the shopping area and led to over thirty arrests after police seem to have lost control of the situation. Such groups are reminiscent of the days of the old National Front in the 1970s and the football 'firms' of the 1970s and 1980s and may represent a nostalgia for a street fighting way of life now reinvented and reinvigorated in opposition to the new 'threat' of Islam. Indeed some of the biggest riots in London have taken place around football matches. One at Bermondsey, South London occurred after Millwall fans, quiescent for a decade, rioted outside their stadium injuring forty-five policemen. Millwall were again at war when they clashed with long-time rivals West Ham at Upton Park on 26 August 2009. This 'pre-planned and organised' riot[20] started as Millwall fans came from Upton Park underground station and were ambushed by West Ham supporters along Green Street, an area almost entirely Moslem. This, however, was definitely white-on-white violence with a history that goes back as far as the founding of the two clubs and which had flared in the 1920s and the 1970s. Such rioting is indeed ethnic in origin and it is both 'religious' and tribal in nature.

What of the future contestation of London's streets, alleys, squares and parks? In 2012 London hosts the Olympics. The Olympic Park, athlete's accommodation and transport infrastructure were a high security risk right from the beginning and plans to secure all the venues and their entry points, including Britain's borders must remain an obvious priority until the event concludes, even after which terrorist elements could have smuggled themselves in as tourists. Such terrorist elements as might be detected threatening the Games are likely (but not definitely) to still be Islamic in belief and possibly foreign in origin.

Environmentalism will certainly not have vanished, but there has been a sharp diminishment of public interest in global issues during 2010. To reinforce the idea that human-induced climate change is a reality and not more government propaganda to increase taxation, climate change protest may become more vociferous and possibly more hysterical and extreme as the 'message' ceases to get through. This means that smaller more targeted and possibly more 'violent' protests will occur at firms who are perceived to be the worst polluters. Where climate change protest may succeed is in the area of restricting air traffic and saving local villages and green belt land. Such protests have a large public base of support and seem to follow the logic of what various governments have preached about the carbon footprint of excessive air travel.

The campaign to stop more air travel was orchestrated, not by left wingers, but by Conservatives and conservative ecologists mainly from privileged backgrounds – the same demographic base effectively as the Countryside Alliance, who do not consider themselves radical. These newer conservative groups are radical. This is the case with the group, Plane Stupid, formed by Tasmin Omond and Richard George during anti-Iraq war protests in 2005. Thus on Wednesday, 28 February 2008, Omond and George as well as Olivia Chessell, Leo Murray and another co-founder Graham Thompson, scaled the Palace of Westminster and unfurled banners attacking the plans for a third runway at Heathrow. The group told reporters that they had entered the Houses of Parliament as visitors, but more likely they were let in like the fox-hunting lobby by 'insider' friends with security clearance. Again, they have been successful in bringing an issue to public notice, although the economic downturn of 2009/10 may have had equal importance in slowing expansion plans. Nevertheless, a third runway at Heathrow, extra capacity at Stansted and even a new airport in the Thames Estuary have now become pipe dreams with the (partial) victory of the Conservatives in 2010, whose policies have been to accept the polluting nature of air travel and to resist the business lobby. An extra runway at Gatwick was dropped in February 2010. In this, protesters, middle-class Tory voters, middle-class defectors and David Cameron himself are seemingly united. A reversal of such policy will prove a flashpoint for demonstrations and probable camp protests such as those at Greenham Common in the 1980s.

With the growth of right-wing and semi-fascist parties and the possibility of right wingers gaining significant power both at local level and in parliament, coupled with the concomitant belligerence of some sections of the Moslem community and the well-organized and practised opposition of political groups opposed to fascism, there is every possibility that there will be a growth of street violence and provocative demonstrations around Britain. 'White' Britishness, now emboldened by its alliances in Europe and by its European and trans-Atlantic networks certainly seeks to make itself felt. Will, such demonstrations come to Trafalgar Square? The answer is yes, if those demonstrating want their message to get into the media and become headlines. Increased nationalism and xenophobia which were effectively moribund at the start of 1997 (the BNP had only 200 paid London members) have risen exponentially since, not in terms of actual votes, but in terms of percentages and general loss of confidence in those elected.

It is not only race hatred that has increased. The murder of Ian Baynham in October, 2009 in Trafalgar Square was a reminder of low level anti-gay attitudes exacerbated by Church prejudice against gay partnerships.* And here may be one source of coming friction: that between a revived 'post-secular' religious authoritarianism which is opposed to the secular human-rights legislation that has been a watchword of recent pluralist attitudes in British democracy. This was made a specific issue by Pope Benedict's polemical diatribe in February 2010, prior to his proposed visit to Britain. The comments, which were intended to be devisive, positioned the government's forthcoming human-rights legislation (the Equality

---

*The women accused of the attack were Rachel Burke and Ruby Thomas. The man was Joel Alexander.

Bill: to tie up anomalies in past human-rights acts) against a broadly Catholic idea of 'natural rights'. The target was essentially the ten years of successful campaigning in Britain of gay-rights activists and the progressive legislation that has legalized gay partnership and adoption, against which the conservatism of some religious groups was legally silenced. The human-rights activist Peter Tatchell, considered the remarks as a 'coded attack on the legal rights of women and gay people. [The Pope's] ill-informed opinions suggests he supports the right of churches to discriminate in accordance with their religious ethos'.[21] The fault line drawn here between the rule of law and the demands of moral certainty which the Pope's comments renewed will be a source of friction for some time to come.

As we have seen there has been a growing criminalization of space and movement since 2007, authority has its grip through sophisticated surveillance against physical protest. Yet such authority remains porous, subject to intense pressure from the media and from watchdogs. Whilst it appears that current protests pit a multiplicity of interests against a stubborn singularity of authority (visible in the ranks of helmeted policemen), this is not the case and the forces of security are themselves divided in their aims and actions; the watchers are now watched by their own surveillance methods (especially CCTV and mobile phones). Will the nature of protest change to meet the new demands of forbidden geography and the importance of mass media? Protestors have for a decade embraced modern methods of communication and organization, but they have also realized the importance of the world's cameras and the possibilities of 'virtual' protest, the 'staging' of an event, whether smashing a bank's windows by a single person or by creating carnivalesque situations that disarm authority and which allow the media the best photo opportunity. All active dissent is marked by an adversarial position and a sequential course of events. Television and newspapers only operate on the latter and as such protest may have to become more photo friendly and less ideological if it wishes to be noticed. Such post-modern protests in which the action stops in order for an 'event' to be properly filmed suggest that simulation rather than participation will create pastiche protest or simulations organized precisely to be 'looked at' later in photographs, on mobile phone videos and on the Internet. The strangest riot of 2010 was the 'Americal Apparel' disturbances on Saturday, 3 April in Brick Lane where after the fashion company had advertised its sale on Facebook but was unable to cope with the crush. Seven policemen were injured and three people arrested.

Preface to the First Edition

The story of London has been told many times. The travel writer H. V. Morton once wrote that 'the great city [is] written to death generation by generation', but the political history of London from its Roman dawn to the present has never been told in full. This book seeks to fill that gap not only by telling of the clashes that occurred between a long line of monarchs, a Parliament that insisted on its rights and a City Corporation that opposed both but also by showing the significance and vitality of the politics that has always taken place on London's street corners. Politicking no longer takes to the streets as it did for hundreds of years and the use of a 'soap box' by John Major in the 1992 election campaign was nothing more than an electoral gimmick. The Labour Party leadership, faced with a general public that harangued or punched them during the 2001 election contest, simply refused to go on the streets for fear of bad publicity. Yet even in our own world of 'talking heads' and presidentially broadcast leaders most of the substance of political change has found its way onto the street and, as often as not, been generated from the genuine concerns of those who have no recourse but direct action. In recent years this has been manifest in the demonstrations against global capitalism, Third World debt and environmental issues. Non-aligned political groups such as the Countryside Alliance or pensioners' associations have marched to Parliament to protest their cause – different causes whose politics are not clearly represented in the electoral system.

This is the story of those Londoners (and others) who took their cause to the streets, and from there lobbied Parliament, opposed monarchs and debated the rights and liberties of a nation. It is also a tale of bitter religious and racial tensions, of extraordinary and vicious retributions and of lingering hatreds. The open spaces, squares and streets of London are a theatre of politics where Londoners have gathered to watch rabble-rousers, great republican agitators, would-be fascist dictators, religious fanatics and brutal executions. This story unfolds not only in smoke-filled rooms where cliques whisper over plots and subversive printing presses or where murder is winked at and bombs hoarded, but also in the open air at Smithfield, Clerkenwell Green, Hyde Park, Trafalgar Square and the streets and alleys of Whitechapel, Brixton, Dalston or Broadwater Farm. Here people harangue, heckle, march, chant, brawl and sometimes murder in the name of a cause or in pursuit of an injustice that needs to be corrected. Here too are to be found the riot police, magistrates, army, secret services and the whole panoply of the state's authority.

In the following pages we find every kind of Leveller, ancient and modern, all sorts and shapes of radicals, republicans, revolutionaries and regicides and every hue of religious, racial and authoritarian bigot. Here also are the causes that motivated them, mostly long-forgotten arguments that came to a violent crisis and vanished away. Some still have lessons for us. Demands for a wider electoral system, more equitable laws, the right to free speech and the defence of the environment are issues that have a long and venerable history which comes up from the pavement orators of the past and the riots, revolutions and political parties they inspired. The nineteenth-century thinker John Ruskin exasperatedly spoke of 'cockney impudence', and Londoners have for many centuries been considered far too 'bolshie' to do what they are ordered for long. This is the story of their political demands and desires. It is a story that continues.

Violent London is organized around a number of major themes – racism, religious bigotry, republicanism and Parliamentary reform – but the book also adheres to a skeleton of chronology, thus allowing the reader a narrative history, though one in which the long continuity of my four themes can be followed with greater clarity. None of my themes is mutually exclusive, but in order to provide coherence I have sometimes separated issues in order to relate them to each other later in the text. Equally, obscure arguments might inspire significant political or religious strife. This is specifically important for the seventeenth century. Therefore, I have laid out the arguments and ideological differences of each conflict and attempted to provide evidence for the evolution of these disputes. I hope in most cases that I have not taxed the reader's patience. Last but not least I have taken London to be the area that extends to its modern boundaries.

1

A Desolation they called Peace

The Destruction of London in AD 60

A thin wisp of smoke curled around the jetty and mingled with the morning mist. Somewhere far off a dog barked and fell silent. Against the shore the lapping waves gave off a faint sulphurous smell as the waters mixed with the mud of the bank. The river slowly drifted by as it always had, steel grey in the dawn light. Here and there, streaked with stains of rust red which clung to them like membranes, alien things were quietly turning in the water, their stomachs oddly distended, their hands limp and black at the fingertips, faces looking intently down into the depths of the water for something they had lost. The river was full of these strange amphibians.

Across the water drifted other smells with the wreaths of smoke and eddies of ashen wafers, a smell somehow both strange and peculiarly attractive, which came up from the sacred grove where they had erected the scarecrows on their wooden crosses. It was the smell of burning flesh . . .

Everything was in ruins, the warehouses, granaries, workshops and marketplaces sent up a dark column of drifting dense smoke; 30,000 men, women and children lay in heaps or hung from trees or floated as corpses down the river. Death was everywhere, the attackers had taken no prisoners, for this was a war of annihilation and at its centre was the woman known to history as Boadicea and to the Romans as Boudicca, the first and most successful political freedom fighter ever to enter London. Yet once it had not been like this at all.

*

It was a land of thick forests and swift-flowing rivers, of rolling uplands and boggy swamps; to the Romans it was a land of red-haired men and women, a source of slaves, corn, tin and hunting dogs: Britannia. The island was densely populated: by peoples inland who saw themselves as indigenous and on the south and east coasts by others related to tribes across the Channel whose myths linked them to previous seaborne immigration. Living in hill forts, on fortified farmsteads, in villages and towns defended by maze-like entrances and ditch systems, the peoples of Britain formed a loose set of alliances and confederations similar to those of the Continental Gauls but more traditional and perhaps (if methods of war are a measure) more archaic. The British had always traded with their Continental partners, especially in iron and tin, knew if only vaguely about the dark-skinned traders from Mediterranean lands, used money as well as goods for payment and if rich enough drank wine and used olive oil bought from regular trade with the Continent. Some Britons had visited their Gaulish cousins, knew the ways of others by custom and by trade. This would change with the coming of the Romans.

By 55 BC Julius Caesar, having marched his legions across Gaul (approximately modern France), felt confident enough to seek new conquests. The invasion of Britain would secure his fame as a warrior, the securing of Britain his fame as a diplomat. During the summer Caesar assembled his legions and auxiliaries and made sure that the Gauls provided the usual diplomatic hostages. The immediate, and clearly factitious, reason for the invasion was to punish the Britons for sending aid to the Gauls who had fought Caesar's legions in the previous campaigning season.

Caesar's forces sailed for Kent but a British allied army awaited them, its warriors wheeling their pony-pulled wicker chariots, throwing javelins and clashing swords, along a stretch of shingle beach against the best trained, armed and organized army in the world. Caesar's forces clung to their boats – the Romans were always poor sailors – but Caesar signalled the warships to beach, the troops to disembark. Still they hesitated. Then, in a famous display of bravado, the eagle-bearer of the Tenth Legion invoked the gods and shouted to his colleagues, 'Jump down, comrades, unless you want to surrender our eagle to the enemy; I, at any rate, mean to do my duty to my country and my general!'[1]

A short, violent and haphazard battle followed on the shingle, but Caesar had his foothold. A Gaulish ambassador, Commius the Atrebatian, having been sent ahead of the invasion and having been taken hostage by the Britons, now returned with news that a peace deal might be concluded. The Britons were buying time. Four days into the invasion a storm caused havoc to the fleet and a foraging party of the Seventh Legion was mauled by British warriors. Caesar was finished in Britain for now and, defeated by the logistics of supply and a hostile population, he returned to mainland Europe. Caesar may have recrossed the Channel but he was still demanding hostages against another attack. The British simply ignored him, sending only two from two disarmed tribes.

By the summer of the next year (54 BC) a huge invasion fleet had been put together and Caesar again set out, reaching the coast without resistance (although shadowed by a large British allied army). This time he brought officials and merchants whose privately built and loaned ships added to the Roman armada. A battle at a fortified outpost sent the British into retreat but left the Romans unable to pursue, night was coming and they needed to camp. Another violent storm damaged the fleet.

At this point the obscurity of much of the campaign comes into focus, for Caesar's forces began their march toward a familiar landmark: the Thames – named for the first time by the invaders. Caesar's intention was now clear. Command of the British tribal alliance had fallen to Cassivellaunus, a tough warlike figure who had spent the previous years fighting his neighbours. For this campaign they elected him supreme commander. Cassivellaunus's own lands were north of the Thames and Caesar intended to cross and invade. Two pitched battles followed, the first in Kent and the second on the banks of the Thames itself.

The allied army retreated but things were now falling apart. The Trinobantes, living in an area from East London to Essex and Suffolk and the strongest of the south-eastern tribes, defected. One of the sons of the royal household went as far as sailing for the Continent (he may have escaped from being one of Cassivellaunus's diplomatic hostages) and put himself under Caesar's protection after the murder of his father by agents of Cassivellaunus. Other tribes, seeing that they might be able to use the Romans as a way of bargaining themselves out of obligations forced on them by Cassivellaunus, also defected, especially the Kentish tribes. Tribute and Roman hegemony then recognized, Caesar tells us he sailed home, perhaps properly revenged. Nothing was settled, however, and the history of the British again returns to silence. Or almost silence.

It seems clear that Caesar's two reconnaissances left a legacy. The first was that by the opening of the first century AD the southern British tribes were becoming accustomed to different ways and tastes. Coinage increased in use and communications and trade between the Roman provinces and Britain also rose. Some southern royal families may have looked towards Roman manners and attitudes, and power had begun to shift towards fewer and more concentrated centres. Of these centres Camulodunum (modern Colchester) in the northeast of Essex was the most significant (quite probably Cassivellaunus had come from the royal household living there). By the Claudian invasion the Romans would have a target to march towards. Conquest had eluded Caesar. It nevertheless attracted others who wished for glory or for wealth. Caligula assembled his legions on the coast of France and, like Napoleon and Hitler, conquered Britain symbolically with a ritual show of force and then marched home again. He had done all he felt he needed to do, smiled complacently to himself and left.

This was not the case with Caligula's uncle Claudius who, despite his fear of public appearances (he had a stammer), still possessed a hunger for glory. Britain seemed ripe for attack, especially since two sons of the house of Cunobelin, Togodumnus and Caratacus, had been fighting a series of expansionist 'wars' (the nature of which is not clear) and destabilizing the tribes of the south and east. The Roman forces led by Aulus Plautius were formidable: four legions and auxiliaries, amounting to 40,000 men. Landing somewhere in Kent, Plautius's army forded the Medway (an alternative theory suggests the Arum in Sussex) and fought a confused series of battles with the forces of Caratacus and Togodumnus that ended with the crossing of the Thames (near its conjunction with the River Lea) and Togodumnus's death.

The death of Togodumnus and the fierce fighting during the campaign stiffened resistance by the Britons and slowed the Romans down. Plautius, with his troops recuperating somewhere around either the south bank or the northern shore of the Thames, waited for Claudius to arrive. The victory had to go to the Emperor. Some six weeks passed and Claudius duly joined the base camp with both Praetorian Guards and a detachment of elephants. His entourage also included a substantial number of senators who saw the possibilities for trade and plunder and who would happily sing Claudius's praises once the conquest was complete.

Claudius advanced across present-day Essex toward Camulodunum, perhaps two or more days' march over non-Roman roads. We know nothing of who ruled the area or who opposed his army. There is no British oral tradition which survived the Roman conquest and no writing of any sort survives by a native Briton living at the time: there are no records of these early encounters written by witnesses and, more to the point, *no written comment* from any Briton in the whole period of Roman occupation (almost four hundred years). The only writing concerning Britannia comes from Roman historians who may or may not have visited the island and occasional almost indecipherable notes from Vindolanda near Hadrian's Wall written over a century later.

The capitulation of Camulodunum marked a turning point in Romano-British relations. It immediately shifted the balance of power. Native leaders who already had good relations with the Romans worked hard to reinforce their fealty whilst others made new alliances to stave off a Roman invasion of their own territories. Some of the stronger rulers tied themselves to Rome in order to strengthen their hand against local enemies, others did so in the mistaken belief that they would be considered as equals by the conquering Emperor. To the west and the north unconquered tribes looked on with disdain, druid priests urgently reading the auguries.

Another change occurred with the fall of Camulodunum. The township had originally consisted of a loose collection of buildings, homesteads, royal houses, stables, outbuildings and workshops, but the Romans rebuilt it on military lines. Laid out as a fortress, with a grid of barracks and headquarters buildings, the whole plan was crossed by two main roadways – the *via principalis* and the *via praetoria*. This military encampment would have added to it a great temple to Claudius, and would epitomize Roman rule and (as elsewhere across the widening empire) provide a blueprint for the new civic spaces of Britain. The native population were allowed to camp around the walls but only under duress. Camulodunum had become Colchester, a Roman colonial administrative capital.

Such changes were the visible civic and political signs of a new order but such development did not end with temples, statues and triumphal arches. Another new type of township was rising on the north bank of the Thames.

London began its life sometime in AD 48 and Colchester in AD 50 as strategic centres for the military. The Roman army that had crossed the Thames had probably camped on the marshlands of Hackney and the Isle of Dogs but needed roads above all to marshal supplies: Ermine Street ran from near where Liverpool Street Station now stands out towards Lincoln via Enfield; Watling Street dog-legged around the city and its bridge and was possibly aligned to earlier crossings of the Thames as it ran through Londinium to St Albans from Richborough, the chief Roman port, in Kent; Stane Street went to Chichester; another road ran from Roman Silchester on an east–west axis via Staines and Brentford to London Bridge and then out again via the modern Roman Road (Bethnal Green) and Old Ford (Stratford) to Colchester.

London's first bridge, key to London itself, was about thirty yards downstream from the modern bridge, which stands at the end of Fish Street Hill. Looking up along Gracechurch Street towards Bishopsgate one is still able to get some sense of the Roman town (and especially its post-Boudiccan look, as so many buildings are in the classical style). The population lived within a rectangular space bounded by the Walbrook Stream (near Walbrook), the juncture of Lombard Street and Bank and the midpoints of Fenchurch Street and Eastcheap. From archaeological finds, much of the population crowded up from the river in the area now defined by King William Street, Lombard Street and Gracechurch Street, with a substantial grouping at the beginning of the Walbrook between Bank, Poultry and Bucklersbury. At the southern end of the bridge, there is evidence of occupation around Southwark. The entire early settlement of Londinium therefore occupied little more than fifteen acres of land, with discontinuous occupation along its trade routes and riverbank possibly adding slightly over twenty more, the tightly packed area around the wharves soon giving way to small open plots and gardens.

This new form of frontier town was not built on the ruins of a British hill fort or settlement nor was it built to house an army, although a marching camp may have been temporarily built at Westminster. It was built for trade and trade alone, fanning out along the banks by the pontoon bridge (later replaced by a trestle bridge) built by the army as it pursed the regrouping Britons. This frontier post was called Londinium, and in many ways it represented the new Roman evils, international money, debt and taxation, for it was here that the Procurator, the Roman tax administrator, made his home and it was here that thousands of strangers, from central Europe, from the Mediterranean, from the Middle East and from Gaul and Rome, came to trade, contract for goods and build their warehouses. To its enemies it was a town of strangers and collaborators.

Tacitus, however, describes this new and bustling frontier town in words that suggest both its sudden rise and its importance. His description of this new *colonia* gave a picture of a rich and major trading centre and one that Romans might like to do business in.[2]

Before there had been almost nothing. The river, wider and shallower, had flowed through gravel and mud and shingle, making islands of the southern shore around what was to become Southwark as well as around the gravelly high ground around Westminster. To the north scattered settlements of ancient origin may have existed on the gently rising land towards St Paul's Cathedral. Rivers like the Lea and streams like the Tyburn, the Walbrook and Fleet flowed into the Thames through marshland or shallow valleys. In the valley of the Walbrook there may have been a sacred grove dedicated by the druids or an even more ancient priesthood. The fact remains that until the Romans threw their bridge over the river the Britons gave the Thames scant attention except, perhaps, as a fishing ground and as a place for fowling. Their worldview took no cognizance of the Thames as the heart of Britain just as their political views saw no significance in the place the Romans chose to place a bridge.

Roman administration did not change this view. The Roman Governor still sited his capital in the east. Roman traders however had other views. The Thames brought all sorts of goods to Londinium – olives, wine, corn, pottery and spices. From its warehouses came the products of the empire for bribery, barter and purchase. Into its wharves came the boats that would carry away hunting dogs, slaves, iron, bronze, gold and corn. Once its strategic importance had been realized Londinium grew at approximately three times the rate of Colchester. Its main road ran up past the wharves and warehouses where most of the traders lived with their goods, past the fish market with its pungent smells, local catches and fish-sauce makers up toward the higgledy-piggledy collection of workshops, houses, small temples, stables, animal pens, slaughterhouses and administrative buildings which were rapidly covering the gentle sloping hillside which led from the bridge out along present-day Gracechurch Street towards the north and north-east. An east–west route already existed and a southern route led back across the bridge toward the south coast, friendly tribes and home. The river provided a lifeline when times were good and trade significant and when times were bad it offered escape.

Aulus Plautius had forded the Thames in pursuit of Caratacus and Togodumnus in the area of the Westminster gravel banks (in the original Claudian invasion and before the building of London Bridge) and pursued his enemy into the marshland of the Lea and Isle of Dogs before retreating back into Southwark to build a camp to await the arrival of his Emperor. Almost twenty years later Londinium was a thriving town with a new bridge, but it had no garrison and the Britons were again on the move.

The seventeen years that separate the Claudian invasion from the great war with the Iceni were not years of pure tranquillity. It is true that after a violent and prolonged campaign Caratacus was captured by the Romans (after he had fled to Queen Cartimandua of the Brigantes who had betrayed him) and been taken in chains to Rome where his last years ended in utter obscurity, the only survivor of a dynasty of great warriors whom some Roman writers had called 'King[s] of the Britons'; it is also true that great swathes of western Britain, Wales and East Anglia had hardly been penetrated by Roman forces and that the Romans still needed a very large army, garrison posts and a fortress system to protect their conquests. Indeed, in the far west the druidic priesthood remained inviolate within its island stronghold of Mona (Anglesey), throwing out threats at the Roman invaders, their new ideas, decadent ways and destruction of traditional tribal values. A new Roman general, Suetonius Paulinus, marched to defeat them.

The druids terrified and sickened the Romans whenever they came in contact. Roman historians recorded of the druids that

[G]ods were worshipped . . . with savage rites, the altars heaped with hideous offerings and every tree sprinkled with human blood. On those boughs birds feared to perch, in those coverts wild beasts would not lie down; no wind ever bore down upon that wood … the trees, even when they spread their leaves to no breeze, rustled of themselves ... The images of the gods, grim and rude, were uncouth blocks formed of felled tree-trunks – their mere antiquity and the ghastly hue of their rotten timber struck terror ...[3]

When Paulinus's army arrived on the shore opposite Mona they were so scared that they were almost unable to act. Tacitus tells us that

The enemy lined the shore in a dense armed mass. Among them were black-robed women with dishevelled hair like Furies, brandishing torches. Close by stood Druids, raising their hands to heaven and screaming dreadful curses.
This weird spectacle awed the Roman soldiers into a sort of paralysis . . . the groves devoted to Mona's barbarous superstitions [Paulinus] demolished. For it was their religion to drench their altars in the blood of prisoners and consult their gods by means of human entrails.[4]

Here lay the religious and sacred heart of the ancient British Isles. To crush this would, the Romans believed, finally cause the collapse of the political struggle as well. Yet the war in the west exposed Rome to its enemies in the east, especially the Iceni in Norfolk and their queen, Boudicca.

The war that followed in AD 60 or AD 61 was no war of subject and colonized peoples, a mutiny or a rebellion in a conquered province by subordinate natives. It was a war waged by people who saw themselves as equal to the Romans – a free people who feared enslavement rather than an enslaved people demanding freedom. So distorted is our view of Boudicca that one pro-Roman modern historian saw her as no better than a malcontent and terrorist working secretly to undermine liberalism and democracy, little more than an ancient version of Ulrike Meinhof.

[T]oleration has little chance of success against certain kinds of religious/political fanaticism, especially when small determined groups are working towards precise but narrow objectives, perhaps not discernible at the time. When toleration in a community degenerates into apathy, there is fertile ground for these small bodies of extremists to plant and nurture their seeds of disruption.[5]

Seen against this background the Boudiccan 'rebellion' is a travesty of a diplomatic and military crisis, only reported by Roman writers and thereafter transmitted in exactly the form the Roman 'conquerors' dictated. This account stems in its original form from the pen of the Roman historian Tacitus and thus, bereft of any British account, we are left with only the tale of the victors.

Tacitus tells us of the disaster that overtook Londinium whilst Paulinus had his forces focused in North Wales. The story began when Prasutagus, king (or warlord) of the Iceni (the tribal grouping in East Anglia), finally died, having built up a prosperous and peaceful kingdom. He left half his kingdom to his wife Boudicca and her two daughters (whom Tacitus fails to name) but for reasons that cannot be clearly explained the Procurator Catus Decianus sent soldiers and tax collectors who plundered the Iceni territory: Roman officers took what they wanted from the area as Roman slaves (presumably administrative slaves close to being independent officials of the state) plundered the household goods of the royal family. Boudicca was whipped as a ritual humiliation; her two daughters were raped before her. Reduced to 'provincial status', Tacitus tells us the tribe 'rebelled' and the Trinobantes (whose former centre had been Colchester) rose alongside them.

> They particularly hated the Roman ex-soldiers who had recently established a settlement at Camulodunum. The settlers drove the Trinobantes from their homes and land, and called them prisoners and slaves. The troops encouraged the settlers' outrages, since their own way of behaving was the same – and they looked forward to similar licence for themselves. Moreover, the temple erected to the divine Claudius was a blatant stronghold of alien rule.

To support the great temple of victory at Colchester, the Romans appointed priests to collect tribal tithes for the imperial deity, doing so with such zeal that they bled the surrounding countryside dry. Yet Colchester was the home of retired legionaries whose interest in soldiering was now fast fading, and who had failed to erect defensive walls. As the Iceni–Trinobante horde descended upon them the omens turned black.

> At this juncture, for no visible reason, the statue of Victory at Camulodunum fell down – with its back turned as though it were fleeing the enemy. Delirious women chanted of destruction at hand. They cried that in the local senate-house outlandish yells had been heard; the theatre had echoed with shrieks; at the mouth of the Thames a phantom settlement had been seen in ruins. A blood-red colour in the sea, too, and shapes like human corpses left by the ebb tide, were interpreted hopefully by the Britons – and with terror by the settlers.

Without support the defenders, who had their families with them, appealed by despatch rider to Decianus, who, ignorant or careless of the situation, sent 200 poorly armed men – possibly auxiliaries (non-Roman troops). It was too late.

Then a native horde surrounded them. When all else had been ravaged or burnt, the garrison concentrated itself in the temple. After two days' siege, it fell by storm. The ninth Roman division, commanded by Quintus Petilius Cerialis Caseius Rufus, attempted to relieve the town, but was stopped by the victorious Britons and routed. Its entire infantry force was massacred, whilst the commander escaped to his camp with his cavalry and sheltered behind its defences. The imperial agent Catus Decianus, horrified by the catastrophe and by his unpopularity, withdrew to Gaul. It was his rapacity which had driven the province to war.

Colchester was only two days' march from Londinium, and it was in ruins, its inhabitants slaughtered, its great temple a smoking pile of ashes. Riders had been crossing London's bridge for the last few days with tales of horror that sent the population running to their household gods and the altars of the soothsayers. Prayers had been offered up, doves, oxen and sheep slaughtered for the messages in their entrails. On every face was a haunted, frightened silence – a grim awareness of coming disaster. Those who could packed and fled south across the mud flats of what would later be Southwark. Others took their families across the Lea marshes to the east hoping to hide in the wilderness of the Lea floodplain. The ships had all departed for Gaul, their captains urging the grain and oil merchants to hurry their loading. Sails hoisted, they silently slipped away towards Thamesmouth. On one such ship Catus Decianus watched for the wind and hoped the Emperor would be forgiving.

Yet it seems that the populace believed the omens to be good even with the departure of the Procurator, with no defences and no soldiers. Tacitus tells us that tens of thousands remained, hoping for a miracle or simply stranded. Then Paulinus arrived. All seemed safe. Recovering from his forced march south, Paulinus cared little for merchants, hucksters and lowly craftsmen and even less for their grasping children, wives and slaves. He had no intention of being trapped defending this rabble of opportunists. He and his men came, took provisions and marched off. Those who could followed him in a long straggling line of refugees and handcarts.

Boudicca must have been very close, possibly close enough to see the raggle-taggle army as it left the town. The attack on Londinium would simply be a massacre of a hated group of colonizing foreigners who had stolen British property. With luck she might enjoy the sight of Decianus himself caught in his own stronghold. She looked forward to the revenge a raped woman might take. With her waist-length red hair, Boudicca appeared a 'giantess' to the Roman opponents – a banshee from hell, leading screaming warriors whose tattooed bodies and lime-washed hair made them almost as terrifying as the tribes of the German forests.

> The natives enjoyed plundering and thought of nothing else . . . Roman and provincial deaths at the places mentioned are estimated at seventy thousand . . . the British could not wait to cut throats, hang, burn, and crucify.

The massacre perhaps took only a single day. Little except a few skulls and a layer of darkened earth remains to tells us of its fury, misery and terror. Boudicca's tribespeople killed or tortured all they found. The dead lay thick in the narrow lanes and alleys of the warehouse area near the bridge, and houses, workshops, temples and villas burned in an area from Ludgate Hill to Mansion House.

In the little wooded valley of the Walbrook Stream (now near Walbrook) the druids may have resurrected their sacred grove, setting up their enemies' severed heads on rows of wooden stakes. We have some archaeological evidence to suggest that this is what occurred but we do not know, just as there are no clues to Boudicca's state of mind or intentions. She had exacted revenge on the object of her hatred, Decianus's headquarters, but she had missed the man himself, now out of her grasp for ever. She had defeated the legions and chased out Paulinus. Druid rule not Roman temples would now prevail. She may have looked south across the Thames but she had no quarrel with the southern tribes and anyway they were already Romanized, already traitors. Did she go to the druids in the sacred grove to find out her fate? We do not know as we do not know if she stayed long in the ruins or even if she chose to chase Paulinus gathering his legions to the north. We do know the warrior queen had one more battle to fight and that the entire British way of life would depend on its outcome.

Finally, some time after the complete destruction of Colchester, London and St Albans, Paulinus was ready to fight. The two sides met on an unrecorded battlefield.

> Boudicca drove round all the tribes in a chariot with her daughters in front of her. 'We British are used to woman commanders in war,' she cried. 'I am descended from mighty men! But now

I am not fighting for my kingdom and wealth. I am fighting as an ordinary person for my lost freedom, my bruised body, and my outraged daughters. Nowadays Roman rapacity does not even spare our bodies. Old people are killed, virgins raped. But the gods will grant us the vengeance we deserve!'

The legions, out for revenge and knowing that retreat might prove more dangerous then advance, steeled themselves for the attack, threw the British back and routed Boudicca's forces, wiping out everything in their path. Tacitus tells us (with some exaggeration) that 80,000 Britons died that day whilst the Romans lost only 400. Boudicca and her daughters poisoned themselves and were buried in an unmarked grave. One Roman commander, unable to aid Suetonius during the war, committed suicide. The miserable British retreated north towards Norfolk and home.

The end of the war was protracted and violent. Paulinus pursued the remnants of Boudicca's army back into the fens and lowlands of their home and some evidence suggests that survivors may have been pursued as they fled north-east. Wherever they went, Suetonius pursued the enemy with an exterminating zeal born of the knowledge of his own earlier failure and loss of honour. The Iceni kingdom was razed and its people dispersed or exterminated. So maniacally did Paulinus pursue his mission that he was recalled. Peace was only partially restored. The coming of Julius Agricola continued the campaign unsatisfactorily concluded in North Wales and then took the war into Scotland. War again flared in the 70s and 80s and disturbances on the northern frontier were never fully settled.

Yet the pattern of Roman rule was established and Roman Britain now became a reality for four centuries, whilst Romanized Britain continued for two centuries more, the memory of Roman ways continuing into our own day. The British aristocracy was drawn inexorably into a Romanized way of life, educated in Latin, dressed as Romans, living in Roman houses and participated in a growing literate culture. The 'benefits' of Romanization now extended beyond the line of the Thames and outside the long-Romanized south and south-east coastline.

Urban landscapes began to appear. Londinium was immediately resettled and rebuilt as the provincial capital (just as Colchester and St Albans reappeared). It was more splendid than before, not only the financial and mercantile capital of the country but also the seat of government – a pattern which has lasted almost unbroken for 2,000 years. An administrative district was built (the basilica) and a forum, theatre, temples, villas, city walls and fortified garrison added to London's splendour. This time the city was built of stone and marble not wood and wattle and it was built to last.

The heritage the Romans left has warped our knowledge of the ancient indigenous people of Britain and for ever obscured their descendants' view of themselves. Almost until the twentieth century it has proved impossible to think of history, art, politics and culture outside Britain's Roman heritage. Indeed it is not possible to think 'history' at all outside this Roman heritage, for history seen in this way did not exist for the indigenous peoples (even if Roman historians made all their foes sound like themselves). Latin informs the religious, medical, legal and political institutions of Britain, housed in buildings based upon classical formulae of order and decorum, built in stone or marble in urban settings. The Roman straight line and angle so greatly replaced the mazy spiral and curve that the latter shapes in landscape and town are considered 'alien', barbarian and 'natural'. For centuries the ideal landscape was classical.

The influence of the Roman legacy left Britain schizoid in mentality and unable to reconcile, because no longer able to notice, the two sides of its national personality. Nowhere does this focus so strongly as in the story of King Arthur and Merlin, the one Romano-British Christian, the other pagan-druidic Celt (the last of his race). The confusion saw Celtic-Welsh leaders appeal to their Scottish and Irish brethren against the English in terms which saw the Welsh as the true inheritors of Rome!

> In 1401, Owain Glyn D'wr wrote for help to both the Irish chiefs and Robert III of Scots, appealing 'on the score of a common descent from Brutus' . . . There were two main forms of the legend: one where Brutus and Albanus (Scotland) were brothers, and one in which all Britain was subsequently divided between Brutus's three sons, Locrinus (England), Camber or Kamber (Wales) and Albanactus (Scotland), Locrinus as the eldest having an implicit claim to suzerainty of the whole, a claim which would prove potentially explosive in Anglo-Scottish politics. Brutus was the ancestor of Arthur, King of the Britons, of whom it was said that he would come again to deliver his people when danger threatened them.[6]

As centuries passed and the dominance of England grew the British heritage mutated into the 'Celtic fringe', something which linked, through mythical and mystical bonds, the Scottish and Welsh to the Irish, Cornish and Manx. Celticism was itself a self-defensive myth to unite those different from the English. To the English it meant wildness, tribalism and savagery exemplified by Irish 'bog trotters', Welsh 'Taffies' and Scottish 'Sawneys' (the name of a notorious, but fictional, family of brigands and cannibals).

In a self-defensive measure 'Celts' found for themselves an ethnic identity which could be celebrated in music and the revival of folk events based on oral traditions denigrated by English literate culture. Yet much of this had to be invented. The destruction of Jacobitism coincided with a new literary taste for all things 'Celtic'. Foremost amongst these writings was the publication of James McPherson's Ossian poetry (*Fingal* in 1761 and *Temora* in 1763). Like Merlin and Boudicca, Ossian too was 'the last of his race' and the toast of London society.

Primitivism was the natural way of life, which Romantics opposed to the stultifying conditions of urban sophistication. Celticism became synonymous with the 'real' religion of Britain. Druidism exemplified this return. The fashion was a creation of eighteenth-century gentlemen and it coincided with the revival of Masonism. In almost no time Druidism had forsaken its sacred groves and was associated with the mystery of Stonehenge and the cult of the solstice. Stonehenge was painted by Turner and Constable and druids were depicted by William Blake.

Druid societies continue to associate with Stonehenge and are now not only associated with summer celebrations on Salisbury Plain or the annual Welsh eisteddfod but form the backbone of New Age anarcho-paganism.

> The late twentieth century has witnessed another renaissance in Druidry, inspired by the renewed interest in alternative spiritualities from the 1960s, by the 'green' movement and by contact with other Nature-based spiritual traditions, notably modern Witchcraft and the 'shamanic' cultures of North American and elsewhere.
>
> There are now some 35 Druid groups in Britain alone, with a further 300 or so worldwide . . . The Mother Grove of the British Druid Order (BDO) was formed in 1979 as part of a personal quest to recreate a native British spirituality.[7]

Anarchist protest of the 1990s took some of its visual cues from pop Celticism, with many protesters combining punk leather jacket with tartan kilt, tattoos and body piercing. In the fight to stop the M11 link road crossing Wanstead, protesters declared the area a 'free republic' aligned along a sacred way or ley line. In March 1994, blockaded by bailiffs and police, protesters warned those that intended to remove them by force to 'Beware the Ides of March', their free newssheet bearing the defiant headline, 'ROMANS GO HOME'. Above all, Celticism has come to stand for anticentralism and, in the extreme case, for Irish and Scottish republicanism. The devolution of power to the Scottish and Welsh assembles in the late 1990s was an attempt finally to shift regional power away from the magnetic centrifuge of Westminster and London.

What of Boudicca's reputation? Gildas the Wise (born AD 416), a scholarly monk, contemptuously referred to her as a 'deceitful lioness' and then all is silence for a thousand years. The Renaissance writer Polydore Vergil called her 'Voadicia'. His contemporary Hector Boece called her 'Voada', and at the connivance of James IV of Scotland set most of the action north of the border, Voada now allied to her brother, the Scottish King Corbrede. Death claims Voada but her daughters marry Romans and live happily ever after. Another Italian visitor to England, this time Pietro Ubaldini, renamed her Bondvica in his illustrated history of the Kings of England and Scotland. Edmund Spenser wrote of Boudicca as Bunduca in *The Ruines of Time* and *The Faerie Queen*. By Queen Elizabeth's reign, Boudicca in all her various spellings was restored as a heroine to complement her illustrious descendant, England's own warrior queen. Ben Jonson put Boudicca in his *Masque of Queenes*, where she appears eighth in a line of great female rulers from antiquity and from legend. John Fletcher and Richard Hopkins produced plays about Boudicca in the seventeenth century and Richard Glover completed his play in the eighteenth as literary taste turned toward the Celtic, barbaric, druidic and Gothic. Milton, in contrast, dismissed her in *Eikonoklastes* (1609):

> The truth is that in this battle and whole business the Britons never more plainly manifested themselves to be right barbarians: no rules, no foresight, no forecast, experience, or estimation, either of themselves or of their enemies: such confusion, such impotence, as seemed likest not to a war, but to the wild hurry of a distracted woman, with as mad a crew at her heels.[8]

By the late eighteenth century Boudicca was reborn in the work of Thomas Cowper, as the 'British warrior queen' (beloved name of so many nineteenth-century public houses), a druidic princess fighting for freedom and independence and founder of the British 'race' upon whom 'Empire is . . . bestow'd'.

By the middle years of the nineteenth century Boadicea, as she now was, had come to epitomize the spirit of Britishness, fair play, independence of spirit and strength of purpose. In a perverse misreading of ancient history she came to stand as the symbol of Palmerston's Pax Britannica (itself a restatement of the Pax Romanum) for empire, order and British womanhood. Boadicea was now as much Anglo-Saxon as Celtic. In 1856 Thomas Thornycroft began the bronze statue group known as *Boadicea and her Daughters*: Boadicea was finally co-opted for the imperialist cause.

The Times correspondent, on witnessing the stupendous statue (as a plaster cast), enthused,

> Mr Thornycroft has given us fine statuary before now, but he has done nothing, as he has attempted nothing, so great as this. It is

not perfect; it has, indeed, faults which at once strike us, but it is not only without doubt the most successful attempt in historical sculpture of this barren time; but it is an achievement which would do credit to any time and any country. The group is nearly twice the size of life, for the figure of Boadicea measures 10 ft. A car, the body of which is wicker-work and the wheels thick circles of solid wood, is drawn at speed by two unbridled horses rudely belted to the heavy pole. They plunge asunder as they sniff battle in the wind; one would dart forward as the other attempts to hold back. In the car, naked to the waist, crouch the Queen's two daughters, and strain their gaze towards the Roman host. The face of one is full of a proud and eager hope, that of the other freezes with horror. Between them stands Boadicea. She lifts her arms high above her head; her right hand is closed round the shaft of a spear, the left is extended, and the whole gesture is of supreme grandeur. Her face and her entire manner finely convey the impression that she is addressing the multitude of the warriors of her tribe. It is the pause before battle, and borne rapidly along the whole array of her people, she calls upon them to take vengeance once and for all and to destroy these Roman soldiers from off the face of British earth. The speed of the car is shown by the incline forward of the figures, the blowing manes and tails of the horses, and the drapery pressed against the outline of the Queen's body. Her face and attitude are instinct with commanding grandeur; she orders the extinction of her foes; she appeals to her people not in frenzy and tears; in tones heart-stirring and eloquent no doubt, but with more pride than rage in them, and her haughty spirit does not dream of defeat.[9]

Thornycroft did not see his work cast in bronze (he died in 1885) but his son completed the work and a public subscription bought it for the nation. But where to put such a grand national monument: Parliament Hill Fields, Hyde Park Gardens or Kensington Gardens 'on a rocky eminence surrounded by water'? In 1902, Boadicea's scythed chariot was unveiled on the approach to Westminster Bridge, the legendary (and convenient) site of her final resting place. Boadicea and her chariot would for ever come to defend the very heart of a city she despised. In bronze she is ready to defend the Imperial Parliament and the approach to London; she stands there today: Queen of the Thames.

2

'Offence – A Londoner'

The Peasants' Revolt to Evil May Day

For over a thousand years the Thames flowed on, indifferent to the lives of those who lived on its shores. As the Boudiccan inheritance was scattered to the winds, London was again occupied and rebuilt, its Roman overlords determined to raise the city in the image of the empire. By the waters of the Walbrook Stream they built a palace for the new provincial governor and thus shifted the administrative capital of Britain. Between Aldersgate and Cripplegate, a great fortress was established from whence the legions might for ever stamp out dissent. Near Cheapside, an amphitheatre saw gladiator games, and a walk away there were baths for London's new citizenry. Up from the stone-built bridge was a great forum and basilica, behind which the road led north-west to the walled fortifications punctuated by gates at Ludgate, Newgate, Aldersgate, Cripplegate, Bishopsgate and Aldgate. At Spittlefields, just outside Bishopsgate, the Romans and the slowly Romanized British buried their dead. At the temple of Mithras, the legionaries may have thought their world would last for ever and their Romano-British subjects may have thought that Roman peace would last a millennium, but Roman London lasted only until AD 410, when the army finally withdrew from Britain. London nevertheless remained 'Roman' and thrived on the trade that still came along the Thames.

By the sixth century, the city was in decline as a major centre of Romanized culture, its buildings decaying and its brick and stone architecture replaced by wattle and daub; nevertheless it was home to a growing immigrant population of Saxons who had no use for Romans, Celts or cities. London was now the central city of the East Saxons, conquerors of Essex, Hertfordshire, Middlesex and the southern shore around Southwark. By the seventh century a new church (St Paul's) was under construction to the east and a great abbey would follow many years later at Westminster. In search of space, the Saxons renewed London beyond its walls, along the Strand, through Aldwych to Tyburn (Marble Arch), but Viking raiders destroyed the city 'with great slaughter' in 850 and left it a ruin for a second time in its history, not to be rebuilt until 886, when King Alfred refortified the old Roman town.*

The new settlements running along the open land towards Westminster that had been Saxon Lundenwic became overgrown and vanished, but within the walls, the Earldorman Ethelred (ruler of Mercia between 886 and 911) rebuilt streets and restored defence works. The centre of the new burgh, still studded with Roman ruins, was slowly reorganized, the new administrative quarter rising over the old amphitheatre where the Guildhall stands today and where the government of the City of London still resides.

In 994 Svein Forkbeard, the Danish king, again attacked London but was thrown back by those on the ramparts built by the legionaries a thousand years before. On his death in 1014 the Danes who ruled the city were forced to yield to the combined armies of Aethelred and his English and Olaf Haraldson of Norway.** For the most part London held, protected by its militia and by its wealth, which its ruler could use to buy off attackers. When Edward the Confessor died in 1066, London was a thriving port and an international marketplace. The great abbey at Westminster proved the growing importance of London's western shore and new roads and streets crowded in upon themselves at Cheapside whilst wooden quays arose at Billingsgate to accept the new trade that flourished between the towns in Germany, Flanders and France. Small churches studded the city but power had shifted to the abbey on the marshy ground beyond Tyburn stream.

---

*In AD 604, London had Mellitus as its bishop. London, said Bede, writing in his *Ecclesiastical History of the English People* was a 'trading centre for many nations who visit it by land and sea'.[1] It was ruled by Ricula on behalf of King Ethelbert and it was here that Ethelbert ordered the building of the first St Paul's. London was sufficiently cosmopolitan for Mellitus to be able to visit Rome, but on the death of Ethelbert the kingdom went to Redwald of the East Saxons who was a pagan. The three sons of client king King Sabert who had followed Ricula were also of the East Saxons, but had all become apostates and Mellitus was driven out. By AD 616, Bede tells us, 'London preferred its own idolatrous priests'.[2] The importance of London, which Bede never visited, was partly to do with the connection to Canterbury and Rochester which were the southern gateways for Christian missionaries from Rome and partly because by the time Bede was writing London was becoming a large, prosperous and sustainable town with international connections.

**St Olave's Street became Tooley Street. St Olave (Olaf Haraldson) is commemorated on the wall of an office block at the southern end of London Bridge and as a statue in Southwark Cathedral.

Here Aethelred built a royal hall accessible from the land and from the ever-essential Thames.

When William and his Norman warlords arrived they found a well-organized and wealthy city, full of the bustle and business of a sophisticated, Europeanized kingdom. The population of 10–15,000 inhabitants would double in less than a hundred years – a real prize for a conqueror. Like the Romans, William knew these subjects could not be trusted and he soon began the building of the great square white keep that became the Tower of London. Westminster, however, remained a more comfortable royal centre giving continuity with the Saxon past, and even if Winchester might become William's capital for a time, it was London that dominated the politics and economics of the land.

By the Conqueror's time, London already had a well-established administration that had evolved from the older *folkmoot* or people's gathering. Later a more select and powerful group called aldermen administered the wards into which the city was later divided under Richard I. Known then as a 'commune' and later as a corporation, this body could negotiate directly with the King. By the fourteenth century the patrician group of aldermen who controlled the Commune had centralized power around a mayor. He was London's principal personality and the most important of England's urban officers. As the 'personification of the city', he had a court in which law, ritual and trade were regulated and on behalf of which he could directly negotiate with the King. Soon, the King's own representatives in London, the Sheriffs, were themselves merely officers of the Mayor. By 1240, the city 'barons' (the aldermen) were in constant dispute with King John at Westminster, claiming that their rights and liberties had been enshrined by Magna Carta (1215). It was at this time too that the King's 'Great Council' started to be called Parliament. When London became England's capital during the 1330s, a strong oligarchy of city magnates already had a long tradition of independence to defend and a London populace steeped in a tradition of self-rule.

This independence was forged in the previous century during the baronial crisis of 1260 to 1270. Widespread concern over corruption had led to Henry III calling a Parliament at Oxford in 1258 to debate state reforms, especially regarding corrupt exemptions from taxation. The Oxford 'laws' or Provisions split the King from his barons, led by Simon de Montfort, who began to propagandize for reform. After much confusion and debate, the old *folkmoot* was recalled at Guildhall and declared for de Montfort to 'save the liberties of London'. Further Provisions of Westminster followed as law and order broke down in factional fighting which spilled over into the murder of Italian monks in the streets near Cheapside.

In February 1261, Henry occupied the Tower and began a programme of pacification much resented by aldermen and populace alike. When rumours spread in 1263 that Henry was dead, London declared again for de Montfort and he entered the city amid rioting against royal supporters. The barons now ruled London. A failed attack by Lord Edward (later Edward I) on the Temple temporarily sealed the fate of London's royal followers; Queen Eleanor, pelted with stones as she attempted to escape, was forced to find refuge in St Paul's.

With their houses burned to the ground, royalists tried to raze the rebellious city, Richard de Ware set fire to Cheapside. Violent anti-Jewish riots followed, as did attacks on foreign merchants. Londoners then marched with de Montfort to Lewes, in Sussex. The victory in which Henry was captured (despite the rout of the London militia) was nevertheless hollow. After de Montfort's death at the Battle of Evesham, Henry marched on London to finish with his enemies. A Suffolk plea roll of 1265 records the expropriation of a London magnate's property and the charge: 'Offence – A Londoner'.[3]

By the fourteenth century, London was confirmed as the capital of England and it was during this time that there emerged the modern idea of a fixed legislative parliament based usually at Westminster. Before this period a parliament or 'parlement' was a gathering of lords called by the king, a type of parley or 'colloquium' of the type called at Runnymede in 1215. In other words, it was an occasion not an institution.

Between 1320 and 1370 parliament was recognized as a fairly organized body meeting regularly – an organ of government not of monarchy. As one law manual put it, 'the king holds his court in his council, in his parliaments'.[4] It was this deepening and complexity which, although not replacing other forms of English governance, certainly showed the growing interrelationship between monarch and people. The large and defined peerage that had emerged during the reign of Edward II after 1325, combined with the representatives of the shires, boroughs and cities constituted this relatively new body.

By 1395, it was so recognized as an independent organization that the Lollards pinned their heretical 'Twelve Conclusions' to both the doors of St Paul's and of Westminster Hall. Apart from certain bishops, parliament was a secular body representing all levels of society and even the 'commons' or 'communes' (originally only shire gentry and burgesses), meeting to make laws and raise taxes which the king could no longer do alone. The institution stood more and more for 'political justice through the law' and its complex legal position as both a court of law and a means to administer the king's writ meant that it soon started to be involved in developing the social fabric of the country. By 1422, parliament was so established that its supremacy was recognized. It was a high court, a great national assembly, a place embodying certain rights and procedures and a place where the commons and the idea of elections would decide power.

London grew and thrived under the Normans and their successors. By 1300, approximately 40,000 people were crowded within the old Roman walls. Most of the inhabitants lived and worked in wooden buildings closely packed along streets that were dust storms in summer and swamps in winter, without any sanitation or recognizable drainage. Thatch, a fire hazard, had been banned from use, but London might be burned to the ground by any stray spark. This city too felt stable and permanent to its citizens. Indeed, older street names were now taking on their modern titles – Candlewick Street became Cannon Street and Westcheap became Cheapside – whilst many medieval street names passed into the nomenclature of the modern *A to Z*. Change there was, however, new waterside docks appearing all along the river with new stairs and landings being pile-driven into the banks to accommodate goods and people, all of whom had to use the river as London's main and only reliable highway.

The Thames was the key to London's success as a centre, first and foremost of trade. Commercial districts lined the road all the way from near Fleet Lane to Grasschurch Street (now Gracechurch Street) and down from Cornhill to London Bridge. Brewing grew up next to the bridge and on the Southwark shore. Tanners, dyers, skinners and butchers worked in districts that reeked of blood and death from East Cheap to Smithfield, night-soil collectors delivering human urine and faeces to the tanners to 'cure' their hides. Cloth and wool merchants did business with all Europe and great annual fairs allowed commerce in fur, precious metals, spices and wine with traders from Bruges or Florence. Wine also flowed in from the English vineyards of Gascony or allied Burgundy.

Everything from soap to spectacles entered London, was traded and exported or sold at a profit. Manufacture and trade was regulated at every level by the powerful guilds under masters whose business acumen was mixed with religious observance and charitable welfare. Nothing could be traded or manufactured within the walls of London without permission of these oligarchical guild bosses, but money talked and medieval merchants were men of practical outlook. It suited them to allow one-third of London's staple export, wool, to be in the hands of foreign merchants, such as those from Flanders, northern France or Italy. German merchants of the Hanseatic League were exceptionally influential in iron, steel and dyes with their own Gildhalla Teutonicum in 1474. Jews from Rouen, the Low Countries or Spain were eagerly courted by English monarchs looking to find banking facilities with those the Church didn't ban from the trade in currency. A great synagogue was built in the quarter still called Old Jewry and it was here in 1189 that thirty Jewish merchants were massacred to 'celebrate' the coronation of Richard I. (A statute of 1275 required Jews over seven years old to wear a yellow badge made up of 'two tablets joined'.) By the fourteenth century, Lombards (after whom Lombard Street was named) were also freely dealing in finance, to the envy and resentment of their English counterparts. When disaster struck the population in 1348 and the Black Death carried off a third of England's inhabitants, foreign merchants and 'profiteers' inevitably became the target for those London factions both resentful of their apparent helplessness in the face of increased taxation and simultaneously aware of their new economic power (their value as labour). Led by wealthy and influential men eager to 'restore' their rights, London was threatened again with invasion and revolution.

The English rising between May and July 1381 which is commonly known as the Peasants' Revolt – a popular and spontaneous refusal by the men of Essex and Kent to be bullied into paying excessive

Anti-Jewish caricature, including depiction of compulsory 'badge', from a medieval manuscript

taxes to a corrupt and vicious ruling elite – began in May when tax collectors found themselves unable to carry out their duties. Heavy-handed use of justices and summary law had further alienated potential taxpayers including a growing group of wealthier (by comparison) and more independent country folk who were not merely farmers but also skilled craftsmen and women.

> These are men who for the most part ply essential trades in any peasant society. Carpenters, sawyers, masons, cobblers, tailors, weavers, fullers, glovers, hosiers, skinners, bakers, butchers, innkeepers, cooks and a lime-burner are found in the Kentish indictments. Much the same is true in Essex, with the addition of a couple of glaziers; and similarly Suffolk, though here the occupational descriptions attached to names are fewer.[5]

A common sense of oppression and a common feeling of lack of fairness (the rich could avoid payment) turned to actual rebellion and a march on London led by Wat Tyler and the priest John Ball. The rebels' aims were clear. These were to 'save [the King] from his treacherous advisers', to kill or remove the advisers and to revenge themselves on John of Gaunt, Duke of Lancaster and Richard II's uncle, who was considered to be behind the corruption.

Violent attacks on property and people now began to occur across south-east England as the main rebel bands gathered at Blackheath,* where John Ball emerged as the radical voice of the rebellion. The King, having intended to meet the rebels for talks at Blackheath, decided eventually not to appear and after the destruction of Lambeth Palace and other properties owned by prominent Londoners the rebels marched into Southwark and across London Bridge where they were welcomed by the London poor. By now London had effectively been abandoned by Richard in order to gain time, although he had tried unsuccessfully to get the rebels to go home on 13 June. On 14 June he again met them at Mile End and talked with Wat Tyler, who presented their grievances. This was followed by the rebels occupying the Tower and executing any advisers or lawyers whom they considered 'enemies' of the King. On 15 June, Richard

---

* In 1450 Jack Cade and a rebel army of Kentish peasants camped on Blackheath for a month. They attempted to capture London by an assault across London Bridge, were repulsed and Cade was beheaded. Blackheath was again the scene of a peasants' revolt in 1497, when Cornishmen camped there on their way to London to protest against taxes for the war with Scotland. Defeated in a pitched battle, their leaders, Thomas Flammock and Michael Joseph, were executed.

met Tyler at Smithfield for another parley but a trap had been set and the rebels were attacked. Tyler was dragged from the sanctuary of St Bartholomew-the-Great and killed. The rebels prudently agreed to leave London only to find themselves the subject of a campaign of reprisals in which John Ball was finally captured in Coventry to be hung, drawn and quartered in St Albans. At North Walsham in Norfolk on 26 June the rebels fought and lost a pitched battle, which effectively ended organized resistance.

It was, however, opening the gates of London that fuelled the crisis and gave the rebellion teeth. London was Britain's largest city, with between 37,000 and 40,000 inhabitants, four times as big as York. The City was prosperous and virtually autonomous with its own ruling body. The suburbs, such as Holborn and Clerkenwell, also thrived. Although full of skilled and semi-skilled workers, those with political rights equalled only a quarter of all men and in the rigid hierarchies of the guilds and mysteries (secular religious fraternities) even fewer exercised power or had choice. There was sufficient organization amongst the London poor (and sufficient fear of their volatility) to force the keepers of London Bridge to open it to allow the rebels to enter the city, where aldermen welcomed them. As shall be seen the aldermen had self-interest at heart. Once in the City the rebels allied themselves with the London 'commons', who now may have made up the majority of the insurrectionists. John of Gaunt's palace at the Savoy was a particular target – Gaunt was blamed by Londoners for the failure of the war in France, corruption and the encouragement of foreigners. It seems likely that the Savoy was destroyed by Londoners before the Kentish and Essex rebels arrived.* Thus it seems that London was *already* in a state of rebellion. Indeed when they entered the city the rebels found there was a massive insurrection of the Londoners themselves, drawing on every element of London society.

> It is by no means easy to separate the actions of the London rebels from those of their allies from the counties. The difficulty is well illustrated by contradictory stories about the burning of the Duke of Lancaster's home, the Savoy, which was between the Strand and the river. The Anonimalle chronicler gives the most detail about London's events. He suggests that the Savoy

---

*The destruction of John of Gaunt's palace at the Savoy left a ruin ripe for rebuilding. Henry IV acquired the land when he declared the Duchy of Lancaster (Gaunt's old domain) to be a personal prerogative. Henry VII rebuilt on the land, when he erected a hospital and three chapels. The chapel of St John the Baptist remains, the personal chapel of the Queen in London.

was burnt by the London commons because of their hatred for the duke before the arrival of the men of Kent. But he also tells us that the commons of Kent passed through London from the Bridge to Fleet Street, presumably through Ludgate, without doing any damage. It was not until they were outside the city walls again that they picked various targets of political or social significance. The chronicler, having told us already that the Londoners burnt the Savoy, describes in detail an attack by the men from Kent on the Savoy, but qualifies this by saying that some people, all the same, blamed the Londoners. In this, the author of the continuation of the *Eulogium Historiarum* agrees with him, emphasising that the Londoners attacked Gaunt's palace before the arrival of the other rebels.[6]

Thomas Farringdon, the most significant London leader and the illegitimate son of a wealthy family, actually seized Richard's bridle at the parley in Mile End and demanded fair play from the King with regard to a property deal that had gone wrong.

Fair play was also their demand when the rebels marched to the prisons and freed their inmates – an act repeated on behalf of *natural justice* in every serious London insurrection thereafter.

The first prison closely associated with London which was opened was the Marshalsea prison in Southwark . . . After opening the Marshalsea prison, the rebels dragged Richard Imworth, its warden, from sanctuary in Westminster Abbey and beheaded him – not in Westminster, but in London, in Cheap. Newgate prison, which had been the city prison, was also broken open. But at this time it was used by the government for all particularly dangerous prisoners, Londoners or not. Another prison from which the prisoners were released was the Fleet prison, once also a London prison but by now in general use by such Westminster courts as Common Pleas and Exchequer, as well as by the King's Council and Chancery. The prison at Westminster Abbey gatehouse, which contained clerical and lay prisoners from the jurisdictional liberties of the abbot as well as from those of the Bishop of London, was also broken open by the rebels.[7]

It is possible that as rebel spokesmen called for justice and fair play they had thoughts of Robin Hood in the back of their minds. Originally recorded in written form by Langland in *Piers Plowman* in the 1370s, it was said that the peasants knew more about the tales of Robin Hood than their prayers. Robin's association with the longbow and the sword spoke of a personality indicative of freedom and nobility – a man really loyal to his King and defiant of usurped power. Robin Hood's appeal crossed classes, and he was popular equally amongst the literate merchants, burgesses and craftspeople and illiterate labourers or villeins.

Yet there were other motives for the activities of the London insurrectionists, informed by far darker designs than the demands of fairness and justice, and all directed at their fellow Londoners – the Brabants and Flemings who had settled in the capital as weavers. This was an economic war against fellow Londoners carried out with extreme ferocity by rival English master weavers and hostile journeymen angered at losing trade and prestige to foreigners. The Fleming master weavers had already successfully petitioned to create a 'gild' – a mixture of trade association, masonic lodge and religious club – and had established themselves along the Thames, in Shoreditch, St John's Street and near the Tower. Opposed to them were the English master weavers and the 'fraternity' of journeymen, a secret and illegal organization, half religious club, half trade union. These 'covins' had already been used as a means of organizing boycotts against the Flemings.

Whether it was because of rival weaving masters, disgruntled journeymen, poor jealous labourers from the lesser skilled crafts or a mixture of all of these, the Flemings saw themselves under attack from the beginning. In Suffolk, for instance, three Flemings were beheaded by local insurgents, and as rebels returned to Manningtree they took their frustrations out by lynching another. The London crowds began by attacking some Flemish prostitutes in Southwark. The pogrom was detailed in blood: thirty-five Flemings were dragged from the shelter of a church. Their fate is unknown, unlike the seven unfortunate craftsmen lynched at Clerkenwell when the Hospital of St John was attacked. In all, it is possible that many hundreds were killed, one chronicler putting it as high as four hundred. The violence of this economic war would be repeated throughout the following centuries, against Italians, Huguenots and Irish.

As early as 1255 the chronicler Matthew Paris had complained about London 'overflowing' with foreigners, whether the merchants of Amiens or those of the Hansa or Bruges. Most deeply resented were the Italian merchants and bankers, the Riccardi, Bardi, Peruzzi and Frescobaldi, families who, through their Paris offices, had established branches in London and upon whom English monarchs grew to depend. As Italian visitor, Andreas Franciscius, wrote a letter on 17 November 1497 recording his suspicions of Londoners. After bemoaning the mud-soaked London roads he continued, 'Londoners have such fierce tempers . . . despise the way Italians live . . . [and] pursue them with uncontrolled hatred'. He too had been the 'object of insult'. Franciscius's fears were not without foundation. Whenever rioting occurred in the city, Italians were often the first to be attacked. During the anti-Jewish riots of 1263, Italians had had to be protected from the mob by seeking protection in the Tower of London. In 1470, after a series of trumped-up accusations by rival English merchants, Italians were attacked in the street and had to temporarily direct their business interests from Winchester.

Not all violence against foreigners succeeded, however, as the riot known as Evil May Day suggests. The attempt to destroy Lombard influence at Henry VIII's court in 1517 was a spectacular failure for its instigator, a broker called John Lincoln. Lincoln had grown increasingly bitter over the alleged stranglehold on money and merchandise by Lombard bankers and their apparent indulgence by Henry. Foreign financiers from Genoa, France and Lombardy were accused of financial chicanery on a massive scale when a number absconded with money loaned by Henry to the Emperor Maximilian. The arrogance of the 'strangers' astounded Englishmen when 'they set naught by the rules of the City' and made it clear that they could act as they wished as long as the King supported them. One Lombard called Francesco de 'Bardi even won a court case against a merchant whose wife had run off to live with the Italian (and had even brought her husband's silverware with her!).

Lincoln, incensed by all this, waited until the Easter sermons were preached at St Paul's Cross and St Mary Spital. These were open-air affairs which formed part of a programme of events including a number of sermons on the theme of the Passion, at which the Mayor and aldermen attended in all their robed pomp. Unable to convince one divine to attack the 'strangers', Lincoln finally persuaded a Dr Bell to include a thinly veiled condemnation of the iniquities of court influence and loss of trade.

> The aliens and strangers eat the bread from the poor fatherless children, and take the living from all the artificers, and the intercourse from all merchants, whereby poverty is so much increased that every man bewaileth the misery of other, for craftsmen be brought to beggary and merchants to neediness.[8]

The preacher then called on 'Englishmen [sic] to defend themselves and to hurt and grieve aliens for the common weal'.

The aggressive language used at the Easter sermons was soon reported to Henry as his court travelled between Greenwich and Richmond, English courtiers and Lombard bankers exchanging veiled threats. As May Day itself approached, Londoners prepared for the extensive festivities and rituals that accompanied it. May Day was a day of licence with a carnival atmosphere, not to be trifled with lightly. During the final days of April foreigners were manhandled and abused but the culprits, men called Petyt, Betts,

Stephenson and Studley, were soon arrested and imprisoned in Newgate. This inflamed rumours of a coming massacre planned for May Day itself.

At this point, Archbishop Thomas Wolsey, the King's Chancellor, who was then installed at his palace at York Place (later called Whitehall), called in the Lord Mayor and Sir Thomas More, the Under-Sheriff of London, to explain what measures they were taking to stop disturbances. More, somewhat discountenanced by Wolsey who was a large, violent-tempered man, was sent off to keep the peace at the last minute, but preventing people letting their hair down on May Day was, to say the least, provocative. Curfews were announced, nevertheless, and householders were required to keep all servants indoors until seven on May Day morning. Information was poorly circulated, however, and left most Londoners unaware of the emergency regulations. Thus when alderman Sir John Murray tried to arrest two boys enjoying a bout of 'sword and buckler' in front of a large crowd of apprentices they took it that the City authorities intended to suppress traditional rights. With a cry of 'Clubs!' poor Sir John was chased off and his quarry left to escape.

Frayed tempers and London gossip soon created a number of street-corner crowds led by both workers and 'gentlemen'.

> Then more people arose out of every quarter, and out came Servingmen, and Watermen, and Courtiers, and by a XI of the clock there were in Chepe six or seven hundred. And out of Paul's Churchyard came three hundred which wist not of the other, and so out of all places they gathered, and brake up the Counters, and took out the prisoners that the Mayor had hither committed for hurting of the strangers, and came to Newgate and took out Studley and Petyt, committed thither for that cause.[9]

More, now in a funk over what to do next, tried to talk the crowds into going home when they reached St Martin's Le Grand but his band of supporters were pelted, abused and forced to retreat, leaving the rioters free to attack property and passers-by in Cheapside, Cornhill and Fenchurch Street. A foreign merchant called John Meantys had his house wrecked. Originating in Picardy, Meantys was not merely the King's French Secretary, he was also well known for sharp practice and illicit wool carding. With things increasingly out of hand the Lieutenant of the Tower took the extraordinary step of bombarding the City. By 3 a.m. the disturbance was over and the forces of the Earl of Shrewsbury and the Earl of Surrey secured the streets and arrested 300 'troublemakers'.

Retribution was, as ever, swift and violent. The charge was not riot but treason (with all that that implied) as the intended victims were from allied countries. Edmund Howard, son of the Duke of Norfolk, had mobile gallows constructed in order to move around the town. Thirteen apprentices were immediately hung, drawn and quartered with such extreme ferocity that chroniclers felt it worth noting the fact that the victims were merely 'poor younglings', perhaps little more than children. Lincoln, having been incarcerated in the Tower, was duly led out with other convicted rioters a week later, to be executed. He met the same fate as those in the previous week but the lesson had now been learned. His fellow traitors were reprieved at Westminster Hall by the King himself, the prisoners throwing their halters in the air in a loud 'huzzah'.

The aggression shown towards Lombards was ineffectual but there were always plenty of other foreigners in later centuries towards whom one could turn one's business frustration and anger.

3
'We'll no need the Papists noo!'

Criminalizing Catholics from the Babington Plot to Guy Fawkes

Everybody knows that it was the divorce that was the cause: the divorce Henry craved to satisfy his desire for an heir. The marriage was already shaky but so was Henry's relationship with God's representative on earth, Pope Clement VII. There already existed deep cracks in the union of Catholic princes and mother Church that could not be mended. Kings, princes, princelings and dukes turned one by one to the new Protestants – Martin Luther, John Calvin and Ulrich Zwingli, who had driven whole nations towards a new Christian interpretation of the gospels and in so doing rewritten the political landscape and language of 'reformed' Europe: the word of God was powerful political medicine. It was a key to new independence, new seductions, new freedoms and new enslavements.

When Henry VIII declared himself the Supreme Head of the Church in England (later Church of England) he not only had to re-establish the absolutism he had rejected in rule from the Vatican but he had to do so by consent. The conflict between a re-established English version of a modified Catholicism (Anglicanism) and the message of dissent that the original break with Rome created were the poles around which English politics would circle for almost 600 years (and Irish politics to the present day). The fight by the Church of England for its rightful place as *the* established Church of the nation was one that constantly involved careful negotiation and the reconciliation between monarchy, the representatives of the law, the archbishops, Parliament and the people. When things went wrong the screams of the tortured, the heretics' bonfires and the sound of gunfire marked the failure. In this cauldron the political freedoms of the English as well as their private consciences were forged.

The establishment of Anglicanism as the religion of the state nevertheless showed quite clearly that *any* group might reconstitute itself as an independent congregation or, if not, object to one or more (no longer divine but simply *routine*) ways of worshipping. In the churches, houses and chapels of London were to be found all sorts of

Dissenters and reformers: Puritans, Independents, Presbyterians and Baptists. The Church was under continuous assault from rebuilders and religious demolishers.

Before Henry's momentous decision to create a national Church everybody in London had been a Catholic; afterwards, apart from foreign ambassadors and their households, every Londoner was, at least nominally, a member of the reformed Church. Many accepted this simple yet fundamental change with equanimity, some with silent resentment and others with open hostility. It was in London that the 'war' with Catholic dissidents was fought at its most intense and savage. By the age of the Tudors, London politics had become the key to power, the seizure of its space and institutions providing effective control of the state and its operations. London was also the key to the kingdom and the focus of those rituals of power that came to dominate English life.

London itself had now spread far beyond its Roman walls into Bishopsgate and out into Clerkenwell, where there were pleasant fresh-water springs, a nunnery and Charterhouse. The road from Newgate led to Holborn, Staple Inn, Lincoln's Inn and Barnard's Inn and Temple, home of the legal profession. There was continuous building and development on a long strip of land following Fleet Street out to Charing Cross and Westminster, whilst to the east the Tower 'hamlets' grew and the 'villages' of Whitechapel, Stepney and beyond slowly began their long coalescence. The river front too had grown (with new suburbs at Deptford, Greenwich and Wapping), its endless activity looking out across London Bridge towards Southwark where the Hope, Rose and Globe theatres offered entertainment alongside the bear pit and brothels clustered near the old palace of the Bishop of Winchester (in Clink Street). The suburbs of London were still leafy and agricultural but inside the city, houses, workshops, grand livery halls and stables jostled in endless confusion from the old Cathedral of St Paul's to Holy Trinity at Aldgate. Bridewell and Greenwich provided new palaces to complement Westminster and the Tower, monuments to Tudor ambition.

London was a place of dense, narrow streets and sudden unexpected open spaces: cottage gardens, vegetable plots, dumping grounds or the empty vistas of the common land and wastes. In the great spaces that still separated the 'villages' of London the public rituals of state control found suitably theatrical surroundings. Used one day as sites for a fair or market and another for a procession or religious celebration, the large open spaces of London were places where public life could be communally expressed and where royal displeasure could be clearly demonstrated.

The great market square of Smithfield enclosed the area between St Bartholomew's Hospital and the ancient church of St Bartholomew the Great, and, just outside the old city walls, was one such venue where cows might be sold for slaughter and men slaughtered for religion. Smithfield had witnessed the quartering not only of sheep and cows but also of William Wallace. It was a suitable place to put fear into a herd of animals as well as a common multitude. When Mary ascended the throne it was a suitable place to burn those heretics who failed to return to the Catholic ways of her youth. Almost 300 years later, Charles Dickens called Smithfield cattle market a place of 'mute agony . . . ferocious men . . . a panorama of cruelty and suffering'.

Henry's eldest daughter Mary, always a Catholic, tried to burn the heretics out of existence from Smithfield to Oxford in her attempt to purge the Church of Protestant 'martyrs', as they became known. Yet the tide had turned already and the religion of the English would never again be Catholicism. Elizabeth, pragmatic and politic, attempted to reconcile private conscience with state duty. It was an act that could hardly be sustained beyond her own death in 1603. With James on the throne London filled with religious reformers and Dissenting heretics.

The Henrician peace was to be sorely tested on his death on 28 January 1547, when various changes to the politics of Europe began to directly impinge on England. Scotland was allied with France and always threatened to squeeze England from a northern invasion backed by French troop landings, whilst the Hapsburgs, rulers of half of Europe might threaten at any time to close the coast or invade. The Emperor looked with half-disguised relish at forming an alliance with a newly restored Catholic England. He might have to wait, but perhaps not for long. The newly established religion was green and delicate, but oddly taking root especially amongst the gentry. Nevertheless, it might easily be deformed or broken from pressures both internal and from without. Few in the mid-sixteenth century had a stomach for revolutions or rebellions, however, despite their occasional appearance. The monarchy rested on stronger foundations than the new religion – political foundations, which were to be tested throughout the 1550s.

Henry's son Edward VI was a minor when he came to the throne and virtually under the tutelage of the Protector Somerset whose mishandling of war in Scotland and France nevertheless did not stop him from having delusions of ultimate power. Feeling that the 'poor commons' would back a *coup d'etat* led by him, his miscalculation cost him the friendship of the king's councillors who seized the Tower of London and barred the gates of London. His supporters had to be told to go home. It was a taste of that hesitancy that marked almost all of the Tudor rebellions in the south. The lesson was not learned quickly in Tudor England and the Duke of Northumberland's

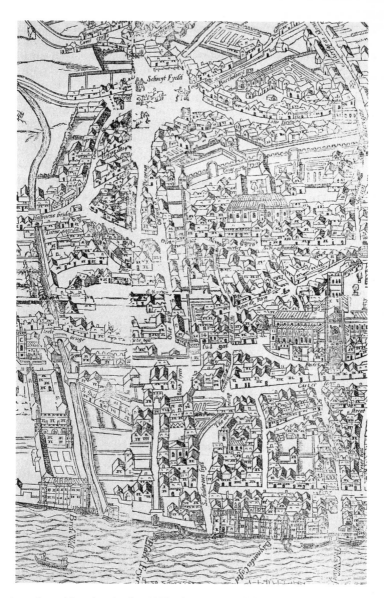

A section of London in the 1550s showing Smithfield: called here 'Schmyt Fyeld' (top centre). (From the 'Civitas Londinium', attributed to Ralph Agas)

attempt to place his daughter-in-law Lady Jane Grey on the throne in 1553 in order to destroy Mary's claim and the possible reversion to Catholicism that Mary threatened gained few followers amongst the Protestant gentry and derision amongst the 'Catholic' poor. Bonfires were lit in London on her execution.

The Tudors it seemed ruled by popular consent and religious indifference. What might change this would be that long-feared reversion to Catholicism which was inaugurated with the accession of Mary. Grumbling there may have been but rebellion in the cause of religious principle there was not. Despite everything this was not the hysterical atmosphere of the next century. There was foreboding, but also resignation and acceptance of the rightful monarch. What would tip this to rebelliousness was the proposed marriage to the Emperor's son Philip of Spain. Such a marriage alarmed not only the French but also those Englishmen who smelt conspiracy, For if Philip became 'king-consort' of a Protestant country would he not reduce England to a vassal state such as was the case in his holdings in Italy and the Low Countries, thereby stifling trade as well as dissent? Was he coming as a king to rule without a parliament or as the mere husband of the queen? There was no precedent for a king-consort. The marriage agreement had to safeguard the line of inheritance, but if Mary died without issue, Philip would be de facto, if not de jure, King of England. On 4 January, he had negotiated a secret agreement that annulled all of the safeguard clauses against this possibility. The deal was brokered on 12 January 1554. Where then would be the power of the English gentry and aristocracy, but broken in the face of an invasion of Spanish diplomats, gold seekers and Jesuits. The fight against Spanish dominance was a political fight dressed in Protestant clothing. England not Protestantism was threatened, but who was to defend it against what appeared to be a perfectly legitimate marriage proposal and perfectly legal settlement amongst princes?

Rebellion was in the air. London's tavern talk buzzed with rumour as discontented forces slumbering for years drew themselves up for a fight. Yet what exactly was the fight and how were they to commit themselves to something that was so ill defined? Was it the legitimacy of the wedding they objected to or the fact that it was to a Spaniard. No one seemed to have raised the question of the 'good old cause'. Protestantism was not an issue and anyway many of the poor who were caught up in the plots were still ostensively Catholic. Any plot would also have to contemplate the possible execution of the monarch and a change of regime to safeguard the return to a strong England able to withstand vengeful invasion, restore Protestantism and protect trade under a settled monarchy. This was quite beyond the resources of any plotter. Only if they acted in concert and hoped the common people would rise and capture London could they hope for success.

So it was that Sir Thomas Wyatt, Sir Peter Carew and the Duke of Suffolk gathered in late 1553 or early 1554 to discuss audacious plans to supplant Mary and put her half-sister Elizabeth in her place. William Thomas, one of the early ringleaders suggested the queen must die and such talk continued throughout the period, regicide being an option that was both quick and easier than nowadays supposed. In December the conspirators had their plan. A fourfold attack on London, the murder of Mary and the enthronement of Elizabeth with the restoration of Protestantism was not only an audacious plan, but also impossible to carry out with their slender means. Farcically, the whole thing began to unravel as soon as it started. The Duke of Suffolk floundered in Leicestershire and Carew and his compatriots caught fright and sailed for France. No one had fired a shot or drawn a sword, but Wyatt, a former soldier was still active in Kent and London might still rise. He raised his standard at Maidstone on Thursday, 25 January, explaining to the gathered crowd that,

> Because you be our friends and because you are Englishmen that you will join us, as we will with you unto death . . . we seek no harm to the Queen, but better counsel and Councillors.[1]

As the London militia trained and prepared, Wyatt recruited and marched uncertainly towards Rochester. He had with him a rag-tag army of Kentish men from across the county, but very few from the coastal towns which considered the pirates of France more of a challenge than those in power at Hampton Court. London was thrown into turmoil, but to her credit Mary stayed and awaited the storm at Whitehall. About 800 troops were gathered in London and although they were well armed, they were ill trained and of dubious loyalty. Special loyalty oaths were also administered just in case one forgot who one was fighting for.

Wyatt was brave and determined. He had little choice as he was now declared a traitor; more of a traitor indeed, given his grandfather's loyalty to Henry VII and the establishment of the Tudor regime. He camped at Rochester and waited for the royalist army to descend. He had some hope for the reputation of his lads, Kent being renowned for trouble throughout the 1540s, but equally the attachment of the gentry to the county was weak, the county gentry being career soldiers and diplomats more attached to London than to their country seat, and therefore less likely to lead trustworthy retainers into a battle where local loyalty would count. Nevertheless, Wyatt had gathered a force of between 2,000 and 3,000 men all of whom had been roused by Wyatt's colourful language of Spanish invasion, rape and pillage which would make the state of 'Inglish men . . . vile'. Wyatt, nevertheless, muddied the waters of rebellion telling his men that they were fighting to save the queen whilst giving others to understand, the 'her hed shall bee chopped off'.[2]

Wyatt waited for the London bands to tramp up to Rochester. Both sides had around 1,200 men ready to fight as they watched each other across Rochester Bridge. As the attack was ordered the Londoners defected and sent the other government troops into headlong flight. Wyatt was now free to march towards Greenwich and Southwark and perhaps get Londoners to rebel en masse. He would be sorely disappointed. The gates were barred, the guns of the Tower trained on the southern suburbs, all shipping sequestered by the government and London Bridge defended. The rebels approached London hungry and tired. Some South Londoners made cause with the rebels, but not enough to count. Even so the South Londoners fed and watered Wyatt's men and clearly felt more affinity with their Kentish cousins than to the rest of London, deserting the government forces they were meant to form part of.

They could not storm the city, so Wyatt searched for a way over from Kingston and the trail back towards Westminster. Some of his followers wanted to march towards Essex to rally the troops to the cause, but were dissuaded. Things had to happen in London, now and no delay was possible. Wyatt's artillery, what there was of it, got bogged down and had to be abandoned, but the crossing was made and the rebels marched into London after staying overnight at Knightsbridge. Londoners gathered to fight Wyatt not because he was ideologically opposed to what they believed but because they feared the idea of the destruction of their city. They were prepared to fight and they were well armed and fed. On the day of reckoning, the Kentish men were straggling and ill ordered. Already the ranks had thinned, Wyatt's troops better able to run than to stand up for their cause met the queen's forces at Charing Cross and were less repulsed that spontaneously retreated. A strange 'battle' now took place in which both sides simply passed by each other in silence and without striking a blow, something which suggests possible collusion between opponents. Blood would be shed.[3]

This was an unreal fight but its outcome was to be decisive. Some of Wyatt's men tried to fight their way out of Westminster, but were surrounded and killed. The rest had followed Wyatt to Ludgate but found the city gate barred and defended, by one of Wyatt's own friends, John Harres whom he expected to join the rebel cause. It was the final defeat and Wyatt knew it. He had fought three small skirmishes and some sixty or seventy men had died and nothing had been gained. Surrender was the only option and execution the only likely result. William Thomas, the man who had proposed the killing of the queen tried to commit suicide but was executed once he recovered. Sir Thomas Wyatt optimistic of a pardon right up until the end was executed on 11 April, dying in the people's eyes as a 'martyr'. Of the 480 convicted with him, 90 died at the executioner's hand and the rest disappear into the obscurity.

Discontent amongst those who went into exile in France after Wyatt's aborted rising continued. Calais was a place of tavern intrigue and again rebellious Englishmen hoped for French help against supposed Spanish expansionism even as they feared a Franco-Scottish alliance. Again the plot was hatched by Protestants but was not overtly religious. The aim of putting Elizabeth on the throne was strategic and political. The chief plotter was Sir Henry Dudley, a malcontent who had been forgiven once already for plotting, but he and a great many others hoped to rob the exchequer, invade England via Portsmouth, seize Yarmouth castle on the Isle of Wight and march on London. The plans were to come into effect during 1556, but despite the careful preparations and the gathering of ammunition and armour, the French king, Henri II, would not be drawn into the plot and the defences of England had time to strengthen against a French invasion. Dudley proceeded no further, the queen eventually died and no action was taken. Indeed he was actually able to gain legal protection against his creditors in spite of his eventual bankruptcy in which state he died plain 'Captain' Dudley in 1558 or 1570.

The Puritans, whose name was a term of abuse as much as a description of aims, sought to reform the Church and purge it of all vestiges of Catholic worship. Most followed John Calvin in their belief in predestination, individual interpretation of scripture (within certain limits), an emphasis on the judgemental side of the Old Testament and a belief that they alone might belong to the 'elect'. Furthermore they took communion as a symbolic (rather than transubstantial) act and in matters of Church rule they denied the 'apostolic succession of bishops'.[4] Puritan-minded vicars sought to 'cleanse' their churches and wrestled with their conscience as to how they might respond to an order from the Archbishop of Canterbury when it came to questions of ritual, the prayer book, the arrangement of the altar, 'superstitious' pictures or objects in church, altar rails and vestments. To hold the Anglican community together was no easy task and an archbishop with Popish tendencies might pay with his life, as did William Laud in 1645.

Within the Puritan tendency were more extreme radicals who wished to reorganize the basis of Church management, ridding themselves of 'Episcopalian' rule (rule by privileged bishops).

> The Presbyterians, finding a model in the magisterial system of the Old Testament, vested authority in the presbytery, a group of ruling elders and ministers. Their churches were not autonomous,

but were subject to a hierarchical control by district and national presbyteries. Their goal was the establishment of an all-embracing national Church – a Church-state like Calvin's at Geneva – in which the civil magistrate, who would be a faithful member of the Church, would punish ecclesiastical transgression in the light of the ruling of the Church elders. Until then they denied the right of the magistrate to interfere with them.[5]

Finally there was a growing number of 'Independent' ministers and congregations where there was no organizational rules or management system but rather a community of believers in each of whom Christ was said to reside. They prayed as equals, falling into trances and speaking their communal visions as they gathered together and looked for God within. In most such congregations men and women were equal and both could preach. Christ was in every member of the group and no bishop or Church structure was needed to find a 'covenant' with 'Him'. From the ranks of the Independents came the more extreme fringes of Protestantism: Baptists, Quakers, Fifth Monarchists and Ranters. Only one enemy united all of these disunified elements – hatred of Catholics. It would be a hatred that had the power to sustain itself over half a millennium, for 'to submit to Rome . . . would be worse than death'.[6]

The fight against Catholicism was a fight of vital national significance and international dimension, taking English armies into the Netherlands and putting English fleets in the Channel. The Catholic threat had both a religious and a political dimension, fought out at the dynastic and at the local level, a matter of both governmental policy and personal salvation. To fight this covert war of shadow play and subterfuge, as much would have to go on under the surface of events as above. There were, for instance, many Catholics at Cambridge University, most being 'recusants' (refusing the Oath of Allegiance and Supremacy and not attending church), and although they could pay for an education they could not qualify for a degree without attesting to the Oath. Many people might take the Oath, attend Anglican services and still be a Catholic or Catholic agent. Nothing might be quite as it seemed.

> The openly rebellious Catholics, who betrayed themselves by their 'malicious and violent speeches', were easy enough to deal with, but the 'other kind of papists', these invisible Catholics, were not. They 'come to church, outwardly conforming, but in secret they do much harm in corrupting of youth'. They 'lurk in colleges, more in number and more dangerous than is commonly thought'.[7]

Catholicism appealed to conservatives and traditionalists at the university as well as to malcontent poseurs, and in 1581 (four years prior to open warfare with Spain) the Catholic English College at Rheims established a secret network of agents in the colleges of Cambridge. The network was organized by Edmund Campion and Robert Persons who reported to Claudius (Claudio) Acquaviva, the General of the Jesuits in Rome.

> In some ways this pull towards Catholicism in the 1580s [was] similar to the flirtations with communism in Cambridge in the 1920s and 30s. It was a gesture of anti-orthodoxy, of going over to the enemy. At its outer reaches . . . lay a career of treason, but for most it was just a dilettante game.[8]

The 'insinuated priest[s]' put in to 'turn' the students were merely the central figures in a long process of surveillance and information-gathering in a world of disinformation and dissimulation. The playwright Christopher Marlowe, then at the university, was already embroiled in this murky world, accused of recusancy whilst actually a government spy. The refusal to award an MA degree to Christopher 'Morley' by the university authorities was based on the evidence of his apparent papist leanings and proposed (or actual) visit to Rheims. The decision to award the degree was on the warrant of the Privy Council itself because, 'It was not Her Majesty's pleasure that anyone employed, as he had been, in matters touching the benefit of his country, should be defamed by those that are ignorant in th'affairs he went about'. Marlowe was just one player in a huge and loose network of spies and informers who watched the Catholics who were watching them.

William Cecil (Lord Burghley), the Queen's Treasurer, and the Earls of Leicester and Essex all ran spies but the greatest was Sir Francis Walsingham, the man responsible for the first centralized and professional spy network in England. Walsingham had fled England when Mary's reign became too dangerous for committed Protestants. He spent his years abroad building contacts and learning foreign languages. On Elizabeth's accession in 1558 he returned and acting on behalf of Burghley was instrumental in breaking up the Ridolfi plot of 1569. Walsingham's new-style 'secret service' was dedicated to intelligence-gathering, disinformation and entrapment. He was only too aware that such work was always dirty and brutal and was equally aware of the risks in employing people you could not trust: 'There be no trust to a knave that will deceive them that trust him, yet such as he is must be entertained. For if there were no knaves, honest men should hardly come by the trust of any enterprise against them'.[9]

Opposing Walsingham in this 'game at chess' were a number of equally canny enemies. There was Claudius Acquaviva in Rome and the militant wing of a 'revived' papacy, also Dr (and later Cardinal)

William Allen, President of the English College at Rheims and cohort of the Duke of Guise, who had ordered the massacre of Protestants in France on St Bartholomew's Day 1572. These men were the fountainhead of English sedition. Yet there was also the Welshman Thomas Morgan, now in exile and chief advocate and proselytizer for Mary, Queen of Scots, who might also call on English Catholic lords (especially in the north) and malcontents such as the Duke of Norfolk. To fight these enemies would take guile and, where necessary, an unpleasant and ruthless opportunism in the employment of poisoners such as Richard Baines, informers such as Robert Poley or Maliverny Catlin, senior code-breakers like Thomas Phillips (or Phelippes), who was Walsingham's closest assistant, counterfeiters and special-effects experts like Arthur Gregory and even the odd playwright on the make like Kit Marlowe.

> The typical Elizabethan spy was a man of middling to low status. He might be a gentleman, more often he hoped to become one. He was often a former servant or page in some prominent Catholic household, who had turned, or had been turned, into an informer. His motivations, in the most part, boiled down to greed or fear, or a mix of the two, with the question of patriotism coming a poor third.[10]

Outside Walsingham's control but at the centre of this spider's web was one of the most revolting, powerful and least-known villains of English history. He was the Queen's chief pursuivant or government interrogator, Richard Topcliffe, a man of sadistic inclination and undoubted psychotic fantasies. Reporting directly to Queen Elizabeth, Topcliffe boasted not only of his power over her with regard to governmental matters but also her enslavement to his sexual allure! One victim of Topcliffe's attentions reported that during September 1591, the government enforcer had boasted

> That he was so great and familiar with Her Majesty that he many times putteth his hands between her breasts and paps, and in her neck; that he hath not only seen her legs and knees, but feeleth them with his hands above her knees; that he hath felt her belly, and said unto Her Majesty that she hath the softest belly of any womankind.[11]

Topcliffe was a professional torturer for a brutal and brutalizing regime. There is no doubt he enjoyed whipping, branding, mutilating and racking as a vocation as much as a duty. One Catholic priest recalled,

> I was hanged at the wall from the ground, my manacles fast locked into a staple as high as I could reach the stool. The stool taken away,

there I hanged from a little after 8 o'clock in the morning 'till after 4 in the afternoon, without any ease or comfort, saving that Topcliffe came in unto me, and told me that the Spaniards were come into Southwark by our means: 'For, lo, do you not hear the drums?' For then the drums played in honour of my Lord Mayor.[12]

From Walsingham's townhouse and London headquarters in Seething Lane near the Tower to Topcliffe's interrogation centres at the Marshalsea and Bridewell, to the dungeons 'known as Limbo, Little Ease and the Pit' and to the gallows at Tyburn and the instruments of evisceration was a winding and ill-lit path.

It was this path that beckoned to the small group of men plotting to assassinate Elizabeth, put Mary, Queen of Scots on the throne and restore the Catholic faith. There was Anthony Babington, whose surname became a byword for the plot; John Ballard, an itinerant priest; John Savage, over from Rheims with murderous intentions; an Irishman named Robert Barnwell; and others like Harry Dunne. During 1586 they came together by various routes at taverns such as the Plough Inn, near Temple Bar. John Ballard was there under an assumed name, Captain Fortescue, a ruse used often by Catholic priests and Jesuits to mask their true intent. With 'Captain Fortescue' was a companion called Barnard Maude. Aware of negotiations between Ballard and Morgan in Paris and also following meetings with Don Bernadino de Mendoza, the Spanish representative in France (he had been expelled from England), the group prepared its plans at Babington's home in Holborn. Don Bernadino had assured Ballard that the Spanish would soon bring England to a reckoning and an internal uprising would certainly help any Spanish invasion plan. John Savage was to kill the Queen. The Counter-Reformation would finally triumph.

Yet this was a classic 'sting' operation by Walsingham, who had infiltrated Barnard Maude into the group as a government spy who himself was backed up by the agent provocateur Gilbert Gifford, and Robert Poley, a double-dealer of epic proportions and one of Walsingham's band of 'projectors' (the name given to agents amongst the Catholics). Tricked by these agents, or merely naive, Babington 'blew' the entire plot to Mary in a letter sent during July. It was, of course, intercepted.

Mary was not in London. She was at Chartley Hall near Burton in Staffordshire in the keeping of Sir Amias Paulet. It was Gilbert Gifford who it is believed came up with the idea that the conspirators correspond with her via empty beer kegs, which were frequently taken away to be refilled by a local brewer. All the letters were intercepted, decoded and replaced. Thomas Phillips was himself at Chartley waiting to intercept the letter which would lead Mary to the block.

On Sunday 17 July the fatal letter went from Chartley in its beer barrel and arrived on Walsingham's desk destined never to arrive at Babington's quarters. Phillips drew a gallows on the packet.

Meeting secretly at various London pubs such as the Three Tuns at Newgate Market, the Rose at Temple Bar and Castle Inn near the Exchange, the conspirators were now firmly in the bag. John Ballard, travelling to meet Babington at Poley's house, was caught first. Others such as Babington and some companions fled north-west of the capital and hid in St John's Wood, then a forested wilderness. Even though they were able to escape to a friendly and safe manor house near Harrow owned by a Catholic family who helped disguise them as labourers, the conspirators were captured on 14 August. It was all over.

Found guilty of treason the group were executed over two days in September on a gallows set up on St Giles' Fields, near Holborn (now Lincoln's Inn Fields). The usual disgusting procedure then took its course. Each man was taken by hurdle (a type of sled) to the place of execution. There they gave last speeches and even engaged with vociferous ministers who harangued them. They were then hanged, cut down whilst still breathing and laid on a table where the executioner cut off their penises and disembowelled them. They were then cut in four, the pieces preserved in pitch to be displayed as trophies in London and across the country in a vicious war of nerves. So violent was the death of John Savage, who was fully conscious when ripped open, that even Elizabeth was shocked.

The death of Mary, Queen of Scots in 1587 shifted Catholic hopes and made them more feverish. Mary's connection with France and with Catholicism had made her a double danger to the government; after her death this double threat was renewed in a slightly altered form. The English exiles who had pinned their hopes on Mary now had to look elsewhere. Two possible contenders, Henry Percy, Earl of Northumberland and Lord Strange (Ferdinando Stanley, later Earl of Derby), neither of whom encouraged this unwanted attention, now provided the focus for the hopes of exiles like Edward Kelley, a necromantic occultist and Catholic fanatic sequestered in Prague, member of a group including Sir William Stanley, commander of an 'English' regiment in the service of Spain, Hugh Owen, the Welsh 'intelligence' agent, the English Jesuit leader Robert Persons and many others who were now in the Low Countries passing intelligence to Madrid. No wonder, wrote Sir Robert Cecil (Lord Burghley's son), that 'The Queen is out of quiet, with her foreign foes and home broils'.

She certainly had cause to be concerned, for the Spanish threat was no paper tiger. With assurances of a home-grown rebellion and the promise of military assistance from the English regiments in Spanish pay, Philip II was already contemplating the vast and disastrous combined operation known to the English as the Spanish Armada. This was no adventure but an extraordinary invasion plan, mustering the largest invasion fleet since the Romans. If it had succeeded, as Protestants long remembered, the flames of Smithfield would have been rekindled and the annihilation of the Church of England and all non-Catholic groups would have followed.

In all the tedium of Elizabethan petty intrigue there was always something real at stake. It could never be forgotten that although the vast majority of recusants, crypto-Catholics and closet Catholics were peaceful, loyal and affectionate towards Elizabeth there were vast areas of the Palatinate of Durham, Lancashire and Wales that were almost totally unreformed and potential areas of sedition and rebellion. London was 'full' of foreigners who threatened trade and worse, threatened the very heart of the state, the Queen herself. The fear of a coup d'état was ever present.

In 1587 an Irishman, Michael Moody, had plotted to put gunpowder under Elizabeth's bed. The plot was already crawling with government agents. Catholic plots were always crawling with government agents and the failure of the Babington Plot in 1586, although striking a cautionary note, never fully educated Catholic plotters in the use of really sophisticated subversive techniques. Walsingham's liberal use of entrapment was so successful that it continued after his death using the same small group of agents.

One plot almost stands for all, in its ruthlessness and connivance and in its success in raising Catholic hopes only in order to trap the plotters in webs of deceit from which there could be no escape. In Prague, seat of the Holy Roman Emperor, Rudolf II, lived a tiny band of exiles. Amongst them was Richard Hesketh, who had come over in 1589. He was sent to England via Hamburg by Sir Edward Kelley to deliver a secret letter to Ferdinando Stanley, in which the plans for a coup d'état were revealed. Derby, appalled, handed Hesketh over to the authorities when he read the letter. He had no need to fear: the government already knew the contents because Robert Cecil's people had forged it initially. Hesketh had, like an unwitting drug courier at airport customs, accepted a sealed note, not in Prague, but at the White Lion Tavern in Islington, via a 'boy of the house'. For his trouble Hesketh was hung and quartered at St Albans and another file could be closed.

Despite the apparent unruliness of London's common people there was far less rioting and disturbance than might be supposed from watching too many Elizabethan plays. The impetus to riot was usually instigated by a discontented lord whose base never extended much beyond his immediate followers and from the aristocracy or gentry who were associated with them through family relations. Indeed, few of the common people wanted to be associated with such dangerous and high politics, a situation which was to change completely in the next century. If a monarch should lose their head in the cause of Protestantism then another must take their place and the order of the world restored.

Plots by Protestants and Catholics pepper the reigns of Elizabeth and James, none were successful and all collapsed, but in their machinations the ground of discontent shifted to religious rebellion. The political and secular manoeuvring of Mary's reign seemed to give way to religious intolerance and religion as a form of politics. This, of course, was to culminate in the Gunpowder Plot of 1605. The question of who would follow the ageing Elizabeth tested both sides of the political divide: a Catholic monarch who tolerated Catholics or a Catholic monarch who winked at Protestantism.

James VI of Scotland was favourite to inherit, but others such as Arabella Stuart and Isabella of Spain were candidates too. Either way, factions grew and one led by the Earl of Essex became a seditious movement. Robert Devereux, Earl of Essex had been a favourite of the queen, but a disastrous campaign in Ireland had ruined his reputation, although it must be said did not seem to dent his ego or ambition. Essex returned secretly to England and threw himself on the mercy of the queen who unceremoniously banished him to his London home, known as Essex House, a large complex of over forty bedrooms, picture gallery, chapel and banqueting hall which stood on the Strand and which had originally been built by the Earl of Leicester in 1575 next to the Middle Temple. It was in this rambling house that Essex would spend a year under a sort of house arrest, plenty of time to brood on his woes and the plots of his enemies. Essex now conceived a hare-brained scheme to seize power and name a new monarch which would also allow him also to destroy his arch rival at court, Robert Cecil.

To succeed Devereux would have to gather men at Essex House, arm them and prepare barricades and send to the army in Ireland to land and join him. The plan, was hatched at Drury House some time between 1600 and January 1601, and the conspirators made elaborate plans for the seizure of the Tower (the key to the City of London) and the immediate calling of a parliament. Like Cecil, Essex also employed a flock of spies and messengers. Yet Cecil's spies were more efficient than those employed by Essex and the plot was discovered. To propangandize for his cause Essex commissioned Shakespeare's *Richard II* to be played at the Globe on 7 February 1601. The point of the play, which tells the tale of the fall of a king whose advisers were corrupt, was not lost on Cecil who went to the queen and exposed the plot. Essex was summoned. He ignored the call. Enough was enough and Cecil saw this as an opportunity not to be missed, although the queen was more affectionate and understanding towards her wayward Earl, but her trust might have been tested by the fact that Essex now had three hundred armed retainers in his house and grounds and a supportive mob outside. What was going on? There was nothing for it but to send a posse of trusted men to find out.

On the 8 February, Edward Somerset, Earl of Worcester, Lord Keeper of the Seal, Thomas Egerton, the Chief Justice of the Court of Queen's Bench, Sir John Popham and Sir Thomas Knollys, the Comptroller of Her Majesty's Household went to find out what was going on. What happened next is not disputed in fact, but Essex's motives are unclear. What happened was that having invited the distinguished guests into his library (or 'back room' next to the library) Essex then locked the door behind them claiming, perhaps truthfully, but probably not, that the mob shouting 'Kill them! Kill them' showed that they intended to murder the visitors. Of course, the subtleties of English were not lost on Essex at his trial where he blamed the mob for their intentions rather than instructions to him! Clearly Essex himself had engineered the fracas and allowed the 'crowd' to swarm up the stairs in the first place. Perhaps it was his intention to scare the queen's councillors to show them he meant business; certainly they might be useful as bargaining counters. Whatever was the cause of the imprisonment, the great seal, sent to show Essex that these were messengers from the queen, was discarded.

Having locked his interlocutors in the library, Essex paraded through London whilst Cecil had his herald proclaim Essex a traitor amid scenes of much confusion. One of the Earl's supporters, William Parker, had tried to prevent the proclamation and failed only to fall or be pushed headlong into the Thames. The Earl with perhaps two hundred of his followers next appear to have gone to St Paul's Cross to hear the Sunday Sermon after which around two hundred to two hundred and twenty followers appear to have paraded though Ludgate shouting 'Murder, murder, God save the Queen!' and other oaths such as might have totally confused an onlooker as to their purpose.

The men marched to Sir Thomas Smythe's house in Fenchurch Street where Essex parleyed with Smythe who was the Sheriff of London and in charge of one thousand men of the London trained bands. Such a force might secure London. The Earl, apparently perspiring, pardoned himself for intruding and asked to change his shirt. This was a little charade to allow for what appeared a pre-arranged meeting, Smythe having secretly discussed the Earl's plans the day before. Sir William Rider, the Lord Mayor may have been in on their plans or Smythe may have been playing for time. As it was he did not hold to the agreement and slipped away by the back door as the Earl changed. Sir John Levenson led the trained bands to Ludgate and began fortifying the surroundings. All London's gates were barred. At Ludgate there was a fracas of some sort and one man (un-named in the trial transcript) was actually killed.

By the afternoon of 8 February, Essex, proud to the end, but still full of self-deluding bravado, admitted defeat without striking a blow and decamped by boat in order to return to Essex House, the house itself having already been broken into and the hostages released. Essex still had around eighty followers barricaded in the grounds who were prepared to defend it against those under the Earl of Nottingham who had surrounded the premises and whose cannon threated to reduce the house to rubble. Essex was not yet spent. He climbed defiantly on the roof and shouted at Nottingham who shouted back that his cannons were loaded and his patience was running thin. Essex came out at around ten o'clock and his followers were arrested with him. Amongst an impressive list of backers were a number of lords and earls, family members, including his sister and members of the lesser gentry. Essex also had covert support from Robert Catesby, Thomas Winter, John and Christopher Wright, Thomas Percy and Francis Tresham, Catholics all. Their far more dangerous conspiracy would have to wait a few more years until 1605.

The Earl of Essex was brought to trial in Westminster Hall on 19 February 1601 and among others on the bench sat Sir John Popham, hardly the most disinterested judge and prosecuting was the triumphant Cecil. Guarding the prisoner with forty halberdiers was Sir Walter Raleigh. Trials were a strange circus in those days with impartiality and orderly conduct unheard of. The prisoner could not cross examine and did not know the indictment until actually in front of his accusers. Essex and the others were accused of conspiring the death of Elizabeth in order to 'make war on London' and change the government. Was Essex guilty? He answered a resolute 'no' to the accusation. Essex finally had his say, but to no avail, whilst others interrupted and heckled. Even Raleigh piped up that the rebellion was 'like to be the bloodiest day's work that ever was'. It hardly added to the weight of evidence, but this was a show trial not a fair trial and the accused knew it.

The cross questioning of Cecil got Essex no further. Essex said (but not really in his defence, rather as a piece of damaging hearsay) that he had heard Cecil say to a third party that 'none on the world but the Infanta of Spain had the right to the crown of England'. This was intended as a slur to muddy Cecil's reputation. Cecil was apparently hidden in an adjacent room when he heard the comments. Cecil charged into the Court unannounced, and, falling on his knees, asked the Lord Steward that he might have leave to answer.

> For wit, wherewith indeed you do abound, I am your inferior; I am your inferior for nobility, for I am not in the rank of the prime nobility, yet noble I am; a sword-man I am not, and here-in also you go before me: yet doth my innocency protect me, and in

this court I stand an honest man, you a delinquent. Wherefore I challenge you, if you dare, openly to name that counsellor to whom I spake those words.

Cecil's reply was to demand 'name him, name him' of the third party. Essex would not give it.

As Essex awaited execution he ponderd that he had been a favourite and might be again. His wife, the Countess of Essex was persuaded to write to Cecil and the queen to plead for his life.

SIR

Althoug the awnswere I receved from you two daies since gave mee small incouragement to flatter my self that anie importunity I could make should bee able to appease the scandall you had conceaved to bee geven you by my unfortunat husband: yet hade it not pleased God to powre uppon mee one affliction after an other, and to add to the immesurable sorrowes of my harte so violent a sicknes as I am not able of my self to stur out of my bed, I had presented unto your vew the image of the importunate Widow mentinoed in the Scriptur, and had never ceased to pester you with my complaines till you had afforded me some assurance that, whatsoever respects might dehorte you from so much as wishinge my husband's good, yet that an aflicted and wofull lady should not wholly loose her labor, . . . I beseech you, that whatsoever new favor you shall now be pleased to add to the old, shall so binde mee to reverence of your vertues as I will resolve to recken my self a bankerout till I have yeelddid some demonstrative testimonie of the best thankfullnes that the honestest harte can expresse for the worthest benefitt. Honorable Sir, I know there bee private causes to discourage mee from movinge you heerin: yet, seeinge the highest providence hath placed you in a callinge mostpropper to bee a mene for my comforte, and that former experiance hath tought me that you are rather inclyned to doe good then to looke allway to private interest, I beseech you, even for your vertues sake, performe this noble oflice for mee . . . in presentinge my humblest supplication to her Majestic Bere Sir, I pray you, with theise tedious blotts from her feeble hand and sad sick harte that is stored with much thankfullnes and infinite best wishes unto you, who will ever rest Your most beeholdinge poore distressed frend.[13]

The inheritance plot of the Earl of Essex was the last great threat to the Tudors, one of a long line of plots stretching from the northern Pilgrimage of Grace in 1536 through the revolt of the northern earls in 1569, to the plots of Ridolfi, Throckmorton and Babbington. Discontent with religious and political dispensations would go deeper underground in the next reign and James would need the services of his spies and informers, perhaps more than ever.

As years and years of failed plot and counterplot frustrated Catholic hopes and aggravated Anglican and Protestant enmity, hopes for a revival of 'the Old Faith' settled on Elizabeth's successor James VI of Scotland, soon to be James I of England. He had encouraged those hopes and appeared liberal and tolerant but on his accession he had casually dashed them with his deadly remark, 'Nah, we'll no need the papists noo.' The scene was now set for the most famous and terrible of all Catholic 'adventures', the Gunpowder Plot of 1605.

The progress James made from Scotland to London for his coronation was an occasion for renewed and hopeful speculation on tolerance. The nominal Catholic figurehead, Henry Percy, Earl of Northumberland, had employed agents to sound James out. He seemed likely to acquiesce. The Act of Uniformity and Act of Supremacy of 1559 had established Anglican Protestantism during Elizabeth's reign. They required allegiance to the Crown and the demand for Church baptism. More to the point, regular Sunday attendance was compulsory, on pain of heavy fines. Non-attendees or recusants were excluded from any public office for almost fifty years. There was even an Act of 1593 forbidding convicted Catholic gentry travelling more than five miles from home. Catholic hopes looked to modify these Acts or perhaps even have them repealed. The dreadful blunder (in English Catholic eyes) of Pope Pius V, who in 1570 had issued the bull *Regnans in Exelcis* that had excommunicated Elizabeth, might now be quietly buried, or perhaps the Vatican might rethink in the light of a rapprochement with England. Even Father Robert Persons's inflammatory *Book of Succession*, published in 1595, which had argued that 'ancestry of blood' was not enough to legitimize a ruler and which therefore made it nothing less than the declaration of a fatwa on English rulers, might be quietly forgotten. There was hope in James. European and English papists felt he would be sensible and tolerant. Philip III had quietly dropped any further plans for an invasion, after another disaster in Ireland, and Acquaviva had urged English Catholics to be patient. Amazingly, although still at war with England, Spain had sent a note of congratulations on James's accession. More pertinently and much closer to home, James's own wife, Anne of Denmark, his affectionately named 'oor Annie', was a professed Catholic with a secret chapel in Somerset House in which she heard mass.

James too needed support. He was the first Scots King of England and the English loathed the Scots, especially when they arrived in numbers at the court in London and in the streets of the city.

> If the newly rich Scots were said to be greedy (as well as unwashed),
> then the attitude to the Scottish lower classes was scarcely likely

to be more enlightened. The poor Scots established a colony in Holborn known as 'little Scotland', but the prospect of immigrants huddling together did not please . . . The beggars with their hateful accent were the most resented of all . . . There were [also] gangs called Swaggerers whose speciality was to prey upon the vulnerable homeless Scots in London.[14]

When James further proposed to Parliament that from now on the island would be called Britain and its subjects 'British' in honour of the ancient Roman appellation, he was howled down by both Houses. In 1604 Parliament rejected the overture, preferring 'our mother England'. James was no fool; he needed the support of the English lords, and with a sense of pragmatism aligned himself with the Protestant ascendancy. In addressing English bishops James commanded that they act with 'a new diligence' against recusants as previously he had declared his 'utter detestation' of the 'Catholic superstition'. On 24 April 1604 a Bill was introduced into Parliament with the intention of outlawing Catholicism once and for all. James would brook no dissent, either from Catholics or from Puritans.

Such an unequivocal line seemed to dash all Catholic hopes, but these had divided before James's pronouncements. Many Catholics had decided that their allegiance to their family religion could be reconciled with their allegiance to the demands of nationality. There were, of course, many Catholic peers and gentry who went along with the status quo as needs dictated. Some great Catholics carried on as if little had changed since Queen Mary's day. Magdalen, Viscountess Montague was one such person who, despite her known affiliations, was favoured by Elizabeth and left alone. So was an un-named 'great' household in Southwark. Others 'happily' swore allegiance and went to church and held office but said mass at home in private. This was an 'honest' compromise for many including the authorities.

The Oath of Supremacy, which acknowledged Elizabeth and now James as Head of the Church of England, nevertheless directly brought up the question of patriotism. The question was stark, King and Country or Pope and Papacy. This has been formulated into the infamous 'Bloody Question' put to prisoners of conscience: 'Whose side would you take if the Bishop of Rome [the Pope] . . . should invade the realm with an army?' The question appeared in disguised form during the 1990s when politician Lord (Norman) Tebbit asked of immigrant families which cricket team they would support should England face Pakistan, India or the West Indies. The racism of the latter question echoed the terror of the former but only the former led directly to execution.

It was the question of patriotism, set out in the most dreadful black and white in the Bloody Question but otherwise fudged or avoided, that polarized patriotic Catholics. One group, probably the vast majority, became 'Appellants' who hoped to create a tolerated *patriotic* Catholicism which would have government approval. Their leader was the 'Arch-Priest', Father George Blackwell. The Appellant wing of English Catholicism believed that James was the lawful monarch and pledged their loyalty to him. On the other side were those who believed that patriotism only began with the restoration of the old religion and that Persons' book had provided the theoretical and theological justification for this position. Assassination and rebellion became the perverse obsession of such unconvinced patriotic Catholics who gathered in the ranks of Sir William Stanley's 'English' regiment in the Spanish Netherlands.

There had already been plots enough. One had been designed to keep James prisoner in the Tower until he relented his hard line against the Catholics. The plot was intended to destroy the real enemy, Robert Cecil. This plot was called 'the Treason of the Bye', just as the next was designated 'the Treason of the Main', a plot to put Lady Arabella Stuart on the throne by killing James and his family, which, of course, again ended in failure and the block. Some of the plotters such as Sir Walter Raleigh were reprieved but the Catholic priests involved were executed. Father Henry Garnet, who had hoped for tolerance, called the whole affair of 'the Bye' 'imprudent folly', the arch-priest George Blackwell forbade patriotic Catholics to join in with any attack on the legitimate government and even the Pope reprimanded his English co-religionists.

One patriot, long in the service of Spain and an ensign in Stanley's regiment, was the ill-fated Guy Fawkes. Fawkes was tough and loyal, tall and red-headed with a thick beard and moustache. Fawkes's family were not outwardly Catholic but he had been schooled at York in the company of others who would help him form the famous 'Powder Plot', as contemporaries called it. Antonia Fraser has called him a 'warrior-monk', a dedicated soldier for Catholicism who preferred a Spanish name to his own, now calling himself Guido. Fraser also suggests he fits the concept of a modern terrorist: idealistic, utterly convinced, acting by faith, daring and unconcerned for self. In the name of the cause Fawkes had tried to convince Spanish officials that England was ripe for rebellion and he may certainly have received encouraging noises from Spain's own intelligence services hoping to stir up trouble at no extra cost.

Fawkes was working on behalf of a terrorist group that had gathered around the charismatic Robert Catesby, who had been born in Warwickshire the son of a family at the centre of English Catholic intermarriage. He was connected to the Throckmortons and Anne Vaux, whose houses (including White Webbs in Enfield) were safe havens for Jesuit priests. Catesby recruited Tom Wintour, Thomas

Percy, Fawkes himself and Jack Wright, who agreed to meet at the Duck and Duke Tavern in the Strand on 20 May 1604.

> The proposition put by Catesby was simple and it was blood curdling. A scheme would be devised to blow up 'the Parliament House with gunpowder' in order to destroy the King and his existing government . . . 'In that place . . . have they done us all the mischief'.[15]

To accomplish their ends the plotters had a plan to capture James's nine-year-old daughter Princess Elizabeth and bring her from the Midlands to a London coronation. How they might justify the murder of her father was not discussed. The Regent would be Northumberland. He could explain.

Further recruits included Jack's brother Christopher 'Kit' Wright, Robert Keyes and Thomas Bates. Keyes was to take charge of Catesby's house in Lambeth whilst Thomas Percy, recently promoted as a gentleman pensioner, could now justify taking a small property within Westminster itself – a honeycomb of buildings and rooms used for official and private purposes and often rented out. Another member, John Grant, was recruited on Lady Day (25 March) 1605, when the plot was outlined to all the gang's members. All were friends or related by marriage or kinship. The conspirators went their separate ways, having ordered new Spanish swords for the day of the coup. The blades were decorated with 'the Passion of Jesus' for fighters in the holy cause. The stage was set.

Every school child used to be familiar with the scene that follows: a desperado with a curling Vandyke moustache, black-hatted with brim pulled down over his eyes, black-cloaked with the collar swept up across his chin, fuse in hand, surprised by guards at the eleventh hour – the classic stage villain in the classic Gothic cellar. Fawkes would set the seal on the moustache-twirling villain, his 'look' and pose the very essence of every spy and secret agent, every bombmaker and assassin, every black-coated villain.

The picture is not quite like that. John Whynniard's 'cellar' was actually on the ground floor, a vaulted room above which sat the Lords. It was one of a number of commercial premises at Westminster, which included wine cellars, warehousing, bakeries, taverns and booksellers amongst a host of privately owned or rented parts of the Palace area. Prostitutes strolled the grounds. In this building Fawkes and the others packed thousands of pounds of surplus gunpowder, constantly increasing the amount as the damp atmosphere caused it to deteriorate. Fawkes now had an alias – John Johnson.

Robert Cecil, Earl of Salisbury had not lost his grip on the intelligence service that he inherited from Walsingham and his own father.

Spies had reported that Hugh Owen was helping Spain organize an invasion for 1605 and an agent called 'Captain' William Turner had already picked up on the activities of Fawkes in Flanders. The government were therefore aware of rumours of a 'plot' as early as the late spring of 1605.

Others also had wind of the plot. Catesby had confessed to Father Oswald Tesimond and he had done so under seal of the confessional to Father Henry Garnet, and, kicking his heels before the conflagration, given a veiled warning to Viscount Montague on 15 October during a meeting outside the Savoy, but the most disastrous leak was contained in a letter delivered to William Parker, Lord Monteagle during the evening of 26 October at his home in Hoxton.

> My Lord, out of the love I bear to some of your friends, I have a care of your preservation. Therefore I would advise you, as you tender your life, to devise some excuse to shift of your attendance at this Parliament; for God and man hath concurred to punish the wickedness of this time. And think not slightly of this advertisement, but retire yourself into your country [county] where you may expect the event in safety. For though there be no appearance of any stir, yet I say they shall receive a terrible blow this Parliament; and yet they shall not see who hurt them. This counsel is not to be condemned because it may do you good and can do you no harm; for the danger is passed as soon as you have burnt the letter. And I hope God will give you the grace to make good use of it, to whose holy protection I commend you.[16]

Monteagle was married to Catesby's first cousin and he knew many of the others involved. The letter, of course, was a forgery, produced as *concrete* evidence of a plot of which Salisbury and others were already fully aware. The letter was written by either Monteagle or a crony but the traitor in the group who supplied the information was never traced. Thomas Ward, Monteagle's servant and a close relative of the Wrights, tipped off Catesby at White Webbs as Monteagle tipped off Salisbury at Whitehall. Monteagle, once imprisoned for his part in the abortive Essex Rebellion of 1601, needed the money from the reward. He was duly paid. Catesby, forewarned in Enfield, nevertheless decided to continue and made his way to the Midlands.

Salisbury now had a private audience with James in which he showed him the letter. James read it twice in silence and ordered that his loyal head of secret police (and the Tudor and Stuart states were 'police states' in the most modern sense) to act. A watch was placed on the Houses of Parliament, as Guy Fawkes was himself handed a watch by his co-conspirators to time his fuses. Meanwhile, Thomas

Percy visited Henry Percy, Earl of Northumberland at his house at Syon, wilfully or foolishly laying a trail to the premier peer, upon whom Catholic hopes continued to centre. Almost like a scene from a spy novel, Sir Thomas Kneweth, Privy Councillor and Justice of the Peace, and a band of soldiers surprised a man in a 'cloak and dark hat' at midnight in Whynniard's cellar. The man looked a 'desperate fellow'. Warrants were issued for the other conspirators.

Things now went from bad to worse. Tom Wintour's inquisitive reconnoitre in Westminster later that day confirmed that the plot was discovered – it was already common rumour. Catesby and the others were now on the road to Dunchurch near Coventry, not far from Ashby St Legers, Catesby's home, and near Coombe Abbey, where Princess Elizabeth, James's daughter, was to be kidnapped. These conspirators were now being hunted by the local posse comitatus. Exhausted by the chase, the gang rendezvoused at another country house at Holbeach on the road to Shrewsbury, where their fortunes worsened when they were blown up by gunpowder that had been carelessly set near a fire to dry! There were serious injuries.

Holed up at Holbeach. The major conspirators, injured, tired, scared but resolute, awaited the arrival of the Sheriff's posse. Two hundred men surrounded the house and grounds and laid siege to the inmates who in the fashion of a classic Western movie charged out with pistols and rapiers only to be shot down in a hail of bullets. The wounded were hauled off to London, the dead ritually decapitated, their heads needed as trophies. On 7 November, the Earl of Northumberland was put under arrest. Conspirators, suspects and convenient victims were now ruthlessly hunted down by the posses, military and priest-takers sent to find them. Ports were closed and the gates of London temporarily sealed. The conspirators and their associates suffered the usual judicial and bloody massacre, their heads displayed on London Bridge on specially commissioned ironwork spikes.*

---

*The display of heads and body parts remained central to governmental policy towards traitors. Such trophies were first covered in tar or boiled in salt to preserve them from birds and the elements and then suitably arranged on the city gates, at the Tower, Westminster or London Bridge. Temple Bar, which formed an arch on Fleet Street and marked the western limit of the City, was used from 1684, its first victim being Sir Thomas Armstrong. The heads of the Rye House plotters were displayed here also. The final victim was Francis Townley, executed as a Jacobite rebel in 1746. Telescopes could be hired to view the remains. A pillory also stood nearby and both Daniel Defoe and Titus Oates spent time in it.

Despite Appellant leaders begging their followers to be patient and *loyal* it was a time of unmitigated pressure and hostility.

> As these disabilities multiplied, Catholics could no longer prac-
> tise law, nor serve in the Army or Navy as officers (on pain of a
> hundred pounds fine). No recusant could act as executor of a will
> or guardian to a minor, nor even possess a weapon except in cases
> of self-defence. Catholics could not receive a university degree,
> and could not vote in local elections ... nor in Parliamentary
> elections . . .
>
> In 1613 a bill was introduced into the House of Commons to
> compel Catholics to wear a red hat (as the Jews in Rome did) or
> parti-coloured stockings (like clowns did), not only so that they
> could be easily distinguished, but also so they could be 'hooted at'
> whenever they appeared.[17]

The ancient celebratory bonfires lit over many centuries on special occasions now had a totem worthy of the blaze. From now on 'Guys' and 'Popes' would fizzle and burn to a background of fireworks, cakes and ale. Every year 5 November would become a day of fun and celebration and the regular search of Parliament for insurgents and dynamiters would itself become a pleasant excursion before a glass of fine port.

4

Free-Born John

Levellers, Fifth Monarchy Men and the Peace Women

For almost 150 years Catholics in London lived in the hope that the British Isles could be returned to the Catholic faith, either by inclination or by force. In this regard they were utopian traditionalists but they were not deluded utopians. The establishment of the Church of England always left open the possibility of reconciliation with Rome. The Established Church retained many 'Roman' features especially regarding vestments, organization and liturgy. Splits over the Eucharist were capable of being healed. Yet Queen Mary's disastrously blood-filled purge had alienated many intelligent people and the excommunication of Queen Elizabeth had been politically disastrous, leading to plots and counterplots, not all of which were products of Walsingham's fevered brain.

Puritanism, the other dissident expression of Christian Englishness, represented an equally problematic version of change. In Puritanism were to be found the roots of the spirit of republicanism and an obstinate renunciation of the state and the established Church. Unlike Catholicism, which looked back to a recent historical tradition based on a strong universal authority, Puritans looked to a future of freedom of faith and local communal autonomy. Just as Catholicism represented a spectrum of opinion from quietist assimilation to outright rebellion, so Puritans included those who accepted the laws and government of England to those who wished to sweep away the King, lords and all. Puritan freedom was predicated on a future in which pre-Conquest liberties would be 'restored' and a 'primitive' Christian commonwealth established awaiting the Final Days. For some these would be imminent, for others more patience might be needed, and according to one or other Puritan group (for there were a large number) individuals might participate in the Second Coming either by faith or by good works.

Puritanism and Protestantism generally might choose to trace a history back to the Lollard artisans of the fifteenth century who gathered in barns to listen to William Wycliffe's English translation of the Bible and to sing psalms, but they more consistently chose to focus on the horrors of the Marian persecution. Completed by John Foxe in 1563 and originally printed in a Latin edition of eighteen hundred folio pages were the recorded lives and last words of the Protestant martyrs. Foxe's book recorded the 'great persecutions and horrible troubles that have been wrought and practised by the Romish prelates, specially in this realm of England and Scotland, from the year of our Lord 1000 unto the time now present'.

The book, soon commonly renamed *Foxe's Book of Martyrs*, became the secular bible of English Protestantism carried around the world by merchants, adventurers, preachers and laymen. Sir Francis Drake even whiled away the hours on tedious journeys colouring in the woodcuts. Henry VIII, Protestant that he now had become, still insisted on the Six Articles of 1539 that maintained many Catholic tenets and he still upheld the right to burn Catholics and Puritans with even-handed disinterest. It was Henry's agents who had secured the arrest and return of the Bible translator, William Tyndale, and it was Henry who considered Tyndale's acts heresy, blasphemy and treason and had him burnt at the stake in 1536. Every word translated by 'Puritans' or their allies into the vernacular was a direct threat to the established order of Church and state, whose control of such matters had to be absolute. Democracy of religious interpretation was not only heretical but a gateway to the loosening of social control, to political democracy and to anarchy. Nearly 100 years after Henry's death, Sir Thomas Trevor, one of the principal judges of England, could still hold as an absolute principle of the English constitution that 'a democratical government was never in this Kingdom'. It was Catholic Mary Tudor, 'Bloody' Mary, whose reign crystallized for ever the heroic martyred history of Dissent and of the Puritan mind. Marriage to Philip II of Spain and Church reconciliation with Rome sealed the fate of Dissenting Protestantism and those of the 'singular sort' either emigrated, went under cover or were caught.

In 1556, thirteen Protestants were burned at Stratford to the east of the City; a woodcut shows the crowd agitated and concerned. A congregation in Islington was surprised and many of its members arrested and later burned at Smithfield and at Brentford. Thomas Thomkins, a weaver, was burnt at Smithfield on 16 March 1555 after Bishop Bonner had failed to get a recantation even after burning Thomkins's hands over candles. Burning was the fate of people like William Wiseman, a cloth worker, Nicholas Hall, a bricklayer, Christopher Wade, a linen weaver, George Takerfield, a cook and others such as John Rogers or Edward Allen, a miller, burnt at Maidstone.

Among the elect it was noticeable that the laity provided most of the martyrs. Besides five bishops and twenty-one divines, one contemporary lists the victims as follows: 'eighty-four artificers, an hundred husbandmen, servants and labourers, twenty-six wives, twenty widows, nine virgins, two boys and two infants . . . Sixty-four more were persecuted for their profession of faith; whereof seven were whipped, sixteen perished in prison, twelve were buried in dunghills'.[1]

Mary's death in 1558 terminated the massacre, thus leaving to following generations one of English Protestantism's greatest symbols – the burning funeral pyres of Smithfield, emblematic of 'papish' tyranny and the martyrdom of *ordinary* English men and women who kept the faith. Despite the growing tolerance of Elizabeth's reign and the careful compromise of the Stuarts, the image of intolerance conjured up in the flames of Smithfield soon came to stand for the loss of English liberties, both of conscience and of political autonomy, which successive regimes seemed to threaten. The smell of burning flesh was the perfume of tyranny. From then on the martyrdom of extreme Dissenters became proof of the truth of the cause, the rightness of self-conviction and of 'election' endlessly debated and scrutinized in order to effect the one true point of existence.

A Puritan congregation did not merely passively hear the sermon, they devoured it like holy bread. Many brought notebooks so they could write down the text. They looked up the preacher's prooftexts in their own Bibles and folded the pages for discussion after dinner. In order to take down the sermon some used the art of shorthand. Timothy Bright, a country clergyman, published his *Characterie* in 1588, which became the first textbook of shorthand to be used widely. Preachers soon observed that women were much faster at shorthand than men, and one even rebuked the ladies in his congregation who had boasted about their superior deftness.[2]

It was this certainty of doubt that upset the established order and frightened its adherents, and it was Puritan refusal to conform that enraged them. Equality in doubt made everyone equally vulnerable and reduced everybody to ordinary mortality. This 'levelling' principle saw no natural preordained right in the alliance of Church and state or such a right in the hierarchy of the 'social orders'. The Puritan Levellers would take an essentially theological message and by degrees secularize it and turn it into a *political* creed of natural and civil rights. The declaration of the Commonwealth in 1649 seemed briefly to Leveller and Puritan an opportunity to eradicate for ever the smell of Smithfield cremation.*

The belief in a divinely ordered universe was certainly important for the seventeenth century, pervading every level of society: 'a chain of reciprocal authority and obedience joined King to humblest labourer in a series of interlocking hierarchies . . . to tamper with any of these hierarchies was to threaten them all, to invite confusion and social disintegration'. Charles I could see his role as nothing other than divinely ordained and the idea went deep into the psyche of the English. The strong sense of order and hierarchy also allowed for ways to let off steam, and this was especially true of local ritual and entertainment. Even though saints' days had effectively vanished with the passing of Catholicism as the official religion many holidays and ritual toasts still clung to an ancient Catholic calendar or even more ancient 'pagan' activities 'accepted' and modified by the Church. Across the country there were all sorts of varieties of festival and feast day; there was bull-baiting and cock-fighting; mummers, jugglers and remnants of ancient processions; there were hobby horses and Morris men and maypoles; there was football and church ales. Puritans attacked licence wherever they found it, their very name becoming the byword for killjoy authoritarians.

The modernizing and reforming zeal of Puritanism paradoxically called upon the *ancient* freedoms of the eroded old English certainties. It imposed a new Protestant calendar of Guy Fawkes bonfires and celebrations marking Elizabeth's accession; highlighted salvation by faith rather than that commonly and traditionally directed through mother Church; it attacked idolatry and painted over the long-revered wall paintings, smashed the sacred stained glass and burned the rood screen that had been the outward symbols of supernatural intervention; took up a new work ethic and created a new model of universal grace in which communal hierarchy was opposed

---

*On 16 May 1649 Parliament passed the following Act.

An Act Declaring England to be a Commonwealth

Be it declared and enacted by this present Parliament, and by the authority of the same, that the people of England, and of all the dominions and territories thereunto belonging, are and shall be, and are hereby constituted, made, established, and confirmed, to be a Commonwealth and Free State, and shall from henceforth be governed as a Commonwealth and Free State by the supreme authority of this nation, the representatives of the people in Parliament, and by such as they shall appoint and constitute as officers and ministers under them for the good of the people, and that without any King or House of Lords.

by the peregrinations of the soul in search of salvation; and at the heart of this system was the concept of the 'self': blind, struggling but protected by faith alone. It was from this that there slowly grew a sense of individual liberty of rights and conscience.

Under pressure from enclosing landlords, a rapacious and centrist monarch, the growing and complex arcana of finance and the new ideology of the levelling tendencies of Protestant ideologies and Puritan sermonizers, the old English hierarchies slowly came unstuck. Nothing was left certain and 'absolute anarchy' had turned the world 'upside down', a phrase never far from the minds or pens of conservatives and traditionalists nostalgic for old certainties. The bastion of those certainties, Parliament, was now to become the crucible in which the temper of the times would be ground. Sir John Eliot, for instance, saw the strength of the King in 'the freedom of his people, to be a king of free men, not of slaves'. When Charles acted on his own authority to collect ship money without the agreement of Parliament he offended this rule. Money demanded by the King from the gentry was greeted therefore by calls for a Parliament and this was repeated by the 'middling-sort of voters' as well. Yet there were other voices too from lower down the social ladder such as the Londoner, 'the prophet Ball', who quoted scripture at his captors after preaching against Ship Money during 1626.

The concept of *deference* was central to the outward signs of hierarchic society, its collapse not merely a symbolic sign of a new age. Recent studies have shown, for instance, that electorates needed wooing in ways that had all but vanished by the nineteenth century and, what is more, there might even be some who would take the monarch himself to task. Such was the case with a letter sent by an Islington brewer, Robert Triplet, in 1629 recommending that Charles surround himself with 'good protestant' and 'commonwealth's men'. The 1640 elections were a rallying point for discussion, pamphleteering, sermons and mob oratory at all levels. At least one candidate found himself dubbed 'Robin Hood'. Thus when Charles and Archbishop Laud tried to mobilize support (especially around the mass, the liturgy and the significance of the altar) they found not merely a lack of enthusiasm but everything from simple mutiny to outward violence, riot and church desecration. By now ancient rites were too closely associated with ancient *rights* to allow a simple return to a golden past. Common rights were now also Protestant rights usurped by Catholic gentlemen, conspiring priests, autocratic aristocrats and misguided monarchs. Robert Triplet's letter had warned of the dangers of the growth of toleration for Catholics and there was a growing identification of the gentlemanly sword-bearing cavalier with Catholicism itself. Against these Cavalier gentlemen stood the 'Roundhead', a term of abuse as much about class distinction as about a religious or political standpoint and one hurled about as often as cavalier. These were fixed terms of abuse by 1642.

The battered peasant's woollen cap, the Puritan's 'steeple' and the cavalier's feathered hat too played their parts in the new crisis in social hierarchy and communal belief.

> We should learn a good deal of the truth about class . . . if we could grasp the whole etiquette of hats. The first principle was that the master of the house, and no one else, had the right to wear his hat in his own home. That is why members of Parliament sat 'covered', and are still supposed to do so. The second principle was that social inferiors 'uncovered' before their superiors – a practice still recalled by the elderly rural labourer's habit of 'touching his cap'.
>
> Against this recognition of class distinctions the Quaker refusal to uncover to any man was a conscious protest. Liberal historians are apt to treat this habit of theirs as a meaningless breach of good manners, a tasteless eccentricity. On the contrary, it meant the boldest thing in social life. It was a revolutionary act. Taken over, like most of the Quaker beliefs and practices, from the Anabaptist tradition, it was an affirmation of human equality, a revolt against class.[3]

The fight between Parliament and King in the Civil War also produced a third group, aligned to neither Cavalier nor Roundhead. This group slowly grew in importance as the war (and the uneasy peace) destabilized English society. Its leader was John Lilburne and its 'party' was called the Levellers. Lilburne was born the son of a County Durham family with connections at court and a second home in the Palace at Greenwich. Whilst his family had land and money, John, a junior member, always had to earn a living and spent his often interrupted working life (for most of it he was in prison) trying to make ends meet manufacturing soap and brewing ale in Southwark. He was not particularly good at either. He never forgot, however, that he was no mere tradesman. 'I am the Sonne of a Gentleman, and my friends are of rancke and quality,' he would insist.

Lilburne's London was a thriving and vibrant city. Its 250,000 inhabitants sprawled across five miles of land on the north bank of the Thames and three on the south. Ferries transported those who could not cross by London's single bridge, and 3,000 watermen (the seventeenth-century taxi drivers) made a living on the river. The wharves were packed with every sort of import and export and ships docked many deep awaiting lightermen to take off their goods. In the east, the old City now joined Westminster by numerous roads and

Charing Cross was no longer an isolated village oasis.* Downstream across the water at Bankside the theatres plied their trade; upstream Westminster Palace sprawled from Charing Cross and a new great building, the Banqueting Hall, was being finished by Inigo Jones. Towards modern Victoria there were still fields; fields still graced Old Ford and Stratford to the east as they did in Moorfields, Clerkenwell and away to Hampstead or Islington, but at the heart of the old City was a maze of buildings, streets and alleys full of the hubbub of Europe's greatest city.

Beyond St Paul's spread the City, a narrow huddle of streets, busy with trade and commerce, wealthy and self-contained. It was still a medieval city, and outside the main thoroughfares the streets were unfit for the passage of carriages, and very unpleasant for walkers. They were mostly unmade, there were few paved foot-ways, down the centre of all but the most important streets ran the kennel which took all waste water and refuse. Sewage disposal was elementary, and often the City's defensive ditch, just

---

*The London village of Charing sat between the City and Westminster and was marked at its extreme western edge by the 'Eleanor' Cross removed to make way for the equestrian statue of Charles I which still marks the meeting of Charing Cross Road and Whitehall and where Oliver Cromwell had his town house. To the east, the great houses of the nobility looked towards the Thames, yet one by one Bedford House, Arundel House, and York House, with their elegant waterfront stairs and private barges, fell into disrepair, were partitioned or redeveloped. Only Somerset House survived, as did the Duke of Buckingham's water stairs at York House. Modern roads recall many of the older palaces and many houses still hark back to the seventeenth century when Pepys lived on the waterfront. In their place arose the elegant and highly fashionable 'Adelphi', built by the Adam brothers as a speculation and soon home to many of London's celebrities, including Samuel Johnson, Sir Richard Arkwright and visitors such as Benjamin Franklin. The Royal Society for the encouragement of Arts, Manufacture and Commerce (RSA) still exists housed in its original building from the 1790s, within the walls of which the Great Exhibition of 1851 was first thought up. It was here also that Charles Dickens worked as a child in the famous 'blacking' factory to the west of the Adelphi at Hungerford Stairs near Hungerford House, itself demolished to make way for Charing Cross Station outside which a new 'cross' was erected. The original complex waterfront was finally destroyed with the coming of Bazalgette's Embankment project, which destroyed the riverside terrace of the Adelphi but left the complex of wine cellars that extends under many of the buildings that still exist. Covent Garden, built by the Russell family after the Great Fire, was intended as an elegant piazza linked to the old Delphi riverside community.

outside the City walls, was the dumping place for refuse of all kinds. Insanitary, evil-smelling, plague-ridden – the coronation ceremonies of both James and Charles had been interrupted by plague – it was nevertheless a city of enormous vitality and great wealth, its population growing, its merchants becoming richer. In spite of the movement west-ward, it was still the home of many men of substance, the hub of trade and commerce, the centre of printing, publishing, preaching, of talk and discussion, and when necessary, of decisive action. Its citizens were vitally alive, conducting their business in Gresham's Exchange in Threadneedle Street, gossiping in Paul's Cathedral, thronging the innumerable churches whose spires were the most striking feature of any view of the town, clustering round Paul's Cross, rushing down the Strand for a spectacle at Charing Cross or Westminster.*,4

Here and here alone was the centre of English political life and English radicalism and it was from here that the radical message would be preached, purified and persecuted. Here too the old Church ways were under attack by Puritans, Presbyterians, Independents and every sort of heathen. 'The Established Church of England – underpaid, pluralist, absentee, inefficient where not corrupt – produced too few protests, too little effort at reform'.5

As an apprentice at the cloth wholesalers in Londonstone, Lilburne listened to radical preachers at Blackfriars, Gray's Inn or Coleman Street and the unlicensed working men like John Trendall the stonemason, Samuel How the cobbler, or Praise-God Barebones, the leather seller of Fetter Lane, who preached from their homes. His education in political ideology came from those men and their fiercely independent sense of justice. Against them stood the established Church and the Archbishop of Canterbury, William Laud, whose papist predilections hastened the Civil War. In the 1630s Laud had his work cut out keeping Puritan preachers and Independent usurpers in line. One opponent was John Bastwick, a Presbyterian preacher imprisoned in the Gatehouse of Westminster Palace whence he published scandalous attacks on Episcopalianism. There was also William Prynne and Henry Bunton, who simply would not keep quiet about Church doctrine and corruption. All three looked to heaven as they were

---

*Whitehall Palace includes the Abbey of St Peter's Cathedral and its grounds as well as Parliament and the original law courts at Westminster Hall. The palace was served by the old Monmouth Stables, Green Mews, Mews Yard and the delightfully named Dung Hill Mews (now lost under Trafalgar Square). It also stretched to Scotland Yard and the Banqueting Hall. In all, here was a complex of 2,000 rooms.

London before the Fire: Blackfriars, where Lilburne listened to radical preachers, is at the bottom. (From the 1658 map 'London' by Richard Newcourt)

pilloried, branded on the cheeks with S L ('seditious libeller') and had their ears hacked off in New Palace Yard during 1637.

Lilburne began his life as a revolutionary by importing forbidden books from Holland. He was trapped by a government spy, arrested by the Stationers' Company and finally sent to the Fleet Prison. When called before the Star Chamber, he made a stand that was to echo throughout the rest of his life and it began with the simple refusal to take the oath required of prisoners. The Oath of High Commission (a lesser procedure) had been refused by Puritans before but the Oath *ex officio* before Star Chamber had not. The oath had ecclesiastical origins that went back into the Middle Ages. Lilburne's refusal to testify on the oath meant he effectively blocked interrogatory proceedings in their initial stages before a trial could be properly convened. It was his first taste of the law and he revelled in it, using every opportunity from then on to face down his accusers with their own rules. Lilburne refused to stand in accusation against himself, demanded due process of law, demanded proper oaths and would not be faced down by the assembled Peers of Star Chamber including Laud himself – who became hysterical with anger as events proceeded. Alongside the aged John Wharton, Lilburne was found 'guilty of a very high contempt' for which he would be fined, whipped and pilloried. This was simply Christ's own passion and Lilburne knew he had won a moral victory.

> The staunch defiance of the old man and the young to this hated court elated the hearts of the London citizens. The news that John Lilburne had stood on his rights as a 'free-born Englishman' to refuse the Star Chamber oath spread like wildfire through the City, and Free-born John, as he was promptly named, immediately secured that place high in the citizens' affections which, in all the many crises of his life, brought them flocking to his assistance.[6]

This victory was essentially that of an idea, based it is true on the false assumption of a usurping Norman yoke imposed upon an Anglo-Saxon sensibility, but so powerful and heroic that even when Lilburne's name was long forgotten his ideas were already deep within that American psyche which would be the true inheritor of the lessons of the English Civil War.

Lilburne took his punishment (1,500 stripes from a three-cord whip from Fleet to Westminster) and was then pilloried where he was harangued by a 'fat lawyer' and gagged to stop his replies, blood spurting from his mouth. In jail he was looked after by an old woman called Katherine Hadley and with her help he smuggled out his libellous, seditious and rebellious pamphlets to be printed in Holland and re-imported through a network of agents. His pen never stopped and he insisted he must 'speake [his] minde freely and courageously'. His father, at the end of his tether, disowned him but Lilburne continued to send out his message of independence from the twilight world of the Fleet. The prison arrangements of the seventeenth century were quite unlike those of a modern jail, being more like a 'badly organised hostelry' with privileges freely available to the wealthy and an open regime based on bribery, which would allow inmates to smuggle in or out everything from prostitutes to seditious pamphlets. Prisoners also retained their weapons and Lilburne, who loved to argue points, was wounded in at least one brawl.

The King was also heading for a brawl. Frustrated in his plans for prayer books and Ship Money and outfaced by the Scots and his own Parliament, Charles saw clearly that his insistence on divine right meant that 'the question is not now whether a Service Book is to be received or not, nor whether Episcopal government shall be continued or Presbyterial admitted, but whether we are their King or not'. To reinforce the point Charles had the following read out in every Church at morning prayers:

> The most high and sacred order of kings is of divine right, being the ordinances of God himself, founded in the prime laws of nature, and clearly established by express texts both of the Old and New Testaments . . . For subjects to bear arms against their kings, offensive or defensive . . . is at least to resist the powers which are ordained of God; and . . . they shall receive to themselves damnation.[7]

Lilburne singled out Laud as the villain behind Charles and through Katherine Hadley put out a pamphlet which got her arrested and so inflamed the London apprentices that they marched from Moorfields to Lambeth Palace and besieged the Archbishop. Lilburne, having urged the seizure of Laud's palace, continued to incite Londoners so that during 1640 when yet another incendiary message was posted at Old Exchequer the trained bands (citizen soldiers) and artillery were mustered in St George's Fields. Something else was also happening. Contemporaries noted that 'common people' were now 'sensible of publike [sic] interest and Religion'.

After years without a Parliament, Charles sniffed the wind and called one for 1641. It was simply storing up trouble by giving official voice to his detractors. 'The People of England', declared Lord Digby, 'cannot open their ears, their hearts, their mouths, nor their purses to his Majesty, but in Parliament'.

In the hectic summer of 1641 the framework of Parliamentary supremacy was completed. Extra-Parliamentary sources of taxation were sealed up: tonnage and poundage and impositions were to be levied only with the consent of Parliament, ship money was pronounced illegal, the boundaries of forest were limited, and Lilburne had the satisfaction of seeing the Courts of Star Chamber and High Commission formally abolished on July 5, while the Councils of the North and of the Marches of Wales, resting on no positive statute, automatically ceased to function.[8]

When war broke out, Lilburne was free and alongside his two brothers joined the Parliamentarians, distinguishing himself (as did his brother Robert) and being captured and almost executed by the Royalists who, like Laud before them, thought 'Free-born John' quite 'mad'. Such madmen would be increasingly attracted to the ranks of the Eastern Association under one of its commanders, Oliver Cromwell, who had begun to create Britain's first professionally organized people's army, most of whom were from a common background of social class and religious outlook. His own regiment was filled with men who had 'sene visions and had revelations' and officered by 'common men, pore and of meane parentage, such as have filld dung carts . . . before they were captaines'. By the war's end Cromwell and Lilburne were 'bosome' friends even if Lilburne was to spend most of his time haranguing Cromwell from yet another incarceration in the Tower.

The aftermath of the fighting found little resolved. The King continued to intrigue and Parliament and the army fell to wrangling as armed groups around the country (the Clubmen) began to resist both. In Parliament the Presbyterians were now in charge and this forced the Independents into an oppositional role, one that soon earned them the name Levellers. Amongst this group were many army officers and rankers as well as Richard Overton, a successful pamphleteer writing under the name Martin Marpriest, Roger Williams, William Walwyn and John Lilburne. Freedom of the press was central to the circulation of Leveller ideas about freedom of conscience (and later republicanism), and secret presses operated in Oxford and in London. Ironically it was now William Prynne who called for the imprisonment of Lilburne as an enemy of the Presbyterian ruling elite in Parliament. Lilburne was now fighting on two fronts – against adventurer monopolies and for freedom of conscience and of printed ideas. Once again in hot water, he stood upon 'the Grand Charter of England' (Magna Carta) and demanded the privileges that 'belong to a freeman, as the greatest man in England'. If his judges were unimpressed the common people of London lapped it up. From 1645 onwards Lilburne spent longer periods in prison (in Newgate and then in the Tower) than at home or at business.

'Justice, liberty and freedom' became his watchwords, using his own situation as the exemplary instance of their terrible decay in England. Prynne found that Lilburne was an 'upstart monstrous Lawyer' and epitome of a 'meere Legend of Lies' but he was already the head of a 'seditious faction' and the 'champion' of the London crowds. By the late 1640s the army was on the brink of rebellion, Parliament was unsure what to do with the King and some of the common soldiers were starting to find a dangerous political awareness. Army councils debated at Putney and presented petitions demanding equality before the law, annual Parliaments, freedom of conscience, freedom of the press, no tithes and no monopolies. Seeing itself as the voice of the people and the symbol of all that was fought for, the New Model Army was dangerously close to becoming a revolutionary machine. Agitators (known only by number) appointed by the regiments corresponded with a secret network of Levellers in London and these in turn appeared to revolve around John Lilburne, incarcerated but defiant and still writing sedition. Called to the bar of the Lords, Lilburne merely poured out invective. 'You . . . Peeres as you are called, merely made by prerogative, and never intrusted or impowred by the Commons of England . . . Magna Charta hath justly, rationally, and well provided that your Lordships shal not sit in judgment . . . upon any Commoner of England either for life, limbe, liberty or estate.' Lilburne appealed, therefore, only to the Commons, his 'competent, proper and legall triers and Judges'. Of course he also refused to kneel to their Lordships. 'I have . . . learnt better religion and manners than to kneel to any human or mortal power . . . whom I have not offended'. Richard Overton summed Lilburne up as, 'Defendour of the Faith and of his Countries Freedoms, both by his Words, Deeds and Sufferings, against all Tyrants in the Kingdome'. When Parliament seemed on the brink of usurping the gains of what had started to look like a revolution Lilburne applauded the army's decision to march on London and purge Westminster; when Cromwell looked like becoming a dictator, Lilburne charged Parliament with bringing him to heel. 'If tyranny be resistable . . . then it is resistible in a Parliament as well as a king', he had told readers in earlier days.

Supporting Lilburne was a whole network of helpers and couriers, many of whom were millenarian in mentality and republican in spirit: Christopher Feake of Hertford, soon to become a Fifth Monarchist, a man named Trevors or Travers, Captain John White and the republican Edward Sexby. There were many others who carried on correspondence in code and used numbers instead of names. From these origins emerged the Fifth Monarchy men and women, whose political education was now taking place. Some women at least were not going to let their menfolk act alone during the years of war and civil unrest. Women challenged men in authority to debate and *to listen*. The Fifth Monarchist agitator Mary Cary, waiting impatiently for the second coming of Christ, worked with a burning zeal to create the right social reforms which would be acceptable to her Lord. These included a stamp tax toward poor relief, a national post office system and wage restraint policies: Christ, it seemed, was a true Leveller, the same spirit abiding in men and women *equally*. Cary was a true revolutionary fundamentalist, happy with the execution of Charles I as a divinely ordained act and equally happy when Cromwell occupied the City. Like other Fifth Monarchists Cary *knew* what would come next. The future was already written in the actions of the New Model Army. In her pamphlet *A New and More Exact Mappe* she had calculated the end of the world to 1701, the date of the 'Full and compleat deliverance of the Church'. By 1653 Cary was still hopeful, still awaiting the end, still prophesying, still reforming. During the same period she married a Mr Rande and vanishes from our sight.

Yet her place was taken by Anna Trapnel, a prophetess and revolutionary preacher whose booming voice, speaking from the depths of catatonic trance, proclaimed the Fifth Monarchy. Anna lived and worshipped in London at John Simpson's Baptist Chapel in All Hallows the Great in Thames Street. From here and her home in Hackney she saw visions of the Last Days and the heroic Cromwell in the glowing clothes of Gideon come to lead his people. Such visions had a strange appeal for political terrorists (as well as for most ordinary people) and Anna received invitations to 'perform' elsewhere. On her way to give her message in Cornwall at the invitation of Captain Langden during 1654 she made two mysterious stops at Windsor and Abingdon.

Captain Langden's Fifth Monarchism had already landed him in jail, as one of a band of extremists too keen to hurry on the end and too disturbing and dangerous for Cromwell's administration to ignore. By the 1650s these fundamentalist men and women were plotting a putsch against the now all-too-regal Cromwell. Trapnel's visit to Windsor allowed her to meet Christopher Feake and John Simpson, imprisoned in the castle but still urging the creation of a 'standing Army for the King of Saints'. At Abingdon there had been a secret convention of Fifth Monarchists. Asked 'whether God's people must be a bloody people?' the answer had been a unanimous 'Aye'. John Thurloe, Cromwell's spymaster, had forewarning of the plot and sent troops. As Fifth Monarchist women screamed, 'Hold on, ye Sons of Sion,' soldiers did the job of breaking up the meeting and arresting the ringleaders. It is quite conceivable that Trapnel was not merely a visionary preacher but that she was also a terrorist courier connecting the far south-west of England to the centre of power at Whitehall and helping to weave the assassination fantasies of God's chosen instruments.

Women might or might not support the revolutionary purposes of war. John Lilburne's wife Elizabeth supported her husband, petitioned Parliament on his behalf, looked after the children, kept house and fought for the cause. Elizabeth was a 'gentle woman' and she expected to be treated like one. Her colleagues, Mary Overton, Mary Prince, Katherine Chidley, spoke and published eloquently on behalf of their husbands and on behalf of their own ideas regarding separatism and freedom of conscience. Katherine Hadley helped John Lilburne in prison at the Fleet during 1638 after his vicious flogging by the authorities. She also smuggled his papers to colleagues and spread his ideas amongst holidaying Moorfields apprentices at Whitsun 1639. When the apprentices rioted the trail led back to Hadley, who found herself imprisoned in the squalor of Poultney Counter Prison. Lilburne quickly came to her defence but she languished in jail for eighteen months. In 1647, Elizabeth Lilburne herself was arrested, interrogated and imprisoned. She followed Mary Overton to jail, Overton having been imprisoned in 1646 for refusing to testify to the House of Lords, a body she and her husband believed an illegal and despotic imposition. Overton had her new baby taken from her. It died later without its mother. The armed struggle and the war of propaganda took their toll; imprisonment, anger and stoicism bred out the tender emotions and made everything taut and brittle. In 1653 John Lilburne writing to Cromwell accused the Protector of crushing Elizabeth's spirit. In the same letter it is clear John and Elizabeth, worn out by fighting others, now no longer loved each other as they used to do. The tone slowly became funereal. At the funeral of Robert Lockier, the Leveller soldier executed in 1649, women dressed in the green ribbons of the Levellers and wearing mourning black followed his coffin in one of the great political demonstrations of the age. It was also the funeral of radical hopes, Cromwell and his son-in-law Ireton now masters of the stage, their opponents dead, imprisoned or exiled.

As times turned topsy-turvy, women of all classes refused to stay silent and marched on Parliament throughout the 1640s demanding an end to war. These Peace Women with their white ribbons came from a variety of backgrounds, 'whores, bawds, oyster-women, kitchen staff women, beggar women, and the very scum of the suburbs',[9] as one acid critic observed. Above all the Irish women stood out, crying for peace and the return of their men, curious bedfellows with papist-hating gentlewomen demanding a return to the old days of King and Church.

On at least one occasion these outraged women demanded peace with menaces and gave as good as they got when the militia attempted to send them on their way. At one demonstration the women kept special lookout for the 'Roundheads', demanding that John Pym,

THE   220

Parliament of VVomen.

With the merrie Lawes by them newly
Enacted. To live in more Eafe, Pompe, Pride,
and wantonneffe : but efpecially that they might have fu-
periority and dominerre over their hufbands : with a new way
found out by them to cure any old or new Cuckolds, and
how both parties may recover their credit
and huxefly againe

London, Printed for *W.Wilfon* and are to be fold by him in
Will-yard in Little Saint Bartholomewes. 1545.

Aug: 14 — London   1646.

A world turned topsy-turvy as women refused to stay silent.
(From a contemporary pamphlet)

leader of Parliament's commitee of safety, be handed over for a 'duck-
ing' in the Thames. When the London trained bands fired blanks to
scare them they were laughed at. 'Give us Pym,' the women cried,
'so that he might be torn in pieces!' Some cavalry charged, shooting
one woman and cutting the nose off another. One old woman was
arrested brandishing a rusty sword and marched off to jail, her hands
tied for fear of the damage she might do.

On 9 August 1643 there were further violent demonstrations at
Westminster, with fighting leading to numerous deaths amongst the
'peace' demonstrators. These included the daughter of a man who
sold spectacles in a shop at the entrance to Westminster Hall, killed
by a disgruntled lover under the pretext of helping to control the
rioters of whom the daughter, it was claimed, was one. Here too, as
on every occasion, said critics, were the oyster-women, 'the sister-
hood of oranges and lemons' and the 'mealy-mouthed muttonmon-
gers'. John Milton, as others, saw the present willingness of women
to express a *public* opinion a symptom of an age gone rotten. The
rot went right up to the way Queen Henrietta Maria 'bossed' her
husband.

How great mischief and dishonour hath befallen to nations under the government of effeminate and uxorious magistrates. Who being themselves governed and overswayed at home under a feminine usurpation, cannot but be far short of spirit and authority without doors, to govern a whole nation . . . most men suspect she had quite perverted him.[10]

Extreme republicanism of spirit often led individuals towards revolutionary forms of social community based on common ownership of property and land and personal relationships based on free association. Millenarianism was both a return to primitive communism as well as premonition of pseudo-socialism. The ascendancy of the New Model Army, especially after the execution of King Charles in 1649, created powerful forces which began to fracture society. Sects and cults grew proportionally as the hopes of labourers and artisans focused on the imminent reign of Christ on earth.

Abiezer Coppe was one follower of the new Free Spirit of the age. Coppe was a Ranter, one of an increasing cult which believed that God 'is in Heaven, Earth, Sea, Hell [and] filleth all things'. This particular view included a belief that God being in everything was in each person, making every individual who believed into God's presence on earth. The attraction to the 'lower orders' was, in the eyes of the gentry, dangerous. Being God, individuals were therefore themselves all-in-all, answerable only to the demand of their own spirit and thus to their own desires. For God there could be no sin and therefore, in freeing the spirit, individuals were free to punish the body or indulge it. Much ranting was attached to the hedonism of drinking, smoking and whoring as a sign of God's grace. Such looseness of morals was as shocking as it was extraordinary.

Coppe's 'damnable and detestable opinions' horrified George Fox, one of the founders of Quakerism, when both were imprisoned together at Charing Cross. Coppe himself had been regularly imprisoned for preaching. 'Adam-style', stark naked, Coppe expressed views which affirmed 'the Free Spirit'.

The urge to apostolic poverty and public self-abasement, normally regarded as characteristically medieval, can be seen here at work in seventeenth-century England. We can also observe . . . how easily such a rejection of private property can merge with a hatred of the rich, and so – as on the Continent in earlier centuries – give rise to an intransigent social radicalism.[11]

Coppe's most significant writing (burned by the public hangman) was apocalyptic, millenarian and socially revolutionary. *A Fiery Flying Roll* was

Word from the Lord to all the Great Ones of the Earth, whom this may concerne: Being the last WARNING PIECE at the dreadful day of JUDGEMENT. For now the Lord is come to 1) Informe 2) Advise and warne 3) Charge 4) Judge and sentence the Great Ones. As also most compassionately informing, and most lovingly and pathetically advising and warning London.[12]

Filled with righteous indignation, Coppe records in this spiritual diary that he was filled with the power of prophecy after four days of hallucinatory visions, which included 'voices' with apocalyptic and revolutionary messages.

The visions and revelations of God, and the strong hand of eternall invisible almightinesse, was stretched out upon me, within me, for the space of foure dayes and nights, without intermission.
    The time would faile if I would tell you all, but it is not the good will and pleasurance of my most excellent Majesty in me, to declare any more (as yet) then thus much further: That amongst those various voices that were then uttered within, these were some, *Blood, blood, Where, where? Upon the hypocriticall holy heart, &c.* Another thus, *Vengeance, vengeance, vengeance, Plagues, plagues, upon the inhabitants of the earth; Fire, fire, fire, Sword, sword, &c, upon all that bow not down to eternall Majesty, universall love; I'le recover, recover, my wooll, my flax, my money, Declare, declare, feare thou not the faces of any: I am (in thee) a munition of Rocks, &c.*[13]

Thus armed with the 'munition' of the Lord he is finally 'ordered' to 'Go up to *London*, to *London*, that Great City' in order to 'write, write, write'. The book however that Coppe begins is turned into a 'Roll' and 'Thrust into [his] mouth' where 'it lay broiling and burning in his stomack' until 'brought forth' with the message.

Thus saith the Lord, *inform you, that I overturn, overturn, overturn*, And as the Bishops, Charles, and the Lords, have had their turn, overturn, so your turn shall be next (ye surviving great ones) by what Name or Title soever dignified or distinguished, who ever you are, that oppose me, the Eternall God, who am UNIVERSALL Love, and whose service is perfect freedome, and pure Libertinisme . . .[14]

God, the great Leveller, has filled him with 'a little spark of transcendent, transplendant, unspeakable glory' that is 'meat and drink to an Angel (who knows none evill, non sin)' now free to 'sweare a full mouth'd oath'. In Southwark, he tells us, 'I am about my act, my strange act, my worke, my strange work, that whosoever hears of it, both his ears shall tingle. I am confounding, plaguing, tormenting nice, demure, barren *Mical* with *Davids* unseemly carriage, by skipping, leaping, dancing, like one of the fools, vile, base fellows, shamelessely, basely, and uncovered too, before handmaids'.

Coppe was clearly an eccentric, but no one, not even his detractors, thought him mad. They thought him dangerously subversive, his thoughts and actions prototypes for later mystical individuals like William Blake or movements like the hippies of the 1960s. Moreover, Coppe had a charismatic personality, which conveyed in action as much as word a new and frighteningly unrestrained individualism – a mirror-image Puritan. After a lifetime of bizarre antics and regular imprisonment Coppe recanted (many thought this a cover) and settled down to practise physic at Barnes under the name Dr Higham. He died in 1672, a man at once out of his time, yet absolutely of his time, for he represented one small part of a whole gamut of religious views and political attitudes which changed later generations' ideas about the nature of the individual and their relationship to the state and to private property. Coppe's pathological desire to 'sweare', against which he 'set a strict guard' until he was twenty-seven, is suggestive of psychological problems which were released as political and religious views once he became a Ranter. Coppe's constant self-vigilance was the psychological cost of religious Puritanism.

The sudden appearance of growing numbers of itinerant preachers, religious charismatics, prophesying women and poor Ranters was certainly not only a phenomenon of town life. It was, if anything, a rural and village problem as small revolutionary groups tramped the countryside or settled in the less inhabited corners of the outskirts of London. The problem such people posed for the local gentry could be acute and induce almost pathological fear. Writing to his friend Francis Manley, in 1666, Henry Eyton could not resist mentioning his fears regarding the 'fanatic party' lurking in the hamlets and glades of the Essex and Hertfordshire borders with the capital, such areas having immediate and relatively easy access to the City and Westminster as London relentlessly spread north and north-eastward.

> We have a restless enemy amongst us . . . I mean the whole fanatic party, the head of which serpent lies in and near London especially upon the confines of Essex and Hertfordshire . . . taking either side of the Ware river from Edmonton down to Ware and particularly those retired places of Epping Forest and Enfield Chase . . . About the road near Theobalds there is a crew of them lie concealed . . . that should there be the least commotion in London we should find to our cost that they would be too ready to second it.[15]

The complex political and religious antagonisms of the war and then the Protectorate were far from confined to the radical publishers and jail inmates of London. Revolutionary ideas and libertarian views spread rapidly across the country through pamphlets, hearsay, travellers and discharged soldiers, some of whom had debated their radical ideas with the grandees of the army. By the late 1640s, even the most extreme views had reached the area now covered by the outer London boroughs. They were of particular importance to the inhabitants of Enfield in North London, where combined with disputes over land ownership they were to produce tragic results.

Enfield Chase was an ancient royal hunting ground some nine miles outside London to the north. Its many acres comprised arable and grazing land as well as a deer park and over the years legal agreements with tenants of the royal estate had granted rights of common such as grazing and wood collecting, which were of great importance to the local economy in an area with a very high rate of poverty, not that such rights benefited the very poor, who were unlikely to be commoners paying rents and taxes. The chase was surrounded by villages and hamlets; Edmonton and Tottenham were close by and the largest was Enfield. There were also estates, manors and farms as well as large mansions and lodges. Small rural communities existed at South Mimms, Hadley, Potters Bar and along the road from Southgate to Cockfosters. Barnet provided the nearest significant town although London was only a day away.

Digger groups soon appeared in both Barnet and Enfield. The Diggers were an extreme group of Levellers, communistic in outlook and shadowy in membership, who had formed around the political activist Gerrard Winstanley. Small groups began digging up common land for squatter communes. Their first venture was St George's Hill, Weybridge but other colonies also appeared elsewhere, to the consternation of locals. Such communities, although very small, were strange and disruptive. They were also made up from the very poor and thus represented a threat to social order and local tradition, as many Diggers were apparently from squatting families who had come to the Chase during the war and just after. They may even had had a blind eye turned to them by Parliament, hoping to disrupt traditionalist opponents of the new regime. Either way, rioting certainly occurred during the Digger occupancy although we do not know if Diggers were involved with the disturbances. It is quite likely they were as local patience ran out. Accused of killing deer and of assault, fifteen men, including a furrier, cordwainer, weaver, butcher and group of labourers, were indicted for the disturbances. These men were almost certainly recently discharged soldiers as all had access to firearms; they also represented the poorest of the area.

The trouble with the Diggers was the least concern for commoners. After the execution of King Charles in 1649, royal lands and property had come up for sale and in the next ten years many areas once owned by the royal family were parcelled out. This was of great importance to the Chase, where commoners on the royal hunting ground had dealt with a relatively untroublesome absentee landlord. Now, under the Protectorate, the land was to be effectively parcelled up and sold. Commissioners had drawn up a scheme based on surveys carried out in 1650, 1656, 1657 and 1658, and in 1659, half the roughly 8,000 acres came up for sale. Locals, seeing the annihilation of long-held rights, were outraged, more so that the grandees of the army were grabbing what they could, men like Adjutant-General John Nelthorpe, Colonel Webb, who was the Surveyor General himself, and the audacious Colonel Joyce, who had seized the King for Parliament. Left with what they considered poor pasture, infertile soil and barren waste, the inhabitants took action by destroying fencing and allowing their cattle to graze the new owners' crops. Troops were called to restore 'order', but after drinking heavily (according to the commoners) they abused and attacked the locals.

The end result of the continuing troubles at Enfield was a pitched battle between local yeomen, yeomen's wives and farm labours and an opposing force of soldiers sent under a sergeant to restore 'order'. The result was a chaotic and very violent confrontation. A pamphlet recording the incident tells the tale.

> An officer of the army having purchased some certain Lands thereabouts, the country people pretend an incroachment upon their Common; and thereupon put many cattle upon his ground, to the great detriment and spoil of corn, which was lookt upon as a great offence and high trespass; insomuch, that thirty private soldiers were selected forth of Colonel Sydenham's Regiment of Foot, viz. Three out of each company by order and command from a superiour officer; the sole command whereof was impowered upon a sergeant of the said regiment: who . . . marched to the place appointed, to secure the corn and grain; but instead of forcing out the cattle in a peaceable and quiet manner, they received a great assault from the country, who fell upon them both with pitch-forks, long sythes, axes, and the like, being about eight score in number, with such inveterate fury and violence, that the soldiers (being but 15 in number, and separated from the rest) were forced to retreat; but ten of them immediately rallying, disputed the place from twelve of the clock till towards one; i3n which desperate conflict, many were wounded, amongst the rest the afore-named Sergeant who commanded the Party, who was run through the thigh with a half-pike, cut in the head, and wounded in the body; so that falling to the ground, the rest being very much cut and wounded, yielded, having neither powder

nor bullet left to defend themselves; and being so mightily over-powered, were made incapable of any further resistance: So that this bloody conflict being ended, a Guard was put upon the prisoners, till they had cleared the field of the dead bodies, which is said to be two men and one woman of the country-mens side; besides many wounded; and one soldier, the Sergeant was carried off in a chair, but in a dying condition. After which, the nine soldiers were guarded up to London, with their wounds bleeding, and on Monday night left committed to Newgate, where they remained in the Dungeon all night, until Tuesday morning about eight of the clock they were removed from thence to the common-side, where Mr Harris the surgeon repaired to dresse them. To which place, divers of the Officers resorted to know the cause, and a Troop of horse is sent to Enfield to secure and bring to London the chief Fomenters and Ringleaders of this high insurrection.[16]

So horrible do these events appear to the pamphlet's author that he concludes that left to their own devices such people as the commoners of the Chase would finally revert to the cannibalism of the Ancient Britons!

To further confuse the issue the soldiers had probably been volunteers paid an extra sixpence per day to defend the property rights of one of the army's resident officers. The country people had set up banners and declared for 'Charles Stewart', defending ancient liberties against the freedom of the property market. On Enfield Chase, ancient rights and liberties came into direct conflict with the new world of contract and finance, and the new sense of the liberty of the person (in conscience, in business, and in politics) conflicted with settled traditions of feudal loyalty, natural order and sense of place. The conflicts engendered by these attitudinal differences were echoed many years later by writers like William Cobbett in his defence of English traditions *and* liberty but even then these antagonisms were not easily reconciled and they reverberate to the present day in the division between town and country exemplified by the BSE and foot and mouth crises of the late twentieth and early twenty-first centuries, and the haulage and hunting lobbies that led to the formation of the Countryside Alliance.

The events of Enfield Chase focused the mind of local republican gentry, men like William Covell of Bulls Cross at the edge of the Chase, an area where 50 per cent of the population were impoverished even by seventeenth-century standards. Covell considered himself a preacher. His antinomian views held that individuals could be saved by grace alone and that this set them free from both the usual and the conventional moral and civil laws. Such believers considered themselves unanswerable to the institutions of the Church as their moral being was unanswerable to the state. This brought him into direct conflict with Cromwell when he expressed his radical, and dangerously 'anarchic' views in front of the General. Finally, Covell found himself court-martialled and dismissed but he continued to preach and publish.

Covell's views were a mixture of extreme individualism and republican constitutionalism. He looked to the army to establish the Commonwealth, and Parliament to uphold the liberty of the individual as the 'people's representatives'. This peculiarly potent Puritan brew of individualist disobedience and political conformism looked to the new order to establish an English utopia. In his pamphlet 'A Declaration Unto the Parliament' of 1659, Covell ferociously attacked the worshippers of 'idols' both religious and financial and called upon '*English* men' (sic) 'to rouse . . . their spirits' on behalf of the army and Parliament ('the people's trustees') so that the creation of a commonwealth would herald 'the restoration of the creation of God'. Looking both at recent Enfield history, the activity of Diggers and the violent local disturbances, as well as reflecting the national pamphleteering and propagandizing of the Levellers, Covell argued that utopia could be created right there on the Chase itself. Covell's constitution for Enfield, its poor villages and local fields, was one of a number of blueprints which led to the Constitution of the United States. In Covell's plea to common sense and decency was to be found a vision which would be increasingly preached on the foreign soil of New England's colonies rather than in the dangerous confines of old England's shires and counties.

5
Murderous Fantasies
The Great Fire to the Popish Plot

Protestant demonology was always full of the inflammatory terrors of papistry. The legendary execution pyres of Smithfield and the everlasting fires of Hell presided over by the Antichrist Pope always gave to Protestant discussions of Catholicism a whiff of ash and sulphur. In 1666 London was still a city of wood and wattle, prone to every spark from every fire. One such spark, from a baker's premises in Pudding Lane, started a conflagration that began at the very heart of the ancient city and burned everything in its path until it reached to within a few yards of Temple Bar. The fire began on 2 September and lasted five days, destroying two-thirds of the old City. St Paul's Cathedral, eighty-seven churches, the ancient Guildhall, over forty livery halls, the Royal Exchange, Customs House and 13,200 houses, shops and workrooms were reduced to ash and rubble as Londoners fled to surrounding fields or over London Bridge to stay with relatives and friends or camp in the open. For urban dwellers before the general use of less combustible building materials a city fire was second only to plague in the terrors it suggested.

Revenue losses to the crown were considerable but also lost were hidden assets. The flames consumed the Post Office, housed in Posthouse Yard off Threadneedle Street. Despite his efforts the Postmaster, James Hickes, was unable to save the 'secret apparatus for tampering with, copying and forging letters in the interests of the State' which had been operated since its creation by Sir Samuel Morland to the 'great advantage to the Crown'.[1]

As the immediate dangers of fire and falling buildings subsided people looked for a reckoning. Some turned to blaming the iniquity of the age and the execution of the late 'martyred' King, Charles I; some recalled the prophesies of Mother Shipton 'that London in sixty-six shall be burnt to ashes'. John Evelyn recalled in his diary entry for 7 September that Charles II spoke to the crowds in Moorfields in an attempt to calm fears and assure his audience that the fire was not an act of foreign insurrectionists:

> Divers Strangers, Dutch and French were during the fire, appre-
> hended, upon suspicion that they contributed mischievously to
> it, who are all imprisoned, and Informations prepared to make a
> severe inquisition here upon by my Lord Chief Justice Keeling [Sir
> John Kelyng], assisted by some of the Lords of the Privy Council;
> and some principal Members of the City, notwithstanding which
> suspicion, the manner of the burning all along in a Train, and so
> blowen forwards in all its way by strong Winds, make us conclude
> the whole was an effect of an unhappy chance, or to speak bet-
> ter, the heavy hand of God upon us for our sins, shewing us the
> terrour of his Judgement in thus raising the Fire, and immedi-
> ately after his miraculous and never to be acknowledged Mercy, in
> putting a stop to it when we were in the last despair, and that all
> attempts for quenching it however industriously pursued seemed
> insufficient.[2]

Yet this was a suspicious age, always open to the likelier suggestion of foreign plots and papist designs. Rumours spread across the coun-try of threats from strangers, fanatics, Frenchmen and the Dutch. The destruction of London was nothing less than the feared (and anticipated) prelude to a general uprising and invasion by enemies of crown and Church.[3]

Thomas Vincent, a contemporary Puritan witness, for instance, believed that anybody who could think up the Gunpowder Plot could easily contemplate the destruction of London. This seemed confirmed when leaflets dated '5 November 1666' were found circu-lating in the City and when a 'planted' broadside was 'discovered' in Temple Church (in the Inner Temple). It was a confession.

> I, who have been a papist from infancy, till of late; and in zeal for
> their horrid principles, had too great a share in the firing of the
> City; and did intend to do further mischief to the Protestants (of
> which I am now, and ever shall be a member) do, upon abhorency
> of that villainy, and religion that hath moved me to it, declare to
> all Protestants the approach of their sudden ruin, that it may be
> prevented, if it be not too late.
>   When I, together with other papists, both French, Irish and
> English, fired the City: others were employed to massacre the
> Protestants, we thinking thereby to destroy the heads of your reli-
> gion: but the massacre was disappointed by the fear of him who was
> the chief agent in this villainy. And the Fire not having done all its

work, they have often endeavoured to fire the remaining part. They intend likewise to land the French upon you: to whose assistance they all intend to come, and for that purpose are stored with arms: and have so far deceived the King, that they have the command of most part of the army and the seaports. The French intend to land at Dover, that garrison being most papists; and the papists in England have express command from Rome, to hasten their business before the next parliament, and to dispatch. Therefore, as you love your lives and fortunes, prevent your ruin, by removing all the papists in England, especially Colonel Legg from the Tower, and the Lord Douglas, and all his adherents and soldiers from Dover, and disarming all papists. I have such an abhorency, that I would willingly undergo any punishment for it, and declare myself openly, were I not assured that I could do you more good in concealing my name for the present. Delay not from following these directions, as you love your lives: and be not deceived by any pretence whatever.[4]

Everywhere, it seemed, foreigners and agents of foreign powers were creeping up to open windows and lobbing in 'fireballs' – whether Dutch, French or home-grown papist no one was quite sure. Catholics remained a sure bet and Parliament demanded that all priests be banished and all recusants forced to take the Oath of Allegiance and Supremacy and disarmed if they refused (a dangerous, dishonourable and vulnerable position). Charles, unconvinced, reluctantly agreed given public distaste for Catholic neighbours. Rumours of Catholic disloyalty were everywhere from Ilford to Soho.

The King's Committee of Inquiry collated everything that came its way: tales of fireballs and lurking incendiaries. A brewer in Southwark whose home had caught fire from floating sparks claimed:

A paper with a ball of wildfire, containing near a pound weight wrapped in it, was found in the nave of a wheel, in a wheeler's yard, where lay a great quantity of timber. How his house was fired he knoweth not: but this he affirmed to the Committee, that it could not be by accident, because there had not been any candle or fire in the house where the hay lay, that whole day: and that the hay being laid in very dry, and before Midsummer, could not possibly be set on fire within itself.[5]

Few Londoners believed that the Fire was anything less than 'maintained by design'. Wearing black became a sign of disaffection and disloyalty reported by local snoops to the nearest magistrate. The apprehending of a Frenchman, Robert Hubert, in Romford, Essex confirmed everybody's worst fears. Hubert seemed indeed to have a worrying knowledge of Mr Farriner's bakery in Pudding Lane where it had all started.

He also had a plausible story of being paid by an agent of the French king to put a fireball into a window of Farriner's house. Despite Farriner denying ever having such a window the obliging Hubert took the entire blame for the fire and was duly hanged. A strange self-destructive 'moppish besotted fellow', he had dined the night previously in the sight of a paying audience. The next day (29 October) he had been preceded to the scaffold by a hollow effigy of the Pope, the head of which was filled with live cats and set on fire. The Pope screamed as the cats burned, to everyone's delight. Hubert was executed by Jack Ketch and his body was torn to pieces by souvenir hunters.

Farriner, desperate not to take the blame but also not to apportion blame, had been caught in a cleft stick. He either had to admit to mistakenly starting the fire (or at least blame his maid), which he strenuously refused to do, or force the blame on Hubert, which the Committee of Inquiry wanted to avoid in order not to get caught in a major diplomatic incident. (Charles would soon come to a secret treaty with his deadly enemy, France.) Sir Edward Harley, a member of the Committee, upheld Farriner's innocence as to the starting of the fire because:

> The baker of Pudding Lane in whose house the Fire began makes it evident that no fire was left in his oven, that the coals were raked up in the chimney, that the faggots left in the oven, and several pots of baked meat as is usual for Lord's Day dinner were not touched by the Fire, and so found entire several days after the City was in ashes, that his daughter was in the bake house at twelve of the clock, that between one and two his man was waked with the choke of the smoke; the fire began remote from the chimney and oven. His maid was burnt in the house, not adventuring to escape as he, his daughter, who was much scorched, and his man did out of the window and gutter.[6]

If this was the case only one conclusion could be reached (even if Hubert was a mere lunatic) and that was plainly that 'it was done by villany'. On the site of Farriner's house and set into the wall of a new building the City placed a commemorative stone. It was unequivocal about the blame for the Great Fire of London.

HERE BY THE PERMISSION OF HEAVEN HELL BROKE LOOSE
UPON THIS PROTESTANT CITY FROM THE MALICIOUS HEARTS
OF BARBAROUS PAPISTS, BY THE HAND OF THEIR AGENT
HUBERT, WHO CONFESSED, AND ON THE RUINS OF THIS
PLACE DECLARED THE FACT, FOR WHICH HE WAS HANGED,
(VIZ) THAT HERE BEGAN THAT DREDFULL FIRE, WHICH IS
DESCRIBED AND PERPETUATED ON AND BY THE
NEIGHBOURING PILLAR.

At Pye Corner in Smithfield was placed another commemorative plaque recording the iniquities of papist plotters. This memorial, a small niche enclosing a naked cherub called 'The Golden Boy', was later re-erected in Cock Street. It remains to this day a few yards from its original site. The accusation, now set in stone, remained a potent reminder of the supposed iniquity of all papists and of the deep prejudices that marked the proceedings of the Popish Plot almost twenty years later.

At no time was the hatred of Catholicism so vehement as at the period of the Civil War and Protectorate. Ironically few Catholics were actually persecuted, as they kept their beliefs secret or went abroad to avoid the new atmosphere of religious fanaticism and millenarian fervour. The Protectorate collapsed in 1660: on 29 May, Charles II returned from France and landed at Dover. Yet Charles had spent his exile at the French Catholic court, his wife was openly Catholic and both Charles and his brother James were suspected of being crypto-Catholics. This would increase tension as any backsliding by the new regime might be interpreted as selling out to the 'Romish Party'. Any sign of traditional festivities was a clear sign of impending doom.

The austere years of the Protectorate, at least in people's memories, needed to be expunged as quickly as possible. Cromwell's ghost continued to haunt the new regime. To exorcize it and to seek revenge for the death of his father, Charles II had Cromwell's body exhumed and ritually decapitated at Tyburn. The head was stuck on a pike on the roof of Westminster Hall, alongside those of others who had condemned Charles I to death. It was said that the head finally fell off in a thunderstorm, was hidden for years until it became a curiosity when it surfaced during the nineteenth century in the hands of an antique dealer who wanted to display it in a shop window in Bond Street. Years later, it re-emerged as the property of a curate living in Woodbridge, Suffolk, the centre of ghostly activity and is now in Sydney Sussex College, Cambridge.

Charles's birthday, coinciding with his restoration, led to nation-wide celebrations and the return of those bonfires, maypoles, Morris men and wassails so long banned. Despite Puritan disapproval maypoles were set up in every town and as fast as the Lord Mayor of London might pull one down in Cheapside another would be set up. Oxford had a dozen despite the Vice-Chancellor of the University ordering the destruction of the 'heathenish' objects.* Drinking,

---

* The outbreak of the Civil War allowed Parliament's Puritan element to close the theatres and in 1647 to pass severe laws against play-acting. Puppet theatres, by contrast, were ignored. It was in the image of the puppet theatre that Henry Cromwell, Oliver's son, reminisced about his father in 1659:

dancing and merrymaking did not, however, disguise the fact that the return of ancient rights would bring with it tensions that would require the centre to wage a permanent 'war' against both Dissenting republicanism and traditionalist Catholicism. The first victims were Quakers whose meeting houses, including Kiffin's Baptist house in London, were attacked and destroyed. Indeed many preachers linked Presbyterians with Anabaptists *and* Catholics as co-conspirators against the one 'true' spirit of the new contract between King and people.

This defence of the centre would, on the whole, look to a quiet and unspoken tolerance toward *private* affairs, an area outside public life and attached firmly to the concept of business and domesticity in which freedom of conscience and action should be left to individuals as long as such freedoms did not interfere with the separate world of governance. Yet this separation also restricted the public realm of state interference and threatened its effectiveness. Thus, paradoxically, the centre became more unstable, seeing threats (sometimes real) in every private word or transaction. Spies were everywhere and rumour continued to be a powerful tool for the propaganda of all sides but especially for the centre attempting to crack down on dissent. The private views of ordinary English people, and Londoners especially, might too easily coincide with the political ambitions of an aristocratic clique at court. It was of paramount importance to keep these two groups from reuniting into any possible oppositional bloc. In such an atmosphere any scapegoat was useful and Catholic scapegoats easily the most convenient.

Anti-Catholic feeling was often genuine and deeply felt. It was also politically significant and could be turned to account when deciding issues of policy. When Charles I dissolved the Short Parliament, anti-Catholic riots took the Queen and her household as their target. Archbishop Laud's overly papist reforms led to his death amid popular applause whilst the threat of Irish invasion would rouse the common people not only to voice their prejudices

---

For though men say he had a copper nose . . . his name still lives. Me thinks I hear 'em already crying thirty year hence at Bartholomew Fair.
'Step in and see the Life and Death of brave Cromwell.' Me thinks I see him with a velvet cragg [collar] about his shoulders, and a little pasteboard hat on his head riding a tittup at tittup to parliament house, and a man with a bay leaf in his mouth crying in his behalf, 'By the living God I will dissolve 'em', which makes the porters cry, 'O brave Englishman'. Then the Devil carries him away in a tempest, which makes the nurses squeak and the children cry.

From George Speaight, *Punch and Judy: a History* (London: Studio Vista, 1955), pp. 37–8.

against papist neighbours but also to join Protestant militias. Petitions to Parliament from manufacturers were often as not as concerned with 'popish plots' as with the threat to shipping by Turkish pirates.

> In 1641 the common system of values was skilfully translated into political language. A national oath of loyalty, the Protestation, was enacted by the Commons during the great fear of a counter-stroke against Parliament by Charles I. Initially the oath was taken only by MPs and by voluntary subscription in a few parishes, but in January 1642 it was sent down in to the countryside and the clergy ordered to administer it to all adult males. Its subscribers swore to maintain 'His Majesty's royal person and estate': the patriarchal, monarchical core of the social and political order. They swore to defend 'the power and privilege of Parliaments, the lawful rights and liberties of the subjects': the ancient constitution and laws from which stemmed the rights of individuals and of the kingdom's component communities. And they swore to preserve 'the true reformed Protestant religion expressed in the doctrine of the Church of England, against all Popery and popish innovation'.[7]

Protestantism (from the late sixteenth century represented as the true religion of England), ancient common rights, the Anglican Church and the monarchy combined to make a complex set of coordinates for any patriotic Englishman. It was Charles II's lifelong business to keep a balance between them or risk gambling his position by allowing one to gain too much prominence. He only had to remember the fate of his father. The fantasies of Catholic-baiters such as Titus Oates threatened to upset the delicate balance of government if not carefully handled. The Popish Plot of 1678 was originally the brainchild of extreme Protestants. Rejected as fantasy by the King and his advisers, it soon proved a way of scapegoating one form of English dissent – Catholicism. Playing both sides against each other provided a useful means for the centre to restore the equilibrium needed to ensure uninterrupted rule and the renewal of the trust between monarch and people. There would, of course, have to be victims and possibly some bloodshed but such sacrifice might happily work, given a certain amount of political 'realism', for the greater good.

As early as the beginning of the seventeenth century the militant Puritan distaste for Catholics offered only three options for their obstinacy. Either they were wicked subversives in the clutches of the devil and the Antichrist or they were mentally deranged lunatics or they were both. The madhouse was filled with recusants as much as the prison when Puritans were on the warpath. Just as in Soviet Russia, dissidents could find their ideological or religious opposition meant they were considered to be literally mad by the authorities. Their punishment was, in such cases, equal to their 'cure'.

> Some are sent to the mad-house, and there bound hands and head to a pillar, then stripped to the waist, and cruelly scourged many times a week, whilst the Ministers stand looking on, endeavouring to pervert them in the midst of their torments, and crying out at every stroke, 'Come, then, to our church.'[8]

The fanaticism of Puritan divines and their allies was equalled by those Anglicans whose 'patriotic' duty it was to root out Catholicism. Such patriots might be genuine reformers or they might equally be 'Church and King' men talking a language that was at one and the same time loyal, reformist and monarchical and also deeply paranoid and inherently subversive. The country was full, it seemed, of such people, half truthful, half insane, but every threat they brought to light had to be weighed and considered. Such vigilante minds set themselves up as defenders against Dissenters and papists (who they equated!) and formed an authoritarian and 'right-wing' bloc that could never be quite dismissed by the King and which had great influence in both Houses of Parliament.

Titus Oates owned one such mind: a man whose obsessively professed loyalty and best wishes to the King and government were matched by a personal and professional deviousness of epic proportions. He was a man without any moral or physical redeeming features. He spent most of his early life a failure trying to make a living in the Church of England, changed horses and went to the English College at Valladolid to train for the Catholic priesthood, offended everybody with his foul mouth, ugly looks and inability to speak any foreign language, and returned to England with a tale of Papal intrigue as revenge. His tale was simple but he was a man fascinated by his own imagination – a gift he also abused. It was, in essence, that a secret 'consort' of Catholics had met in London to plot the shooting of Charles II at Windsor and the firing of London in another uprising. Oates peddled his tale to Israel Tonge, a fanatical anti-Catholic pamphleteer, who took it to the King. Charles was not impressed by this lunatic but referred the whole thing to the Privy Council who, for their own reasons, took things more seriously even though the tale was too close to all sorts of older plots hatched by Fifth Monarchists. Indeed 'Captain' Oates and Thomas Tonge, both Fifth Monarchist revolutionaries and both executed in the early 1660s, may have been related to the present heroes of the hour.

Oates was called to testify before King and Council but he was an inept liar and a puerile forger. Nevertheless, having convinced Tonge of his tale he took his carefully written document of forty-three articles (it grew and changed over the period of the Plot) to be sworn before the magistrate Sir Edmund Berry Godfrey.* As yet little credence was given to Oates's tale by Charles and James but the Lords of the Privy Council, who were always alert to plots (there had been a number of assassination rumours), were more suspicious. They waited for news. They did not have to wait long. Godfrey was found murdered on Primrose Hill and the belief soon spread that it was because he had told Edward Coleman about the deposition which had been sworn before him. All London was now looking for Papists to hang and chapels to burn.

Edward Coleman was Suffolk-born but had ended up in London a 'fanatical' Catholic and personal secretary to James, Duke of York, the King's brother. He was also rumoured to be plotting to put the Catholic James on the throne. As Godfrey knew Coleman it was presupposed that not only Coleman but James (a closet Catholic) had been in on the murder. When Coleman was arrested indiscreet letters were found in which he suggested that James was simply biding his time to restore the true faith. Coleman was as stupid in these letters as James was ignorant but it reinforced calls by the followers of the Earl of Shaftesbury that James had to be *excluded* from the succession. Moreover Shaftesbury may have been behind Oates, Tonge and the other conspirators and secretly bankrolling them.

Next on the scene, having waited patiently in the wings, was 'patriot' William Bedloe, a con artist and fraudster who had met Oates at the Jesuit College in St Omer in France. Bedloe was soon peddling a fantasy about Catholic conspirators killing Godfrey at night in Somerset House and then faking his death as suicide – a man who knew too much. Bedloe's genius was to place Godfrey's death in the home of the Queen and thus implicate James and all those who surrounded Charles as papists and traitors. By avoiding mentioning her by name he neatly sidestepped accusations of treason whilst letting the mud stick. A wholesale roundup of Catholic plotters and Irish murder teams (one for Charles, one for Godfrey) now led to a series of show trials.

---

*It was not until the Middlesex Justices Act 1792 that the modern magistrates' court came into existence in London. Before this time justices worked in their own homes, which they used as offices, holding quarter sessions in shire halls and taverns. The Westminster Sessions were held at the Hell tavern near Westminster Hall until 1763, when a courthouse was built in King Street. The Middlesex Sessions were held at Hicks Hall. Bow Street, home of Sir John Fielding, was the first to look like a court, the result of a new sense of judicial space and gravitas by the representatives of the law.

Political trials, especially trials of suspected traitors, could have only one single and terrible conclusion. This was especially true when the Lord Chief Justice was Sir William Scroggs, a mean-mouthed Catholic-baiter with a holier than thou attitude who could castigate Oates or Bedloe as fools even as he convicted (usually without any evidence) those they accused. Scroggs was nothing less than a thug in a wig but he was a loyal 'Church and King' man who knew the law and his duty and mistook political expediency for justice. Complementing Scroggs was Sir George Jeffreys, sometime Recorder of London and then also Lord Chief Justice, a man of supercilious humour with little time for idiots like Oates but loyal and fierce in his determination to serve the state. Between them they despatched over twenty innocent people – not one a Protestant.

Charles and his brother were no fools; their Catholic sympathies would not cloud their support of Anglicanism and certainly did not stop them courting Dissenters when necessary. Certainly Charles could reconcile his Catholic leanings with the acceptance of Catholic persecution by his ministers and senior judges. Umpteen Catholics had been judicially murdered (the word can hardly be too strong) for a plot 'uncovered' by liars, cheats and psychopaths. For example Peter Talbot, Archbishop of Dublin, was executed on 1 July 1681 even though Charles had happily agreed with the French Ambassador that he was quite innocent.

On his deathbed, Charles, a Catholic 'in everything except outward observance', was reconciled to the Church and handed James a reliquary (his own crucifix) containing a relic of the True Cross. For years he had kissed the painted portraits of martyrs hanging in the Queen's rooms; James too had long been suspected of a continuous correspondence with Rome. As early as 27 April 1678, Sir John Player reported to the Committee of Secrecy on Coleman's correspondence with John Leyburn, who lived in Rome:

> Some time ago I saw considerable papers and transactions betwixt the Duke and the Pope. I did scarce believe it till I saw it. Some from his Highness to his Holiness gave him occasion of so great joy (and surely they must be considerable letters that made his Holiness so merry) and yet they made the old man weep; and that bespeaks excess of joy. Some time before there was notice given of such letters coming, but they gave great trouble at Rome that they came not, but when they were received, his Holiness returned the Duke a most kind and obliging answer, and her Highness the Duchess was presented from the Pope with a holy token of consecrated beads, and other fine things, which I do not understand, and I hope never shall.[9]

The Ambassador of Modena despaired at the folly, '[The English] regard themselves now more than ever as being on the brink of ruin and destruction, on account of a Plot in which there has never been seen, either before or after it was revealed, one single overt act of treason'.[10]

The answers are clear when it is recognized that state policy did not necessarily coincide with state principle. Charles had not only the memory of his father's fate but also the fear of his brother's future with the growth of Whigs and ultra-Protestants.

> If we do not something relating to the succession [said Lord Russell], we must resolve, when we have a Prince of the Popish Religion, to be papists or burn, and I will do neither. We see now, by what is done under a Protestant Prince, what will be done under a Popish. This is the deciding day betwixt both religions.[11]

With all the bluster he could manage and all the awe he could produce, Charles delayed and equivocated but dared not cancel the decisions of law courts and Commons. In balancing the religious oppositions and tensions of his reign, Charles used pragmatic subtlety to subvert challenges directed either at James or at himself through the Queen. It was essential, if the House of Stuart was to survive, to placate the central body of Englishmen dedicated to 'Church and King' and the Constitution and laws that reinforced that concept. All else and everybody and everything else could be ditched – Catholics, Presbyterians, ultra-Protestants, Scots, Irish, former and present Lord Chief Justices and anybody who might come in the way. Charles's reign may have been 'merry' but it was certainly as brutal and murderous as any before.

Charles was acutely aware that Church and state were not one but had to be seen *as one*: appearance was all and any breach of appearance which brought an overtly *political* challenge could not be tolerated. The murdering cabal of high court judges, which included Scroggs and Jeffreys, were all political appointees and politicized animals with a sincere but perverse sense of justice. Scroggs was obsessed with taking 'innocent' blood, but did not restrain himself. Their concept of the law was itself determined by their absolute obedience to the concept of 'Church and King'. The protection of this principle against all challenges was essentially political – a judge would work for another monarch as long as the principle was left intact. What counted were absolute allegiance and the constant proof of allegiance.

For many people, taking the 'test' was a pragmatic and sensible way to proceed with their lives and for English Catholics a way to get ahead or at least be left alone. At least one wing of influential Catholics had accepted the Oath of Allegiance as we have seen and no more than a third of professing Catholics were said to have a problem. French bishops in 1682 unequivocally decided that

> Kings and sovereigns are therefore not by God's command subject to any ecclesiastical dominion in things temporal; they cannot be deposed, whether directly or indirectly, by the authority of the rulers of the Church, their subjects cannot be dispensed from that submission and obedience which they owe, or from the oath of allegiance.[12]

No pope would interfere with a crowned monarch and a Catholic Englishman was an Englishman first, or, if a Catholic first, one who would keep that fact as quiet as possible in a hostile climate.

The 'political' nature of the prosecutions was evident in the fact that those Catholics (especially the tradesmen and women of London) who took the Oath were, in general, simply ignored. A man named William Staley was the first alleged plotter to be sentenced to death. The attendees at the masses and burial held for Staley in November 1678 were not harassed although they presented an excellent target for 'priest-takers'. Of course, government scruples may have played a part but it was certainly scruples that left most London Catholics alone. When two Bills were introduced into Parliament designed to banish all Catholics from London and forcibly transplant Catholic landowners there was uproar. The defeat of the Papists (Removal from London) Bill and the Papists (Removal and Disarming) Bill were shrewd moves by a House only too aware that City trade would be shaken and that dire disruption would follow depopulation.

The political nature of events revealed the real enemy to be the Jesuits and lay-clergy fifth columnists. Jesuits were 'famous' for prevaricating, lying, subterfuge and every sort of villainy. They also went under many assumed aliases and used coded language, forming a secret Masonic brethren whose ideology was the utter annihilation of Protestantism. Their famed secrecy made mild men appear duplicitous: fanatics with a smiling face. This was the origin of the random accusatory voice, the zeal of priest-takers, the intemperate language of those who believed there was a Jesuit behind every plot, hiding behind a mask of compliance.

Edward Coleman had fuelled the belief that the royal household was a hotbed of Jesuit secret-servicemen ready to ferment all sorts of anti-Protestant mischief. Heneage Finch, the Lord Chancellor, could not restrain himself in summing up in the trial against William Howard, Lord Stafford when he asked rhetorically, 'Who can doubt any longer that London was burnt by papists?' Jeffreys himself was clear in his own mind about the difference between 'honest' English Catholics and Jesuits.

I do not speak this to you, as intending thereby to inveigh against all persons that profess the Romish religion; for there are many of that persuasion that do abhor those base principles of murdering kings and subverting governments. There are many honest gentlemen in England, I dare say, of that communion, whom none of the most impudent Jesuits durst undertake to tempt into such designs; these are only to be imposed upon silly men, not upon men of conscience and understanding.[13]

A French Jesuit visiting England at the time noted that

The name of Jesuit is hated above all else, even by priests both secular and regular, and by the Catholic laity as well, because it is said that the Jesuits have caused this raging storm, which is likely to overthrow the whole Catholic religion.[14]

Such deep distrust lay dormant for hundreds of years. Even the historian John Kenyon, writing in 1972, described the Jesuits as Catholicism's 'Waffen SS shock troops'. Many sober men including MPs believed quite sincerely that there was a *shadow* Jesuit government just waiting for the right moment to spring the trap that would finish England with a coup d'état, the razing of London, the massacre of Protestants including mass burnings in Smithfield and an inevitable invasion of an army of occupation assisted by the fifth-columnist 'night riders'. This was the seventeenth-century version of the Cold War.

Fanaticism is only useful as long as it remains politically expedient but by the summer of 1681, Oates, Bedloe and crew were falling out of favour. Things seemed to have changed when Stephen College, a colleague of Oates, was tried and executed for high treason. Times were becoming more precarious for informers and Oates found his official allowances so reduced and his hopes of a bishopric or pension so quickly fading that he was moving towards penury. Now becoming an embarrassment to the establishment, Oates found himself arrested for a previous indiscretion against the Duke of York. The trial which followed saw him convicted of slander and James awarded £100,000 compensation, a sum so vast that it could only have been thought up to keep Oates in debtors' prison for ever.

Charles died on 6 February 1685 and James seemed ready to complete his revenge when Oates was arraigned for perjury. Jeffreys presided, free now to bring Oates to book and to complete the growing opprobrium which was sticking to him.

Is it not a prodigious thing [he said] to have such actions as these today defended in a court of justice, with that impudence and unconcernedness as though he would challenge even God Almighty to punish his wickedness, and blasphemously blesses God, that he has lived to do such wonderful service to the Protestant religion, and is so obstinate in his villainy as to declare he would venture his blood for the confirmation of so impious a falsehood? And, indeed, he makes no great venture in it, for when he has pawned his immortal soul by so perjured a testimony, he may very easily proffer the venturing of his vile carcase to maintain it . . .

My blood does curdle and my spirits are raised, that after the discoveries made, I think, to the satisfaction of all that have attended this day, to see a fellow continue so impudent as to brazen it out as he has done this day; and that there should appear no confusion and shame than what was seen in the face of that monstrous villain that stood but now at the bar. The pretended infirmity of his body made him remove out of court, but the infirmity of his depraved mind, the blackness of his soul, the baseness of his actions, ought to be looked upon with such horror and detestation as to think him unworthy any longer to tread upon the face of God's earth.[15]

Jeffreys, and all the judiciary implicated in the gross distortions of justice over which they had happily presided not too long ago, were now intent on treating the Plot as solely Oates's invention and themselves and Parliament as unwitting dupes. The active complicity with which the judicial system played along with Oates's and Bedloe's fantasies meant that a volte face would have to be accomplished with care – political expediency 'that the Plot must be howled as if it were true, whether it were so or not' (Lord Halifax) would now require an *ad hominem* solution: one wicked man. Jeffreys summed up:

When a person shall be convicted of such a foul and malicious perjury as the defendant is, I think it is impossible for the court, as the law now stands, to put a punishment upon him any way proportionable to the offence, that has drawn after it so many horrid and dreadful consequences. We do therefore think fit to inflict an exemplary punishment upon this villainous, perjured wretch, to terrify others for the future.[16]

The punishment was severe. Oates was fined a huge sum, defrocked and, with a plaque proclaiming his offences, paraded and whipped from Aldgate to Newgate and from Newgate to Tyburn after which he was pilloried and imprisoned for life. This was as near as possible to actually executing him but he did not die, surviving instead to petition for a pardon which he received from William III although the count of perjury stood. By this time Jeffreys himself was a spent force, dying of gallstones while imprisoned in the Tower for backing the wrong monarch.

Two other judges who had sat with Jeffreys and passed judgement on Oates were themselves hauled before the Lords to justify their decision. Oates survived it all, settling in Axe Yard in Westminster, attending the Courts of Law, writing religious squibs, staying with friends, with other Whig extremists and even marrying (although his known homosexuality got him into court on two occasions accused of buggery – he was acquitted twice with costs). He took to preaching again at the Baptist chapel in Wapping although a few of the congregation murmured when scandal called. Finally he got his pension from William III but he was not to enjoy it for long, dying aged fifty-six in 1705.

Israel Tonge, Oates's old crony, died in 1680 after flooding London with works including *The New Design of the Papists Detected*, *An Account of the Romish Doctrine in Case of Conspiracy and Rebellion* and numerous others intended to expose Catholic conspiracy. Charles donated £50 towards his funeral costs. William Bedloe also died in 1680, having received the £500 reward money for the 'discovery' of the murderers of Sir Edmund Berry Godfrey and various other amounts including a payment for the maintenance of witnesses. Stephen Dugdale, another useful informer and fantasist, continued to fleece his employees of large sums for dubious expenses and he also received a small allowance for life, which ended in June 1682. All in all no conspirator became fabulously rich and none seemed to be able to survive without the enjoyment of an informer's pay; imaginative invention was their only real source of income, the national good weighed in pieces of silver during an age which considered such payments quite normal.

It was one thing to live in fear of fictional Catholic plots and quite another to experience the reality of Protestant republicans. If Charles has come down to us as the 'Merry Monarch', to his Puritan and Dissenting subjects he was certainly debauched, a wily absolutist and a closet Catholic; his brother was nothing less than an absolutist and papist through and through. Republicanism and aristocratic power politics meant that Charles was far more likely to fall the victim to the pistol or poison of Fifth Monarchists or Green Ribboners than to Catholic rapiers or gunpowder.

Fifth Monarchists did, perhaps, pose the single most dangerous threat from Dissenting groups, believing as they did in a millennial and apocalyptic future in which they alone would act as caretakers until Christ's return. Their fanaticism was a threat to King and Protector alike and at least two uprisings in 1657 and 1661 led by a wine-barrel maker, Thomas Venner, showed the danger they posed to the state. Although finally destroyed, their ideas

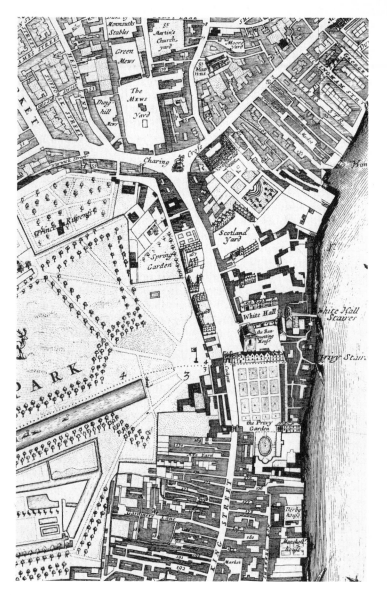

Westminster in 1682, showing Whitehall, Old Charing Cross, Scotland Yard and Axe Yard. (From 'London Etc Actually Survey'd' by William Morgan)

continued to haunt politics into the 1680s and beyond in Green Ribboner conspiracies.

Venner was one of a new type of man, born of the lower orders, bred in the fulcrum of the civil wars, reasonably educated, fiercely republican and deeply religious. The medieval period suffered its usual share of bread riots and work-related scuffles no doubt, but large scale political questions were beyond the common folk and generally passed them by. This changed during the Peasant's Revolt, but such an upheaval came at a peculiarly traumatic moment in the fourteenth century which was not to be repeated and which was, in any case, confined geographically. This was really the last time for three hundred years that those 'below' were able to make their economic grievances into a coherent political argument. It was only the upheaval of the Civil Wars in the seventeenth century which allowed ideas from below, about freedom of conscience, religious toleration, removal of tithes, reform of the law, republicanism and the destruction of the 'class system' to finally surface, that the common people gained a political voice. With the beheading of the king, previously seditious thoughts could be openly spoken. For a short time the grip of authority was loosened and rebellion might be contemplated by those lesser folk who had been taught for years to hold their tongue in front of their betters. Such ideas, circulated by the printing press and by word of mouth meant that the immediate worries about food, shelter and taxes could be put aside for long-term goals which might be striven for by the lower orders acting in concert as a body with only ideology or religion to guide them.

Waiting impatiently for the Fifth Monarchy of the Apocalypse when Christ himself would reign, men like Venner gathered congregations and preached the coming end of the world. They were convinced by the signs of recent history and by extrapolating from their own circumstances to the rest of the world that the End of Days was near. After the Civil War they had gained political strength and convinced many in the army including Cromwell of their position, but the various parliaments that followed failed to deliver the republic they demanded before Christ's coming. There was no wish from those in charge of the country to get rid of taxes, lawyers and tithes nor to hand over government to a self-appointed group of 'saints' who would convene a Sanhedrin to administer law just as in ancient Israel. The saints had a model of patriotism in which England was both the home of the twelve tribes, but also the holy land itself. They were to be disappointed in everything – with Cromwell, with the peace with the Dutch, with parliament and its lawyers and with the betrayal of the army and final royal restoration.

There would be nothing left to do, but give in to fate and admit the time was not propitious for the Second Coming or rise and make history bend to their will. One of the first attempts was the aborted rising at Farnley Wood near Leeds in October 1663. Its leader was one Thomas Oates of whom little is known except that he may have been a relative of Titus Oates who emerges later in the Popish Plot.

Before and after the restoration of Charles II, Protestants feared that their position would always be precarious once a monarch with Catholic sympathies was back on the throne and with that lingering doubt went the suspicion that fuelled rebellion or outright republicanism. Indeed, the belief in a Catholic plot which would effectively handover the crown to French domination was not just a silly rumour but was backed up by proof of secret bilateral agreements. Protestantism needed to arm itself in self-defence. There were already rumblings in Scotland where the Covenanters feared destruction. They gathered, fought and died in the Pentland Rising of 1666, at Drumclog and Bothwell Green in 1679 and Ayrsmoss in 1680, setting up their fiery crosses against the hidden tides of Catholicism. Back in England, the saints gathered to restore what had been 'promised' before the execution of Charles I.

Unlike the Levellers with whom they sometimes mixed, Fifth Monarchists were committed, not to an egalitarian tolerant republic under the army, but to an intolerant religious republic ruled by a religious elite and with no army to interfere. John Lilburne himself would be betrayed by Fifth Monarchy men and Levellers had no reason to support religious fanatics whose aims were opposed to theirs, They thought Ranters and such like religious fanatics, ridiculous.

For the most part the Fifth Monarchists were gathered in London and had rebellious congregations at Blackfriars, Southwark, St Mary Overy's Dock, in a cellar near London Bridge and at Venner's Swan Alley, Coleman Street meeting house, where having returned from New England he filled his listeners with ideas of rebellion. The congregations which were filled with both zealous men and many women were hotbeds of sedition and closely watched. Their preachers were in and out of jail, but it did not stop them, nor did it stop their printing presses.

Venner, like many of the Fifth Monarchists in London was a revolutionary. At one time he planned to blow up the Tower of London and chop off Cromwell's head. No opportunity arose for action until a Fifth Monarchist by the name of John Pendarves was buried at Abingdon. The funeral turned into a rally and Venner returned to London ready for war. By the opening months of 1657 he had a secret organization in London made up of cells of enthusiasts. There was little enthusiasm elsewhere in the country. His plan was to attack some horse troops and then parade through Epping Forest and eastwards gathering recruits. Eighty followers gathered at Mile End Green in Shoreditch on the evening of 9 April, but were interrupted by soldiers, their arms taken and Venner whipped off under guard to the Tower. He cooled off in there for a time.

The affair warned the government, but fired the saints, women spreading the word in secret, distributing pamphlets and even wearing armour and fighting alongside the men. These men and women were the chosen people and could not be thwarted. They planned assassinations and risings anew. When Charles II was finally restored it would be now or never. Some thought never and made accommodation, but others thought not. In May 1660, a preacher at Venner's meeting house was preaching regicide and on Sunday 6 January 1661, Venner and fifty followers armed and in armour, marched to St Paul's and waved their manifesto, which declared for 'King Jesus' alone. A fight with troops left them unexpectedly victorious, but with little idea of what to do next they retreated towards Highgate where they hid and trained, being well armed and ready for more action. There may have been up to three hundred followers by this time but it appears only fifty were ever seen together. These marched back to the City three days later and fought a very ferocious battle with soldiers where they lost twenty six men for twenty soldiers killed. At least one woman wore armour in the fight. The end of the rebellion came when Venner, his fury expended was arrested and put on trial alongside fifty others. Venner and twelve conspirators were hanged and their heads placed on spikes on London Bridge. The Fifth Monarchists were almost finished, but they fought on in minor skirmishes during 1661 and more plots were discovered both in 1661 and 1662 and scares were frequent.

In July 1671 a cow broke into the Palace Yard at Westminster and, by a series of misadventures metamorphosized into a radical come to kill the lawyers in the law courts; 'the fifth-monarchy men were up and come to cut the throats of the lawyers who were a great plague of the land', it was said. The cow perhaps mooed. It was enough to panic the legal profession who abandoned their calling and their dignities with rare speed. William Scroggs, later Lord Chief Justice, a sufferer from gout, 'was' apparently, 'perfectly cured' and stripped himself of his gown and hairpiece, and 'with great activity vaulted over the bar'.[17]

Thomas Blood, the most famous and notorious renegade of the late seventeenth century was a confederate of the Fifth Monarchists, a believer in their doctrines and an active participant in their conspiracies and battles. He recorded the fact that he was wounded in the Pentland Rising in his diary and he was active in plots both in Dublin and London. At least one meeting in Petty France was the scene of assassination plans which were thwarted by a spy, John Atkinson, whose attempts to seize the 'phanaticks' failed. This did not stop Blood plotting with a close friend called John Mason, who ran a tavern. Around 1670, Mason had thought up a scheme to attack Whitehall with fifty men, but nothing came of that particular dream, instead another scheme was about to come to fruition. This was the bizarre attempt to assassinate James Butler, 1st Duke of Ormonde, for reasons that are obscure, except that he was virtually the most powerful man in England after James II, a fierce royalist, had virtually ruled Ireland for years and had come to terms with Irish Catholics. Either he would be shot or hauled off to Tyburn to be hanged. He was hated by the Duke of Buckingham who may have paid Blood and Mason to do the deed in broad daylight. So this would be a political, rather than a religious act in every sense.

It was to be achieved thus. Shortly before seven o'clock on the evening of the 6 December 1670, five armed men entered the Bull Head tavern in Charing Cross. It was a popular place, Samuel Pepys enjoying the dinners there. The men drank heavily and waited for the Duke to arrive on his way from a banquet held to honour William, Prince of Orange and Charles II's nephew who was at the Guildhall that night. At around seven o'clock the Duke's coach and entourage approached the pub on the way to his home in St James's. Blood and his accomplices bought three pipes, paid and left.

Moments later the highwaymen had stopped the coach and were struggling with Ormonde, who although sixty, was tough enough to escape, avoiding two bullets as he did so. Blood, meanwhile had gone to get a rope to hang his captive at Tyburn. By now the plot was in disarray, the Duke's household and footmen were now in the fray and success was impossible. The gang retreated to the Fulham ferry which they took to the safety of Southwark and freedom. They were declared 'assassinates' and a reward of £1,000 was offered for their capture.[18] A House of Lord's committee identified the main culprits as a Dr Thomas Allen, Thomas Hunt and Richard Halliwell as 'desperate Fifth Monarchy men', Allen was one of a number of aliases of Blood and 'Thomas Hunt' was none other than Blood's son Thomas.[19] There were others too in on the plot, Samuel Holmes, John Hurst, a cook by the name of John Washwhite, a butcher called Thomas Dixey who came from Southwark and Fifth Monarchy radicals William More and William Smith.[20] In the end there was not enough evidence to prosecute any of them. Blood was free and safe. He rewarded himself for the deed by a promotion from 'Major' to 'Colonel' Blood in accordance with his own growing notoriety. Finally, he retired from revolutionary activities and turned to spying for the king.

Republicanism ran like a thread through the seventeenth century. During the early 1680s disaffected Anglicans and republican assassins met to plan a coup d'état at Rye House near Hoddesdon, Hertfordshire, the home of Richard Rumbold, who years before had played his part at the execution of Charles I. Rye House itself was a large manor house on the edge of a marsh through which Charles and James would have to travel when returning to London from the races at Newmarket. Here the road narrowed, a perfect spot for a double murder. The plan required the overturning of a farm cart and the ambush and annihilation of the royal party and its escort. Monmouth, Charles's illegitimate son, would then be declared head of a new government.

Needless to say, the plot misfired when a fire prevented further racing and the royal brothers returned too early, but amongst the forty conspirators there was no reprieve. Those implicated by association fled or were imprisoned, the most senior of all, the Earl of Essex, cutting his own throat whilst in the Tower. Throughout 1683 and 1684 trials and executions ran their course but some of the most significant conspirators lived to fight another day. Monmouth was indicted but escaped punishment, Rumbold escaped to Holland ready to lead another rising in Scotland and the ever-conspiratorial Earl of Shaftesbury only escaped implication because he was already dead. The Rye House Plot was singly one symptom of a long quarrel with extreme Protestant Dissent, which would lead to rioting, revolution and terror.

Anthony Ashley Cooper, Earl of Shaftesbury, was the last great republican conspirator, and with his death in exile went a real possibility that a republican government would finally triumph. And yet, with the abortive rising of the Duke of Monmouth, it became clear that republicans were doomed to fail and that the fight of Levellers, Fifth Monarchy men and Diggers had all finally come to dust, fifty years of struggle wasted in the coming of the so called 'Glorious Revolution'.

Shaftesbury's plotting and his attempt to control parliament and the City aldermen came to nothing and there was little to do except accept exile and defeat. Shaftesbury nevertheless, with his taste for oligarchy, lack of mysticism and acute political sense effectively forged the first political party and created the first mass political programme and that programme was republican at heart. 'The rights and liberties' of the people were to be tested against a free parliament which 'cannot enslave the people' for at bottom, 'Englishmen's minds are free and better taught in their liberties'. Shaftesbury, despite his wealth was an 'Englishman' from choice and not merely a parochial 'little Englander' despite never having been abroad. By slow degrees, parliament revoked every progressive ruling, turned back all the gains of the Civil War, virtually criminalized dissenters and made the way clear for a possible Catholic succession. Shaftesbury was out of favour. Finally at odds with the monarch and the ruling elite, stripped of all his offices and forced to surrender the 'Great Seal' of the realm he said 'it [was] but laying down my gown and putting on my sword'. He was up for a fight and he knew why. It was, he told the Lords for them alone to maintain an independent position, neither pawns of a tyrannous king nor dupes of an anarchic democracy, but the safeguard of English liberty. 'My Lords', he declared, 'it is not only your interest, but the interest of the nation, that you maintain your rights; for, let the House of Commons and gentry of England think what they please, there is no prince that ever governed without nobility or an army. If you will not have one, you must have the other, or the monarchy cannot long support or keep itself from tumbling into a democratical republic.'[21]

No one in power listened and Shaftesbury was further marginalized as a result. He threw in his hand with the Duke of Monmouth, Charles's son. Shaftesbury maintained his party through the close knit poorer communities of London. The importance of the printing press, his 'feminine part of revolt', having long been acknowledged. His followers printed and circulated pamphlets such as the one which reproduced the dying words of the Regicides. This was treasonable by the Licensing Act of 1662 which banned publications which attacked the Crown or Church. What emerged from government repression was the 'New Country Party' and it was a thoroughly revolutionary movement.[22]

Shaftesbury made his headquarters at the King's Head at the edge of the City and around him he gathered his 'Green Ribbon' men, demographically egalitarian and raffishly defiant, wearing their green cockades at a defiant angle called the 'Monmouth cock'. The Popish Plot, that nonsense dreamt up by religious fools and condoned by monarchy, began a situation that might favour the Country Party with the introduction of the Exclusion Bill into parliament. James thought it merely a manoeuvre to get a 'republike'. The Scots covenanters were at war and in London Justice Godfrey lay murdered. Now to whip up the populace Shaftesbury arranged a show of strength to frighten his enemies – it would be a type of masque, the first real political rally, although it wore the clothes of religious bigotry. Through the City came a lone horse with the carnivalesque corpse of Judge Godfrey upon it, the body stained with blood and held up by a 'Jesuit'. Behind this nightmarish vision came the real nightmare, a wagon bearing an effigy of everything Catholic and terrifying – the pope as Anti-Christ.

There was, for a short moment, an apocalyptic air to London. It did not last long and the royalists regained their supremacy through three subsequent parliaments. Shaftesbury was finally arrested and put in the Tower. The Country Party held the City, but their grip was illusory and broken by the king's perogative. There was nothing left but to declare a republic, rebel or shut up for good. The conspiracy started with a thought which found its voice in Londoners who felt a grave injustice. They demanded nothing less than the political programme of the original Levellers. To achieve it they would barricade the City and 'fight not to change persons only, but things' where a constitutional monarchy might reign if a republic could not. The rising was ambitious and unlikely, but if it had succeeded Shaftesbury would be 'prime minister' to the crowned Duke of Monmouth with James excluded and exiled. They argued and debated and they delayed until too late. The royalists had won and Shaftesbury was a marked man. He and his confederates left for Amsterdam and oblivion. Whilst in exile he died suddenly on 21 January 1683 – 'Milord Shaftesbury [était] mort'. [23]

Charles died in 1685 having converted to Catholicism on his deathbed. All his fourteen children were illegitimate. James, Duke of York succeeded his brother on 6 February 1685, as James II, King of England and Ireland (and, as James VII, of Scotland), sovereign over a growing empire of eleven American colonies, seven Caribbean islands and Bermuda. He was also a long-time Catholic.

Handsome, heroic and a true Prince of Protestantism, James, Duke of Monmouth, Charles II's most prominent son, now chose to seize the opportunity of restoring a 'free' Parliament from an 'obviously' Catholic absolutist, something to be achieved by a swift and effective invasion from the Netherlands. Unfortunately, Monmouth had no real idea of how to achieve his mission, or what he would do once he had restored Parliament's lost prerogatives. He landed in England at Lyme Regis, in Dorset, far away from London, his target. Accompanied by a mere eighty-two supporters he had to hope for a spontaneous rising, especially as the Earl of Argyll's rebellion (aided by Richard Rumbold) had given clear warning of trouble. Entering Taunton, Monmouth did rally support and his small army of West Countrymen did defeat a force sent to check them but all in vain. At the Battle of Sedgemoor, which was more a massacre, Monmouth's hopes were dashed. Now began the famous 'Bloody Assizes' of Judge Jeffreys as he rooted out the last vestiges of rebellion. Monmouth forfeited his head in London. The doomed champion of the English Protestant cause and the Whig Party had not only to suffer the horrors of execution but also to suffer them at the hands of one of England's truly incompetent executioners – Jack Ketch. When the Duke remarked upon the dullness of the axe he was reassured with a little too much complacency.

> The executioner had five blows at him. After the first [Monmouth] looked up, and at the third he put his legs across, and the hangman flung away his axe, but being chid took it up again and gave

him t'other two strokes, and severed not his head from his body
till he cut it off with a knife.

After the gruesome deed, Monmouth's head was sewn back onto
his neck for a last portrait!

The struggle that ensued between Anglicans jealous of their privileges
and Dissenters disqualified from power did little to allay Catholic
fears of reprisal once James II could no longer control Parliament, his
peers or the army. Years of 'no popery' propaganda, which demonized
the Pope as Antichrist and reinforced at every opportunity the notion
that 'papists' had split loyalties, were secret conspirators and were
ever in the pay of Jesuitical plots to land a foreign army or lead a
Catholic crusade, meant that, sooner or later, all political problems
would find a way to Catholic doors. If monarchy and nation were
one and that unity was Protestant then what hope for tolerance once
the natural centre for toleration and clemency was removed? James's
toleration seemed to Anglicans and patriots a sign of weakness and
a proof of conspiracy. How could James continue a Catholic monarch but Defender of the Faith? Between 1679 and 1681 the political
grouping under the Earl of Shaftesbury known as the Country Party
and then the Whigs had tried repeatedly to bring in legislation to bar
James from the succession. The defeat of the Exclusion Bills, mainly
due to Charles's intervention, had led this alliance of ultra-Protestant
republicans, Dissenters and 'low' Church Anglicans to the desperate
measures which had failed at Rye House. Now James was King and
he had a son and heir.

Even though Titus Oates and his vile colleagues had been exposed,
antagonism continued between Protestants and Catholics. It took little to reignite it. Thus when James II, in his last act as monarch, put
his name to the Declaration of Indulgence of 27 April 1688, the consequences were inevitable. Narcissus Luttrell, a contemporary commentator, witnessed the disaster, and recorded it in his diary,

DEC. 11th 1688
and accordingly searches are everywhere made to disarm the
papists, and several popish soldiers are disbanded.
   The 11th, in the evening, the mobile [mob] got together and
went to the popish chapel in Lincolns Inn Fields, and perfectly
gutted the same, pulling down all the wainscot, pictures, books
etc. and part of the house and burnt them; and proceeded to
Wildhouse, the Spanish ambassadors, and did the same, and continued in a great body, several thousands, all night . . . Father Ellis,
a popish bishop is lately taken . . . This night (the 12th) the mobile
[mob] were up again in a numerous body, and proceeded to pull

down several popish houses; they carried away in books, pictures, goods, money and plate, of his own and others, which were carried there for shelter, to the value of near £100,000; they would have plundered and demolished the houses of several papists, as the Lord Powys, the late Judge Allibons etc. if they had not been prevented by the trained bands which were out; a party of horse were also out, who did at last disperse them.[24]

Monmouth may have been willing to gamble his head but James's son-in-law William of Orange certainly was not. Before arriving in England he conducted lengthy diplomatic negations and after hesitation and delay secured the loyalty of men like John Churchill who along with the established Tory–Anglican hierarchy hoped to see a Protestant back on the throne and their abused rights restored. When James fled London in the face of defection and an unreliable royal army, William, a rather dour Calvinist, took his place in an almost bloodless coup, creating at once a northern Protestant bloc. When James returned with an Irish–French army he was roundly defeated at the Boyne (1690).

With the arrival of William of Orange in England and his advance towards London, and fearing the defection of those around him, James secretly fled from the capital by boat on 11 December 1688. It was a precipitate and disastrous move, which left Londoners 'astonished' at 'the surprising news'. What could this portend other than an attempt by James to seize the capital in order to massacre its Protestant citizens or raze its buildings or both, using as his instruments the fifth column of Catholics living in London and secretly hoarding weaponry in foreign embassies and chapels? Such fantasies, which seemed to confirm the fantastic machinations of the papacy and suggested a dramatic and apocalyptic attempt to bring in 'popery' via a royal coup, brought masses of Londoners out onto the streets. With the unspoken (if temporary) connivance of magistrates and militia the City and its outlying villages both sides of the Thames could safely be seized by the mob on behalf of the 'old cause'.

Made up of apprentices, youths, labourers, servants, disbanded soldiers and deserters from James's army, 'the mob consulted to wreak their vengeance on Papists and Popery' in a carnival of hatred directed at Catholic sites which locals identified with the deepest fear, loathing and suspicion. Even before James's departure, in November the mob had found in the chapel in St John's, Clerkenwell 'gridirons' so large they had to have no other purpose than the torture of Protestants! A violent 'pitched battle' with soldiers assigned to protect the building and its goods left many of the crowd dead or injured but also resulted in the utter destruction of their target, trophies being carried to Holborn for the bonfires there.

James's ultimate act as ruler was to close all 'mass-houses' except those belonging to foreign embassies and the Royal Family in December 1688 as a last-ditch attempt to save the Catholics of London from a restless majority. Wealthy Catholics, fearing for their property and their lives, left London or hid 'in holes', sending their belongings and children to sympathetic Protestants or foreign ambassadors. Poorer Catholics simply waited to become targets. There was little or no chance of protecting chapels or objects of Catholic veneration too large to hide. The mob was at work, but its work was purposeful, directed and thorough.

> They began their brutal purgation with the most conspicuously placed of the 'mass-houses': the Franciscan chapel, near the Arch, in Great Lincoln's Inn Fields, which was one of the largest and had been open for less than a year. The 'enraged multitude', having assembled 'to a prodigious number', went to their work with relish. Using their bare hands, and such sticks and staves that they had with them, they 'gradually from top to bottom pulled down' as much of the fabric as they could. Working through the night, they 'took out the timber and all that was combustible', not only wainscoting and floorboards, but beams and joists 'and burnt it in the Fields', leaving the chapel 'perfectly gutted'.[25]

The small Catholic population was unable and too terrified to intervene. The Protestant aggression in London was without opposition both in the City itself and across the London suburbs. This was nothing less than a very English *Kristallnacht*. 'They first broke into all these places, and whilst some plucked down, and threw out all the goods, pictures, and furniture out of the windows, others without and below set them on fire; this being begun in several places at one time, the whole town seemed in a flame'.

Only the Great Fire of 1666 had seen more fires: the Benedictine monastery and chapel at St John's, Clerkenwell burned, so did the Jesuit chapel in Lime Street, the Carmelite house in Bucklersbury and the residence of the Spanish Ambassador, Don Pedro de Ronquillo, which was looted and fired partly because of its resident and his unpaid extravagancies, partly because Spaniards were fair game and partly for his open patronage of Catholic activities in the City. The embassies of Venice, Tuscany and the Palatinate followed. Judge Jeffreys was himself caught by the crowd in Wapping as he attempted to escape in disguise. A contemporary print shows him terrified of being torn 'to peeces'. Unable to enter the royal palaces, the mob was able to destroy the convert Henry Hills' (Catholic) publishing house on Ditchside at Blackfriars after Hills had fled across the Channel forewarned by royal hand. Destruction in all cases was thorough.

On 12 December 1688, roughly twenty-four hours after the violence began, and satisfied that it had secured London, destroyed the signs of Catholicism and created a huge propaganda success, the provisional government of peers and privy councillors ordered magistrates and militia into action to restore order for the triumphant appearance of William of Orange, Defender of the True Faith. On 29 January 1689, roughly a month after James had fled, the House of Commons accused him of abdication of government and subversion of the Constitution and concluded with a certain clarity and brutality, 'that it hath been found, by experience, to be inconsistent with the safety and welfare of this Protestant Kingdom to be governed by a Popish Prince'.

The accession of William III on 13 February 1689 brought with it more rows between high and low Church, Anglicans and Dissenters following the limited broadened toleration that William needed to secure his throne. For almost twenty years Catholics could breathe a freer air simply because the state and Church were no longer aggressively looking their way. Legal toleration of any sort still ignored them and resigned acquiescence was the best way for safety. For a moment at least the fury of the mob would be directed elsewhere.

Frustrated by the machinations of the grandees, blocked in their desires for an equitable commonwealth and ever hopeful of the second coming, extreme Dissenters and republicans became ever more violent and conspiratorial. By the latter half of the seventeenth century those who had not embarked for the New World were beginning careers as terrorists. The Rye House Plot was simply one of a number of increasingly desperate moves by a shrinking body of militants. One of these extremists had tried to assassinate Oliver Cromwell for betraying the Commonwealth and revolution and becoming too monarchical. The attack that occurred in Hyde Park was frustrated as was a desperate plot to raze London during the months before the Great Fire itself. In this gamble an ex-colonel in the Parliamentary Army called John Rathbone and half a dozen other conspirators intended to kill the King and the Duke of York, blockade the Horse Guards in their barracks, capture the Tower, shut the city gates and fire its buildings. The conspirators were, as always it seemed, found out and executed. It is quite possible that Fifth Monarchist incendiaries helped fuel the Great Fire once the blaze (however started) took hold. Papists, however, made better scapegoats.

The Catholics were to the sixteenth, seventeenth and eighteenth centuries what Communists were to the twentieth, a combination of real enemies and occasional traitors with a convenient chimera for the establishment and government to spy on, cheat and ultimately control. They also provided a convenient excuse for a spy network which watched threatening elements that came from the extremes of the Catholic 'right' and the republican 'left'. Nowhere did this show more obviously than in the Popish Plot, manufactured out of the imagination of an ugly snitch and a gaggle of conmen. Central to that intrigue was the murder of Sir Edmund Berry Godfrey, which remains one of the great unsolved crimes of British history and, perhaps, a gateway into the murky world of Fifth Monarchist intrigue and Protestant republican terrorism, into the mentality of the forces of opposition as they attempted to manipulate the political process.

Godfrey's body was found on Primrose Hill, then a deeply rural area far from the City, just in time to legitimize a set of accusations which became ever more strident as ever more unbelievable: Charles saw through the whole charade and left a growingly hysterical Privy Council to debate itself hoarse whilst he and his brother went to the races. The plot devised by Titus Oates, William Bedloe and Israel Tonge was flawed by the obvious falsity of the documents and their hints about the treason of the Queen and the Duke of York. Charles was only too aware that some of the accusations had a validity as surmises of fact but the conclusions were spurious and noxious. He knew all about his wife and his brother's sympathies. He was for sensible silence and avoiding stirring up a hornet's nest that was intended to trap his brother, his wife and, perhaps himself. Charles was, however, a pragmatist and the murder of Justice Godfrey forced him to follow opinion whilst pretending to lead it. Yet he was something more than just dismissive of the Plot, for although he could quite easily judge Tonge's and Oates's characters and take on an air of insouciance in face of imminent assassination, in fact he was more ambivalent, granting audiences, listening carefully, avoiding trouble, remembering his father's fate and bearing in mind his brother's likely fall. Godfrey's death clinched the case against the Catholics and on Godfrey's skewered carcass was inscribed the treason Oates's narrative could not supply.

Charles had been unconvinced by Tonge and his tall tales of Catholic plots and so Tonge, left without an option, turned to Oates to swear to the truth of his story and then go back to whoever in government would listen. Oates and Tonge therefore went looking for a magistrate. They did not go to William Waller, a staunch anti-Catholic. Perhaps they felt he would look too obviously a prejudiced choice. They chose instead Sir Edmund Berry Godfrey and visited him during September, on the recommendation of a group simply referred to as 'very honourable friends'.

Godfrey was not shown the deposition that Oates left with him but he was made aware that it referred to the 'firing of . . . towns' by Jesuits, especially by John Grove, a friend of Godfrey and indeed a Jesuit, but also in the forefront of fighting the destructive fire that broke out in Southwark in 1676. Godfrey now knew he was open to being charged with misprision (or concealment) of treason, which was a major offence. A further expanded version was later sworn and deposited with him. Now he was becoming seriously alarmed at his involvement. 'When I went with my depositions to him, he was so frightened, that I believe he beshit himself; for there was such a stink I could hardly stay in the room,' Titus Oates remembered. The next weeks saw Godfrey go about his business as a magistrate and parish dignitary but his meetings with colleagues were littered with odd innuendoes. To one he said he would be the first 'martyr' of the Plot and to a woman friend that he would be 'hang'd' or worse. A depressive person by nature, Godfrey seemed more distracted than usual. He only had weeks left to live.

Some five weeks after his conference with Oates, Godfrey went missing. He had gone walking and various people had greeted him but then he had vanished. Rumours quickly spread that he had been murdered and like a self-fulfilling prophecy his dead body was discovered on Primrose Hill near a local tavern. He had been run through with his own sword, but he was also extensively bruised and showed signs of strangulation. Also his pockets were still full of money and his shoes were clean even though the area was muddy.

Culprits had to be found and quickly and it was William Bedloe who happily obliged. According to him, in a long convoluted tale, Godfrey had been lured to Somerset House, the home of the Queen and the centre of Catholic hopes, and there murdered in order to shut him up as he now knew too much of Popish plans. Bedloe's evidence was hopeless – there were no real corroborative facts – but a number of convenient suspects were rounded up and duly framed and executed. According to Bedloe and a number of other dubious witnesses, Godfrey was killed by strangulation then ferreted away at night by use of a sedan chair and a cart and dumped with his sword thrust through his body to make it all look like suicide. However clumsy the story it was needed and was used to great effect. Even Samuel Pepys, no fool, swallowed the tale. The result was an anti-Catholic pogrom.

A number of theories have attempted to answer the enigma of Godfrey's 'suicide'. There are, of course, the obvious ones. Godfrey may have been killed by his two brothers, who themselves appeared a little too eager to find a corpse once he had vanished. Another explanation suggests an attack by footpads that was disturbed. Neither of these explanations may be quite as plausible as the one put forward by Stephen Knight in his 1984 book, *The Killing of Justice Godfrey*.[26]

According to Knight, Godfrey's death was central to plans under the direction of the Earl of Shaftesbury (Anthony Ashley Cooper). Attitudes towards Shaftesbury differ greatly. For the historian John Kenyon, writing in the 1970s, the Earl was both 'enlightened and patriotic', whereas from Shaftesbury's contemporary, the poet and dramatist John Dryden, there was little but contempt. Dryden called him a 'bag pipe', 'bart'ring venal wit for . . . gold'. Shaftesbury had been dismissed in 1676 and had gone into permanent opposition against the court party. His opposition focused every dissident Protestant group and channelled funds to various espionage and terrorist groups. It was certainly Shaftesbury's money or that of his colleagues that paid some of Oates's expenses and helped offset costs for Bedloe to look after witnesses. Shaftesbury's name, if not his person, was also linked to the Rye House Plot. Around the Earl grew a legitimate opposition party (that would become the Whigs) and an illegitimate covert group working towards a coup. Shaftesbury's followers began meeting at the King's Head Tavern in Chancery Lane in 1675.*

Information about Shaftesbury's complex and clandestine operations emerge from government surveillance and the work of Colonel Thomas Blood (famously pardoned for stealing the Crown Jewels). In a secret report to Sir Joseph Williamson, the Secretary of State, Blood claimed he was working in 1677 to uncover a plot by Fifth Monarchists, atheists and the 'Robert Peyton Gang'. These were ultra-Protestants, who combined militant republicanism with millennial dreams and 'free-thinking' dissent (atheists might also, as with Christopher Marlowe, be occultists or 'humanists'). All were violently opposed to Catholicism. These forces had combined in the Yorkshire Plot of 1677, which had the usual ingredients of an armed uprising and march on London, the seizure of the Tower, assassination of all the royal family and the reinstatement of a Puritan Commonwealth under Richard Cromwell. Government agents ruined the plans, which were abandoned.

This left, nevertheless, the tantalizing problem of the identity of Peyton's Gang. These men may have represented 'the honourable friends' who suggested Oates get in touch with Godfrey in the first place. We certainly know something of Robert Peyton, MP for Middlesex and a vehement opposition figure. He and his friends were also certainly known to the security forces, for many were men in authority, whom the Lieutenant of the Tower Hamlets, Sir John Robinson, believed formed a secret and high level 'masonic' group. A secret communiqué named the Gang, some of whom were then stripped of their positions. On a scrap of paper Robinson sent to Williamson during 1676 and headed 'Paiton's gang' are listed

---

*Much of London's political life has centred on public houses. In the eighteenth century, Robert Walpole's conservative opponents met at the Fountain in Fountain Court near the present Savoy Hotel and Simpsons, whilst many years later, both Karl Marx and Lenin drank toasts to revolution in the radical Pindar of Wakefield (now the Water Rats public house, Gray's Inn Road).

Sr Edmund Berry Godfrey Sr Robert Peyton
Sr Reginald Foster
Sr William Bowles
Sr Edmund Berry Godfrey
Georg Welch Esq
William Barker Esq
Richard Adams Esq
William Hempston Esq
Peter Sabbs Esq
Samuell Buck Esq
John Barker Esq
Charles Umphreville Esq

If this paper is authentic then Godfrey may have been an extreme republican. Given that he did not lose office he may have been useful in other ways as a 'turned' seditionist. Other evidence suggests that a dinner held in 1674 at the Swan Tavern in King Street, Hammersmith, then a suburb, was one of a number that led to the formation of the Green Ribbon Club. This particular one was abandoned for fear of arrest but the venue might always be convenient as the freehold was held by Godfrey. Peyton was ostensible leader of the Green Ribboners, helping to orchestrate anti-papal propaganda and Pope-burning processions. (These still continue in Lewes in Sussex each 5 November.) Peyton was a supporter of Monmouth should it be necessary to keep a king but he also nurtured hopes of being 'Chiefe for London'. Having been accused of being 'turned' by James's agents, expelled from the House of Commons and imprisoned in the Tower, he was back in action in 1679 implicated in the Meal Tub Plot.

The swirling shadows of intrigue swamped Godfrey when he was 'set up' to take the depositions. Godfrey, like many of the Catholic victims, was to be the patsy for the Exclusionist cause to remove James from the succession. The reason, Stephen Knight suggests, lies in his mysterious and clandestine meeting with a man calling himself Clark (or Clarke) at a Colonel Weldon's house on 28 September after the depositions had been sworn. Clarke, it was revealed to the Lords Committee of investigation into the murder, was the alias of Edward Coleman, the Queen's Catholic confessor. This may or may not have been true. If true, it would certainly make Godfrey a double agent and traitor to the cause; if untrue, it was a good way to damn the Catholics and thereby hide the real villains. Godfrey was dead either way. Coleman led straight to James, but Godfrey, with cold feet, had warned him to destroy his papers, which he almost did, and he had sent a copy of the depositions to James as a warning. In other words Godfrey had become a government man attempting to defend the status quo. A bizarre twist also suggested that French money, filtered *through* Coleman, may have gone to the Opposition!

Godfrey was now at the centre of the web and he knew it. It is quite possible that his brothers knew it also and were now enemies. If Knight's speculations are correct then Godfrey was being shadowed by republican terrorists and had no hope of reprieve. Indeed, they already had a murder squad put together under the leadership of a man called John Johnson, who may have been brought over from America. Johnson's real name was John Scott, a republican agent and fraudster. As with so many others, he called himself 'Colonel' for good measure. Blood had an inkling of his connection with Peyton and murder but was frustrated as to details. As the last hours ticked away Godfrey took delivery of a secret letter after which he burned papers and settled his debts as if he would be free of it all soon.

Then Godfrey was dead. His bruised, battered, strangled and stabbed body was found outside the White House tavern, Primrose Hill, a venue for a regular Catholic Club, his death mysteriously reported before its discovery by a man in a 'grey suit' who swore the murder had taken place at Leicester Fields (now Leicester Square). This mistake may have been an unwitting clue given by an agent provocateur not clear on the correct line or it may have been an intended clue designed to make it clear that the murderer was untouchable by government forces, for such a person did live in Leicester Fields.

This man was Philip Herbert, Earl of Pembroke, who owned a town house in the area. He was an opposition supporter and a probable republican (republicanism was conceived as based on an aristocratic plutocracy). He was also a psychopath, nicknamed 'the Mad Peer'. A 'giant' of a man, he kept fifty-two mastiffs, thirty greyhounds, bears, a lion and sixty 'bestial' servants at his country seat at Wilton. He was also a man of quick and deadly temper, duelling at any opportunity, kidnapping and abusing where possible and latterly murdering at the least provocation. Imprisoned in the Tower for the kidnap and abuse of a parson (as well as for atheistic blasphemy), he was soon released to fight another day. Philip Ricant came to London to visit a friend but met Pembroke instead: he was attacked and beaten black and blue, strangled and near-fatally stabbed. The day before his appearance in front of the Lords Pembroke killed Nathaniel Cony after a drunken binge: Cony was beaten, strangled and stabbed. Dreadful bruising had been caused by the famous 'Pembroke kick', a form of violent stamping. These were, of course, all symptoms noticed at Godfrey's autopsy, recorded in the coroner's report.

Pembroke certainly had the correct modus operandi to have murdered Godfrey, the sword thrust after death a means to avoid the obvious suspect. He continued on his savage way without respite, he and his men brawling with local constables and murdering when it was convenient. An assassination attempt having failed to stop him, he finally fled abroad after an indictment for murder. It was not the first: that had been some years before and Godfrey had been Chairman of the Jury. He therefore had a personal score to settle with the magistrate. He was, nevertheless, a staunch Protestant, a member of Monmouth's supporters and a peer. Charles granted him a pardon on 22 June 1681. He was dead of alcohol poisoning (or worse) at the age of thirty. What of the American, Colonel Scott? He escaped, and narrowly missing detection told his interlocutors with the cheek of a professional that his name was 'Godfrey'. He took a boat and sailed away.

Stephen Knight's explanation of Godfrey's death brought to a seeming conclusion the history of re-examinations of this famous murder case. It also had the merit of tying together the many conspiratorial factions of the period and of bringing into focus notorious double agents such as Thomas Blood and John Scott, the man who claimed to be Godfrey when stopped on the road to Dover.

Knight's explanation remained unchallenged for only thirteen years. In 1999, Alan Marshall, reviewing the evidence, concluded that Godfrey had indeed committed suicide by self-strangulation, being discovered by his servant and the whole episode made to look like a conspiracy by the two remaining brothers, Michael and Benjamin, prominent London merchants, whose political ambitions fed City and Whig aspirations and who needed to cover up a suicide which would lead to the loss of Godfrey's estate. Thus the death of a manic-depressive would ultimately serve the cause of Protestantism and the magistrate end his life as a martyr.[27] The case remains unsolved to this day.

6

George's War

From the Jacobites to the Gordon Riots

It is said that London is demolished and rebuilt every fifty years, as much an imaginary space as a geographical location where old place names record the almost forgotten byways and livelihoods of another age. The Thames flows through a landscape of almost continuous metamorphosis. Nowhere was this metamorphosis more evident than in the rebuilding of the city after the Great Fire.

The pre-fire city still retained its medieval-Tudor look, a great, boisterous, dirty and plague-ridden metropolis where 70,000 people had died of 'pestilence' in 1665. The committee that decided on London's future looked to reconcile public need with private property, modernization with the old medieval web of streets. The committee of the Corporation of London ordered over 100 streets to be widened, new roads such as King Street and Queen Street to be built, new parish churches, a grand new St Paul's Cathedral and the rebuilding of the Guildhall. Houses and most other buildings were to be of red brick, and timber was not to be used. Nine thousand houses were rebuilt and St Paul's was completed in 1711. The city remained crowded and insanitary, however, great poverty huddling next to great wealth.

Outside the old city boundaries, new suburbs arose. Merchants grown rich on American, West Indian or Asian trade built elegant town houses along Oxford Street and Mayfair. Islington, Hackney, Edmonton, Blackheath and Twickenham grew as satellite villages. New town squares also appeared in Soho, Leicester Fields (Leicester Square), and on sites that took on the name of a builder or aristocrat: Bedford Square, Cavendish Square, Grosvenor Square and Portland Square. London was a consumer city, too, fed in its desires as much by the watchmakers of Clerkenwell as by the furniture manufacturers of Camden or the tailors of Westminster. Great wealth was slowly moving west in order to separate itself from abject poverty, but both still existed side by side whilst the new 'middle class' became the lawyers, shopkeepers, petty merchants, publishers and a host of other professions and trades that fed the appetites of the powerful and avoided the foreboding presence of the squalid multitude.

The rebuilding of the new city was achieved with the money of the old. The inheritors of the great corporate and financial world of the medieval merchants still ruled London as they had done in the days of the Commune. The Corporation of London was the mightiest financial power in England and rapidly overtaking those powerful groups in Europe against which they would divide the world. Financial and mercantile power was also political power.

The ancestors of the livery companies were the guilds of London. In the twelfth century there had been craft groups of saddlers, bakers, weavers, goldsmiths, pepper dealers, cloth workers and butchers amongst a host of others formed into nineteen guilds. In a further two centuries this had risen to over a hundred, using their power to regulate trade, property, religious donations and welfare. No ruler could afford to alienate the guilds or their masters and each guarded its fraternity against all newcomers. No tradesman or craftsman could set up within the City without joining a guild. The growth of suburban trade and craft centres around London reflected the need to escape the grip of city regulation. By the time of the Tudors further groups had been founded within the city to regulate and expand foreign trade: the powerful Muscovy Company was one. The Hudson Bay Company, founded in 1670, followed the Tudor tradition. Small guilds as well as powerful livery companies built lavish halls and traded in the Royal Exchange. The seventeenth and eighteenth centuries saw the further tightening of the city's grip on finance and trade with the building of the Bank of England and purchase of a building for the newly created Stock Exchange.

Members of the older guilds and later livery companies were 'freemen' of the City and no tradesperson could work independently within the old Roman walls unless they became a freeman. This privilege was acknowledged by the use of a parchment certificate sometimes called a 'copy of freedom'.

The 'Square Mile' controlled by the Corporation of London stretched from Fleet Street and Holborn to the east to Aldgate and across to Liverpool Street, and remained unchanged until boundaries were renegotiated in 1994. Southwark, despite being partially under Corporation control, resisted the incorporation foist on it in 1550. To all intents and purposes, the Corporation of London was the government of London. The City was divided into twenty-six wards (reduced to twenty-five in the late twentieth century) and freemen could vote in local elections until 1867. Each ward had an alderman and several common councillors according to the size of the area. The aldermen met as a court, which was later expanded to include councillors and called the Court of Common Council, which had both a civic and a judicial function. Twice a year, Common Hall met to elect the city sheriffs and Lord Mayor, City MPs, town clerk and other officers. During the eighteenth century Common Hall (made up of all the senior livery men of the companies) was the centre of extreme political manoeuvring. Jealous of its control of finance, the Corporation fought a contrived battle to renew its right to license brokers including those on the Stock Exchange and in so doing restrict the influence of French, Dutch and Jewish dealers. From the Billingsgate porters to the watermen and lightermen of the Thames, to the lowliest widow or orphan of a freeman to the highest city dignitary, the Corporation was central to their lives.

The group of senior wardens and masters who controlled the Corporation effectively controlled London and then the empire. Yet politically the Corporation was a strange mixture of loyal monarchists and republican-minded oligarchists. It was a club made up entirely of true 'Church and King' men whose members had no love for democracy yet whose very existence encouraged liberal marketeering and individual entrepreneurship. The freedoms so coveted by this club when they were allied with property nevertheless sowed the seeds for the liberty necessary to all people under a universal and disinterested legal system. Always opposed to the tyranny of strong monarchs, it was also always watchful of Catholic aristocrats, an overly zealous Parliament and a turbulent populace. The Corporation pragmatically traded with everybody: when necessary it might bring out the London apprentices to demonstrate its true Protestant dislike of an overly autocratic Stuart or Hanoverian, demanding liberty and law, or it might fete the very same monarch at the table of the Lord Mayor in order to show who was boss. By the late seventeenth century the Corporation was preparing to fight a long series of legal and ideological battles with Parliament and King, from which a modern market economy (and its legal and philosophical premises) eventually emerged. It was a struggle with its roots in the obscure religious debates and state politicking of the time of Charles I.

By the eighteenth century the old exclusion debates had polarized the country into two distinct parties, Whigs and Tories, both trying to prove their greater loyalty to 'King and Church'. Few trusted the new German rulers, the Hanoverians who had inherited the throne after Anne's death in 1714 and whose origins, language and inclination were all Continental; and with one side of the Stuart dynasty alive and well and living in exile few could reckon on their permanence. (Permanent they were. The last Hanoverian was Queen Victoria.) The Whigs, nevertheless, aligned themselves with the House of Hanover and accused the Tories of plotting a return of one or other of the Pretenders who would instantly restore absolutism and 'popery'. If Toryism hedged its bets it also believed in a strong King, a strong Anglican Church and an establishment based firmly on Anglican values.

The continuous threat posed in the first fifty years of the eighteenth century by the deposed Stuarts (especially the Jacobite rebellions of 1715 and 1745) destabilized London politics, and threatened the new dynasty and its Whig supporters. Toryism, with its adherence to monarch and Church and its opposition to commerce and Dissenters, would always be 'touchy' regarding the legitimacy of the new German royal family. With the imprisonment or exile of the Stuart's supporters the old guard was clearly under threat. On Queen Anne's birthday Jacobite royalists noisily and publicly drank her health, while on 28 May, the birthday of George I and the anniversary of the restoration of Charles II, the London justices kept continual vigil.

The factional differences between London Jacobites and Hanoverians came to a head in November 1715, and for eight months fighting broke out on significant royal (or other) dates. Jacobites (or 'Jacks') regularly attacked houses and properties of Hanoverians, and loyalists happily fought back after a night at the tavern. Support for the deposed Stuarts lingered long and dangerously. On 10 June, the birthday of James II's son (James Edward Stuart – later called the Old Pretender) was celebrated by Jacobites gathered at a tavern in Drury Lane. Having enjoyed a number of toasts to his health, the celebrants were said to have rushed into the street with flags and drums and forced passers-by to drink a 'loyal' toast to the deposed family. There was a swift reaction and fighting broke out between the drunken revellers and local people, leaving the pub in ruins and the Jacobites beaten, bruised and taken prisoner.

These disturbances were called the 'mug-house' riots because of their association with tavern drinking. The loyalist Roebuck Inn on Ludgate Hill was the scene of continuous brawling and even on one occasion a massed assault by Jacks, which was met by murderous musket fire from the pub itself that killed or wounded a number of attackers. Another loyalist tavern, Read's in Salisbury Court, off Fleet Street, was attacked the following year by Jacks shouting 'High Church and Ormonde' but the tavern's occupants over-retaliated by shooting dead one of the hooligans, named Daniel Vaughan. The dead man's funeral was reason for further rioting and the new regime, having had enough, finally decided to act, hanging five of Read's attackers next to the pub. This sobering episode brought to an end the opportunity open to Jacobites in London to express their opposition to the new ruling elite after a night's heavy drinking.

The fear of Jacobitism was present in London throughout the first fifty years of the eighteenth century. The Old Pretender's birthday was celebrated again on 10 June 1720 by the open display by 'many people of white roses in their hats' and during 1736 it was believed a 'sett of low Jacobites' had been responsible for a phosphor-bomb attack on Westminster Hall. The riots against Irish labourers during 1736 were certainly fuelled by lingering suspicions that the Irish in London were closet Jacobites.

The appearance of the Young Pretender, 'Bonnie Prince Charlie', at Derby in December 1745 threw these fragile alliances into turmoil and produced official hysteria in London itself. The House of Hanover was built on too precarious ground to be able to ignore the threat from the north. Indeed, John Murray, Charles's secretary, when examined after the Pretender was defeated at Culloden in 1746 suggested that 'there were many Persons in the City well affected to the Pretender', a comment full of suggestive possibilities regarding Tory aldermen whose relationship with Parliament was becoming more complex and combative. To fearful supporters of the fragile peace the Hanoverian regime had caused the advance of Charles's army and portended nothing less than the utter ruin of Parliament, trade and the Protestant cause: a Catholic army was poised to take the city, a set of incendiaries would burn it to the ground, a cabal of Jesuits were about to rule at the crowning of Charles III! The government had eyes and ears everywhere, took every rumour and alarm at face value and every minor comment as high treason.

On 3 October, Charles Cavendish mentioned that one of his friends was 'a good deal alarm'd at the number of Irish that have for some time resorted to this town, of whom he has met upon ye Hertfordshire road'. Two weeks later, the London alderman Robert Ladbroke reported to Newcastle [then First Minister] that he had received an anonymous letter claiming that the Jacobites were about to set fire to the capital, an episode widely reported in the press. And at the same time a merchant told his son there had been 'fears and suggestions of the rising of ye Papists today to masicry [sic] the Protestants in this Citty'. These reports were aggravated by the discovery of small arsenals. Twenty chests of cutlasses were seized at the Saracen's Head in the City; a hardware shop in Leadenhall Street was searched for musket ball; and several witnesses came forward with stories of ominous packages stored in Catholic houses in Clerkenwell. Furthermore, on 19 October, thirteen Catholics and a priest at the Portugal Coffee House in St Katherine's Lane were arrested by the Tower Hamlets militia. A week later, a Catholic priest named James Corbet was apprehended for throwing a seditious broadsheet at the King as he reviewed the City trained bands; and within days, the Government rounded up several hawkers who publicized the incident and arrested the printer, William Fowler of Shorts Gardens, Drury Lane. In November, news leaked out that a Scottish Romish priest named Gordon had been apprehended at his house near Red Lion Square for distributing several thousand pounds to the rebels; and early the following month another hawker and printer were arrested for circulating the Pretender's declaration. The capital appeared to be ridden with conspiracy.[1]

Rumours and fantasy (often begun by drunkards at taverns in the hearing of 'patriots', spies and those who eavesdropped for a quick reward) suggested, 'that the Pretender . . . would be in London in less than four Month's time' and that, as Charles Haydon, a Spitalfields dyer, bragged, he would have a rebel army of 120,000 to do his bidding. John Rivers and Daniel Smith from Shoreditch and St Giles-in-the-Fields were indicted like many others for getting drunk and toasting the Pretender's health. They were both fined twelve pence and sentenced to nine months' imprisonment. Joseph Payne, a common labourer, got drunk, toasted the Pretender and found himself informed upon, arrested, tried at the Old Bailey and sent to Newgate for two months having been fined five shillings.

After the '45 Rebellion those convicted of treason were hanged at Kennington Common. In August, Donald MacDonald, James Nicholson and Walter Ogilvie were all taken there by sledge from Southwark New Gaol. Each was hanged, decapitated, disembowelled and quartered. In this instance, individual hanging lasted fourteen minutes, nine minutes longer than that afforded to those executed in July, consisting of Francis Townley, Geoffrey Fletcher, Thomas Chadwick, James Dawson, Thomas Deacon, John Barwick, Andrew Blood, Thomas Siddall and Thomas Morgan. In November Sir John Wedderburn, John Hamilton, James Bradshaw, Andrew Wood and Alexander Leith also travelled the short distance from Southwark to Kennington. Having all been decapitated and quartered, their body parts were then returned to Newgate for display across London and the country. Manchester, Carlisle and London's Temple Bar were considered the best places for these trophies of war.

> Mr Townley was cut down, his body (not being quite dead) being stripped and laid on the block, the hangman with a cleaver severed his head from his body, which were put into a coffin; then taking out the bowels and heart, threw them into the fire: he then proceeded to the next, cutting them down, beheading and

disbowling [sic] them one by one, in the same manner as the first; when the heart of the last was put into the fire, the executioner cried out, *God save K. George*, at which the multitude of spectators gave a great shout . . . the heads and bodies were convey'd in coffins to the prison from whence they came.[2]

Vigilantes could always be relied upon to procure a stream of traitors and Catholics for the courts. As the militia roamed the London streets anyone drinking too much or talking too freely could be trapped and arrested, as were groups of Catholics in Holborn and Soho. Drunk but sincere supporters of the Stuart return might find themselves arrested after tavern or street brawls often with soldiers, who themselves vied to act a prosecuting witnesses.

What remains fascinating about these aggressive purges of loose tongues is the nature of those arrested. They were tradesmen, weavers, pedlars, chapmen, fruiterers, tailors and labourers, many with Irish names or possible origins: Delaney, Donnelley, Doyle, Farrell, Flanagan, Maloney and Murphy, for instance. Many if not all were probably Catholics living in known papist colonies in the East End, Southwark and (urban) Surrey, Holborn, Bloomsbury, St Giles and Marylebone. Many worked in the traditional Catholic trades of labouring, victualling and weaving, although there were also tanners, costermongers and peruke makers. In the Protestant, Tory heartland of Clerkenwell and Westminster prosecution fell away, as it did in the West End where Catholic servants could be protected by the wealthy and where Catholic craftsmen in the luxury industries were seen as necessary by clients.

The violent orchestrated war against 'papists' that marked the sixteenth and seventeenth centuries had boiled and then subsided by the late eighteenth. By then the very idea of persecuting Catholics was anathema, something from a barbarous age. Believing such hatred to be a dead letter, Parliament proposed a Catholic Relief Bill in May 1778, which aimed to free Catholic Scots Highlanders from the old draconian Oath of Allegiance brought in during William III's day and allow their recruitment into the army. It was a cynical move. The annulment of the 1699 Act would effectively allow for the creation of extra regiments to be sent to fight the growing strength of rebellion in America.* Yet ancient passions, it seemed, had only slumbered, and when the Act was finally passed it caused immediate rioting in Scotland and the prospect of worse to come in London. Eventually the furore brought the capital to the brink of revolution.

---

*In effect, one regiment was created, the Royal Highland Emigrants.

Opposition to any Catholic relief began in Scotland and soon caught hold in London. The Protestant Association was formed and in its turn chose a minor Protestant aristocrat as its President, the long-haired, hatchet-faced, vociferous George Gordon. He was the sixth child of the Duke of Gordon, born into a family that Horace Walpole dismissed as 'all mad'. In 1774, at the age of twenty-two, Gordon became an MP. He was from the beginning a libertarian and part republican, setting himself up as an opposition party of one, 'the party of the people' whose voice was the 'voice of God'. In this he followed a more famous and notorious Member of the House, John Wilkes.

> John Wilkes, the demagogue, the most 'wicked and agreeable fellow' that William Pitt had ever met had also voiced his respect for the opinion of the people in similar terms. 'I firmly and sincerely believe', he once declared, 'the voice of the people to be the voice of God. I wish always to hear it loud and distinct. When I do I will obey it as a divine call.'[3]

Gordon's own voice was hectoring and shallow. He was long-winded and less than popular in debate, and never likely to find governmental preferment. Nevertheless his anti-slavery, pro-reform and libertarian views were often far-sighted and intelligent. He also opposed the war in America, seeing much that was right in the Americans' cause.

The circumstances to which Gordon would for ever have his name attached now came to a head with the extension of the Catholic Relief Act to Scotland. The Act already covered England and Wales without any fuss. News quickly spread that this was a plot to put Catholics in power, a rumour particularly liable to cause discontent amongst the 'middle classes', artisans and apprentices. The Catholics, as usual in such allegations, were amassing a 'secret army' ready to emerge from long years of tunnelling under London's streets – the Thames would be rerouted in order to flood the City when Catholics detonated gunpowder hidden on its banks! Even John Wesley ranted about 'the raging fires of Smithfield'. Rioting broke out in Edinburgh and Glasgow. The Act would certainly have a rough ride.

To counter Parliament's apparent neglect of Protestant rights, a solemn League of Protestant Associations was formed and these carried on a propaganda war of some ferocity.

> Let us call to remembrance the massacre at Paris; there Popery appeared in its true colours with the blood of the saints and with the blood of the martyrs of Jesus. Whilst Popery has existence upon earth, let it be remembered though to the disgrace of humanity,

let it be remembered with horror that on Saint Bartholomew's day thousands and tens of thousands of Protestants were murdered in France in cold blood. Smithfield, Oxford, Cambridge . . . have a voice crying aloud 'Beware of Popery, O Britons'. Let not the blood of the martyrs be forgotten . . . To tolerate Popery is to be instrumental to the perdition of immortal soles . . . and is the direct way to provoke the vengeance of a holy and jealous God . . .[4]

Gordon's own involvement came after his parliamentary speeches became well known north of the border. Gordon was both an unimpeachable Calvinist and, in his love of trews and Scots folk music, an unimpeachable Scot. His visit to Scotland was triumphant and on his return to London he was visited by James Fisher, Secretary to the London Association, who asked him to become its President. Effectively he was now leader of the 'People', and embodied their 'will' as President of the most significant 'lobby' group. As President he was dispatched to see George III but only ended up by being ill tempered and alienating the 'ill educated elector of Hanover', as he insultingly called the King.

The next stage was a monster petition and march – a classic form of protest since the time of the Civil War. A series of meetings of the Association Committee ended without result, partly perhaps because Gordon had misgivings about Fisher, a lawyer who spent (at least for Gordon) too much time defending the criminals of Whitechapel, and who was 'A very fluent orator, specious and crouching and submissive with a plentiful command of crying and whining about religion in his speeches; and no lack of buffoonery and low gesting'. Gordon's commitment to the Protestant cause had been neither obvious nor necessary but he soon took to it with zeal both inside and outside Parliament. Spies reported the growth of the Association and this in turn sparked an attempt to 'buy off' Gordon with a huge government pension. Gordon, the bit between his teeth, would not be bought and his attitude now became more threatening.

One day as a fellow Member presented a petition in Parliament and unfolded it on the floor of the House to show how long it was and how many signatures it contained, Lord George jumped up and called out in derisive indignation: 'Pooh! What is all this? With a great deal of pulling, this petition seems to extend from your chair Mr Speaker to the door of the House. In a few days, Sir, I shall present you the Petition of the Protestant Association. It will extend, Sir, from your your chair to a window at Whitehall that Kings should often think of.'[5]

Gordon and his committee finally agreed to hold an open-air rally on 2 June 1780 in St George's Fields.* This was a vast area of open waste and light industry stretching from Lambeth Palace to what is now Waterloo Station. After the rally a march on Westminster would produce the great petition Gordon had threatened. Petitioners were to be distinguished by blue cockades given out on the day, which proved hot and sultry with bursts of summer lightning.

Across the fields at least 60,000 people gathered, vast numbers coming from Westminster and Southwark and a major contingent from Scotland led by pipers (a banned symbol of independence). There were flags and banners and the singing of hymns and psalms as Gordon arrived in triumph ready to lead the march. Singing more hymns and waving blue banners the people's army, marching in ranked disciplined files and led by a protester carrying the roll of 100,000 signatures, proceeded in deadly (if still peaceful) earnest towards Westminster. 'The whole city was amazed, the house-tops were covered with spectators and every person awaited the event with anxious expectation', wrote Gordon's biographer, Robert Watson, in his memoirs of 1795.

Gordon's army represented two types of protester. On the one hand there were the middle orders, tradesmen, aldermen and merchants, who marched direct to Westminster over the new toll bridge (they could afford the fee). On the other hand, there were artisans and apprentices who took the long route via London Bridge and proceeded to march through the East End back towards Westminster. Frederick Reynolds, then a schoolchild, later a dramatist, reported,

> Then we witnessed the most novel and extraordinary proceedings . . . The mob, shortly receiving the addition of many thousands of disorderly persons, occupied every avenue to the Houses of Parliament, the whole of Westminster Bridge, and extended nearly to the northern end of Parliament Street, the greatest part of it, however was composed of persons decently dressed, who

---

*St George's Fields was crisscrossed by lines of street lamps marking the roads into London. The effect at night surprised and delighted many foreign visitors. Building slowly encroached on the open spaces as speculators attempted to reproduce the elegance of the north bank. Their failure left the area shabby if sometimes genteel. The area still remains associated with vinegar production, which was part of the original local brewing industry. Bethlem Hospital moved from Liverpool Street to the area in 1815. Devoid of its wings it now exists as the Imperial War Museum. The obelisk that marked the confluence of the roads to London can still be found in Kennington.

appeared to be incited to extravagance by a species of fanatical phrenzy . . . They talked of dying in the good cause . . .[6]

The situation soon degenerated when the crowds arrived at Westminster itself. Lords identified as 'enemies' of the people were jostled, abused or attacked, barricading themselves against attack once inside Parliament. Anti-papistry was soon anti-aristocracy; Tories and landed gentry were attacked as much for their undeserved privileges as for their political or religious beliefs. Thus the Chief Justice, Lord Mansfield, was attacked in his carriage (he had recently acquitted a priest) and was only narrowly rescued by the Archbishop of York who raced (he was an athlete) to his rescue! The Duke of Northumberland and General Grant were jostled and had their watches stolen. Other lords were also attacked and soldiers had to be used to help Lord North (the First Minister) escape, his hat liberated from his head by the crowd, torn up and sold at a shilling a piece. In contrast, Members of the House of Commons received a much lighter drubbing; only two were attacked.

As the lobby of the House of Commons filled with protesters Gordon could be seen shunting back and forth between the clamour of the crowd and the debate inside, whipping attitudes up by reporting that Lord North considered the lobbyists a mere 'mob'. Alarm was now spreading amongst middle-class Londoners. Sarah Hoare, wife of the Quaker banker Samuel Hoare, wrote to her mother,

> Everyone is anxious to hear the conclusion of an affair, which has made great noise in the city all this day. Thou hast most probably heard of the meeting which was advertised to be held in St George's Fields, to proceed from thence in procession to the House of Commons to deliver a petition from the Protestants. Accordingly 50,000 men, divided into companys [sic] of 8000 each, with Lord George Gordon at their head, assembled at the hour appointed and marched through the city. The Guards were ordered out, and many feared that would produce great confusion What reception they met with on their arrival I have not heard. I must own I have seldom felt my fears equally awakened.[7]

Poor Sarah had little time to wait. Rioting began when troops tried to free the members of the House of Commons. The crowds opened, and then surrounded the soldiers and began pelting them with stones and faggots, but the worst violence was to fall upon Catholic masshouses (chapels), one especially drawing attention in Lincoln's Inn Fields. As with so many anti-Catholic disturbances, the crowd first turned on the chapels of foreign diplomats. The Sardinian Chapel was systematically and comprehensively demolished, its attackers both organized and disciplined. Soldiers finally arrived and arrested, apparently rather indiscriminately, anyone caught near the action. So terrified was one lady, Mrs Mary O'Donald, that she 'fell into fits which occasioned for her death!' The crowd moved on to Golden Square and destroyed the house of the Bavarian Ambassador, Count Hasling, long considered a 'fence' for all sorts of contraband goods. Finally exhausting foreign targets, the crowd made for the Irish population of Moorfields. Meanwhile, the army headed in the opposite direction for the squares of the West End in order to protect aristocratic property.

By the evening of 3 June a crowd had marched to Rope Maker's Alley, Moorfields, to attack the chapel there. This was near to Mr Malo's silk business, where 200 looms kept 2,000 men at work. Malo, believing (correctly as it turned out) that disaster was at hand, hastened to see Lord Mayor Kennet, who appeared confused and could only talk in a riddle still not fully explained: 'I can assure you', he told Malo, 'that there are very great people at the bottom of the riot.' The Mayor did nothing, avoided contact and refused to authorize immediate action to read the Riot Act or bring out the military. It is certainly possible that he was in cahoots with the Protestant Association or was simply unwilling to protect rival Catholic or Irish merchants. His inactivity would certainly hurt the King, whose ineptitude in the American War had caused the Colonists to boycott tea and thus to ruin sales for London merchants like Alderman Frederick Bull, a central figure in the Association and a major Catholic-baiter.

By 5 June, various parts of London were under siege, with gossip providing regular updates of the destruction.

> . . . We have just received intelligence which gives us equal concern and surprise, that there is actually a riotous meeting at Moorfields, and that a great number of seditious persons are employed in demolishing different dwelling-houses, and all this is done in broad day without the least interposition of the civil magistrate.[8]

From Wapping to Leicester Fields various mobs, often led by well-dressed and 'mysterious' gentlemen, were attacking Catholic homes and businesses and building bonfires with the contents. Groups of soldiers gathered to protect property found themselves hampered by the irresolution of the magistrates, disinclined to protect Catholic citizens. Yet things were clearly out of hand and Gordon put his name to a public disclaimer.

> Resolved unanimously, That all true Protestants be requested to shew their attachment to their best interest by a legal and peaceable Deportment, as all unconstitutional proceedings, in so good a

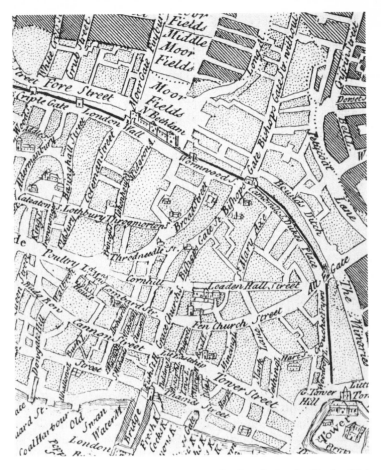

Moorfields, shown on this 1744 map, was under siege during the Gordon Riots. (From 'A Plan of the Cities of London & Westminster' by Robert Dodsley)

cause, can only tend to prevent the Members of the Legislature from paying due attention to the United Prayers of the Protestant Petition.[9]

Later that night Malo went once more to the Lord Mayor.

At a late hour on Monday evening Mr Malo went for the last time to the Lord Mayor. He represented to his lordship his dangerous situation, entreated in the strongest terms his protection and begged his lordship to permit him to bring his wife and daughters to his house. His lordship was as little moved with these as with any of the former applications. He did not condescend to give Mr Malo any answer, but turned his heel, and went to an inner room. He soon after returned and said 'Surely, sir, you are a Papist?' Mr Malo said he was of the religion in which he was educated, the Roman Catholic faith. 'I always thought so', replied his lordship and retired.[10]

Mr Malo would get no protection. Catholic families now sought to leave London and head for the suburbs or local villages; poor Irish simply hid in cellars.

Things had degenerated further by 6 June with houses being destroyed without any judicial or military intervention. Charles Jenkinson (then Secretary at War and later First Earl of Liverpool) now sent the following to Lord Stormont:

I have now the honour to enclose to your Lordship the copy of a letter and report transmitted to me by Major-General Wynyard of what happened in the course of yesterday and last night, and must beg in the most serious manner to call your Lordship's attention to some parts of that letter and report wherein it appears that in one instance the Civil Magistrate having called for the Troops was not ready to attend them; that in another instance the Troops having been called out were left by the Magistrate exposed to the fury of the Populace when the Party were insulted in a most extraordinary manner, and that in two other instances after the Troops had marched to the places appointed for them, several of the Magistrates refused to act. It is the duty of the Troops, my Lord, to act only under the Authority and by direction, of the Civil Magistrate. For this reason they are under greater restraints than any other of His Majesty's subjects, and when insulted are obliged to be more cautious even in defending themselves. If, therefore, the Civil Magistrate after having called upon them is not ready to attend them, or abandons them before they return to their quarters, or after they arrive at the places to which they have been ordered, refuses to act, I leave it to your Lordship to judge in how defenseless and how disgraceful a situation the military are left, and how much such conduct as this tends even to encourage Riots, and how much the public service as well as the Troops must suffer by it.[11]

Legal opinion was that the military could only intervene if called upon by the civil authority (a magistrate) and although this ruling was later challenged it meant that on 6 June any soldier killing a civilian was liable to be indicted for murder The military was therefore impotent.

Meanwhile Protestant pamphlets began circulating in the City. One read:

> In this paper will be given a full account of the bloody tyrannies and inhuman butcheries exercised on the Protestants in England by the See of Rome; highly necessary to be read at this important moment by every English-man who loves his God and his Country. To which will be added some reasons why the few misguided people now in confinement for destroying the Romish Chapels should not suffer, and the dreadful consequences of an attempt to bring them to punishment.[12]

Mr Malo was soon to feel the opprobrium of a Protestant mob.

> On Tuesday morning Mr Malo removed some of his valuable stock of silks, but the utensils of his trade and the furniture of his house he had not time to shift. At noon several large bands of rioters came to his house, from different avenues about Moorfields, at almost the same time, assembling at back and front. They knocked and threatened to murder the people inside if the door was not opened immediately. Two of Mr Malo's servants made their escape over the leads of the house. Mr Malo his wife and daughters fled, but the eldest son fainted the instant the mob rushed into the house and was for many days so affected that both his life and his intellects were in danger. The mob demolished everything in the house; they tore down the wainscot, broke all the furniture, threw it out of the window and made a bonfire of it. Among the things they heaped on the bonfire were some canary birds with their cages. Passers by wished to deliver them from their fate and offered to purchase them but the mob said they were Popish birds and should burn with the rest of the Popist goods. Some of the birds were rescued, but the rest were kept screaming on the fire until they were consumed.[13]

So helpless was the military that one 'charge' only succeeded in knocking down a number of rioters who 'lay in the most ludicrous manner . . . Like a pack of cards'. Far from being intimidated, the incident was treated as a huge joke by the crowd, many of whom were milling about Parliament attempting to scare the two Houses. The two Houses, finally resolved to stand up to the mob, would also have to decide on the nature of the disturbances, for riot was apparently turning to rebellion.

By now Leicester Fields was ablaze, as was Covent Garden and Bloomsbury Square. Fanny Burney's father only assuaged the mob outside his house by crying out 'No Popery' and raising his hat to which his would-be assailants shouted, 'God bless your Honour!' St Martin's Lane was filled with rubble when the violence seemed to take on a different and more deadly nature. It was not that Catholics were forgotten, far from it; to religious outrage was now added a revolutionary and quasi-republican libertarianism generated from the passion of the moment. Waving a black and red flag, a man called James Jackson, possibly a discharged or retired seaman (or a weaver disguised as one), rallied those with him by shouting, 'A hoy for Newgate.' On the way the crowd collected all sorts of bystanders, of whom one was the twenty-two-year-old William Blake, not yet a mystical revolutionary. As the crowd passed Sir John Fielding's police offices at Bow Street the building was effectively flattened in retaliation for the imprisonment there of some of the rioters. Newgate Prison was next.

The mob came to Newgate and Publickly declared they would release the confined rioters. When they arrived at the door of the prison, they demanded of Mr Akerman, the keeper, to have their comrades immediately delivered up to them; and upon his persisting to do his duty, by refusing, they began some to break his windows, some to batter the doors and entrances into the cells with pick-axes and sledge-hammers, others with ladders to climb the vast walls, while others collected fire-brands, and whatever combustibles they could find, and flung [them] into his dwelling house. What contributed more than anything to the spreading of the flames was the great quantity of household furniture belonging to Mr Akerman which they threw out of the windows, piled up against the doors, and set fire to; . . . A party of constables, to the amount of a hundred, came to the assistance of the keeper; these the mob made a lane for, and suffered to pass till they were entirely encircled, when they attacked them with great fury, broke their staffs, and converted them into brands, which they hurled about wherever the fire, . . . had not caught . . . all the prisoners, to the amount of three hundred, among whom were four ordered for execution on the Thursday following, were released . . . they dragged out the prisoners by the hair of the head, by legs or arms, or whatever part they could lay hold of . . . so well planned were all the manoeuvres of these desperate ruffians, that they had placed centinels [sic] at the avenues to prevent any of the prisoners from being conveyed to other jails. Thus was the strongest and most durable prison in England, . . . demolished . . . in the space of a few hours.[14]

Frederick Reynolds reported, in somewhat more purple prose,

> The mob fired the jail in many places before they were enabled
> to force their way through the massive bars and gates, which
> guarded its entrance. The wild gestures of the mob without, and
> the shrieks of the prisoners within, expecting an instantaneous
> death from the flames, the thundering descent of huge pieces of
> building, the deafening clangor of red hot iron bars, striking in
> terrible concussion the pavement below, and the loud triumphant
> yells and shouts of the demoniac assailants on each new success,
> formed an awful and terrific scene.[15]

These events, of which the attack on Newgate and every other
London prison presented exemplary instances, suggested nothing
less than armed revolutionary insurrection, a rehearsal for the demolition of the Paris Bastille and the destruction of the French monarchy. American libertarian republicanism suddenly seemed too close
to home. It was for one witness, 'as if the city had been taken by an
enemy'.

By now, the troubles had lasted four days. The authorities might
tolerate a riot, they might have a hand in helping one along, they
might stand by as Catholic merchants were roughed up, but Lord
Mansfield's town house was ablaze and prisons from Southwark to
Clerkenwell were blackened empty shells. It would be now or never
to reimpose order and it was now time for magistrates to toe the line
as military reinforcements began to muster on London's outskirts and
as rumours of the imposition of martial law began to circulate. When
it came to manning the barricades, both John Wilkes and George
Gordon offered their services and their rifles to the government and
both were prepared to defend the institutions of the City.

The massive destruction around Holborn and Barnard's Inn produced, perhaps, the longest-lasting of all images from the riots and
the definitive image of mob rampage for later generations. This centred on the explosion at Thomas Langdale's gin distillery at the Black
Swan. Langdale, a Catholic, had attempted to placate his tormentors
with gin and cash but his premises were going to be a target with
or without bribery. The scenes that followed impressed contemporaries more than anything else with a belief that the lower orders
were essentially unthinking and demonic brutes if not kept under
control. Even twentieth-century authors continued to be shocked by
the scene.

> By nine the buildings were enveloped in smoke and flame, while
> there flowed down the kennel of the street torrents of unrectified

and flaming spirit gushing from casks drawn in endless succession from the vaults. Men and children, followed by women with infants in arms, emerged from courts, lanes and alleys and hastened to the latest outrage. From the windows of burning houses men tossed furniture into the all-devouring flames below. Ardent spirits, now running to pools and wholly unfit for human consumption, were swallowed by insatiate fiends, who, with shrieking gibes and curses, reeled and perished in the flames, whilst others, alight from head to foot, were dragged from burning cellars. On a sudden, in an atmosphere hot to suffocation, flames leapt upwards from Langdale's other houses on Holborn Hill. The vats had ignited, and columns of fire became visible for thirty miles round London.[16]

As Langdale's burned, the military organized and the civil magistrates braced themselves. The first major bloodshed occurred as crowds attempted to destroy the newly installed tollgates on Blackfriars and found themselves under fire from defending troops. Troops had already tried to disperse crowds at Newgate, leaving a hundred dead. At Blackfriars the dead were piled up and thrown into the Thames. One observer recollected:

> We were informed that a considerable number of rioters had been killed on Blackfriars Bridge, which was occupied by troops. On approaching it we beheld the King's Bench Prison completely wrapped in flames. It exhibited a sublime sight – we stood at a central point from whence London offered on every side, before as well as behind us, the picture of a city sacked and abandoned to a ferocious enemy.[17]

The new ferocity of the action combined with the determination of the crowds to destroy the symbols of City power, Mansion House and the Bank, lent urgency and hysteria to both sides. Colonel Twistleton, who commanded the Bank detachment, was confronted not with a mere mob of apprentices but by 'many decently dressed people' who urged on the poorer sectors of the crowd but pretended not to be involved when challenged. At least one leader was identified as a sailor (or a disguised weaver), who waved his cutlass in defiance. The troops fired, killing eight or nine including at least one innocent bystander, and continued firing as the threat seemed to continue. It was here that Wilkes and Gordon offered their services to the military. Civilians on both sides were now arming, some of the rioters having weapons despite all gunsmiths being required by law to shut up shop and secure their goods.

As the riots subsided Militia volunteers (vigilantes) found themselves pursuing their prey deeper and deeper into the rookeries of London, coming face to face for the first time with the real slum conditions of the city and their complex criminal complexion.

Attended by peace-officers, one of our detachments visited Chick Lane, Field Lane and Black Boy Alley. From Chick Lane we escorted several persons to Prison. These places constitute a separate town calculated for the reception of the darkest and most dangerous enemies to society, in which when pursued for the commission of crimes they easily conceal themselves. The houses are divided from top to bottom into many compartments, with doors of communication in each and also with the adjacent houses, some having two to four doors opening into different alleys. In many of the rooms I saw six, seven, eight to ten men in bed, in others as many women . . . Into one apartment we crept through a trap door, our bayonets and pistols in our hands . . . The peace-officers and the keepers of these houses appeared to be well-acquainted with each other, and on terms which rather shocked us.[18]

As cinders cooled and the riots subsided in the face of determined and overwhelming force the inquest began. Who had *really* been rioting rather than protesting? Many pointed to unruly apprentices and girl prostitutes, others pointed to religious fanatics tanked up on brandy and obsessed with violent disorder in the name of Protestantism, but some also noticed the well-dressed agitators and speculated on who these mystery men were. Charles Stuart, writing to his father, recollected a strange incident at the massacre at the Bank.

A very well dressed man was killed whose face they [the rioters] took great pains to hide, but after most of them dispersed a curious watchman looked at the body, expressed some surprise, and said he knew the Person. Upon which they seized the watchman and dragged him to Moorfields, where they swore him in the most sacred way to secrecy. As they also took off the body, nothing has been discovered.[19]

Hearsay and rumour turned the anecdotal reminiscences into hardened facts.

Many had no doubt that they were agents paid by the Opposition to bring down the Government with accusations of anarchy. 'Depend on it', Richard Cumberland wrote to his brother, 'the rioters were encouraged and supported by that abandoned Party who have long been diffusing the Seeds of Insurrection'. Many others were certain that the French and Americans were to blame. 'I am convinced', Lord Mountstuart wrote to his brother, 'that tho' the beginning of the tumults was entirely owing to the Fanaticks [sic], yet they had no notion of the outrages being carried so far, and that the American emissaries took the advantage of the mobbery once begun to carry their diabolical purposes to the great extent they did.'[20]

It is convenient to see the burning of Langdale's Distillery as the last scene of a first act, the second act being that of a revolutionary march on the Bank of England. The image would however be incorrect as confusingly complex acts of disorder were happening *simultaneously* across London, none of which had greater or lesser precedence. Thus the riotous uprising of feeling against Catholics was never abandoned in favour of a revolutionary programme of jail breaking, and the systematic demolition or firing of houses and buildings whose occupants represented authority was carried out alongside wholesale looting and petty theft. At no time throughout the disturbances did the rioters unite as a *coherent* body and directly threaten the destruction of Parliament or the monarch, even if proto-revolutionary voices seem occasionally to have been heard to direct the action of various sections of the milling crowds. More tellingly *no* contemporary talks of the revolutionary interest of the crowds but all talk of the *religious* element. The rioters lacked the foundation of independence to be found in the American colonists. The entire ideological and legal basis of the American cause was not only lacking but so was its driving force, the mercantile-legal professionals who led it and the rational egalitarian philosophy that backed it.

Observing the disorder which seemed to flow nearer every minute, Ignatius Sanchez, a black African ex-slave, and now a famous author and respectable middle-class shopkeeper, wrote in haste to a friend (John Spink) on 6 June:

In the midst of the most cruel and ridiculous confusion, I am now set down to give you a very imperfect sketch of the maddest people that the maddest times were ever plagued with. – The public prints have informed you (without doubt) of last Friday's transactions; – the insanity of Lord George Gordon, and the worse than Negro barbarity of the populace; – the burnings and devastations of each night you will also see in the prints . . .

There is at this present moment at least a hundred thousand poor, miserable, ragged rabble, from twelve to sixty years of age, with blue cockades in their hats – besides half as many women and children, all parading the streets – the bridge – the Park – ready for any and every mischief. Gracious God! what's the matter now? I was obliged to leave off – the shouts of the mob the horrid clashing of swords and the clutter of a multitude in swiftest motion drew me to the door when every one in the street was employed in shutting up shop. It is now just five o'clock the ballard-singers are exhausting their musical talents with the downfall of Popery, *Sandwich* and North. Lord *Sandwich* narrowly escaped with life about an hour since; the mob seized his chariot going to the house, broke his glasses, and, in struggling to get his lordship out, they somehow have cut his face. – The guards flews to his assistance the light-horse scowered the road, got his chariot, escorted him from the coffee-house, where he had fled for protection, to his carriage, and guarded him bleeding very fast home. This is liberty! genuine British liberty! – This instant about two thousand liberty boys* are swearing and swaggering by with large sticks – thus armed, in hopes of meeting with the Irish chairmen and labourers.[21]

Horrified by the collective madness and affected by a sense of order, law and culture which came from his Christianity, compassion and belief in human goodness, Sanchez added a postscript.

The Sardinian ambassador offered 500 guineas to the rabble to save a painting of our Saviour from the flames, and 1000 guineas not to destroy an exceeding fine organ: The gentry told him, they would burn him if they could get at him, and destroyed the picture and organ directly. – I am not sorry I was born in Afric. [sic] . . . There is about a thousand mad men, armed with clubs, bludgeons, and crows, just now set off for Newgate, to liberate, they say, their honest comrades. – I wish they do not some of them lose their lives or liberty before morning. It is thought by many who discern deeply, that there is more at the bottom of this business than merely the repeal of an act which has as yet produced no bad consequences, and perhaps never might. – I am forced to own that I am for an universal toleration. Let us convert by our example and conquer by our meekeness and brotherly love!
    Eight o'clock – Lord George Gordon has this moment announced to my Lords the mob – that the act shall be repealed this evening: Upon this, they gave a hundred cheers – took the horses from his

---

*Liberty boys were 'Journeymen weavers living in the Earl of Meath's liberties adjoining to the city' – *Annual Register*, 1765.

hackney-coach – and rolled him full jollily away:– They are huz-zaing now ready to crack their throats.[22]

Sanchez's strong sense of outrage when it came to slavery abroad was more reserved when it met mob rule at home making it 'vain to think of attending any business while . . . anarchy last[ed]'. Sanchez's 'universal toleration' was rational, law-abiding and constitutional. With his fellow property owners and tradespeople – the rising middle classes – Sanchez had a hatred of destruction and spontaneous uncontrollable crowds. His fear of anarchy (sweeping away 'reason and principle', to quote Thomas Paine) aligned him with a nostalgic conservatism.

> Government is sunk in lethargie stupor – anarchy reigns – When I look back to the glorious time of a George II and a Pitt's administration, my heart sinks at the bitter contrast. We may now say of England, as was heretofore said of Great Babylon – 'The beauty of the excellence of the Chaldees is no more'.[23]

Part of the rising (and radical) middle class, Sanchez feared the uncontrollable (and revolutionary) potential of the labouring orders ('there is more at the bottom of this business than merely the repeal of an act'). His London neighbour, Hester Thrale, owner of one of the great breweries of London (and a patron to Dr Johnson), had deeper hatreds that saw people like Sanchez (the black nouveaux-riche) actually in an unholy *alliance* with the mob itself – here was the soul of anarchy!

> Well! I am really haunted by *black shadows*. Men of colour in the rank of gentlemen; a black lady covered with finery, in the Pit at the Opera, and tawny children playing in the Squares, – in the gardens of the Squares I mean, – with their Nurses, afford ample proofs of Hannah More and Mr. Wilberforce's success in breaking down the *wall of separation*. Oh! how it falls on every side! and spreads its tumbling ruins on the world! leaving all ranks, all custom, all colours, all religions, *jumbled together*.[24]

Mrs Thrale's apocalyptic racist nightmare of a multi-ethnic, multi-cultural and truly democratic London was the most dreadful and wondrous vision of all.

7
The Ape-Like Irish

The Aftermath of the Gordon Riots, the Catholic
Emancipation Act and the Garibaldi Riots

The cost of the Gordon Riots was enormous. By 1783, after years of
petitions, new legislation and lawsuits, the bill for the various parts
of the city came to almost £42,000, for Middlesex, almost £21,500
and for Surrey £7,000. Damage to prisons added £30,000; in all, it
was the equivalent of several billions today. Property damage apart
from attacks on chapels and prisons amounted to approximately 150
houses and shops with damage to all sorts of goods including clothing, furniture, money, valuables, books and pictures. Approximately
50 homes had to be demolished. Most of the victims were either prosperous gentry or manufacturers but many were small but comfortable tradespeople living in areas such as Bethnal Green, Spitalfields
or Bermondsey. Property owners were potential targets and Catholic
or Irish property owners likely targets throughout the disturbances.

The insurance companies were soon scrutinizing their policies in
order to avoid paying their clients. The Sun Fire Office included a
clause excluding damage by rioting or 'civil commotion' and other
companies tried to avoid fire-damage payments to those who furniture had first been *removed* from their properties, thus voiding the
claim. That said, the insurance companies found themselves pursued
for thousands in compensation, which they slowly but duly paid out.
To cover any shortfalls, and in accordance with provision under the
Riot Act of 1715, local parishes could levy a riot tax to pay for local
damage. This they duly did.

Compensation, however, was the last thing on John Eliot's mind
when at ten at night he wrote in haste to his wife, whom he had sent
to friends for safety from their home in Bartholomew Close. With
soldiers flooding London and rioters on the street he could only wish
for the safety of 'the ladies' and the hope that the Lord will stop the
rioters' 'monstrous wickedness'. Something else would need to be
done to restore the peace of mind of Eliot's wife and daughters.

The first step had been a royal proclamation, issued on 5 June, calling on all the officers of the civil law to enforce the law, especially with regard to foreign embassies, and offering a reward of £500 for anyone willing to give evidence towards a conviction of those demonstrators who had demolished the chapels of foreign dignitaries. This proclamation was met with universal contempt. No one ever claimed a penny of the reward, although many must have known the guilty parties. The temper of the times was quite different from that of Oates. The nonchalance of the City aldermen, magistrates and Lord Mayor and their clear acquiescence in the troubles was a sign of confrontation with Parliament, executive and monarch and was only likely to be stemmed when trouble got out of hand. It was rapidly doing so as the property of Catholics, both foreign, Irish and English, was joined in destruction by those of Protestant landlords and tradespeople.

Troops and militia were now visibly on the streets twenty-four hours a day. Horse patrols could be found in the area from Guildhall to Moorfields and across from Bishopgate Street, over London Bridge as well as at Shadwell and Wapping and from the Royal Exchange to Old Street. Patrols of troopers were also concentrated in the West End, at Green Park, St James's Park, Grosvenor Square, Pall Mall, Soho Square and around the palaces. Grenadier Guards marched in Piccadilly, Curzon Street, Chesterfield Street, Hanover Square and at various other locations whilst hourly patrols of the 3rd Dragoon Guards kept a watch around the Artillery Ground, through Barbican, Moorfields, Broadstreet and all streets in between until three each morning. The 4th Dragoons were in Bermondsey and on Westminster Bridge, the 16th Light Dragoons were in Holborn and at Newgate, St Paul's and Cornhill; Colonel Twistleton's Detachment were at Royal Exchange, Threadneedle Street and Tower. These forces were supplemented by Light Horse volunteers, Foot Guards and Northampton Militia who were stationed at Lambeth, Vauxhall, Bloomsbury Square and 'Gray's Inngate [sic]'.

London was now an armed camp but the relationships between civilians and military authority were immediately strained as rumours spread that the huge encampments in Hyde Park meant London had been placed under martial law by secret meeting of the Privy Council. It had not however and emphasis was quickly placed on the civil law and the role of the magistrates to whom the soldiers had to answer. For the moment this would have to pacify the City fathers, whose control of London life seemed to be slipping into the hands of Westminster and the King. Jealous of their privileges, the Corporation had no intention of yielding an inch of ground to a 'usurping' authority against whom ancient Protestant 'liberty' was preferable even if London was left in rubble. John Wilkes and his colleagues turned out only in extremis, defending the Bank of England on the night of 7 June with zealous ferocity.

The self-assurance of the City aldermen was nowhere more evident than in the relationship between the Corporation and the monarch. This came to a head on 23 May 1770, when William Beckford, the Lord Mayor (and father of William Beckford Junior, author of *Vathek*), headed a deputation that handed in a remonstrance to George III. After the usual pleasantries and formalities, Beckford added, 'Permit me, Sire, to observe that whoever has already dared, or shall hereafter endeavour, by false insinuations and suggestions, to alienate your Majesty's affections from your loyal subjects in general, and from the City of London in particular, is an enemy to your Majesty's person and family, a violator of the public peace, and a betrayer of our happy Constitution, as it was established at the Glorious Revolution'.

This small (and to later generations) innocuous speech was for Beckford's contemporaries like a lightning bolt, combining over-familiarity with a reminder to George that what was compacted in the Glorious Revolution could be revised if necessary. One observer, writing to the Duke of Bedford, was appalled at the sheer effrontery of Beckford's words. 'This is the first attempt ever made to hold a colloquy with the King by any subject, and is indecent to the highest degree'. William Pitt, however, was overwhelmed with praise for the independent spirit that Beckford represented: 'The spirit of Old England spoke that never-to-be-forgotten day . . . *true Lord Mayor of London*; that is first magistrate of the first City in the World! I mean to tell you only a plain truth, when I say, Your Lordship's mayoralty will be revered till the constitution is destroyed and forgotten.'

Beckford's limited demands for more equal representation, the end to rotten boroughs and the reduction of pensioners and 'placemen' stood for the new equality demanded by merchants and the 'middle classes'. As a representative of the City and the greatest West Indian absentee slave owner of his time, Beckford was the spokesman for businessmen and men of finance who were only too well aware that political gain would bring economic gain. London itself was changing and as it grew the City elders would have to take on a *political* role for the greater metropolis if they were to continue to exert influence. Southwark, Westminster, the counties of urban Middlesex, Surrey and Essex had all greatly expanded and conglomerated and turned London into the giant 'Wen' so deplored by William Cobbett. The City was becoming a *part* of London instead of its centre.

The City's programmatic radicalism (as opposed to mere dislike of governmental ministers per se) was a partially self-aware articulation of the new as yet unfranchised but highly political 'middling' sort who made up the bulk of London's expanded property owners. It was these people who regularly met at coffee house and tavern to promote a radicalized agenda, represented by City aldermen and MPs such as John Wilkes and William Beckford.

During 1769 Beckford's parliamentary speeches had been directed at the destruction of corrupt boroughs that gave undue influence to the aristocracy and by 1770 he had helped formulate a programme of reform to produce shorter parliaments, a place and pension Bill and equalization of representation. Such reforms were part of the social and intellectual life of radical clubs such as the Supporters of the Bill of Rights who met at the London Tavern, the Sons of Freedom, drinking at Appleby's in Westminster, the Society of the Anti-Gallicans and numerous others. May Feast at Southwark in 1771 was also an occasion of political debate. The demands of these clubs united property with representation and were expressly intended to exclude a mob who, because they were propertyless, were without those responsibilities felt imperative for enfranchisement. Radicalism would soon clash therefore with mob 'anarchy' once bricks flew through Protestant property.

To emphasize their independence the various wards continued to pass anti-Catholic motions even at the height of the 1780 disturbances. At Lime Street Ward on 30 May 1780, local aldermen petitioned for the repeal of the Act that had provided for the partial social and economic enfranchisement of Catholics.[1] The Court of Common Council passed a similar resolution on 31 May and on the fiercest day of rioting was still composed enough to petition the House of Commons against the Act.

Meanwhile, the City and the parishes were preparing for a little self-help. Lords, property owners, housekeepers and tradespeople impatient with the military (and suspicious of it) began to form vigilante groups to protect themselves. Armed and drilled, these groups of volunteers were soon assigned army officers to lead and guide them. Uniforms and equipment would be provided by subscription once the volunteers had learned to march in step. From Whitechapel to Islington and from Rotherhithe to Bethnal Green local inhabitants were joining together 'to acquaint themselves with the military exercise'.

Foremost amongst these volunteer groups was the (St) Marylebone Association, formed after a meeting called by the Duke of Portland, Viscount Mahon, Viscount Townshend, the Bishop of Ossery and the Dean of Windsor. A publicity campaign, requiring 5,000 leaflets to go to local households and numerous newspaper advertisements, helped create a self-help force of gentlemen, bakers, apothecaries, victuallers, undertakers, butchers, coffeemen and a sculptor (Ian Bacon of 17 Newman Street). Membership was restricted to property owners only and Catholics were absolutely denied admission unless they took a prayer oath. Catholics were therefore unprotected by these self-help toy soldiers but as the rioting had long ceased before the associations really got under arms these groups soon petered out.

The Protestant hatred for Catholics which soon dominated the various deadly rivalries of Scots and Irish also encouraged the hardly suppressed suspicions of a growing number of liberals and democrats. It was common and convenient shorthand to call authoritarian government 'papist', and it was an argument of American Liberty and French republicanism: 'monarchy in every instance [was] the Popery of government' was Thomas Paine's opinion, and it was 'popery' that the 'Norman Yoke' had made the cornerstone of arbitrary rule and divine right. Thus, as he stated in *The Rights of Man*,

> Government, like that of William the Conqueror, was founded in power, and the sword assumed the name of a sceptre. Governments, thus established, last as long as the power to support them lasts; but that they might avail themselves of every engine in their favour, they united fraud to force, and set up an idol which they called *Divine Right*, and which, in imitation of the Pope, who affects to be spiritual and temporal, and in contradiction to the Founder of the Christian religion, twisted itself afterwards into an idol of another shape, called *Church and State*. The key of St Peter, and the key of the Treasury, became quartered on one another, and the wondering cheated multitude worshipped the invention.

Paine's brilliance was to harness the language of paranoia to the philosophy of 'common sense' after which he named his most famous political pamphlet, published in 1776 in the cause of the American Revolution. For Paine, as for other republicans and rationalists, papistry was a peculiarly English disease made up of an unholy alliance between Dissenters, Presbyterians, High Tories and Catholics. Paine's rhetoric happily invoked 'papistry' as an *English* political disease from which Europe was free, hence

> Britain is the parent country, say some. Then the more shame upon her conduct. Even brutes do not devour their young, nor savages make war upon their families; wherefore the assertion, if true, turns to her reproach; but it happens not to be true, or only partly so, and the phrase *parent* or *mother country* hath been jesuitically adopted by the [King] and his parasites, with a low papistical design of gaining an unfair bias on the credulous weakness of our minds. Europe, and not England, is the parent country of America. This new world hath been the asylum for the persecuted lovers of civil and religious liberty from *every part* of Europe.[2]

This strange and obtuse reversal of language was nevertheless symbolically triumphant – a clear argument for seeing the colonies as quite separate from Great Britain and therefore constitutionally and militarily enslaved. This was language direct from the lexicon of eighteenth-century conspiracy theory and it 'proved' beyond doubt the complicity of outwardly orthodox Protestants like Paine's former friend and now opponent, Edmund Burke, whose famous *Reflections on the Revolution in France* had pricked him into writing *Rights of Man.*

> Mr Burke takes his seat in the British House of Commons! From his violence and his grief, his silence on some points, and his excess on others, it is difficult not to believe that Mr Burke is sorry, extremely sorry, that arbitrary power, the power of the Pope, and the Bastille, are pulled down.

English Liberty (exported to the United States and even France) was the realization and exposure of this very British conspiracy.

But what of the fate of Lord George? To his contemporaries George Gordon was a trouble-making enigma much like the later Lord Byron; 'mad, bad and dangerous to know'. Thomas Paine thought him quite mad, turning prison into 'Bedlam', and most biographers since have followed a similar line, one going so far as to accuse Gordon of being 'feeble minded'. In a way that was hard for his contemporaries and impossible for later historians to understand, Lord George seemed to be *too* visible, too strange, thus making what he was almost invisible.

Gordon's was a strange but not 'mad' personality and it was a personality in which political idealism was part of a lived experience inseparable from it. Here was a libertarian who had toasted the American rebels and discoursed against slavery and its iniquities, and who was quite prepared to 'beard' the King, hector his council and harangue Parliament on behalf of Protestantism and patriotism. He enjoyed being lionized by the mob, but he caught a fright when they became dangerously belligerent. He was a classic libertarian individualist whose idealist strain (and revolutionary potential) was always at war with his conformism. His 'patriotism' inflamed the incendiary possibilities for revolution without equipping the revolution with a creed. No wonder he had nowhere to go but back once the violence got out of hand. It would be Tom Paine's *reason* that inflamed passions three thousand miles away and that would give a sense of purpose to Protestant patriotism. For Paine and others Gordon was the worst of incendiaries – one who seems to have care for neither self nor property, the very opposite attitude to Paine's own.

Without a clear sense of purpose but with a permanent sense of outrage (he never forgot the injustice of his inability to get a promotion in the navy), Gordon continued to campaign on issues of liberty and conscience after his acquittal of the charges of high treason. He was, for instance, to be found leafleting Oxford Street against the shop tax and inducing shopkeepers to put up the shutters and put out banners reading 'This shop to be let. Enquire of Billy Pitt'. Indeed, he had campaigned against window tax, candle tax, stamp duties, postage duties and the taxation of distilleries. He had also worn Highland plaid banned since the '45 and he had championed the 'working people' against taxation on linens, 'Scotch' gauze and cotton proposed by Pitt's Tory government. Sailors goaded on by Lord Sydney and going to Gordon's house to cause mischief ended up shouting 'Gordon and Liberty!' Lord George talked them into reason and sent them off with the suggestion that they 'pull down Mr Pitt's house' instead.

Gordon remained a noisy pest so that when he libelled the Queen of France in 1786 the government finally had a good excuse to put him away, although they waited first to trap him in a double libel. His first mistake had been to befriend the dangerous figure of Count Cagliostro, a magician, confidence trickster and social radical who had been banned from France after the strange 'case of the Diamond Necklace' (which later had implications for the Revolution). Gordon then took out a notice in the *Public Advertiser*, which also suggested libel against the French royal family. His second mistake was to make a libellous attack on the 'Laws of England' after he had replied to a petition from prisoners about to be transported to Botany Bay. Enough was now enough and Lord George was hauled in front of the Bench to answer the charges.

To avoid incarceration Gordon did a flit, only to be found some time later in Birmingham living the life of a devout Jew under the name Israel bar Abraham George Gordon. For Paine, a man not unhappy with anti-Semitic imagery especially in his pamphlet *Common Sense*, this clearly made the fickle Gordon no more than a lunatic. But this last twist was not bizarre at all. Gordon had always been a man torn between the carefree life of company, drink and women and the austere and ascetic life of an idealist. Gordon became an orthodox Jew precisely because it offered an *organized* and *purposeful* world in which his Protestantism (never necessarily 'ultra') and his politics found a moral home. He was, noticed one observer, 'constitutionally religious'. Gordon became, of course, more Jewish than a Jew, refusing the company of any Jew except those who strictly adhered to the Torah. He ate kosher food, covered his head and observed Saturday as the Sabbath. Yet he remained an affable egalitarian whose prison rooms were always full of visitors and guests and where there was no bias of religion, race or class.

> His guests had beer or wine, but he himself never had a single glass of porter . . . After dinner he lit his pipe and started a discussion on social problems, religion or more often politics . . . The quiet conversation lasted until 6 o'clock, when his guests and his two little maids, one Gentile and one Jew, had to leave the prison and go home. When he was left alone he had some tea, a plateful of salad, lit his . . . pipe . . . and spent an hour or two in quiet contemplation and prayer . . . Sometimes to break the monotonous pattern of the days, there would be a party . . . Dukes would meet Italian barbers, ladies of fashion would dance with Jewish shopkeepers, soldiers would drink with Members of Parliament, Polish noblemen with American merchants, Rabbis with infidels.[3]

Gordon was the first person to seriously tap into the emotionalism of republicanism, egalitarianism and reformism and the heady contradictory brew that mixed anti-Catholicism with the 'Good Old Cause' and both with growing class consciousness. John Wilkes had stirred the sentiments, Gordon had shown how close they were to the surface and Paine would harness them toward a revolution in America, as justification for one in France and, *by implication*, one in Britain. For the last few years of his life Lord George Gordon continued a prodigious correspondence with the French National Assembly and with the representatives of the newly created United States, Benjamin Franklin, Henry Laurens and Gouverneur Morris, warning them of the dangers of imperial usurpation and the monarchically directed desires of 'enemies' of the new republic like John Adams.

After the Gordon Riots fears of Catholics and of 'popish' designs slowly faded. By the reign of George IV (1820–30) they were little more than memories, or at least memories that Parliament felt confident in finally laying. The Catholic Emancipation Act was passed on 13 April 1829. The Act definitively annulled the Oaths of Allegiance, which for 250 years had disqualified from public office Catholics who openly professed their faith.

The new Oath of Allegiance bore, however, the inevitable and paranoid history of its evolution: the fear of Catholic conspiracy, assassination, dual allegiance and the Papal Bull *Regnans in Excelsis* which had originally declared open season on the English monarchy. It tied Catholic officials, requiring them to accept their minority status within a Protestant country with a Protestant government and Protestant Church establishment whose head was the reigning king or queen.

I . . . do sincerely promise and swear, that I will be faithful and bear true Allegiance to His Majesty King George the Fourth, and will defend him to the utmost of my Power against all Conspiracies and Attempts whatever, which shall be made against his Person, Crown, or Dignity; and I will do my utmost Endeavour to disclose and make known to his Majesty, His Heirs and Successors, all Treasons and traitorous Conspiracies which may be formed against Him or Them: And I do faithfully promise to maintain, support, and defend, to the utmost of my Power, the Succession of the Crown, which Succession, by an Act, intituled *An Act for the further Limitation of the Crown, and better securing the Rights and Liberties of the Subject*, is and stands limited to the Princess *Sophia*, electress of *Hanover*, and the Heirs of her Body, being Protestants; hereby utterly renouncing and abjuring any Obedience or Allegiance unto any other Person claiming or pretending a Right to the Crown of this Realm: and I do Further declare, That it is not an Article of my Faith, and that I do renounce, reject, and abjure the Opinion, that Princes excommunicated or deprived by the Pope, or any other Authority of the See of *Rome*, may be deposed or murdered by their Subjects, or by any Person whatsoever: And I do declare, That I do not believe that the Pope of *Rome*, or any other Foreign Prince, prelate, Person, State, or Potentate, hath or ought to have any Temporal or Civil Jurisdiction, Power, Superiority, or Pre-eminence, directly or indirectly, within this Realm. I do swear, That I will defend to the utmost of my Power the Settlement of Property within this Realm, as established by the Laws: And I do hereby disclaim, disavow, and solemnly abjure any Intention to subvert the present Church Establishment, as settled by Law within this Realm: and I do solemnly swear, That I never will exercise any Privilege to which I am or may become entitled, to disturb or weaken the Protestant Religion or Protestant Government in the United Kingdom: And I do solemnly, in the presence of God, profess, testify, and declare, That I do make this Declaration, and every Part thereof, in the plain and ordinary Sense of the Words of this Oath, without any Evasion, Equivocation, or mental Reservation whatsoever. So help me GOD.

By the same Act, British Jesuits were also recognized and protected.

Ironically the passage of the Catholic Relief Bill almost cost the Prime Minister his life. The Bill had had a particularly stormy passage at almost every stage; George IV was strongly opposed and the Duke of Wellington, the Prime Minister, only lukewarm. Nevertheless, after continuous goading by the rabidly anti-Catholic Earl of Winchilsea, who accused Wellington of 'disgraceful and criminal' motives for the 'infringement of our libertys and the introduction of Popery into every department of the State' he decided to make the whole thing an affair of honour.

Realizing his quarrel with Winchilsea was a matter of principle and a direct consequence of the government policy he embodied, Wellington, who had never duelled in his life, met his opponent on 20 March 1829 on Battersea Fields. In this he followed a line of recent ministers who were willing to jeopardize the country and take pot shots at each other for matters of personal honour. These included Charles James Fox, who fought William Adam on 29 November 1779 in Hyde Park, William Pitt, who met George Tierney on Wandsworth Common on 27 May 1798 and Viscount Castlereagh and George Canning, who blasted away at each other (to no great result) on 21 September 1809, again at Wandsworth. After a hesitant start when Wellington and his opponent had to dodge passing field hands both fired to miss and Winchilsea agreed to make an apology; the whole affair when made public made the Duke a popular hero (having been a popular villain) and delighted George IV.

Anti-Catholic aggression was always sporadic and fed by crises brought on by fear of foreign wars and foreign governments. Catholics were symbols and scapegoats, always a permanent fifth column. The Irish were a different sort of fifth column, willing to take lower-paid jobs and peasant-like in attitude (to Protestant cockney neighbours). The 'low Irish', as they were contemptuously called, were also likely to live in the slum ghettos of the West End, St Giles, Holborn, St Pancras and Clerkenwell. Not only were the labouring Irish considered brutish drunkards by the middle classes (Charles Kingsley, author of *The Water Babies*, thought they were 'apelike') but they were implacably Catholic. Anti-Irish feeling, which was often economically determined, was always mixed with anti-Catholic resentment and anti-papist ideology. By the middle of the nineteenth century therefore anti-Catholic disturbances in London were overtly anti-Irish in nature.

During the Popish Plot, Irish priests had been left alone for fear of provoking a rebellion. Only at the end were certain priests put on trial. The fantastic plot to murder Charles II and James at Windsor was blamed on 'Irish ruffians' and in the Gordon Riots the populace had targeted the Irish as the special enemy. Economic, political, religious and cultural prejudices and concerns went hand in hand to make of Irishmen a permanent 'alien nation'. Visible by accent, livelihood and looks (as well as by surname) first-generation Irish Londoners were easily identified. Their children, blending in with those of neighbours, could increasingly be seen as an *invisible* threat of the half-assimilated.

A whole army of imported Irish had built the roads, canals and railways. The central feature of all these major engineering achievements was the appearance of camps and shanties, and vast groups of Irish lodgers in areas being developed. Pay day was usually a time of high spirits and brawling, and sometimes sporadic riots. Often it was the Irish labourers who were attacked, especially if locals became resentful – as they did in Wales in 1846 at Penmaenmawr or during the navvy 'civil war' of 1845 when Irish workers were attacked by those from Lancashire and Yorkshire. The image of the hard-drinking, hard-fighting Irishman became the standard for Irish navvy communities and neighbourhoods such as Navvies Island in Hackney where labourers had decided to put down permanent roots in the capital.

By the 1850s, the 'Catholic' question was no longer one of religion per se but of the perceived *cultural* difference between sober Englishmen and Irish rowdies. These differences came to a head during the long-forgotten rioting which accompanied radical agitation on behalf of Garibaldi and the Italian 'Risorgimento' during 1862. Support for Garibaldi and for Italian nationalism came from radicals, working-class unionists and pro-republicans who saw in these events a blow against the authoritarian empires of Austria and Russia as well as a decisive step against French connivance in European affairs and papal superstition and control. George Holyoake and the secularists joined forces with the Workingmen's Garibaldian Committee to raise a pro-nationalist fund and equip an English legion of volunteers. To further the cause they decided to hold a rally in Hyde Park on 28 September.* By 3 o'clock in the afternoon approximately 10–20,000 people had gathered to hear Charles Bradlaugh, the outspoken republican freethinker, and others give their speeches atop a mound near Grosvenor Gate (the mound, later flattened by order, was nicknamed the 'redan' after the defensive position at the Battle of the Alma during the Crimean War).

Suddenly, a group of Irish, including women, armed with sticks and rocks surged through the crowds, attacked the speakers and occupied the redan. They then sang 'God and Rome'. A large contingent of off-duty Grenadier Guards then joined 200 Garibaldian supporters in an assault on the Irish who fled only to regroup and attack again later. Rain stopped play at 3.30 p.m. and five Irishmen found themselves on charges. No soldiers or Garibaldians were arrested. The papers next day, somewhat confused about the demonstration and the intervention of the Irish labourers, took to the most convenient anti-Irish cant, accusing the arrested of using knives, which they had not (but which Italian monarchists and absolutists were to use in the coming battles in Hyde Park). On 5 October the disturbances

---

*There were 'Garibaldi' meetings at places such as Primrose Hill.

were repeated. The police were taking no chances and assigned 410 officers and six plainclothesmen under Assistant Commissioner (Captain) Harris to patrol the Park and provide continuous reports to the Commissioner Richard Mayne, who had turned his home at Chester Square, Belgravia into police headquarters.

By early afternoon, approximately 200 Irish occupied the redan waiting for a fight. The Garibaldi Committee failed to oblige but a large crowd, including soldiers from the Coldstreams, Grenadiers, Life Guards and Buffs, were happy to 'mix it' with the Irish enemy and their Italian allies. An original 2,000 rioters had, as Mayne reported, metamorphosed into 15,000 by 3.20 p.m. Mayne considered the off-duty troops as extra police. At least one Italian was convicted of a stabbing offence. On 12 October, despite a ban on a further rally, fighting broke out between Irish and Garibaldians and brawls spilled out of pubs in London and in Birkenhead. By the end of the disturbances all the royal parks were under police guard and Sunday meetings had been banned.

Why though had hundreds of Irish labourers, both men and women, felt the need to march on Hyde Park to protest against supporters of a foreign war? The answer is far from clear but suggests that working-class Irish people felt *directly threatened* by agitation on behalf of Italian revolutionaries. Commissioner Mayne had put the violence down to a mixture of 'Chartism, Socialism and Infidelity', the use of 'seditious and blasphemous language' and ill-disciplined soldiers, the papers blamed Mayne, the reading public remained confused and that seemed to end the matter.

Yet Mayne's outburst was not mere petulance, for in the working-class radicalism that supported the demands of Chartist reform,* the new class-awareness of working people and the growth of working-class scepticism could be found a serious challenge to authority which in extreme form had caused the trouble in the Park that autumn. But the Irish saw something else. Conservative and Catholic, the Irish working man was profoundly different from his English Protestant colleague. Perhaps the working class were not one. Irish workers heard in the calls of the Workingman's Garibaldian Committee the

---

*On 1 August 1840, the *Northern Star* published 'the principles requisite to secure . . . representation of the people'. These were:

The right of voting for Members of Parliament by every male of twenty-one years of age and of sound mind; Annual Elections; Vote by Ballot; no property qualifications for Members of Parliament; Payment of members; and a division of the kingdom into Electoral Districts; given to each district a proportionate number of Representatives according to the number of electors.

old anti-papist rant echoing down the centuries. It was now only a faint echo but it was still there. Despite Irish Chartist leaders and the demands of Irish radicals in the embryonic British working-class movement, the causes of reform, equality and liberty of conscience were inextricably tied to the Dissenting tradition of which secularism (infidelism) and socialism were an expression.

Mainland prejudice against Catholics slowly lost its hold as the nineteenth century progressed and remained high only in Glasgow. Official prejudice, however, fuelled by fears of Irish Home Rule, lasted into the twentieth century where the deeply religious head of MI5, Vernon Kell, kept a watchful eye and, it was said, barred Catholics from his spying network. During Kell's period of office at MI5 official attitudes also hardened in Unionist circles at Stormont. Lord Craigavon assured Ulstermen that his government was made up of 'loyal men and women' whilst Sir Basil Brooke, a minister (and later first minister of Northern Ireland), appealed to industrialists only to employ 'good Protestant lads and lasses'. He also exhorted all 'loyalists not to employ Roman Catholics, 99 per cent of whom are disloyal'. Such sentiments would fuel the long-simmering hatreds that would have tragic consequences for the people of London, during the bloody days of the struggle for Irish independence.

8

'Wilkes and Liberty'

The Political Riot

The eighteenth century long ago lost its image of order and powdered wigs. The extraordinary propaganda exercise begun by the Augustan classicists and reinforced in the popular mind for the next 200 years disguised a long century of disturbance and social disaffection. Without adequate local organizations or a national voice the common people regularly took to the streets and lanes to make their protests; without a local police force or real magisterial power the authorities called out the troops. The riot became both an expression of discontent for the lower orders (the mobile, or mob) and a valuable safety valve for those above. The riot was *the* final political resort of unenfranchised groups once recourse to law or to parliamentary petition failed. It also provided a means whereby those in power got the common people to fight their political battles in the London streets.*

This was certainly the case with the complex set of arguments and events that led to the impeachment of Henry Sacheverell and the riots that followed in 1710. The whole affair was sparked by a debate over monarchical legitimacy following the settlement of the 'Glorious Revolution' of 1688 and the accession of William III. Every government has to establish its legitimacy and every revolutionary government must do so with decisiveness. The definition of treason suddenly becomes a pressing issue. On 17 July 1649, for instance, the new government of the Commonwealth had declared in Westminster Hall that,

> Whereas the Parliament hath abolished the kingly office in England and Ireland, and in the dominions and territories

---

*The years leading towards the Gordon Riots were constantly disturbed by mob rule, much of which was determined by a mixture of economic, religious and political concerns. Fear of Catholic autocracy and economic change led, however ironically, to debates about liberty and democracy.

thereunto belonging; and having resolved and declared, that the people shall for the future be governed by its own representatives or national meetings in Council, chosen and entrusted by them for that purpose, hath settled the Government in the way of a Commonwealth and Free State, without King or House of Lords.

Nevertheless, it continued,

. . . if any person shall maliciously or advisedly publish, by writing, printing, or openly declaring, that the said Government is tyrannical, usurped, or unlawful; or that the Commons in Parliament assembled are not the supreme authority of this nation; or shall plot, contrive, or endeavour to stir up, or raise force against the present Government, or for the subversion or alteration of the same, and shall declare the same by any open deed, that then every such offence shall be taken, deemed, and adjudged by authority of this Parliament to be high treason.

The legitimacy of the settlement with William of Orange was one of the most violently debated of all issues in an age characterized by violent legal, religious and constitutional debate. The problem, at least in part, was the status of the new Oath of Allegiance, which to many in public office was in direct contradiction to their oath to James and therefore an obvious undermining of all oaths and a questioning of the nature of governmental legitimacy. The need for an immediate settlement that left the Church of England in place as the supreme authority, the King its head, and Parliament its defender, nevertheless left many clergy in serious doubt as to the value of their new loyalty and, more importantly, it left open the question of who might ascend the throne on the death of William's daughter Anne – a Stuart or a Hanoverian? The question was quite capable of creating serious public disorder.

At least 200 tracts had been written on the subject of loyalty and legitimacy when in 1691 the Tory clergyman William Sherlock (then Master of the Temple, later Dean of St Paul's) published *The Case of the Allegiance due to Sovereign Powers*. Hoping to square a difficult circle, Sherlock, who had previously refused to swear the new oath and now wished to re-enter public life, produced what many saw as the ultimate surrender document to *any* authoritative regime. Sherlock's intellectual problem was simple – were William and Mary legitimate or just de facto rulers? His answer was straightforward and pragmatic.

Looking back over an age of revolutions and constant fear of revolutions, Sherlock's argument, framed in the language of a litigious age, was one in which stability and order were the central concerns.

First he laid out the Jacobite case in detail, with its central tenet that

> a rightful prince only has right to our allegiance. That though he be disposed of his throne, if ever he had right to it, he has right still; and therefore our duty is still owing to him, and to no other; and our oaths of allegiance to him still bind us: and that no other prince, who ascends the throne without a legal right, has right to our allegiance; and that to swear allegiance to him, while we are under the obligation of a former oath to our rightful prince, is perjury.

Against these views, Sherlock placed the authority of God's will who puts monarchs on thrones and also removes them in ways not to be questioned.

> If these principles be true, it is plain, that subjects are bound to obey, and to pay and swear allegiance (if it be required) to those princes whom God hath placed and settled in the throne, whatever disputes there may be about their legal right, when they are invested with God's authority.
>
> And then it is plain, that our old allegiance and old oaths are at an end, when God has set over us a new king: for when God transfers kingdoms, and requires our obedience and allegiance to a new King, he necessarily transfers our allegiance too.

Against the legal qualms of churchmen and constitutionalists for whom the Church of England represented the supreme institution attached to the legitimate monarch, Sherlock posed 'natural allegiance' to settled kings and governments. Moreover, this was clearly also a matter of pragmatism.

> To venture our lives and fortunes to preserve the kings person and government, while he is in possession, is reasonable enough; because it is a real service to our king and country, to prevent unjust usurpations, which overturn the government, and often unsettle or destroy the laws, and with them the rights and liberties of subjects, as well as the right of the king; but to swear to do our utmost to restore the king, when he is dispossessed, is to swear never to submit to usurped powers, but to take all opportunities to overthrow such governments to restore our king, which is contrary to our duty, when God removes one king and sets up another.

The matter did not end there and considerable antagonism built up between those who supported the new regime and those who remained loyal to their old beliefs. All this formed another link in the growing polarization of Whig and Tory politics in which a very considerable number of the population took an interest, especially in London. At least a quarter of all males could vote, and if they might be royalist and traditionalist they were also not to be toyed with by the establishment, only too well aware as they were of any infringements on their 'ancient' rights. As Daniel Defoe pointed out, 'Passive obedience, Non-resistance, and the Divine right of hereditary succession are *inconsistent* with the rights of the British nation . . . inconsistent with the Constitution of the British government . . . and inconsistent with the *declared*, essential foundation of the British Monarchy'.[1]

The establishment of the Bank of England (first in Mercer's Hall and then in Grocer's Hall) in 1694 had helped create a new world of international money which circulated in ways disliked by the landed elite and distrusted by ordinary people. The threatened Jacobite invasion of 1708 had put the Whigs in power under a 'Junto' of 'five tyrannising Lords', the cost of the War of the Spanish Succession had been borne by Tory lords paying the land tax and to top it all the government had passed a General Naturalisation Act allowing 10,000 Calvinist Bavarians to enter the country. Foreigners seemed to be doing very well out of all this, Tories pointed out, especially those Huguenot, Spanish Jewish and Dutch merchants, thirty of whom were represented in 1709 as stockholders of the Bank itself.

It was the 'overbearing, ill-natured, shallow, hard drinking, High Church, Oxford Clergyman' Dr Henry Sacheverell[2] who became the spokesman for Tory discontent, giving a thundering sermon (in the days when all sermons were potentially political) on 5 November 1709. The irony of Guy Fawkes' Day was hardly lost on his audience, in front of whom he attacked every Whig, Dissenter and Catholic, with the Lord Treasurer, Sidney Goldophin, liberally slandered. Sacheverell had been invited to offer his inflammatory peroration by Sir Samuel Garrard, the Tory Lord Mayor, with the intention of creating a panic in which the Church of England was seen to be in immediate danger of infiltration by 'clamorous, insatiable and Church-devouring malignants and dissenters . . . begot in rebellions, born in sedition and nursed up on faction'. Any toleration was a direct attack on High Tory and High Church hegemony and Sacheverell's central argument regarding the 'utter illegality of resistance' whilst a clear attack on Whig triumphalism was also a clear threat to challenges to the established order by Dissenters.

The Court of Aldermen, under control of the Whig faction, having been tricked by the Mayor into allowing the sermon, nevertheless forbade publication, were ignored and prosecuted Sacheverell for seditious libel. Sacheverell was, however too canny to lay himself open to the charge, not least because his sermon was ambiguous, and the impeachment which followed was foolhardy, giving Toryism a platform. The questions involved were clouded by further questions regarding the definition of resistance and against whom.

> The ideological issue was from one point of view clear – for or against 1688 and by what right the monarch ruled . . . In fact, as the Whigs alleged at his trial, Sacheverell was evidently in favour of non-resistance only to James III, while the Whigs believed in the right of resistance but not to themselves. The only upholders of the doctrines of absolute non-resistance and passive obedience were Jacobites, but those doctrines would become operative again only when the Pretender was restored. And if resistance was always wrong and the Revolution was unjustified, then clearly he, not the Hanoverians, should succeed the Queen.[3]

As delay piled on delay before the trial, High Church clergymen rallied to the cause of the 'Church in danger' and Sacheverell found himself with a black-clad bodyguard of militant churchmen. Angered at the Whigs and suspicious of local Dissenters and foreign merchants, the 'mobb' voted with its feet to follow Sacheverell's banner. On 27 February 1710 a large crowd of 400 armed supporters marched alongside Sacheverell as he made his way from Temple to Westminster Hall. In the Hall itself, he was accused of offering a veiled threat to Queen Anne by suggesting non-resistance was actually code for resistance to the House of Orange. The second day of the trial opened with the clergyman now protected by a 'hired company of butchers' who were there to intimidate opponents. Concerned that he might be imprisoned, Sacheverell slipped away for the day.

Things now became more ominous and on the third day of the trial huge crowds gathered at Westminster threatening to continue the attack on the Dissenters' hall they had attacked the day before. They cheered the Queen and the Doctor and looked for an opportunity to attack any Dissenters' meeting hall or chapel, an opportunity already being engineering by Sacheverell's close aides. Equipped with crowbars and hatchets the crowd systematically demolished meeting-houses in New Court, Covey Street, Holborn and Drury Lane. The contents were piled up at Lincoln's Inn and set alight. One paper found on a rioter read, 'Down with the Bank of England and the Meeting in Houses: and God damn the Presbyterians . . .' After hours of (convenient) delay, the Guards were called out, and order was restored with no one killed.

The Sacheverell riots made plain certain irreconcilable differences in the attitudes to the type of society England should be and what it had become. The perception amongst the 'middle sort' that London was rapidly becoming a lawless frontier town was confirmed not only by the activity of the mob but also by the disdain for the law shown by the aristocracy. During the 1710s there were continual rumours of a secret aristocratic gang of Whig lords called the 'Mohocks' (after the North American Indian warriors) who roamed the poorly lit streets at nights poking out eyes, slitting noses and assaulting women.

There was, for instance, Lord Mohun, who had been commissioned to look into certain aspects of the Sacheverell disturbances at Westminster. Mohun was, like the Earl of Pembroke in the century before, one of a self-selecting band of aristocratic psychopaths who had spent most of his time in hard drinking and street fighting and had managed to kill at least two people in brawls. Acquitted, as he always was by a House of Lords which acted, in all such cases, as an exclusive club there to protect its members, he went on to fight a duel with the Duke of Hamilton in Hyde Park. Not only were Mohun and Hamilton at drawn swords, so were their seconds, and a general melee ensued, conducted with 'uncommon ferocity' in which the 'blood flowed freely'. By the end, both the main protagonists, having fought with the 'supernatural strength' of 'madmen', lay dead with multiple stab wounds and Mohun's second had fled for Holland. His body brought home to his wife, Mohun's widow simply complained that her husband's corpse had ruined her new sheets with its blood! Curiously, both this incident and the whole Mohock affair were considered by many people in London, including Jonathan Swift, to be part of a shadowy and ill-defined plot to assassinate members of the government and cause anarchy on the streets – a *political pattern* always seemed to lurk just below the surface of random and commonplace violence.

There was every sort of riot possible during the eighteenth century. Sometimes these were local and spontaneous, sometimes they were whipped up by tradesmen, gentry or aristocrats with a grudge and an eye for pressurizing Parliament. Against a background of major outbreaks of typhus, dysentery and smallpox the countryside suffered rural food riots during 1729, 1740, 1756–7, 1772–3, 1795 and 1800.* During 1757 Cornwall was virtually under martial law. Food riots broke out in Leicester, Northampton, Nottingham, Coventry, Derby and Leeds as well as twenty other areas from Morpeth to Norwich. Anti-Militia riots amidst fears of invasion by the French also occurred during 1757 in Bedfordshire and the East Riding of Yorkshire as well as across Lincolnshire, Cornwall, Dorset and Northumberland.

---

*There were further riots in the West Country in 1801, caused by a combination of poor harvests and antagonism at the overwintering of sailors in Torbay which pushed prices above local pockets.

Events turned violent in towns as distant as Enfield in Middlesex and Padstow in Cornwall.

It was the centrality of London and the volatile nature of the London 'mob', however, that most exercised the minds of the authorities in their permanent neurosis over security in the capital. This was partly due to the shifting nature of crowd disturbances.[4] Rioting pockmarks the entire century. There were, for instance, numerous disturbances at the Haymarket Theatre and Covent Garden, ranging from a riot following a bad play in 1738 to riots following increases in ticket prices in 1744 and 1763, and there was a major outburst at Garrick's Drury Lane after the audience objected to French dancers during the period leading to war with France. But there were also other causes for a good fight. There were riots against the import of calico by Spitalfields weavers in 1719 and 1720 and continued anti-Irish rioting (over the fear of cheap labour) throughout 1736; there were marches and protests by merchant seamen over wages during 1763 and these were accompanied by demonstrations of Thames watermen over the threat of new bridges: there were strikes by hatters and a 'Gang of Hatters' roamed Southwark in 1763 at the same time as Charles Dingley's sawmill in Limehouse was demolished by 500 sawyers concerned at his use of mechanization; glass grinders, barrel makers and journeymen tailors also went on strike, the tailors providing an early instance of a nascent trade union 'formed into a kind of republic'.

Wages and tariff disputes went on throughout the century. Hat dyers were on strike during 1770, hatters were again on the streets in 1775 and merchant sailors were demanding higher (actually restored) wages in 1772, gathering at Tower Hill to protest, as did naval seamen discharged after the American War who rioted in 1783. During 1773 coal-heavers, watermen, car-men, porters and silk weavers combined to petition the King, sometimes so threateningly that any march was instantly banned (with varying success) for fear of serious trouble.

The worst outbreak of industrial violence, however, occurred in 1768, first among weavers and then amongst the East End coal-heavers. London was fuelled by coal that was unloaded from colliers in the Thames and taken ashore by lightermen and coal-heavers. This was a very tough and dirty industry using Catholic labourers from Shadwell and Wapping. The authorities were on the alert as such men could become volatile and unpredictable. The troubles of 1768 began when the coal-heavers demanded both an increase in payment per load and a regularization of working practices. In 1758 a Parliamentary Commission had agreed to set up a proper organization for the industry including a registration scheme, which paid sick benefit and a widow's allowance as well as funeral costs.

William Beckford (then a Billingsgate Ward Alderman) administered the scheme but it was thwarted by the criminal fraudulence of his deputy, Francis Reynolds. Another scheme was immediately set up by Ralph Hodgson in Shadwell, which gave a style of trade union power to the coal-heavers who joined him and which pushed up wages. Hodgson also supported the coal-heavers in their wage claim and strike which shut the Port of London in April 1768.

Beckford now advertised for blackleg labour. One of the organizers was John Green of the Round About tavern in Shadwell. Armed with cutlasses and clubs, the striking coal-heavers besieged the pub until driven off by gunfire from the (now broken) windows. Next day the men returned and attempted to 'cut [Green] to pieces and hang him on his sign'. Green retreated but retaliated by shooting dead two (or three) of the attackers. The justices did for the rest, condemning seven assailants to the gallows which had been erected on Stepney Green but not before Green's sister had also been brutally murdered ('torn to death') in retaliation. By May, the masters had decided to refuse the pay rise and engaged sailors to load and unload their coal. This was a very dangerous mistake and when opportunity arose coal-heavers boarded a collier as it unloaded and told the sailors that if they remained on the ship (the *Thames and Mary*) they would be killed. Next day sailors taking leave from unloading another vessel were attacked. Two were wounded and one, John Beatty, stabbed to death. Violent street fights continued between sailors and striking coal-heavers and two ship's masters were also severely beaten the following week. Inevitably and with the dull predictability of all bloody reprisals the magistrates and the army were called in, caught the ringleaders and executed them. The strike collapsed but not until the sailors themselves had decided to blockade the Port of London.

In 1756, Lord Tyrawley, in command of the Coldstream Guards in London, had sent a memorandum to the Duke of Cumberland, the Commander-in-Chief, outlining a plan for the imposition of martial law. Ignored at the time, it formed one link in the chain leading to the partial military occupation of London during the Gordon Riots of 1780. London, with its significance as the capital, the largest city, the seat of government and home of royalty, would always be the key to the security of the nation. 'London is of all places in the island the most attentively to be watched, on account of the many actively desperate and ill-affected people who are in it. I need not say how little, the magistracy of the City is to be trusted, or how much to be feared', wrote Lord Barrington, the Secretary at War, in 1776. His concerns were coloured by a real sense of urgency.

It is not many years, since a mob at Madrid forced the King of Spain to fly from his capital; or many months, since another alarmed the King of France at Versailles: at the same time it was necessary that every baker's shop at Paris should be protected by soldiers. The governments, in almost all the provinces of North America, were overturned by insurrections last summer, because there was not a sufficient force to defend them.

If an insurrection in London should be attended with the least success, or even to continue unquelled for any time, (a circumstance much to be apprehended, as the City Magistrates will not call for the assistance of troops) it is highly probable, there would also be risings in many parts of the kingdom. The present apparent quiet should not make it forgotten, that there is a very levelling spirit among the people.

Repeated experience shows that no stops can be put anywhere to these risings, without the intervention of troops; and if there are not, within reasonable distance, sufficient troops to check them at the beginning, a large force becomes necessary for the purpose.[5]

As Sir John Fielding in Bow Street ruminated on the need for a permanent civilian police force, Barrington and others considered the possibilities for the rapid deployment of troops. He had had ample opportunity to study strategic and tactical military decisions in action during the London weaver riots of 16 to 21 May 1765. So serious were the initial troubles that Horace Walpole considered the real possibility of a 'rebellion in the heart of the capital'.

The trouble had started when disaffected silk weavers, feeling yet again the pinch of trade, had gathered in Moorfields, broken the windows and attacked the houses of master weavers and marched on Parliament. The following day a crowd of 8,000 weavers again marched on Parliament then later in the evening went off to attack the Duke of Bedford's town house, targeting him for his refusal to support restrictive duties on Italian silk. A large body of troops were already attempting to quell rioting in other parts of London such as St Pancras and Islington but sufficient troops were mustered in front of the Duke's house to prevent his capture and death and the destruction of the building. Dragoons and troops were now stationed throughout London from Hoxton to Kensington, Paddington to Tottenham Court.

The military had acted with speed and some decisiveness against the weavers, opening fire on crowds without compunction. This was hardly surprising. The weavers were one of a number of artisan groups (such as shoemakers) in the capital who had a strong sense of their own *collective* value and a real sensitivity to economic charges. They constantly rioted and marched against foreign imports, especially cheap Indian calico, in the early years of the century, and both wool and silk weavers were acutely aware of their status under continued threat from cheap labour. The fear and hate felt towards Irish weavers became a feature not only of local disputes with master weavers but also an irritant in wider anti-Catholic agitation (as in 1780). The Irish could be relied upon to undercut English wages by anything up to a half. In 1736 a builder in Hackney called Goswell found that employing Irish labour considerably cut his wage bills, but it also provoked a riot from his English ex-employees (he had sacked them in order to employ the Irish) and disgruntled English weavers, who, in a body of approximately 2,000, attacked a local Irish drinking den. It took fifty soldiers, a week's negotiations, and the 'retirement' of Goswell's Irish workers to fix things.

To the authorities of London the defeat of the weavers was one blow in a continuing war that was *political* as well as economic. For their part, the weavers were rapidly developing a *politicized* will in which economic demands could easily be converted into insurrectionary actions. It is of some significance that the swift action used against the weavers did not occur during the first few days of the Gordon Riots where clear political demands were backed both by respectable elements of the Protestant Association and by the City Aldermen opposed to the Tory aristocracy. Even so, the weavers of Spitalfields, as elsewhere, remained steadfastly anti-Jacobite, anti-Irish and anti-Catholic.

For the whole of the eighteenth century the handloom weavers of London proved a defiant and virtually unassailable body: they might march to Parliament one day with black flags flying to petition against foreign imports and another offer oaths and pledges of loyalty; they might happily arm themselves with pistols and cutlasses, disguise themselves as sailors and in the dead of night go to the homes of blacklegs and smash looms; they might demand increased wages and form themselves into a trade association called the Bold Defiance; they might pick up guns, as they often did, and fight running battles with soldiers and magistrates hunting for cutters (loom destroyers). No government could afford to antagonize the weavers for long, only the coming of water and steam power would finally prove fatal to their aristocracy. Quite forgotten, the last loom weavers in London were Mary and Charles Waite of 45 Cranbrook Street, who stopped in 1938.

No one person divided political opinion so violently or created such expectations and disturbances at elections as John Wilkes. The husband of a nice but dull heiress, Wilkes was a member of the Hell Fire Club, a club formed under the leadership of Francis Dashwood and committed as much to the revolutionary and republican aims of many of its members as to heavy drinking, satanic ritual and sexual extravaganzas. Wilkes was also a libertine and a man who always lived above his means. Those determined to dislike him from reputation found instead an amiable, intelligent and astute personality who carried out his official functions with due sincerity and discipline. Wilkes hated George III, who returned the distaste, considering him a 'rascal' and below contempt. Aristocratic enemies disliked Wilkes's attempts to rock the constitutional boat and his aping the libertine ways of the very upper social levels. Throughout his life Wilkes was a 'third' party in Parliament, too independent to be simply tied to the Whigs. He remained a conviction politician and refused the enticements of party pragmatism, resting as he always would on the causes he espoused and the support they found amongst the poor and 'middling' folk and amongst the tradesmen and 'parcel of low shop keepers' (to use George III's words) of the City. Wilkes was always impatient with the 'set of idle, listless, loitering, lounging, ill-informed gentlemen of Westminster'.

He entered Parliament in 1757 just prior to the accession of George III, whose attempts to bring together political antagonists and unify the country terminated in both greater divisions in and out of the House and the disastrous years of the American Revolution, by the end of which George's rule was seen as both arbitrary and despotic even by opponents whose credentials were neither violently republican nor overtly radical. Things could hardly have been worse for the King when he chose Lord Bute, his former tutor, to be Secretary of State and First Lord of the Treasury. Bute was duly attacked wherever he went by mobs out to get all 'Scotch rogues'. Even a bodyguard of 'bruisers and butchers' failed to save him. Bute's Chancellor of the Exchequer, Sir Francis Dashwood, was reputedly so poor with numbers that he even found difficulty with 'tavern bills'.

The aggression shown by the populace against Bute was matched by adulation for his opponents. William Pitt and William Beckford were politicians held in high esteem by the artisans and tradespeople of London. Pitt was instrumental in courting public opinion and was a hero of the City, so that when he resigned having failed to get a declaration of war against Spain he became even more the hero for London patriots. Bute found himself pelted and abused on Lord Mayor's Day (9 November 1761); Beckford had organized the demonstration, which while falling short of an actual riot succeeded in making the people's displeasure quite clear to both the King and his new First Minister.

Such corruption was meat and drink to the reforming mind of Wilkes, whose political paper the *North Briton* attacked the King's speech of April 1763 in issue No. 45 for being the 'most abandoned instance of ministerial effrontery ever attempted'. George took the comments as a personal insult but Wilkes pointed out he had simply attacked the ministry, and claimed parliamentary privilege.

He was, nevertheless, prosecuted for seditious libel and general and specific warrants were issued for his arrest.* General warrants allowed the authorities any and every sort of forced entry and seizure they deemed fit (they were specifically protected against in the American Constitution) but were considered at variance with British principles of liberty. Every sort of abuse followed as the authorities attempted to stop Wilkes and his publication. Forty-eight other people found themselves arrested whilst Wilkes, who lived a few yards away from the Secretary of State, Lord Halifax (who had signed the warrant for his arrest), went scot-free. Those sent to arrest him came up with ludicrous excuses and Wilkes's challenge to the writ against him bought more time. Finally Halifax invited Wilkes to his house along the street, which Wilkes refused as being rather rude until offered a sedan chair. Having enjoyed his little charade and made idiots of his enemies he gave himself up and settled himself into the Tower awaiting trial.

On the second day of his trial Wilkes made a brilliant and incisive speech on general liberty of conscience. 'The liberty', he told the court, 'of all peers and gentlemen and what touches me more sensibly, that of all the middling and inferior set of people who stand most in need of protection – is in my case this day to be finally decided upon; a question of such importance as to determine at once whether English liberty shall be a reality or a shadow.'[6]

The speech had little to do with the case and much to do with Wilkes's astute sense of his political position. Finally acquitted, he was escorted to the cry of 'Wilkes and Liberty' by a crowd made up of people of 'far higher rank than the common Mob'. He was now 'the life and soul of the Opposition'. All the others accused with Wilkes were acquitted and set to suing for damages.

Once free, Wilkes began reprinting the notorious No. 45 and once again George III and his ministers determined to rid themselves of him. This almost succeeded when Samuel Martin, whom Wilkes had called 'a mean, abject, low lived and dirty fellow', taunted him into settling the remark as an affair of honour in Hyde Park. Wilkes was no coward and had experience of duelling. He threw down the gauntlet only to be seriously wounded in the groin by his opponent who, it seemed, had cooked up the affair after a long period of target practice. It is possible that this was, therefore, a bungled assassination attempt. When the public hangman attempted to burn No. 45 near

---

*The general warrant was used 'to search for authors, publishers and printers' when a book or article deemed libellously seditious was produced anonymously. Once the authorities had established Wilkes's identity he was sought under a specific warrant.

the Royal Exchange he and the City Sheriffs were pelted with mud and attacked whilst the Lord Mayor, in nearby Mansion House, went quietly on with business and whilst coffee-house gentlemen shouted approval and echoed the chant of 'Wilkes and Liberty'. The Speaker of the Commons expressed his outrage at the insult and Wilkes was expelled from the House, tried in absentia for libel and convicted. So hated was the foreman of the convicting jury that he was hounded into suicide.

Wilkes had skedaddled to France and when he failed to return was declared an outlaw. He did return, however, after a change of ministry to stand for one of the seats in Middlesex in 1768 and was duly elected, to the consternation of his opponents, the bitter anger of George III and the joy of the middle and lower ranks. Wealthy merchants helped pay for the mobs that attacked the houses of Lords Bute and Newcastle. The streets rang with 'Wilkes and no King' and impressed Benjamin Franklin as he stood a spectator. On 20 April, having petitioned the King for clemency and having received no reply, Wilkes surrendered himself – an outlaw and one of the MPs for Middlesex.

Wilkes's victory in the Middlesex elections was celebrated from 'Temple Bar to Hyde Park' and the crowds that revelled in the streets that night found their own suitable symbol of his ascendancy.

> The rabble was very tumultuous; some persons who had voted for Mr Wilkes having put out lights, the mob paraded the whole town from east to west, obliging every body to illuminate and breaking the windows of such as did not do it immediately. The windows of the Mansion-house, in particular, were demolished all to pieces, together with a large chandelier and some pier glasses, to the amount of many hundred pounds. They demolished all the windows of Ld Bute, Lord Egmont, Sir Sampson Gideon, Sir William Mayne, and many other gentlemen and tradesmen in most of the public streets of both cities, London and Westminster. At one of the above gentlemen's houses, the mob were in a great measure irritated to it by the imprudence of a servant, who fired a pistol among them. At Charing Cross, at the Duke of Northumberland's, the mob also broke a few panes; but his Grace had the sense to get rid of them by ordering up lights immediately into his windows, and opening the Ship alehouse, which soon drew them to that side.[7]

Wilkes believed in the importance of individual liberty, property and law. He was closer to the American revolutionaries than to any British party and held out for complete freedom of conscience, a secular state, a reformed Parliament and just laws (of which general warrants were a clear abuse); a republican in spirit, Wilkes epitomized in his demeanour the opposition to the landed court interest and the championing of trade; his model, if anything, was a new federal union of Britain and America with a constitution bereft of any place for despotic and arbitrary rule; his means were peaceful and judicious even if crowds pulled his carriage to court huzzaing as they went and shouting for Liberty and even as violent disorders swirled round his prison near St George's Fields whilst he remained on remand.

On 27 April 1768, Wilkes appeared in court to answer charges but was released by a mob who took him to the City. Wisely, Wilkes again gave himself up to be sent to the King's Bench Prison, around which rioting on his behalf continued sporadically until early May. Faced with a coincidental blockade of the Port of London by striking sailors and violent coal-heavers the military were unable to restore order around Southwark, let alone anywhere else. The growing crowds milling around the King's Bench Prison in St George's Fields were swelled by those expecting Wilkes to be triumphantly taken to his place in the House of Commons when it opened on 10 May. Lord Weymouth, the Secretary of State responsible for keeping order that day and a man considered by at least one contemporary to be 'idle' and 'debauched', decided that only draconian means – bloodshed – would teach a mob proper manners. He ordered more troops to guard Wilkes's prison and told the local JPs to look lively when reading the Riot Act.

A vast crowd (estimated at 40,000) had now grown around the prison walls, but passers-by and people just going on their way in a crowded area had added to the number. Little occurred until some soldiers, being too demonstrative, were pushed and shoved. Then a libellous rhyme was found on the prison wall. It was all too much, and Justice Samuel Gillan (or Gillam) read the Riot Act twice, the only effect of which was that he was hit with a stone by a man in a red waistcoat. Gillan then ordered the soldiers to fire, which they did to deadly effect, killing between five and eleven people (according to different accounts) and wounding many others. The day, 10 May, became known as the Massacre of St George's Fields. During the disturbances soldiers pursued the man in the red waistcoat down some side streets. One Guardsman, Donald MacLane (or Maclean), had cornered a man he believed to be the culprit and had bayoneted and shot him to death. The dead man, William Allen, had been quite innocently working in the yard at his father's pub.

MacLane was one of three soldiers accused of murder even though following orders: the government had caught a temporary fright. After appearing before 'packed' (i.e. rigged) juries all were acquitted. Justice Gillan was indicted by supporters of Wilkes but defended successfully by the government. Wilkes was now a greater hero: the martyr of despotism who had *willingly surrendered* to defend his case, a case he won when Lord Mansfield gave judgement in an extra-ordinary and, perhaps, panicked volte face and reversed the verdict of outlawry.

Wilkes was never a rabble-rouser in any real sense and although crowds followed him throughout his political career he always tried to conduct his affairs within an honourable (if sometimes Machiavellian) framework. Apart from his parliamentary seat, the City always supported him. He was elected Alderman of one of the two Farringdon wards, then Sheriff and finally Lord Mayor of London. His reforming influence led to the formation of the Society of the Supporters of the Bill of Rights, the first parliamentary lobby group seeking to influence electoral change and reform, but once back in power Wilkes remained a respectable and orderly member of the establishment whose stand on behalf of liberty, 'rights' and freedom of speech made him the hero of the new entrepreneurial middle class, tradespeople, shopkeepers and lawyers whose voice was now to be heard in Boston, Philadelphia and London. On the whole, Wilkes's 'mobs' were self-disciplined, intelligent and made up of sufficiently large numbers of respectable, literate petty tradespeople and workers that little damage was ever done. One twentieth-century Conservative historian conceded that 'without Wilkes and the crowd, government would have become more arbitrary'.[8]

Wilkes proved himself the inheritor of a long tradition of antagonism between the City and Westminster and the Crown. Charles James Fox, during the 1760s a firebrand Tory, called Wilkes 'a profligate libeller', making it quite clear at the same time exactly who it was who took the responsibility for and decisions on behalf of the nation. 'What acquaintance have the people at large with the arcana of political rectitude, with the connections of kingdoms, the resources of national strength, the abilities of ministers, or even with their own dispositions?' he demanded. 'Sir, I pay no regard whatever to the voice of the people: it is our duty to do what is proper, without considering what may be agreeable; their business is to chuse us: it is ours to act constitutionally, and to maintain the independency of Parliament'.

Fox's conception of parliamentary rule was quite clear: the people chose their representatives and were thereafter to abide by the decisions of their representatives (and betters). Fox hated Wilkes's mob oratory and 'democratic' attitude, which he saw as a perverse attempt to undermine Parliament through abusive publications and compliant City aldermen. It was ironic therefore that Fox himself metamorphosed from a Tory traditionalist into a 'Man of the People' who strongly supported the American Revolutionaries.

George Washington he described as 'my illustrious friend'. Washington's talents and virtues were 'the best possible apology for this freedom'. Buff and blue, the colours of Washington's army, were adopted as uniform of the Fox Club, and the cover of the *Edinburgh Review* . . . and . . . became, during the war with the colonies, the badge of the entire Whig party. Fox and the Whigs supported the Americans, because they believed that if George III succeeded in imposing despotism in America, he would surely follow up that success by doing the same in England.[9]

By the mid-1780s, Fox had aligned himself with radicalism and with anti-monarchical feeling. It was 'enough to make one sick', he told friends, 'how ruinous everything done by Tories is always destined to be'. The Tories were 'the tools of monarchy'. Fox's new interests in liberty of trade, united with his concern for property rights, placed him in opposition to George III (who he called 'Satan') and the King's supporters, 'for, had the present king any hereditary right? Parliament, indeed, had made him, the successor to the throne, but hereditary right he had none. He was . . . the mere creature of the people's instituting, and held nothing but what he held in trust for the people, for their use and benefit. There is no man who hates the power of the crown more, or who has a worse opinion of the Person to whom it belongs than I'.

Despotism appeared a real threat during the 1780s, and whilst deploring the Gordon rioters' mob action Fox approved their motives. The riots exposed the real intent of monarchy and allowed Westminster reformers their legitimate role. As 'King of Westminster' (his constituency) Fox came to advocate many of the reforms later taken up by the Chartists, mixing as he did with reformers such as John Jebb and John Cartwright, the outspoken advocate of universal suffrage. As with Gordon and Wilkes, Fox also emerged a populist radical opposed to 'despotism', and the ancien régime. Only complete victory in America by the revolutionaries would send a clear message to George III about imposing despotism at home. It would, of course, also liberate binational trade.

The war with British 'despotism' was a game for serious players and Fox was a gambler with a strong stomach. He had no intention of letting 'Satan' George outplay him. George, long angered by Fox's dubious friendship with his son (the Prince Regent to be), was also in implacable mood. The crisis occurred during 1782–4. Lord North's ministry fell in March 1782 to be followed by a Whig administration led by the Earl of Shelburne and the Marquis of Rockingham. Fox was the éminence grise of the party, and prepared to act as 'kingmaker', especially when Rockingham met stony silence from George III over Whig promotions. George was implacably opposed to anyone but Lord North. Fox saw this as pure despotism and looked to a moment of crisis to destroy George's influence. The opportunity appeared in the summer of 1782 when Rockingham died and Fox backed the Duke of Portland as his successor, leaving no place for Shelburne. Fox, however, in forcing the Duke on the King had himself turned Parliament into the creature of party. Shelburne warned, 'in truth, it is taking the Executive, altogether out of the King's hands, & placing it in the hands of a Party, which however, respectable, must prove a compleat Tyranny to everybody else'.

Fox's initiative showed his hand too clearly (he should have known better as a great gambler!) and seemed to threaten the very prerogatives of the crown and the King's constitutional position. If, as Fox feared, everything had been stitched up behind closed doors ('in the closet') and Shelburne had been given 'the Treasury' by George there was a total 'End of *Whig Principles*', the King would have won and Fox would now be a pariah. It was clear that Shelburne had been offered the premiership. Fox was furious and reprimanded the King and then Shelburne. Fox had failed and the King and Toryism had triumphed for the moment. His defeat suggested another rebuff for the forces of Parliament, ill matched against the worst excesses of the old order.

> Alternatively, a contest between a king and the Whig aristocracy could always be characterized as an attempt at oligarchy on the part of a few great families. Horace Walpole saw the threat to the constitution not in terms of a royal despotism, but as Foxite exclusiveness: 'I hope we shall have a codicil to Magna Charta produced, for we are certainly to have a new War of the Barons, a struggle between the King and some great peers in which the people are to go for nothing'.[10]

Eighteenth-century elections were noisy, chaotic and often violent. The Middlesex elections had only been one extreme example of the processes surrounding the hustings. There was, however, also an element of farce, which all classes appreciated and which found expression in the bizarre annual ritual of the election of the Mayor of Garratt. The hamlet of Garratt itself was a dusty and neglected heap of cottages between Wandsworth and Tooting with no significance whatsoever and certainly no parliamentary representative. The origin of its 'mayor' lies in a local drinking and anti-enclosure club, which needed a chairman and decided to elect him as the Mayor of Garratt. Local innkeepers saw that the joke was a way of attracting crowds who would drink all day (which is exactly what happened) and they sponsored an annual event which was said to attract as many as 100,000 people out for a holiday in the country.

The election itself was a satire on the political process, the world turned upside down for a day to allow comic speeches, vulgar banter and political impersonation. The entire lampoon was designed to get people to drink as well as to relieve tensions over political questions and class divisions. Candidates were amongst others watermen, cabbies, gravediggers, fish sellers, barbers, a fruit seller and a wig dealer, and were all given aristocratic titles or knighthoods, becoming Squire Blow-me-down, Lord Twankum, Squire Gobbins or Sir George Comefirst for the period of the hustings. Speeches were at a premium and candidates might be offered squibs written by David Garrick or even John Wilkes.

After a procession with everybody dressed in ridiculous costumes, the company arrived at Garratt Green. Here candidates took a vulgar oath, their right hand resting on the sign of the mob – a brickbat! The oath was too rude to be repeated by Victorian folk historians, it seems. It scrutinized voters' property qualifications in the language of sexual innuendo.

> That you have admitted peaceably and quietly, into possession of a freehold thatched tenement, either black, brown or coral, in hedge or ditch, against gate or stile, under furze or fen, on any common or common field, or enclosure, in the high road, or any of the lanes, in barn, stable, hovel, or any other place within the manor of Garratt; and, that you did (Bona fide) keep (ad rem) possession of that said thatched tenement (durante bene placito) without any let, hindrance, or molestation whatever; or without any ejectment or forcibly turning out of the same; and that you did then and there and in the said tenement, discharge and duty pay and amply satisfy all legal demands of the tax that was at that time due on the said premises; and lastly, did quit and leave the said premises in sound, wholesome and good tenable repair as when you took possession and did enter therein. So help you.[11]

Interestingly, the licence granted to the Mayoralty came to an end in 1793 when satire turned to sedition in the speeches of the deformed wig maker 'Sir Jeffrey Dunston'.

> He was a foundling who took his name from the parish of St Dunstans-in-the-East in the City of London, where, in 1759, he was discovered on the step of the churchwarden's house. He was brought up in the workhouse, had knock-knees and a disproportionately large head, and only grew to a height of 4 feet . . .
>
> Although deformed he was a wit, and his lively sallies made him popular with the crowd, who twice more returned him to office. A man fond of his drink, he became too outspoken against the establishment and in 1793, at the height of the French

Sir Jeffrey Dunston

Revolution, he was tried, convicted and imprisoned for seditious expressions.*,12

The violent career of the eighteenth century called for violent measures. The country seemed to teeter on the brink of anarchy, threatening always to fall into the hands of 'the mob' – the 'fourth estate'. Henry and John Fielding, the magistrates at Bow Street between 1754 and 1780, had long been convinced that it was only the use of the Riot Act that kept a barrier between good order and mere chaos. It was, they thought, 'the most necessary of all our laws for the preservation and protection of the people'. Unfortunately, the magistrates and local constables went in constant fear of reprisals. After

---

*Mock-elections and mock-Parliaments did not end with the Mayor of Garratt. During the 1880s working-class debating societies called themselves 'parliaments'. One group was the South Lambeth Parliament, which met at an evangelical mission hall between 1887 and 1890. Such clubs allowed the still unenfranchised a chance to debate parliamentary issues and imitate the ways of the Members of the Commons.

all, these were local men living in a community that resented them. One justice of the peace quailed,

> We shall have a total relaxation of justice if something is not immediately done by the Government to put a stop to these riotous proceedings, for the gentlemen of these parts cannot do it by the civil power as none of the peace officers will obey us, being intimidated by the threats of the mob to pull down their houses.[13]

The Riot Act itself was one of the most muddled and problematic pieces of legislation ever to get on the statute books, having been brought in during 1715 when, with the death of Queen Anne in 1714 and the accession of George I, the government feared street demonstrations by Jacobites. The Act put a duty on those in authority such as magistrates and mayors to read out a prepared proclamation if twelve or more persons were 'unlawfully, riotously and tumultuously assembled together to the disturbance of the public peace'. The magistrate was to proclaim with a 'loud voice':

> Our Sovereign Lord the King chargeth and commandeth all persons being assembled, immediately to disperse themselves and peaceably to depart to their habitations or to their lawful business, upon the pains contained in the Act made in the first year of King George for preventing tumultuous and riotous assemblies. God save the King.

Should a 'mob' ignore the warning they had one hour before the magistrate could call on law-abiding citizens, constables, militia, yeomanry or regular army to break up the meeting and apprehend the participants who would henceforth be treated as common 'felons'. If the authorities killed anybody then it was simply too bad, the culprit being indemnified for carrying out his lawful duty.

The Act was intended to strengthen the hands of magistrates, who were the local executives of the authorities but who had little power to enforce their will. It was true that they had always been able to call upon locals to help quell disturbances but the Act made the duration of *assembly* rather than riot the focus of attention. This confused the situation regarding common law and the continuing rights of the magistracy.

> Magistrates after 1714 behaved as if the Act had submerged the common law right of dealing with rioters, and believed their hands to be tied for one hour after proclamation. In fact the position at common law was still intact as it was before 1714; a crowd could become felons by statute after the expiry of one hour, but could also become felons at common law if within the hour they

proceeded to acts of felonious violence, such as pulling down houses. This position was explained in the judgments in the case of Rex v. Gillam (1768) and again by Lord Mansfield in the House of Lords and by Lord Loughborough in the trials arising from the 1780 riots. The Riot Act has a poor record, and better drafting at the time to make plain the intention of the legislature, or a clarifying statement later, would have saved much difficulty. A great deal of damage was done within the statutory hour on many occasions during the 1780 riots, because the authorities believed themselves unable to interfere. The law was no better understood at the time of the Bristol riots in the next century and further explanation was necessary.[14]

Even more significant was the ambiguity of certain phrases. When would it be 'absolutely necessary' for the magistrate to read the Act and call upon military assistance (there was no other to call upon until the founding of a regular police force)? Edmund Burke saw this as tantamount to a licence to impose martial law – 'the military', he argued, 'can never be employed to any constitutional purpose at all'.

The army itself was always in a quandary as to its role. The very first use of the Act had, ironically, been to quell an army mutiny in Ireland in 1717 but the army had been introduced to the tangle in which it might find itself in 1736, when Captain John Porteous, who had ordered troops to open fire on a crowd after an execution in Edinburgh, was charged with murder and jailed, only to be dragged out by a lynch mob and hanged from a lamppost. Nevertheless, and despite the appearance of a regular police force, the military (often Yeomanry volunteers) were regularly called upon by magistrates for almost 250 years. The original Riot Act itself survived until 1968, when regular troops long since absent from mainland disturbances found themselves embroiled in the growing disaster of Northern Irish politics.

The rising levels of crowd disturbances during the eighteenth century and the increase of criminality due to poverty were accompanied by ever more aggressive criminal laws. These were not, however, a simple response to events uncontrolled by police forces, rather they were often pre-emptive in their attempt to proscribe activity and punish malefactors. The major Act from which all else stemmed was the Waltham Black Act of 1722, an attempt to stop forest raids by armed poachers on newly enclosed land. The law, however, went much further, and covered a vast universe of criminal acts, its original limited existence of three years made permanent in 1758. Under the Black Act, as it came to be called, almost any trivial act of theft or disturbance became a capital offence. The Act, observed Lord Hardwicke in 1735, was the 'only bulwark against the degeneracy of the times'. To reinforce the message, execution was to be as humiliating as possible, with bodies offered for surgical dissection. At the same time, juries and judges could avoid ultimate sentences by either lowering the estimation of an amount stolen (to avoid the penalty) or commuting the sentence to one of transportation. The first fleet sailed to establish a colony in New South Wales in May 1787 with 778 convicts aboard.*

---

* At the same time, the growth in the criminalized population meant that old naval ships, 'hulks', had to be used as semi-permanent jails for those awaiting transportation. The entire system, which did not get scrapped until long into the nineteenth century, was an attempt to export criminals or, where necessary, simply kill them off. Such draconian attitudes, which often included the transportation of political dissidents, immediately created large and homogeneous criminal communities on board hulks and transportation vessels. As might be expected, they too rioted or mutinied. Convicts bound for Halifax, Nova Scotia mutinied on board the *Swift* in 1783 when it sailed from Blackwall. Thomas Bradbury, mate of the *Swift*, testified at the Old Bailey to the events on 10 September. Under cross-examination he recalled:

The prisoner [David Hart] and the rest of them, who had been confined between decks, made what they called a rush; they came all at once into the cabin [sic], and secured the captain and myself, and all the ship's company, and the fire arms.
Did you see the prisoner amoungst [sic] them? I did.
Did you see them come on deck? No, I was in the cabin, and in about a minute afterwards they rushed into the cabin.
Tell us what yourself [sic] saw? I saw them secure the arms, I saw them with the arms in their hands, the prisoner was amongst them, and had either a musket or a blunderbuss in his hand.
How long was this a doing? It was done in a minute.
How did they get their liberty? The night before, they had sent a letter to the captain, desiring he would take their irons off, he said he would not, they said if he would not they would take them off themselves, he said he would fire on them, they said fire and be damned, and then went to work, and everyone took their irons off with as much ease as if they had none on.
Did you know on board the ship, that they were taking off their irons? Yes. Could you prevent it? No.
How many did your crew consist of? Eighteen; after they had secured us, they bore away, and went a little to the east of Dunganness [sic] between that and Rye, they let go the anchor, and hoisted the boats out, and went on shore, as many as could cleverly get into the boats got on shore, with the arms along with them; that was on the 29th the same day they made the rush, it was six o'clock in the evening that they went on shore. [John Cobley, *The Lives of the Lady Juliana Convicts – 1790* (Sydney: Library of Australian History, 1989), p. xii.]

Forty-eight people escaped only to be rounded up later, and, like David Hart, reconvicted and transported.

The likelihood of armed mutiny was forever present. On 24 September 1778, the *Gentleman's Magazine* reported a riot by 150 convicts in the Woolwich hulks, which led to the death of two convicts and the wounding of seven others. Riots continued into the nineteenth century. There was rioting on 5 August 1802, again at Woolwich.

> Several of the convicts who are to be transported to New South Wales formed a plan for an escape, which they endeavoured to carry into execution this day. They were all on shore, to the number of about 170, and were confined within a building near to the waterside, where they are accustomed to work, and which is fenced round with a high wall. On a sudden they rushed out and seized some of their keepers, and others they knocked down. The ringleader had armed himself with a large knife, and on finding that the convicts had secured the keepers, proceeded to the outer gate, where a centinel [sic] was placed. To him the armed convict, with several others, addressed himself, and insisted upon the gate being opened, or he would instantly run him through. The soldier fell back a few paces, and shot the ringleader through the head. At the instant he saw the centinel about to fire, he turned away his head, but the ball entered the back part of it, and he died immediately. Another of the convicts was attempting to scale the wall, and was shot by an other soldier. – it was their intention to have seized those boats which are generally in waiting to take the convicts on-board the hulks; when many of them would have got clear off.[15]

By the 1850s, such rioting and onboard communal disobedience had taken an ironic tone. The *London News* of 3 January 1852 reported under the heading 'Convict Demands for Transportation to Australia' that

> It would appear as though the news of the gold discoveries in Australia had penetrated to the wretched inmates of the hulks who have been sentenced to the penalty of transportation, and that they regard themselves as unfairly dealt with because they are not sent out at the public expense to the 'land of promise' where, furnished with the convict's passport – a 'ticket-of-leave', they may apply themselves to the pleasant task of literally 'reaping a golden harvest' as some compensation for the sufferings they have hitherto endured at the hands of society, by whom they have evidently, in their own estimation, been misunderstood. Indeed, these ill-treated gentry feel so indignant on the subject, that they

have not recourse to violence, in order to mainifest their sense of the grievance; and asserting . . . 'the right of insurrection', they have risen *en masse* on board the *Warrior* at Woolwich, and, armed with knives and other weapons, have mustered together in one part of the ship in a body numbering upwards of 100, and demanded to be immediately conveyed to the 'diggins' . . . The whole affair speaks trumpet-tongued as to the light in which the criminal classes regard transportation to Australia, and the government can have no pretence to pass unheeded so evident a testimony as this and other recent occurrences exhibit, that their present system of transportation to the Australian colonies, by holding out reward instead of punishment, serves but to foster crime at home, and utterly corrupt beyond redemption the stream of social life in those most important dependencies of the empire.

Deportation to the antipodes is, in fact, considered a magnificent boon by the criminal, who is quite as well aware as the honest man is, that, joined to its fine climate, New South Wales now presents the additional attraction of speedy wealth in its most concentrated form to the man with strength of arm to dig or daring enough to rob the digger.

9

The United States of England

The English Jacobins to the Cato Street Conspirators

Of all Britain's radicals, Tom Paine was either the most revered or the most reviled, according to one's political position. Indeed he was either the greatest patriot or the vilest traitor, an 'incendiary' whose effigy would be burnt in public squares by anti-republican mobs. For Solicitor General Wedderburn, Paine was nothing less than the equivalent of 'an enemy in the bowels of a Kingdom', in other words, the 'enemy within'.

Tom Paine was born Thomas Pain on 29 January 1737, the son of a Quaker staymaker married to the daughter of a local lawyer. He was locally schooled but when it came to earning a living he proved disinclined to continue long in his father's craft and little inclined towards a sedentary life. His parents' religious beliefs also went by the way as he travelled looking for work. After a few years as a merchant seaman, he settled in Sandwich and opened a corset shop and later a general grocery and tobacco business, all of which failed. He also became an excise official but found himself first dismissed for mismanagement and then, after reinstatement, sacked for leading a pay dispute that had led him to a winter in Westminster lobbying MPs.

By 1774, Paine was bankrupt and jobless but his political activity had brought him into contact with Benjamin Franklin, then London agent for Pennsylvania. Arriving in London, Paine persuaded Franklin to write to his son-in-law in America to see if he could provide a job for 'an ingenious, worthy young man' possibly as a schoolteacher or surveyor. Thus arriving in Philadelphia, Paine began teaching but was soon persuaded to write for the *Pennsylvania Magazine*, which he edited as well as providing articles on antislavery, scientific and political topics. At the same time, the deepening political divisions between Great Britain and the colonies were ripening into crisis. On the one hand an economic war had begun when the First Continental Congress had passed a measure known as 'the Association', an agreement to ban all British goods after 1 December 1774. Britain responded with a Restraining Act restricting New England's trade to Britain, Ireland and the West Indies. On the other hand, political debate had greatly increased, so that by 1776 everything hinged on whether a full declaration of independence would be required.

Early in 1776 Paine left the *Pennsylvania Magazine* to write a pamphlet on behalf of independence – *Common Sense*. He also changed his name from Pain to Paine, now a reborn American citizen.

Common Sense first went on sale on 10 January 1776, selling 120,000 copies immediately and eventually more than 500,000. On 14 February a second edition appeared with Paine's name appended. It was the greatest and last of all 'Leveller' pamphlets, making Paine the first true English professional revolutionary.

His call for a revolutionary consciousness amongst Americans was a summary of many republican English views whose origins preceded the English Civil War, but it was born of the rational humanist traditional of eighteenth-century radicalism. Paine combined them to create a powerful message, which appeared obvious or common sense. It was based on an attack on privilege, tradition and government. Such common sense recognized that where government (or the state) had to exist it did so only to restrain the wicked, but that government was also the only guarantee of freedom and security: 'Here then is the origin and rise of government; namely, a mode rendered necessary by the inability of moral virtue to govern the world; here too is the design and end of government, viz. freedom and security'. This being the case, Paine turned to examining the constitution of 'England'.

> I know it is difficult to get over local or long standing prejudices, yet if we will suffer ourselves to examine the component parts of the English constitution, we shall find them to be the base remains of two ancient tyrannies, compounded with some new republican materials.
>
> First – The remains of monarchical tyranny in the person of the king.
>
> Secondly – The remains of aristocratical tyranny in the persons of the peers.
>
> Thirdly – The new republican materials, in the persons of the commons, on whose virtue depends the freedom of England.
>
> The two first, by being hereditary, are independent of the people; wherefore in a *constitutional sense* they contribute nothing towards the freedom of the state.
>
> To say that the constitution of England is a *union* of three powers reciprocally *checking* each other, is farcical, either the words have no meaning, or they are flat contradictions.
>
> To say that the commons is a check upon the king, presupposes two things.

First – That the king is not to be trusted without being looked after, or in other words, that a thirst for absolute power is the natural disease of monarchy.

Secondly – That the commons, by being appointed for that purpose, are either wiser or more worthy of confidence than the crown.

But as the same constitution which gives the commons a power to check the king by withholding the supplies, gives afterwards the king a power to check the commons, by empowering him to reject their other bills; it again supposes that the king is wiser than those whom it has already supposed to be wiser than him. A mere absurdity!

Such government created a 'house divided against itself'.

Paine's next target was the monarchy itself and the concept of hereditary kingship. His argument was both viciously satiric and caustically accurate.

England, since the conquest, hath known some few good monarchs, but groaned beneath a much larger number of bad ones, yet no man in his senses can say that their claim under William the Conqueror is a very honourable one. A French bastard landing with an armed banditti, and establishing himself king of England against the consent of the natives, is in plain terms a very paltry, rascally original. – It certainly hath no divinity in it . . .

The most plausible plea, which hath ever been offered in favour of hereditary succession, is, that it preserves a nation from civil wars; and were this true, it would be weighty, whereas, it is the most barefaced falsity ever imposed upon mankind. The whole history of England disowns the fact. Thirty kings and two minors have reigned in that distracted kingdom since the conquest, in which time there have been (including the Revolution) no less than eight civil wars and nineteen rebellions.

Paine's diatribe could lead only to one conclusion – separation from Great Britain leaving 'England to Europe' and 'America to itself'. With a plan for 'peace for ever' Paine's final words were unequivocal, supporting as they did, 'THE RIGHTS OF MANKIND *and of the* FREE AND INDEPENDENT STATES OF AMERICA'.

The pamphlet, with its sense of outraged justice, was extraordinarily influential in tipping the balance of American views towards revolution and ensuring the virtues of freedom of conscience and freedom of trade, new 'middle-class' attitudes that would strike at the heart of the ancien régime and British monarchical 'tyranny'. Only full republicanism could ensure the appropriate setting for a community that believed in law, commerce, private property and freedom of conscience. Such a society would be egalitarian, ruled by contractual equality rather than feudal obligation and by individual desire rather than hierarchic requirements. Such freedoms would nurture spiritual development only if the state became fully secularized and religion became a matter of private conscience. Nowhere do the Dissenting voice and the republican spirit of Paine's predecessors echo more than here, but the religious 'commonwealth' they longed for was now ironically turned into the inevitable result of their desires: the first democratic and constitutional republic in the world. Paine eulogized in defence of 'the natural rights of all Mankind' that 'we have it in our power to begin the world over again'. The Stars and Stripes flew at many subsequent demonstrations in London alongside the red flag of socialism and the black flag of anarchy. At the demonstration at Cold Bath Fields in 1833 there was a black flag with a skull and crossbones bearing the motto 'Liberty or Death', the French tricolour, a Liberty Cap on a pole and the American flag.

Paine's rallying cry made him the most read English author since Bunyan and his pamphlet the most significant Dissenting document since *Pilgrim's Progress*. Its message quickly struck a chord with British revolutionaries and pro-Jacobins. The 'Rights of Mankind' made it clear that being an 'American' could be a *state of mind* towards which British men and women might aspire without actually emigrating to the United States. When Paine published his highly influential *Rights of Man* (1791) in defence of the French Revolution he had helped to create, he quickly became the quintessence of revolution for his supporters in Britain and a folk demon for the Tory establishment. Paine's work is the first to fully articulate the ideology of the British revolutionary tradition.

The powerful sentiments crystallized in Paine's *Common Sense* flashed and fizzled in the sharp climate of the 1780s and 90s, rekindling 'the good old cause', if only for a moment, on British soil. It took the heated debate over the French Revolution begun by Edmund Burke in his *Reflections on the French Revolution* (1790) written during the 'Terror' and Paine's reply, *The Rights of Man*, to rekindle the republican spirit. It was not only home-grown English Jacobins that the forces of order had to fear but the powerful conjunction of republicanism and *nationalism* found in Ireland and there made more potent by its message of liberation and anti-imperialism. It was only in Ireland that republicanism consistently aligned itself with a demand not only for democracy but also for national independence. The republican struggle in Ireland and exported from Ireland (in its war with England) is itself the longest struggle for both independence and republican government in the history of the United Kingdom. It is also a struggle which for 200 years scarred not only Ireland itself but also the very fabric and people of London.

Aligned against these powerful forces during the 1790s was a rapidly enlarged British army prepared not only to defend the mainland and

Ireland but to take the war against revolutionary France across into Europe and the Middle East. This much-increased military presence was only possible with the raising of part-time and volunteer units. Forces of gentlemen cavalry and their servants (the Yeomanry) were soon on parade in their new uniforms across Britain. The Yeomanry was first used to quell a civil disturbance in spring 1795. The incident occurred in Leicester when rioting accompanied the assault on Leicester jail to free prisoners. In 1801 there were slightly over twenty-four thousand such armed amateurs enlisted.* At the same time, infantry volunteers, often called 'Loyal' or 'Armed' Associations, were being drilled. These consisted of tradesmen and 'honest' or 'respectable' workers who were town-based rather than the rural Yeomanry regiments. Even radical Clerkenwell had an Association once invasion by Napoleon seemed imminent. These new 'amateur' soldiers were only too aware of their volunteer status and maintained themselves as armed clubs with their own codes for dress and discipline quite distinct from the harsh and brutal world of the regular army. Moreover, they created an esprit de corps – a snobbish clannishness – maintained by the fact that each company or battalion was kept going by members' subscriptions. Even volunteer's blue coats were considered smarter than regulation red.** Quite different from the volunteer soldiers were the impressed militia, a type of national guard required to fill garrisons and do home duty and quite capable of savagery and cowardice in equal measure. Upon these volunteers and impressed men the government hoped to fight the tide of sedition.

Thomas Paine's pamphleteering was the most extreme form of English support for the new spirit of republicanism. The French Revolution brought a chill wind to aristocratic privilege on both sides of the Channel and home-grown republicans looked to a swift invasion of the French sans culottes to overthrow the King and Lords. Hectic correspondence with French diplomats as well as a revived network of corresponding societies and secret unions suggested rebellion might turn into open revolt. Spies working for the government reported suspicious midnight meetings on lonely Yorkshire moors and clandestine trysts at Lancashire taverns. Caches of arms, especially pike heads to defeat the Yeomanry, were reportedly being

---

*To this nominal figure should be added the Provisional Cavalry, raised under the Provisional Cavalry Act 1794 for counties in which there was no Yeomanry, since although they were not volunteers, by 1802 they outnumbered the Yeomanry.

**The return for Volunteer Infantry and Artillery (c. 1,530 companies) was 123,000 NCOs and men, plus the Voluntary Associations for Defence (500 companies), for which there is no return; for the Militia, including Supplementary Militia, and Fencibles in the three kingdoms, 104,000 men.

organized and hidden (indeed, one was actually discovered in the 1830s) in anticipation of French landings.

Nowhere were things more in a state of flux than in Ireland, where negotiations between Irish patriots such as Theobald Wolfe Tone and the French promised swift delivery from the English. Tone had no qualms about French republican help.

> I am sure a great many of us make use of these words that do not know the meaning of them. But suppose they are levellers and republicans and suppose that these words mean everything that is wicked and abominable, still I say, what is that to us? If a Republic is a bad form of government, in God's name let them have it and punish themselves; if it be a good form, I do not know what right we have to hinder it.[1]

Open warfare in Ireland following an abortive rising proved a dreadful disaster with a campaign of state terror, agreed by Pitt, used to utterly demoralize the Irish opponents of Dublin Castle. Torture was frequently and systematically applied. This included flogging, 'picketing'* and the pitch cap, a brown paper 'helmet' covered in pitch and set alight on the victim's head! A nice variation was the gunpowder cap. Lord Clare, the Lord Lieutenant, speaking for the authorities, thought 'the example necessary' and a 'mercy' to deter others. Whilst these outrages continued loyal Protestants in the north split Irish nationalist ranks with the creation of the Orange Order founded in 1792 and galvanized at the Battle of the Diamond (21 September 1795). In so doing they plunged northern Ireland into a civil war.

It is of considerable interest that the extraordinary violence meted out to the Irish was anathema when dealing with the captured French invaders. When they arrived under escort in Dublin in 1798, huge crowds gathered to watch:

> there was found only one man who betrayed any other feeling than curiosity . . . [who] walked up to a French Officer and spit in his face! The Frenchman drew his sword (the officers were suffered to wear their swords) and aimed a blow at the wretch who insulted him, which would have proved fatal, but for the interposition of the halbert [sic] of an English Sergeant. A member of the Merchants Cavalry, who witnessed the transaction, rode up

---

*'*To Stand upon the Picket*, is when a Horseman for some Offence, is sentenc'd to have one Hand ty'd up as high as it can reach, and then to stand on the Point of a Stake with the Toe of his opposite Foot; so that he can neither stand, nor hang well, nor ease himself by changing Feet.' – Edward Phillips, *The New World of English Words* (6th edn, ed. J. Kersey), in *OED*, sv Picket.

and apologized to the Frenchman, and then turning to the mean offender, dealt him such a blow with the flat of his sword as set him reeling, at the same time damning the scoundrel for daring to treat a captive enemy in such a manner. The honest indignation of the army, yeomanry, and the people, was loudly and strongly expressed on the occasion, and the rascal slunk away amidst the hootings and execrations of the crowd.[2]

Captured French officers were treated with politeness and respect and were allowed the liberties of any person of 'quality', only being required to be on their honour not to escape. General Joseph Humbert, who had led the French invasion, for instance, was so well entertained that his hosts were glad to see the back of him on his exchange, as he and his staff had indulged themselves so effectively that they had eaten their captors out of house and home.

The revolutionary fervour that swept Europe had actually begun to subside by the late 1790s when growing fear of French despotism replaced democratic hopes. Nevertheless, there was already in place a secret network of United Irish, United Britons and United Scots whose corresponding societies kept the revolutionary flame alive. Their hopes included manhood suffrage, annual elections, equal electoral districts, removal of property requirements, payment of MPs, the abolition of tithes, the enfranchisement of Catholics and Dissenters, the abolition of the Lords (and the disestablishment of the aristocracy) and the end of monarchy. 'Liberty' was too frequently spoken of to be taken lightly and a monster 'peace and bread' rally held in 1795 in London's Copenhagen Fields (near the modern Caledonian Road, Islington) and organized by the London Corresponding Society (LCS) suggested a direct threat to authority. Authority acted without compassion. Thomas Hardy, the working-class (shoemaker) leader of the LCS, was arrested for treason (exposing the use of government spies in the process), habeas corpus was continuously suspended, the laws on treason were extended and meetings of over fifty people were banned without permission (never to be granted). The introduction of the 'gagging acts' (Treasonable Practices Act; Seditious Meetings Act) meant the LCS was effectively silenced, leaving its extreme elements to go underground. The 'physical force' radicals now organized.

These revolutionary elements came together around the Irish Colonel Marcus Despard and his followers, who hoped to ferment revolution in 1801 and 1802. They had their headquarters in or near Soho Square, where a mixture of United Irish and United Britons met to plot. A large London Irish contingent were part of this group who alongside a number of (secretly) seditious soldiers drew up a plan to seize London.

The soldiers presented the Committee with a Paper which consisted of Six Articles. 1st That the Tower should be delivered at such a time as may be thought convenient. 2d That the Bank of England should be seized. 3d. that Woolwich should be seized 4th. That it was the Opinion of the Army that both Houses of Parliament should be seized when sitting (This was not agreed to) 5th. That all Soldiers engaged in this business shall receive one Guinea per Week, and if the Point be carried shall be at Liberty to retire and to have ten Acres of Land with a Proportion of Money to cultivate it with. That the Army should do all in their Power to bring over the Seamen if possible.[3]

The plotters convinced themselves that Londoners and garrisoned soldiers would rally to the cause, and

That the Tower and the Bank should be seized first but not until Parliament is dissolved and then as soon as it may be thought convenient and all Towns . . . concerned in this business shall have timely Notice, so as to have the Flags of Liberty ready to hoist and all must join their own Standard; and that no private property must be meddled with on any pretence whatsoever.[4]

Others in Leeds, Sheffield and elsewhere would also be called to arms. Pike heads were being produced, it was alleged, and 'conductors' (agitators in charge of cells) were to drill and prepare their men.

As with all such conspiracies during the period Despard's group was foiled by spies and captured, the London populace left relatively indifferent as to his fate. Elsewhere others had waited eagerly for the signal and the promised French invasion but government control was absolute despite naval mutinies and war in Ireland. A further attempt at revolution in 1803 by Robert Emmet was also successfully foiled due to the government's efficient system of 'police' and spies.

The government acted with decision once the French Revolution turned to terror. The main legislation was the Alien Act of 1793, designed to monitor and register all foreigners entering Britain, the information being sent to a central index at Whitehall. In charge were three 'Alien' officers at the Home Office: John King, Charles Flint and William Wickham, all of whom ran spies. By 1800 there was a call by Wickham to make the service 'regular' as work expanded and new premises were found. The Alien Office was now the centre of Britain's spy network, watching subversives through the apprehending and copying of letters sent through the Post Office. This practice had been legitimized in 1711 in order to 'create intelligence'. If letters were in code then 'Maddison' the code breaker would be called in. This 'mainstay of the Secret Office' was opening and deciphering letters such as one to a Mr Dechumes of Lincoln's Inn Fields and a Mr Anthony of St Giles in 1798. The London police were also involved from their headquarters at Bow Street from where Richard Ford sent 'Runners' to act as plainclothes detectives across the country, liaising with informers or acting as spies themselves. 'Secrecy, intrigue and conspiracy [were] the hallmarks of politics in the nineties, the network of intelligence gathering so sensitive that all the papers of the Alien Office were finally "lost" by 1850'.[5]

As we have seen, the government, unable to offer conciliation for fear of looking weak, tightened laws on combinations and assembly and effectively crushed unenfranchised and labouring political dissenters. The details of such laws are of particular significance as, for instance, the law against assembly demonstrated, aimed as it was towards crushing demonstrations by main force.

> Whereas Assemblies of diverse Persons, collected for the Purpose or under the Pretext of deliberating on public Grievances, and of agreeing on Petitions, Complaints, Remonstrances, Declarations or other Addresses to His royal Highness The Prince Regent, or to both Houses or either House of Parliament, have of late been made use of to serve the Ends of factious and seditious Persons, to the great Danger and Disturbance of the Public peace, have produced Acts of Riot, Tumult and Disorder, and may become the Means of producing Confusion and Calamities in the Nation . . .

If such a crowd assembled, it was to disperse once an authorized person with a 'loud voice' had proclaimed:

> Our Sovereign Lord the King chargeth and commandeth all Persons here assembled immediately to disperse themselves, and peaceable to depart to their Habitations or to their lawful Business upon Paine of Death.
> GOD SAVE THE KING

The consequences of non-dispersal were dire:

> If any such Persons shall, to the Number of Twelve or more, notwithstanding such Proclamation made, remain or continue together the Space of One Hour after such Proclamation made, that then such continuing together to the Number of Twelve or more shall be adjudged Felony without Benefit of Clergy, and the Offenders therein shall be adjudged Felons, and shall suffer Death as in cases of Felony without Benefit of Clergy.

Moreover, threats to the King, Prince Regent or Parliament by marches or rallies were utterly proscribed.

And Whereas it is highly inexpedient that Public Meetings or Assemblies should be held near the Houses of Parliament, or near His Majesty's Courts of Justice in Westminster Hall on such Days as are hereinafter mentioned. Be it therefore enacted, and it is hereby enacted, That it shall not be lawful for any person or Persons to convene or call together, or to give any Notice for Persons to convene or call together, or to give any Notice for convening or calling together, any Meeting of Persons consisting of more than Fifty Persons, or for any Number of Persons exceeding Fifty to meet in any Street, Square, or open Place in the City or Liberties of Westminster, or County of Middlesex, within the Distance of One Mile from the Gate of Westminster Hall.

If any such meeting did occur and the constables or Militia were called effective force was to be used and the demonstrators dealt with severely. The Act specifically indemnified authorized 'officers of the peace' from prosecution in the event of their killing or maiming civilians.

The influx of discharged and unemployed soldiers and sailors, shortage of bread and economic hardship revived the sense of outrage that had been felt by radicals in the 1790s. To many radicals Napoleon was still a revolutionary hero and Britain still a sink of corruption. There were mass meetings and renewed talk of revolution, which led to rioting and arrests after a meeting at Spa Fields, Clerkenwell (see below). A mass meeting in Manchester on 9 August 1819 led to a general rampage by the local Yeomanry and, taking its ironic name from Wellington's great victory, the event became known as 'the Peterloo Massacre'. The government, headed by Lord Liverpool and Lord Sidmouth as Home Secretary, was tough and aggressive. The cabinet had been in power a long time and led the most experienced British government in over a hundred years. They refused to concede anything to 'rabble rousers' and brought in an even more draconian set of laws, known as the 'Six Acts', which consisted of the Training Prevention Bill to prevent drilling of civilians, the Seizure of Arms Bill which allowed for general warrants, Misdemeanours Bill to speed up prosecution, the Seditious Meetings Prevention Bill, the Blasphemous and Seditious Libels Bill and the Newspaper and Stamp Duties Bill to silence editors like William Cobbett (who fled to the United States).

The temper of the time could be gauged by the popular emotional rejection of George IV on the death of Queen Caroline, against whom many thought he had acted with simple and vicious malice. Indeed considerable public disquiet had already led to violent disturbances in the summer and autumn. So violent was the crowd at the funeral that the hearse was diverted from its course several times, abandoning the original route eastward to Harwich, avoiding the City, and now moving west towards Hyde Park. A Bow Street patrol led by George Avis reported that it was on hand at Cumberland Gate on the day of the procession, Tuesday, 14 August 1821. Avis was hit in the head by a stone. Patrolmen John Mason, hit by a stone in the knee, and William Godfrey, also hit by stones, were both injured, Godfrey severely. As the crowd was stoning them another patrolman was being pelted with mud. Avis's attempts to calm the crowd which amounted to 'begging of them to desist' met with further attacks from 'brickbats and stones' the crowd shouting 'butchers and murderers' and 'Bloody Murdering Rascals' at the Bow Street patrols and soldiers alike. As things got worse the patrolmen drew their staves to 'protect' the procession which had arrived at Hyde Park Gate. Nevertheless, as they attempted to arrest a man throwing stones at patrolman John Blakesley, the assailant was rescued by a man on horse and whisked to safety. At Tyburn Gate, near the site of the original gallows,* people reported gunshots and rumour spread that someone was hit. The Life Guards then drew carbines, fired in the air and cleared the Edgware Road for the mourners. Things were clearly out of hand, the cavalry hitting people on their 'hats' with the flats of their swords. Two men 'dressed in black' (Avis reported) then came from Cumberland Street with a flagstone and hurled it at a Life Guard who toppled from his horse, 'the People crying out Murder him but some said let the bugger go'. From then on Avis had his own life to save, that moment hit on the back of the head by a brickbat.

Avis and his little band were part of the Bow Street foot patrol, a civil 'police force' that was a forerunner of the Metropolitan Police, organized with rudimentary discipline. Dressed in civilian clothes (the foot patrol was not uniformed until 1822) and armed with staves, it was the complement of the similar (but uniformed) horse patrol and night patrol. Since the mid-eighteenth century, Bow Street had a small police office with eight detectives (the Runners) as well as being the headquarters of the day and night patrols. Sir Robert Baker was resident chief police magistrate at Bow Street and had neither the force of will nor the actual personnel to deal with the violent disturbances he was now entrusted to quell. Poorly paid, poorly trained

---

*Tyburn gallows were erected on the corner of Tiburn Road (now Oxford Street) and Tiburn Lane (now Park Lane). Tiburn House and turnpike stood in fields near the fatal spot, which was linked by hedgerows to Hyde Park. Stands were built for those with a pocket as large as their appetite for death and entertainment, a source of great profit for the local woman who realized the potential of grandstands where crowds of 10–14,000 might come for a hanging. Samuel Pepys recalled paying a shilling simply to stand on a cartwheel to get a better view.

and ill equipped to deal with rioters, Avis and his patrol found itself part of Sir Robert's plan to keep the peace.

It was not only the London 'mob' who were furious. So angered were some members of the radical elite that they also took the dead Queen's side. Sir Robert Wilson, radical MP for Southwark, was heard to offer five shillings and quantities of drink to anyone willing to oppose the original route of the funeral. Alarmed, Baker changed the route but only after an altercation with Captain Richard Oakes of the Life Guards escorting the hearse and who was concerned not to encourage 'the mob'.

Major General Sir Robert Wilson was himself part of the funeral procession and his 'words' may well have been invented by the government in order to find scapegoats for those who did not go along with the brutality of the times. Wilson was a hero of the Egyptian and Peninsular campaigns as well as being in Ireland during the 1798 Rising. He later became a secret agent in Russia and Prussia and was no coward. He greatly disapproved of the deliberate and indiscriminate firing of the Life Guards. Two people were killed after the Guards panicked when they became surrounded and had half their men injured. Opening fire without permission of a magistrate was plain murder – Wilson knew it. 'Damn you, go along with you,' he yelled, 'are you murderers or what?' One trooper, protesting it was his duty to obey his officer, was severely threatened by Wilson whilst another was told he had blotted his performance at Waterloo. Wilson's bravery was rewarded by a demand for his immediate resignation from the army. He did so but fought the decision, and after four years was reinstated and promoted and in a further career lasting over twenty years rose to the highest rank and was buried at Westminster Abbey.

Poor Sir Robert Baker was dismissed from Bow Street for allowing the procession to enter the city and by so doing resign his authority to the mob. Henry Hobhouse, Civil Under-Secretary, knew only too well what Baker's failure of nerve would mean. 'I dread the moral effect of this day. The Mob glory in having carried their object by force, and in having beaten the Military. Neither of these is the Fact, but the public Impression is the same'. Sir Robert Wilson remained a hero in radical Southwark.

The years following the end of the Napoleonic Wars were frantic ones for would-be revolutionaries. The day of insurrection seemed tantalizingly near and plans, plots and counterplots marked the actions of rebels and authorities alike. The mob orator Henry Hunt, who was at the centre of troubles at Peterloo, was put on trial in 1819. His trial followed others where desperate men or radical MPs found themselves indicted for 'seditious libel' or worse – treason.

No more dangerous and extreme group existed than those who called a meeting at Spa Fields in Clerkenwell in 1816. Henry 'Orator'

Hunt was to speak on the necessity of universal political enfranchisement as the only cure for the economic slump following the war. The
organizing committee were a group of Spencean Reformers who met
at various public houses to discuss ideas that were forms of primitive agrarian communism – 'The Land is the People's Farm' was an
indicative slogan. The leading lights of this little band of some forty
or fifty committed republicans were a tight-knit group consisting of
'Dr' James Watson,* his son James (Jem) Watson, Thomas Preston (an
alcoholic), John Castle, John Hooper (a labourer) and John Keens.
Alongside Dr Watson there was another leading member, Arthur
Thistlewood, the illegitimate son of a Lincolnshire farmer. He had
come into money and lost it, tried farming and failed, joined the
British army, gone to Paris during the Revolution, and become a soldier of fortune in a number of uprisings; he was an expert swordsman and liked women too much. Information linked him to Marcus
Despard's attempted coup of 1802. A friend described him as only 'fit
for a straightjacket'. If Thomas Paine was Britain's first professional
revolutionary, then Thistlewood was its first professional terrorist.

On 15 November 1816 John Castle carried the banner into the
first of two meetings at Spa Fields. A second meeting was called for
2 December. Surrounding the first demonstration were large numbers
of police directed by the Chief Magistrate of Bow Street, Sir Nathaniel
Conant, who had been warned in advance of serious trouble by his
spies. Conant's position effectively made him chief police officer in
the capital, and, as a police magistrate, his own judge and jury.

An anonymous note to the Home Office declared: 'The meeting
in Spa fields is aware of the Collection of Soldiers in this vicinity.
The appearance of Troops will occasion the destruction of London.
Twenty thousand Englishmen can set any city in such flames as no
Engines can extinguish.'[6]

The police were less prepared than they might have been and the
crowd, strengthened by curious people returning from a public hanging, began to swell as Henry Hunt spoke of government wickedness
from a window in the Merlin's Cave pub. From a wagon outside Jem
Watson made another speech considered by the police commander
John Stafford (Conant's second in command) to be incitement and a
general tussle began in order to arrest the leaders and seize their flags.

The police failed to stop the rioters marching towards Newgate and the
Royal Exchange on their way to seize the Tower. Here John Hooper was
arrested. He was armed with two loaded pistols. As the crowd marched
towards the Tower they broke into gunsmiths and looted their shops.
When one looter argued with Jem Watson, Watson shot him in the

---

*Not to be confused with the Scottish radical Dr Robert Watson.

stomach at point-blank range. At the Tower a man climbed the railings and waving a cutlass called upon the troops to join the revolution. They ignored him, he vanished and the crowd, now bored, went home.

Lord Sidmouth, as Home Secretary, now authorized Conant to organize a manhunt for the ringleaders: the charge, treason. Slowly the leaders were picked up but Jem Watson made good his escape to America after shooting at a patrol in Highgate. Only Thistlewood remained at large, a man unknown to police records and travelling under a set of pseudonyms. All the police had to go on was that he was more like a gentleman than the rest. James Watson and the others kept silent under interrogation but John Castle squealed. He was living in penury and needed the reward (by 1817 he was a paid spy). Working for the government were spies like William Oliver, who was the most successful of all agents, fermenting rebellion in the north and using his entrapment techniques to draw out dupes like the Nottinghamsire revolutionary Jeremiah Brandreth. He claimed to have been at the centre of the entrapment of Despard and may possibly have helped Jem Watson escape. Radicals and Tories alike saw the hand of Oliver everywhere, the exemplification of government double-dealing. Then there was the Irishman ('Spy B'), John Shegoe, the sailor ('Spy C'), John Williamson and George Edwards, a modeller of plaster busts and eventually Thistlewood's lieutenant. All these agents infiltrated and reported on Watson's and then Thistlewood's plans for armed rebellion – 'their plans are desperate' reported one observer. Too close to exposure, John Williamson finally fled, working his passage to America as a ship's cook. Thistlewood was arrested as he boarded a ship bound for America. Once safely incarcerated in the Tower of London he was put in an identity parade and picked out by a man called Richard Heywood. The only other man in the line-up was a Beefeater in full uniform!

From evidence, it appeared that Thistlewood not the Watsons was the guiding light of the revolution, with a plan to liberate Napoleon from St Helena and seize London. To do this he had been able to purchase a few old pistols and cutlasses. Yet it seemed others were willing to begin an uprising. On 8 June 1817 there was a muster of several hundred Yorkshiremen and on 9 June an attempted march by insurrectionists led by Jeremiah Brandreth ('the Nottingham Captain') to seize Nottingham itself. People like Brandreth and Thistlewood may have been in contact through secret networks of corresponding 'cells' preparing for zero hour.

As Thistlewood and the others came to trial at Westminster Hall, Brandreth was being executed as a traitor: hanged until dead, his head then cut off and displayed to the crowd. The conspirators caught fright and Dr Watson decided that survival meant keeping a low profile. As Castle was a poor witness, being a former brothel-keeper and a banknote forger, all the accused found themselves at liberty. When Thistlewood later said, 'We shall all be hang'd,' only Watson didn't see the joke.

Conspiracy was indeed back in the air and as years went by and Thistlewood became poorer and more determined, his fantasies took flight until at the head of a 'Committee of Public Safety' he saw himself master of London with an army of 40,000 armed workers at his side. In 1819 rumours of rebellion had led him and Henry Hunt to Manchester; both returned in triumph after the 'massacre', their carriages decked out in ribbons. Thistlewood smelled out rebellion wherever he could, plotting endlessly to ferment rebellion amongst the London garrisons, finding out how to work artillery, learning how to make 'fireballs' and grenades. More meetings at Spa fields and more rumours of insurrection kept spies working twenty-four hours a day on Thistlewood's case. As his entire group was riddled with spies and agents provocateurs he knew he played a very risky game.

'These infatuated men had fully persuaded themselves of their competency to rule the nation', wrote a spy in their midst and by 1820 they were ready to try their hand. Thistlewood knew the entire Cabinet would be having a dinner together. The hated Sidmouth and Lord Castlereagh would be there, between them responsible for the gagging acts and the carnage in Ireland twenty years before. Wellington would also be there. A new gang of revolutionaries soon formed which included Richard Tidd, a shoemaker, William Davidson, the 'mulatto' son of the Attorney General of Kingston, Jamaica sent to Britain to study law but considered by his neighbours a man of psychotic tendencies with, as he boasted, a plate in his head, and James Ings, a rough butcher who thought all Ministers 'buggers'. Their bible was Thomas Paine's *Common Sense*.

The 'West End Job' needed a place to make and store weapons near the target in Grosvenor Square and a fake coffee shop was set up. Here every conceivable weapon was made and stored. As the day approached one conspirator boasted, 'We are going to kill His Majesty's Ministers and will have blood and wine for supper!' Premises in a run-down alley called Cato Street were also taken and here, armed and in their greatcoats, the gang was surprised by Bow Street Runners and soldiers and after a short fight captured. The events were described next day by the *Morning Chronicle*.

Yesterday evening the West-end . . . was thrown into the utmost confusion, the streets were lined with soldiers and spectators, and the greatest alarm prevailed . . . Information having been received at Bow-street, that a meeting of persons armed was to be held at a house in Caton-street [sic] Marylebone.

They were all armed with guns, swords, daggers, and other weapons, and appeared ready to leave the place, which was a hay-loft at the top of the house. On the officers going up the steps they demanded entrance, which they were refused. Wescot [Westcott], one of the officers, went up first, [actually John Ruthven] and was followed by several others, on which the persons assembled made a most desperate resistance, and the officers were fired on. Wescot received three shots through his hat, and Smythers [Smithers], an active officer, received a stab in his right side, and he was carried away quite dead. A desperate affray took place, in which several of the officers were wounded, some most seriously. Gill [Gibbs], one of the officers [Ellis], upon going up the steps was met by a man of colour, named Davison [Davidson], who was armed with a loaded gun, which after threatening the officer he fired off, but fortunately missed his object, on which Gill took out his staff and belaboured him over the wrists until he let go. Davison then seized a sword, which he was prevented using. In consequence of this resistance most of the officers were prevented from entering the loft in which these persons were, but were obliged to remain below while some of the party escaped by means of a ropeladder, [actually, it did not exist] which they (it appeared) had cautiously placed out of a back window in case (it is supposed) they were detected. As they escaped the resistance became less, and the whole of the officers, except those injured, endeavoured to enter the place, and to secure nine of the offenders, who had received much injury; one of them, a butcher, [not Ings but Thistlewood] is supposed to be the man who stabbed Smythers; he had a desperate black eye, and his hands were much cut. – To enter into particulars of the injuries received by the officers would be tedious, suffice it to say, that scarcely one of them escaped without some injury. By this time Captain FitzClarence, arrived on the spot with a party of the Guards, the soldiers were dreadfully injured by stabs, &c. On searching the place, guns, pistols, swords, bayonets, &c. were found which together with the rope ladder were brought to Bow-street Police Office in Hackney coaches, in custody of the officers, and they were escorted by a strong body of the soldiers, who surrounded the coaches.

On their arrival at Bow-street, it was filled with soldiers, and the prisoners were placed at the bar. Statements of what had occurred being related by each of the parties, Mr. Birnie put several questions to each of the prisoners, who were chiefly shoemakers and carpenters, but could arrive at no satisfactory point as to the object of their meeting. Davison denied the charge. They were all remanded to Friday next for further examination.

Mr. Birnie ordered that they should be conveyed in hackney coaches to the House of Correction. They were handcuffed together;

two were placed in each coach, with resolute officers, and, according to the directions of Mr. Birnie, two soldiers sat on the box of each coach, and two behind, in which way they went along, guarded by the rest of the soldiers, who had their bayonets fixed. They were followed by a vast concourse of persons, and the utmost good order was noticed. The instruments of destruction found by the officers were ordered to be kept in their custody until Friday next.

Sermon [possibly a civilian called Sarman], another of the Bow-street Officers who was wounded upon this occasion, is, we understand, in a very dangerous state; he received a pistol-shot in the head. The person, whose stab proved fatal to Smythers, has escaped. This person was stated at Bow-street to be Arthur Thistlewood.

Mr. Birnie, the Magistrate, accompanied the officers to Caton-street. Government is understood to have had previous information of this extraordinary meeting.[7]

There could be no mercy now and after finally being apprehended, Thistlewood, Davidson, Ings, Tidd and their gang were duly hanged, beheaded and declared traitors to the huge crowd that came to watch at Newgate on 1 May 1820. The *Sunday Observer* noted earlier (3 March 1820):

The interest excited by the discovery of the diabolical conspiracy to assassinate his Majesty's Ministers has, throughout the last week continued with unabated force. The premises in Cato Street, which will be ever memorable for the events of which they were the scene, was visited by several thousand persons. Among whom were many individuals of the highest rank.

The blood of poor Smithers was still visible on the floor, and seemed to be avoided with a sort of reverential awe. Lee, one of the officers who was there when the assault took place, was present, and explained the whole operation from the commencement to the conclusion. Among others attracted to the spot, we remarked several of the fair sex, who braved the inconvenience of the difficult ascent to the loft for the gratification of their curiosity.

A contemporary historian, George Theodore Wilkinson, recorded the details of the hangings.

Thistlewood struggled slightly for a few minutes, but each effort was more faint than that which preceded; and the body soon turned round slowly, as if upon the motion of the hand of death.

Tidd, whose size gave cause to suppose that he would 'pass' with little comparative pain, scarcely moved after the fall. The struggles of Ings were great. The assistants of the executioner pulled his legs with all their might; and even then the reluctance of the soul to part from its native seat was to be observed in the vehement efforts of every part of the body. Davidson, after three or four heaves, became motionless; but Brunt suffered extremely, and considerable exertions were made by the executioners and others to shorten his agonies.

Amongst the crowd was a young Charles Dickens. It was the most disgusting thing he had ever witnessed.

With the execution of Arthur Thistlewood and his co-conspirators the puny extreme British republican movement was effectively destroyed. The great agitations that led to the 1832 and 1867 Reform Acts, though often violent and bloody as in the insurrection of Chartists in Newport, Wales, were nevertheless essentially channelled into movements that were cooperative, reformist and religious in nature and union-organized in practice. It was from these beginnings that the labour movement, the trade union movement and the Labour Party rose.

Anarchism, which in its broadest sense had considerable appeal amongst workers (rather than property owners) before the 1830s, lost its appeal as cooperatives and unions gained ground and as the concept of the 'working class' began to emerge as a unifying term for the labouring poor. Anarchism, intellectually appealing to the artisan class of the late eighteenth century and Regency period, continued to have great appeal in the mid-nineteenth century when self-help individualism and cooperative organization united various utopian schemes and pastoral visions. Rioting and arson throughout the Victorian age could still excite farm labourers, but by the 1880s only unionization and socialism seemed to answer obvious needs for improvements in working conditions and political democracy.

Thus extreme republican anarchism never moved beyond the small cadre of revolutionaries of the Regency period and never appealed to the anarchist 'movement' as a whole. It was finally associated with 'foreign dynamiters'. Only one republican revolutionary group survived in sufficient numbers to worry and harass authority – the Irish. The English insurrectionary tradition was not entirely forgotten, however.

The dangerous idealism of the Cato Street Conspirators or of the armed revolutionaries of the Chartist uprising continued to inspire idealists who wanted to make their mark in history. Edward Oxford was only nineteen when he took a shot at the newly wed Queen Victoria and her consort Albert as they were being driven in an open carriage in Hyde Park. When questioned, Oxford claimed his pistol had never been loaded but was used merely to frighten the Queen. Yet he had also issued a 'proclamation' claiming an army of revolutionary republicans would rise on his orders. He had drawn up a set of rules for his version of 'Young England', which included arming all members, an oath of allegiance, the use of fictitious names and the need to travel in disguise. Found guilty of high treason, he was acquitted on grounds of insanity and sent to Bethlem Hospital and then to Broadmoor from whence he was conditionally discharged twenty-seven years later on 27 October 1867. Warned in no uncertain terms to quit the United Kingdom or be returned to Broadmoor, and taking the hint, he sailed on 30 December 1867 aboard the *Suffolk* bound for Melbourne, Australia, and obscurity.

The incident has a strange epilogue. In May 1907 Edward VII was sent a letter from two religious Sisters (Agatha and Anne), working at the West London Mission based in Chalton Street off the Euston Road, in which they claimed that they were petitioning the King on behalf of Priscilla Houghton (née Lowe), the daughter of Joshua Reeve Lowe, who it was claimed had seized Oxford when 'he ran across the road', helped by his nephew Albert Lowe, who had taken away the pistol. The letter claimed that Joshua Lowe had been given a pension of some sort as a reward for saving the Queen but dying six years earlier had left his daughter (now aged sixty-one) nothing against her old age and she, after years of earning 'a hard livelihood by book binding in the City of London', was now reduced to a 'poor lonely widow'.

A reply from Sir Dighton Probyn on behalf of the Palace stoutly denied the Sisters' claim that Priscilla should be saved the indignity of 'the workhouse' being the daughter of 'so brave a subject', denying even the knowledge of the pension given to her father. An indignant typed letter was sent back to the Home Office on 9 July 1907 on headed paper from Reverend Sylvester Horne (Whitfield's Central Mission of the London Congregational Union) reminding the original correspondent (Lord Carrington) of the matter of Priscilla's claim as supported by her birth certificate and articles about the attack in *The Times* of June 1840. The letter, like Priscilla, was disregarded.

10
Monster Rallies

The War with the Chartists, the 'Sally Army' and
the Rebellious Schoolchildren of London

The poet travelling across Westminster Bridge in the early dawn on
that quiet September morning in 1802 was a man with a murky past.
William Wordsworth had fled France during the Terror leaving a pregnant girlfriend and revolutionary idealism behind him. Wordsworth
was one of a new breed of artists whose 'Romanticism' matched the
democratic fervour of the European Continent. His sonnet 'Upon
Westminster Bridge' recorded the city one early autumn dawn as a
'mighty heart' on the brink of fulfilling another day's potential. For
Wordsworth, as for the revolutionary artists he inspired, men such as
North Londoner John Keats, the city was a living entity suffused with
the life of the multitude.

London too stood on the brink of revolution. The great industrial
revolution of the late eighteenth century brought a new urgency to
the trades of the city and the bustle of London's docks. The Pool
of London, just above what is now the site of Tower Bridge, was
already overcongested with barques and brigantines, schooners and
East Indiamen burdened with tobacco, timber, coal, furs, wines,
rice, cotton, cocoa and iron. By value, over 7 per cent of Britain's
imports came from America, both Canada and the United States;
over 11 per cent from British commercial holdings in South America;
another 11 per cent from Britain's African colonies; over 17 per cent
from the West Indies (sugar, rum, nutmeg), and over 50 per cent
from Europe, the Baltic and Russia.

New wharves and shipyards soon spread along the Thames, its
waters now brown and polluted, to ease the burden of loading,
unloading and shipbuilding. The London Dock was built in 1805
near the Ratcliffe Highway in Wapping. Surrey Commercial Docks
followed in 1807 built next to meadows in a line from Rotherhithe
down along the south bank opposite the Isle of Dogs. The West India
and East India Docks, built between 1802 and 1806, were strung
along the east bank and bisected the Isle of Dogs, effectively turning
the peninsula into an island. St Katherine's Docks next to the Tower

opened in 1828. Between all these great docks there were commercial and royal yards where the Royal Navy had many of its warships constructed.

Across the dark and swift-flowing Thames new bridges appeared: Westminster (1750); Vauxhall (1816); Waterloo (1817); Southwark (1819). The old water taxis of London along with the ferrymen were soon without a living. The construction of new roads such as the Marylebone–Euston 'bypass' built during 1756 to 1761 joined the City Road (1761), the New North Road (1812), Caledonia Road (1826) and Camden Road (1825). Such roads linked the old coaching roads from the north bringing poets like Wordsworth along dusty or muddy highways to inns such as the Grove in Hendon, the Green Man in Finchley and the Red Cap or Race Horse in Holloway, finally to clatter to a grime-laden halt at the Adam and Eve in St Pancras or, if coming from the south, the George in Southwark. The canal craze and the great railway building mania soon also traversed London, making the coach routes redundant.

In the first quarter of the nineteenth century, London was firmly established as the centre of industry and empire. It also stood on the brink of revolutionary new ideas such as republicanism, democracy and liberalism imported along with the timber and wine that came from the United States and France.

The passage of the first Reform Bill in 1830 and 1831 was accompanied by countrywide disturbances and a particularly violent street battle in Bristol in October 1831. The whole thing threw the ruling class into a state of apoplexy. The Duke of Wellington believed the passing of the Bill would 'render the ordinary operations of government difficult and the protection of the institutions of the Country and its property by the Government as nearly impracticable'. Indeed the Act itself was nothing less than the first enactment of 'the revolution' when 'that power is transferred from one class of society, the gentlemen of England, professing the faith of the Church of England, to another class of society, the shopkeepers, being dissenters from the Church, many of them atheists'.[1] In one sense, the Iron Duke was premature in his fears. The men demanding the reforms of 1831 were from the middle classes who whilst growing strong economically still needed a say in the political decision-making process that would stabilize and advance their own position. They had no desire to enfranchise the propertyless labouring classes.

The embourgeoisement of culture during the early nineteenth century was crowned not by revolution but by the triumph of middle-class political aspirations with the reform of Parliament following the introduction of the three Reform Bills of 1832 also known as the (first) 'Great Charter'. Respectable newspapers saw the proposals as a triumph for common sense, a rejection of despotism and a rebuff to the extremes of radicalism that had bubbled away since the French Revolution and that had created demands for full democratic participation which no one in power would entertain for a moment. 1832 was the final recognition of the capitalist class – the class of trade, laissez faire, individualism and self-improvement. It represented a safety valve against revolution and a widening of participation for those very communities who would have most to lose from a challenge to their economic and *moral* control by the 'lower' orders. 'England', one paper noted, 'had been snatched from the very brink of anarchy'.[2] Furthermore, this was a triumph for 'the people'. The agitation (later to crystallize as Chartism) which began in the late 1830s and continued until its leaders were imprisoned in 1848 was the direct result of the frustrations at exclusion from participation by the great mass of the people.

Against the rising tide of revolution stood a new force dressed in top hats and swallow-tailed blue coats and armed with wooden staves: the Metropolitan Police. Opposition to Sir Robert Peel's* newly proposed police force, which had both preceded and followed the passing of a Bill for 'Improving the Police in and around the Metropolis' on 19 June 1829, was as vehement amongst working-class radical leaders as conservative traditionalists. In September 1830 posters addressed to the 'grievously oppressed and overburdened Parishioners of St. Pancras' announced a meeting to petition the new king, William IV, for the immediate 'abolition of the present military and grievously EXPENSIVE SYSTEM OF POLICE'. Further fly-posting proclaimed the arming of the populace against a thoroughly un-English system.

Peel's Police, Raw Lobsters, Blue Devils, Or by whatever other appropriate name they be known. Notice is hereby given That a subscription has been entered into, to supply the PEOPLE with STAVES of superior Effect, either for Defence or Punishment, which will be in readiness to be gratuitously distributed whenever a similar unprovoked and therefore unmanly and bloodthirsty Attack be Again made upon Englishmen by a Force unknown to the British Constitution, and called into existence by a Parliament illegally constituted, legislating for their individual interests, consequently in opposition to the Public good.

Before the disturbances on Lord Mayor's Day 1830, the following notice was pasted up.

Liberty or Death, Englishmen! Britons!! And Honest Men!!! The time has at length arrived. All London meets on Tuesday. Come

---

*Benjamin Disraeli once quipped that Peel's smile was like the 'silver fittings of a coffin'.

Armed. We assure you from ocular demonstration that 6,000 cutlasses have been removed from the Tower, for the use of Peel's Bloody Gang . . . These damned Police are now to be armed. Englishmen, will you put up with this?

Such passionate views were always to remain part of the anti-police rhetoric of those who saw the traditional rights of the community put under state ban or who saw the direct use of police as a weapon to proscribe future demands. Whether seen as a force abrogating existing freedoms or prohibiting future justice, the police were evidently an *extension of the state* into private lives and communal disputes which had been free from the monitoring of the authorities (at least in theory). For most radicals, the police were neither 'of the people' nor 'for the people' but a new third political force (after government and judiciary) working on behalf of a class besieged by franchise and industrial demands. In a word, the police were the enemy. The very concept of *order* embodied in the idea of a *standing* police force was entirely dependent on a new network of power relations and state-led rhetoric opposed to the interests of the ordinary lower orders and the demands of social democrats (communists, anarchists and reformists alike). The police were, quite simply, 'the minion and paid servant of the Government'.[3] Rioting against the 'plague of blue locusts' was endemic in the North when police forces were established there during the 1830s.

The role of the police in protecting *property* only seemed to confirm the worst fears of radicals that here were indeed the servants of the landowners and freeholders. That at least two policemen had died violently on duty by the end of 1830, the first trying to stop a fight and the other burglary, recommended them only for the jobs of preventing theft and assault. When it came to public order that was a different matter – after all, police training, let alone discipline or ethical code, was virtually non-existent.

According to P.C. 149K Henry Wood, in his written report dated 29 April 1834, he joined the Force on 25 March that year. He was issued with his uniform at Scotland Yard and then walked to Poplar police station to which he had been posted. He was there instructed in his duties and the next night found him walking his beat from the Ferryhouse Mill wall as a fully-fledged constable.[4]

Even more to the point, almost half the constables of the newly formed force were dismissed for drunkenness or disorderly behaviour.

On 13 May 1833 the National Political Union called a meeting at Cold Bath Fields, off the Gray's Inn Road, close by Cold Bath Prison and the Clerkenwell House of Detention, to call for the 'Rights of the

People' and a 'National Convention'. Handbills and fly-posters called for armed revolution and recommended that protesters came armed. On the previous day a meeting had been held at the Jolly Gardeners public house in Lambeth at which it was declared:

> . . . and so, friends, the time has come, the hour has struck. You are the workers, the producers of the taxes, not the squanderers. We do not give a fig for the Whigs and the Tories, or . . . the German King. Down with the hereditary aristocracy and up with the aristocracy of the working classes, already united in our National Union. Tomorrow will be your day of glory. Let every man resist the oppressors to the death. Every one of you must go armed. Rally to the flag – Liberty or Death – you and your families have endured starvation and poverty long enough. Arm, arm against the foe. Tomorrow we meet near the new Bedlam and march over Blackfriars Bridge to triumph!

Memories of Arthur Thistlewood briefly flickered amongst the assembled crowd of forty working men of the Lambeth 'class' of the National Union of the Working Classes as weapons were handed round, admired and concealed. Other meetings were being held in Bethnal Green, Hammersmith, Camberwell and Islington. Government spies reported that the 'Union' members marching in support of the National Political Union would certainly be armed. The police spy 'Popay' kept a watchful eye on proceedings in Clerkenwell, the march's destination.

Many of the marchers certainly did come ready to fight, carrying knives, cudgels, sticks and Maceroni pikes, also called 'marcaroni lances' (daggers on poles). Lord Melbourne, as Home Secretary, immediately ordered Colonel Charles Rowan to disperse the crowds that had gathered despite the government ban. Rowan had 500 police concealed in the neighbourhood and 70 on site and decided enough was enough when speeches became inflammatory. The inevitable brawl began and the police were left battered and disordered. At least two policemen were badly injured and one, Constable Robert Culley, was killed. He was on patrol with a group of constables but becoming isolated, was surrounded and stabbed. Crawling into a nearby pub just off Coldbath Street, he died in the arms of the barmaid. 'Oh, poor lamb,' she exclaimed. Culley was the first policeman to die in a riot, something not repeated until the death of Keith Blakelock on Broadwater Farm over 150 years later.

Few radicals mourned his death and the coroner's court brought in a verdict of 'justifiable homicide' due to the failure to read the Riot Act. Furthermore, the police were accused of being 'ferocious, brutal and unprovoked by the people'. The jury was, moreover, feted on its 'glorious verdict', and treated to a torchlit procession, a pleasure cruise on the Medway and inscribed silver loving cups! Although the verdict was overturned on appeal, radicals such as William Cobbett (MP for Oldham) stood by it and its implications. 'It was something new', he mocked, 'to see peace officers in uniform embodied in companies and battalions marching in rank and file, commanded by Sergeants and Colonels – under the mock name of Superintendants'. If such drilling continued what was left but 'the people must arm themselves'.

William Cobbett was a man who strongly believed in the traditional vision of a rural England, its rights and obligations epitomized in the farmstead and yeoman farmer. The police represented the appearance of a human version of the industrial process – a *machine* to oppress the people. Such fears regarding the appropriate social position of the police with regard to the public were not to be resolved in either the nineteenth or twentieth centuries. One hundred and fifty years on from PC Culley's death at Cold Bath Fields the institutional nature of the police and its role as a key instrument of the executive was still unresolved even amongst Commissioners. In the 1970s, for instance, Sir Robert Mark of the Metropolitan Police could assure his audience that the force had a 'long tradition of constitutional freedom from political interference in our operational role . . . the police are not servants of government at any level. We do not act at the behest of a minister or any political party, not even the party in government. We act on behalf of the people as a whole'. It was a claim so hollow that it was almost disingenuous. 'This notion of the political neutrality or independence of the police cannot withstand any serious consideration', suggested one leading twentieth-century commentator.[5]

Political agitation, meetings and insurrections during 1837 to 1840 and 1842 to 1843 seemed to confirm the Duke of Wellington's fears that 'atheists' were in charge of the revolution. The Reform Act had given enough to frustrate rather than satisfy general hopes of real parliamentary change towards democracy. In 1839, angry crowds in Todmorden, Lancashire attacked the property of mill owners and destroyed cottages in retaliation for the passing of the New Poor Law, whilst in Birmingham violence was provoked by the suppression of Chartist meetings and the town had to be abandoned to rioters. Forty London constables sent by train to aid the authorities were themselves besieged by crowds and had to draw cutlasses and fight their way out with the aid of mounted dragoons. The Chartists roundly condemned the new *mobility* of the police as 'an unjust outrage . . . upon the people of Birmingham, by a bloodthirsty and unconstitutional force from London'. Around the same time crowds attempted an arson attack on Bolton Town Hall.

In the early 1840s strikes and picketing were used in the North, the Midlands and Scotland to bring factory owners to heel and when unsuccessful were accompanied by the destruction of boilers (the aptly named 'Plug Riots'). In Wales the Chartists fought a pitched battle in Newport and the Rebecca Riots rumbled on. These were centred on Narberth in South Wales, the scene of much activity by local organized protesters who targeted tollgates, salmon weirs and the local workhouse. The level of hostility to the loss of local rights and the imposition of new road 'taxes' and poorhouse regimes required the presence of the 14th Regiment of Foot to keep the peace. At least one leader is known, Thomas Rees (Twm Carnabath), whose use of a dress borrowed from a 'tall . . . maid called Rebecca' may have given a name to the local disturbances (or it may have come from the biblical Rebecca). The activities of Rebeccaites lasted across the late 1830s and early 1840s. A few quiet years in the mid-1840s were followed in 1848 by revolutions abroad and a resurgence of Chartism at home. Kensington shopkeepers complained that the West End was 'swarming with French Revolutionary Propagandists'. There were 'Swing' riots across rural areas of England. On 5 March, a month prior to the 'monster' Chartist rally at Kennington Common, an armed mob took over Glasgow, giving notice to the government of what might occur in London.

Kennington Common was not only the scene of highway robbery, it was also the place where such acts were duly punished, as in the case of the execution of John Thompkinson, caught for robbery on the highway in 1766.[6] Such executions were always hazardous affairs, as was the case with the execution of Matthew Dadd, a coachman, whose friends threatened to rescue him, forcing the gaoler to call for a military escort.[7] Even after death the body of the executed might become the focal point of clashes between the authorities and the 'common' people. Such tussles might indeed end in unforeseen and bizarre ways, as the *Gentleman's Magazine* observed of an execution at Kennington on Friday, 6 April 1739.

> Were executed, at Kennington-Common 3 Highwaymen and a Housebreaker, condemned at the Assizes for Surrey. The Surgeons fix'd on the Body of one of them, a Shoemaker, but it was rescued by a great Number of the Craft, and carry'd home in Triumph to the Widow, who, to avoid Reflections, having withdrawn herself, they were so exasperated that they hawked about the dead Corpse for some Hours, offering it to sale to all the Apothecaries from Horsflydown to Rotherhith[e] at a very cheap Rate; and at last meeting with no Purchaser, they pitch'd it all over, and bury'd it in St George's Fields.

Kennington Common had long been used to political rallies and since 1832 had been significant for radical working-class agitation. It was not, however, a pretty place for a meeting of any sort. It retained its lawless reputation from the previous century, being half rubbish tip, half footpad heaven, bounded by ugly cottages and a ditch filled with 'dead puppies and kittens' which was 'green and purple' from 'putrefaction'. A vitriol factory poured out 'a black offensive muddy liquid'. The Chartists resolved nevertheless to hold on 10 April 1848 a monster rally on the Common.

In 1848 revolution was in the air and Victoria and Albert quietly slipped away to Osborne on the Isle of Wight for an extended holiday. The magistrates caught fright and ordered the appointment of special constables so that they 'might check any attempt at depredation' and provide for the dispersal of the crowd who might attack the area 'for the purposes of plunder'. A huge force of specials was sworn in to back up the police. The Duke of Wellington, hero of Waterloo and still Commander-in-Chief, prepared to defend London from insurgency.

> All in all, Wellington deployed 890 cavalry, eleven pieces of artillery, including three 12 lb howitzers, nine brigades of Infantry (that is 5,000 men) and 12,000 enrolled pensioners. Besides St. George's Barracks and the stables, he [used] Hyde Park. Bethlehem Hospital, the Royal Mews, the Tower of London and the grounds of the Royal Palaces to station troops in the centre of the Metropolis. Not since the Civil War had London been so 'fortified'.[8]

It was diplomacy that defeated the Chartists on this occasion. The government quite simply tricked the leading Chartists, including Ernest Jones and Feargus O'Connor, into making their rallying point Kennington Common. The large groups coming from north of the Thames were trapped in South-West London away from Westminster and trouble. The Commissioner of Police, Richard Mayne, then informed the organizers that only the men taking the Petition to Parliament could recross the river to deliver it. Thus the mass of perhaps 30–40,000 people were left to mill about aimlessly; any order to march to Westminster would now bring police and soldiers instantly into action in what could only turn into a bloodbath. No Chartist leader could take that responsibility. Palmerston, the Foreign Secretary, recorded the day as 'the Waterloo of peace and order'. The entire affair, utterly peaceful as it was, marked the nadir of Chartist agitation. Humiliated, they went home as 'God Save The Queen' was heard being sung in the West End.

The rally earned its fame for quite another reason, however, as it was the first political meeting to be photographed. The photographer was William Kilburn, and his picture shows one corner of the rally, a wagon full of speakers and delegates, its banners blown out like the sails of a galleon pulled by great black shire horses and standing at the centre of a well-dressed and peaceful crowd: top hats, pork-pie caps and the occasional bonnet distinguish sex and class. In the background can be seen the rows of low cottages and the vitriol factory that offended so many. In the foreground a pony and trap and a brougham stand idly as their drivers watch the proceedings. In the middle ground, standing in a patch of open space, two small boys stare at the gingham-draped wagon of radicals. It is an extraordinary and powerful image. And what of the noisome radical common? It was soon to become a public park dedicated to Victorian promenaders and strictly off limits to political agitators who wanted to march on Westminster.

Chartist agitation was already nine years old when these forces gathered, with little achieved and no compromise offered by either side. Nevertheless, despite sabre-rattling, the London Chartist disturbances never grew to the ferocious level that led to a virtual insurrection in Newport in Wales during 1839. Instead London papers reported:

> An attempt has been made to get up a Chartist meeting in this town, but every effort failed, and it was then manoeuvred to obtain a few signatures to a Chartist petition, but this was also entirely unsuccessful, and the only result of the reconnaissance has been to expose a silly fellow of the lowest station in society to the taunts of his fellow townsmen, whose derision has been excited by his being the only inhabitant of Woolwich, either high or low, who would join, or even listen to the ravings of the Chartist Bobadils [braggarts].[9]

There was nevertheless growing interest amongst ordinary working people. Almost ten years later and some months after the Kennington Common fiasco, Chartists again gathered in Bethnal Green. A chairman called 'Page' addressed approximately 500 people on open ground outside the Birdcage tavern. Amidst applause and cheers, he told the crowd:

> They were met together to show Government that they were determined to rest neither night nor day, not even on the Sabbath, without the charter (Cheers) . . . and they would soon convince the . . . Government that they must make the charter, and nothing else, the law of the land. (Loud cheers). He admired their enthusiasm, but working was better than preaching. From what had appeared in the papers he had no doubt that the police would

Westminster Police Court.

To Mr. *William Forster 4 Belgrave Street South*
in the Parish of Saint *George Hanover Square*
in the County of Middlesex.

WHEREAS it has been made to appear unto Me *William John Broderip* Esquire, one of the Magistrates of the Police Courts of the Metropolis sitting at the Westminster Police Court within the Metropolitan Police District, and usually acting for the said District, upon the Oath of Henry Hatchard Sugg, a credible Witness, that Tumults and Riots have lately taken place in the City and Liberty of Westminster, within the said District, and may reasonably be apprehended to take place again;—And I, the said Magistrate being of opinion that the Ordinary Officers appointed for preserving the Peace in the said City and Liberty are not sufficient for the preservation of the Peace and for the Protection of the Inhabitants and the Security of the Property in the said City and Liberty, do hereby, in pursuance of an Act of Parliament made and passed in the Session of Parliament holden in the First and Second Years of the Reign of his late Majesty William the Fourth, intituled " *An Act for* " *amending the Laws relative to the Appointment of Special Constables, and* " *for the better preservation of the Peace*," nominate and appoint you the said *William Forster* — as and to act as a Special Constable for the Preservation of the Public Peace, and for the Protection of the Inhabitants, and the Security of the Property within the said City and Liberty. Such appointment to continue in force during the period of Three Months from the date hereof.

GIVEN under my Hand at the Westminster Police Court aforesaid, this *Tenth* Day of *April* in the Year of our Lord One Thousand Eight Hundred and Forty-eight.

W. J. Broderip

Special Constable warrant

attempt to put down their meeting. Would they succeed in their vile purpose? (Cries of 'No'). Then let them all be determined to a man, and show the vile police, if they came there, that they were not afraid of them (Cries of 'We will'). Well, then, he would tell them how to do it. If they saw the police coming, instead of making infernal asses of themselves by running away let them form into a military square, and he would answer that not one of them would be injured. If on the contrary, they commenced running away, so surely would they be butchered by the blue monsters.[10]

With the arrival of Inspector Tarlton from M Division, the crowd nevertheless began to run away but a small group stood their ground and pelted the 'bloody police' with stones. Tarlton and a police sergeant were soon wounded by bricks as the crowds retreated into the nearby neighbourhood of Turk Street and Castle Street, shouting abuse at the officers.

> The houses there are tenanted by the lowest characters in Bethnal Green, who began to throw out from the windows brickbats and ginger-beer bottles at the police. Police constable N. 169 was severely cut on the mouth by a brickbat, and was obliged to be taken away to the station-house. Though the mob received a very rough handling, crowds continued to assemble in Virgina-row, and other places, when a party of mounted constables came up with swords drawn, and by using the flats of their weapons succeeded in getting the streets tolerably clear. They had barely done so and gone off to another part of the neighbourhood, when being informed another attack was made on the officers, they set to work again, and many heads were broken before the mob would disperse.

As disturbances were quelled in Bethnal Green, a potential 'monster meeting' was prevented by a large body of police being sent to London Fields in Hackney under a superintendent and two inspectors. On the same Sunday (4 June 1848) crowds began to arrive in Victoria Park, near Bethnal Green, and by eight in the morning approximately 300–400 people had gathered. As speakers addressed the crowd the meeting was broken up by mounted police with drawn swords, whose presence and precipitate action did little to calm an already agitated assembly. At least two policemen were attacked in Virginia Gardens during the afternoon in a revenge attack, which nearly ended in their deaths.

During the afternoon of the same day another meeting gathered at Bishop Bonner's Fields in Bethnal Green to hear a number of speakers including Ernest Jones condemn the recent 'banishment' to

Bermuda (fifteen years' transportation) of John Mitchell, the editor of the *United Irishmen. The Times* reported Jones's speech.

> Brother slaves, and men of the Tower Hamlets, I am sorry I could not be here before. I have been attending a large meeting at Paddington, where, although the police tried to prevent it, we had a glorious meeting. My friends, I know the b—y Government are mad, but they are not mad enough to put down these meetings. If they did I would hurl defiance at them, their police and their military. I hope you will stand fast by your colours; for the whole of the country is now looking to London to ascertain the state of feeling here . . . I hope you will not desert your posts if a few policemen come amongst you, for there is danger for those who run, safety for those who stand; and, whatever may be the consequences, Your [sic] business now is to organize. Appoint your class leaders, make your classes; divide yourselves into wardmotes: get in so thorough a state of organization that you may at any moment be ready to act if called upon. I have heard from a very good authority that the men of Dublin have already commenced, and I have also been informed, that the Government have requested the newspapers not to insert any accounts of the Irish outbreaks. We therefore require funds to send a man to Dublin to ascertain if such is the case. It is no use for the government to put me down, for I shall never cease agitating until I have procured for the poor man his rights and brought the nose of the rich to the grindstone. On Whit-Monday we shall have another display – another Kennington-common meeting, but not at Kennington. ('Hear, hear', and cheers). Will London do its duty? (Cries of 'yes, yes') Mr. Jones concluded by advising them to organize, and in a few days the green flag would float over Downing-street . . . and Lord John Russell and Lord Gray on their way to Baffin's Bay. (Loud cheers).[11]

The crowd, many of whom apparently came from Bethnal Green and Victoria Park during the morning's melees, now found their attention drawn to a lone policeman on his way toward the nearby church. Pelted with cobbles and stones picked up from a pile put aside for road resurfacing, the policeman escaped as his attackers turned their attention to the church windows in the belief that the building was full of police or soldiers.

The police had indeed been concealed, but not in the church, and this left them free to march onto the field. The crowd, now angry but also hesitant, were assaulted so violently that several men and boys were left casualties on the ground. At least one policeman was stabbed in the hand as men with cudgels and knives fought police truncheons. Meanwhile, the Honourable Artillery Company was put on guard in the City Road and police occupied Smithfield Market. *The Times*'s conclusions about the London working classes were as sanguine, wrong headed and ill conceived as the tetchy irritation shown by the Duke of Wellington in the comments they reported.

The Duke of WELLINGTON complained on Friday evening [2 June], in very forcible terms, of the inconvenience to which the troops and police were exposed by being kept for many nights under arms, and in a state of preparation. This is in itself an evil of no ordinary magnitude. It is a reason for taking some active measure to prevent any future assemblage of those gangs of peripatetic pickpockets who have of late infested our squares and thoroughfares, even if we leave out of the question the alarm and annoyance constantly caused by the rioters to the inhabitants of those quarters where these disorderly meetings have taken place. We see that the Duke of WELLINGTON gave it as his opinion that there were two ways of dealing with such gatherings as those, which have lately been seen on Clerkenwell-green and elsewhere. One mode (said his Grace) is to prevent the assembly of such persons – to forbid their meeting at all. Another method would be, to make those persons who called such meetings together responsible for the evil consequences attendant upon them, either by the spoliation of property or otherwise. With yesterday's experience [4 June] we will not complain of the first of these two means of dealing with these riotous bodies. A score or two of broken heads, administered by the truncheons of the police to a crowd of pickpockets and London thieves, is not, perhaps, a very unsuitable remedy. As to the second method proposed by the Duke of WELLINGTON we can only say, if it can be discovered who is the actual convener of any one of these meetings, and he should turn out to be a person beneficially interested in half-a-crown, by all means let him be mulcted [fined] in that amount.

There is, however, a third method, which we should be happy to see adopted by the police with the least possible delay. The fear of the hulks deters from other criminal offences, why not from this? Let them select any one – such a sanguinary-spoken fellow as the man [Joseph] FUSSELL, for example – and have him instantly put on his trial under the late act, and, if convicted, sent to . . . Bermuda. The benefit arising from such a prosecution would be twofold. In the first place it would, we are convinced, have the most calming effect upon the London streets, and in the second it would leave the Irish hucksters of sedition without a word in their mouths. Whether in Dublin or in London, let ruffianism meet with its appropriate punishment.[12]

The humiliating failure of 10 April 1848 had backed the Chartist leaders into a corner. Peaceful protest seemed to be at an end but violent insurrection was hardly an option; the government had played its ace and gained a strategic and psychological advantage over reformists looking into the abyss of long prison sentences for offering even the slightest hint of sedition. The demonstrations in June ended in scuffles and the government got wind of a 'plan' to seize the capital. More troops arrived in London, now using the train system for ease of movement, and were deployed in the West End and in Victoria Park and Bethnal Green. Very heavy artillery was also brought into the capital, the sort used to bombard military defences.

> 10,000 troops were secreted in the centre of London, special constables manned streets, and many public buildings were fortified (often with nothing more substantial than bound copies of *The Times*). The Police were busy occupying the places in advance where the meetings were to be held, ensuring that when the marchers did arrive they had to disperse . . . In the ensuing days, more people (nearly five hundred) were arrested and were to follow Ernest Jones and the other Chartist leaders in spending the next two years or more in prison.[13]

Ernest Jones was finally arrested with his colleagues and sentenced to two years for sedition. Two years' imprisonment might easily kill a man living in insanitary conditions and forced to do hard labour as a means of paying for his keep. Luckily for Jones he had sufficient friends to stump up the five shillings a week for food and 'lodgings', at least at the beginning of his sentence.

Jones was only too aware that he was not a common criminal but, in his own words, a 'political prisoner' (letter, 27 October 1848). Constant petitioning by his wife Jane and loyal associates emphasized the political (non-criminal) nature of his activities, 'as there is no standard of political criminality' and as 'political offences (unlike crimes) in one age are in many cases deemed virtues in succeeding ages'. The petitions were ignored: two years in a British prison was intended to kill, enfeeble or humiliate the seditious. As a political prisoner, he refused to wear the prison uniform, deeply objected to being part of the 'silent system' and refused to mix with the other *criminal* prisoners. At the end of April 1849, his food money having run out, he found himself under orders to 'pick oakum'. He refused, complaining of the 'tyranny' of prison. By this time too his supply of information about the outside world, and Chartism in particular, had dried up, and the prison governor had refused permission for Jones and the other Chartist prisoners to read 'political' books, although they were allowed to read the classics.

Jones was only one of a number of Chartist prisoners who expected to be treated with respect for their moral and political position. They were, after all, respectable men, but they were all treated eventually (when their money ran out) as common criminals. Alexander Sharpe, William Vernon and Joseph Fussell (whom *The Times* had singled out for particular opprobrium) were jailed alongside Jones. From Westminster Gaol, Sharpe wrote a secret letter to Vernon, which he tried to hide under his bed. 'I will publish an account of this infamous system,' he wrote, 'which will Create a great sensation in the country than they imagine By God' [sic]. The letter was finally read by Sharpe's warders on 1 July 1849, Sharpe having no opportunity to send it. On hearing of an assassination plot against Queen Victoria (see Appendix 2), he caustically remarked that the would-be killer was a 'fool' whose real target should have been 'those in Downing Street'.

With agitation in tatters after ten years of futile battling and its leaders locked up, Chartism collapsed and in doing so seemed to prove the truth of the respectable and rational refutations of the conservative press. With the threat removed, the press debated the problem of the 'masses', a problem highlighted by the recent revolution in France. *The Illustrated London News* (23 September 1848) noted that the pressing question of the moment was 'the Condition-of-the-people-of-England'. After considering the disastrous recent history of France, the paper considered 'it was the Poor Law that had preserved the British constitution and its institutions . . . amid political convulsions'. Indeed, the revised Poor Law, despite the immense unpopularity it produced, was considered as the only *welfare* provision commensurate with a greatly expanded population and a free society. It was, in short, the only 'safety valve' between freedom and state control.

> By acknowledging the right of all men to live, without, at the same time, recognizing the duty of the state to provide work for all men . . . we solved, if not quite effectually, at all events, temporarily and safely, the problem of modern society in Europe.

By preserving the free state of 'competition' against the 'Organisation of Labour', Poor-Law welfarism preserved Britain from the danger of political fanaticism by preserving English institutions from Continental state control. Thus, concluded the article,

> Commerce and manufactures cannot be forced. We can no more make a prosperous manufacturing nation in a day, than we can raise an oak from an acorn in the same period. The Communists and others in France, pretending to the title of social philosophers,

have imagined other and more sudden remedies. They have seen, as we all see, the danger of allowing large masses of the people to increase in numbers and in poverty at the same time, and have thought to remedy the evil by a rapid process which they call Communism, . . . Icarianism, Owenism, or Fourierism. All these 'isms' differ widely in some respects, but agree in their praises of co-operation or union as the new bond of society, and in the anathemas they launch against 'Competition'. The result of the 'errors of Communism' and the 'beehive school of humanity' proposed by revolutionaries such as Proudhon would inevitably lead to the dictatorship of the State.

Every bargain has two sides. If the workman be master of the State to compel work, the State must be master of the workman to compel the kind of work and the locality of its exercise. In other words, the workmen must be slaves; and the world would once again behold such a state of slavery as that which existed among the nations of antiquity, and by which every man was converted into a machine in the hands of the ruler or rulers of the people.[14]

The solution for the editor of the *Illustrated London News* was as natural as it was simple: the diminishment of pointless expenditure on a European arms race and 'more work and more trade, and the emigration of large masses to new countries which shall in their turn become customers for the produce of this increased work and trade – these are the practicable remedies for the sufferings of the masses'.

Chartists became more strident as they became more frustrated. Working-class Chartist radicals were the least likely to compromise over issues and turned towards a more apocalyptic vision of struggle. This increased as pressure from reformists in the middle class came to claim the attention of radical opinion. This was especially so in areas such as the repeal of the Corn Laws and in issues of public virtue such as thrift and temperance. Political extremism was snuffed out by reformist successes in union organization and parliamentary agitation on behalf of a mobilized working class. Religious extremism too was slowly forced out of working people's lives by the growth of a respectable Nonconformism and gentility. Political extremists remained isolated and disorganized, offering no threat to the new unionism or the rising political organizations that would go towards the formation of a Labour Party.

Quite different was the growth of working class anti-religious militancy in the form of antagonism towards William Booth's Salvation Army. Booth was an old-fashioned 'charismatic' preacher and the 'Sally' Army a militant form of Methodist (primitive) revivalism. Its mission was to reach 'the submerged tenth' of the rookeries and slums for which the message of respectable working-class Nonconformism had no relevance. Without intellectualism or deep theology, the Army promised personal redemption and instant salvation to all who heeded the call and renounced former wickedness (including drink). Hell was replaced by Heaven in clear and understandable language.

In 1878 the previously named Christian Mission donned the uniforms and adopted the official titles and marching bands of a regular army. Evangelism would take God to the slums just as it would to the ends of empire (indeed the Salvation Army was at the forefront of evangelizing in Africa). Marching into towns with brass bands and banners, playing 'Onward Christian Soldiers' and holding open-air meetings outside public houses, near factory gates and on street corners and singing hymns on Sunday in the parks, the 'Sally' took the fight against sin into the poorest towns and districts. Bastions of propriety, Salvation Army 'citadels' soon appeared in major towns and cities. Unlike anarchist republicans, the Army stood for the preservation of 'the country from mob violence and revolution', as Catherine Booth explained in books like *Aggressive Christianity* (1880).

The communities in which the Army evangelized were, however, only too well aware that primitive revivalism was an authoritarian form of conservatism deeply opposed to traditional rights. For instance, dislike of temperance groups sometimes included suspicion of public water fountains, which were often 'donated' to an area by evangelists for a cause that remained unpopular.

A working man resented being told to forgo his pint of bitter and drink alongside his horse, so these monuments to middle-class concern for working-class sobriety were regarded as particularly offensive. In 1903, when the Battersea Council was run by Progressives, it flatly turned down an offer from the Metropolitan Drinking Fountain and Cattle Trough Association to donate a drinking fountain and dog trough with the terse response that 'the Council regret that they have no available site'.[15]

Trouble first broke out in 1880 when a Captain Payne reported to his superiors that sales of *War Cry* had been disrupted by the appearance of opponents formed into 'the unconverted Salvation Army' and by 1881 'Skeleton Armies' of riotous youths playing 'rough music' and marching alongside the Salvationists had sprung up in a number of southern provincial towns. Wearing elaborate costumes and processing in parody of the 'Army' itself, these mock armies were often paid for by local brewers, thought of as 'defenders' of their districts and treated leniently by local magistrates. Sometimes Salvationists were abused, occasionally pelted with manure, mud and sewage. By 1893 these ragged and raucous disturbances were over but they expressed a side of working-class life that would be increasingly under pressure from political and moral conformism.

Anger against evangelical, temperance or sabbatarian interference with the traditional pastimes of ordinary people was not always merely local or reactionary. In such actions some saw the seeds of revolution. Such was the case with Karl Marx, living in London and looking for a clear manifestation of proletarian consciousness and revolutionary fervour. For Marx the Sunday Trading disturbances of the summer of 1855 suggested a new and more organized spirit amongst the wakening working class.

What had created this new spirit was the introduction of a Sunday Trading Bill by Lord Robert Grosvenor, a sabbatarian measure designed to end shopping on Sundays. Combined with the Wilson–Patten Act of 1854, which meant that working-class excursions would return too late by train for passengers to get a last drink before going home, it would restrict all entertainment, including closing public houses early and stopping most clubs. All such measures were clear attacks on traditional Sunday enjoyments and declared war on ordinary working people's relaxations. Not since the Protectorate had 'the religion of England [been] preaching and sitting still on Sundays', as one seventeenth-century Frenchman wryly observed years before. The growing evangelism and Puritanism of the mid-nineteenth century was sure to be opposed not least because, although Sunday laws existed, they had been winked at since the time of Charles II, acknowledging it as a 'right' of the people to relax or shop on the one free day of the week. What made matters worse was that the Bill would create hardship by making it impossible for working people to get provisions for the week as many were not paid until Saturday night, going to the market or grocer's next day. The richer classes of course could shop whenever they wished, and the restrictions on drinking did not affect *private* West End clubs. It seemed obvious that the legislation was aimed at the enforced moral education of the working class and it seemed equally obvious the police would be required to make the law work on behalf of only one sector of the population – the rulers. The Police Act of 1839 already restricted drinking over Saturday night so that churchgoers might not meet with drunken rowdies on Sunday morning. When combined with the proposed new legislation these Acts were bound to find an angry reaction.

Riotous crowds soon gathered in Hyde Park to protest against the new Bill and running fights with the police became a feature of that long hot summer. What gave the whole affair a more than merely fleeting interest was its naked antagonism towards the 'toffs' who took the air on Rotten Row (the carriageway) and whose intimidation was matched by their own willingness to goad the crowds whenever possible. At the same time, the police seemed only to act in the interests of the 'carriage-class'. Indeed Superintendent Samuel Hughes, second in command of the police in the Park, not only encouraged surges by his own men but also hit out violently with a riding crop which, he later told the Royal Commission called to investigate police brutality, he had used as he would a sabre! *The Times* even talked of the 'outrageous conduct of the police', which it considered the cause of the riots in the first place.

Lord Grosvenor quietly left the capital before a crowd descended on his house to break windows and also quietly dropped his Bill, but not before further scuffles and even a punch-up between Grenadier Guards and the police. *Reynold's Newspaper* (8 July 1855) considered the riots a battle 'between the aristocracy and democracy', the *People's Paper* (7 July 1855) was sure 'that the men of London have accomplished a successful revolution', *The Times* reported 'that Hyde Park . . . was the Champ-de-Mars of the English race' whilst Karl Marx proclaimed, 'Do not think we are exaggerating in saying that the English Revolution began . . . in Hyde Park' (25 June 1855). During fighting in July, Karl Marx had wandered along with other émigré revolutionaries to see the fun. Some had shouted 'Bravo, Englishmen! A republic! A republic', an English artillery officer had reported; others had led stone-throwing mobs of boys in Belgravia whilst others had suggested overturning cabs to make barricades. No doubt they would have been amused by the catcalling of the crowd and especially the shouts of 'Go to Church!' directed at the aristocrats on the carriageway or the marching chant 'Where are the geese? Ask the police', a reference by demonstrators to the theft of some geese by a constable on duty in Clerkenwell. All this had inflamed one writer for *The Times*, who had suggested that 'nothing will frighten a mob more than the crash upon the pavement of a ten pounder', a comment whose echo would later resound in Lord Harris of Hackney's call for the use of rubber bullets during the May Day Monopoly 2001 demonstrations.

The gathering of protesters in Hyde Park during 1855 created a venue for popular demonstrations that the Royal Parks Commissioners hardly intended and vigorously resisted.

> With the rapid growth of London, the traditional venues of demonstrations, Coldbath Fields, St George's Fields, and Spa Fields, had been covered with bricks and mortar, leaving Trafalgar Square and the royal parks as the only adequate central grounds. Kensington Gardens, Hyde Park, Green Park, St James's, and Regent's Park were popular and convenient for the West End, and people in other parts of London were willing to travel considerable distances to use them.[16]

Yet something even more significant was also taking place. As the second half of the nineteenth century progressed the lower orders were slowly coalescing into the industrial working class, literate, articulate and politically aware. This was especially visible in the growth of newspapers and their ability to create national issues where only local ones existed before.

By the 1860s it was certainly true that in many areas literacy rates, meaning the ability to read and write at a functional level, were near enough universal. The educational reforms of 1870 formalized an already thriving elementary system and solidified gains in literacy levels determined by informal and semi-formal processes in education that had existed a good half century previously. By the 1880s the solidly literate base produced by the 1870 reforms meant that a vast potential market lay ready to exploit. Led by London, literacy throughout the country reached at least 90 per cent for both sexes in all areas at the beginning of the twentieth century.

If the British working class might not be able to write as well as their betters they could certainly read, and for most people in the nineteenth as well as the twentieth century *reading* was the decisive measure of literacy. Writing was a *skill*, reserved for others, rarely needed formally and usually practised informally and haphazardly (diaries, letters, postcards, etc.). This was clearly attested to throughout the nineteenth century by the growth of ephemeral printed material, ranging from fly-posters to newspapers and recorded in the extraordinary rise in postal correspondence. The readership and appetite for newspapers was clear indication of the new reading habits, creating a reading *public* (educated to take information second hand and deliberate upon it to create a mass opinion) rather than an active mob (acting on impulse through local, visual stimuli). By the 1870s, although *The Times* was the only national newspaper, there existed a public of perhaps 5–6 million readers. The appetite for newsprint was insatiable and newspapers were consumed on trains (the carriages were littered with abandoned newspapers), the omnibus, in public houses and in the newly created 'newsrooms' of public libraries. On the occasion of the opening of Bancroft Road Library in 1902 Canon Barnett (of Globe Town in East London), recalling the Boer War, called libraries 'blockhouses against hooliganism'. Newspapers were read out loud to the family, to work colleagues and to servants as well as being consumed in silence in public or in the library reading room. Thus was a *national* political consciousness formed.

If in the 1860s most papers catered for middle-class readers, by the 1870s there were the half-penny *Echo*, *News of the World*, *Weekly Dispatch*, *Reynold's News*, *Morning Post* or *Daily Telegraph* to cater for the lower middle classes, working classes and servant classes. The *Illustrated London News* (launched 1842) combined words and pictures and found a large readership in the 1880s and 1890s. The *Strand Magazine* combined articles and pictures in a 'pot pourri' style, reaching a general readership of between 300,000 and 500,000 – especially when a new Conan Doyle story appeared. At the turn of the twentieth century, the penny dailies catered for the lower middle-class 'respectable' reader with family and responsibilities whilst manual labourers found interest in the ha'penny press. Such newspapers reached into slum homes as well as cottages.

The raison d'être behind newspaper production had already changed, and this was linked to readership demand. Previously newspapers had been largely political in nature, local in kind and educational in requirement, and agitation throughout the country for the removal of governmental taxes (stamp duties) on print and paper had focused on the fact that cheaper print created a better educated population which would have earned the right to participate in democracy. In the mid-1800s the newspaper was seen as a moral force but by the end of the century the literacy/democracy campaign had largely been won and newspapers turned increasingly to entertainment. Thus the notion of 'cheap' in the 1830s and 1840s became a byword for 'nasty' by the 1900s. The 'new journalism', as it was dubbed, relied on sport, sensation and personality, much of which it took from the style and content of working-class Sunday newspapers, which were voraciously consumed in preference to or as an accompaniment to going to church. Thus the British Sunday of church, sex, scandal and gossip took its peculiar shape led by papers such as the *News of the World*.

The working class in London was growing but it was also splitting into the reforming and respectable craft- and skills-led artisan groups (the so-called 'aristocracy of labour') living in new terraced houses in suburbs as distant as Walthamstow, Forest Gate, Peckham or Brixton, and the large and ill-educated group of labourers, dockers, costermongers and casual labourers still living in the inner slum of Whitechapel and Bethnal Green eventually to be joined by waves of Mittel-European immigrants. Rioting would now be accompanied by organized mass rallies, marches, and the formation of new political allegiances. Even so,

> While the riot was becoming less and less the tool to express popular demands, the events of 1855 showed that 'outdoor' working-class pressure was nonetheless effective, even without more sophisticated institutionalised procedures. The public meeting, the independent newspaper, the petition, the reforming campaign, the steady democratisation of Victorian life, all represented at least a change in the way in which working-class pressures were applied, if not an absolute gain in the political power of the masses in mid-nineteenth century Britain.[17]

Spontaneous rioting also remained a powerful form of protest but was more and more confined to the *local* level. The radical Reform League agitation of 1866 which sought again to democratize Parliament led to one of the last of the old-style mob riots. Having had the meeting banned by the Home Secretary, Spencer Walpole, the League went ahead regardless. Sir Richard Mayne as Commissioner had no choice but to begin to organize a police presence – in this case just over 1,600 officers. A peaceful march to Trafalgar Square from Speaker's Corner left sufficient crowds for a violent battle to ensue in Hyde Park. A war then seemed to engulf the police, who were faced with crowds armed with knives and cudgels as well as the uprooted railings of the Park which were now used as spears. Mayne was injured alongside 265 other officers, twenty-eight of whom were crippled. It needed two companies of Guards (one battalion of approximately 400 men) to restore order. Six other battalions were put on standby. The day was the first of a number of 'Bloody Sundays'.

Food riots, the most acute and long-lasting of all riot protests, were always local and specific and continued throughout the nineteenth century even if at less and less frequent intervals. In very poor areas such protest would always be considered legitimate.

Typical in this regard were the bread riots in Deptford during the winter of 1866–7, a period of some shortage and rising prices. In February 1867 the Deptford Relief Committee reported 3,430 people being offered some form of parish relief. On 23 January that year, Mr Patte, the relieving officer of the local Board of Guardians, reported being 'besieged' by 'disreputable . . . individuals' from Greenwich and Deptford. Frustration boiled over into destruction and a rampaging crowd of about 2,000, who one victim called a 'rabble', attacked every baker in the area. These included a Mr Mager, whose shop in Deptford High Street was looted, (the wonderfully named) Mrs Cracknell's Bakery, which was attacked, and Mr Urry's shop, saved by locking the doors. Mr Sammond's bakery was only saved by the owner throwing out loaves of bread to the crowd. A linen draper was also looted. Local businessmen were outraged at police inactivity and angry letters appeared in the local paper.

> Can any of the numerous readers of your valuable paper inform me why the lawless mob of about twenty roughs, apparently unarmed, that sacked shop after shop in the High-street and Broadway of this town a few weeks since, were not arrested. It is a general opinion, had prompt measures been taken and a few of the worst secured, the so-called riots would have been at an end. If the police can excuse themselves by saying they were not strong enough when it commenced at Mr. Mager's shop, they certainly cannot say so when it reached Mrs. Cracknell's as there

were a party of mounted, as well as other police, who evidently were afraid. Had they only but called on the crowd, the majority of whom were attracted out of curiosity, they would undoubtedly have aided and assisted in securing the roughs, which statement is corroborated by several of the unemployed having offered to be enrolled as special constables.

If you, Sir, will do me the favour of inserting these few lines; it may be the means of ventilating this subject, my only object being to find out if the police did their duty, and are able to protect our property should another raid be attempted, or must we still remain at the mercy of the mob?

I am, Yours respectfully, A. TRADESMAN[18]

Richard Mayne sent detachments of A Reserve and put Chief Superintendent Walker in charge. Yet violence continued on the second day when butchers were attacked, one of whom saved himself by waving a cleaver at the crowd. Another was pushed aside by one ringleader who proclaimed to the assembled crowd, 'There you are; walk in and help yourself.' The crowd duly did so without the police interfering. A tobacconist was then burgled and the crowd marched off to Greenwich.

Once the disturbances calmed down, local businesspeople and magistrates were quick to vindicate local people. 'The hardworking individual classes took no part in this disgraceful movement', and J. J. Barker of the Council made it clear that non-locals caused all the trouble. A convenient whitewash would thus save High Street business. That notwithstanding, sentences for those caught were harsh and clearly motivated by personal animosity towards 'bolshie' indentured apprentice boys. On 25 March the magistrate Mr Traill handed down a sentence of three weeks on 'bread and water' to fifteen-year-old William Yarnell, an apprentice of a Mr Russell of New Cross who had accused him of being 'obstreperous' and being 'a perfect terror'. The actual offence was the careless leaving open of a door!

From the 1880s, the working class began to coalesce rapidly as a political force. Unionization entered already close communities and gave them new directions as labour came to a sense of its own discrete needs. The growth of self-awareness through increased literacy, union propaganda and information as well as through the newly flexing muscle of the growing Labour Party (formed from an alliance of many diverse working-class strands) also led to increased stridency in disputes.

Such stridency and self-confidence became a legacy for working-class children as well as a pattern for their own fight with the authorities over compulsory schooling. In 1889 and in 1911 there were waves of national school strikes, led by pupils often after incidents in which friends had been punished too severely. Strikes at schools centred on issues such as corporal punishment, the school day, holidays, the school leaving age, exploitation of 'monitors', unpleasant teachers and bullying headmasters or mistresses. In 1889 there were strikes in Finsbury Park, Homerton, Woolwich, Plumstead, Kennington, Charlton and Lambeth; in 1911 these were repeated at Enfield, Islington, Hoxton, Fulham, East Ham and Deptford. The London strikes provoked imitations across the twentieth century and certainly were a notable feature up to 1939, as strikes in Haringey (1914), East Ham (1929) and Chatham (1938) suggest.

Educationalists and teachers, middle class and respectable, soon recognized that working-class children were not merely copying their trade union parents, they were using organized working-class militancy to articulate the deepening rift, not only between young and old but between middle-class authority (the teachers) and working-class demands (the school children). The *Educational News* of October/November 1889 declared:

> Schoolboy strikers . . . are simply rebels. Obedience is the first rule of school life . . . School strikes are therefore not merely acts of disobedience, but a reversal of the primary purpose of schools. They are on a par with a strike in the army or navy . . . They are manifestations of a serious deterioration in the moral fibre of the rising generation . . . The ringleaders are probably few in number – not more than half a dozen in any school. It should be the business of the teacher to find them out and expel them. They will prove dangerous centres of moral contamination wherever they have the opportunity of posing as heroes . . . Freed from their presence, their erring dupes would speedily forget their folly and settle down to work.

Schoolboy rebels would use pickets, marches in the street and demonstrations to make their point. Contemporary illustrations show them marching through the streets carrying flags emblazoned 'NO CANE', to the amusement of police and shoppers alike. When the Chairman of the London School Board received a warning that the schoolboys of Lambeth and Kennington were to meet at the Embankment to demand free education, one free daily meal, no homework and no caning (demands finally realized only during the reorganization of education in the late 1960s), he read the letter 'amidst laughter'. Sometimes a school picket would end with window-breaking, but always the punishment was severe with boys being lined up to be beaten in front of the school. Some children were publicly birched or sent to the workhouse. Reprisals were carried out which were greatly out of proportion to the crime and clearly meant to intimidate the children who looked on and might sympathize, as well as their parents who might take the 'revenge' punishments as a covert message about their own demands.

And the authorities were rattled. In Bethnal Green the schoolboy ringleaders were seen to carry red flags and wear 'scarlet liberty caps'. The *Dundee Advertiser*, commenting on continued disturbances at schools in Scotland, smelled conspiracy.

> It has not yet been ascertained through what medium schoolboys received the signal for united action . . . Such movements as this do not spring up spontaneously. They are always evidence of a deep conspiracy against social order . . . It is perfectly evident that the schoolboys from Land's End to John O'Groats could not without organisation arrange to strike simultaneously. The doom of the Empire must be near at hand if the country is honeycombed . . . with Secret Societies of schoolchildren.[19]

After a strike at a school in East Ham during 1929, one paper sourly noted the growth of 'active resistance to discipline' amongst 'the unmoulded minds of . . . children' which had 'in most cases' occurred at 'the instigation and approval of the parents'. Strikes at school were swiftly suppressed and soon forgotten, but as the authorities had feared they left an indelible trace in the personality, a trace that would be one first step in many people's political education.

On 19 March 2003, the Stop the War Coalition organized another school walk out. Approximately 5,000 pupils in Birmingham, 3,000 in Manchester, 1,000 in Sheffield and 300 in Swansea and numerous others from Edinburgh, Leeds and Bristol missed school to protest against the war in Iraq. In London a rally in Parliament Square resulted in scuffles and arrests. On the same day, the Stop the War Coalition held a 'die-in' outside the south London home of Jack Straw then Foreign Secretary. The protest organized by Nick Buxton, used fake blood, gravestones, recordings of air raids and a lie-in to make its point. The protests were part of a number of protests against the war, including various marches on 19, 20 and 29 March and the giant Hyde Park rally on 22 March of between 100,000 and 200,000 supporters. A hundred teenage protesters also blocked Oxford Street singing 'Give Peace a Chance'.

11
Persecuting Pigeons
Trafalgar Square and Bloody Sunday

As the nineteenth century progressed the old wastes and commons of London where the people traditionally met to protest a government measure, a national injustice or local heavy-handedness by the parish or vestry were rapidly diminishing, and those left were being rationalized into parks and gardens. Victoria Park had sufficient open space to accommodate large protest gatherings, but it was too far to the east. Brockwell Park in the south would serve as a space for a rally before a protest march to Westminster but it too was some distance from the centre. The vast open tract of St George's Fields on the south bank was inexorably covered with factories, houses and the new Waterloo Station. The buildings that had originally dotted the area – a prison, a madhouse – were hemmed in, demolished and forgotten. Clerkenwell Green still survived to the north as a politically unruly if small area, but house building had crept across the old grassy slopes up to Islington and swallowed Spa Fields and Cold Bath Fields. Smithfield was still there but it had lost significance, whilst to the south-west Kennington Common, scene of the Chartists' great rally in 1848, was enclosed, tidied up and turned into a park. Hyde Park remained the protest ground of choice, near Westminster as well as next to the wealthy districts of the West End.

Any open space was, at least potentially, a site of rebellion and sedition and for the authorities the fewer the better. As the traditional open spaces of London were shut down, built over or landscaped for healthy recreation another rose in their place, which was close to Buckingham Palace and Parliament, adjacent to the long built-over Leicester Fields (Leicester Square) and at the centre of London's web of major roads. Trafalgar Square constituted not merely a new open space for protest but became *the* open space for national radical debate, right next to Westminster.

Proposals to create a new road scheme and grand monument in what is now Trafalgar Square began to be submitted at the beginning of the nineteenth century. Such ideas had been sparked by

John Nash's report to His Majesty's Commissioner of Woods, Forests and Land Revenues in 1812. In an attempt to remodel Charing Cross, considered the 'hub' of London life, Nash proposed new roads and grand vistas where a hotchpotch of roads and alleys then existed. An Act of Parliament in 1813 ensured the Nash scheme, for a major new road for the north of the capital and from the area around Haymarket and Charing Cross, would go forward. The rebuilding work would create great sweeping crescents such as Regent Street, designed by Nash specifically to separate the 'Nobility and Gentry' in their 'streets and squares' from the 'narrow streets and meaner houses occupied by mechanics and the trading part of the community', the new roads organized in such a way as to 'cut off' access by the poor who might want access for whatever terrible reason as they journeyed out of their ghettos in St Giles, Porridge Island, Seven Dials and the mean streets near Haymarket and Westminster.

The Commissioners considered Nash's proposals but suggested that part of this grand scheme (and the schemes to improve access to the west of the city) would be new roads to the Houses of Parliament and to the British Museum and a greatly increased 'space' approaching Whitehall. It was finally agreed to clear the area in front of St Martin's Church in order to create a square bounded by the National Gallery, the Union Club Houses and the College of Physicians as well as St Martin's itself. The Commissioners now set about the work of moving inconveniences such as St Martin's Workhouse (finally relocated 1864), a school and a library, determining that the buildings around the square would be in the grand manner. It was George Ledwell Taylor, one of William IV's naval architects, who claimed to be the first to call 'the Charing Cross Quadrangle' by its new name of Trafalgar Square, a fitting tribute to Nelson's great victory, a victory that had ensured the unchallengeable rise of the British Empire and British trade in the defeat of the Napoleonic invasion threat of 1805.

The long-drawn-out war with republican and imperial France did little to enhance the prestige of the ruling class, whose military strategies had proved disastrous, Jacobinism was on the rise at home and West Indies trade was under threat. Nelson's crushing defeat of Napoleon's Egyptian fleet at Aboukir Bay made him the darling of the elite as well as a popular hero. His tragic-heroic death at Trafalgar made him a legendary hero, the victory ensuring British naval and imperial supremacy up to the First World War.

Nelson's status had yet to be recognized in a public monument of sufficient grandeur to capture the nation's (and more especially, the aristocracy's) appreciation of his importance; nevertheless, a start was made when the Nelson Memorial Committee met at the Thatched House Tavern in St James Street on 22 February 1838 to organize a national subscription (and a competition) for a monument. Twenty years previously, William Wood had argued for the need of a gigantic monument to those who 'proudly stemmed the torrent of revolutionary frenzy'.

> The ordinary feelings of men are not adequate to the present crisis. They must be sublimed from the domestic apathy in which they now contemplate the approaching storm, to a state of active patriotism and manifest their love for their country by a gigantic effort to *preserve* it.[1]

Wood's own ideal monument was a 250 foot pyramid tomb guarded by four giant lions. Such a sublime national monument was (despite its Egyptian design) to act as a reminder of the martial virtues of the Greeks and Romans and the centrality of British patriotic valour and steadfastness in the face of rising republicanism.

> Who loves his Religion, his King, his Country, and its law cannot be insensible to the present awful crisis; a juncture in which not only our own existence as a nation, but the continuance of rational liberty on the earth is about to be decided.[2]

Despite the bluster and the grandeur of the designs, at least on paper, no effort was made to build a permanent monument to Nelson for another thirty-five years and five years after the original meeting at the Thatched House. Wellington now had a grand statue in front of Mansion House; why not Nelson and why not at the centre of the square at the centre of London? The resolution to build a monument was proposed by Admiral Sir Pulteney Malcolm and seconded by Nelson's flag captain, by now Vice Admiral Sir Thomas Hardy. As the most significant members of the Houses of Parliament deliberated on the final design it was clear that it had to contain an unequivocal message, one which reinforced the established order and authority of the state and the ruling class. If the chosen form was to be classical, it would be imperial rather than republican, for which recent London statuary might act as an inspiration.

One suggestion was

> that of the Memorial to the . . . Duke of York, one-time Commander-in-Chief of the British Army . . . in Waterloo Place, . . . The choice in 1829 by the Duke of York Memorial Committee (which counted among its members the Duke of Wellington, Lord Palmerston, Lord Shaftesbury, George Canning and Sir Robert Peel) of Benjamin Wyatt's edifice modelled almost exactly on the Emperor Trajan's

Column in Rome was quite deliberate. Trajan's Column, it will be remembered, was erected to illustrate two successful military campaigns which in themselves marked the moment when the Roman Empire had reached its vastest extent.

Other suggestions included a 'Temple' dedicated to 'military virtue' surrounded by a Roman imperial eagle. The final design by William Railton was itself modelled on a Corinthian column found in the temple of Mars Ultor (Mars the Avenger) in the Augustan Forum at Rome.[3]

Despite the intentions of the various designers, the Column and the Square (and its pigeons) have become the symbols of London, the grandeur of the space subverted by its very openness, attracting not only crowds of tourists but also political crowds whose sentiments could be at once patriotic and radical. Landseer's gruff, monumental and somehow cuddly lions have been climbed or sat upon by generations of children, pigeons sit on Nelson's hat and every radical and protest group has happily used the Column's podium as a platform to attack any and every orthodox political opinion or government programme for nearly 160 years.

The first use of Trafalgar Square as a rallying point for a demonstration came in March 1848, when protesters gathered to hear speakers denouncing the increase of income tax from 3 to 5 per cent. The plinth of Nelson's Column was still covered by hoardings as building work slowly progressed. Scared by police threats of prosecution, the rally's organizer, C. Cochrane, declined to speak for fear of arrest, leaving the platform to G. W. M. Reynolds, then a young Chartist and a republican. Speaking of the events in France which had toppled Louis Philippe and proclaiming, 'A Republic for France – The Charter for England', Reynolds was catcalled by someone in the crowd (an agent provocateur it seems) asking what he would do if he had Philippe in his grasp – would he kill him? Cleverly avoiding a charge of treasonable sedition, Reynolds answered that he would put him in the zoo as an exhibit! This was enough for the police, who attacked the crowd and battered several of them. Such a crass act only created a riotous response, and the police now had to contend with a pelting of stones from the Column's base, after which the hoardings were torn down and thrown. Builder's sheds were also set alight as a section of the crowd made its way to St James' Park with the cry of 'To the Palace! Bread and Revolution!', smashing windows and lampposts on the way. Between 6 and 8 March, 103 arrests were made at or around Trafalgar Square, with 73 of those arrested convicted.

The Times lamented, '8,000 to 10,000 persons assembled in the Square, belonging entirely to the working classes [some estimates say as few as 1,500], and the great mass of them apparently out of employment . . . judging from appearances, not a dozen probably were subject to tax.'[4] At least, however, the 'respectable classes' (as *The Times* referred to them) might now have seen the back of 'this senseless, and in a political sense, ridiculous movement'. The author was, of course, referring to the demands of the Chartists whose 'monster' rally was to be held on 10 April on Kennington Common and against whom 100,000 special constables had been recruited in London alone.

By the 1880s, the virtues of free trade and liberal politics sat uneasily with the demands of organized labour and poverty. The London United Workers' (or Workmen's) Committee (LUWC) was a *Tory* union dedicated to fighting free trade and creating tariff barriers against foreign manufacture. They intended to hold a rally in Trafalgar Square on Monday 8 February 1886 and prepared to go ahead when the Social Democratic Federation (SDF), the most radical and republican wing of the socialist movement, decided to hold a counter-rally. The SDF intended to protest peacefully but the police prepared for problems. Many unemployed people were also attracted to the square as demonstrators, and spectators made ready to mix it or simply watch.

The police, leaving the LUWC to its own devices, ordered the SDF to march off to Hyde Park. The leaders agreed but the procession found itself being abused by the 'clubmen' of Pall Mall shouting from upstairs windows. In return, they were pelted with stones and bricks and the march collapsed into a street brawl. Looting began and spread from St James's to Piccadilly and Oxford Street. *The Times* described the whole affair as being orchestrated by 'concealed leaders' and carried out by 'the vagabondage of London'. The leaders of the SDF were all arrested. The group included Henry Myers Hyndman, its founder, who had rejected the life of a Tory stockbroker for the path of socialist reform; John Burns, a fiery agitator and founder of the Battersea branch of the SDF (in 1881), later to find fame in the London Dock Strike of 1889; Henry Hyde Champion, the editor of the SDF's paper *Justice*; and John Williams, a full-time agitator and a man long associated with anarchist causes.

Next day, London was shrouded in a 'peasouper' fog, the thick yellow 'pestilential' fog that swirled around coal-burning London and that by the Victorian period had already been called 'smog', and rumours soon spread that an angry mob was preparing to descend on the West End out for revenge. A telegram was even sent to *The Times* from residents in the Old Kent Road warning of '30,000 men moving on Trafalgar Square' and small groups of Londoners actually gathered to welcome them as shopkeepers boarded up their premises and the police and military turned out. Nothing happened. William

Morris's belief that the rally was 'the first skirmish of the Revolution' was plainly grossly overstated, as Friedrich Engels pointed out. Hyndman's revolutionary vision of land and industrial nationalization and universal suffrage coupled with his bombastic attitude to his personal leadership of the radicals had, in the end, simply failed to ignite interest.

'Black Monday' or 'Bloody Monday' was a serious failure for the SDF, which failed to animate the poor, unemployed and socially disenfranchised and was not able to crystallize the socialist conscience or organize copycat action elsewhere. Instead, other agencies came into play: Nathaniel L. Cohen, for instance, set up a 'labour exchange' in Eltham. The police meanwhile came under the particular criticism of the Parliamentary Committee looking into the disturbances. Police problems included

1. Insufficient number of officers of superior rank and education.
2. Want of a more efficient telegraphic system.
3. Absence of an adequate force of mounted police.
4. A defective chain of responsibility among the superior officers of the force.
5. A want of published police regulations for dealing with large meetings.
6. The position and duty of officers in charge of meetings.
7. Absence of a proper system of communication with the Home Office in the event of emergency.

Colonel Sir Edmund Henderson, the Commissioner of the Metropolitan Police, had certainly botched some of the operation. Neither he nor District Superintendent Robert Walker (then seventy-four years old) had covered themselves in glory. Henderson had foolishly left his headquarters, and Walker, directing tactical operations, had not only misdirected reserves *away* from the fighting in Pall Mall but, arriving dressed as the gentleman he was, in *civilian clothes*, had been mistaken for a rioter by his own men and had his pocket picked.

Although Henderson resigned he was feted and rewarded. To some the entire event suggested a government trap where the police were intended to be caught off guard in order to bag the SDF leaders. Henderson was replaced by Sir Charles Warren, a noted archaeologist and administrator from South Africa who was an enthusiastic supporter of Gladstone and had stood (unsuccessfully) as a Liberal candidate for Sheffield. Warren was clear who the enemy were. They were the same 'loafers' who had destroyed 'Imperial Rome' by expecting the state to provide constant welfare provision: 'We all know the history of Rome, that before it fell there were loafers and other bodies who did not work, who were fed by the state . . . soon after that Rome fell'. Was the British Empire to suffer the same fate?

Social deprivation was central to the concerns of people like Henry Mayhew, Friedrich Engels and Charles Booth. Booth's monumental seventeen-volume analysis of London social division – pink for comfortable working class, red for middle class, yellow for upper class, black 'the lowest vicious scum animal' – helped map London's poorest inhabitants. Accompanied by George Herbert Duckworth, half-brother of Virginia Woolf, Booth would walk the streets noting the class and ethnicity of those he met. For these jaunts he was often accompanied and protected by a local policeman who knew the 'patch' or 'manor'. One such policeman was PC Moss, a 'bucolic beefy and provincial' man who took Booth's assistants round South London (and who incidentally was involved with the 'One Tree Hill' disturbance – see Chapter 25).

The loafers were all around. Unemployed people slept rough on the Embankment, on London Bridge, in Covent Garden and most conspicuously in Trafalgar Square. Their presence was a horrible reminder of the seamier side of Victorian success (to reformers) and an emblem of moral turpitude and decline (to the authorities). Proposals were made to fence Trafalgar Square, which was now surrounded by the most prestigious buildings in London, and Queen Victoria was written to by Lord Salisbury to ask her approval – after all the Square was part of the Crown Estates. Warren, mindful of his officers turning a 'blind eye' to the homeless and also aware that the SDF were organizing them under the slogan 'Not Charity, But Work', decided to revoke marches by the poor who, with their red and black flags, smacked of 'an insurrectionary temper' which could not be allowed to continue. He also noted the poor seemed 'organised' and able to employ tactics to avoid arrest. There was clearly a secret conspiracy.

To meet this 'conspiracy', the force that he could call upon as Commissioner was quite different from the small, beleaguered and motley crew that had been the Bow Street Police. The Metropolitan Police District comprised an area up to fifteen miles in any direction from Charing Cross (nearly 700 square miles), excepting the City, which had its own police. It covered parts of Essex and Hertfordshire as well as Surrey and Kent and it covered all the area of the expanding boroughs. There were twenty-one land divisions plus a river force, using about 200 police stations, each headed by a superintendent. It was a complex bureaucratic machine that included officers dealing with finance and property administration, the detectives of the Criminal Investigations Division and the 'secret police' known as Special Branch, set up originally to work against the Fenian threat.

The force, through the Commissioner, was answerable to the Home Secretary and thus to Parliament.

Throughout the nineteenth century the entire machine was steadily expanded. According to one estimate, in 1829 seven Acts of Parliament related to the duties of the Metropolitan Police; by 1861 there were seventy-five; between 1861 and 1868 'scarcely a session of Parliament' ended without further duties being added relating to 'the supervision . . . of a vast multitude of details of more or less importance' on 'an immense variety of . . . subjects'; between January 1868 and January 1878 a further thirty Acts were passed 'entailing new duties and responsibilities'; and the trend continued until 1914.[5]

This hardly went unnoticed. The Royal Commission of 1908 saw the expansion of police provision as 'so extensive' that it limited 'in almost every direction the freedom of action of every Londoner'. Some people saw this as entirely a good thing, restraining the mob and preserving civilization.

> Governments are plainly unable to keep a mob in check, and are afraid to try unless they have twenty thousand shopkeepers as special constables to back them . . . A centralized bureaucratic system gives a great resisting force to the hand that commands the Executive. Our Executive has nothing to fall back upon. There are practically no reserves. The bayonets and sabres here and there are perfectly powerless before the masses, if the people really took it into their heads to move; beside which it is an instrument that they dare not in practice rely on. A few redcoats may be called on to suppress a vulgar riot; but the first blood of the people shed by troops in a really popular cause would, as we all know, make the Briton boil in a very ugly manner . . . Men with heads on their shoulders know that an appeal to force would be the end of English society; and what is even more to the purpose, that there is no force to appeal to.[6]

The danger from Fenian bombers in 1867 and 1868 had also led to the drilling of police in the use of revolvers, selected officers going to Wormwood Scrubs in West London to train. By late 1868, 400 pistols were under lock and key in London police stations, and officers (suburban only) were entitled to the protection of guns or sabres on night duty. Luckily few took up the offer and since most were quite unable to handle firearms gun drill it rarely affected practice on the street. If guns were needed on the streets of Victorian London the army would provide them, and although they were brandished, they were never used. It was not until the terrorist campaigns of the early 1900s that police found themselves confronted with armed revolutionaries whose fanaticism was matched by deadly skill.

By the 1880s the role of the police in catching criminals was all but accepted amongst the respectable classes. What the public was never reconciled to was the role of the police in keeping civil order, a role which often put them into the role of aggressors in the fight for free speech and a democratic franchise. Although Commissioners protested their independence and *neutral* position it was clear that they acted as both moral guardians and a paramilitary force working to suppress anti-government activity.

The first use of aggressive (rather than reactive) crowd-control tactics had occurred in 1830 after a Lord Mayor's Show had got out of hand. The anti-income tax disturbances of March 1848 had proved the inadequacy of equipment and tactics when attempting active intervention and prevention and the continuing need for *military* support. By the late nineteenth century the police still needed to prove themselves in public-order crises and they needed to demonstrate decisive control. Warren stood ready with a drilled and well-equipped force which could bring overwhelming numbers to bear at key points and at key moments of a melee.

Sir Charles Warren was determined to keep the centre of London clear of the homeless and unwashed and he was equally determined that no more demonstrations on their or anyone else's behalf would take place in Trafalgar Square. The red and black flags of communism and anarchy would, he hoped, never again flutter next to Landseer's lions. On 8 November 1887 Warren posted notices stating that 'no Public Meetings will be allowed to assemble in Trafalgar Square, nor will speeches be allowed to be delivered therein'. The notice outraged the left, who saw the Square as a prime venue (in a rapidly shrinking pool) for their protests. Freedom of speech was clearly threatened as was the ancient right of the people to meet to consult.

The occasion of Warren's notice, a ban on a proposed meeting on behalf of William O'Brien, an imprisoned Irish Home Rule advocate, was now to be made into a protest over the gagging of freedom of speech and freedom of assembly. The rally would take place on Sunday 13 November. All the socialist and union groups would march to the square, as would the Metropolitan Radical Association, the recently formed Law and Liberty League and the Irish National League, formerly the Land Reform League (LRL). The march would be headed by prominent union leaders and socialists such as John Burns and Annie Besant. William Sanders of the National League notified Warren on 9 November that he would hold a meeting and was arrested in what everybody saw as a test case. W. T. Stead, watching events closely, saw the problem as one of 'defend[ing] the legal liberties of the Londoner from the insolent usurpations of Scotland Yard'. *The Times*, however, saw such liberties as 'an absurdity' and backed Warren. Warren set his face and his reputation against any march and the supposed liberties of the London population.

Warren massed his blue ranks and turned London into an armed camp. On the morning of the march, which the organizers had no intention of calling off, he had 1,500 men positioned around the Square. They stood in phalanx around the plinth of Nelson's Column. Horse police patrolled the streets nearby as 2,500 others closed all roads around the West End. He also had the services of two squadrons of cavalry mounted on large black chargers and equipped with brass helmets and breastplates. These troops would be used to accompany the magistrate, a Mr Marsham, described as 'a sort of country-looking imbecile' who would read the Riot Act. A detachment of Grenadier Guards, in full uniform of scarlet jacket and bearskin and armed with twenty rounds per man and fixed bayonets, completed Warren's army of professionals. Behind them stood hundreds of special constables sworn in at local police stations and made up of tradespeople, middle-class professionals and students who feared putting London 'under the auspices of the red flag' and 'placing control of the streets in the hands of the criminal classes' (as *The Times* put it).

Meanwhile the various groups that were preparing to march met at prearranged open spaces around the City and in the suburbs. Clerkenwell, traditional starting point for so many radical meetings, saw crowds gather to hear Annie Besant (later triumphant in the Match Girls' strike of July 1888), Edward Aveling (Karl Marx's son-in-law) and William Morris talk of the need for free speech and socialist principles. With red banners unfurled and led by the Finsbury Radical Club and St Peter's brass band, 5,000 protesters, all of whom were respectable besuited artisans, marched via the Clerkenwell Road down Theobald's Road into Bloomsbury and towards St Martin's Lane. Morris had warned there would be trouble. They found it in aces. In St Martin's Lane stave-wielding mounted police stationed in side streets assaulted them. The battle had begun. Morris later recalled how easily the authorities routed the workers.

At the same time South London contingents from Peckham, Bermondsey, Deptford, Greenwich, Woolwich, Southwark and Battersea were approaching Westminster Bridge. They linked arms to show solidarity and create a protective barrier as they saw the police at the Parliament Square end. They were attacked as they crossed under Big Ben, the police swapping blows with their staves with demonstrators using their flag and banner poles to defend themselves. The western contingent had already marched without incident from Paddington and Notting Hill, their flags and banners fluttering and their own bands playing. At the Haymarket they too were stopped and found themselves embroiled in a street melee, brawling with police who were determined to allow no demonstrator near the square. Some marchers did inveigle their way into Trafalgar Square, where a vicious street fight continued all day.

At four o'clock, Warren still held the Square but at that moment 400 men led by John Burns (later Liberal MP for Battersea) and the socialist MP Cunninghame Graham (North-West Lanarkshire) made a strike for the Column's plinth. Both Graham and Burns, surrounded by police and standing still, were violently beaten up by their captors. Graham's wife noted they 'stood perfectly quiet to be murdered' and a witness in the nearby Morely Hotel (the site of South Africa House), Sir Edward Reed MP, confirmed the unnecessary force used, which amounted to assault by police officers. At this point the cavalry with the magistrate and the soldiers with their bayonets entered Trafalgar Square. They were jeered at by the crowd but the soldiers pushed protesters into the police who pushed them back against the rifle butts of the soldiers. By early evening 200 people were injured, of whom three died, two soon after and one a few days later of injuries sustained that day. 'Bloody Sunday' had been an unmitigated disaster for socialism and a triumph for police order.

Opposed to the SDF and the revolutionary politics of its leaders, Hyndman and Morris were the Fabians. The Fabian Society, founded in 1884, was an offshoot of the Fellowship of New Life, which had been created in the early 1880s by a group gathered around the Scottish 'wandering scholar' Thomas Davidson. This group, consisting of idealist thinkers and emancipated women, included Havelock Ellis, and Oliver Schreiner, who wrote *The Story of an African Farm* (1883). They were joined by Annie Besant, Edith Nesbit (the children's author) and her husband Hubert Bland, future Prime Minister Ramsay MacDonald, George Bernard Shaw, a cockney socialist called Sidney Webb and the freethinking daughter of a capitalist Beatrice Potter (not to be confused with Beatrix Potter).

The difference between this 'evolutionary' group and the revolutionaries could not have been clearer, Shaw going so far as to declare that the Fabians 'have never advanced the smallest pretensions to represent the working classes'.[7] The rioting of 13 November 1887 was roudly condemned by the group who thought the populace cowardly. When in 1892 Beatrice Potter announced her intention to marry Sidney Webb, her socialist colleagues abandoned her, and her reforming (but antisocialist) friend, the great investigator of poverty, Charles Booth, castigated her future husband as 'an undersized, under bred, and "unendowed" little socialist'.[8]

According to where you stood on the matter, Sir Charles Warren had saved Britain from communism, or had effectively murdered freedom of assembly and free speech. The subsequent official inquest into the events merely suggested that the police should order stronger truncheons. So many had broken that experiments began to find a better material and an easier method of carrying them, as protesters had twisted the scabbards in the policemen's belts in order to 'pinch' their opponents.

William Morris was deeply affected by the setback: 'the mask is off now, and the real meaning of all the petty persecutions of open air meetings is as clear as may be. No more humbug need be talked about obstruction . . . The very Radicals [i.e. the Liberals] have been taught that slaves have no rights'. Even as he lamented, large hampers of food and donations of money poured into police coffers from the grateful citizens of the 'respectable' and upper classes. A protest meeting held on Sunday 20 November 1887 was treated to the same Warren style. One protester, Alfred Linnell, having left the meeting to look at the police lines in Trafalgar Square, was unlucky enough to be trampled by a police horse. He died two weeks later. A huge funeral procession followed his coffin to Bow Cemetery. The hearse was covered in 'Irish, Socialist and Radical flags' and accompanied by a shield inscribed 'KILLED IN TRAFALGAR SQUARE'. The pallbearers were Annie Besant, Cunninghame Graham, William Morris, W. T. Stead (the campaining journalist who died on the *Titanic*), Herbert Burrows and Frank Smith of the Salvation Army. Cunninghame Graham, recovering from his injuries, was sentenced to three months' imprisonment.

His counsel was Herbert Asquith, a rising star in the Liberals, and it was under Asquith, Home Secretary in 1892, that the right of assembly in Trafalgar Square again became an issue, only to be fudged by a compromise allowing discretionary regulation to replace outright prohibitions. The compromise was supported by John Burns, now an ILP MP, but rejected by the SDF. The regulations remain in place to this day. Throughout the nineteenth century the continual use of Trafalgar Square as a meeting place for protesting and disgruntled groups and the vulnerable nature of its location as a hub of numerous roads led the police to devise ways of observing it without being noticed. One solution was the building of a small stone tower at the south-east corner, which gave the appearance of a sewage access tunnel or vent but was, in fact, an armoured observation post housing three policemen. It was connected to Scotland Yard (just round the corner) by telephone. The little stone tower, topped by a large lamp, but long disused by the police, remains to this day situated opposite South Africa House.

12

'Good Old Dynamite'

London's War with the Bombers

7 January 1911 started wet. Despite the relentless drizzle that had fallen since the night before, an ever-growing group of spectators had been gathering all day at the Rising Star; every window had been thrown open with gaggles of men and boys peering eagerly out. In the road outside, a crowd of working men, cloth-capped and lounging, pressed forward to get a view, drawn by the commotion. Two women, muffled against the cold and tugging skirts up to avoid the muddy doorway in which they huddled, peered anxiously out, somehow finding themselves beyond the armed soldiers lined up across the cobbles.

The soldiers had just arrived and deployed on the corner where dozens of helmeted police constables, station officers and assorted government officials had stood all day blocking the street and informing the curious 'Nothing to see here, son'. Scots Guards now formed a grey line as a barrier. One soldier leaning his rifle against his thigh had paused a moment from his sentry duty and was quietly smoking. The action was too far away, no one was quite sure what to do or who, what or where it should be done. Gathering its own energy, a rumour had started suggesting that the artillery was on its way. For once, this was not just hearsay. The artillery was on its way and so was a heavy machine gun.

Further down the street men with rifles, shotguns and bulldog revolvers crowded into the limited shelter of the doorways, yards, entrances and alleyways of Sidney Street; in puddles, the wet detritus of the life of the East End: broken bottles, strewn soggy cardboard packing, rotting vegetation and the debris of siege – empty small-arm shell cases, hundreds of them, rolled and dully glinted in the gutters and on the cobbles. These would be collected next day by the local street children, as trophies of war.

With an eye for timing and a sense of the dramatic, the man with the astrakhan collar and shiny silk topper had been drawn to the siege by an irresistible and inherent desire to be in the thick of the action. Next day the press would make him regret his folly and his arrogance; after all, he was the Home Secretary not a policeman or a soldier. He had called for a double-barrelled shotgun and been given it – it felt like the old days in South Africa – Winston Churchill was having a good day . . .

*

During the latter years of the nineteenth century the working class may slowly have been coming to what Marx believed was a sense of self-awareness; they may slowly have been coming to regard their needs as to be met only by socialist principles; but working-class political views were still tied to the radical and reforming wing of the Liberal Party. Dreaming over his books in the British Library Reading Room, Marx might well have hoped for the spontaneous combustion of capitalism and the rise of a workers' culture but the truth was that he would be dead long before the Liberal Party collapsed, and the capitalist system he so abhorred would long outlast the consequences of the theory and principles he created. Despite the long march of republican orators and agitators, would-be assassins and terrorists, the ideals of the republic were essentially the pipedreams of a few professional 'street' politicians. Nowhere is this more evident than in the rise of a parliamentary and constitutional Labour Party out of the various socialist groups of the 1880s and 1890s and it is equally clear in the retreat from spontaneous or violent street confrontation towards clubs, debating societies and socialist presses.

The London Patriotic Society was typical of such clubs. Formed from republican, democrat and Fenian supporters, the club represented 'the head-quarters of . . . ultra nonconformity [and] treason'. It met in pubs such as the Hole in the Wall, where republicans could book private rooms, but after somewhat lavish praise of the Parisian Communards the police had got publicans to ban all such meetings. The 'provinces of liberty' then called a meeting at the Robin Hood, Leather Lane, to form a society and rent premises. The rooms they finally found were at 37a Clerkenwell Green (now the Marx Library) in an area notorious with the authorities for its reputation for protest, Sunday speakers, rallies and general political troubles. Spa Fields was round the corner, as was the Clerkenwell House of Detention, built on the ruins of a prison destroyed by Gordon Rioters. The London Patriotic Society's Club and Institute soon changed into the London Patriotic Club, with members meeting to discuss science, social justice, foreign revolutions and votes for women.

The nineteenth century wore on with economic crises in 1873–4, 1878–80 and 1890–93, and radicalism grew stronger as trade unionism started to make headway with the Master and Servant Act of 1867, the Workman Act 1875 and the Conspiracy and Protection of Property Act 1875 giving legal protection to unions. Skilled workers were now more settled and prosperous and were debating the significant issues of the day, whilst the very poor grew in number and in destitution. The London Patriotic Club was one of a number of groups that attempted to form alliances between the more extreme elements demanding votes for women, anti-imperial legislation and Irish Home Rule. The Russian revolutionary Peter Kropotkin was, for instance, a guest during his stay in 1881 to 1882 and the Club members were supporters of Narodnaya Volya, the Russian revolutionary group that had assassinated Tsar Alexander II. By the second half of the 1880s clubs such as the London Patriotic were breaking up under the pressure of debates over how social change might best be effected. More radical socialists had joined the Social Democratic Federation (SDF) led by H. M. Hyndman to put forward a Marxist programme for change. Although not part of the SDF, the club cooperated over a number of issues and the Twentieth Century Press, a radical publisher, transferred to the club's premises in the 1890s.

Of considerable interest was the association of Lenin with the Clerkenwell premises. He had arrived in April 1902 with his wife Krupskaya and other revolutionaries on the editorial committee of *Iskra*. Harry Quelch, one of the hard-line Marxists of the SDF (derided by Engels as a 'sect'), had offered his press to Lenin, who printed issues 22 to 38 from Clerkenwell. Lenin left London during May 1903 but he did not forget the help he had found. In 1913 he wrote Harry Quelch's obituary and years later, when Quelch's son Tom visited in 1920, Lenin asked 'How [is] everybody at Clerkenwell Green?'

For the most part, the visitors to the London Patriotic Club had no desire to follow the old violent revolutionary path of Arthur Thistlewood or the Chartists but contented themselves with the belief that socialism would inevitably triumph. The growth of the trade unions and the rising tide of colonial subjects who refused to do what they were told, not to mention Irish nationalist elements and a growing politicization of the whole working class (including women), lent credibility to the belief that capitalism would collapse with only the slightest push. How this might eventually be achieved split aged Chartists from Marxist-Communists and the creators of the embryonic Labour Party from anarcho-socialists. Socialism might be the future of humankind but would it appear by revolutionary or constitutional means? Whilst the old republican spirit survived it found itself unable to excite the masses or their new organizations: trade unions were there for limited and often local aims and their members, to a man, were conservative, respectable and royalist.

Indeed, *reformism* rather than revolution informed the radical agitation of the 1860s. The reformists, usually tradesmen or self-employed, were backed by leaders whose inclinations were in tune with the Liberal Party. Thus the Club and Institute Union of 1862 spanned such groups as the Commonwealth Club of Bethnal Green and the London Patriotic Club in Clerkenwell. The founders of both clubs had been original members of the First International, a small group of socialists who met in a pub. Later the Metropolitan Radical Federation was formed to coordinate these reforming clubs, with their dedication to temperance, constitutionalism and respectable protest. Such clubs formed the 'left' of the Liberal Party in the 1870s and 1880s.

Revolutionary and republican socialism was reimported into British politics by European émigrés and those with European connections, such as Frank Kitz, who was born in the revolutionary year of 1848 to an English mother and German father. Settling in Soho in the early 1870s, Kitz joined a group called the Democratic and Trades Alliance, in which poor but skilled manual workers could discuss the issues that interested them. Kitz spoke on communism. By 1875 he had helped create the Manhood Suffrage League, an alliance of both radicals and republicans that publicized the heroic action of the Parisian Communards. 'Kitz was committed to revolutionary rather than electoral action and by *his* use of the phrase he clearly meant a revolutionary democratic socialism. The distinction was between a total *social* democracy and a partial *political* democracy. At that time 'social democracy' was not reducible to parliamentary reformism.'[1]

Other German and Russian émigrés swelled the numbers of such groups, especially after the German anti-socialist laws. Many joined the English Revolutionary Society, itself part of the Social Democratic Club which met at pubs in Soho. Here they would plot their return home and dream in exile. Alternatively they might plot more violent action, known as 'propaganda by the deed', essentially campaigns of bombing or assassination. At the same time the club issued *Freiheit*, a revolutionary paper that was illegal in Germany and smuggled by sailors. Pursued to Britain, one of these revolutionaries, Johann Most, found himself on the receiving end of an eighteen-month prison sentence for incitement to murder heads of state. It was only in 1882 that *Freiheit* was closed down, for printing an article approving the recent murder in Phoenix Park, Dublin of Lord Frederick Cavendish, the Irish Chief Secretary. This was the last straw for the moderates, who decamped leaving the more revolutionary group to form the Anarchist Club in St Stephen's Mews, Rathbone Place, in 1883.

There were, however, British working men who instinctively moved towards the position of the foreigners. One was Joseph Lane, who founded the socialist Homerton Social Democratic Club in Hackney. He also attended the Social Revolutionary and Anarchist Congress in July 1881 at a pub in Euston. Most of the forty-five delegates there were from Europe but five British socialists attended – at least one,

C. Hall, was a police spy. From this Joseph Lane formed the Labour Emancipation League (LEL), itself a development of activities in East London where the Stratford Dialectical and Radical Club had been formed after a split in the National Secular Society (NSS). In its turn the NSS was led by Charles Bradlaugh, an opponent of Christianity, royalism and class privilege, who had a great following amongst working men and was the British voice of republicanism and the 'infidels'. He had been born in humble circumstances, the son of a solicitor's clerk from Hoxton, and influenced by the radical atheist Richard Carlile, he became a free-thinker, setting up the National Secular Society in 1866. By 1877 he was working on a book on birth control with the socialist reformer Annie Besant. For the publication of *The Fruits of Philosophy* he was jailed along with Besant for six months, the book being considered obscene. Elected in 1880 as an MP for Northampton, Bradlaugh asked to 'affirm' the oath of office instead of swearing on the Bible. He was refused by the Speaker and expelled from the House of Commons. In June 1880 he attempted to take his seat again, was expelled and imprisoned in the Tower of London! He could not take his seat lawfully until 1886. In Parliament he supported republicanism, redistribution of land and Irish home rule as Carlile had done all those years before. Yet for all his efforts he still proved a disappointment to socialist radicals, who demanded a clean sweep of political and social institutions and not gradualism.

The socialists of the 1880s were neither clearly Communists of the Bolshevik model nor anarchists in a modern sense. These were times when such ideas were still fluid and theoretical divisions still hazy. Cooperation was, nevertheless, always difficult between groups whose own lack of identity and clear direction put them into conflict with others who seemed to oppose their views. Added to this, clubs were often infiltrated by spies working for the police or for foreign embassies. Although surprising, the fact remains that even amongst hard-line terrorists from Russia and Germany theoretical and ideological issues were still a matter of debate right up to the early years of the twentieth century.

Such debates were soon taken to the streets of the East End and the Mile End Road. Leading the discussions was Joseph Lane, paying for the necessary propaganda out of his own small wages as a cart driver. He demanded:

> Equal direct adult suffrage; direct legislation by the people; aboli-tion of the standing army, the people to decide on peace or war; free secular and industrial education; liberty of speech, press and meeting; free administration of justice; the nationalization of land, mines and transport; society to regulate production and wealth to be shared equitably by all; the monopoly of the capitalist

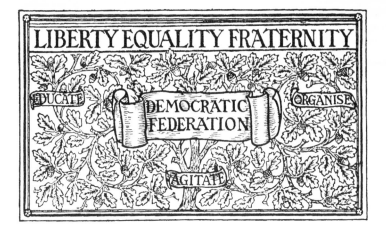

William Morris design for the Democratic Federation

class to be broken and the means of production transformed into collective or public property.[2]

The most surprising convert to this agenda was Henry M. Hyndman, the stockbroker whose political leanings began as those of an independent Tory. After meeting Lane he came round to the idea of forming an Independent Labour Party, and held a meeting to that effect at the Westminster Palace Hotel in June 1881. He went on to create the Democratic Federation, an alliance of revolutionaries and reformers, but Marx, whom he courted, dismissed him as 'self-satisfied' and a jingoistic nationalist. Yet Hyndman was a genuine convert to socialism, if an autocratic one, who did hold radical views on Ireland, capitalism and social reform. A convert too was William Morris, the great artist and designer, who turned to 'practical socialism' as a way of restoring the medieval craft society he so loved. His socialism was only tangentially linked to the theoretical intricacies of Marxism: 'I have tried to understand Marx's theory but political economy is not in my line and much of it appears to me to be dreary rubbish'.

These many conflicting 'socialisms' made central leadership impossible and as the Democratic Federation changed into the Social Democratic Federation (SDF), members began to break away to form more radical forces. The Socialist League, for instance, was created by disenchanted 'ultras' and the old LEL. Edward Aveling and his wife Eleanor Marx drafted a constitution at Friedrich Engels' prompting. It was William Morris who drafted *The Manifesto of the Socialist*

League. His position was neither constitutional, parliamentary social-istic, nor communistic anarchist, but the strong state socialism of what became known as Marxist-Leninism.

> As to mere politics, Absolutism, Constitutionalism, Republicanism have all been tried in our day and under our present social system and all have alike failed in dealing with the real evils of life . . . No better solution would be that State Socialism, by whatever name it may be called, whose aim it would be to make concessions to the working class while leaving the present system of capital and wages still in operation: no number of administrative changes, until the workers are in possession of all political power, would make any approach to Socialism . . .[3]

Against these demands should be placed the rival pronouncements of Henry Seymour, whose paper the *Anarchist* called for the abolition of the state and its functions, and whose personal attitudes fed into the early debates of the Fabian socialists. The SDF was now home to many Fabians whose brand of socialism was essentially intellectual and unprogrammatic. On the periphery of these groups were maver-icks like the poverty-stricken Dan Chatterton of Seven Dials whose *Chatterton's Commune: the Atheistic Communistic Scorcher*, published between 1884 and 1895, made him a political party of one.

> Who does not remember . . . a pale haggard old man who used to climb the platform at meetings of the unemployed, or in the closely packed Socialist lecture halls and pour forth wild denun-ciations of the robbery and injustice that flourishes in our rotten society, mingled with fearful prophecies of the terrible revolu-tion that was coming? He looked as he stood in the glare of the gaslight, with his ghostly face and flashing eyes, clad in an old grey overcoat and black slouched hat, a red woollen scarf knotted around his neck, like some grim spectre.[4]

Frank Kitz joined and met Morris when the SDF was created but Morris thought him too anarchistic and destructive, although he did recognize the strong anti-state, anti-capitalist organization Kitz and others had created in Mile End and Stratford. These social-ist groups never numbered more than a few dozen to a few hun-dred members, but while the SDF had only 400 London recruits in defence of civil liberties or parliamentary reform it could call upon thousands of sympathetic supporters, as happened when they pro-tested against police raids on the Anarchist International Club and the breaking up of open-air meetings in Stratford. Even more to the point, the SDF and the other militant organizations could organize large independent rallies such as those during February 1886 against a Tory 'fair-trade' demonstration and the riotous disaster of 'Bloody' Sunday.

By the 1880s, squabbling, personal feuds and ideological differences had begun to paralyse action. Morris complained that the 'Anarchist element . . . seem determined to drive us to extremity' whilst Kitz complained of the affliction of 'anaemic respectability'. When British anarchists did turn to 'propaganda by the deed' in imitation of their Continental brethren the attempts were woefully inadequate to the occasion. One group was caught supposedly planning a bombing campaign in Walsall. This was a classic piece of police provocation undertaken to 'draw out' dangerous elements and using a long-term double agent, Auguste Coulon. Coulon had come into the Socialist League during the 1890s but was always too rich and too eager to be trusted. 'One would think he lived on bombs,' commented one colleague, the soon to be entrapped David Nicoll, whose life of abject poverty was dedicated to fighting for civil liberties. Coulon's career as an agent provocateur (he wrote one letter to the anarchist paper *Commonweal* which concluded 'Good old Dynamite') was undertaken under the wings of Special Branch operatives such as Inspector Melville.

> A Spy of the School of Fouché, he speaks French and Italian like a native. In person he is a very big man, extremely stout, with a fine forehead, a clean-shaven face, slight moustache, and two cold, enquiring, grey eyes. He is on terms of perfect intimacy with the police agents of foreign governments. Melville and his gang have dogged the steps of the foreign refugees for years. It is only lately that English police agents have followed the example of their foreign associates in manufacturing plots.[5]

In 1892 a series of raids in Walsall and London (near the anarchist Autonomie Club in Tottenham Court Road) bagged a number of conspirators who, it was alleged, intended to manufacture bombs for export to Russia using Johann Most's book *Revolutionary Warfare* as a guide.

> If a man had a copy of this book in his possession, he would have been a conspirator, no matter how innocent he might be of the conspiracy at Walsall. Another simple enthusiast in the country was recommended to collect ginger beer bottles 'for bombings'. The day of Revolution was at hand, and it was necessary to strike terrible blows at the enemy.[6]

Once imprisoned Nicoll actually became deranged. British anarchists and their émigré colleagues lived in an atmosphere of suspicion and double agents were a daily hazard in such cloak-and-dagger
proceedings, proceedings often closer to Gilbert and Sullivan than to
grand opera.

> If anybody was thinking of examples of 'individual action' immedi-
> ately before the Walsall case broke, they would probably be mostly
> concerned with the rather farcical action of John Evelyn Barlas
> (a poet whose collection of poems, *Phantasmagoria*, was published
> under the pen-name of Evelyn Douglas). On 31 December 1891,
> a policeman first heard and then saw him discharging several shots
> from a revolver at the Houses of Parliament at about 9 o'clock
> in the morning. The policeman ran towards him. 'Seeing wit-
> ness [i.e. policeman] he [i.e. Barlas] handed him the revolver says,
> "I am an Anarchist and I intended shooting you but then I thought
> it is a pity to shoot an honest man. What I have done is to show
> my contempt for the House of Commons". Magistrate, "was the
> prisoner sober" Witness, "Perfectly".'[7]

The revolutionary propagandist H. B. Samuels was a tailor by trade,
whose introduction to radical politics led him to become a man
'obsessed with violence' who saw in the American anarchist movement, in the Spanish massacre at the Liceo Theatre in Barcelona and
in the French, Belgian and Russian 'dynamitards' (especially the terrorist Ravachol) perfect models for his own revolutionary fervour.

> I claim the man who threw the bomb at the theatre as a comrade.
> We must have our own some day, they murdered our comrades
> and we must murder them. Twenty-three killed, how sad? . . . An
> eye for an eye. Aye, twenty eyes for one eye. I claim that unknown
> comrade has done better work than any philosopher. That
> unknown comrade . . . has caused such a terror that the rich dare
> not walk the streets of Barcelona for fear of the bombs. I don't
> believe in organizing bodies of men to meet the Gatling guns. We
> will fight the bloodsuckers by any means. I don't blame these men
> because they are bloodsuckers. I don't blame a dog but I will kick
> him damned hard if he bites me. We expect no mercy from these
> men and we must show them none.[8]

Samuels, who finally became editor of the radical journal
Commonweal in 1893, acted as apologist for bombings at the
(French) Café Very and Café Terminus (1894). He also applauded the
self-sacrifice of Martial Bourdin, who had blown himself to bits in
Greenwich Park in February 1894, but failed to act in anything other

than words himself. The Greenwich explosion was later reworked in Joseph Conrad's popular novel *The Secret Agent*, and it is this novel that provides the classic picture of a 'dynamitard' of the late nineteenth century.

> And the incorruptible Professor walked too, averting his eyes from the odious multitude of mankind. He had no future. He disdained it. He was a force. His thoughts caressed the images of ruin and destruction. He walked frail, insignificant, shabby, miserable – and terrible in the simplicity of his idea calling madness and despair to the regeneration of the world. Nobody looked at him. He passed on unsuspected and deadly, like a pest in the street full of men.[9]

If British anarchists dreamt of bombs but did little, this was not the case with the more ruthless terrorists who came to Britain from the Russian Empire (especially the Baltic region) and settled, temporarily at least, in the East End. These dedicated revolutionaries were social democrats (Mensheviks and Bolsheviks) as well as nationalists and anarchists. Entry into Britain was easy and the import of weapons or even bomb-making equipment was virtually ignored. Revolutionaries escaping the harsh regime of the Tsars, especially Latvian and Lithuanian revolutionists had taken flight from the Tsarist secret police, found a welcome in London where socialist groups supported those dedicated to democratizing Russia.

At the beginning most groups were anarchist, later they included Bolsheviks but in both cases they adhered to the doctrine of 'expropriation' by which robbery (in order to finance further revolutionary activity) was dressed up as reappropriating the already 'stolen' profits of the capitalists. Theft was the chosen method of income for such groups, who moved between Britain and Russia in a number of disguises and under a variety of names. For the most part these desperados went about armed with the latest machine pistols, expecting no mercy from the British police whose methods they mistakenly took to be the same as those of the Tsar's Ochrana.

The waves of bombings and assassinations that had terrified Europeans in the 1880s and 1890s merely made newspaper headlines in Britain until the first decade of the twentieth century. In 1907 an abortive attempt to assassinate the President of France killed the bomber, 'Strygia'. 'Jacob Lepidus', his brother, and 'Paul Hefeld', his fellow accomplice, fled to Britain. In January 1909 they plotted the armed robbery of the wages desk of Schnurmann's Rubber Factory in Tottenham. The raid was badly bungled, however, and both men found themselves pursued by police and civilians across Tottenham marshes towards Walthamstow and then Chingford, at that time one of London's countryside villages. In the pursuit they commandeered a milk cart and even a tram, shooting at anybody and everything that threatened them. Exhausted and corned the two fought it out. Hefeld shot himself and was captured (he later died); Lepidus committed suicide. The day was a bloodbath. A stray bullet killed a young boy, and over twenty others, including policemen, were wounded.

Anarchists in France gloried in their heroes of 'the Tottenham Outrage'. The anarchist paper *Le Rétif* reported the deaths of 'our audacious comrades' (both had been members of 'Leesma' or 'the Flame'). The paper then turned to their victims.

> Haven't you any remorse? – No! Because those who pursued them could only have been 'honest' citizens, believers in the State and Authority; oppressed perhaps, but oppressed people who, by their criminal inertia, perpetuate oppression: Enemies! For us the enemy is whoever impedes us from living. We are the ones under attack, and we defend ourselves.[10]

A year later, an even more violent confrontation occurred after a bungled robbery at a jeweller's shop in the East End. A number of Bolshevik expropriators had planned the robbery for some time but in silent streets their handiwork made too much noise and attracted the attention of the police. The gang were all seasoned in revolutionary warfare, all members of the 'the Flame' (they would send any monetary gains from the robbery to Lenin and the Bolsheviks) and all heavily armed, being determined that if caught they would fight to the death. The police closed in on the house from which the gang were trying to break into the jewellers not knowing the danger they were in. The terrorists simply shot their way out, killing three policemen and wounding another. One terrorist was wounded – 'George Gardstein', a man with eight other aliases – and dragged off by his colleagues to bleed to death in a poky bedroom in a poky lodging house nearby.

The 'Houndsditch Murders' were shocking because of their cold-blooded indifference and a massive hunt soon got under way. Gardstein's body was discovered with ammunition and papers linking him to the Lettish Anarchist Communists and with guides on how to make bombs. In one letter to his brother he asked mysteriously, 'Have you written to the finger of God in Libau?' His passport called him Schafshi Khan. In January 1911 a roundup of suspects started to bag the main culprits and the police made progress. Two however had bolted and were holed up at 100 Sidney Street, a three-floored tenement built in a back-to-back square near a brewery. It was a fifteen-minute walk along Whitechapel Road from where the robbery had gone wrong. Inside were two men armed to

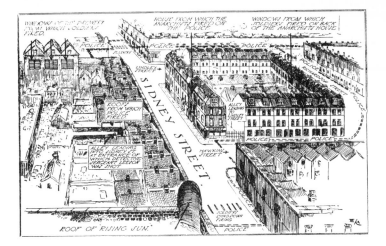

Sidney Street

the teeth: Fritz Svaars and a man called 'Joseph' or Yosef. Both had numerous aliases.

The police, coming from both the City (independent of the Met) and elsewhere, began surrounding the area and evacuating those that lived there. This took some time, as some residents who spoke only Yiddish in this predominantly Jewish area were frightened and disturbed. As this operation went on the terrorists opened fire, killing one policeman and wounding another. They were armed with German guns of the highest technological quality and could fire rapidly and accurately for up to a thousand yards. Against these, the London police had virtual blunderbusses.

Unable to make any headway, the police asked the Home Secretary, Winston Churchill, for military reinforcements. The military – a detachment of Scots Guards – duly arrived, as did Churchill, who could not resist coming, the whole thing being 'so extremely interesting'. As he arrived the chant of 'Oo let 'em in?' came from onlookers, who disliked the new immigrant presence in the area. Churchill was given a shotgun as the five-hour siege played out its tragic story. Eventually the terrorists' house caught fire. Svaars and 'Joseph', unable to escape, kept up a rapid and deadly barrage until one was finally shot and the other died in the burning building. When the roof collapsed it trapped and killed the firemen sent to put out the fire.

A vast amount of ammunition had been used on both sides. The artillery were even on their way. Churchill, overenthusiastic, had been caught on newsreel. When it was shown the audience catcalled and shouted, 'Shoot'im!' The French press thought the episode amusing. The Russians said too bad and the Germans offered to show the British how to run a proper police state. As for those still held in custody little could be proved and it was convenient to blame the dead for everything that had occurred. The accused were all acquitted. One, Nina Vassilleva, worked for the Russian trade organization in London (and spy 'front') Arcos; she died in 1963 having lived all her life near Brick Lane only a few hundred yards from the tragedy of 1911. Another of the accused was Jakob (or Jacob) Peters, a cousin of Fritz Svaars. He too operated under a series of alter egos including Jacob Colven or Kolnin. In Russia he was known as Svornoff. Also acquitted, he journeyed back to Russia to take part in the Revolution of 1917, rising to become Deputy Chairman of the Cheka, the Bolshevik secret police. He finally vanished in 1939 or 1944, purged by Stalin.

With the passing of the centenary of the Tottenham Outrage in 2009 and with the hundredth anniversary of the Siege of Sidney Street due in January 2011, there has been much renewed speculation as to the identity and intent of the various groups of 'expropriators'. A casual look at the incidents of January 1909 reveals certain problems which may never be resolved. One is simple. By what means did the robbers have access to such sophisticated weaponry and such supplies of ammunition? May we assume that all or some of it was imported when they landed in England or were they supplied on arrival by whom and where? The pair themselves are shadowy and although we know something of them, we do not yet know if they were part of the wider group based in the East End who finally broke into Harris the Jeweller. Was the Tottenham robbery an opportunist affair or planned and if planned where in Tottenham, amongst fellow anarchist or elsewhere? Why was the raid so bungled and why stage it in front of a police 'barracks'!? And finally, why did the inquest record all the comments by the gunmen (which were heard by the pursuers) in English when neither was talking in English and no one there could understand Latvian or Yiddish? Were the two connected directly or otherwise to the mysterious raid on a bank in Motherwell in 1908? Who was the mastermind? There is much research still to be done.

This then clearly brings us on to the serious questions remaining after the attempted robbery in Houndsditch a year later. Why for instance did the gang target an apparently seedy back-street jewellers that, given its location, could have been little more than a pawn shop and trinket dealer? Why make elaborate plans to crack a safe when a short journey would have taken the robbers to Bond Street and the pick of jewellers? There spectacular goods in diamonds and gold might more easily have been smuggled or fenced, a getaway undertaken in the luxury of a purloined motor vehicle (as did the Bonnot Gang in France in the same years).

The peculiarities mount. Was there something unique in that safe that was worth more to the robbers than jewellery and if so what? Perhaps it was negotiable Tsarist bonds that might be sent back to feed Lenin's coffers, but then why were they secreted in an East London jewellery shop? Perhaps the shop was itself a front for nefarious dealings, but if so why would the agents of the Tsar or the merchants of the Russian Empire favour it against Garrards or other royal jewellers? If this was the case it might explain the extraordinary wealth of the family some time later. Either way, there must have been something special about the shop as the raid was at least a year in planning and seemed to account for the whole active cell of revolutionary Latvians living in the East End.

Whatever it was they were after would have to be smuggled out of England using couriers and fences and this would have meant that the revolutionary movement abroad would have been spiced with all sorts of criminal elements who might give the game away for a reward. At any rate the deaths of the main protagonists drew a line under the affair; those rounded up and tried were freed and others fled although the authorities never ceased surveillance on those acquitted and who stayed in London, as the later 'Arcos' raid signifies.

Of those who escaped one particularly stands out. He was the notorious 'Peter the Painter', the shadowy mastermind blamed for the raid and its aftermath, whose legendary status began when his body was not recovered from the house in Sidney Street where he was supposedly holed up with his compatriots. For fifty years his name conjured up the strange atmosphere of the East End and the shadow of Jack the Ripper.

It was only in 2009 that the mystery of Peter the Painter was finally solved. The investigator Philip Ruff, having got access to the Latvian archives was able to piece together the life of Janis Zhaklis a revolutionary organizer active after the 1905 revolution, and a vicious street fighter who was dedicated to the Bolshevik cause and founded the revolutionary group 'Leesma' (the Flame). He had already robbed and shot his way across Latvia, before having to escape to Britain. He was young, well dressed and with a striking resemblance to the footballer David Beckham. He was also ruthless. Was he in charge of the raid, but not present, and left straight after its failure on a boat to Australia and anonymity? Did he later work for the Soviet secret services only to be 'purged' in the 1930s or was he the strange prisoner of the gulag who could retell the story of the revolutionary mission in London in minute detail as late as the 1950s? Did he just start a new life, leaving the grime of London and the cause for which he fought behind?

Propaganda by the deed seemed more and more attractive to some and had already proved its effectiveness in the hands of the Irish. The attraction of getting what you wanted by waging a new type of guerrilla war using dynamite and pistols had precedents not only in obscure bombings in Berlin or Paris but also in the effective campaigning of the Irish Republican Brotherhood (IRB) during the 1860s and 1880s. The IRB, funded and aided by expatriate Irish, was founded in Dublin in 1858 but many of its 'soldiers' went to fight in the American Civil War, which kept them out of Britain until the late 1860s. At the Civil War's end, the IRB leader, Colonel T. J. Kelly, having quit the Union Army, began plotting an Irish revolt for 1867. Captain Richard O'Sullivan Burke, who had also seen service in Chile, aided him. The plot required the seizure of arms at Chester Castle and an immediate insurrection. Both were foiled, first by the fact that Burke's train was late, second by the obvious presence of large numbers of suspicious Irishmen and third by the crucial intervention of a police spy, John Corydon.

On 11 September 1867, Kelly and his associates including a Captain Derry were arrested but during their transfer to jail in Manchester their van was ambushed, and a police sergeant (Brett) shot, which allowed the Fenians to make a getaway. On Friday 28 September three Life Guard bandsmen enjoying a drink were also attacked in Bloomsbury. It is possible that this was a revenge attack on a Fenian informer and one of the soldiers, Eddie McDonnell, was shot and later died of his wounds. Meanwhile, the Metropolitan Police had put James Thomson on the case. He was a multi-linguist and one of the new breed of professionally minded and scientific detectives. He soon arrested John Groves on suspicion of the murder of McDonnell after finding the gun and Fenian papers at his lodgings. Extreme measures were taken to secure Bow Street and the route to Clerkenwell House of Detention to avoid any more rescues. The *Illustrated Police News* reported that hordes of Fenians had been spotted lurking around Bow Street, recognizable by their peculiar 'walk and attire'. To avoid problems Thomson and his men were armed and escorted by mounted police with guns and sabres.

Despite Thomson's care, police methods were haphazard and forensic capabilities merely a wish. Groves was acquitted when it was clear that one prosecution witness showed signs of being mad and that the gun in his possession was *not* the murder weapon. Thomson, thwarted and humiliated, did not have to wait long to gain an arrest that would stick. An informer named Devany led him to Burke's hiding place in Tavistock Street near Tottenham Court Road. Burke was with an aide, Casey. Thomson and a passing police constable arrested the two. When Burke attempted to escape, Thomson drew a gun on him exclaiming, 'By God, Burke, if you don't stop I will fire on you.'

Burke, having stopped, replied with dry good humour, 'Don't do anything desperate.' Finally a cab was hailed and the police and the bagged terrorists went to Bow Street. They were then sent on remand to Clerkenwell House of Detention.

Being sent to Clerkenwell was a gift for the Irish Nationalists. It was in a strong pro-Irish area and one known for its sympathies for radical causes. Burke, ever resourceful, got word to Kelly and others to spring him whilst he exercised in the prison yard. Sir Richard Mayne, however, had had word of the plot from informers in Dublin. Having informed the prison governor, Mayne nevertheless was foolish enough to fail to increase security properly. The Nationalists' first try at blowing up the prison wall was a failure as the gunpowder was damp and failed to go off. They were also lucky as a policeman (one of only two or three keeping watch) saw them but failed to act. The next attempt was to be a spectacular success. On 13 December 1867 two Irishmen, Allen and Despond, and an Irish woman named Ann Justice wheeled a barrow full of explosives up to the prison wall. They were part of a 'cell' led by tough Irish fighters Barrett and Murphy from Glasgow and another man called Ryan who had been accidentally wounded when Barrett had waved his pistol about.

The explosion, at 3.45 in the afternoon, ripped the prison wall apart and demolished a row of houses (Corporation Row), killing six local people (of whom two were children) and injuring forty others. Incompetent bombers, the terrorists had used 548lb of explosive, far too much for the job. The explosion was heard up to forty miles away. The explosion caught Inspector Thomson (he had been promoted) just as he left the prison with a witness but he had been able to warn the governor to move Burke to a safer place the night before. This did not, of course, prevent a mass breakout when the wall was blown up. Frantic activity over the next few weeks did, however, round up most of the culprits, and Ann Justice attempted to hang herself in her cell. The little group of conspirators appeared at the Central Criminal Court on 20 April 1868 but results were mixed and only Michael Barrett was found guilty and executed on 26 May 1868. His was the last public execution to be held in Britain.

Official recriminations began almost immediately, with Thomson accusing Captain Codd, the prison governor, of pompous and unwarranted self-confidence, and the Under-Secretary at the Home Office (a Mr Liddell) reporting to friends that Mayne had been told in no uncertain terms that he had made a 'damned fool of himself'. The House of Commons, in a funk, had sanctioned the Home Secretary to recruit 50,000 special constables and increase the Metropolitan Police at the same time. A week after the explosion selected policemen gathered at Wormwood Scrubs for professional arms training, the first such course to be organized. Sir Richard Mayne, this disaster unforgotten, died on 26 December 1868.

The Irish bombers, having achieved little in the 1860s, returned to England during the 1880s. It was this campaign that showed anarchists the possibilities of 'propaganda by the deed' when armed with dynamite. The wave of attacks orchestrated during the 1880s were the work of Clan-na-gael, a secret Irish-American society founded in 1870 and dedicated to all-out war with Britain. The dynamite gang itself arrived in Liverpool in early March 1883, having crossed on the Cunard ship *Portia*. They consisted of a Dr Gallaher (or Gallagher) and his brother Bernard Gallagher, Henry Wilson, John Curtin, Alfred Whitehead (who ran a Birmingham bomb factory), and men called O'Connor, Dowd and Norman.

The first bomb was placed at the *Times* office on 15 March 1883 but did little damage. A further bomb exploded on the same day at the Local Government Office in Whitehall. In October bombs went off at Charing Cross and Westminster (Bridge) underground stations as well as Praed Street Station (now closed). Here sixty people were injured, the dynamite lobbed out of a train window as a type of grenade. In 1884 mainline stations were targeted. These included Victoria Station, where a deposited bag hid the device. Other clockwork-timed bombs were tracked to Charing Cross, Paddington and Ludgate Hill after the arrest of an Irish-American called John Daley at Birkenhead. Whitehead's Birmingham 'bomb factory' was also raided and a bomber called Lynch (a.k.a. Norman) arrested in Southampton Street in London.

The bombers were undeterred and well organized, and having regrouped they continued their campaign. On 30 May 1884 an attempt to blow up Nelson's Column with sixteen sticks of dynamite was foiled by police but revenge followed when a large section of Scotland Yard was demolished by a bomb placed in a lavatory. It took six months to catch up with the bombers, Burton and Cunningham, who had also exploded a bomb at the Tower of London. Further explosions occurred at the Junior Carlton Club and at the base of Tower Bridge (where the bombers died in the explosion) but an attack on Westminster Hall failed when a policeman carried the smoking dynamite to safety! Even then there were serious casualties.

The rise in public disorder, armed crime and terrorism between the 1860s and 1880s meant that the police would have to change in order to cope. By the time of the era of the 'dynamiters' and anarchist demonstrations during the 1880s, the force began to evolve new departments and functions. Even so these were often inadequate to the task of monitoring subversive activity or investigating rising (often violent) crime. Sir Edmund Henderson, who replaced Mayne, quickly recruited over 200 detectives of whom 180 were stationed around Central London. Those at Scotland Yard were placed under the control of Superintendent Adolphus Williamson. Yet even Henderson was unsure if he had unwittingly damaged the status of the police by the creation of a 'secret' detective force, which was 'viewed with the greatest suspicion and jealously by the majority of Englishmen [sic] and is, in fact, entirely foreign to the habits and feelings of the nation'. He might have added that his detectives were also not to be trusted, because some of their chief officers were taking large bribes from criminals. Reform came through centralization of all detectives in the new Criminal Investigations Department (CID) of 1878.

By the 1880s the corruption of the 1870s had been dealt with but bribery and corruption was small beer in the face of bombs and insurrection. The 'Met' had no expertise in those areas. Once the bomb attacks began in the 1880s the authorities had to act. The Home Secretary not only promoted an Explosive Substances Bill which became the Explosive Substances Act but also approved the use of Royal Irish Constabulary (RIC) officers in London. This was a force which had long fought terrorists and foiled James Stephens's Fenian rebellion of 1858. The bombing campaign of 1883–4 following the assassination of Lord Frederick Cavendish, Chief Secretary for Ireland, and his Under-Secretary in Phoenix Park in May 1882 left the government little option but to act. A 'Special' Irish Branch was duly set up whose secret police force was soon being called by the embarrassing name of 'the Political Branch'.

Countersubversion in the late nineteenth century had evolved from a civilian (if effective) spy network into the professional work of a police cadre. In the mid-1880s there were five such bodies: uniformed police on guard duty at public buildings; port of entry officers including plainclothes detectives; special duty 'Irish Branch' men stationed at Central Office; two intelligence sections; and the RIC. With changes to this organization came James Monro, known semi-officially as 'the Secret Agent'. With Monro came a growing bureaucratization of these forces, with a central group of senior detectives recruited in the war against the Fenians. These detectives would now be paid secretly from imperial coffers rather than be on the Metropolitan payroll. The complexities of the system can be seen by the fact that Scotland Yard's Special Branch was separate from the Irish Branch, known as 'Section D' and recruited from special duty CID personnel until 1911. To confuse matters further the original Special Branch consisted simply of the four senior officers recruited by Monro in 1887. This was quite different from the 'Special Irish Branch' of CID officers, which was counted as a separate unit. Moreover it suffered from a distinct lack of identity being variously called the Special Confidential Section, Special (secret) Branch and Home Office Crime Department: Special Branch.

These new groupings, which became 'Special Branch', were highly secret and made every effort to frustrate enquiries into their purpose and organization. They were secret too because they were a *national* police force, which carried out political surveillance and arrest when no such force was meant to exist, being against Victorian principles of policing. Lastly they reported directly to the Home Secretary, their remit to destroy Fenian and 'anarchist' networks.

It was not until the successful outcome of long police surveillance and the arrest of John Daley that the general public heard of the new police organization, which was first reported as existing on 24 March 1884 in *The Times*. By now there were 600 detectives in the Metropolitan Police and a network of agents, spies and agents provocateurs deep inside anarchist, socialist and Irish organizations. From the late 1880s until the early twentieth century the war with Irish Nationalists was fought in Ireland rather than on the mainland. This culminated on 21 November 1920 when Michael Collins effectively wiped out British intelligence (and its operatives) in Ireland, but this did not rule out taking steps to assassinate leading members of the Irish Establishment resident in London.

One target was Sir Henry Wilson, Chief of the Imperial General Staff during the First World War, an Irish MP and an outspoken opponent of Irish republicanism. On 22 June 1922, Wilson had unveiled a plaque to the war dead of the London North-eastern Railway at Liverpool Street Station and after the ceremony had caught a cab back to his home at 36 Eaton Place in Chelsea. As he left the cab he was approached by two Irishmen using aliases: James Connolly, or Connelly (actually Reginald Dunn), and Joseph (or John) O'Brien who was also Joseph (or John) O'Sullivan. Their identities were more hidden than their guns and Wilson, lacking Special Branch protection, was gunned down. He drew his ceremonial sword and fell dead.

An epic chase followed and Dunn, hobbling because of a wooden leg (some sources state the other assassin as the owner of the wooden leg), attempted to stop a van and a cab but both sped off. Nevertheless the killers did commandeer an open-topped brougham complete with liveried coachman in which they made their escape as far as West Eaton Place where a car driver attempted to ram them but crashed when he was shot at. Police were now also in on the chase and PC Walter March attempted to wrestle the guns from the cornered killers but was shot in the groin and the car owner who had run to help was shot in the leg.

As the killers ran they turned into Gerald Road and by horrible ill luck passed a police station which was also a barracks. More police poured out, some armed. In Ebury Street the gunmen fired again but missed. The police threw truncheons and milk bottles, their armed officers being too far back. One policeman, PC Skilton, actually got in a taxi and attempted to get near enough to the fugitives to hit them on the head with his truncheon, Keystone Kops style. Finally cornered, the two exhausted gunmen advanced on the crowd of police and civilian pursuers, shot and injured a detective constable but were overpowered when one gun aimed at the head of an advancing policeman failed to fire. Although the *Daily Herald* campaigned for clemency as it claimed the men were 'prisoners of war', both assassins were executed. Large crowds of whom many were Irish stood outside Pentonville and Wandsworth prisons singing patriotic Irish songs, but were kept deliberately uncertain about the place of execution (for fear of a rescue attempt).

In Southern Ireland, however, things had gone badly for the Irish Republic Army (IRA). The Irish government had imprisoned 12,000 activists and executed 77 others thus effectively crushing the movement. On 24 May 1923 the IRA declared a ceasefire, an act tantamount to surrender. Opposed to partition, the IRA fighters were now enemies of both the British government and de Valéra's Irish Free State.

It was not until 1937 that IRA elements again regrouped and plotted new campaigns against London. At least one was an aeroplane bombing raid on the Houses of Parliament. The most militant of the new leaders, Sean Russell, now advocated a new anti-British bombing campaign which would bring the 'war' to civilians. His opponents, Sean MacBride and Tom Barry, were prepared to take a team to assassinate the Prime Minster and his cabinet but not use terror tactics and the two sides parted company, allowing Russell to start planning in earnest. Using money from America, and the veteran bomber Jim O'Donovan to instruct his new recruits, Russell's plan required two dozen 'soldiers' to infiltrate London and elsewhere. IRA women, in the Cumann na mBán, would act as couriers and provide safe houses.

On 12 January 1939 the IRA delivered an ultimatum to Lord Halifax, the Foreign Secretary, demanding 'troops out of Ireland', and as the campaign got under way pro-IRA fly-posters on the walls of St George's Church, Southwark reiterated IRA demands.

> Withdraw her armed forces, her civilian institutions and officials and representatives of all kinds from every part of Ireland as an essential preliminary to arrangement for peace and friendship between the two countries. Ireland is still tied, as she has been for centuries, to take part in England's wars. The time has come to make a fresh fight – that is, a fight to make effective the 1916 Proclamation which sets up the Irish Republic.[11]

By now the bombings had begun across the country, with particular attention paid to London. On 17 January, bombs exploded in Manchester, Birmingham, Liverpool and London. The Central Electricity Board Offices were destroyed in Southwark in South London, whilst in the north-west suburbs a bomb exploded near power cables in Harlesden. Another bomb damaged power cables in Brimsdown near Enfield, but the most damaged area of all was British intelligence whose frantic liaison with Dublin had failed to stop even one incident. The bombers seemed to have carte blanche, a position gained only after police stopped but failed to arrest two Irish labourers transporting explosives along Green Lanes, Ilford, East London.

In February, the bombers had created sufficient devices for explosions at Tottenham Court Road and Leicester Square stations. Then, in late February, the IRA sabotage plan, the 'S-Plan', was put into effect across Britain. Bombs in Leicester, Liverpool, Birmingham and Manchester were matched by attacks in Aberdeen and Lancaster. In London coal sidings were blown up at King's Cross Station as was the goods depot at St Pancras next door. The bombers were now using a number of devices including gelignite, incendiaries and fertilizer, often sending their packages through the mail in order to cause mayhem at sorting offices. The mail campaign finally got Eamon de Valéra to act from Dublin and on 14 June his government passed the Offences Against the State Act, but this was hardly likely to terrify the idealists operating in Britain and it had no effect.

As summer deepened the bombers concentrated on central London. On the night of 24 June, in response to Dublin and as a warning to London, the IRA exploded a series of bombs at Piccadilly Circus (10 p.m.); Baker Street and Euston Road near Madame Tussaud's (10.05 p.m.); at the Strand and the Aldwych (10.50 p.m.); again at Piccadilly (10.55 p.m.); at Aldford Street at the corner with Park Lane (12 p.m.). Thirteen people were injured including two boys. This brought to a temporary climax the campaign that the *News of the World* had noted during February after the bombs in the underground:

> Sensational bomb outrages and acts of sabotage in the Tottenham Court Road and Leicester Square Stations have convinced the authorities that a ruthless campaign of terrorism is now in the process of execution in Great Britain. Scotland Yard has ten thousand men engaged in the most extensive and intensive roundup in London's history.[12]

The passing of the Prevention of Terrorism Act 1939 did little to dampen IRA spirits and bombs continued to explode. The Act itself was the result of yet more bomb attacks, this time at King's Cross and Victoria, that left many wounded and one dead. By the end of 1939 there had been 242 'outrages' reported and the police had rounded up 128 people, of whom 62 had been arrested in London.

It was not the police who found the first clues of the terrorists' whereabouts but a Manchester plumber called Charles Heap, who had grown suspicious after working at a house in Chorlton-on-Medlock. He had spotted bomb equipment in a bedroom wardrobe and reported it to the police after returning to the house to check. The servant girl living in the house, Mary Glenn, provided more evidence and an address in Kilburn was turned up once the owners were arrested. As police combed the North and the Midlands, arrests followed in London: Peter Stuart (Peter Walsh), an IRA intelligence officer, was picked up, as was George Kane, the IRA commander for Sutton, Cheam and Ewell. At the Central Criminal Court, Peter Stuart, Charles Casey, Michael Mason (aka Cleary), Michael Preston, John Healy, Jane Lyons, Michael O'Shea and George Kane were all found guilty of bombing and conspiracy and given long sentences. Only one defendant, Joseph Walter, was acquitted. Trials continued throughout 1939.

The continuing detentions and trials were only a prelude to the IRA's biggest explosion. This occurred in the middle of the afternoon on 25 August in Broadgate, the shopping centre of Coventry, and it killed and injured scores of people. A tip-off, nevertheless, led Scotland Yard to the centre of the conspiracy, and a whole series of IRA operatives were arrested beginning with Peter Barnes, who lived in Westbourne Terrace in West London, and James Richards in Coventry. Unfortunately this proved a red herring as the actual bomber, a killer so psychotic that he was under treatment as late as the 1980s, had already escaped to Dublin. Although Barnes and Richards did not plant the bomb, outrage was sufficient to have them sentenced to death for their part in the action. 'Balloon' bombs exploded at Euston as a fanfare for doomed IRA youth as the two prepared for the scaffold.

Meanwhile, the IRA, hated in Britain and proscribed in Southern Ireland by the Offences Against the State Act, began negotiations with the Abwehr, Hitler's military intelligence. Sean Russell at General Headquarters had already began meetings with Eion Duffy (Oscar Pfaus) *before* the mainland bombing campaign had got fully under way and was content to take Nazi money and information in return for promises of help from the Germans who might find uses for extra agents as war approached. On 22 February 1940 and under cover of the blackout, the IRA exploded bombs at Marble Arch and in Oxford Street, killing and maiming soldiers as well as civilians.

This was the end of a long campaign for now. Such actions were becoming counterproductive. De Valéra had already declared Éire neutral and closed Irish ports to the British. Churchill, furious at being frustrated, had plans drawn up to invade Ireland. De Valéra, concerned not to let neutrality make Éire a safe home to Nazi spies and determined to finish with the IRA, began interning and imprisoning IRA activists. The IRA was considered simply a criminal gang and hunger strikers demanding political status were allowed to die. The IRA had become little more than a bunch of dangerous bandits. In the North, the newly created Royal Ulster Constabulary (RUC) rounded up the separate IRA command as German bombs devastated Belfast. In one raid alone half of Belfast was destroyed. The IRA's men and women still free in the North nevertheless killed B Specials (Ulster Special Constabulary) and RUC men when possible.

The hope that Nazism would help unite Ireland was as forlorn as Wolf Tone's expectations of speedy delivery at the hands of a French army almost 150 years before. German spies were not successful in Éire; most were picked up after they had secretly arrived via U-boat. In August 1940, Sean Russell was in Berlin negotiating guns, explosives and radio equipment with Foreign Minister, Joachim von Ribbentrop and Admiral Canaris, Head of the Abwehr. He was to return to Ireland via U-boat and left Wilhelmshaven on 8 August hopeful of prompt support. Somewhere on the journey he fell 'sick' (was shot or poisoned) and was buried (dropped overboard) at sea, a dangerous liability to a German High Command that could not afford to bring Éire into the Allied camp.

From the beginning of the 1950s to the late 1960s the IRA continued to lose support and was reduced to a rump of enthusiasts. Its desire for a united Ireland was muddied by internal wrangles between right-wing orthodox Catholics and their nationalist, socialist rivals. In 1962 Cahal Goulding became Chief of Staff and started a policy of creating a 'socialist' IRA, but his leadership proved weak and he started trading IRA arms to Welsh Nationalists. Meanwhile to counter the IRA a new force of Protestants appeared, the Ulster Volunteer Force (UVF), which took to the streets in 1966 and was named after the patriotic volunteer army that opposed Home Rule in 1912.

Things remained quiet until 1968 when a peace march in Derry was attacked by the RUC. At the same time a student organization called the People's Democracy marched in Derry, but at Burntollet Bridge they were attacked by the RUC and the police reserves (B Specials). The Burntollet March made it clear that the police and the Catholic community were enemies. In 1969 with things getting out of hand 500 soldiers were now posted to help the Irish garrison. The situation continued to degenerate and with the 'marching season' rioting flared again in Derry. On 12 August 1969 Apprentice Boys, Orangemen, RUC and B Specials fought in the street with Catholics defending the Bogside. The RUC used CS gas and armoured cars. On 14 August the army was called in to bring peace, but the peace the army brought to Derry was countered by the extreme violence that was brought to Belfast's Shankhill Road on the same day. B Specials and Protestant hooligans caused such devastation that next day, 'the Falls was a scene of devastation, with whole streets of burning homes. Hundreds of Catholic families, their belongings piled on handcarts, made their way to safety.'[13]

Even with the deployment of the army the situation continued to deteriorate. By now, however, they had a new hardline version of the IRA to deal with. These were the Provisionals, advocates of physical force and opponents of Dublin's Marxist version of nationalism led by Sean MacStiofain. They came into existence during January 1970. Along with the 'official' IRA they brought the campaign to Britain during the 1970s after the introduction of internment and the disastrous events of 'Bloody Sunday' on 30 January 1972 when the 1st Battalion of the Parachute Regiment opened fire, killing thirteen people.

This was clearly an attack that called for IRA revenge, and after due preparation at houses in Muswell Hill in North London and Holloway the bombers led by Seamus Costello were able to plant devices in the Parachute Regiment's barracks in Aldershot. The explosion mainly killed women kitchen staff. The perpetrators were all caught except Seamus Costello, who escaped only to be gunned down when he broke away from the IRA and started the Irish National Liberation Army (INLA). The campaign produced poor publicity for the IRA and they called a moratorium on British bombing and left the Provisionals to it.

Both the Provisionals and the official IRA had secret meetings with Edward Heath's ministers in 1972, but the situation did not improve and the Provisionals organized a cell to bomb targets in London. This group included two sisters, Dolours (sometimes Dolores) and Marion Price, who with the PLO's Leila Khaled and the Red Army Faction's Ulrike Meinhof seemed to confirm the belief that the most feared terrorists were the women. The group planted four car bombs on 8 March 1973. Two were defused but the others exploded, the one outside the Old Bailey injuring 180 people. Yet the group was not so efficient as to be able to escape and they were caught in various locations, including the departure lounge at Heathrow. When Commander Robert Huntley of the Anti-Terrorist Squad had mobilized his forces he had issued the order 'Close England' that had led to the downfall of the sisters and their colleagues. Once imprisoned the two sisters went on a 205-day hunger strike and Harold Wilson's government, fearful of martyrs, finally sent them to a less draconian prison. They were released in 1981. The use of the hunger strike and the use of faeces to cover cell walls by protesting prisoners did not appeal to Mrs Thatcher's sentiments. When Bobby Sands and nine of his colleagues tried the tactic again in 1980 and 1982 her government refused to intervene and instead let them die.

The Provisionals had lost a cell but regrouped again, and during 1973 and 1974 continued the war in England. (The Scots and Welsh were exempt as 'true' Celts, which did not prevent them from being killed in English towns.) Bombs exploded in the Midlands and at Chelsea Barracks and an incendiary was left at Harrods. Other bombs went off in Manchester, Birmingham and at the Tower of London and Westminster Hall. During the same year bombs blew apart public houses in Guildford (October), Woolwich (November) and Birmingham (November), killing over 20 people and leaving over 160 injured. Two groups of Irish men were arrested some time later. Both groups were given heavy sentences.

The British authorities knew they did not have their men but they also needed to restore confidence. Sir Michael Havers, the crown prosecutor in the Guildford Four trial, commented at the time, 'accusations of the most appalling kind have been made against the police during this trial. If true, there has been a really gigantic conspiracy . . . through officers of all ranks . . . if the allegations are true there has been a most appalling perversion of justice'.[14] His fears allayed and the two sets of conspirators' accusations of a police conspiracy dismissed as paranoid delusions, the cases concluded in the only possible way. It was not until many years later that the cases of the Birmingham Six and the Guildford Four were finally reviewed and the miscarriages of justice overturned.

The actual bombers, Henry (Harry) Duggan, Martin Joseph (Jo) O'Connell, Edward Butler and Hugh Doherty (or Docherty), were a dedicated and single-minded group of killers. The group moved to England, lived respectable lives in respectable neighbourhoods and made bombs. They were part of a supply network that linked London and Belfast to Amsterdam, Brussels, Italy, Lebanon and Spain. The 'Provos' dealt with the Palestine Liberation Organisation (PLO) and Euzkadi Ta Askatasuna (ETA) and used Italian terrorists in the Lotte Continua organisation in a worldwide and highly secretive terrorist web where violence and mistrust were endemic.

This dedicated group attempted to assassinate Edward Heath, but the bomb failed to explode. Nevertheless, they bombed and machine-gunned their way across London. From Crouch End and Stoke Newington they bombed Kensington Church Street, the Hilton and the Portman Hotel. They also targeted 'upmarket' restaurants in a class war, attacking Lockett's in Westminster and Scott's in Mayfair, which was bombed and later shot at. A second attempt on Heath failed but a murderous attack on Ross McWhirter, co-editor of the *Guinness Book of Records* and an avowed opponent of the IRA, did not. McWhirter had put a 'bounty' of £50,000 on the heads of the gang. Duggan said later, 'he placed a bounty on our heads. He asked to be killed' and so he was by Duggan at his Enfield home as he answered the door.

Disaster caught up with the gang as they 'shot up' Scott's in their second attack. The police by now had more men on the street and a number of unmarked armed patrols cruising London streets. The shots, from a Ford Cortina, were heard by police and a chase began with the gunmen's car pursued by unmarked police 'Q' cars. Deciding to abandon the car in Marylebone, the gang began a firefight in the street as they searched for cover. This they found at 22b Balcombe Street, where having burst in they took the owners, Jim and Sheila Matthews, hostage.

Police soon surrounded the building and Sir Robert Mark, the Commissioner, put Chief Superintendent Nigel Read of Enfield CID and Commander Roy Habershon of Scotland Yard's Bomb Squad in charge of the siege. Mark himself viewed the besieged men as 'vulgar criminals' and certainly not freedom fighters in a war of liberation. Nevertheless, an old armoured car owned by a local enthusiast was wheeled into place (it had no engine) as an added piece of cover. It was only after painstaking discussions conducted mainly with Chief Superintendent Peter Imbert (later Commissioner: 1987 to 1993) that the IRA men gave themselves up and freed their hostages. The operation had been a resounding success for the police who had previously brought another hostage crisis to a peaceful conclusion in the Spaghetti House siege, where a group calling itself the Black Liberation Front led by Franklyn (or Franklin) Davis had held Italian waiters hostage after a bungled wages snatch. In both sieges only one person had been slightly hurt, but the police triumph was also a judicial disaster, for although some of O'Connell's gang admitted to the bombings in Guildford and Birmingham their confessions were suppressed.

The loss of one active service unit still left plenty of operatives in place and with the Provisionals taking charge of the war in Britain a new group was soon formed. This was the 'England Department', with a core of dedicated men such as Patrick Magee, Gerald Tuite, Paul Kavanagh and Thomas Quigley. Across Britain small groups or 'sleepers' were available when needed.

The 1981 campaign targeted Chelsea Barracks and Sir Michael Havers QC, who had been leading counsel for the prosecution in the Guildford, Birmingham and Balcombe Street cases. The campaign started in the autumn so it was not until 1982 that operations began in earnest with Margaret Thatcher a priority for assassination. Meanwhile, on 20 July a massive explosion killed a mounted group of the Household Cavalry as they rode through Hyde Park. Two hours later, six bandsmen of the Royal Green Jackets were blown up as they played to civilians in deckchairs in Regent's Park. In December Harrods was the scene of further carnage with six people killed and nearly one hundred wounded. In 1984 Patrick Magee had an assassination mission to fulfil. Using a long timer fuse, he planted a bomb at the Grand Hotel, Brighton where Thatcher and her cabinet were staying during the Party Conference. The bomb exploded in the middle of the night of 12/13 October, and despite the intense heat of the subsequent fireball and the fact that the hotel was demolished, the Cabinet and Prime Minster survived. Magee was in Belfast when he saw his handiwork on the news. In September 1989, ten Royal Marine bandsmen were killed at their Deal Barracks and a bomb had killed at least one senior Conservative, Sir Ian Gow (in 1990).

By the 1990s the IRA squads who bombed Britain were more sophisticated in their methods than their predecessors and were able to hide their tracks amidst London's sprawl and bustle using safe houses, 'sleepers' and operatives who lived quiet suburban lives for years. The replacement of Margaret Thatcher by John Major robbed the IRA of the coup they hoped for but still left the possibility of hitting Downing Street with mortar bombs that might just kill one or two of the Cabinet. The chance came on 7 February 1991 when the War Cabinet met to discuss progress in the Gulf War. The Cabinet Office was filled with the most significant members of the Conservative Party from John Major to Douglas Hurd, Peter Lilley, Tom King and others as well as Chief of the Defence Staff, Sir Percy Craig, when missiles hurtled into the nearby garden and shattered Number 10's windows.*

---

*No. 10 Downing street is now part of a fortified block which it has been ever since Margaret Thatcher barred the approach to the building. The gates, which do not even give a glimpse of the house are now guarded by armed police. It was not always so. Originally, there had been three houses: a mansion, a townhouse and a cottage, but these were latter joined together. The townhouse was actually owned by Sir George Downing who combined landowning and spying for Oliver Cromwell and Charles II. The mansion or 'House at the back' was older, built in the 1530s, and was owned by Thomas Knevett who captured Guy Fawkes. For some time royalty lived in the house as did aristocrats such as George Monck, Duke of Albermarle, George Villiers, Duke of Buckingham and the Earl of Litchfield, but after 1720, the house again reverted to the Crown and was rebuilt. George II gifted the 'House at the back' to Sir Robert Walpole, his first minister, but Walpole did not want the expense of living there and the house became the temporary residence of any First Lord of the Treasury. It was Walpole who got the tenant of the cottage to move so that the buildings could be combined, being redesigned by William Kent. Walpole moved in in 1735, but his successors disliked the house and stayed away, although there were exceptions such as Lord North and Pitt the Younger. Nevertheless, it was not the prestigious residence it is today and was virtually abandoned after Pitt, the house being far less grand than the normal homes of statesmen. The area declined in the nineteenth century until the house was derelict and most of the rest of the street pulled down although

The home-made mortar launchers had been placed in an old white Ford Transit van and parked at the junction of Whitehall and Horse Guards Avenue. The missiles, inaccurate though they were, severely shocked the Prime Minster and proved again the impossibility of stopping determined people. Two weeks later bombs exploded at Victoria and Paddington Stations. By now the previous two decades' constant hoax calls and repeated closures of streets and stations were making life in London increasingly aggravating, although the sporadic stoppage of trade and transport often left Londoners merely bemused or resigned. Either way, the attacks *did not* undermine morale or cause mass disaffection because Oxford Street was shut yet again. Londoners remained firmly on the side of the police.

The attack on the financial heart of Britain was another matter and the enormous explosion on Friday 10 April 1992 that demolished the Baltic Exchange, a nearby medieval church and many other buildings, killing three and injuring ninety-one, was a blow that threatened the working of the City and capital itself. Another blast, this time at Bishopsgate on Sunday 24 April 1993, using a ton of high explosive, confirmed the danger to City finance and a 'ring of steel' consisting of roadblocks on major routes was put in place. The ring of steel was the first 'wall' to be built round London since Roman times and it remains in place into the twenty-first century. Needless to say, during the 1990s the IRA might simply have chosen other targets or have already penetrated the City defences so that the network of roadblocks proved as effective as the Maginot Line. Penetration of the roadblock system was also sure to make the police look stupid. Further bombs in 1993 were aimed outside the ring of steel, however, and culminated with a set of mortar bomb attacks at Heathrow.

By the early 1990s the Official and Provisional IRA and their enemies, the British army, MI5, MI6, RUC and UVF, had bombed, shot, gassed, petrol-bombed, assassinated and double-crossed their way into a standstill. Both sides were exhausted and under the pressure of the City financial institutions, the insurance companies and finally Bill Clinton the two sides began secret talks. Precarious though it was, John Major's gamble paid off and Sinn Fein/IRA, in the persons of Gerry Adams and Martin McGuinness, prepared to take their place in a devolved Northern Irish Parliament meeting at Stormont. The temporary breakdown of talks and the end of the IRA ceasefire, however, resulted yet again in a bomb attack. This time a massive

---

government buildings had grown around it. In 1877, Disraeli moved in, but Lord Salisbury disliked the place. It was Arthur Balfour who started to restore the house's fortunes, No. 10 becoming more associated with the residence of the prime minister through its media appearances during the twentieth century.

explosion on 9 February 1996 destroyed an office block in Docklands and killed a newsagent and a passer-by, Inam Bashir and John Jeffries. Four years later, one of the bombers, James McAndle, was released by Tony Blair as a goodwill gesture towards further peace, a move that caused consternation amongst his victim's families.

The inclusion of Sinn Fein (the political party of which the IRA is the military wing) in legitimate Northern Irish politics was a particular if ironic coup for British ministers, who had put limited power into Sinn Fein's hands without the loss of one inch of Ulster territory. Suspicious, the IRA kept its guns hidden as Sinn Fein took its seats at the Assembly. For others this was nothing but a sell out. A splinter group called the Real IRA again took the war to the streets. First there was a massive and deadly explosion in Omagh on 15 August 1998 and then the beginnings of a campaign in London. In early summer 2000 an explosion damaged girders on Hammersmith Bridge. Then, on the night of Wednesday 20 September, an audacious rocket attack was targeted on MI6's headquarters near the Albert Embankment. Little damage was done to the building but considerable proof was offered of the power of the Real IRA to continue a campaign in London. In 2001 some of the worst riots in Irish history broke out during the Protestant marching season with rioters using 'blast' and petrol bombs. On Thursday 2 August 2001 a grey Saab car liquefied in a ball of flame in Ealing High Street. The never-ending war with the Irish extremists entered yet another bloody phase. This time it did not disrupt the fragile peace that was now enjoyed in Ulster and on the streets of London.

13
Women Behaving Badly

The Suffragettes

Of all the political movements of the early twentieth century it was the fight for women's suffrage that proved the most unnecessarily unpleasant and bitter, revealing, as it did, that the Edwardian sense of a civilized society hid the fact that imprisoning and torturing women with force-feeding was a necessary adjunct to good manners. It was a fight that brought stones and broken windows to Horse Guards and Whitehall, that caused chaos in Mayfair and Piccadilly and took reform to the very chambers of the Houses of Parliament in a revival of the revolutionary fervour of the London women of the seventeenth century.

The fight to *regain* women's suffrage (some wealthy women could vote before the Civil War, a right later withdrawn) began, however, in Manchester during the nineteenth century. The first suffrage society was founded in 1865 and hoped to succeed in putting through legislation as part of the 1866 Electoral Reform Bill.* The attempt failed but the fight was continued by women such as Millicent Fawcett, Flora Stevenson and Lydia Becker. It was, however, Dr Richard Pankhurst who successfully gained the municipal vote for women in 1869 and pioneered the Married Women's Property Act in 1882. In 1879 he married Emmeline Goulden and they went on to have two sons, and three daughters: Christabel, Sylvia and Adela.

The family was thoroughly political and soon Emmeline and her daughters were involved with suffrage agitation. In 1903 the daughters and their mother founded the Women's Social and Political

---

*From 1867 to 1905 women's suffrage was debated eighteen times in the House of Commons. Three of the Bills, Bright's (1870), Begg's (1897) and MacLaren's (1904), even got to a second reading. Twenty-seven Bills were debated between 1906 and 1914 but only five gained a second reading. There were also two Resolutions and over 900 parliamentary questions on the subject. (See especially Marian Ramelson, *The Petticoat Rebellion* (London, Lawrence & Wishart, 1967), p. 162.)

Union (WSPU), the most militant of the many suffrage groups. Most of the WSPU members were also members of Keir Hardie's Independent Labour Party (ILP), which proved a source both of strength and friction as women's suffrage was not always comparable with working men's rights or the fight for better wages and conditions.

Trouble for the WSPU began almost immediately when, in 1904, a debate in the House 'talked out' the reintroduction of the 1866 clause (proposed by the ILP). A women's lobby group was pushed and shoved by police outside Parliament and police took the names of WSPU supporters. In Manchester, Christabel and her friend Annie Kenney, a strong-minded and highly intelligent working-class mill hand from Oldham, went off to barrack a Liberal Party rally and unfurl a banner declaring 'Votes for Women'. Christabel had already decided passive protest was useless and she engineered her arrest by pretending to spit at the policeman who had grappled her to the ground when taken outside the hall. This was a new world where nice middle-class 'gels' spat a policeman who manhandled them, pushed them and arrested them. The 'angel of the house' was now a devil.

It was also first round of a long and of vicious battle between suffragettes and the Liberal Party, whose spokesmen and leaders became the target of women's wrath – Winston Churchill (a Liberal until 1923) was regularly heckled at his meetings for his opposition to the women's vote – and with the victory of the Liberals at the general election of 1905, women and socialists made common cause. Annie Kenney was sent to London by the WSPU to 'rouse' the capital and she lodged with Sylvia Pankhurst in Chelsea. Here she met socialists such as Will Crooks, Dora Montefiore and George Lansbury. Thus the suffragists (renamed by the *Daily Mail* as the suffragettes) and socialists held a meeting in Caxton Hall and marched (illegally) on Parliament at its opening on 19 February 1906. It was to be the launch of militant suffragette activity in London.

Accompanied by new members such as Emmeline Pethick Lawrence and her husband, the WSPU organized a deputation to Downing Street.

> 'Freedom for English women!' called Irene Miller, banging on the door [of number 10]. Annie jumped onto the step of the Premier's car which stood in front of the house and began to address the crowd. While police struggled with Irene Miller on the door step, Mrs Drummond pulled at the little brass knob in the centre of the door and to her amazement the door flew open. She rushed inside, but was hastily shown out again. Soon all three ringleaders were arrested and taken off to Cannon Row Police Station.[1]

George Bernard Shaw, with more bravado than sense, suggested that women should have a revolution. They 'should shoot, kill, maim, destroy until they are given the vote'. Rioting in the Ladies' Gallery of the Commons proved too much for more conservative suffrage groups, however, and they distanced themselves from the WSPU from then on.

Meanwhile, the WSPU itself was changing character. Its upper middle-class leadership was now broadening out to include a large working-class *unionized* women's membership, as another march on 19 May demonstrated.

> Members of trades' organisations and Suffagette groups from all over the country had arrived to march in procession with their delegates. Women weavers, winders, reelers, shirtmakers, chair-makers, iron-workers, cigar-makers, book binders, college gradu-ates and pit-brow women all stood waiting in ranks. A group of mill girls were conspicuous in their clogs and shawls.[2]

By now the pattern of future events had begun to become clear: marches, protests and outrages followed by violent arrest, harsh sentencing and seriously brutal prison treatment. It also took on a sense of class division: a march to Herbert Asquith's house in which the usual arrests were made was marked by a policeman pointedly telling Annie Kenney that she 'knew jolly well Mr. Asquith would not see a person like her'.

Emily Emmeline Pethick Lawrence recalled at Kenney's trial,

> The three prisoners presented a sorry spectacle. All were working women and poorly dressed. Apart from her flaming eyes, Annie Kenney looked an ordinary north-country mill girl, Mrs Sparboro was the wife of an Italian workman resident in east London and Mrs Knight was lame and insignificant.[3]

The women were sentenced to six weeks in Holloway. Such sentences began quite lightly with suffragette women finding themselves in the relative comfort of 'the first division' (akin to open prison) but as the years went by the sentences became harsher and the women were increasingly criminalized rather than being treated as only 'technical' criminals for their political beliefs.

In 1906 the movement gained a headquarters, situated at 4 Clement's Inn, from where it made its banners, printed its propaganda and dealt with the press until 1908. The Pethick Lawrences became the organizational dynamos behind the office whilst poor Mrs Sparboro was reduced to the office 'tea lady'. At the same time the WSPU split over its relationship with the Labour movement. Emmeline and Christabel Pankhurst, disillusioned with Keir Hardie and the ILP, broke from Labour whilst Sylvia and Adela kept a socialist line. This would bring conflict to the Labour Party itself and cause considerable conflict where suffragettes and working men saw their causes as opposed.

Meetings at Hyde Park and elsewhere were now continuously closed down and the speakers arrested. These were upper middle-class women unused to rough handling. Mrs Pethick Lawrence felt her 'heart die within [her]' as she entered Holloway and Mrs Montefiore had a nervous breakdown. Marching and petitioning became an almost continuous habit of both the WPSU and the 'constitutional' suffrage leaders of the National Union of Women's Suffrage Societies (NUWSS), which formed later. With the Women's Enfranchisement Bill coming up for debate on 19 March 1906, pressure increased. From Caxton Hall, where the 'Women's Parliament' was meeting, Christabel organized groups of women, many working-class north-erners who had arrived by train, to go and try and break through police and enter the chamber of the House of Commons. 'Seize the mace and you will be the Cromwells of the twentieth century,' she proclaimed to those whose assaults would end in inevitable arrest. After continuous agitation fifty-three suffragettes from the WPSU and NUWSS were sent to Holloway. 'Holloway is full up', commented the *Daily Mirror*. The unofficial opposition was also growing and women's meetings were attacked or broken up by groups of youths or middle-class rowdies. The Bill did not even get to a vote – it was talked out by the Opposition.

1907 was a year of reorganization and reconsideration. The year was devoted to literary propaganda rather than marches or assaults and the creation of a publicity department in the Women's Press. By the end of the year, a lobby group fighting for a place for women in the political system had transformed itself into a full political party with its own organizational machinery. They were also used to their opponents in the Liberal Party using their fists to make their point, as Mrs Pankhurst found out when she was beaten up at Newton Abbot in 1908.

Suffragettes meanwhile enjoyed aggravating the Cabinet by chain-ing themselves to the railings of 10 Downing Street, as Edith New and Olivia Smith did in January 1908. To the *Daily Mirror*, New and Smith were 'naughty' suffragettes. It continued,

> These are new WSPU tactics. Among the methods which the Suffrage Movement has so far introduced into political war fare are: Bell ringing – door knocking – police court protests – voluntary imprisonment – chain and padlock tableaux – systematic minister baiting – the pantechnicon – megaphone and taxi appeal.[4]

Votes for Women poster, Hyde Park rally

Suffragette pressure began to tell when a by-election at Peckham ended with the Liberal candidate's defeat after women speakers had saturated the area. Churchill testily remarked that Peckham was a 'capricious little London slum'.

In the summer of 1908 the suffrage movement held a great meeting in Hyde Park. Despite scuffles, 50,000 people (half a million claimed) listened to a variety of suffrage speakers. Then on 9 October, the Pankhursts held a meeting in Trafalgar Square in preparation for the introduction of another women's suffrage bill. The leaflets called for women to 'rush' the House of Commons on 13 October. After the event arrests were swift and sentencing brutal. Throughout 1909 agitation was followed by arrest and imprisonment. Meanwhile, the WSPU and other groups were not prepared to allow themselves to be picked off on marches and a self-defence group was formed around volunteers from Edith Garrud's ju-jitsu classes whilst a sabotage group of 'Young Hot Bloods' was created by Mary Home.

The frustrations of the previous year became the violence of 1909. An extraordinary volume of meetings (1,000 a month nationwide) had resulted in no change of government policy and a hardening of attitudes towards protesters. The demonstrators too were at the end of their tether and on the evening of 29 June parties were sent out from Caxton Hall with bags of stones to break the windows of the government buildings in Whitehall whilst others went on their usual fruitless pilgrimage to lobby Parliament. One volunteer stone thrower recalled, 'To women of culture and refinement and of sheltered upbringing the deliberate throwing of a stone, even as a protest, in order to break a window, requires an enormous amount of moral courage.'[5]

That night alone 108 arrests were made. Asquith, attacked by stone throwers in his own home in Kent, was now protected by Special

Branch and detectives on the lookout for bombs. Christabel declared, 'This is war.' Forcible feeding was again added to the miseries of prison life. Keir Hardie, having asked a parliamentary question about the process, was 'horrified at the levity displayed by a large section of the Members of the House. Had [he] not heard it, [he] could not have believed that a body of gentlemen could have found reason for mirth and applause in a scene which . . . has no parallel in . . . recent history.'[6] When asked in America about her imprisonment, Mrs Pankhurst replied laconically, 'I am what you call a hooligan.'

In 1910 Herbert Gladstone was replaced as Home Secretary by Winston Churchill. Elevated to the peerage, Gladstone became Governor General of South Africa. The imperial mentality, far from benevolent, was revealed in its dealings with the suffragettes as brutalist and violent. For all intents and purposes, women *were* colonial subjects and would be treated as such if they got 'uppity'. One Liverpool doctor involved with forced feeding 'slapped' women in his care to prove the point.

Other 'hooligans' also made their voice heard when, during the National Anthem at the Lord Mayor's Banquet (10 November 1909), Amelia Brown and Alice Paul smashed panes of stained glass and shouted 'Votes for Women' until wrestled from the nearby staircase. Nothing had resolved itself a year later when Parliament was to reassemble during November.

On 18 November, suffragettes again made their way to Caxton Hall and prepared to march on Westminster, some wearing white satin badges which marked them out for more dangerous volunteer duty. After speeches, Emmeline Pankhurst, Elizabeth Garrett Anderson, the eminent doctor, her daughter, Hertha Ayrton, an eminent scientist, Princess Sophia Duleep Singh and Mrs Brackenbury and Miss Neligan, two leaders now in their seventies, as well as other leading women of the WSPU, led a determined body of women towards Whitehall to hand in a petition. An equally determined police force under Churchill awaited their arrival. Ayrton recalled,

> Before any of us could get into the House, we had to run the gauntlet of organised gangs of policemen in plain clothes, dressed like roughs, who nearly squeezed the breath out of our bodies, the policemen in official clothes helping them . . . I nearly fainted . . . [one protester] was seized by the breasts and thrown down. Women were thrown from policemen in uniform to policemen in plain clothes literally until they fainted.[7]

Pandemonium now broke out as women struggled with police who were determined to put paid to their aggravating inability to give up. As the police were under orders to bar the way to Parliament, the provocation provided by the demonstrators (who quite happily attacked government property) would have to be met with equal force. Nevertheless, the police were frustrated and taunted and soon casualties were returning to the Caxton Hall as others sallied out. Ada Wright remembered the day's proceedings too.

> When we reached Parliament Square, plain-clothes men . . . kicked us, and added to the horror and anguish of the day by dragging some of the women down side streets. There were many attempts of indecent assault. The police rode at us with shire horses . . . a policemen grabbed my arm and twisted it round and round until I felt the bone almost breaking and I sank to the pavement, helpless . . . Each time I got up, and once more made a show of advancing to the House of Commons only to be thrown to the ground once again . . . As I leaned against the railings after one of these episodes, a sense of the humiliation I was undergoing came over me . . . I said to myself with a shudder: 'What a sordid day.' The next morning I found I had been photographed lying on the ground . . . and the photograph occupied the front page of the *Daily Mirror* . . . There were headlines: BLACK FRIDAY.[8]

The horror felt at their abusive handling was also felt by male sympathizers. At this time the Men's Political Union (MPU), a Liberal lobby group, joined the fight and opposed their own party. One member of the MPU, Hugh Franklin, even attempted to horsewhip Churchill as he travelled on a London-bound express train. Agitation and occasional violence continued, to little effect, throughout 1910.

1911 saw a re-elected Liberal government but with a tiny majority, thus increasing constitutional pressure for a widened franchise. A new Conciliation Bill passed a second reading in May under the impetus of a new alliance of suffrage groups, the National Union of Women's Suffrage Societies (NUWSS), but to everybody's astonishment Asquith, again Prime Minister, brought in a *Manhood* Suffrage Bill and refused to countenance women's inclusion. The women again took up their stones.

Window-smashing expeditions were now organized in Oxford Street, Piccadilly and Tottenham Court Road. When chased, the offenders would scuttle back to Garrud's ju-jitsu school, hide their weapons and pretend to be participating in a class!

Police raids on Clement's Inn and arrests of most of the WSPU meant that the organization had to be flexible and organic, each arrested women passing on her responsibility to those outside jail. By now a number of medical figures were even trying to prove that women were physiologically predetermined towards mental instability and therefore biologically unsuited to the vote. Mental torture was, however, a regular occurrence for a number of suffragette prisoners who had determined to go on hunger strike. Force-feeding (a tube forced down the throat and into the stomach) was now such a scandal that people as diverse as Marie Curie and Upton Sinclair were protesting from abroad, whilst George Lansbury had actually accused Asquith of being a murderer and torturer. The scandal of imprisonment was exacerbated by the new 'Cat and Mouse Act' of 1913, which released women who became dangerously ill in prison on a 'ticket of leave' system but which also allowed for immediate rearrest once the woman recovered and was deemed to have re-offended. The system was abusive, cynical and bypassed normal procedures. It also allowed for constant surveillance and meant women could be reimprisoned at a moment's notice.

During 1912 and 1913, the militants of the WSPU stepped up their campaign, which included window-breaking raids, postbox arson and burning down (or attempting to burn down) a variety of government buildings (and the occasional cricket pavilion). Events again came to a head when a plucky head tailoress decided to make her mark. Leonora Cohen had travelled to London from Leeds, a representative of the Leeds tailoresses. She stayed in London a week wondering how to do 'her bit' and came up with an ingenious and scandalous scheme: to attack the Crown Jewels.

> I pondered the matter very carefully, went out and bought a guide of the area giving the places of interest – museums, art galleries, etc. I then decided I would go to the Tower of London, remembering Colonel Blood, who once tried to steal the Crown Jewels. My hostess was much against the idea, but I was determined. Having no missile, I took out a bar from a grate, filed it down, packed it in a small parcel and started out for the Tower.[9]

Arrested by two Beefeaters (an occurrence not usually in their line) Cohen was duly charged and jailed.

She was luckier than Mrs Pankhurst, who soon found herself looking at three years' imprisonment (with suggestions that she be deported to St Helena!). Such a sentence would kill her and her supporters knew it. As she was sentenced on 3 April 1913 at the Old Bailey her supporters sang the 'Marseillaise'. Those not imprisoned now started a new arson and bombing campaign which included all sorts of wrecking and destructive expeditions. No one was injured or killed, however, despite the destruction of property, which the suffragettes had decided was the key to attacking the property-owning class where it hurt them most. On the whole, the women activists had been the main victims of their campaigns, this being nowhere more obvious than when Emily Wilding Davison, exasperated at the lack of progress made by the cause, threw herself under the hooves of the King's horse at Epsom Races and was fatally wounded. Her funeral was accompanied by the arrest of a number of leading suffragettes and the editors of the *Suffragette* itself on charges of conspiracy. They were to be treated as common criminals and once sentenced were hurried to a variety of prisons where bromide was used to keep prisoners docile.

As 1913 turned autumnal, the suffragettes marched and organized afresh. Emmeline was back in prison, having been arrested yet again on her return from America and France (where she visited Christabel), and Sylvia was now ensconced in a new headquarters in Bow, having split from the Pethick Lawrences, her mother, sister and main group of the WSPU. Sylvia moved towards a more left-wing position (many suffragettes were conservative and patriotic), seeing the fight for women's suffrage as part of a wider remit to help the poor. She later helped found the Communist Party of Great Britain (CPGB). From the East End she led working-class women to Trafalgar Square and Downing Street. At Bow Baths she once had to jump from the stage into the crowd to avoid arrest. Lansbury's sons had helped her to escape once before hidden in a cartload of firewood. She was arrested, starved, released, rearrested.

Thus things continued into 1914. Mrs Pankhurst was now on her ninth hunger strike and every letterbox, government building and cabinet minister's home was under threat. Even Buckingham Palace had become a legitimate target, and on a pleasant afternoon the undaunted WSPU, some in disguise, some wan with hunger and fatigue, others fresh from trains from Preston or from Leeds, Manchester and cities and towns across Britain, gathered to show defiance before the monarchy itself. Around the pale figure of Mrs Pankhurst was the newly formed 'bodyguard'. Yet the police broke up their opponents despite the bodyguards' use of Indian clubs, the women's tactic of cutting the police horses' bridles and the rain of cricket balls and stones that were flung at windows and assailants. 'King's Thursday' proved another costly failure and police now began to raid houses for caches of stones brought to London in heavy suitcases from Brighton and Southend.

The summer activities of the WSPU were abruptly curtailed when war was declared on Germany. On 10 August Mrs Pankhurst issued orders to suspend action for the duration. Almost at the war's end, on 11 January 1918, women secured the vote for all over thirty. On 14 June 1928, as the royal assent was given to the Act giving equal voting rights to men and women over twenty-one, Mrs Pankhurst died. Sylvia had already found Communism within which to continue the struggle and Christabel had found religion.

The national suffragette movement could not have been sustained without the support of its local branches who supplied the activists and militants for 'the cause'. This is especially true of South London, where there were branches in Lewisham, Woolwich, Blackheath and Greenwich. The WSPU held meetings at Catford Town Terminus, on Blackheath Common, at Deptford Broadway, Plumstead Common and Beresford Square as well as propagandized by talking on street corners, handing leaflets to football supporters, selling their newspapers and marching on Parliament. Across the area they were often opposed by 'roughs', by medical students (of which more below) and Labour Party supporters who saw them as middle-class 'Conservatives' playing with working-class sympathy. To all this activity must be added non-WSPU societies such as the London Society for Women's Suffrage, Lewisham Women's Franchise Club, the Church League for Women's Suffrage and the Free Church League for Women's Suffrage. Although all were part of a general association by 1914, many women in these clubs were opposed to the militant tactics of the WSPU or to the nascent socialism of leaders such as Sylvia Pankhurst.

In Lewisham as elsewhere, the WSPU held large outdoor meetings, often attracting 2,000 or 3,000 people. One meeting on Blackheath was said to have attracted 6,000 and certainly by 1914 the papers could speak of three parties: Conservatives, Liberals and Suffragettes! Nevertheless, suffragette rallies were lively affairs and heckling and abuse quite common. Both Edith New and Christabel Pankhurst were able by wit and intelligence to counter intrusive hecklers although invasion of the podium by medical students, 'rowdies' and socialists might lead to scuffles and disruption. In 1912 Sylvia Pankhurst was physically assaulted and knocked down by Guy's Hospital students on Blackheath, although this diverted attention from other speakers who were left in peace. Violence also flared at Catford Tram Terminus in 1913 when police got the suffragettes to abandon their meeting and retreat on a bus.[10] The crowd had already started shouting that Mrs Pankhurst (then in prison) should die and that the women should be 'whipped and boiled'. The suffragettes were equally happy, however, to disrupt their opponents' political meetings. Often these were Labour Party meetings, because the socialists were accused of abandoning women's suffrage in their alliance with the Liberals who were imprisoning and force-feeding activists. During March 1913 a very violent scuffle at a Labour meeting ended with one woman being held down and repeatedly punched in the face and another having her face cut open. In fact, in 1913 the WSPU had decided to break up local Labour Party meetings as a matter of policy.

Other militant tactics were also adopted by the local branches and by individuals willing to carry on one-woman campaigns: Edith New received two months for stone throwing at Downing Street in 1908, the latest of a number of sentences she had received for public disorder; Eugenia Bouvier, a Russian émigré, broke windows of government buildings in 1909; in 1911 Mrs Aldham received her third prison sentence for window breaking and later damaged a picture in the Royal Academy; chalking and graffiti campaigns were common across the area throughout; in 1913 St Alfego's Church in Greenwich had a service disrupted by banner-waving women; in January 1914 the activists undertook an arson attack on a cricket pavilion and in both 1913 and 1914 set fire to Dulwich College. The destruction of St Catherine's Church on Telegraph Hill was also laid at the door of the suffragette arsonists.

The most remarkable of all these local women was May Billinghurst, who participated fully in all the suffragette activities but also carried on her own one-woman 'terror' campaign even though her legs were paralysed and she was confined to a crude tricycle wheelchair. Her speciality was pillar-box 'outrage'. This consisted of blowing up pillar boxes, setting fire to letters or spoiling letters. Miss Billinghurst was an expert. She would pull up to a box, purple and green streamers attached to her 'bath chair', and deposit leaking parcels of brown sticky glue, molasses and oil (it was not clear what the ingredients were) into the pile of letters. If she was spotted, the woman who pushed her would do the deed once suspicion had become centred on the occupant of the wheelchair. When she died in 1953, a fellow activist recalled:

> She was responsible for many of the letters which were damaged in pillar-boxes. Of course, she was caught – so blatantly did she go about it, it could hardly have been otherwise, but perhaps that very blatancy enabled her to do much damage before she was suspected. She would set out in her chair with many little packages from which, when they were turned upside down, there flowed a dark brown sticky fluid . . . She went undeviatingly from one pillar-box to another, sometimes alone, sometimes with another suffragette to do the actual job, dropping a package into each one.[11]

Despite her severe handicap, May used her tricycle to charge police lines and cause trouble. On 'Black Friday' 1910 she was treated with extraordinary barbarity by the police when arrested outside Parliament.

> At first the police threw me out of the machine on to the ground in a very brutal manner. Secondly, when on the machine again, they tried to push me along with my arms twisted behind me in a very painful position . . . Thirdly, they took me down a side road and left me in the middle of a hooligan crowd, first taking all the valves out of the wheels and pocketing them so that I could not move the machine . . .[12]

Arrested and sentenced in South London to a period in Holloway Prison (in North London), she complained of the fact she had no means to take herself to jail

> unless a policeman pushed her chair all the way, so one was detailed for the job. On the journey she saw that she was passing a friend's house so she asked him if he would mind waiting whilst she called on the friend. He agreed and she went inside leaving him on the pavement in charge of the chair, until she came out twenty minutes or so later. Further on they found themselves passing the abode of an acquaintance of the policeman's – I have a suspicion that it was a public house but surely he would not drink on duty! – and he said to her: 'Look here, Miss, I did you a favour. Will you do me one? Wait outside here until I come back.' This she did but eventually they reached Holloway, where, of course, she went on hunger strike.

Once on hunger strike, she was force fed which resulted in

> the most awful torture. I coughed and gulped . . . would not let the tube pass down my throat . . . tried the other nostril . . . too small . . . jammed it down again. I could see tears in the war-dresses eyes . . . then they gagged my mouth open . . . the doctor jammed a pair of iron fingers between my clenched teeth and chipped a piece of my tooth . . .[13]

May Billinghurst was not dismayed by her harsh treatment and continued to work for the women's movement into the 1950s, joining the Women's Suffrage League, the Suffragette Fellowship and offering cash aid to the Equal Pay Film Fund.

The suffragettes were not just interested in demanding political enfranchisement. They concerned themselves with all levels of women's lives and interests. Most significant of all was education around women's health issues and those of sexual ethics. In Lewisham there was a Women's Health Society, and suffragettes in Woolwich who had affiliated to the Labour branch had begun to meet as a separate caucus to discuss health and other issues during 1908. Moreover, women read pamphlets about explicitly sexual matters: Christabel Pankhurst's *The Great Scourge*, a pamphlet about the problem of venereal disease, was widely debated, and in 1914 Lewisham walls and hoardings openly advertised it. Health issues almost immediately made suffragettes the target of male medical students jealous of their expertise and paranoid about any attack on their privileged status. The war between emancipators and students reached its climax during 1907 and it was all over a small bronze statue of a dog in Latchmere Recreation Ground, Battersea, the radical working-class borough upriver from Lewisham.

The attack of the statue and the subsequent Brown Dog Riots, as they came to be called, centred on the ethics of animal experimentation and its value to research. Battersea itself was the home of the old hospital the 'Anti', whose doctors did not perform vivisection, which was much loved by locals but also considered hopelessly old-fashioned by the medical profession. Battersea Dogs' Home was also in the borough and when approached for dogs for experimentation flatly refused cooperation. Allied to the 'moral' radicalism of the borough inhabitants and institutions was a strong political sensibility. The whole area had grown from just over 6,000 inhabitants in 1841 to 168,000 by 1901; factories had sprouted on once green hills and replaced the older cottages, whilst Nine Elms had been reduced to one of the poorest areas in London.

Nevertheless, there were enclaves of professionals around Battersea Rise to Clapham Common, and although somewhat genteel, the better areas could also look to a tradition of anti-slavery evangelism. The radical council saw itself as the most 'democratic' in Britain and boasted of its programme of building housing estates and amenities. It also elected Britain's first black mayor, the Pan-African John Archer in 1913. In 1922 Battersea North was the first constituency to elect an Asian as a Labour Member of Parliament. Shapurji Saklatvala's campaign was run by Archer (for Saklatvala's story see pp. 368–70). The Liberal MP for Battersea from 1892, John Burns, had led London dock workers to victory in their strike of August 1889 to raise their hourly rate from 5d to 6d, 'the full round orb of the docker's tanner', in which he was supported by the Battersea gas workers, whose own strike for shorter working hours had been successful in the spring. In 1902, the borough council in effect acted treasonably by refusing to sign the loyal address to Edward VII. Under Labour and trade council control it also refused to accept a donation for a library from Andrew Carnegie, who was considered 'tainted with the blood of Pittsburgh striker'.[14]

And so to the cause of the riots: one small statue of a dog erected in a local recreation ground. The immediate cause was the publication of an anti-vivisection book called *The Shambles of Science*, a transcription of the diaries of two physiology students at University College. The students in question, Louise Lind-af-Hageby and Liese Schartau, had enrolled in order to expose the cruel practices of the physiology laboratory and especially the use of improperly anaesthetized animals. The experiment on an improperly prepared brown dog by Professor William Bayliss had been performed whilst the dog was fully conscious and struggling. As with women's franchise so too with anti-vivisection – one group was in favour of gradualism, another for a single piece of legislation which would ban animal experimentation once and for all. Backed by Stephen Coleridge of the radical National Anti-vivisection Society, the publication of the diaries would serve not only to alert the public but also to bring a court case against Bayliss for breaking the 1876 Act relating to cruelty to animals. Bayliss would, of course, counter-sue and thereby bring more publicity and opprobrium. Bayliss duly did so, won £2,000 damages and thus started a war between the suffragettes, Socialists and the world of medicine.

The death of the anonymous dog at the hands of a system both cruel and contemptuous of public opinion seemed to symbolize the casual indifference of the establishment to women and the working class. Against the hopeless gradualism of the Liberal radicals, the leaders of the Social Democratic Federation (SDF) and the militant suffragettes demanded immediate legislation which alleviated the poverty caused by capital, the political exclusion caused by men and the cruelty practised on animals. The brown dog crystallized opinion and defined a clear enemy – the male students of the medical profession, young privileged 'hooligans' with the power given them of life and death. Indeed *The Times* actively called Bayliss's victory 'medical hooliganism' and the *Daily News* opened a subscription fund to pay the damages he had won. Hopelessly mixed up with the betrayal of the brown dog was the 'betrayal' of the working class by Battersea's hero, John Burns (elected on an ILP ticket), when he became a minister in the Liberal government, having been elected for Battersea without the need of support from either his union or from the more radical groups in the area.

A number of militant WSPU suffragettes, including Charlotte Despard (sister of General Sir John French), lived amongst the poor of Nine Elms and they joined with non-violent suffragettes who were also anti-vivisectionists, people like Louise Woodward of the Church Anti-Vivisection League. Together with Louise Lind-af-Hageby they presented Battersea Council with a drinking fountain topped by the statue of the dead dog. It was inscribed:

> In memory of the Brown Terrier Dog done to Death in the Laboratories of University College in February 1903, after having endured Vivisection extending over more than Two Months and having been handed over from one Vivisector to Another Till Death came to his Release. Also in Memory of the 232 dogs Vivisected at the same place during 1902. Men and women of England, how long shall these Things be?

The memorial was duly unveiled on 15 September 1906 before a crowd which included George Bernard Shaw. The University of

London on behalf of University College threatened legal action. Battersea Council told them to 'mind their own business'. The erection of the statue in a recreation ground facing new council houses was intended by the Mayor, J. H. Brown, to emphasize the link to the council's own action on behalf of the working classes. Things would not remain calm, however, once 'The Anti' found itself under threat from a new government act.

> In Battersea the Socialists were still complaining about John Burns and threatening to run their own candidate against him in the next elections. They were joined by the antivaccinationists, who were outraged when Burns voted in favour of the Vaccination Act, which made inoculation a condition of employment in government service. 'The Old Anti' had always served the working folk of Battersea, but now abruptly it was refused funds from the Metropolitan Hospital Sunday Fund. The Battersea Council saw John Burns's influence at work here and organised carnivals to raise money for the hospital and what it stood for – an institution where every doctor was pledged not to engage in any form of vivisection.[15]

Thirty University College medical students, under the leadership of a young tyro named William Lister, sallied across the Thames and attacked the monument on 20 November 1907. Unfortunately, the night was exceptionally foggy and after one blow with a sledgehammer the students were arrested by plainclothes policemen lurking in the vicinity. Council house tenants also helped arrest their dismayed opponents, who were finally bound over with a threat of hard labour if they were caught again. Medical students were now routinely attacking suffrage meetings, including those held by gradualist agitators, such as Millicent Fawcett (sister of Elizabeth Garrett Anderson) who did *not* disapprove of vivisection. Lister and his chums attacked the statue again and found themselves counterattacked by locals. On 10 December Lister and his followers marched to Trafalgar Square shouting, 'Down with the Brown Dog.' Beaten by police, they returned to attack Battersea again where they were beaten by the locals once more; forced to seek aid at the 'Anti', they found the doors barred. When Louise Lind-af-Hageby addressed an anti-vivisection meeting at Acton Central Hall on 16 December 1907 she needed a guard of Battersea workers but fighting still broke out when a hundred students got in.

By this time the police were fed up with the time spent defending the statue and they asked Battersea to foot the bill. Its new Mayor, Fred Worthey, a temperance Congregationalist and anti-vivisectionist, bluntly told the Commissioner to make his officers do the job the police were paid to do. The Council, in no mood to compromise, recorded:

> That the inscription on the memorial being founded on ascertained facts, the Council declines to sanction the proposal to remove it, and that the Chief Commissioner of Police be informed in reply to his letter that the care and protection of public monuments is a matter for the police and any expense occasioned thereby should be defrayed out of the public rate to which this Borough contributes so largely; also that the Council considers more strenuous efforts should be made to suppress any renewal of the organised ruffianism which has recently taken place in the Metropolis in connection with the Memorial.[16]

But time had run out. In February 1908 the Municipal Reformers under Sir Herbert Jessel gained control of the London County Council, the Progressives had had their slogans appropriated and lost. Battersea also went to the Reformers. The 'Anti' was closed for 'neglecting its patients' and on 10 March 1910 the little statue was taken away by council workers protected by 120 police, hidden in a bicycle shed and finally broken up. For the Reformers the little drinking fountain had come to represent the worst excesses of a socialist council pouring money into the pockets of 'wastrels and loafers'.

The affair of the Brown Dog was a strange one, in which the normally hostile trade union movement united with its arch-rivals, the suffragettes, to fight aggression by class enemies; the working class, accused by the Royal Society for the Prevention of Cruelty to Animals of cruelty to their animals, nevertheless stood by anti-vivisection and stood by their hospital – the 'Anti'. Causes blurred and coalesced.

Women's suffrage had very little in common with anti-vivisection, but the two had become confusedly entwined through the accident of circumstance: the image of the vivisected dog blurred and became one with the militant suffragette being force-fed in Holloway Prison.

14
Huns and Hashish
The Yellow Peril to the German Pogrom

The First World War put a temporary halt to the demands for women's suffrage, but it gave rise to other previously unconsidered and darker fears shared by suffragettes and opponents alike. From all sides the empire appeared to be under threat. It was in London, centre of imperial might, that these fears crystallized around two quite different immigrant groups who were now the target of Londoners' deepest suspicions: the Chinese and the Germans.

The Chinese population of London, small and ever discrete, did not start to settle until the middle of the nineteenth century, when British and American merchant shipping began to create major trade routes to the Pacific and South China Sea. Even so, only seventy-eight Chinese were recorded as living in Britain in 1851. Thereafter numbers increased, divided between a professional group who entered British universities from 1901 onwards and a labouring group typically working as casual seamen. It was this latter group who took the abuse of East End locals in the areas adjacent to Limehouse where Chinese laundries, boarding houses, groceries, meeting places (*fongs*) and opium dens created a sense of a closed and mysterious ghetto. West India Dock, Limehouse Causeway and Pennyfields were shrouded in strange tales of white slaving and drug addiction. The reality was more mundane but sailors from China and the East Indies (lascars) were sometimes abused or pelted with horse dung if they strayed too far from the safety of their own neighbourhood.

Yet the Chinese were also a little scary to middle-class Britons, to be abused with caution. This may account for the fact that violence was often limited to literary expression rather than physical attack. The 'yellow peril' was extraordinarily potent as an ingredient of the 'shocker', the forerunner of the modern thriller. The image of the inscrutable Chinaman provided a living for writers such as Arthur Sarsfield Ward, who as Sax Rohmer created the monstrous Dr Fu Manchu, hell-bent on conquering the British Empire from his fog-bound lair in Limehouse.

> that accursed Chinaman! . . . If that Satanic genius were not indeed destroyed, then the peace of the world may be threatened anew at any moment! . . . What became of his band of assassins – his stranglers, his dacoits, his damnable poisons and insects and what-not – the army of creatures? . . . imagine a person tall, lean, and feline, high shouldered, with a brow like Shakespeare and a face like Satan, a close-shaven skull, and long magnetic eyes of the true cat green. Invest him with all the cruel cunning of an entire Eastern race accumulated in one giant intellect, ... and you have a mental picture of Dr. Fu-Manchu, the 'Yellow Peril' incarnate in one man.[1]

The Chinese, or at least their literary version, became a symbol between the First and Second World Wars of 'the enemy within'.

Aggression against the Chinese community was, on the whole, confined to literary fantasy. This was not the case with the German community, which had been steadily growing during the nineteenth century to the point where it represented the largest immigrant group before the arrival of the Polish and Russian Jews. The German population in Britain in 1861 was just over 28,000 but that had risen to over 50,000 by 1911, made up of part of a vast exodus of Germans looking for work in other countries. Immigrants arriving in Britain soon created their own infrastructure of churches, clubs and shops but it is worth noting that at least half of these new arrivals were from Britain's old German allies Hanover and Hesse (Electoral Hess and Grand Duchy Hesse). Others came from Prussia, Wurttemberg, Nassau, Bavaria and a myriad of lesser states and principalities.

Many chose to settle in the East End of London, in Whitechapel, St George-in-the-East and Mile End, whilst at least one area, bounded by Whitechapel Road, Leman Street, the Highway and New Road/ Cannon Street Road, was known as 'Little Germany'. Still others gathered in communities in East and West Ham where sugar, chemical and fertilizer work gave factory employment. Germans were especially known as bakers and butchers, and it was certainly claimed that bakeries in the East End were a German monopoly, but others pursued trades as diverse as cooperage, coffee roasting and even waxfruit making. By all accounts, the German population of the East End and elsewhere settled down to a prosperous and enjoyable life (for many of the men one of clubs and drinking) and by the outbreak of the First World War many considered they were British in everything but name.

The war changed this with brutal force and created a wave of Germanophobia, which effectively reminded immigrants that they could never relax their guard. The first consequence of hostilities was an Aliens Restriction Act that required all Germans to register with the police and restricted movement to a radius of five miles other than with a permit. Domiciled Germans who had long seen themselves (or at least their children) as British were humiliated, especially as their sons went to fight for King and Empire on the Western Front. The government also interned 32,000 Germans and Austrians and threatened German women with deportation. All Germans, especially in industrial areas, were considered potential spies. So famously panicked was the Royal Family that it changed its name from Saxe-Coburg-Gotha to one named after its home: Windsor. One public house in Stratford diplomatically changed its name from the King of Prussia to the King Edward.

Attitudes quickly hardened towards German families and businesses in East End neighbourhoods.

A correspondent writes suggesting that there are several German barbers in East Ham, Manor Park and Forest Gate, and he pleads for Englishmen to patronise English barbers. He suggests that there should be pickets near the doors of all German barbers, whether they are naturalised or not, and that it should be the duty of such pickets to put the case of England and Englishmen very plainly to customers patronising such people.[2]

Germans were soon 'forced' to show clear signs of loyalty such as the following remarkable advert:

The present titanic struggle between Germany and the Allies [is] proving immensely disastrous and deplorable and Mr. Reidmuller, of Albert-road, North Woolwich says: I have been domiciled in England 38 years, resident in West Ham, East Ham and North Woolwich; all my children have been born in one or other of these districts, educated amongst British children, learned to love and respect them, and to be loved and respected in return . . . I have long been really and truly a 'Britisher' at heart . . . No British-born subject can possibly feel more grieved and horrified at the revolting tales of the inhuman atrocities perpetrated by the enemies [sic] troops – would that I could forswear my nationality. The extensive spy system which has been revealed has aroused an immense hatred against my fellow countrymen, to which I also am a partial sufferer. I defy any living individual to quote a single instance of my having given the slightest cause for suspicion of my entire trust, and honest respect, for the British, and my earnest desire is to still retain their full confidence as one of them.[3]

The war, deaths on the front, Zeppelin raids and economic hardships made living in Britain more than a little awkward for German families; the sinking of the British liner the *Lusitania*, on Friday 7 May 1915, an act nothing less than a sign of Hunnic barbarity, created a pogrom.

The riots of May 1915 remain some of the worst widespread London disturbances since the Gordon Riots of the eighteenth century. Anything and everything 'German' was fair game for destruction, looting or harassment. The local newspapers reported in great detail rioters' progress during the days following the *Lusitania*'s loss. The *East Ham Echo* reported,

The feeling of resentment against Germans . . . reached its highest pitch . . . the scenes which occurred in the district and neighbourhoods surrounding were such as have never been witnessed before.

The cowardly act of our inhuman enemy of Friday last, in sinking the Lusitania with its load of humanity, followed on Monday by the incendiary bomb dropped at Southend, were the popular excuses given for the curious scenes. Persons of German birth at Canning Town, suffered severely at the hands of the crowd on Tuesday night, and on Wednesday morning further attacks followed, the excitement and indignation spreading at midday to North Woolwich.

Women at North Woolwich were in the forefront of the rioters, and mainly at their hands shops were utterly wrecked and pillaged of the entire contents, the sufferers in every case carrying the businesses of either butchers or bakers, with one exception. In one case the 'Echo' representative saw a few people gathered round a shop which soon swelled into a muttering crowd. A policeman or two tried to disperse the people, but a stone thrown caused a cheer to ring out. The next minute stones innumerable were being hurled at the house and the police were powerless to stay the bombardment. To the accompaniment of more cheers, pieces of glass smashed on the pavement, until only the framework of both the shops and living rooms were left.

Those occupants who had not already left, hurriedly departed trembling and weeping. What could the few available police do? As a constable turned his back some of the crowd rushed forward, scrambling through the window frame, and raided the shop. In less time that it takes to tell, the shop was full of a mob, tearing, wrenching, straining at the fittings, stealing, destroying the goods . . . Yells, cheers and cries were incessant and the police struggled and sweated in vain to check the rush.[4]

Rioting in Woolwich, where butchers, bakers and tobacconists were looted, was equalled by activity further upriver in East Ham. The *East Ham Echo* continued:

> The law-abiding [sic] inhabitants of East Ham were startled on Wednesday night by further scenes of destruction. The feelings of the thousands of persons who collected in various parts run as high as at other places'.
> The district is well known for the behaviour of a certain section of its boys, and it was they who started the riots. Just after the children left school in the afternoon, boys assembled round the shop of Mr G. Bollman, hairdresser, of 85, Barking-road, and commenced stone throwing. That drew an older crowd, and for an hour the shop was pelted. Soon after it started the occupiers are stated to have discreetly left.[5]

Once the crowd had finished its destructive entertainment they left the smashed-up premises to be found by an unawares postman delivering birthday cards to Mr Bollman's children.

Greater violence against 'German' property followed in Stratford and in Manor Park, where the shops of Mr Bachmeyer, Mr Menzler, Mr Krantz and Mr Streitberger had their windows smashed by a crowd, whose demeanour was reported as 'good humoured and easy to control'! Indeed, they did not disrupt tram operations or bus timetables, reported the local press. Mounted police were stationed opposite Streitberger the Butcher and Krantz the Jeweller in Romford Road, Manor Park but did not prevent the looting of the shops or the destruction of the shop owners' houses.

> Showers of missiles of all descriptions shattered the windows, and excited by the damage, the crowd attacked the shop fronts. The jeweller's premises gave way first, and the contents of the shop were in part thrown into the street and in part appropriated by the raiders. Clocks, watches and other articles disappeared as if by magic. Meantime persistent onslaughts on the door at Streitberger's had resulted in its breakdown . . . Clothes, chairs and other articles of furniture were thrown into the street, many persons in the crowd outside making off with the articles. The same process was then gone through at Krentz's house, the household effects being thrown indiscriminately into the streets, to be captured and carried off by anyone so inclined to profit by the excitement. It was noticeable that quite respectable people appropriated parts of the loot . . . The 'Echo' representative saw one apparently respectable man with a purloined clock under his arm almost inviting the attention of the police. One man got off with an armful of plates

in a butcher's apron, and several women walked off with all the airs of innocence with such of the chairs as had survived whole the descent from the upper floors to the pavement.

Some local papers actively encouraged the violence. The *Kentish Independent* pompously intoned that day:

> The apathetic British public has yawned, stretched itself and opened its eyes. The cloak of lethargy, which seems to have been its mantle of late has suddenly been thrown off. Throughout the country the people have taken if only temporarily, the law into their own hands on the alien question. The sinking of the Lusitania has kindled the smouldering fires of indignation throughout the land.[6]

'Stolid Britains' finally roused to indignation by 'German bestiality and fiendishness' nevertheless soon found themselves crowded into police courts for offences ranging from theft to disorderly conduct. One rioter, Richard Smith of Manor Park, was even apprehended carrying off a suspicious piece of cheese. Terrifying one's German neighbours was treated by many not as criminal behaviour but as a good-hearted, if rambunctious, way of letting off steam.

> The destruction throughout was proceeded with a spirit of good humour, and there was not, as perhaps one might have expected in some quarters, any display of acerbity or bitter animosity. By many, undoubtedly, the demonstrations were regarded as fitting outlets to their animal spirits, and young lads and girls were quick to seize upon the opportunity as a 'safety valve' to their effervescent energy. One man boasted 'I've worked my way from Barking to-day, and I've been throwing pianos out of windows all the way down'.[7]

One attack was only aborted when the crowd had it explained to them that the shop owner had just lost a son fighting for Britain. The crowd magnanimously sang 'For He's a Jolly Good Fellow' and marched off looking for other victims.

Meanwhile rioting continued across Canning Town, Leyton, Hackney and Tottenham. One resident of Tottenham recalled that as a child,

> Dad sent me just across the road from our house in Seventh Avenue to Rhumbke's, the barber, with a note saying that my hair should be cropped short. When I got back home with no hair left except for an inch fringe in front I told anybody who would

listen that I was not going to the barber again because boys had to wait until there were no more grown-ups in the shop, even if they came in after we boys had come in. Some days later I was pleased to see that the barber's shop windows were all smashed. When Dad came in to dinner I asked him why and he told me that since the sinking of the Lusitania there had been rioting and that Rhumbke was a German. There had been lots of bad feeling. The barber disappeared, his shop being taken over by Hooper to open as a newsagents.[8]

Trouble in North London included rioting and looting in Seven Sisters and Wood Green. The Jolly Butchers public house in Wood Green also displayed a notice warning that 'No Germans will be served in this establishment'.[9] Sylvia Pankhurst, suffragette and socialist, believed the crowds were motivated by hunger but it is quite clear that this was an attempt to put a sociological gloss on a week of activity that many commentators called a 'pogrom'. Crowds acted in a leisurely and definite manner and were encouraged by a valueless police presence and by a jocular good humour that hardly speaks of desperation. This was plain German-baiting for fun and patriotism with many women and children encouraged to partici-pate. Isolated attacks on the property of Jewish bankers or premises owned by Scots or Irish with foreign-sounding names were, in this regard, peripheral.

Police attitudes and actions are also of interest as many fewer uni-formed police were available to keep order, their numbers thinned by army recruitment and their replacements provided by 'amateur . . . police' or 'Specials'. These had been created after a meeting at Scotland House during the afternoon of Saturday 8 August 1914 and were intended as temporary replacements for regular officers, not to be confused with the special constables of the nineteenth century. An emergency meeting had concluded that a force of 20,000 'citizen volunteers' would be needed to police Britain's cities for the dura-tion. The honorary Special Constables were not required to put on uniform, instead strapping on an armband whilst on duty, 'its origi-nal brightness ameliorated by previous wear on the brawny arm of some regular policeman'.

Suspicion of suspected spies ran high when *all* resident Germans, some who had lived thirty or forty years in Britain, were considered 'enemy aliens', and the Specials seemed capable of finding innocent people to accuse whenever possible. One German reported to be walking too near a London waterworks during September 1914 was treated to the following when accosted by a (rather well-educated) police officer 'tipped off' by a Special on sentry duty.

'You don't appear to be British,' remarked the officer, running his eye over the visitor – not unkindly, yet in something of the fashion, which makes Englishmen so beloved abroad . . .

'Don't you speak English?'

The mouth of the exile – it was plain by now that he was an exile on a strange shore – twitched convulsively, but no sound came from it.

'Ah I see', said the officer encouragingly, 'vous parlez français, sans doute, monsieur. N'est-ce pas?'

Still no luck, but the questioner never lost heart.

'Entshuldigen Sie, mein Herr', he murmured gently. 'Sie sprechen deutsche, nicht war?'

That did it. It was as though the rod of Moses had again smitten vulnerable rock. The foundations of the mighty deep of the sad-faced exile's silence were broken up in a preliminary, 'Ja, mein Herr, ja'. Then the parts of speech streamed out in a profusion, which filled the air with guttural sound and even a good simulation of fury. And the wealth of gesture that accompanied it was like a semaphore gone mad. The sharply challenged and close-pursuing ear of the attentive Englander did its best, but was quite unequal to the task of making what may have been essential distinctions between accusatives and datives, to say nothing of catching and joining on the spot the far-from-each-other fragments of separable verbs.

Out of the tumult of it all presently emerged some of the data on which to found a judgment. It seemed to show that the exile was merely out for fresh air and with not the least intention of impairing the water-supply of London; that he had been only two months in this hospitable country; that, although a quasi-professional man in his native land, he had not yet acquired enough of our language for the working purpose of life; that he had been registered as an enemy alien, according to law, but that he had changed his address and had not given the required notification to the proper authority.

The subsequent examination showed that the man's papers were in order. By those who ultimately dealt with the case, it was not thought necessary to do more than regularise the change of address and let 'the poor chap' go.

There was a parting suggestion that persons who said 'jah' for 'yes' had better in the existing circumstances keep away from the waterworks and their adjuncts.[10]

At best police attitudes to Germans living in Britain were the same as colonial administrators towards the natives of the Empire, patronizing and paternalistic and coloured by an unshakeable belief that all foreigners were slightly simple and in need of British discipline. Yet the war unleashed more visceral responses amongst police as well as the general public: that all Germans were barbarians and that Germans in Britain were war profiteers and spies. Colonel W. T. Reay, commander of the Specials, recorded the sinking of the *Lusitania* opened people's eyes to the enemy within.

> It is important to recollect that prior to the *Lusitania* crime there was no such rioting. If the people of London did not suffer the Germans gladly, at least they did not interfere with them or their property. Indeed, these enemy aliens were treated with a consideration amounting in many cases to a chivalrous compassion and tenderness which – judging by the reports of those lately liberated from Ruhleden – was in marked contrast with the treatment of British citizens whom the war caught in that home of kultur, Berlin. Germans here carried on business as bakers, barbers, and what not, without let or hindrance, and found more profitable than ever a field from which British trade rivals had removed themselves by volunteering for the fighting services. It was an anomalous state of things; but, as we heard one greatly tickled and cynical German express it, 'so like the English'! That is how the Teuton regards kindness. With him it is the sign either of weakness or stupidity.[11]

This was only slightly more temperate than Horatio Bottomley's call in his paper, *John Bull*, to annihilate all resident Germans whether British citizens or not! Furthermore, the Specials (and regular police) assigned to quell the disturbances shared the attitude of the rioters towards the ordinary and *innocent* people they were sent to protect.

> For it may well be doubted whether amongst the thousands of Special Constables who did their duty so splendidly, 'who combated the fury of the crowds' and protected the assailed Germans and their property, it would have been possible to find a man who did not heartily share the wholesome anger which provoked these riots.[12]

What motivated the Specials was not the protection of innocent foreigners but the knowledge that compensation would have to come from the local rates, that is, the pockets of the Specials amongst others. It was this aspect of the disturbances that the commanding officers emphasized.

Specials were rushed hither and thither, to Poplar, Limehouse, West Ham, Plaistow, East Ham, Forest Gate and Ilford in the east; Stoke Newington, Islington, Tottenham, Holloway Road, Walthamstow and

Edmonton in the north; Battersea, Clapham, Borough, Tooting and Brixton in the south-west; Deptford, Greenwich, Woolwich and Plumstead in the south-east; Chiswick, Hammersmith and Shepherd's Bush to the west; Lambeth and the Borough; Putney and Wandsworth. The final 'suppression' of the riots coincided with a general exhaustion in the participants but left 1,100 cases of 'damage and theft', 250 'looted' properties, 60 'wrecked' buildings and 70 'looted and wrecked' homes and shops. Nearly 2,000 people claimed compensation and although no one had been seriously hurt, 250 people had been injured. In Bethnal Green 50 people had been treated in hospital on 14 May. By the end, 866 people had been arrested. Utterly without compassion for the victims, and with a cynical reference to military injuries, Colonel Reay put German 'casualties' as 257 people.

Germans were again the victims of rioters when Kitchener drowned and when Zeppelin raids took their toll. On 5 June 1916 violence broke out in North London when news of Kitchener's death suggested he had been the victim of a fifth-column espionage ring. By 1917 North Londoners had started to form lynch mobs, when during July,

> Moved to anger by the murderous effects of air-raids, there was, first open talk of taking reprisal measures against an internment camp in Cornwallis Road, Holloway, and next a hostile move on the camp. It is fortunate for the Germans there that the police were not caught napping. The angry crowd found themselves opposed by a strong force of Regular and Special Constables. There was some stone-throwing – amongst those hit on the head being Superintendent Evans – but no German suffered damage. Four evenings in succession the police protected the camp, and it was then left to its usual military guard.[13]

By the end of the war, Germans living in London either disguised their origins and hoped for the best or were interned, harassed and made homeless. A once thriving community, including many men who fought for Britain *against* Germany, was now decimated never to recover.

15
Comrades All
Red London to Red Ken

The legacy of republican socialism bequeathed by the Social Democratic Federation (SDF) was taken up by the later British Socialist Party (BSP) and this, in turn, became the core of the Communist Party of Great Britain when it was formed just after the First World War, in 1920. The CPGB was born on a cold summer's day when a dedicated group of socialist revolutionaries held a meeting at the Cannon Street Hotel near St Paul's. The delegates, 160 in all, were from a variety of backgrounds; many had fought in the First World War. Arthur McManus chaired the meeting. He was the son of a Fenian and had helped turn the Clyde 'red' before coming south to England. There was also Sylvia Pankhurst and her Workers' Socialist Federation (WSF) from the East End. The WSF and the Socialist Labour Party (SLP), McManus's Scottish group, were meeting in this London hotel to make acquaintance and forge alliance. Lenin himself, who put £55,000 at McManus's disposal, had primed them. Lenin waited on results and accepted the SLP's recommendation that the ILP be excluded for being too revisionist whilst a revolutionary and politically stable core of support was built up. The CPGB began life with 3,000 dedicated members including hard-line trade unionists like Arthur Horner and Willie Gallacher, self-taught workingclass activists like Harry Pollitt and intellectuals such as the rather austere and aloof Rajani Palme Dutt. They were all revolutionaries, antiparliamentary in their political aims and violently opposed to the 'capitalist' class. The Communists were never gradualists or reformists, and their enemies who were – the trades union movement, the Liberals and, above all, the Labour Party – were all vilified in turn.

In their manifesto of 1935, *For Soviet Britain*, adopted at their thirteenth congress, the CPGB made their revolutionary plans quite clear: Britain was under the thrall of capitalist fascism.

> Britain today is in the hands of millionaires – owners of the biggest trusts, the biggest banks, the biggest steamship companies; in

short, owners or controllers of the big monopolies. Nearly every-thing we use or need pays toll to them: soap and milk, cigarettes and cinemas, newspapers and wireless are in their grasp, as well as mining, chemicals, transport, etc. These millionaires, these monopoly capitalists, not only own or control the chief means whereby we work and live, but, in fact, control the whole govern-ing machine. They pull the strings. And they use their power to make themselves richer and richer – at our expense . . . Fascism is the weapon of the millionaires against the working class. Fascism is the dictatorship of the most ruthless, reactionary and jingo sec-tion of monopoly capitalism.

The only way to defeat these powerful forces was by social revolution.

The Communist Party declares it is not possible to end capital-ism and establish socialism in Britain by the election of a majority in the House of Commons . . .
How the Workers Can Win Power
The answer is that a workers' revolution can do it . . .
Nor has the Communist Party ever denied that this overthrow must be a forceful one.

The overthrow of capitalism, which would lead to 'true' Communist democracy, was to be achieved through workers' councils or sovi-ets reporting to a national council under the leadership of the party itself. The model, of course, was Russian and, as in Russia, the 'dicta-torship [of the proletariat] over the defeated capitalist class' was to be 'severe'. Once such a victory was won, Britain would become a true soviet democracy run by an efficient state machine on 'scientific' principles.

This utopian vision required, however, a crisis in capitalism, a series of disasters in the Empire, the appearance of armed workers at the factory gate and on the streets and the dissolution of Parliament (including the 'removal' of the monarch and his family and the pun-ishment or re-education of plutocrats). The programme was one of creeping and increasing class war. Such open advocacy of revolution was clearly a threat to the status quo and to the forces of liberal democ-racy, and the secret services were inevitably going to see the CPGB as the greatest internal threat to Britain since the Catholic menace of the sixteenth and seventeenth centuries. The fears of the authorities would be exacerbated by the fact that the CPGB was always in receipt of Soviet money (as British fascists were of Italian cash) and that a large number of subversives were working for the successful outcome of the 1935 programme by spying on behalf of Soviet Russia. These

The aftermath of Boudicca's attack on London: three skulls found in the Walbrook Stream bed. (Courtesy of The Museum of London)

Wat Tyler is killed by Sir William Walworth in the presence of Richard II. (Engraving by Harris from *Froissart's Chronicles*, courtesy of Mary Evans Picture Library)

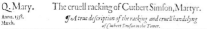

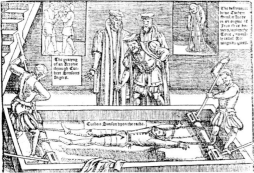

The racking of Protestant martyr Cut[h]bert Simson in Queen Mary's reign. (A woodcut from Foxe, Acts and Monuments, II, 1576. Author's Collection)

The conspirators
in the infamous
Gunpowder Plot.
(Author's collection)

John Lilburne in 1641, from an engraving by George Glover
(Bodleian Library, Oxford — Firth.e.63 (2).Frontispiece)

The House of Commons as
it was in 1624. (Contemporary
engraving)

John Lilburne in 1641. (From
an engraving by George Glover.
Author's collection)

The Golden Boy memorial, now on Cock Street. (Courtesy of Debra Kacher)

Titus Oates. (Contemporary engraving)

JEFFREYS AS LORD CHIEF JUSTICE OF ENGLAND
Aetat 36
(Engraved from a Portrait by SIR GODFREY KNELLER)

Judge Jeffreys, Lord Chief Justice. (Engraved from a portrait by Sir Godfrey Kneller. Author's collection)

SIR EDMUND BERRY GODFREY'S MURDER
AND THE PRETENDED ASSAULT ON JOHN ARNOLD
(From a contemporary cut in Ussher's "Protestant School")

A contemporary illustration of the murder of Sir Edmund Berry Godfrey and the assault on John Arnold. (Contemporary cut in *Ussher's Protestant School*)

168 The pillory, like the stocks, was a familiar feature of town and village before imprisonment was introduced as a punishment rather than temporary restraint. Its purpose was public humiliation; but its effect was arbitrary. The victim might be pelted with offensive but harmless rubbish; or he might be stoned to death, as happened to Egan the thieftaker at Smithfield, shown in this print from the Newgate Calendar. The pillory was last used in London in 1830; the penalty was abolished in 1837.

Egan the thieftaker is pilloried at Smithfield, and stoned to death. (From the *Newgate Calendar*. Author's collection)

INDUSTRY AND IDLENESS—PLATE XI—THE EXECUTION OF THOMAS IDLE

An eighteenth-century hanging at Tyburn, from a contemporary print entitled *The Execution of Thomas Idle*. (Author's collection)

The burning and plundering of Newgate during the Gordon Riots, 7 June 1780. (Unnamed artist, published by Fielding and Walker 1 July 1780, courtesy of Mary Evans Picture Library)

A contemporary caricature of the eighteenth-century politician John Wilkes. (Author's collection)

Charles James Fox. (An engraving from a picture by Sir Joshua Reynolds. Author's collection)

Arthur Thistlewood, leader of the Cato Street conspirators, at his trial.
(Author's collection)

BREAK UP OF THE TRAFALGAR-SQUARE MEETING.

'Black Monday' – the break up of the Social Democratic Federation meeting
in Trafalgar Square, 1886. (From the *Illustrated London News*, 13 February
1886. Author's collection)

MR. H. M. HYNDMAN.

Henry Hyndman, founder of the SDF. (From the *Illustrated London News*, 13 February 1886. Author's collection)

MR. JOHN BURNS.

John Burns, founder of the Battersea branch of the SDF. (From the *Illustrated London News*, 13 February 1886. Author's collection)

The police observation post in Trafalgar Square, built in the late nineteenth century. (Courtesy of Debra Kacher)

THE "HOLE IN THE WALL"—A MEETING OF THE LONDON REPUBLICANS

Anarchist meeting as imagined by *Illustrated News* in the nineteenth century. (Author's collection)

'X' marks the spot: cottage in Chingford where 'Jacob Lepidus' died during the events of the Tottenham Outrage in 1909. (Courtesy of Vestry House Museum, Walthamstow)

Winston Churchill attends the Sidney Street siege in 1911. (Courtesy of Hulton Getty)

Mrs Pankhurst is arrested outside Buckingham Palace, 21 May 1914. (Courtesy of Mary Evans Picture Library)

An anti-German mob attacks a shop in the East End in 1915.
(Courtesy of Hulton Getty)

The Indian MP Shapurji
Saklatvala, from *Punch*.
(*Punch*, 14 June 1926.
Author's collection)

ASSIMILATION: "We don't let our dogs do that"

Anti-Jewish propaganda published by Arnold
Leese. (Author's collection)

A pre-war Mosley rally – the black shirts had been banned by this time.
(Courtesy of *Searchlight*)

William Joyce, 13 March 1940.
(Courtesy of *Searchlight*)

Geoffrey Hamm leaving court
after being arrested for rioting.
(Courtesy of *Searchlight*)

Arnold Leese of the Imperial Fascist League. (Courtesy of *Searchlight*)

Police disperse a 'Keep Britain White' demonstration at Waterloo,
1 September 1960. (Courtesy of *Searchlight*)

A camping trip for British fascists, 1962. (Courtesy of *Searchlight*)

Hitler's birthday is celebrated in Lewisham in the 1970s. (Courtesy of *Searchlight*)

A clash between police and demonstrators in Red Lion Square. (Courtesy of *Searchlight*)

Tariq Ali and Ted Knight speaking at an anti-Fascism demonstration at Wood Green. (Courtesy of *Searchlight*)

The IRA bomb the Palace of Westminster in 1970 (Courtesy of Hulton Getty)

This is not a protest...

A leaflet advertising the Guerilla Gardening May Day 2000 event. (Author's collection)

The monument to the victims of the 7 July 2005 bombing attack in Hyde Park. (Author's collection)

G20 protester in ubiquitous 'V for Vendetta' mask symbolic of everything antigovernmental. (Courtesy of Jonathan Bloom)

'Eat the bankers': an effigy, later set on fire in front of Mansion House. (Courtesy of Jonathan Bloom)

Bishopsgate Climate Camp. (Courtesy of Jonathan Bloom)

2010: Anti-capitalist protest at empty property in Bedford Square, Bloomsbury, (Author's collection)

men and women, dedicated to the sovietization of Britain and also to preventing Britain opposing Soviet international interests, were *never* overt members of the CPGB and were unknown to CPGB members (they were always to keep their interests secret) but infiltrated the British secret services or intelligence organizations wherever possible.

This is not to say that many of the CPGB leadership, showing as they did clear affection for the Soviet Union and making frequent (if sometimes secretive) visits to Moscow, were not also clearly 'agents' of Soviet policy. Jack Murphy, for instance, certainly acted as a courier for Soviet money and was lectured by the Bolshevists on the correct line and tactics to follow.

> The Russians seemed incapable of exhaustion by discussion. We had got to learn that a Communist Party was the general staff of a class marching to civil war, that it had to be disciplined, a party organised on military lines, ready for every emergency, an election, a strike, an insurrection.[1]

He also had Russian contacts in London such as 'Mikhail Borodin' (Mikhail Grusenberg), who, working under the name George Brown, was the Comintern's British agent. Others also had contacts direct to Lenin. One was Andrew Rothstein, the son of the Lithuanian revolutionary Theodore Rothstein, who had fled to Britain in 1891, became the London correspondent of Pravda and acted as Lenin's London agent. After serving Lenin for many years, he returned to senior diplomatic work in Russia. Andrew, a rather cringing, if highly intelligent, party functionary, also frequently couriered money but remained secretive about the role he and his father played in the control of the CPGB.

> Smuggling cash in this way was a dangerous and uncomfortable business. It was even more dangerous to be a Comintern agent – the people who travelled secretly from country to country, helping and advising Communist Parties, making sure they worked efficiently, spent Moscow's money wisely, and followed the Moscow line. Police surveillance was close and Comintern agents kept their identities secret even from CP members. Mikhail Borodin was at a meeting in Glasgow with Bob Stewart, Willie Gallacher and others when the room was raided by a dozen or so policemen . . . Borodin found his six months in Glasgow's Barlinnie Prison hard. It was colder than Siberia, he said, and he knew what he spoke about. The food – almost exclusively porridge – was excruciating. He scalded his legs badly with boiling water in the prison laundry

and could hardly wait for the six months to be over so that he could be deported.[2]

Controversy dogged the CPGB from the start because of its overly close ties to Moscow. MI5 and Special Branch had already begun surveillance operations on the party's leading members when a letter was published in 1924 by the *Daily Mail* which showed that Grigori Zinoviev, the President of the third Comintern, had been in correspondence with Arthur McManus discussing the possibilities of initiating a revolution. The letter greatly damaged the Labour government and helped in its defeat in the general election four days later, even though it was generally accepted that the letter was black propaganda created by White Russians, paid for by the Conservative Party and published by the *Daily Mail*.

The damage done, the unmasking of the fraud was an accepted fact years later and there the matter rested – except, as Cabinet papers later revealed, the probable *authenticity* of the letter was disguised by government censorship and mismanagement. This was a particularly touchy area as many of the secret service's sources were unreliable or acted as double agents. Lord Curzon, the Foreign Secretary in 1921, had already been embarrassed having used false documents against the Russians that he had believed authentic. These documents, the 'Sisson' Papers, were sold to American intelligence in 1918 through the agency of the secret service or Foreign Office using Sidney Reilly (so-called 'Ace of Spies'). They showed the Bolsheviks to be agents of the German Imperial Headquarters, but they were fakes used by the British to trick the Americans into action against the Soviets! The truth of the matter was that both sides in the Russian Civil War used black propaganda and that the sympathies of dockers (where Communist local organizers were strongest) hampered operations. As the CPGB were de facto a revolutionary party dedicated to Bolshevizing Britain they were de jure acting seditiously when acting to support the Russian Bolsheviks. The party sincerely believed it was engaged in a war for social democracy in which Soviet Russia was being victimized. Many ordinary people agreed.

On 14 October 1925 the authorities decided to act against the CP Executive and arrest warrants were made out at Bow Street. This time the charge was sedition and incitement to mutiny. The decision for the arrests had been reached through the pressure of Sir Wyndham Childs, Assistant Commissioner CID, who had declared war on Communism and looked for a showdown.

I spent the seven best years of my life trying to induce various governments to allow me to use the full force of the law . . . I have never been able to comprehend why the successive Governments I served always refused to strike one overwhelming and final blow against the Communist organisation.[3]

There had already been portents. In May 1921 Sir Basil Thomson, Head of Special Branch, had organized a raid on the CPGB offices and seized mountains of paperwork and publications. Prosecution followed as the government tried to prove the seditious nature of the journals and pamphlets. In 1924 the party was also prosecuted after publication of a 'mutinous' open letter to the armed forces published in the *Workers' Weekly* (July). Albert Inkpin, the one-time secretary of the BSP, was sentenced to six months' hard labour for fermenting 'civil war', as the Lord Mayor put it.

The raid in October 1925 was prefaced by intensified surveillance. The new Home Secretary, Sir William Joynson-Hicks, was eager to prove his government was tough on Communists. The warrant, taking its legality from the Incitement to Mutiny Act of 1797, accused the whole Executive of 'conspiracy', 'sedition' and incitement to mutiny. Simultaneous raids went to the CPGB offices in King Street, the Young Communist League (YCL) offices at Great Ormond Street and the *Workers' Weekly* office near Temple. Albert Inkpin, now Secretary of the CPGB, was again arrested as was Ernest Cant, the London organizer of the Party. Tom Wintringham and Johnny Campbell were arrested at the *Worker's Weekly* and Harry Pollitt and William Rust, the Secretary of the YCL, also found themselves cautioned and taken away. In Scotland, Thomas Bell and Willie Gallacher were picked up and sent to Euston to be collected on arrival. Gallacher was used to being arrested. He had been arrested in 1919 for making speeches inciting the crowd to riot. After searching the offices, police then went to the homes of those arrested and less than a week later they arrested the remaining members still at large: Arthur McManus, John ('Jack') Murphy, Walter Hennington and Robert Arnot.

The group were charged with incitement and 'conspiracy to publish seditious libels'. As the case proceeded there emerged proof that the CPGB received its money through 'secret channels' (these continued into the late 1950s), but most of what emerged as evidence proved innocuous and consisted of little more than CPGB wish lists. Notes toward subverting the army and navy were to be taken seriously (the mutiny of eight ship's companies of the Atlantic fleet at Invergordon in 1931 proved their importance) but were not backed up by any real proof of infiltration. The defendants were, however, sent to the Old Bailey, where the trial began on 17 November. The jury found the twelve members of the Executive guilty and without much debate all were sent to jail. Those with previous convictions were given twelve months. The trial's significance lay not in the defendants' actions but in their unlawful desires. As such the whole affair was the most important *political* trial in Britain during the twentieth century, a point not lost on Sir Travers Humphreys, part of the prosecution team, who observed:

> This is not a prosecution of an individual for an individual act. The case for the prosecution is that all the accused are engaged with others – many others – in an illegal conspiracy – a conspiracy to do an act, or achieves an end by unlawful means. They are concerned in different capacities in teaching the doctrines of what they call Communism.[4]

The subterfuge detected in the CPGB was evident in equal measure in the activities of the recently established Russian Trade Delegation in London, whose premises in Moorgate Street housed their cover operation, Arcos Ltd. These premises were also a convenient place from which to run spies and couriers, with rooms reinforced with concrete as well as steel doors. Special Branch had information that Moscow was supplying funds to the CPGB as well as militant unionists plotting after the failure of the General Strike through Arcos Ltd, and when stolen RAF documents were said to be apparently on the premises a raid was organized. On 12 May 1927 police breached Russian diplomatic immunity and went into the building in search of evidence of subversion. Instead they found piles of burnt papers and useless information. The Russians had been warned in advance. Yet the police were satisfied that aid to the CPGB was coming from the Arcos office and that Arcos was one of the most serious security risks of the 1920s, even if, as it transpired, they found little to carry away except ashes and embarrassment.

Despite all protestations to the contrary, the CPGB and the Soviet spy agencies were part of a large and complex network of open and secret stratagems, which included everything from trade-union activism (usually at shop steward level only), trades council leadership, affiliation to the Labour Party (before wholesale expulsion) and parliamentary 'entryism'. In every case, secret or open, the CPGB acted largely under the directing hand of Soviet needs, breaking with the Soviet Union only after his invasion of Hungry in 1956. As late as 2000, Arthur Scargill (a one-time member of the Young Communists) and the historian Christopher Hill both excused Stalin's purges of the 1930s as necessary expediencies and refused to condemn them as atrocities. It was Stalin and his people's republic that had, after all, single-handedly defeated fascism; the CPGB itself was the product of the catalyst of the 1917 Revolution. This link could and would never be fully broken by men and women whose *personal* life as well as their public activities had been so intimately joined to a cause for so long. One ex-member recalled bitterly that

> We grouped ourselves on chairs and hassocks about his living-room. Kerrigan sat in the centre, his arms folded on the table below his open-necked shirt, a big man, a massive man with closely-cropped hair. No smile on his face, his eyes looking down at the papers before him. The accused was told: 'This is a Disciplinary Committee, comrade. Certain charges have been laid against you'... In his clipped emotionless voice Kerrigan read out a fourteen page document listing the man's crimes. They were not charges at all as the man in the street would understand them, but wild accusations and abuse: 'Unreliable, opportunist, deviationist, provocateur, bourgeois thinking, fractionising . . .'[5]

The years leading to the formation of the CPGB were driven by continual union actions across a number of heavy industries as well as in the growing electrical industries. The debates in working men's institutes and on factory floors as well as in the homes of middle-class supporters, not forgetting a growth in socialist proselytizing by newspaper and pamphlet, had given rise to a whole spectrum of socialist programmes and groups: the BSP, the Socialist Labour Party, the syndicalist movement, the Independent Labour Party, the Plebs League and the SDF. Only the SDF was overtly Marxist, but split when the Scottish SDF fragmented into a rump SDF and new Socialist Labour Party (SLP). In England the Fabians had also drifted to the ILP and new Labour Party. Many of these groups were very small and their active membership only counted in tens or a few hundred. Nevertheless they had big ambitions. The ILP South Wales Conference of 1918 gravely concluded that 'The time is ripe for the ILP to extend its activities to the Economic, in addition to the Political Field, seeing that it is in the field, factory, workshop, and mine that the real issue with the capitalist class is met, and that only by the workers organising industrially as well as politically will the overthrow of Capitalism be brought about.'[6]

For the nascent Communist groups such sentiments were simply that – sentiments – if the ILP intended to dally with parliamentary procedures. Equally the view of anarchist syndicalists was to be rejected when they refused to accept the *vanguard* role of the party as explained by Marxist-Leninist doctrine.

> Leadership: implies power held by the leader. Without power the leader is inept. The possession of power inevitably leads to corruption. All leaders become corrupt, in spite of their own good intentions. No man was ever good enough, brave enough, or

strong enough, to have such power at his disposal, as real leadership implies.[7]

'Rank and fileism' was also to be rejected as mere 'lobbyism'. The CPGB had no intention of merely being a pressure or 'ginger' group. It intended to seize power and the events of 1917 showed those with local or national radical attitudes the *international* level of their struggle. The CPGB was a Bolshevik party dedicated to its own central authority and leadership. The hesitation of the forces of revolution in 1919 when Britain seemed on the brink of 'civil war' and the later disastrous refusal of the CPGB to involve itself in the General Strike of 1926 paralysed its leading role almost at once. The party never recovered from the mistake of ignoring 1926 and although membership soared by the end of the Second World War and Willie Gallacher and Phil Piratin were both returned as MPs the party had lost prestige and membership even before the duplicity of 1956 was revealed.* It was the significance of certain key Communist shop stewards (TUC leadership by and large deeply distrusted Communists) that was of significance from the late 1950s to the middle 1970s, not the general political activities of the party as a whole. Left-wing student activists of the 1960s, like Tariq Ali, were not attracted to the CPGB and its old men, but formed a broad Left front without CPGB approval. The International Socialists (IS) Group (later SWP) also grew from this period.

By the late 1980s the CPGB had fallen from a peak membership of over 50,000 in the middle 1940s to near its original number of between 3,000 and 5,000. The last congress of the party ended in sadness and what was left fell apart leaving only those dedicated enough to pursue a Euro-Communist line either as the Democratic Left or as the Communist Party of Britain, formed during 1988 around the *Morning Star*.

The formation of the CPGB effectively created a single British Communist revolutionary bloc. Those organizations that had participated in its formation either subsumed their interests and were amalgamated or were left unable to function, bereft of many of their members or of any larger organization except the CPGB with which to form an alliance. The Labour Party was considered by many to be beyond redemption but the CPGB, under instruction from Lenin, willingly entered into a convenient alliance. Lenin's pragmatism hid an ideology that was unforgiving. His idea of a vanguard 'party of a new type' with its rigid hierarchy, adherence to Moscow's latest line, and belief in a central proletarian state which acted *on behalf*

---

*The CPGB found it difficult to reconcile their 'Moscow' line with the Soviet Union's invasion of Hungary.

of the workers was quite opposite to those anarchistic Communisms that had provided a broad revolutionary left alliance from the 1880s onwards. The complex and fluid relationships of a number of organizations whose Communist credentials were not Bolshevist were bulldozed into a monolithic unity by Maiden Lane (CP headquarters). For the middle forty years of the twentieth century anarchists were barely able to get quorate meetings as the CPGB battled Trotskyist recidivism. No wonder that the revival of anarchism during the 1980s and 1990s and the collapse of the CPGB was met with such undisguised glee by anarchist opponents.

> Well, what of the CPGB? Its collapse recently was reported in 'the Guardian'. Stalinism discredited throughout the world, the only option for the remaining parliamentary Stalinist parties was to change names. The CPGB's long lingering death had been delayed due to bad weather in the Winter of 1990–91 disrupting its AGM. The organisation survives for the time being under the name 'The Democratic Party of the Left', or 'The Communist Party in Transformation'. An analysis of how the CPGB came into existence and its subsequent behaviour is long overdue. The CPGB has recently published a series of pamphlets under the heading 'Our History'. In them there will be no mention of their real behaviour. We look forward to more publications about the CPGB in different periods of its existence. We have been discredited by the spectre of the Comintern for too long.[8]

Londoners did not need the CPGB to remind them how to be militant. Even the administrative structure of local government in the capital seemed uncompromising, independent and republican – in the words of its opponents, 'red'. The very nature of London's identity was itself a matter of urgent political debate in a protracted and sometimes vicious battle between conservatism and socialism. London itself would now gain a *political* identity of its own from which to challenge the ancient hegemony of the City and the self-regarding privileges of Westminster and Whitehall. For most of the hundred years between 1888 and 1986 the 'government' of London would never be anything other than controversial – a quasi-socialist conspiracy, too cockney, independent and 'bolshie' by half.

*

As Victorian London sprawled along the network of railway lines and tube train routes that led to its tangled centre it became increasingly apparent that no one spoke for the metropolis and nobody represented its interests. The old core of the City of London and its Corporation still sat at the heart of business and finance but it had no role to play in decisions regarding infrastructure in housing, roads, education, sewerage, lighting and the myriad requirements of a great metropolis. For many, London would not be able to play a full role in the world until it centralized its administration and until the local authorities, a motley gathering of boards and vestries and parishes, worked towards one goal. In the mid-nineteenth century at least 250 local Acts of Parliament were passed relating to London administration and 10,000 commissioners exercised varying degrees of control and responsibility. Finally it was agreed that one body might administer sewage. The Metropolitan Board of Works grew to take control of roads, clearances and open spaces but this was never adequate enough.

Changes did little to affect the pyramid of City institutions that still survived. Apart from the Corporation itself, forty-one vestries and district boards survived, as did 'The Metropolitan Asylum Board, thirty-eight Boards of Guardians, The Burial Board, The Thames and Lea Conservancy Board, and The School Board'.[9]

The London County Council (LCC) was the result of a fudged compromise to set up a single authority and it came into existence in 1888, the decision of a Conservative government under reforming pressure and the spectre of growing poverty, urban unrest and administrative confusion. London had finally followed the example of civic pride in Manchester and Birmingham. 1899 saw the creation of twenty-eight self-administering local boroughs with mayor, council and town hall. These related to the old vestries and district bodies. The creation of the LCC gave London a *voice* in the political life of Britain, which was neither that of the government nor of the City aldermen. Such a voice was from the beginning radical and vocal.

So long as London was managed by the Metropolitan Board of Works, it could not canalise its discontents through constitutional channels nor could it provide its citizens with the opportunity of participating fully in the politics of social control. A County Council would be a forum. The leader of its dominant party, the Conservative critics of their own government feared, might become more powerful than 'any prime ministers and some monarchs'.[10]

The LCC meant centralization, organization and order against the sprawl and 'anarchy' of the old village London mentality. Such an attitude was inevitably managerial, bureaucratic and centralizing, that is, it tended willy-nilly towards *socialism*.

The first LCC had a clear Progressive (i.e. Liberal) majority when elected in January 1889, and the Progressives soon demanded greater and greater powers. From 1889 to 1907 the Progressives ruled the LCC, making it a hot-bed (at least for opponents) of 'Reds, Cads and Fads'. The LCC did not prove inadequate to the needs of London until the mid-1960s, by which time it seemed unable to deal with the pressing problems of transport, housing and centralization of London governance. It would be reviewed by the Herbert Commission, set up by a Conservative government hoping to break Labour's thirty-year hold on London's political life, but the recommendations (published in 1960) were ignored.

The complexities of London meant that an adequate governing body suitable for all occasions would be most difficult to create. When the London Government Act 1963 established the Greater London Council (GLC) and thirty-two boroughs it left intact the old City Corporation and it left much duplication and uncertainty over administration especially regarding roads. Housing was equally confused, the GLC and the local boroughs *both* being the local housing authority.

As problematic as housing was the new political geography of the capital, including better off Tory suburbs now drawn into the Greater London Borough map. Not only boroughs but the GLC itself would now mirror the political polarizations of the rest of Britain; moreover, 'the Conservative boroughs of outer London suspected the GLC of reducing inner London's problems by exporting Labour-voting council tenants to the suburbs. Bromley and Redbridge were not alone in virtually refusing to co-operate with the GLC's efforts to re-house Londoners in their areas'.[11] Such political redrafting of the map was of serious constitutional importance in the late 1970s and early 1980s.

The first move to disestablish the GLC (and thereby rid the country of a 'quasi-socialist organisation' ruling London) was in 1974 when Geoffrey Fineberg, then MP for Hampstead, but Tory Leader of Camden Council between 1968 and 1970, produced *A Policy for London*, which was designed as a blueprint for virtual abolition. 'The Abolish the GLC Campaign' then fought thirty-one out of ninety-two seats at the GLC elections of 1977 and although they did not succeed they sent a clear message to their Tory colleagues who had won a third term in office. Thus they exposed the contradiction of a *centralizing* Conservative authority. Nevertheless, Horace Cutler, the GLC Conservative Leader, had already commissioned a report from Sir Frank Marshall (previously Conservative Leader in Leeds) which concluded as late as July 1978 that a central authority that 'transcends that of its constituent parts' was still necessary. The May 1979 election of Margaret Thatcher as Prime Minister would set Westminster in direct opposition to London's own 'parliament'.

On 7 May 1981 Labour again won back control of the GLC. The Labour Leader was the moderate Andrew McIntosh, a man happy to make alliances with Tory opponents, but his rival Ken Livingstone immediately replaced him in a palace coup. The victory shifted GLC politics into a central place in the country's political concerns, and for 'Thatcherite' Conservatives it finally unmasked the revolutionary nature of 'far left' political organizations. Ken Livingstone was, along-side Arthur Scargill of the miners and Derek Hatton in Liverpool, Thatcher's classic example of an 'enemy within'; a fifth columnist of the left willing to abuse any and every dearly held political value – an institutionalized political terrorist now head of the 'loony left' republic of County Hall!

Livingstone himself soon declared 'war' on the right and centre of his own party as it disintegrated into factions. In March 1981 four former Labour Party members, Shirley Williams, David Owen, Roy Jenkins and William Rogers, formed the Social Democratic Party (SDP). In June the SDP formed an alliance with the Liberals, challenging the Labour Party to reform or get out the way. Councillors in Southwark, Islington, Tower Hamlets and Hackney left Labour and joined the SDP–Liberal Alliance. Such groupings recruited not only from decent but alienated traditional Labour voters but also from 'old guard' Labour revolutionaries and elements of the racist white working-class. 'Liberal focus' directly profited from right-wing racist recruitment and had considerable success as its ideology evolved in areas such as the Isle of Dogs. Nowhere were attitudes more polarized than in Bermondsey, an 'old guard' Labour seat now contested by the middle-class intellectual gay activist Peter Tatchell, who deliberately goaded the local Labour Party 'gerontocracy' and local 'right-wing Catholic dockers' into political suicide. Simon Hughes was duly elected in Bermondsey on an SDP–Liberal Alliance ticket, 10,000 votes ahead of Tatchell.

And it was significant that the 'infiltrator' Tatchell should claim that he was the true inheritor of that radical socialism which had once flourished in Bermondsey's soil but had been allowed to wilt and atrophy by an old guard who had let down both the cause and local people. Reclaiming the past to legitimise the present was a powerful motif in the war torn Labour politics of the 1980s. During the rate-capping fiasco of 1984–85, when Labour parties across London (led, if that's the right word, by Lambeth, Hackney, Camden, Islington and Livingstone's GLC) competed to hold out longest against setting a legal rate, the ghostly shroud of Poplar, 60 years dead, was proudly waved once more. Although no one this time went to prison for the pains, councillors in Lambeth were surcharged and disqualified. When, in the wake of rate-capping and other bloody defeats, a new realism was espoused by Labour, a photograph of Herbert Morrison was dusted off, recovered from the basement of Hackney Town Hall and hung in the leader's office: Morrison may have been mayor of Hackney in 1920–21 and an alderman till 1925, but 'Good Old 'Erb' had been a non person in Hackney Labour Party for almost 20 years. Yet these were not fake symbols. They reinvented for modern times a London Labour heritage around which meanings could cluster and identities could be forged and recognized, even if there was much debate over just what were the 'true' traditions they represented.[12]

Exaggerated by the media, the extremities of Livingstone's administration outweighed its achievements. Anti-racist education, careful land development, a commission on food standards and the encouragement of multi-cultural living was set against clique-ism, grants to fringe groups, flirtation with Sinn Fein, dislike of the Royal Family and overt involvement with sexual politics, all of which alienated most voters and sent out confusing messages about the role of the GLC. By the time Thatcher had decided to destroy Livingstone, it was clear that he had every intention of creating opportunities for *direct* confrontation with central government, pitting County Hall against Westminster.*

Overwhelming public support for the retention of the GLC, 74 per cent in one poll, and even vociferous opposition to its abolition by Conservatives such as Edward Heath were to no avail. The GLC elections were cancelled in 1985, thus cutting off their use as a plebiscite, and it ceased to exist on 31 March 1986 amid the crackle and whiz of a great firework display.

Red Ken, however was neither down nor out. Elected to Parliament as the Labour MP for Brent in West London, Livingstone resigned in order to fight as an independent for the new position of Mayor of London in 2000. Still regarded with affection by many of the capital's voters, a man who no longer represented the 'loony left', but was rather someone whose integrity seemed impeccable given his rivals, he was elected in a poll so low in turnout that it reinforced the realization that Londoners have little interest in who governs their town.

---

*Not everyone was an enthusiastic supporter of the GLC. Thatcher had odd comrades. On 10 June 2003 the *Evening Standard* broke a story regarding the planned assassination of Ken Livingstone whilst he had been Leader. Michael Stone, the convicted killer of three mourners at an IRA funeral, revealed how Loyalist paramilitaries, angered at Livingstone's apparent favourable treatment of the IRA, had stalked him in preparation for the murder on the London Underground which would have been carried out by a hooded gunman. The plan was aborted because of its possible adverse repercussions.

16
Brave Boys of the BUF
The Origins of London Fascism

In the early years of the twentieth century one antidote to the Communist menace and the spectre of a 'red' London was fascism. Many of the groups that coalesced to form the core of London's fascist parties had their origin in the covert war fought over wages between industrialists and workers. The crisis in Liberal politics during the period around the First World War was defined by a growing and apparently unstoppable challenge from socialism on the one hand, and on the other a determined and intransigent rejection of compromise in industry, and over empire or Ireland by the ultra-Conservatives known as the Diehards. In Liverpool and elsewhere, industrialists such as the Cunard family were paying spies to inform on Communist or anarchist troublemakers, and the Cunards' man, J. McGuirk Hughes, was only one of a number of infiltrators and agents provocateurs used by the right to disrupt left-wing opposition. Some union leaders also subscribed to having Communists watched or sacked.

Men like Hughes belonged to patriotic 'volunteer' agencies such as the British Empire Union (BEU), which had grown from the Anti-German Union begun in 1915. The Central Economic Council and the National Propaganda Fund coordinated anti-Communist efforts. Meanwhile such groups soon took on a more aggressive attitude that included the use of arms. Nowhere was this more obvious than in the support of the Ulster Volunteer Force (UVF) in 1913, but it also can be detected in the National Security Union, the Liberty League, the Anti-Socialist Union, the National Citizens' Union and the British Commonwealth Union (BCU). Created by ex-military men, generals and admirals, these organizations were military in outlook. Some were hoping to 'mobilise the patriotic element in the country' into military units, and the BEU created 'a perfectly well known gang of bullies'. From these groups British Fascisti (BF) formed its own protection squads, called Q Divisions, in the 1920s and Mosley recruited his Biff Boys. The BEU indeed recruited from ex-servicemen and reservists who attacked meetings of which they disapproved. Strike-breakers and blackleg protection squads were also formed.

When it came to recruitment into the BF, the initial members came from these vigilante origins. Prominent were retired officers, and aristocrats such as Alan Percy, Duke of Northumberland whose paper, the *Patriot*, announced the creation of the BF. Northumberland was a Diehard ultra-patriot who saw fascism as the *only* solution to Britain's decline. Indeed, shortly before the Fascisti was launched Northumberland had written that 'all those brutal attacks on Christianity, individual liberty, patriotism and loyalty to the throne, under which – but for the coming of Fascism – Italian civilization had perished, are to be reproduced here'.[1] The BEU meanwhile, with whom Northumberland was also linked, had by 1923

> become deeply paranoid about the prospect of a constitutionally elected Labour government which, it believed, would be secretly controlled by 'alien' Bolshevik agents 'trained in Moscow'. Its annual report for 1922 warned that 'all sections of the Socialist Party, from the most moderate to the extreme Communists . . . were devoting themselves with redoubled efforts to propaganda . . . and electoral strategy', and that anti-socialist forces had to pre-pare themselves for a possible Labour victory at the next election and organise to fight and destroy Labour's attempts to 'Bolshevise' Britain.[2]

Fear of political disorder was such that even George V made contact with the National Fascisti (wound up 1927) through Lord Stamfordham, who spoke to their President, Lieutenant Colonel H. Rippon Seymour, about their preparedness for patriotic duties.

Fascism's hour seemed to have arrived when on 1 May 1926 the Trade Union Council (TUC) met at Memorial Hall in Farringdon and ratified its decision to call an all-out strike in support of the miners. The General Strike brought 100,000 volunteers into the government's control, including aristocrats such as Lady Astor, the 460 under-graduates known as the 'plus-four brigade' and the membership of National Fascisti who considered the entire affair was a Communist plot led, in part, by their favourite hate figure Shapurji Saklatvala, MP for Battersea North and nicknamed 'Parsee Pawnee-Wallah' in extreme-right propaganda.

Fascists busied themselves in Hyde Park, where the government had organized a food distribution centre, helped as volunteers on buses and trains and generally made as much fuss as possible about their new role fighting the CPGB, who they considered at the bot-tom of it all. Nevertheless, despite their bluff and bluster, and despite their acknowledged *official* role as part of the government's machine, fascists never got to mix it with Communists on the streets of London despite the fact that there were sporadic scuffles with police when demonstrators gathered at Elephant and Castle, along the New Kent Road, Newington Causeway or at Newington Butts. Although volunteers were blacklegging in docks at the Pool of London, and armoured cars and troops had to escort food convoys down the East India Dock Road and Commercial Road, almost no violence occurred in London and crowds remained jovial. Close to the docks Leyton trades council reported a 'very pleasant relationship with the police' throughout.

Occasional attempts to label the General Strike a 'revolution' were suppressed by both the government and the TUC; the CPGB leadership were already languishing in prison, jailed under the Incitement to Mutiny Act, 2,500 members had been arrested during demonstrations and all this *without* the CPGB endorsing the actions of the TUC. Unlike Coventry, London never had a 'soviet' (workers' council) to direct operations and thus the fascists did not have the chance, which later came their way, to confront Communism directly on the streets. For National Fascisti, the General Strike proved little more than a 'phoney war'.

Many of these groups moved inexorably towards more and more extreme solutions as they identified their enemy as the (Jew-) Communist. These solutions had their roots in the collaboration between Special Branch and hardline Diehards during the First World War. The National War Aims Committee (NWAC), set up in June 1917 and put under the control of Sir Edward Carson, was intended to counter pacifism. The NWAC used the BEU and British Workers' League, and the Cabinet instructed Special Branch to supply confidential information on meetings and individuals opposed to the war effort. 'Spontaneous opposition' was then orchestrated by gangs of right-wing volunteers and pacifists and Communists were harassed and beaten up. The army's intelligence unit A2 also used the services of the BEU. These vigilante groups were a ready recruiting ground for the volunteers who flocked to help break the General Strike. The networks built up from 1912/13 onwards by such organizations, and especially by their leading members, made them useful to British intelligence. Admiral Hall, formerly Director of Naval Intelligence, was Director of the National Security Union (NSU), National Propaganda and Chairman of the Economic League. Sir Vincent Caillard, first Director of NSU, Patrick Hannon of the BCU, George Makgill of the BEU and the Duke of Northumberland, amongst many others, cooperated with MI5 and supplied agents. This had considerable significance when two former members of the BF, William Joyce of the BUF and Charles Maxwell Knight of MI5, found themselves on opposing sides during 1940 (see below).

The vigilance committees and ad hoc partisan clubs of the 1920s found political expression in the appearance of Rotha Lintorn Orman's British Fascisti (BF) during 1923. Lintorn Orman was an early recruit for the Girl Guides (as a troop leader) and served with the Women's Reserve Ambulance Corps during the First World War where she showed conspicuous bravery. Her new organization, made up from admirers of Mussolini and of strong government, paraded in their blue uniforms and protected ultra-Conservatives at party meetings or hustings. Their enemy was Communism but Lintorn Orman's was the alcohol to which she finally succumbed during 1935 after her organization went bankrupt. The appearance of the BF with their blue uniforms was often a cause for amusement for their opponents. In October 1928, Captain Robert Smith, its General Secretary, complained to the manager of the Metropolitan and District Line at Victoria because the booking clerks had whistled 'The Red Flag' when he asked for a ticket.

The organization had been military in style from the beginning with its discipline enforced by a Grand Council of retired colonial officers and military types including Brigadier General Blackeney, former general manager of the Egyptian State Railway. Such a group provided a *political* focus for every sort of patriot and imperialist and gave a platform to those who believed the 'Red Menace' was Jewish inspired. Such people included Arnold Leese, a former vet from the Middle East whose book on diseases of camels was a standard in veterinary circles. He was one of two councillors in Stamford in Lincolnshire but he was also an extreme anti-Semite whose influence would far outweigh his own personal value to the BF or his activities with his own organization, the Imperial Fascist League (IFL). Alongside Leese were other committed Jew haters, the most significant being William Joyce.

William Joyce was attracted to the fascist ideal as an enthusiastic seventeen-year-old and he joined the BF during 1923. What attracted him was what attracted young people to the YCL, a sense of belonging and of purpose and a community of like-minded friends whose idealism suffused their leisure time and personal habits. Fascism (like Communism) in Britain engendered a club-like bonhomie and camaraderie for those whose sense of outrage at social decline could be matched to a sense of purpose.

Joyce had been brought up in Ireland, the son of an Irish Catholic builder who had tried to make good in America, failed and returned, even if with an American passport. Like his parents the young Joyce believed in law and order and took pride in his patriotism even though he too had an American passport. The family always saw themselves as British and he insisted upon it even though the father always had only an American passport. The American episode would be the one incident that might have saved Joyce junior from the hangman, but he always reiterated his Englishness. Despite being a Catholic, William Joyce was a Unionist and he despised the gunmen of the IRA whom he claimed he had fought as an 'irregular' with a knowledge of 'bayonet fighting'. This had led him to apply to the Officer Training Corps in the hope of a place in the Regular Army. His letter of application, written at age sixteen, already repeated the myth that he was a British citizen. With Lloyd George negotiating away part of the Union with Sinn Fein and the subsequent creation of the Irish Free State, the Joyces moved to the heart of Empire – London. For William the old order was not only corrupt but also traitorous.

Meanwhile Joyce began to study at Battersea Polytechnic, where he sat the intermediate examination for entry to London University in order to study at Birkbeck. At Birkbeck he gained a first-class degree in English Literature; at Battersea he gained skills in boxing, fencing and riding and became quite an athlete. By the time he joined the BF, he was already, as the fascist traitor Norman Baillee-Stewart put it, a 'thug of the first order'. Joyce's ability with his fists made him an ideal candidate for the BF's I Squad of toughs who 'protected' Diehard meetings from Communist disturbances. During the election campaign of 1924 and after the publication of the Zinoviev letter, antipathy to socialism verged upon paranoia. Fighting at the hustings was a regular feature of the campaign and Joyce and I Squad were deployed wherever Communists threatened disruption.

A week before the elections (22 October 1924) Joyce was on duty at Lambeth Baths. Fighting broke out during the evening and Joyce was slashed across the face with a razor. He claimed he had been fighting bravely against overwhelming odds but was more probably 'jumped' and held down. Either way, he acquired a very long scar on his right cheek that extended from his ear to his mouth. This was confirmation enough of the appalling levels of violence the 'Jewish Communists' and 'Jewish organisers of the Left' would stoop to. Joyce was never in any doubt that he had been attacked by a '*Jewish* Communist' not just a left-wing ruffian. His hatred of Jews, which one biographer describes as 'near hysterical loathing', also extended to his tutors, Joyce insisting his 'Jewish' tutor at London University plagiarized his master's degree (a bizarre and deluded accusation).[3]

By the late 1920s, Joyce was a disillusioned fascist but an experienced street-corner orator with an ability to hold a crowd and a street fighter with an ability to use a knuckleduster. He left the BF and joined the Conservatives but he was only marking time until 'the Leader' appeared. Sir Oswald Mosley was, for Joyce, 'the greatest Englishman I have ever known' and he was soon a devoted disciple. Mosley, in return, thought Joyce 'intensely vain . . . a very small man'.[4]

Mosley was a man in a hurry – dashing, handsome and an expert swordsman. Born in 1896, his rise to prominence and his maverick nature soon made themselves evident in the Commons. He began his political career as Conservative Unionist MP for Harrow, holding the seat from 1918 to 1922, but he crossed the House over Ireland and the treatment of Sinn Fein prisoners in 1922. He kept his seat as an Independent until 1924, when he joined the Labour Party as MP for Birmingham, Smethwick. In the ranks of Labour he was a rising star and soon became Chancellor of the Duchy of Lancaster with promises of the highest rank beckoning. But Mosley was impatient and when Ramsay MacDonald, the Prime Minister, rejected his economic and social plan for reconstruction, known as the 'Mosley Memorandum', he resigned his office.

Mosley had a mission to revive British fortunes and prestige and finally provide the 'home fit for heroes' promised after the First World War. The democratic process had failed, it seemed, as the 'old guard' refused to see the coming disaster and Labour refused to act out its promised socialist programme. On the other hand, Mosley was enthused with a vision of a new Britain, with first and foremost a return to full employment and an end to industrial decline. To put forward this 'steel creed of an iron age', he proposed a controlled economy with central direction. The corporate state that would emerge would use the Empire and Dominions as a self-sufficient, closed or 'autarkic' economic zone with both public and private ownership in a managed economy. Africa would form the bottom of this pyramid, Britain's African colonies providing cheap labour and raw materials. The market would be manipulated to the advantage of 'our own race'. At the same time, although there would be no Parliament there would be an 'occupational franchise' to select a body of citizens to provide plebiscites when an 'election' was needed. Such elections would determine the oligarchy that would manage the economy alongside an upper house of 'Notables'. Mosley's pattern was Italian and his model fascistic and authoritarian. Vision and leadership would be provided by a vanguard party (the party Mosley would now create) and a visionary hero: Mosley himself. Mosley may have had a background of privilege but his distaste for the 'old gang' brought him close to the revolutionary socialism of the Communist Party of Great Britain. Unlike the CPGB's essentially material view of culture seen in the cold light of economic determinism, Mosley's attitude was predominantly mystical and transcendent. In short, he was a romantic who felt the future of Britain was embodied in *his own personality* and that therefore the future could not take place without him.

His rejection of Labourism was reinforced when he felt his position vindicated at the Labour Party Conference of 1930, some time after his resignation. His solution was the creation of a third party to challenge the collapse of will that resulted in the National Government of 1931. The New Party (NP) put up twenty-four candidates and with tension rising between NP and Labour supporters and Communists, he also organized the Biff Boys, who relied on 'the good old English fist' to keep order. The Biff Boys were organized and trained by Ted 'Kid' Lewis, a Jewish boxer from the East End, and Mosley was backed by the Jewish publisher Paul Hamlyn, but both withdrew once Mosley's fascism was financed by others of a more overtly anti-Semitic nature: Lord Nuffield the car magnate and Lord Rothermere at the *Daily Mail*.

The campaign proved a disaster despite Mosley's powerful backers, and no candidates were returned. More extreme solutions beckoned and Mosley relaunched his party as the British Union of Fascists (BUF) on 1 October 1932. By this time he had been deserted by John Strachey (who joined the CPGB and then found Catholicism), Harold Nicolson and any Jewish support. By early 1933 people like William Joyce saw in Mosley the promised light. With a clear rejection of socialism, a new 'military' barracks called the Black House in Chelsea and an egalitarian black uniform, the BUF were reactionary revolutionaries who were going to break the mould. Fascism's new race men and women was intended to be heroic and athletic; their symbols were the racing car and the aeroplane whizzing along in a futurist vision of speed and steel. Thus, when Sir Malcolm Campbell recorded a land-speed record at Daytona on 7 March 1935 he carried the pennant of the BUF London Volunteer Transport Service. Like fascists across Europe, Mosley was only too well aware of the power of spectacle and the use it could be put to at rallies. He was a master of the mass meeting, NP having held one at the Albert Hall. In 1931 NP had its own film unit, and set about making a film for the times. *Crisis* was shown at a screening in Birmingham in October but was banned by the censor and finally lost. The BUF were always concerned with the use of cinemas for their propaganda as cinema chains were a 'monopoly' of their 'implacable opponent, the Jew, Isidore Ostrer [sic]' – a reference to the Odeon chain's chairman. Now Mosley intended to use Olympia to stage a great meeting in June 1934, with a seated audience of 12,000 including guests and dignitaries. It would make use of arc lights which would swamp the hall with their beams finally coming to rest on the great man himself at the podium.

The plans for the meeting were, from the start, seen as a provocation to the CPGB, who were determined to break it up. They had cause to be alarmed, as Lord Rothermere of the *Daily Mail* had thrown his weight behind Mosley and given him a voice in the media. Special Branch reported that trouble was brewing, and by late May it had information to show that CP members disguised as Blackshirts would infiltrate the audience. The CPGB also organized a counter-demonstration to be held outside Olympia on the evening of the rally, advertised on 17 May by the *Daily Worker*. A large Jewish contingent would also be present. Five hundred Communists, disguised as Blackshirts, duly took their seats as a demonstration of 2,000–3,000 people gathered outside. Meanwhile the Blackshirts had marched from the Black House in the King's Road, Chelsea in full uniform to provide the 'honour guard' of 2,000 with 1,000 acting as stewards. The audience began to arrive amidst scenes of increasing hostility and some had to force their way through the crowd, which booed and jostled.

The class nature of the confrontation comes out clearly in a letter sent by one member of the audience to Lord Trenchard, the police commissioner, complaining that he and his wife had been 'pushed by a gang of roughs' at the entrance, that he had heard the phrase 'bloody murderers' shouted at ticket holders of 'high rank in society', and that 'ladies and gentlemen of gentle birth' had had 'horrible faces thrust in their carriage windows'.[5]

Mosley could be pleased with himself as his organization was now the toast of society and a large number of Britain's socialites and establishment figures graced the guest list. The whole thing would be a coup de théâtre. At 8.30 the meeting got under way as fifty-six standard bearers preceded him to the platform swept by the powerful searchlights the BUF had hired.

'Ladies and gentlemen,' began Sir Oswald, looking no doubt with satisfaction on the organizational machinery that now put him under the spotlight. 'This meeting . . . is the culmination of a great national campaign' . . . but he hardly got the next few words out before chanting and fighting broke out in the audience. 'Fascism means murder: down with Mosley!' came the shouts as black-shirted stewards ran towards the interrupters and fighting erupted in the auditorium. Mosley called for calm and after some further interruptions, he finished his speech, everybody sang the National Anthem and went home. The sergeant at Hammersmith police station recorded that the event went off 'without any serious violence'. He was less than truthful.

What occurred grew with the telling but it is quite clear that both sides used extreme violence. Twenty-three people were arrested outside for carrying offensive weapons, others were arrested as known 'troublemakers'; many were Jewish. Inside the hall searchlights had played on the fighting amongst the audience in which, as *The Times* reported, 'wholly unnecessary violence [was] inflicted by uniformed Blackshirts'. The whole affair was 'a deplorable outrage on public order' with the Blackshirts acting like 'bullies and cads', said Geoffrey Lloyd reporting on events to Stanley Baldwin next day. Mosley went on to the BBC to defend free speech but the BBC had had enough of him and he broadcast again only in 1968.

Violence in the hall itself and in the surrounding corridors was clearly disproportionate to the disturbances and considered by many witnesses, including Aldous Huxley, to be 'sadistic'. Women were beaten and stripped and men debagged or left naked from the waist down having been attacked with knuckledusters, razors and coshes.

> Both sides allege use of weapons. Mosley produced a collection of them which he said he had captured from the 'Reds' after Olympia, including a hatchet. Philip Toynbee and Esmond Romilly had knuckledusters. Miss Pearl Binder, on the other hand, specifically states that she saw 'several Blackshirts using knuckledusters'.[6]

The Communists were also armed but claimed disingenuously that they only acted passively when confronted by their attackers. They were, of course, greatly outnumbered and reasonable opinion did not put the blame on them. The Very Reverend Dick Shepherd, who had officiated at Sir Oswald's first marriage, to Cimmie Curzon, and also officiated at her funeral, confirmed the level of Blackshirt thuggery in an interview for the *Daily Telegraph*.

There were those, however, who saw Mosley as a champion of free speech and the man who would stand up to the Communists and Jews. Lloyd George approved of Mosley's spirit. 'You are having a very exciting time and I envy you your experience. At your age I went through a period of riot and tumult in my endeavour to convey my ideas to a resentful public.'[7]

Others, such as the former editor of the socialist *Daily Herald*, Hamilton Fyfe, condemned the counter-demonstration and hecklers and blamed the whole thing on Jewish 'young men . . . in fighting mood'. Mosley's biographer, Robert Skidelsky, reflected on the *political* significance of the rally.

> Why, then, all the furore? First, there is no doubt that many violent acts took place which were deeply shocking to those who witnessed them. Secondly, although political violence on the scale of Olympia had occurred in the nineteenth and early twentieth centuries, it had virtually disappeared by the 1920s. People relatively new to politics or those unconnected with politics were shocked at this echo from half-forgotten times which seemed so 'unEnglish'. Politicians with older memories, like Lloyd George, or those with more recent experience of violence, such as the I.L.P. or left-wing labour groups, were less shocked and outraged. There was little sense of outrage in the *Daily Worker* report after Olympia: the tone was very much that of the good fight well fought. It was only

after Olympia that the communists fully realised what a valuable ally they had in the liberal conscience.[8]

Whatever occurred inside Olympia that day, whether thirty protesters were reasonably ejected or were beaten up, whether the CPGB brought the whole thing on their own (provocative) heads or even whether Mosley revelled in the brawls highlighted by the lights; whatever occurred profoundly affected future feeling on both sides. Mosley lined up firmly against Jewish opponents and Communists; trade unionists and Jews in London, Leeds and Manchester prepared for a long street war.

The rally at Olympia was declared a victory by both sides but it was clearly a propaganda victory for the Communists and anti-fascists. Mosley needed another venue and better stewarding but his meeting at White City in August 1934 had had to be cancelled and so the BUF prepared to march to Hyde Park on 9 September. Lord Trenchard was only too aware by this time of a new element that had crept into fascist mass rallies – the use of technology. On 2 July 1934 he offered his advice on the White City booking.

> It is unquestionably a new element of danger in these meetings that by means of loud speakers one person can address a crowd of people five or six times as large as was previously possible. A big Fascist demonstration, with Communists and Socialists present, is, in the present state of public feeling, an explosive mixture of a highly dangerous kind, and if, as I gather, the view of the Government is that such meetings cannot be prohibited altogether, I must ask them to consider what the results are likely to be.[9]

By the mid-1930s Mosley had already purchased five big loudspeaker lorries, at least one of which (AXL 591), survived the Blitz and was reused by the BUF's successor organization, Union Movement, in 1948.

The counter-demonstration, which would also head for Hyde Park, was planned as the culmination of the greatest political campaign against fascism that had been organized in this country 'and it consisted of various communist controlled bodies, co-operatives and trades council organisations, and a . . . number of trades union branches'. Its coordinating secretary was John Strachey and although a large number of Jewish protesters joined those marching they were not represented as a specifically Jewish group. This is of some importance as it is too easy just to see fascists as merely anti-Semites and anti-fascists as 'only' Jews.

Before the marches, Special Branch reported,

Hundreds of thousands of leaflets etc., were distributed at meetings, thrown from buses in crowded thoroughfares, from the top
of Selfridges and other buildings; large posters were displayed,
without authority and taken down on being discovered, from
the Law Courts, Broadcasting House and Transport House; and
attempts, which were sometimes partially successful, were made
to broadcast anti-fascist slogans through 'outside' microphones
used by the B.B.C. In addition the communists followed their
usual practice of painting and chalking slogans on walls, pave-
ments etc.[10]

On the day, anti-fascist contingents came in from the Edgware
Road and Marylebone Road (North and North-West London),
Stepney Green (East London, led by Harry Pollitt of CPGB and John
McGovern MP) and Exhibition Road (West, South-West and South-
East London contingent) whilst printers, busmen and railway work-
ers came along the Embankment (despite police refusal) and Lambeth
Palace Road. Collections taken in the East End, it was reported, 'were
well supported by the Jewish community'. By late afternoon 10,000
anti-fascists gathered at their four speakers' platforms where nine-
teen speakers prepared to shout their message to those willing to
hear. Many marchers and spectators drifted off to heckle the BUF.
Mosley's 2,500 men and 450 women assembled at Victoria
Embankment (the trade union opposition had been refused a meeting here previously) at 2.40 in the afternoon having arrived by
underground or bus, many direct from the BUF Headquarters, the
Black House, in Chelsea. All were dressed in their black uniform and
Mosley's 'guard' were dressed especially smartly in knee-high boots.
At 4.40 p.m., Mosley duly arrived and drove along the assembled
legion giving the fascist salute from an open-top car after which
the group marched three abreast through Northumberland Avenue
and Piccadilly to Hyde Park. Police noted that the appearance of the
Blackshirts led not to fear but mirth amongst spectators. Inspector
Harold Keeble reported to his superiors that, 'The assembly was witnessed by about 2,000 onlookers, many of whom showed much
amusement at the quasi-military movements of the Blackshirts'.
As the fascist military-style band entered Apsley Gate the crowd
began booing and 'catcalling'. Finally the speeches from platforms
1 to 5 ceased and attention focused on Mosley at platform 4 but his
speech like those of all his colleagues was drowned out by a hostile
crowd only yards away. A bodyguard surrounded Mosley for protection as he told anyone who could hear that

[he] knew that an organised attempt would be made to interfere,
but it had failed. Blackshirts were attacked by street terror and

by corrupt power in parliament, which sinks to mob terror and underhand methods. From Baldwin to Pollitt the front against fascism is unbroken. To-day they seek to suppress us. They will fail, but to-morrow we shall succeed in suppressing them. They fight, they yell, they howl against Fascism, because they know the red flag is going down and the Union Jack is going up. The fury and force of the opposition against us is the greatest tribute to the Blackshirt movement.[11]

He had been preceded by John Beckett, who had joined the BUF in 1934. Earlier that afternoon Beckett had spoken of the BUF's loyalty to 'king and country . . . the British nation . . . and the British Constitution'. Only minor speakers used any embarrassing attacks on Jews and Mosley re-emphasized his crusade against Communism.

For their part the CPGB emphasized that the BUF were the lackeys of the capitalists and that Lord Trenchard was himself a fascist and friend of Mosley. John McGovern was clear as to Mosley's 'real' agenda:

Mosley is in his position at the present time representing all that is rotten in British political life today, trying to get support for fascist politics in Britain by the same method that Hitler got them in Germany. You may have been impressed by Mosley's 'Ten Points'; may I remind you that Hitler achieved his popularity also on the basis of ten points.[12]

Yet it was McGovern who advocated violence, not Mosley:

War would have come a year ago if the ruling class had not been afraid of the people. They were afraid to place rifles in the hands of the common people. They are capable of shooting down members of the ruling class. Bullets are no respecters of persons. Bullets have been known to despatch kings and empires. I am not telling you to shoot them, but I am telling you they have been known to do it . . .[13]

Despite the heady language of revolution and of patriotism, almost no one was hurt and everybody went home satisfied. The anti-fascists believed their disciplined and restrained show of force had won the argument and fascist activity would now diminish, exposed as the charade they believed it to be. They were wrong. The fascists believed their iron will and sheer presence lent strength to their message of unity. They too were wrong but they certainly felt like they might be winning even if they were not quite ready to challenge their real enemy, the Communist–Jewish conspiracy, head on. This would not occur until October 1936.

Mosley might enjoy a large rally but he was best on the street or out in a large open space speaking from the roof of a loudspeaker lorry. He might be a baronet, at ease amongst the Mayfair and Chelsea sets, but for over thirty years he remained London's leading street orator and the East End's own demagogue. He was always at home amongst the disenchanted indigenous white working class of the old East End – one of a tight-knit pantheon that would later include the Kray twins. Mosley's maverick 'bolshie' aristocratic attitude perfectly complemented the aggressive cockneyism of Whitechapel or Dalston with its paradoxical combination of fierce patriotism, hatred of the establishment, self-regarding superiority and sense of rightness. His East End supporters felt a real sense of self-containment and at-homeness with a person recognized as one of their own. The *Daily Mail* (having dropped Mosley but still friendly) reported a typical East End meeting held in June 1936 in Victoria Park.

A mob, a multitude, of men and women and children surging round three black loud-speaker vans drawn together under the evening sun of a typical English park. Ringing the mob posses of mounted police and little knots of foot police.

The crowd is orderly, for the most part a middle-class assembly in its Sunday clothes, but here and there are sections of more ugly-looking customers.

On the roofs of the vans stand four or five uniformed men, some in black shirts, others in a German-looking uniform of black tunics and peaked hats. These wear brassards of red with a white circle on which is shown the streak of forked lightning, which is the Mosley equivalent of the Hitler swastika.

There is a roar of cheering and the sudden outburst of hoots and hisses and the singing of the 'Internationale'.

Mosley has suddenly appeared, as if sent up through a pantomime trap, and is giving the Fascist salute. It is answered by hundreds of hands clustered around the vans, and the familiar standards rise above the ragged level of human heads.

The speech begins. It is a forceful exposition of Britain for the British. It attacks internationalism and Jewry. He then embarks on a sea of simple economics.

The Reds are congregated in one corner of the huge terrain, and the speech is not heard there over the hooting and the singing. Every little while the police ride into the thick of the crowd, a little cruising police van comes to the edge of the mob, and some more vicious interrupter is thrust within, but for the most part of the audience is partly good-humoured, after the manner of people having a free show on an idle evening, and partly intent upon hearing the exposition of the credo.

Within an hour it is over. The Fascist marching song is sung and the National Anthem played.

Police appear from everywhere to protect the column, which marches off to the objurations and insults of angry Communists, spitting obscenities at the women's sections.

But organisation is triumphant. The unruffled police and the equally unruffled Blackshirts ride and march away to martial music – and the show is over.[14]

The ordinary men and women who joined the BUF because it gave them a cause and a purpose were opposed by equally ordinary people who saw the cause and purpose of fascism as inherently evil – its anti-Semitism part of a capitalist conspiracy to divide the working class. There were people such as Frank Frankford who came to live in Hackney and joined the YCL in the 1930s. He was born the illegitimate son of a wealthy factory owner in Slough in 1913 but drifted towards socialism and joined the Hackney Branch of the CP. Membership of the CP did not last and Frankford ended up in the ILP, which met at the Salmon and Bull pub in Cambridge Heath Road, where the wide pavement was a good place to attract a crowd to debate issues of the day and tactics for beating the fascists. On one occasion BUF members coming from their meeting in Bethnal Green found a ready target in ILP members coming from theirs when it closed at ten. The result, with BUF boys shouting 'Jew bastards', was a fracas that required police. Later Frankford was set upon by Blackshirts in the Whitechapel Road. Fired up with the need to defeat fascist oppression he finally travelled with the International Brigade to Spain.[15]

Many women joined the struggle against fascism. Kathleen Gibbons was a single mother earning a living selling encyclopaedias in St Pancras. She began attending CP meetings on the street of Mornington Crescent where the party erected platforms for its speakers. One speaker, Joe Kennedy, wore a kilt and was as 'good as pantomime'. By 1933, she was already aware of the coming plight of German Jews from reading about Nazi propaganda and she was determined 'to fight it' as fascism 'was no friend of working people'. St Pancras was, however, 'very anti-fascist' and showed 'real working-class solidarity'; indeed 'half Camden Town' had 'turned out' to attack the BUF 'scum of London'.

Gibbons was first arrested at a demonstration during the middle 1930s (1935 or 1936, she thought [actually 1937]) outside the Stanley Institute in Tufnel Park and taken to Holmes Road police station. Here, as elsewhere, she was struck by the fact that the police 'were fascists' and were sympathetic to the Blackshirts. One day in 1936 after attending her co-op's quarterly meeting, Gibbons went to shout at the fascists. Whilst bawling 'What about Guernica?' she was arrested by a local sergeant, 'a white-faced bastard, [a] real fascist himself', and charged with disturbing the peace. At Clerkenwell Court, the magistrate fined her *all* her co-op savings: £4.

Alongside Frank Frankford and Kathleen Gibbons were dedicated Jewish socialists who were in the forefront of the fight. These included people like Phil Piratin, who went on to become one of the CP's two MPs after the war (1945–1950). Piratin and hundreds of thousands of anti-fascists found an opportunity for action on 4 October 1936, the day Mosley had scheduled for a march into the heart of the East End.

Mosley could always count on a large and consistent constituency of East End voters, most of whom were disaffected, 'lower middle class, semi-agricultural people' whose cultural conservation split them from their Labour-voting neighbours and moulded them into a reactionary Liberal position convertible into fascism. These 'islands' of voters remained loyal to Mosley and fascism from the 1930s to the 1990s. Mosley intended to play to these interests and march from Royal Mint Street to Shoreditch, Limehouse, Bow and Bethnal Green. Knowing that his decision to march would cause a massive reaction, Mosley was soon faced with the problem of where he should actually march with his 3,000 supporters. He decided on a relatively 'neutral' route away from the centre of the Jewish population, and chose Cable Street near Ratcliffe Highway.

As usual the Blackshirt leaders were dressed in their uniforms, not this time the utility 'fencing' uniform usually worn at meetings and intended to prove fascism's egalitarian nature, but instead the full-dress marching version of black peaked cap, black military tunic with brass buttons, black leather Sam Browne belt, black jodhpurs and jackboots; on the arm, a brassard with the fascist symbol: a circle enclosing a lightning bolt. Mosley would take the measure of his men from an open-topped car giving the fascist salute as they paraded. Between double rows of police they then marched east.

Philip Piratin was born in Coke Street, Stepney in 1907 of Russian Jewish parents who came to Britain in the 1890s. Although his father and mother both spoke Yiddish they brought their children up to speak English and although Piratin went to religious classes his family entered the first quarter of the twentieth century 'Anglicized'. When his brother went to war in 1917, Piratin 'felt English. No question at all'. Socialist in outlook, he became a socialist in action when he heard of the dumping of oranges from a boat in Liverpool, which could have been given to the poor but were wasted to save profits. During 1929 or early 1930 and whilst in his early twenties, Piratin joined the Friends of the Soviet Union and started to read economics, finally joining the CPGB in 1934 once the clash with fascism was seen as inevitable.

> And then there was the particular event in June, the summer of 1934, at the [sic] Olympia, where Mosley held a big rally; where there was a lot of violence. So that he already indicated he was following in the steps of Hitler. And that was the final stimulant [sic]. And the next week, I joined the Communist Party.[16]

Piratin joined the cell known as the Blackwell Buildings Group and then the Fulgate Mansions Group who boasted of a membership of 100–140 members in the borough but could rarely muster more than seven for a normal meeting. Nevertheless they felt Stepney was so radical that (like Lambeth many years later, or Poplar earlier) it had become an 'autonomous republic', a joke often repeated by CP members. In the local streets of the East End, fascists and Communists vied for the approval of local people and both groups were involved with the fight to improve tenants' rights. Where they differed was in their treatment of the Jewish population, who had now formed a Jewish People's Council against Fascism and many secular young Jews were active in the local CP.

Although Piratin was both Jewish and a Communist he regularly opposed the policy of 'see a fascist, bash him' until he learned of the violent scuffles at Olympia, when he realized his mistake. However, he was still under the restraint of the CP leaders, who wished to avoid a direct confrontation with the BUF in the East End, preferring instead to mount a rally in Trafalgar Square. It was not until the situation began to slip out of their hands that they declared for a defence of the area through which Mosley intended to march.

Piratin's own house at 65 New Road became headquarters and a new telephone line was put in by the Post Office. From here Piratin and others organized the erection of barricades and the stopping of trams, the provision of a medical and legal unit and the distribution of a million leaflets cancelling the rally at Trafalgar Square and calling for a mass demonstration on 4 October. With the slogan 'They shall not pass' (used by Republicans in the Spanish Civil War), a frenzy of activity, including wall and pavement chalking and leafleting as well as the distribution of the CP paper, brought vast numbers of anti-fascists to the area of Gardiner's Corner and Cable Street. Gardiner's Corner was the site of a famous local department store (later it burned down and the area was redeveloped) and Cable Street, slightly away from the real area of Jewish concentration, was a dingy narrow byway of old eighteenth- and nineteenth-century houses long subdivided into tenements and inhabited by dockers and others, including some

Jewish families. Here as elsewhere shops were shuttered (with the heavy wooden boards of the previous century), roadblocks were built using an overturned lorry and household furniture, and four trams (with the connivance of the CP Tramway Co-op) stopped before their terminus in order to constrict Gardiner's Corner, Commercial Road and Whitechapel, difficult to block because of their width. In Cable Street the barricades were hastily erected by CP members and others from East and West Ham led by a man called Ronnie Sell who was responsible for finding a suitable lorry to overturn.

> And Ronnie Sell was in charge of the barricades and so on. And there was a lorry which had to be pushed over. And they got hold of the wrong lorry. And these are the things we chuckled over for weeks. You make cock-ups, don't you? It's inevitable. But it was done.[17]

Such 'cock-ups' provided a 'giggle' and for Piratin and his CP colleagues the entire day was good humoured if sometimes aggressive. Meanwhile as the wrong lorry toppled into place Piratin and a friend travelled around on a motorbike checking the various barricades and the spirit of the groups behind them, including the Labour League of Youth, who had defied the main Labour Party and joined the CP for the action. Yet the CP were not the only group organizing. The ILP was there, but in small numbers, the largest component of the coalition belonging to the East London People's Council Against Fascism (ELPCAF) and Jewish Council, the latter acting against the advice of the Board of Deputies of British Jews. ELPCAF was made up of trades councils and local groups whilst the Jewish Council was essentially Bund (Friendly Society) based. Number Nine Branch of the Jewish Circle of the Jewish Council, based in Hackney, was also a 'revolutionary' cell. Elsewhere places were assigned to groups from as far afield as Stepney and Hammersmith. 'Bill' Fishman (later Professor William Fishman) marched along to Aldgate with the Hackney Branch of the YCL despite the Labour Party ban. He recalled,

> From out of the narrow courts, alleyways and main thoroughfares came the steady tramp of marching feet, growing in intensity as the columns were swelled by reinforcements. A forest of banners arose, borne aloft, with the watchwords THEY SHALL NOT PASS emblazoned in a multi-variety of colours, with red predominating. Youngsters clustered at the rear of the marchers chanting 'Mosley shall not pass!' and 'Bar the road to fascism!' Loud speaker vans . . . patrolled the streets booming out the message for all to rally to the defence lines at Cable Street and Gardiner's Corner. Mass battalions, mobilising spontaneously from the ranks of mainly local folk.[18]

Cable Street barricades were organized like a 'military operation', recalled Piratin afterwards, reminiscing about the Popular Front's 'intelligence' on the day.

> And the work which the intelligence section did was very effective. And we had two leaflets. All secretaries had been told that they'd got to have someone in a position where we could make contact with them. And then the cyclists would get through.
>
> One [type of leaflet] was in I think pink: one was in white. So that it made it clear. If the information was that [the fascists were] going to march, then our cyclists were ready to get down – New Road from Aldgate is half a mile – to Aldgate in no time, and distribute the white ones. And each white one had bundles of two hundred little leaflets, about that size – two hundred of these which you can put in your pocket.[19]

Piratin, his home now turned into CP headquarters, did not find himself in the fighting that followed.

The police, both on foot and mounted and supported by a radio-linked autogyro (an early form of helicopter), were soon attempting to clear a path for the BUF. The police, treating the crowds as ruffians, were intent on dispersing what they saw as a mere mob. The fighting therefore took place exclusively between protesters and police and as police horses charged along Cable Street and elsewhere the crowd surged and swayed and lapped around them. Marbles were flung on the street to send the horses flying, stones and insults were hurled as the police riders repeatedly charged but the mounted police themselves were unable or unwilling to draw their long batons. 'The mounted [police] were surrounded by such masses of people, that had anyone of them taken his baton . . . out, he could have been killed. They'd have torn him to pieces,' Piratin recalled.

The police, nevertheless, did baton charge the barricades along Cable Street and elsewhere. This was a day the police had hoped to avoid, being only too well aware that a violent confrontation was inevitable especially as the sheer numbers of protesters (300,000–500,000) would be impossible to disperse despite the use of 6,000 police officers and the entire mounted division. Equally the police were aware that they would run the gauntlet from attackers pelting them from upper-storey windows along the route. Sir Philip Game, the Metropolitan Police Commissioner, was in no doubt that he could *not* protect the route which the Home Secretary, Sir John Simon, had approved. Piratin recalled the to and fro of 'battle'.

The fascists were due to march at 2pm. The police, aiming to keep Leman Street clear, tried to hew a path through the crowd, estimated at at least 50,000, that blocked the whole of Gardiner's Corner. At the junction of Commercial Road and Leman Street a tram had been left standing by its anti-fascist driver. Before very long this was joined by others. Powerless before such an effective road block, the police turned their attention elsewhere. Time and time again they charged the crowd; the windows of neighbouring shops went in as people were pushed through them. But the police could make no impression on this immense human barricade.[20]

It was not long before fights had broken out amongst isolated groups of fascists and anti-fascists but it was the police who would face the crowd as they attempted to clear Leman Street and Gardiner's Corner and the area around the abandoned trams.

The protesters milling about consisted not only of Jews and Communists but also Irish dockers, professional people from Hampstead, shop workers from across the East End and busloads of people down from other cities.

Then, like a scene from a film someone called out 'the dockers are coming' and they swarmed into the street in their hundreds. Many of them carried pick-axes and they used them to pry up the paving stones – some they broke into pieces to use as missiles and some they used to build a barricade; they also had marbles to roll under the feet of the policemen's horses and fireworks to scare 'em.[21]

Most people recalled the aggression of the mounted police and the fear they engendered.

They were pushing us on to Gardiner's window. There were people going straight through the plate glass windows. There were horses coming straight into the crowd, and the police were just hitting anyone indiscriminately. We never saw a fascist all that day. We were fighting the police. They were just hitting everyone, there were women going down under the horses' hooves. Absolute terror . . .

People were knocked to the ground and the horses didn't care who they trod on. They tried to push them back. Of course, they went so far and no further. I went to help this chap who the horse had jumped on – his stomach, see? He was in terrific pain. I went to help him but the police were saying 'Get back, get back.' They were going to hit me, I had to go back, I couldn't help the man. But Mosley never got past. It was a heavy atmosphere. Many people were afraid, they stayed in their houses and wouldn't come out. But a lot of us did.[22]

Others saw things differently. The BBC covered the rioting for its programme *Radio Gazette*, which was broadcast a week later on 10 October. Its reporter Philip Wagner, an American journalist, was standing at the corner of Leman Street and Whitechapel Road and witnessed for himself the activities of 'the mob' who had '[lost] their head'. Watching the surge and retreat of the crowd, Wagner concluded that the only 'heroes were the cops'.[23] Faced with this disastrous build-up of civil disorder, Sir Philip Game advised Mosley to cancel his initial plans. Mosley, a stickler for law and order, did not demur, and led his march and rally westwards where he took the salute from his Bentley and disbanded his Blackshirts.* Although an extraordinary and significant achievement the 'victory' of 4 October was purely mythic and ideological. Mosley's men were back almost immediately smashing windows of Jewish property and preparing to march again.

During the months after Cable Street there was an intensification of street-corner speaking and local rallies. The BUF was hardly defeated. Police records show that between December 1936 and November 1937 the fascists held 3,094 meetings, and the anti-fascists 4,364 meetings, in the London area alone. The brawling and casual violence that accompanied such affairs was, however, rarely conveniently timed for police arrests and between 1 July 1936 and 30 June 1937 only 63 fascists and 140 anti-fascists were arrested in the area, and these were only for minor offences. Amazingly no one died in the entire period of the conflict.

On 2 May 1937 Mosley marched from Limehouse to Victoria Park Square in Bethnal Green, across the heart of the East End but avoiding Stepney and Whitechapel. The Blackshirt uniform had been banned by the Public Order Act 1936 and Mosley marched in a double-breasted suit and black sweater behind a bagpiper.** The march was neither banned nor attacked. On 3 October he marched from Westminster to Bermondsey, an area where he could expect a reasonable reception, and was again left alone by the opposition. In 1938, the women's corps of drums was formed to capitalize on the increased recruitment of women in the previous year. On 28 July 1938 the fascists organized a 'Britain First Campaign', which culminated in a rally at Ridley Road, Dalston. Mosley had previously toured London

---

*Mosley took the salute from his Bentley (GU2511), which did not resurface until spotted in Cannes in the 1980s.

**The Public Order Act (Section 5) made it an offence to use 'abusive' or 'offensive' language and to wear uniforms. It was first used against strikers at Haworth Colliery for creating a disturbance. Uniforms were actually banned on 7 January 1937.

on his loudspeaker lorry and may have addressed over a quarter of a million spectators in all. In July 1939 he held a vast peace rally at Earl's Court, claimed by his followers to be the largest indoor rally ever held, and in November he was back marching the streets of Bethnal Green, proclaiming 'We Demand Peace'. Finally on 5 May 1940 Mosley spoke to his last public audience at Victoria Park. It was the last outing for his girl drummers and (almost) all his loudspeaker lorries.

Just two weeks later (22 May 1940), Winston Churchill activated Regulation 18b of the Defence of the Realm Act, which allowed for suspension of habeus corpus and detention of enemies of the state and hostile aliens without trial and for the duration. Over 400 men and women were picked up, including Sir Oswald and Lady Diana. Most were sent to the Isle of Man, where they petitioned for their release as patriots. Mosley and Diana spent a comfortable imprisonment and almost all their followers were released relatively quickly. For the duration of the war, at least, the struggle was suspended.

Mosley was a patriot in an old-fashioned (if perverse) way and had no intention of acting as an agent for Hitler. He often protested his willingness to die opposing an invasion, although he never decided on his position given an *imposed* peace. The same could not be said for a handful of rabid Nazis who eagerly joined the minuscule and laughably useless British (or 'English') Free Corps. After the war they faced the consequences of their decision at the Old Bailey. Of these traitors, William Joyce (although technically an American, and never a member of the British Free Corps) was the most notorious.

Joyce escaped the police roundup and made his way to Germany. Here he became 'Lord Haw Haw' (as he was dubbed) and alongside John Amery he broadcast to Britain, where he found an audience denied to Mosley but which was now universally bemused or hostile. On 30 April 1945, as the Russians approached Berlin, Joyce made his final radio broadcast. In a slurred and syrupy voice, broken by long pauses and the thump of the table to emphasize a point, Joyce addressed his 'English listeners' who wished to 'live their own simple lives' just like their fellow Germans with whom they must now join to defeat the Soviet Union. The theme was the 'threat from the east' and 'the Bolshevik attack': only the 'German Wehrmacht stood between Soviet hordes and the British army'. Joyce signed off with 'Heil Hitler and farewell'; he went on the run only to be wounded, captured and identified. The British government passed the Treason Act the day before he was escorted back to Britain, and in the Old Bailey he stood trial for treason committed between 3 September 1939 and 2 July 1940. Given his actual nationality, he should not have been indicted but he was found guilty and sentenced to death. The Law Lords rejected his appeal and he was hanged on 3 January

1946 at Wandsworth, still the hero of many 18b detainees. He concluded his last letter to his wife 'Sieg Heil! Sieg Heil! Sieg Heil!'.

There were also a number of other fascist and pro-Nazi groups who joined together just before the war to form a 'leaderless and formless' confederation called the Nordic League, whose figure-head was Captain Ramsay MP. These included activists from the Militant Christian Patriots and the Liberty Restoration League, who met regularly in Lamb's Conduit Street to discuss issues of the day. The concept of the League, 'a free association of kindred spirits', brought together in 'an association rather than an organisation' had its origins in a British version of the Ku Klux Klan: the White Knights of Britain, known as the Hooded Men. For the most part the association was dedicated to upholding the Empire and defeating the Jewish conspiracy, debated regularly at various meetings: 'Race and nation' were the primary points of allegiance for those fighting 'International Zionism'. The 'mole' planted in its ranks by the Board of Deputies of British Jews (an ex-Special Branch inspector) reported that 'the speakers must be strongly anti-Semitic in their utterances. This is a proviso insisted upon'. Furthermore, the League claimed that 'every member . . . [was] fully prepared to commit acts of violence against Jews'. The Liberty Restoration League (LRL), a group led by Captain Bernard Acworth, avoided overt anti-Semitism in its lobbying of Parliament for greater economic freedom through privatization, but used such efforts to reinforce a covert message about Jewish monopolists and sovietizers. The secretary of the LRL, Captain Arthur Rogers, met Ramsay once a month to coordinate policy.

At meetings of the Right Club attended by a host of ex-army officers including naval commander E. H. Cole, Captain Eldwin Wright, Brigadier General Blackeney, General J. F. C. Fuller and Captain Ramsay were also representatives of the Arab Propaganda Bureau, an Australian 'professor', Serocold Skeals, a Unitarian preacher called Coverdale Sharp, a German, a Japanese and A. K. Chesterton (later to found the National Front). In a room full of anti-Semitic posters and books, Ramsay regaled his listeners with his forebodings.

> Having lost Germany, Italy, Hungary, Czechoslovakia and now Spain, the Jewish High Command were concentrating on Britain and France. A world war, and that very soon, was the only way to the fulfilment of Zionist ambitions. It must be brought about by fair means or foul.
>
> One man at the moment frustrated their plans. That man was Neville Chamberlain. Eden, Churchill, Hore-Belisha and a host of others would respond to the call immediately, but they were held in leash by the Premier.

It may be a revelation to some . . . but it is a proven fact that the Irish Republican Army is a Moscow controlled body, financed by Jewish gold.

It is no more coincidence that the I.R.A. is at this particular moment letting off squibs [!] in England. They will bomb a few more tube stations perhaps, a few more generators and pylons and in a short time, we shall become quite used to them.

But there is a far more sinister and more subtle motive for their presence here.

Watch Mr. Neville Chamberlain. If in the blowing up of another tube station or a public building, the Prime Minister is blown up too – well, it would be just another crime attributed to the wicked I.R.A., another blow for Irish freedom.

But remember that peace or war depend on Mr. Chamberlain, and the Jews are determined it shall be war.[24]

Applause and congratulations would be followed by drinks at 'the paying' bar and the toast of 'P.J.' and 'Perish Judah'.

The eventual roundup of British fascists, which took place during 1940, was precipitated by the actions of the Nordic League rather than the BUF. It was the aggressive pro-German line of the Nordic League that worried MI5 on the eve of the Second World War. More significantly German agents such as George Arnold Pfister, who worked for Otto Bene of the Ausland Organisation, had infiltrated the BUF and were in touch with Joyce in 1935. Although Pfister was expelled and exposed, émigré Germans met BUF members and members of the Nordic League more discreetly. Although Mosley did not go to Germany until 1935 it is noteworthy that from September 1934 his anti-Semitism became more marked, a possible push given by the success of Hitler, whose style of oratory he also began to copy.

Mosley certainly admired the corporate 'socialism' of the Third Reich, and the BUF became the British Union of Fascists and National Socialists in 1936 in imitation of the Nazi Party. After the war, the Walthamstow activist Charlie Watts castigated fellow BUF members in a circular letter (1 December 1945) for their tolerance of 'Hail [sic] Hitler' supporters, 'cranks and fanatics'.

Extreme Mosleyites and suspected Nazi sympathizers were interrogated by MI5 at Latchmere House on Ham Common. After a regime of 'semi-starvation' and psychological pressure, prisoners were meant to crack under interrogation. Some, however, like Charlie Watts, saw themselves as defiant heroes in enemy hands. At the end of his ordeal, Watts had breath enough to spit out, 'Hail Mosley – fuck 'em all!'

When hostilities were finally declared in 1939 Leese and Ramsay and most other pro-Germanists immediately declared their patriotism, disbanded their groups and suspended activity. Yet patriotism and pro-Germanism might actually be synonymous, as Mosley (a pan-Europeanist) was quite aware.

> We have said a hundred times that if the life of Britain were threatened we would give again, but I am not offering to fight in the quarrel of Jewish finance in a war from which Britain could withdraw at any moment she likes, with her Empire intact and her people safe.
>
> I am now concerned with only two simple facts. This war is no quarrel of the British people, this war is a quarrel of Jewish finance, so to our people I give myself for the winning of peace.[25]

Mosley was not a member of the Nordic League, but on its disbandment he immediately began to hold secret meetings with Ramsay and others.

Ramsay continued to intrigue to no great effect until his internment, but he had recruited a number of women to his ranks who were more sinister in intent. These included Mollie Hiscox, the mistress of Jock Houston (the rabble-rousing working-class agitator), Anna Wolkoff, a rabidly anti-Semitic pro-Hitlerist, and at least three MI5 plants, including Joan Miller (as 'Miss X'), who reported to Maxwell Knight, Head of Political Counter-Surveillance.

At the Russian Tea Room in Harrington Gardens, South Kensington, Anna Wolkoff presided over an essentially Nazi salon, using the restaurant as a cover for Right Club activities. The restaurant, with its caviar and cocktails, was geographically at the heart of the aristocratic and upper middle-class fascist world – Ramsay lived in Onslow Square, the Black House had been situated in Chelsea, Mosley had a flat in Dolphin Square and most of the other members had homes in or near Chelsea and Kensington. From here, Wolkoff arranged 'sticker' raids (the use of sticky labels) to spread anti-Semitic propaganda.

> Walk on the dark side of the road. Prepare your sticker in advance, it will stick the better and you will not miss your object. Don't stop walking while sticking if possible. Look out for dark doorways; police usually stand in them at night. Stick on Belisha Beacons, lamp posts, Church boards, hoardings, bus stops, phone kiosks. Don't stick on walls as the glue is not strong enough for rough surfaces . . . As danger signal talk of the weather, for instance. Colder from the East means someone is approaching from the right. Read your road indication by torch-light and memorise at least two streets in advance. Take turns in sticking, look-out and route reading. As we leave this house we do so in pairs at a few seconds' interval and are strangers until we meet at midnight at Paradise Walk.[26]

Yet these were little more than adolescent pranks compared to her other activities.

In the early months of the 'phoney war' Wolkoff and the other fascist women built up a number of useful connections through the use of neutral or Allied embassies. Contacts existed in the Belgian, Romanian and Yugoslavian embassies and legations, which enabled messages to get to Germany. Wolkoff was communicating with William Joyce through the Italian Embassy. During the commencement of actual fighting in 1940, Wolkoff was in contact with a London-based American cipher clerk, Tyler Kent. He had access to coded correspondence between Roosevelt and Churchill and passed this to Wolkoff and Ramsay at the Tea Room; they passed this information on to the Germans. This was clearly treasonable and when Wolkoff approached Joan Miller she was able to help spring a trap on behalf of Knight and MI5. Wolkoff and Kent were caught, tried and imprisoned. On 22 May 1940, two days after Kent's arrest, the War Cabinet looked again at its defence regulations and decided to use its power to round up *all* known fascist activists. The necessary amendment to the legislation 'Allowed for internment without trial of members of organisations which were subject to foreign influence or control, or whose leaders had or had had associations with leaders of foreign governments, or who *sympathized with the system of government of enemy powers.'*[27] Ramsay and Mosley were soon arrested (23 May). Ramsay was out of prison by 26 September 1944, however, and remained an MP until Parliament was dissolved. He continued to write and speak on the dangers of Jews and Communists. The obsessional and maverick Arnold Leese went into hiding, only to be arrested once he returned home in secret. He made himself known by kicking a detective's backside! After the war he continued his anti-Semitic attitudes until his death in 1956. His final home in Notting Hill Gate became the centre for the revival of Nazism (rather than Mosleyite fascism) and virulent racism.

*

One mystery remains. There is an odd and still unexplained event that occurred during the roundup of BUF members (and other leading fascists) from 23 May 1940 – the escape of William Joyce and his subsequent re-emergence in Germany and re-invention as 'Lord Haw Haw'. Joyce had already escaped in August 1939.

Although Mosley had marginalized Joyce, by 1939 Joyce's obvious sympathies for Hitler's policies clearly made him a security risk and it should have been relatively easy to track him down alongside people like Leese. Instead, a day before the swoop, he was tipped off and vanished. Much speculation remains as to who made the call.

The accusatory finger points to Knight in MI5 or one of his close associates. Knight was head of a political subversion unit under Sir Vernon Kell, having been recruited in 1924. From Department Bg(b), he ran a network of spies, informers and political (and actual) saboteurs who were known as Knight's 'Black Agents' and who knew him as 'M' (a codename later borrowed by Ian Fleming for his James Bond books). Knight had moles in the CPGB, unions and various fascist groups, especially the BUF. His agents would report back to him so that he could alert Special Branch to carry out arrests. During the late 1930s Knight himself operated out of 308 Hood House, Dolphin Square, later moving his secretary, Joan Miller, to Collingwood House. Mosley too had moved to Dolphin Square in 1940 and it was here that he was arrested as Knight's neighbour.

> Outside the block of flats Diana noticed four or five men standing on the pavement 'aimlessly staring into space': my father recognised one or two of them as policemen who had been on duty at his meetings. They said they had a warrant for his arrest. He was allowed to go up to the flat to pick up some clothes. Then he was taken to Brixton Prison.[28]

Knight, however, had darker connections and his interests in subversive techniques can be traced to his *private* clandestine work. This began when John Baker White, who ran a private security agency, recruited him to work for Sir George Makgill in the BEU. Through Makgill, Knight was introduced to Sir Vernon Kell and through John Baker White to BF (British Fascisti). During the 1920s Knight was therefore a fascist working in a private capacity for MI5 on surveillance and subversion of the CPGB and union militants. His own silence, the deposition of Makgill's papers in the Vatican and the destruction or loss of BF records for the relevant period obscure his role in the BEU. John Baker White, who died in 1989, left no useful record of the period either. William Joyce on the other hand had joined the BF in 1923 after it had been going for seven months. Both Joyce *and* Maxwell Knight were therefore in the BF at the same time and it is unlikely that Knight did not know of the little man with the boasted first-class degree and a long razor scar across his cheek. He would certainly have realized the connection in the 1930s. We do not know, however, if the men spoke to each other or knew each other during the early 1920s.

There is another way back to link both men (although equally tantalizing and fraught with snares). The connection begins with the occultist Aleister Crowley. Crowley (self-titled 'the Great Beast 666' and by the press 'the most wicked man in the world') was part of the new wave of occultism and romantic nationalism sweeping

Europe on the tail of the emergence of paganist, Thule-ist, theoso-phist and spiritualist secret societies at the end of the nineteenth century. Crowley was widely travelled and in Moscow had helped Sir Robert Bruce Lockhart, who ran 'anti-communist agents', to search for show girls. Lockhart had tried to recruit Crowley but failed. It was Lockhart who instead fell for Crowley's occult interests. So did Knight, who met Crowley through the author Dennis Wheatley, who also had an interest in the occult, and whose strange adventure *The Devil Rides Out* (1934) is a thinly disguised roman-à-clef regarding Crowley. Crowley had long since been a friend of Germany, actually taking a pro-German stand during the First World War. He visited the Third Reich too and sent Hitler a copy of *The Book of the Law*, believ-ing the Führer to be a great magician. As Lord Haw Haw, Joyce even joked about Crowley holding a black mass at Westminster Abbey to hold off the Luftwaffe.

What is possible is that a number of activists from the days of the BEU and BF now recruited by or close to MI5 retained fascist and occult connections from a period when romantic fascism (both pan-Celtic and Aryan) attracted almost all Europe's intelligentsia on the right. Paganism was both revolutionary and patriotic, as Action Français tried to show in France before the emergence of BF in Britain. The roots of fascism and pan-Germanism in Britain *cannot* be clearly separated from a belief in mysticism and an emerging *völkischer* men-tality that saw Jews as alien precisely because they were believed to be conspiratorial occultists.

> Self-defence has compelled him [the Jew] to rely upon craft and cunning, always the weapons of the weak, and to enter into alli-ance with every subversive movement. In these Jews see power – power to avenge their wrongs, and power to gain world domi-nation under an avenging messiah – as foretold by Talmud and Qabalah.[29]

Mosley's belief in the 'Thought-Deed' Man comes from occult messianic philosophy, and Joyce's own jibe that Jews were 'sub-men with prehensile toes' was not simply unpleasant social Darwinism but an idea from German occult thinking which saw human affairs in the light of a *cosmic* war between a 'troglodytic' and an 'Asiatic' race.

It is true that attitudes were divided in fascist circles as to the nature of the occult. Sir George Makgill wanted to root out 'the cult of evil of which Aleister Crowley was the centre' but George Baker White's mother, Katherine Atkinson, was a member of BF's Grand Council alongside the occultist and leading theorist of the BF, Nesta Webster. By whatever means, Joyce had threads that joined him via a number of routes to Knight at MI5 and Knight had a tangle of connections going back to Joyce, possibly including the return of a favour for some past service. Whatever the case, when police arrived at Joyce's home in Earl's Court he had packed and gone. His sister claimed he received a phone call before the raid from an MI5 officer.

In a letter to the fascist circular *Comrade*, the author Bryan Clough claimed that between 1923 and 1927, Knight was a 'senior officer in the British Fascisti', as was his first wife, Gwladys. Knight, claimed Clough, was a 'friend of William Joyce' and 'tipped off Joyce about his imminent arrest'.[30] We do not know for sure who phoned Joyce from MI5 as the trail goes cold here. The likelihood is that either through an old go-between or by a carelessly leaked piece of information left in the right place it was possible to contact Knight's old Communist-fighting, Jew-hating colleague and give him time to escape. Knight could then pursue other fascists to whom he owed nothing. The plot, like a whiff of smoke, remains intangible.

17

Not Quite Kosher

The Jews of London, Jeffrey Hamm and the Return of Oswald Mosley

Between 1861 and 1901 the population of London grew from over three million to six and a half million people, overflowing into the newly expanding suburbs made possible by improvements in transport. As early as 1881 administrators were using the term 'Greater London' to express the extraordinary nature of the metropolis. The restless, misshapen, bubbling mass of London was something new and contemporaries recognized the fact. Here was the 'world city', not only the culmination of city development but also an arena where the events of the world were reproduced in miniature. The First World wealth of the capitalist West End starred disbelievingly at the Third World poverty of the 'socialist' East End, and in the East End the revolutionary politics of the European poor played themselves out in a miniature version of the events in France, Prussia and Russia. The Jewish population, defending itself against the iniquities of local anti-Semitic groups and still with its roots (and relatives) in the hated Tsarist police state, was often drawn to the 'communist' and anarchist groups that British patriotic parties believed typified the Jewish alien and his or her subversive *anti-English* nature.

Anti-Semitism in London was largely a twentieth-century phenomenon caused by the concentration of poor Eastern European Jews in the East End,* the rise of fascist parties and the creation of Israel. It reached its zenith in the 1930s and sporadically reignited just after the Second World War and in the very early 1960s. Long before the General Strike, proto-fascist groups had noted an apparent symbiosis between Jews and Bolsheviks. It took little time for such conspiracy theorists to believe that Communism and capitalism were Zionist

---

*The original Jewish merchant community of the East End gathered around Goodmans Fields, a large area below the Whitechapel Road. The ancient Jewish cemetery is still to be found to the east along the Mile End Road.

plots intended to destroy the Empire and that all Jews were undesirable aliens.

Christian Britain was always ambivalent about Jews. On the one hand they were stereotyped as Shylocks and (in the nineteenth century) as Fagins but on the other someone like Disraeli (albeit after conversion) could become leader of the reformed Tories and forge them into the modern Conservative Party. It was never in doubt for Disraeli's contemporaries that he was still 'Jewish' in habit, attitude and culture. Disraeli popularized the hybrid term 'Caucasian', which he used in the modern sense precisely to avoid the distinction between the 'Anglo-Saxon' and the Semite. At the same time the circumstances of immigration during the first half of the nineteenth century which had effectively created two Jewish communities, one old Sephardic and settled, the other modern Ashkenazi and mercantile, created tensions which the Reform Movement of 1841 tried to remould into 'British Jewry' in order to 'efface' differences. It was the appearance of poor Jewish immigrants from the 'Pale' (Russian-ruled Poland), Russia, Germany and elsewhere that triggered modern anti-Semitism in 'patriots' defending London's labouring classes.

By the latter half of the 1880s, widespread immigration by Polish Jews especially into the East End of London had led to growing tensions, especially with local Irish communities. This led to accusations in 1888 that a Jewish slaughterman known as 'Leather Apron' was in fact Jack the Ripper. Graffiti accusing the 'Juwes' was removed on police orders to avoid rioting in Whitechapel. By the early years of the twentieth century this cultural and social fear had been turned into a political platform for extreme 'conservative' groups fighting elections in London's poor boroughs.

The formation of the British Brothers League (BBL) marked a turn towards organized anti-Semitism. Founded in 1901 by a clerk called William Stanley Shaw, it appealed to the conservative core of the old 'inner East End'. It was backed by Sydney Buxton, MP for Poplar (and later Governor General of South Africa), Samuel Ridley, MP for Bethnal Green South West and Major Sir William Evans Gordon, Conservative MP for Stepney, and attracted many respectable City bankers as well as the popular novelists Sir Arthur Conan Doyle and Marie Corelli. Many of the BBL leadership lived in Stepney and local meetings demanding the restriction of alien entry were attended by up to 4,000 people, the BBL claiming a membership of 45,000 on the strength of one of their petitions. A mixture of Primrose League Tories (ultra-patriots) and working-class Liberals, the BBL attacked Jewish 'sweated labour' and demanded economic protection for non-Jewish business people. Rent rises and increases in the density of the Jewish population in very poor tenement areas such as Whitechapel led to rioting and looting in June 1903. Despite their anti-alien stand, East End locals were not automatically allies of Tory Diehards. Walter Besant noted that cockneys were not particularly keen on nationalism: 'the Union Jack is never seen in East London', he wrote at the start of the twentieth century, 'the children are *not* taught patriotism', an ironic comment given the liberal use of Union flags by later parades of East End racist groups.

The crusade against socialism, anarchism and Bolshevism and the Communist Party of Great Britain (CPGB) was soon led by the fear that Communism was a 'front' for a worldwide conspiracy of Jewish bankers and socialists working in a destructive and *secret* alliance in order to 'take over' Christian countries and destroy their culture.

On the eve of the First World War there were approximately 150,000 Jews who had escaped from Russia and come to Britain (many hoping to get to America). They joined another 150,000 Jews who had already come forcibly from Germany and Poland from the 1880s. Many of the new immigrants were attracted to the possibilities offered by the radical socialism of the Latvians, Lithuanians and Russians in their midst. Brought to fear and hate the secret police forces of the Tsar, enforced military service and the poverty and hardships of sweated labour, many East Europeans, especially Jewish workers, were drawn to the belief that they might create a more equitable world either in Britain by unionizing sweatshop workers or by returning to Russia and fighting Tsarism. Most became firm supporters of the Labour Party and its parliamentary reformism, some were anarchists and others (often Anglicized sons and daughters) became Communists and joined the Young Communist League. The catalysts for these affiliations were twofold – the rise of fascist parties with anti-Semitic programmes and the Russian Revolution.

The Times characteristically charged in with accusations of a Jewish conspiracy as soon as the Russian Revolution began: the Bolsheviks, it declared, 'are adventurers of German-Jewish blood'.[1] Jews also turned out to be capitalists as well for those inclined towards overt anti-Semitism.

> And please take note that the Red Shield (of Rothschild) and the Red Flag (of Communism) are not only of the same colour, but are one in essence, and the colour is the colour of blood. 'Judaism' says Professor Sombart, 'is identical with Capitalism.' But it is equally true to say that Judaism is identical with Communism.
>
> The question is often asked; how can it profit the Jewish Capitalists to have revolutions? Whatever answer may be given to the question of the 'How', the fact remains that it does.[2]

Robert Cecil, deputy Foreign Secretary to Lord Curzon during the period of the Russian Revolution, glossed the disaster in Russia as

Jewish 'revenge', not merely on Tsarist Russia but on European society in general.

> Nor is the action of Jewish revolutionaries confined to Russia . . . there is scarcely a dangerous revolutionary movement in any part of Europe which has not at the back of it a Jew, driven into enmity of the whole existing order of things by the injustice and outrage which he or his relatives have suffered from the hands of the old Governments of Russia and other states in Central Europe.[3]

In St Petersburg, Robert Wilton, who had been the *Times* correspondent in Russia since 1903, even went so far as to report that the Jews had erected a statue of Judas Iscariot in Moscow. Although a rabid hater of both Germans and Jews and finally ensconced on the staff of a White Russian general, Wilton's reports were taken as fact by *The Times* back in London. Furthermore, in order to boost the British intervention on behalf of White Russian counter-revolutionaries (who killed 100,000 Jews during the Civil War period), not only was the British government prepared to publish the Emmott Report, detailing Bolshevik atrocities during the Revolution, but it was also willing to peddle the lie that the Bolshevik leadership was Jewish and working on behalf of the Germans. These accusations were compounded by the publication of an even more notorious document.

In February 1920, the strange forgery known as *The Protocols of the Elders of Zion* was published in English. It purported to be the report of a secret cabal of Jews making plans for world domination. The work had existed prior to its English publication and circulated amongst European anti-Semitic groups, having been extensively used by the Russian Tsarist secret police to foment trouble. On 8 May 1920 *The Times* ran an article entitled 'The Jewish Peril', in which the Protocols were dismissed so half-heartedly that it only added to the possibility of their being authentic after all.

> What are these *Protocols*? Are they authentic? If so, what malevolent assembly concocted these plans, and gloated over their exposition? Are they a forgery? If so, whence came the uncanny note of prophecy, prophecy in parts fulfilled, in parts far gone in the way of fulfilment? Have we been struggled these tragic years to blow up and extirpate the secret organisation of German world domination only to find beneath it another, more dangerous because more secret? Have we, by straining every fibre of our national body, escaped a 'Pax Germanica' only to fall into a 'Pax Judaeica'?[4]

The author's rhetorical tone suggested just that, saying just sufficient to provide room for a useful (and much needed) disclaimer which might be needed later (in fact in August 1921).

The success of the (Menshevik) Russian Revolution suggested a new dawn for Jewry. The Chief Rabbi, Dr J. H. Hertz wrote in jubilant mood to the *Daily Chronicle*,

> The Jews of the British Empire . . . are thrilled by the glorious tidings . . . for 150 million human beings the sun of Freedom and Righteousness has risen with healing in its wings, and a government of the people, by the people and for the people is now and for all time breaking the political, racial and religious fetters of the old despotism . . . In such a free and regenerated Russia, the martyrdom of my Jewish brethren . . . is at an end.[5]

Yet such letters only tied British Jews *closer* to their Russian cousins. The Chief Rabbi's forlorn belief that Russia would now be an American-style democracy ('by the people and for the people') suggested to Jew-haters simple connivance – the 'people' nothing less than the Jews themselves. The Bolshevik coup d'état destroyed the hopes of people like the Chief Rabbi, for the Communist Jews were Communists first. The Jewish sections of the Communist Party ruthlessly pursued their co-religionists in Russia who could not or would not submit to the party creating a state of 'Jewish Civil War', which was further proof to anti-Semites in Britain that Jews were behind all the trouble.

Jews in Britain were not willing, however, to be the passive targets of their accusers. From the clutch of Jewish MPs to the Yiddish-speaking East End revolutionaries, Jews were both politically sophisticated and well organized. The thousands of Eastern European immigrants who crowded into East London might know little about British politics, but they had first-hand experience of the harsh regime they'd escaped in the Pale of Settlement, the area between the Ukraine and Poland where most of Russia's Jews lived. Here, the more progressive amongst them had formed the Jewish Workers' Bund of Russia, Lithuania and Poland in 1897 – 'the Bund' for short.

The Bund was an attempt to create an overarching union to defend Jewish cultural and political identity in almost intolerable conditions. Its ideology was broadly revolutionary socialism, believing that the best defence of Jewish identity was a strong (socialist) democracy which recognized ethnic diversity. It found adherents from the factories, created an armed defence force, produced a newspaper, *Di Arbayter Shtimme*, and upheld the idea of a secular, Yiddish-speaking Jewish community. As such, it was opposed by the orthodox as well as by Zionists who looked elsewhere for salvation. The Bund also helped organize the Russian Social Democratic Workers' Party, which finally split into Menshevik and Bolshevik camps. The Bolsheviks saw no need for a Jewish identity and Trotsky emphatically refused his own Jewish identity: 'I am a Social Democrat, and only that,' he told an enquirer.

By 1905 the Bund was an organization of 30,000 people, many of whom had started to leave for New York and London looking for a new life. Yet the Bund grew. It had an uneasy relationship with the Communists during the 1920s but continued to reject Zionism right up to its annihilation in the death camps and on the barricades of the Warsaw Ghetto. Yiddish, as a European language, was then virtually extirpated. Jewish socialist hopes transferred themselves to Palestine and the Bund reorganized to continue from New York. In London, the old life of the shtetl was gone, as was its politics, and the new English-born generation took its radicalism to the Labour Party or Young Communist League.

In 1910 there were sixteen Jewish MPs sitting in the Commons, and some, like Herbert Samuel, advanced to take up prominent government positions, Samuel himself becoming Home Secretary. Yet despite the numbers of Jews in the East End during the First World War, no Jewish MPs represented them and none of the sitting Jewish MPs bothered much with specifically Jewish issues. The representatives of established Anglo-Jewry and especially those from long-assimilated families were often embarrassed by their dirty 'schnorrer' co-religionists in the ghetto of the East End. For the most part immigration controls when proposed by the TUC (1892 and 1895) and when passed by the government (1905) went unopposed. Almost all supported alien conscription during the First World War and backed internment legislation against Russian immigrants. It was better to have a settled middle-class and prosperous community than the influx of Yiddish-speaking 'aliens' who did not attempt to assimilate and whose presence increased anti-Semitism.

These MPs were looked upon suspiciously by patriotic 'ultras' from the Tory backbenches, including Tories affiliated with the Primrose League, British Empire Union, National Democratic Party and National Party. In the general elections of 1918 the two latter parties gained eleven members between them on an ultra-patriotic ticket. Such patriots used Parliament to spread anti-Jewish/Bolshevik propaganda. On 7 August 1918 the MP for Islington East, Alfred Raper, actually questioned the Under-Secretary of State for Foreign Affairs, 'whether he has any information as to how many Greek Orthodox priests have been done to death by the Soviet Government in Central Russia; and whether a single instance is known of the said Government having dealt in the same way with any Jewish rabbi?'

To defend themselves against Jew-baiters, exploitative landlords and bosses, and against the lack of support from Jewish MPs, many immigrants with radical backgrounds looked to local self-help or affiliation to revolutionary republican groups. This was especially true when defending Russian immigrant men from forced conscription or deportation. Patriotic Englishmen and women could not see (so the newspapers fumed) why 'friendly' aliens proved so hostile to coercion, not understanding that the immigrants saw such tactics as exactly the same as the police-state actions of Tsarism which also enforced conscription.

Anti-Semitism always used Jewish customs and attitudes to prove the Jew was inherently un-English, either because of accent, alleged success in business, political affiliations or most consistently dietary habits. Nowhere was this platform more violent (and more veiled) than in its attacks on *shechita* (the Jewish method of slaughtering animals), which affronted modern 'rational' attitudes adopted during the 1930s. The novelist Hamilton Fyfe demanded of Jews that they abandon '*kosher* meat and their worship of a bloodthirsty, revengeful, anthropomorphic deity'. Animal rights were at the heart of both German Nazism and *British* anti-Semitic attitudes. The RSPCA's attitude before and during the Second World War was intended to create a moral and political cordon sanitaire around Jews in Britain, using objections to *shechita*.

> Opposition to *shechita* was a common cause of anti-Semitism in the 1930s and 1940s. Nazi groups in Britain such as the Imperial Fascist League and the Nordic League gained some success amongst the public and animal welfare groups in trying to link *shechita* to the basic evilness and cruelty of the Jews . . . Organisations such as the RSPCA were not worried about accusations of anti-Semitism; in fact they exploited anti-Semitism to try to reach their goal of banning *shechita*. In 1939 the chairman of the RSCPA warned the Board of Deputies that 'in the last couple of years there [has been] growing up a very strong feeling of antagonism toward the continuation of the Jewish method of slaughter in the country'.[6]

The RSPCA has renewed its attack on Jewish slaughterhouses sporadically ever since.

Veterinary objections to *shechita* were and remain too clearly aligned with anti-Semitism and fascism for this to be a mere coincidence: decency to animals is matched by hostility to Jews per se. This could be clearly seen in the National Front resolutions on ritual slaughter during the 1970s and the involvement of far-right activists in the Animal Liberation Movement during its formative years. This tendency crystallized around the virulent anti-Semite Arnold Leese, who as a practising vet (and expert camel doctor) campaigned against Jewish methods of slaughter before the Second World War.

A convinced believer in conspiracy theories regarding Jews and Communists, Leese became the leader of the Imperial Fascist League

St George, Our Guide!

An anti-Jewish cartoon published by Arnold Leese

in 1930, immediately introducing a pathological anti-Semitism to the organization's patriotic authoritarianism. Using his newspaper the *Fascist* to spread propaganda, he has been likened to 'the nearest equivalent in outlook to an English Hitler'. Leese's final solution for the Jews was to put half in a zoo and exterminate the other half. Indeed so violent were his views that he thought Sir Oswald Mosley's black-shirted British Union of Fascists, which he referred to as 'Kosher Fascists', was a Jewish-backed conspiracy! Leese continued his anti-Semitic ways after the Second World War and became an active influence on Colin Jordan, to whom his widow willed his home in Notting Hill Gate to be renamed Arnold Leese House and used as a headquarters. Like many anti-Semitic 'humanitarians', Leese reserved his pathologically destructive attitude, not for the sick animals in his care but for the Jewish 'race' to be 'put down' as if they were themselves incurable animals. 'A more permanent way of disposing of the Jews', Leese wrote in his paper the *Fascist*, 'would be to exterminate them by some *humane* method such as the *lethal chamber* [emphasis added]'.

As Jewish servicemen and women returned after the Second World War from fighting fascism abroad they were dismayed to find that British Hitlerists were back on the streets and protected by a government which had a misguided belief in free speech, however inflammatory its contents. Thus Germans held in de-Nazification camps, could, on ticket-of-leave passes, go and listen to British fascists arguing the greatness of Hitler and the iniquity of Jewish parasitism and watch as Britons gave the Nazi salute. All this, as news of the Holocaust filtered into people's consciousness via newspaper and newsreel.

Even before the end of the Second World War, the members of the old BUF detained under Regulation 18b were back on the streets. They had kept loyal to each other in internment and they had kept loyal to Sir Oswald Mosley. Amongst them were Alf Lockhart, coordinator for Mosley Publications, aimed at Right Book Club members. Lockhart enjoyed the cultural side of fascism and its camaraderie. He organized dances, parties and reunions and even got the 18b Detainees Fund registered as a charity (in later years he even visited Israel). There was also Victor Burgess, who had championed fascism at Speaker's Corner in 1944 and founded the Union for British Freedom from whence he published *Unity*. His shop was in Edgware, which was in the centre of a large Jewish community: the Corporate Bookshop was, of course, full of hate literature. Burgess was also a regular street orator. Raven Thomson had been senior to Lockhart and Burgess and had acted as Mosley's Director of Policy during the 1930s. One of Mosley's closest friends, he too set up as a publisher, finally taking over the leadership of Mosley's Union Movement. John Beckett and Jeffrey Hamm completed the old guard. Beckett had been an Independent Labour MP for Peckham but his interest in fascism led him to the anti-Semitism of the Duke of Bedford. With William Joyce he finally broke with Mosley and founded the National Socialist League, later joining the Duke of Bedford's British People's Party. By a quirk of fate, his own son, Francis Beckett, later married a Jewish woman and had a barmitzvah for Beckett's grandson.

Of all the post-war BUF fascists Jeffrey Hamm was the most significant. He was born in 1915 to a working-class family living in Ebbw Vale, Wales. When he was nineteen he chanced upon a BUF meeting whilst having a holiday in London. He liked what he heard and marched alongside the Blackshirts as they return to their headquarters. He joined the party in March 1935, quarrelled with his father over the decision and left home. In 1937 he holidayed in Heidelberg and returned a supporter of Hitler; he attended the huge Mosley peace rally on 16 July 1939. Looking for a job, he finally landed a teaching position in the Falkland Islands (which he had thought were in Scotland) and was there arrested under Regulation 18b and imprisoned with Germans in South Africa. Released, he returned to Britain and joined the army.

Discharged from war service in 1944, Hamm went about gathering ex-BUF members together and by the time Mosley launched Union Movement on 7 February 1948 Hamm was already a seasoned street orator. He was especially fond of attacking Jews and after a short period in detention he joined the League of Ex-Servicemen and Women and then started his own similarly named (but *fascist*) British League of Ex-Servicemen and Women. So concerned with Hamm were the Board of Deputies of British Jews, they commissioned a secret report.

> Repeatedly, but for the presence of police in numbers, Hamm's highly provocative, Jew-baiting speeches, would have resulted in open street fighting, in which the outnumbered Jews would have been badly handled . . . Hamm is adroit and quick both in speech and repartee, and his personality has won favour and brought support . . . from many old time Fascists who have eagerly awaited an orator of his type. Also, there is little doubt that Hamm has to be some extent established himself amongst those East-Enders who, while not active or professing Fascists, dislike Jews, . . . Hamm is now regularly welcomed.[7]

The lack of positive action by either the (Labour) Home Secretary, James Chuter Ede, to bring in legislation against inflammatory racist language or the Board of Deputies led young Jewish ex-servicemen and women to set up the 43 Group (named after its original membership) in order to combat fascist speakers on the street. This was especially important as Hamm and his colleagues were using the British war with terrorist fighters in Palestine to justify an overall denunciation of all Jews – a patriotic theme as British soldiers were then engaged in a messy conflict they could not win. By April 1946, 300 Jewish volunteers had joined the 43 Group organized from a large house in Bayswater Road rented out by a German-Jewish couple who had been refugees, and whose home was now converted into the 43 Group headquarters.

Using a variety of tactics, from street heckling and attacking meetings to assaulting fascist leaders (Hamm was beaten up on his doorstep), the 43 Group (and the CPGB) harassed the burgeoning fascist movement. It was even suggested that Mosley should be kidnapped and dumped naked in Piccadilly Circus! The situation soon grew more threatening, however, as both sides armed themselves with razors and coshes, the 43 Group 'commandos' quite aware of the stakes. 'I see this fascist in front of me and I think of the newsreels. I automatically put the bastard into a Nazi uniform in my mind and I go mad. I just want to hurt him!'[8] On 24 December 1947, two 43 Group members, John Wimbourne and Gerald Flamberg, were arrested for trying to shoot the fascist agitator John Preen whilst he sat in his car. Preen, the founder of the British Action League and the owner of a race-hate bookshop, was, however, the only witness to the alleged attack and under the cross-examination of Sir David Maxwell-Fyfe his testimony crumbled. That there was a possible conspiracy as Preen alleged seems quite likely, however the most significant confrontations took place on the streets.

The brawl on 1 June 1947 that saw seven commandos arrested as well as one fascist brought the issues into a courtroom. The summing-up by the magistrate, Daniel Hopkin, showed a clear understanding of the underlying issues and a real sense of outrage that the claim of freedom of speech was used as a cover for racist propaganda.

> This . . . case . . . deals with a matter vital to Britishers and that is the question of free speech . . . This court is going to support every action that is taken to uphold public order and if speakers come into this district, essentially a Jewish district, to talk anti-Semitism in this kind of way, to stir up racial hatred, to insult and abuse the people here and to provoke them, then they must take what is coming to them.[9]

On 7 February 1948, Mosley announced the inauguration of his new party, Union Movement (UM), at a rally held at St Wilfred's School in Victoria. The booking had been unknown to the school's governors and kept secret. At the announcement there were chants of M-O-S-L-E-Y and fascist salutes. Mosley then began a campaign which aimed at recruitment in the north of England, the East End and Essex. To defend his meetings he also authorized the creation of a tough bodyguard under the direction of a man named Dickie Bird, and with the aid of a Maltese gang (from Romford) was able to keep 43 Group attackers at bay. Times, however, were changing and the withdrawal of British troops from Palestine denied fuel to Union Movement accusations of Jewish terrorism against soldiers doing their duty. The creation of the State of Israel and its subsequent fight for survival was viewed by the British people and the media as admirable and so Union Movement had to look for other targets. With the failure of Union Movement's anti-Semitism and its turn to racism the 43 Group ceased to have a clear enemy and it disbanded in 1950.

By the early 1960s, Mosley believed his star was again on the rise. He still had a close following of old BUF men and a growing group of younger people were attracted to his stand on immigration.

Reiterating the 'corporate' agenda of his young years and the convenient racism of his maturity he went on the stump hoping to capture North Kensington and return to Parliament. He came to the electorate with two visions – one idealistic, the other merely gutter politics. The vision was a planned economy and a new Europe. He had long since become an ardent Europeanist but he sought out his own ilk. In 1962 he joined a pan-European fascist alliance which included many SS men and Mussolini's former advisers, who were 'passionately European' and 'advanced'. On 1 March 1962 they jointly issued the Declaration of Venice, signed by Mosley for Union Movement, Gionvanni Lanfre and others of the Italian MSI, the German Reichspartei and Belgian Jeune-Europe Group. Mosley's 'journal of opposition', the *European*, begun by Sir Oswald and edited by Diana, included contributions by the American poet Ezra Pound, admirer of Mussolini and ardent anti-semite, Henry Williamson (author of *Tarka the Otter*) and Otto Strasser (significant for his highly influential brand of 'progressive' socialist Nazism) amongst others. As with the concept of Empire, so with that of Europe. Mosley believed in a corporate and managed federated Europe directed centrally and driven by economics. Africa would supply the raw material for Europe's advance.

The vulgarity in his vision was his racism (which replaced his anti-Semitism) regarding the 'coloured immigration problem': he advocated repatriation and hinted at the rise of crime in immigrant areas. Although he thought all black people deserved respect ('courtesy and kindness') nevertheless he was prepared to make jokes about black people eating Kit-E-Kat (cat food) where necessary if such comments found votes. Mosley always looked for crisis and the familiar surroundings of the street was where he usually found it. Early in 1962 members of UM were beaten up at their headquarters by the Jewish 62 Group, which had been formed by Jewish activists worried about the re-emergence of British fascism, and on 22 July a UM meeting in Trafalgar Square had to be aborted after scuffles. Finally on 31 July, on the old turf of Ridley Road, Dalston, Mosley himself was severely beaten to the ground as he prepared to speak.

The question remains as to Mosley's own attitude towards the Jewish population. Was Mosley really an anti-Semite? Some recent writers have chosen to see him as an idealist whose buccaneering personality led him into dangerous liaisons. One recent historian of the BUF has even suggested that

> Mosley would have liked his movement, when compared with its continental cousins, to be 'fascism minus violence'. His militant opponents, the Communist Party of Great Britain (CPGB) and radical Jewish working class organisations, ensured that there

was never any likelihood of the BUF being perceived in that light despite the much lower level of political violence in Britain than on the continent.[10]

This is a dangerous conclusion and clearly flawed. Mosley *united* a variety of fascist groups into a coherent political body: his New Party metamorphosed into the rump Nu-Party (NUPA) and thence into the BUF and later UM. Mosley would have been in no doubt that his allies were not just patriots and his willingness to lose backers who disliked the BUF's overt anti-Semitism suggests he was prepared to allow his pro-Nazi Director of Propaganda, William Joyce, a relatively free hand. Joyce did not force Mosley into overt anti-Semitism in 1934; Mosley already knew of Joyce's background and sympathies. Mosley removed him far too late for any moral scruples. Equally Mosley's choice to march through predominantly Jewish areas, wear a black fascist uniform (clearly, closer to the German model rather than the Italian) and use a flash symbol reminiscent of that of the SS cannot be dismissed as useful political bravado. Mosley always intended to *provoke*. This was his personality: a man of action and decision who needed an *enemy* whether Communists, the National Government, Ramsay MacDonald, economic decline or Jewish interests. Sponsored by Mussolini (but avoided by the Germans, who felt he was a liability) Mosley nevertheless chose in 1936 to marry Diana Mitford in Goebbels' house. Hitler was a witness and presented them with a framed photograph. At a press conference at his home at 38 South Eaton Place on 28 November 1947, Mosley refused to countenance the Holocaust and blamed it on Allied bombing. The gas ovens were needed to 'get rid of the bodies of typhus victims', he said. Information on the death camps, he insisted, 'proves nothing'. Indeed, he never fully repudiated the 'biological' Final Solution anti-Semites who supported him. As for the end of the British Empire, his opinion was clear: 'I don't believe the Negroes can develop or govern Africa'. Back in the political arena after the Second World War Mosley again chose to back the overt anti-Semitism of Jeffrey Hamm in the 1940s and the anti-immigration propaganda and anti-black hate of the late 1950s.

In 1948 he also had a meeting with the White African supremacist Oswald Pirow and by the late 1950s he was openly mixing with ex-members of the SS. At best, it might be said that he was an anti-Semite only through expediency. Anti-Semitism seemed naturally to connect in his mind with the concept of a beleaguered group (his BUF) fighting for a purer world in which Jewish 'pollution' was just one strand of the overall corruption in the old order. Mosley's anti-Semitic speeches fitted this self-defensive model and then become a self-fulfilling prophecy as Jewish groups allied themselves with Communists to defeat him.

The vision which drove Mosley was supported by a belief that only he offered salvation, and this was driven by a restless impatience that aligned itself with others who suffered from that same sense of urgency and irritation. Such people had first to acknowledge Mosley and his cause, which was one of reactionary revolution: the politics of right-wing modernism. Since he fused together the elements of the old 'ultra-patriotic' right, and these were intimately involved with anti-Semitic behaviour, it would clearly follow that he would have no choice but to incorporate their beliefs. To secure support from colleagues such as Joyce meant that Mosley had to speak out as an *overt* anti-Semite in order to keep their allegiance. Pushed too far, Mosley split with Joyce because the latter was impolitic and a challenge to his sense of the party's destiny, which could only emanate from himself. Joyce compromised this position with his speeches and actions during 1934, clearly showing that Mosley's arguments of 1933 (that he was a victim of Jewish aggression) were disingenuous. Joyce was a metropolitan petit-bourgeois ideologue, modern man in essence – Mosley was a country-house aristocrat; Joyce had no attachment to the established order and loathed it – Mosley was an intimate part of the fabric of a social world that led all the way to the Royal Family. Mosley's problem was that the failure of NP only left him a choice of appealing to people like Joyce and the rump of a disaffected white working class. Only with his pacifist position taken against the coming of war could he hope to widen his base beyond the street brawling violence he thrived upon and Joyce could whip up.

Even more particularly, Mosley was always attracted to parliamentary politics and reasoned argument. He was an Englishman steeped in the traditions of the English and looked back with fondness to his family's origins in the Tudor period – a time which appealed for its sense of buccaneering civilization: the quintessence of the English spirit. Count Dino Grandi came to such a conclusion in January 1934:

> He wants to bring back Tudor England, the England of Henry VIII and Elizabeth, the England that wasn't 'natural' but sectarian, that ate oxen roasted on the spit, chopped off people's heads, tilled the soil and committed piracy on the high seas. I remember the historian Cesare Baldo's definition of strong peoples – 'peoples possessed by civilised barbarism'.[11]

Mosley's dismissal of Joyce put him out of sight and out of mind – an embarrassment. Joyce, instead, embraced the cause more vigorously than ever and saw Mosley as the dilettante.

Joyce rejected the need for any dilettantism and saw his patriotism as encapsulated in the need for a national socialist Britain – a dictatorship on German lines with Mosley as the Führer. Mosley never took the final step into violent revolution and his discussion in 1931 with Harold Nicolson, Robert Boothby, Oliver Stanley and Walter Elliot as to the need for a 'Fascist Coup' was never more than talk. Unlike Joyce, Mosley could not take the final step into revolution as Joyce was effectively to do and which led him inevitably to the gallows.

It is of interest to speculate on the possible repercussions of an enforced or mutually agreed peace between the British Empire and Germany. Mosley would certainly have been at the forefront of such an arrangement, as would leading members of the Nordic League and Right Club, such as Archibald Ramsay. In the background there would have been numerous secondary figures such as William Joyce and John Beckett as well as churchmen and aristocrats who saw their patriotic duty as defending the 'race', fighting the Jewish–Bolshevik menace and upholding the crusade of Christians against the ungodly.

Mosley's corporate British Empire with its autarkic self-sufficiency would have had no place for its Jewish citizens. As late as his peace rally at Earl's Court in July 1939, he continued to blame Jewish interests for the world situation. The hall, filled with 30,000 adherents, was attended by numerous old 'patriotic' anti-Semites including Admiral Sir Barry Domvile who recalled, 'We have lovely seats at 10/6 – . . . The hall was laid out à la Nurnberg. Packed. About 30,000. Masses of the Press all giving Fascist salute – but no Press Reports in the organs of our Free Press!! O.M. spoke . . . perfectly splendid'.[12] Another listener, Francis Yeats-Brown, recalled that Mosley was 'as good as Goebbels'.

All fascist groups and many sympathizers blamed Jewish interest alone for the war. Hitler was simply defending German interests, they declared.

> It was a Jews' war . . . that we should be asked to fight. Hitler had sworn to destroy the world's No. 1 enemy. He was succeeding beyond measure. The Jews and their rotten Masonic institutions were disappearing under the Crusader's hammer blows – and we should be asked to stop them. It was unthinkable.[13]

The *growth* of upper-middle class and aristocratic anti-Semitism immediately before and during the early months of the war coincided with the populist appeal of Mosley's BUF and the violently anti-Semitic agitation of Arnold Leese and others in the Nordic League or around its periphery. If this had halted the drift to war on a 'peace' platform, which had brought Mosley to power, then life would have been intolerable for Jewish Britons.

It is quite likely that Mosley would have had to purge the likes of Joyce, Beckett (both of whom deserted Mosley to found the National Socialist League (NSL) in 1937), Leese and even Ramsay had he decided to pursue a policy of 'soft' anti-Semitism. He could, however, have tolerated a 'revolutionary' wing of the Party dedicated to finishing the Jewish problem on German lines. This would have *excluded* the possibility of just enforcing emigration to a 'Zionist' state, as most pre-war anti-Semites were also ardent Arabists. The pressure from people such as Leese or Joyce and the clear views they held about a possible final solution might have opened the way to extermination camps in the United Kingdom. Britain's crusade against Bolshevism as an ally of Germany would have silenced American opposition, which could be ignored by a self-sufficient Empire with London or York as its capital.

The registration of Jewish businesses and their enforced sale to 'real' Englishmen would certainly have followed. Mass Jewish emigration would have been a problem but some thousands of Jews might have been able to leave (minus their cash, perhaps) for the United States, although even there anti-Semitic immigration laws might have proved a barrier. Leading left-wing opponents and Jewish or liberal voices would have been silenced, locked up or liquidated – the latter a real probability for the executive of the CPGB or Jewish anti-fascist organizers. The extremes of the fascist right would have certainly pressurized Mosley towards a 'German' solution to the Jewish problem, as actually occurred when the German army occupied the Channel Islands during the Second World War.

18
Alien Nation
Indian Assassins and Black Radicals

Similar to the Jewish experience, the Indian presence in London from the eighteenth century onwards was always one of uneasy equality. After all, the vast subcontinent might be home to untold millions of peasants but it was also home to extraordinarily wealthy and powerful princes with an infinitely rich culture and religious life. India not only provided the capital with cheap (but fashionable) cloth, new spices and foods and even the use of shampoo (brought by Sake Deen Mahomed during the 1820s), it also brought artists, religious sages and intellectuals who accounted for much of the small elite group who chose to make Britain their home or split their life between living in India and living in London.

Central to this double life that the Indian intellectual lived was the question of an independent India free from British rule, or, at least, free from direct British control. Rajah Rammohan Roy, called the 'father of Indian nationalism', was the first in a growing line of Indians and Britons to submit papers to the Parliamentary Committee on Indian Affairs calling for an independent India. In July 1839, he joined a group of British sympathizers who had formed the British India Society, which began political and economic activities aimed at pressurizing the East Indian Company and raising awareness in India itself. By 1865, the London Indian Society had appeared and by 1866 this had metamorphosed into a parliamentary lobby group called the East Indian Association. Its failure led one of its leading radicals, Dadabhai Naoroji, to form the London Indian Society in 1872 in which a number of Indian students living in London soon found a more radical home. In its fifty-year existence it drew the attention of Irish Home Rulers, who saw the potential for joint agitation, which might be beneficial to both sides. Irish MPs spoke up for India in Parliament and *Indian* candidates were put up by the Liberals for Irish constituency seats or radical constituencies in England. In the election of 1883, Lalmohun Ghose stood (unsuccessfully) for Deptford, paving the way for the first Indian MP, Dadabhai Naoroji, who became MP for Finsbury Central in 1892.

Naoroji was born into a poor Parsi family on 4 September 1825 but he was able to study and graduated from Elphinstone College in Bombay, later to become its first Professor of Mathematics and Natural Philosophy before moving to London to take up the post of Professor of Gujerati at University College. He also founded the London Zoroastrian Association and acted as its president between 1861 and 1907.

By the 1880s, Naoroji had begun agitation for Indian Civil Service reform, demanding a proper share of involvement for Indians in all civil administration and the removal of barriers to Indians sitting as judges. The Ilbert Bill of 1883 had tried to bring this about but had been modified to avoid allowing an Indian judge to preside over a case with a European defendant. This blatant racism aroused support for Naoroji from British radicals including John Bright, better known for the Anti-Corn Law League, Keir Hardie and Ramsay MacDonald. In an effort to get working-class support, Naoroji and his colleagues set up the British Committee of the Indian National Congress in 1889. By 1892 Naoroji was Britain's second black candidate and about to be the first black MP. The Tory Prime Minister, Lord Salisbury, was horrified.

> But then Colonel Duncan [the Tory candidate] was opposed to a black man, and however great the progress of mankind has been, and however far we have advanced in overcoming prejudices, I doubt if we have yet got to that point when a British constituency will take a black man to represent them . . . at all events he was a man of another race who was very unlikely to represent an English community.[1]

Attacking Salisbury for his blatant racism, the *Newcastle Leader* pointed out that, 'by far the larger proportion of the British subjects are black men [sic]' and the *Star* suggested, somewhat ironically, that the Prime Minister was actually darker skinned than the Liberal candidate! Nevertheless, more extreme Conservatives were unbending in their antagonism. Sir Lepel Griffin, Chairman of the East Indian Association and a long-standing Indian administrator, fumed that Naoroji was

> An alien in race, in custom, in religion; destitute of local sympathy or local knowledge, no more unsuitable representative could be imagine or suggested. As to the people of India, Mr Naoroji no more represents them, than a Polish Jew settled in Whitechapel

represents the people of England. He is a Parsee, a member of a small foreign colony, probably Semitic in origin, settled in the west of India. The Parsees are the Jews of India; intelligent, industrious, and wealthy . . . But they are quite as much aliens to the people of India as the English rulers can possibly be.[2]

Even the local Liberal Association eventually baulked at their choice and Naoroji was finally unseated. An Indian successor, Manmath Mallik, who stood as a Liberal for St George's Hanover Square in 1906 and Uxbridge in 1910 was also unsuccessful. As an MP Naoroji had not only kept his word to the Irish and voted for Home Rule but had also come to see that the 'working classes' were the key to real reform. Having lost his seat he retired and returned to India in 1907, where he died on 30 June 1917 at ninety-two.

Naoroji bowed out of British politics as another Indian found a parliamentary seat. This was Mancherjee Bhownaggree, son of a rich Parsi family from Bombay who had also graduated from Elphinstone College and had become a newspaper owner. Unlike Naoroji, whose views of the British were always mixed, Bhownaggree was a staunch loyalist and imperialist, showered with honours by the British government and feted by the Tory Party. Put up as a 'stooge' to prove the Tories could also muster black support, Bhownaggree nevertheless won the seat of Bethnal Green Northeast, an area of poor working-class white voters. His luck did not hold but he remained a popular figure whose lasting legacy was as a benefactor of the Imperial Institute (later the Commonwealth Institute). He also began a long association of Asian voters with the Conservatives.

Whilst an older generation of mainstream Indian activists living in London might argue for an accommodation with the British, others looked to an amiable but clear separation. Such thinkers included Krishna Menon, who arrived in Camden Town in 1924 and, like many others before him, saw socialism and spiritual regeneration as a way forward. He was both a theosophist and a socialist, whose intellectual abilities brought him to the notice of Allen Lane, whose Penguin paperbacks had first appeared in 1935. Menon was appointed overall editor of the new Pelican list, dedicated to contemporary and serious issues. His first commissioned title was George Bernard Shaw's *Intelligent Woman's Guide to Socialism, Capitalism, Sovietism and Fascism*, published in 1937.

Annie Besant, the radical and theosophical campaigner whose spiritualist ideas had first attracted Menon, had set up a Home Rule for India Association as early as 1912. Under the leadership of people like Menon, it slowly became the India League, dedicated to 'freedom and self determination'. Menon's agitation, both as a councillor for St Pancras and, alongside Jawaharlal Nehru as a campaigner for independence, was tireless: for his borough, he helped create what became the Camden Arts Festival; for India, he continued to work for the Congress Party, being rewarded in 1947 with the position of High Commissioner, a post he held until 1952.

Whilst many Indians saw a constitutional accommodation reached through a change of political will at Westminster as the likely way forward to dominion status or even full independence, others of a younger generation looked to immediate independence brought about by revolutionary means. From 1905 onwards an Indian revolutionary cadre planned and plotted at India House, a hostel at 65 Cromwell Avenue, Highgate. India House was the brainchild of Shyamaji Krishnavarma, the son of a poor family in Cutch State who nevertheless had been educated at Elphinstone and Balliol and then called to the Bar. In 1897, he finally left India for Britain and settled in London.

From the hostel, Krishnavarma issued an anti-imperialist penny monthly called the *Indian Sociologist*, which preached a policy of open antagonism to British rule and Indian cooperation. The journal attracted socialist agitators such as H. M. Hyndman, who had long been associated with anti-parliamentary propaganda and who officially opened the premises, which could house sixty-five students, on 1 July 1905. At the time there were only about fifty Indian students living in London but these included revolutionaries such as Vinayak Savarkar and Madho or Madan Lal Dhingra. It was Dhingra who on 1 July 1909 decided to take action on behalf of his country, assassinating both Sir William Curzon Wyllie, political ADC to the Secretary of State for India, and Cawas Lalcaca, an Indian doctor who tried to help him.

India House had already invited police attention by its 'seditious' debates such as that offered by a 'Dr Desai' in 1908 on the problems of bomb making. Furthermore, Scotland Yard spies might also be treated to discussion on the need to infiltrate and subvert the Indian Army or the necessity of creating alliances with Egyptian nationalists. Vinayak Savarkar also bought guns and supplied bomb-making instructions to his brother Ganesh in India and India House students began to take shooting lessons at a gun club in Tottenham Court Road.

On 23 July 1909, the government ordered the seizure of the *Indian Sociologist* and arrested its printers for 'sedition'. Guy Aldred, the prominent anarchist, took over its printing but was also imprisoned. Krishnavarma fled to Paris and was promptly disbarred. Meanwhile, Savarkar, already considered a dangerous problem in India and now living in London, had formed a new nationalist organization called the Young India Party. When Dhingra assassinated Wyllie, Savarkar became the prime suspect as the murder plot's 'mastermind', engineered in order to exact revenge for Savarkar's brother's arrest. On 17 August 1909 Dhingra was hanged at Pentonville Prison and Savarkar was a wanted man. He was finally arrested seven months later at Victoria Station, having returned from self-imposed exile in Paris after the police raids on the *Indian Sociologist*. He was promptly put on board a ship headed for India but escaped through a porthole at Marseilles where unfortunately for him he was again arrested by French police and deported. Tried for 'abetment of murder', on 10 December 1910 he was deported and imprisoned on the Andaman Islands, where he spent fifteen years of a fifty-year sentence.

At his trial, Dhingra spoke of the obligation of patriots to throw off the hand of invaders, if necessary by the gun. The issue was clear, for no 'Englishman' would allow 'Germans walking with the insolence of conquerors in the streets of London', and so it was with Indians 'working for the emancipation of [their] country'. British Social Democrats, Liberal radicals, Irish Home Rulers and working-class propagandists saw in Dhingra's action a laudable aim emanating from real despair. In Ireland Keir Hardie even helped publicize his 'bravery' by getting posters printed and distributed. It had long been apparent to many revolutionary socialists that the ending of the exploitation of the British working class was *directly* involved with the ending of all imperial exploitation; the need for an independent Ireland and an independent India being the equivalent of freeing the workers from the control of capital, landed privilege and an aristocratic Parliament.

Many Indians hoping to liberate their country by revolutionary means turned to the newly formed Communist Party of Great Britain (CPGB) as the result of momentum in two different political worlds. The first was the struggle between British reformist socialists and the more militant anti-parliamentary Social Democrats, who were themselves slowly differentiating between anarchists and Communists within their ranks. The second was excitement generated by the crisis in Russia and the vanguard Party Communism of the Bolsheviks (Marxism-Leninism). Soviet Communism stood for a new workers' state run by local soviets and a strong proletarian 'dictatorship' under control of the party of revolution. The heart of the problem in Britain was the stranglehold of capital and the support it gained from a parliamentary democracy based upon liberal (property and free-market) economic policy. CPGB policy (until the Second World War) was for direct, *violent*, revolutionary action against capitalism and imperialism, one of the creators of its programme being the Indian author Rajani Palme Dutt.

Actually, the huge armed forces, and the colossal imperialist apparatus of the British capitalists is only made possible by the oppression and robbery of the colonial peoples. It is the plunder of India and other colonies that enables the ruling class to wage the class struggle in this country. And this is also the reason why the struggle of the British workers must be bound up with the struggle of the colonial masses.[3]

Such ideas were immensely attractive to a number of Indians in Britain who were keen to change both Indian *and* British political life from *within*, but who believed that real democracy was directly opposed to parliamentarianism.

The contradictions inherent in being a Communist *and* a parliamentarian were nowhere better exemplified than in the figure of Shapurji Saklatvala, Britain's second Communist MP. Saklatvala was a Parsi, like many radical Indian politicians, born on 28 March 1874 into a merchant family from Bombay who eventually moved to Manchester. Touched with a social conscience, the young Saklatvala worked in the plague hospitals of Bombay whilst also acting on behalf of his family's industrial interests. In 1905 he came to live in Manchester, and married a poor English girl called Sarah Marsh in 1907.

On his arrival Saklatvala joined the National Liberal Club but realized that his political convictions, which were those of a determined anti-imperialist, were more to the left. He then joined the Independent Labour Party (ILP) but his convictions brought him to the attention of Special Branch, who named him 'one of the most violent anti-British agitators in England'. By the beginning of the First World War he was active in union work and had decided to join the British Socialist Party, the forerunner of the CPGB. As a member of the People's Russian Information Bureau, Saklatvala was prominent in attempting to counter British anti-Soviet propaganda. Alongside people such as Palme Dutt, Saklatvala helped to create a strong Marxist caucus in the ILP and hoped to see the party join the Communist International of 1919. Defeated in their resolution to affiliate, Saklatvala, Palme Dutt and their colleagues then resigned and re-formed as the CPGB. By now, Saklatvala was considered a real menace to the authorities, a position exacerbated when he helped set up the Workers' Welfare League of India (later the All-India Trades Union Congress) and organized the Indian Seaman's Association and lascar lodging houses. MI5 quite correctly believed the Association and the lodging houses were bases for Communist cells.

In 1922, Saklatvala stood as a candidate for Battersea North, an enclave of popular radical politics and home to many progressive thinkers such as Palme Dutt himself. John Burns, although considered a turncoat by many local socialists, represented the constituency for many years and was still a working-class hero. Although a Communist, Saklatvala stood as a Labour candidate and won with a 2,000 majority and while he lost in 1923 he returned in 1924 as a representative of the CPGB but *backed* by Labour. He was now the second Communist MP (after Walter Newbold) and the only Asian ever to be so. The *Daily Graphic*, covering his victory, reported that he was a mixture of 'fakir' and 'Svengali', who had women 'kissing his portrait' and 'solid . . . taxi drivers' supporting his cause.

Saklatvala's victory was seen by the establishment press as a defeat for constitutionalism, reason and 'law and order' (the ticket of the Conservative candidate) and a licence to turn the area into 'Red Battersea' under the 'flagrant Communism' of the 'avowed apostle of Bolshevism'. Only 'chaos and ruin' could follow, suggested the *Daily Telegraph*.

Saklatvala's 'entryism' was never going to be an easy thing to handle and by 1929 the difficult relationship with the Labour Party had ceased to suit anybody. Of most concern was his increasingly non-party-line rhetoric, which irritated his constituents and angered Labour Party headquarters. Dual-party membership was ended in 1924 and so Saklatvala had to choose the Labour Party line or leave and declare his position as one of open hostility. Either way he lost support and in 1929 he was dropped by the local party and polled less than one-fifth of constituency votes. He was never re-elected either in Battersea or elsewhere.

Hounded by the press and by Special Branch, in 1925 Saklatvala was banned from an Inter-Parliamentary Union visit to the United States by American officials paranoid about Communist influence and 'tipped the wink' by MI5. Such a ban, against a sitting MP, was illegal and protests occurred in New York. Saklatvala was used to harassment; police had searched his house in 1921 and he would be thwarted in his attempts to visit Egypt in 1927 on his way to India. Afterwards he was refused further entry into India. During the general strike of 1926 he was arrested for a seditious speech urging the army to side with the workers. He was arrested and after refusing to be bound over spent two months in Wormwood Scrubs.

Another group of immigrants long resident came from other imperial colonies. The African-Caribbean presence in Britain has been an area of intense interest for historians of ethnicity. As long ago as the sixteenth century there were sufficient black people in England that intermarriage and inter-racial sexual relations became accepted as commonplace in many areas. By the late 1590s there were calls to expel black people from England, repeated by royal decree in 1601, but by the early eighteenth century there were as many as 10,000 black Londoners. Indeed, 'Queen Charlotte, the wife of George III, was directly descended from the illegitimate son of an African mistress in the Portuguese royal house. She was portrayed in state portraits as dark and described by her physician as having a "true mulatto face"'.[4]

None of this prevented continued and regular calls for the expulsion or segregation of the black community. The *London Chronicle* of 1773 recorded,

That it is humbly hoped the Parliament will provide such remedies as may be adequate to the occasion, by expelling the Negroes now here, who are not made free by their owners, and by prohibiting the introduction of them in this kingdom for the future; and save the natural beauty of Britons from the Morisco [sic] taint; and remove the envy of our native servants, who have some reason to complain that the Negroes enjoy all the happiness of ease in domestic life, while many of those starve for want of places.[5]

Fears of miscegenation and of economic competition were also fears about the property rights of slave owners who brought servants into Britain. The verdict on such property rights was delivered in the Yorke Talbot judgement of 1729, which stated,

We are of the Opinion, That a Slave by coming from the West-Indies to Great Britain or Ireland, either with or without his Master, doth not become free, and that his Master's Property or Right in him is not thereby determined or varied: And that Baptism doth not bestow freedom on him, nor make any Alteration in his Temporal Condition in these Kingdoms. We are also of Opinion, that his Master may legally compel him to return again to the Plantations.[6]

This did not stop disputes continuing, the most celebrated being the case of Somerset versus Stewart. Charles Stewart (or Stuart) had brought his slave James Somerset to London when he quit America in 1769. In 1771 Somerset escaped into the black population of the capital but he was found and sent in chains to be press-ganged for a ship called the *Ann and Mary* bound for Jamaica. Rescued by a writ of habeas corpus, Somerset was brought to the Mansion House before Lord Mansfield, the Chief Justice, who referred the matter on to the Court of King's Bench. Somerset's counsel was Granville Sharp who, though white, fully sympathized with the black population of the capital. Mansfield's judgement freed Somerset in June 1772. The *Public Advertiser* recorded that,

On Monday near 200 Blacks, with their Ladies, had an Entertainment at a Public-house in Westminster, to celebrate the Triumph, which their Brother Somerset had obtained over Mr. Stuart his Master. Lord Mansfield's Health was echoed round the Room; and the Evening was concluded with a Ball.[7]

The victory was, however, only partial as the judgement left in abeyance the question of the legality of slavery, substituting the illegality of forced repatriation abroad. Indeed, Mansfield himself had a slave whom he had brought to London, who was *his own niece*, Dido Elizabeth Linsay, with whom he lived at Kenwood House, Hampstead, until his death in 1783 when she was freed under the terms of his will.

Granville Sharp himself had become involved with black affairs by accident after helping a teenager, Jonathan Strong, who had been beaten up and abandoned and then rekidnapped by his master. Sharp fought and won the case on behalf of Strong and thereby made himself a focus for black aspirations. It is indicative of the precarious position of the black British population not only that they had to act with extreme caution but that this caution was always to be tinged with abasement when dealing even with their allies, this for example the letter of gratitude sent by the 'Sons of Africa' to Sharp on 15 December 1787.

Honourable and Worthy Sir,

Give us leave to say, that every virtuous man is a truly honourable man; and he that doth good hath honour to himself: and many blessings are upon the head of the just, and their memory shall be blessed, and their works praise them in the gate.

And we must say, that we, who are a part, or descendants, of the much-wronged people of Africa, are peculiarly and greatly indebted to you, for the many good and friendly services that you have done towards us, and which are now even out of our power to enumerate.

Nevertheless, we are truly sensible of your great kindness and humanity; and we cannot do otherwise but endeavour, with the utmost sincerity and thankfulness, to acknowledge our great obligations to you, and, with the most feeling sense of our hearts, on all occasions to express and manifest our gratitude and love for your long, valuable, indefatigable labours and benevolence towards us, in using every means to rescue our suffering brethren in slavery . . .

And now, honourable Sir, with the greatest submission, we must beg you to accept this memorial of our thanks for your good and faithful services towards us, and for your humane commiseration of our brethren and countrymen unlawfully held in slavery.

And we have hereunto subscribed a few of our names, as a mark of our gratitude and love. And we are, with the greatest esteem and veneration, honourable and worthy Sir, your most obliged and most devoted humble servants.

Ottobah Cugoano	Jasper Goree
John Stuart	Gustavus Vases [Vassa] (Equiano)
Geo. Rob. Mandeville	James Bailey
William Stevens	Thomas Oxford
Joseph Almaze	John Adams
Boughwa Gegansmel	George Wallace[8]

The black signatories of this letter had in the back of their minds the sort of inflammatory language that appeared in the *Morning Post* the previous year and was itself a commentary on the expulsion of black people from France.

> The oppositionists have converted numbers of the *black* poor into zealous *patriots*. They assembled, it seems, in Whitechapel, where they held, what the Indians term a *talk*; the purport of which was, that they had 'heard of an intention of introducing the *arbitrary French laws*, with respect to *black people*, as part of the new French Treaty; and they looked upon the *arts* now practised to inveigle them out of a land of liberty, with the utmost jealousy'. In this instance, as in many others, the lenity of our Government operates to the detriment of the nation. Are we to be told what articles in a treaty should be adopted or rejected, by a crew of reptiles, manifestly only a single link in the great chain of existence above the *monkey*? Should a sooty tribe of Negroes be permitted to arraign, with impunity, the measures of Government? A few constables to disperse their meetings, and a law, prohibiting *blacks* from entering our country, would be the proper mode of treating these creatures, whose intercourse with the inferior orders of our women, is not less a shocking violation of female delicacy, than disgraceful to the state.[9]

The slave owner and Jamaica planter John Gardner Kerneys, in a pamphlet of 1783, was clear that 'Negroes imported from Africa partake of the brute creation . . . a few degrees removed from the ourang outang . . . from which many Negroes may be supposed . . . to be the offspring'.[10]

By the late eighteenth century, despite the viciousness and power of the anti-black, pro-slavery lobby the black community had established itself in both the fashionable middle-class squares and in the artisan communities around Soho, Clerkenwell and St Giles. There may have been between 10,000 and 20,000 black people in London in the late eighteenth century and contemporary prints of the Gordon Riots record the faces of black axe-wielding protesters! One black woman, Charlotte Gardener, was hanged on Tower Hill for her part in the violence.

For Sir John Fielding, London's most famous eighteenth-century magistrate, black slaves who came to London were liable to be infected with the desire for liberty and if able to learn to read and to use firearms might then export revolution or, with 'the mob on their side', join in a class war at home. Fielding believed,

> They no sooner arrive here, than they put themselves on a footing with other servants, become intoxicated with Liberty, grow refractory, and . . . begin to expect wages . . . A great number of black men and women . . . have made themselves so troublesome and dangerous to the families who brought them over as to get themselves discharged; these enter into societies, and make it their business to corrupt and dissatisfy the mind of every fresh black servant that comes to *England* . . . It gets the *mob on their side* [emphasis added], and makes it not only difficult but dangerous to the proprietor of these slaves to recover the possession of them, when once they are spirited away . . . There is great reason to fear that those blacks who have been sent back to the plantations, after they have lived some time in a country of liberty, where they have learnt to write and read, been acquainted with the use, and entrusted with the care[,] of arms.[11]

Fielding was concerned not only for the slave masters of the Caribbean upon whom Britain's wealth rested but also for the ruling elite in London (often the same people) who might be threatened by an insurrection by armed and educated working people – the 'mob'.

The campaign against slavery would indeed, as Fielding predicted, have an impact on emergent artisanal demands in London where republican sentiments re-emerged during the French Revolution. Despite the final refusal of the French to accept the end of slavery in their colonies (having first abolished it), the sentiments of the Revolution appealed to black freedom fighters and artisan democrats. Throughout the late eighteenth century and then into the Napoleonic Wars, black slaves in the Caribbean rose in revolt. The Haitian victories of Toussaint L'Ouverture inspired an uprising in Grenada in 1795, which by 1796 had almost achieved black republican status until crushed by an invading British army. The slaves had adopted the tricolour flag and the slogan 'Liberté, égalité ou la mort'. St Lucia followed, as did Dominica and St Vincent, and sporadic revolts continued in the nineteenth century with war in Demerara and in Jamaica. Between 1841 and 1905 there were twenty-one rebellions and these continued into the late 1930s, even though slavery in British colonial possessions had been abolished on 28 August 1833 and had finally come to an end in 1838 (the close of the indenture system that had replaced slavery itself).

The spirit of anti-imperial insurrection was a consequence of the emerging attitudes towards liberty and democracy to be found in both black middle-class intellectuals and white artisan republicans. In 1789, Olaudah Equiano, a former slave and now a respected black Londoner, produced an autobiographical account of his years as a slave. It was also a polemic against the very institution. The work was an immediate and outstanding success and it strengthened his friendship with the radical Scotsman Thomas Hardy who, although a shoemaker by trade, had founded the London Corresponding Society (LCS), a working men's agitation group. Equiano probably joined the LCS and he certainly helped them with contacts and information. Hardy soon realized that the fight against slavery was the corollary of the fight for democracy. To one correspondent he wrote:

> Hearing from Gustavus Vassa [Olaudah Equiano] that you are a zealous friend for the Abolition of that accursed traffick denominated the Slave Trade, I inferred from that you was [sic] a friend to freedom on the broad basis of the Rights of Man, for I am pretty persuaded that no Man who is an advocate from principle for liberty for a Black Man but will strenuously promote and support the rights of a White Man & vice versa.[12]

Indeed, Sheffield radicals during a meeting of artisan cutters in 1794 recognized the equal rights of 'our Negroe Brethren', and John Thelwall of the LCS continued throughout 1794 and 1795 to link the issue of slavery to the issue of artisan rights. 'Here we have a two-pronged tradition: black people playing a part in the emerging British radical working-class movement, and British workers, especially after the Haitian revolution, making the abolition of slavery one of their central aims'. Of the thirty-three most feared 'reformers' (i.e., dissident agitators) in the police reports of 1819, two at least were identified as black men. One was William Davidson, originally from Jamaica, who had become a revolutionary republican. He was secretary of the illegal shoemakers' union and was later hanged and beheaded for his part in the Cato Street Conspiracy of 1820. The other was Robert Wedderburn, also from Jamaica and also a revolutionary, who had organized a debate on the right of a slave to kill a master. The debate had found in favour of the slave and Wedderburn found himself subject to surveillance and imprisonment. The authorities could take no chances with the man who had sent the revolutionary journal *The Axe Laid to the Root, or a Fatal Blow to Oppressors, being an address to the Planters and Negroes of the Island of Jamaica* to the West Indies. Wedderburn even advocated a joint uprising by black slaves and European white workers. He also enlisted Irish nationalists to the cause.

At least three prominent black men were associated with the Chartist agitation for parliamentary reform in the 1830s and 1840s. Two leaders of a Chartist rally in Camberwell were the 'men of colour' David Anthony Duffy and Benjamin Prophitt; both were sailors and both suffered draconian punishments for their actions and ideas. Duffy was transported for seven years and Prophitt for fourteen. The third was William Cuffay, a leading London Chartist, who had been born in Chatham in 1788. He had been a tailor whose father was an ex-slave from St Kitts. By 1848, he was the focus of anti-Chartist opprobrium, *The Times* referring to the 'Black man and his Party'. Accused of 'levying war on Queen Victoria' on the evidence of two police spies, Cuffay's destruction was central to the authorities' attack on Chartist demands and a bogeyman for Victoria's own horror at the idea of 'democracy'. Transported for life to Tasmania, Cuffay died there in 1870 aged eighty-two.

19
The Tiber Flowing with Much Blood
Enoch Powell, Notting Hill and Hackney

The vast majority of black immigrants who arrived in London after the Second World War dragging their cardboard cases and letters of introduction down dingy back streets in Notting Hill, Brixton and Lewisham were neither intellectuals nor radicals, but found jobs as hospital porters, bus drivers, London Underground workers or casual labourers. At least one commentator thought the new bus drivers and 'clippies' brought a refreshing chaos to London Transport.

> The pre-war bus crews were men who loved the lash. Highly paid, and cocks within their own working class areas, they took a perverse pride in their subservience. They were the men who loved to stand to attention, wear their gleaming, white coats on the correct day of the year and who knew their well-paid place within their semi-military organization. But undisciplined labour from overseas has made a fortunate havoc of many stupid rules. The bare headed men and women, the coloured scarves, open necked shirts, brown shoes, the occasional punching of a passenger, skirts of their own choosing instead of the official uniform-wear, are small comforts that have been won against the employer and without any assistance from the official union by people who are indifferent to the prized humility of the old guard busmen.[1]

Immigration from the West Indies rose dramatically, from 15,000 in 1951 to 238,000 at the beginning of 1962. All the West Indian islands contributed to the flow eastwards: this represented nearly 10 per cent of Jamaica's population, 8 per cent of Barbados', 13 per cent of the Leeward Islands' and 8 per cent of the Windwards'. Many wives and daughters also travelled east and as early as 1951 made up 37 per cent of West Indian immigrants and by 1961 just under 40 per cent. (Interestingly, these figures, for both male and female immigrants, are often different according to which statistics are consulted.) One woman recalled the situation of the new arrivals.

> I've been here since 1954 and during the Notting Hill riots of 1958 I lived in Shirland Road in North London. My husband was so scared as soon as he came in he hid in the bed, nobody would get him out. But we were happy living in this house, we all lived in one room. We could afford two and I had heard about another room in West London. So I went out to use the phone to find out about this room. I was so shocked the next morning when I passed the phone box, the Teddy Boys had thrown stones and its windows were in splinters . . . There were riots on, our lives were in danger, they were getting at us and we had to be very careful. Then you had the younger boys, they really used to fight back, and it was from those days we really got the impression of how prejudiced the police were, because the Teddy Boys would attack the Black boys and then they would go back at them, and the police would keep blaming the Black boys when we know that they weren't the attacker, they were the attacked. Then the Black boys, more or less, went into groups, they made sure that they didn't walk alone; it was dangerous to walk alone. Of course they walked in gangs, wouldn't you?[2]

From 1955 settlers were also arriving from India, Pakistan and other areas known as the 'New Commonwealth'. In all, Indian immigration rose from 5,800 to 19,050 by 1962 and Pakistani immigration from just under 2,000 to over 25,000. In the same period 18,000 immigrants arrived from other areas and these included white families. Concentration of immigrant groups, especially those made up of single men in poor areas and in a limited number of bed-sits and run-down houses, soon attracted unwelcome attention from white neighbours and teenage gangs. Jamaican and Barbadian clubs and restaurants were often obvious and conspicuous. Nevertheless, the rioting that broke out in Notting Hill, West London, in 1958 was entirely manufactured by white racist groups and not a spontaneous reaction of disgruntled locals. The Notting Hill riots occurred over a number of days in August 1958: Colin Jordan's White Defence League (WDL) had joined with elements of John Bean's National Labour Party (NLP) and Oswald Mosley's Union Movement. Their actions were coordinated from Arnold Leese House in Notting Hill (now Jordan's headquarters). The result of the alliance was not only the terrorization of local black people but also the death of Kelso Cochrane, who was murdered a year later. Bean's NLP and Jordan's WDL eventually came together to form the original British National

Party (BNP) and, alongside other elements, these again merged to form the National Front in 1967.

Despite the violence that flared during 1958, most of Notting Hill's black residents were determined to make a go of things in London and create an atmosphere which echoed that which they had left in Trinidad and Barbados.* The concept of the Notting Hill Carnival turned a little piece of grey rundown west London into a colourful facsimile of Georgetown. Steel bands and floats transformed drab streets into an open-air party, whose amorphous nature was more reminiscent of Mardi Gras than the usual British garden fete. The event soon started to draw big crowds (by the late 1990s it was the largest street event in Europe) but whilst the days went off happily the petty criminals and drug dealers attracted to the area made it a potentially dangerous and violent venue at night. This was the case, at least as far as the police were concerned, and there is no doubt that they were genuinely concerned with the potential lawlessness of a gathering which could not easily be patrolled and which ran to codes of licence they did not understand. For the black community out enjoying itself, the police presence always remained simply a provocation. The violence of the bank holiday weekend of 29–30 August 1976 seemed to confirm the worst fears of both sides.

> The mob attacked with an assortment of weapons ranging from coping-stones to ammonia sprays, and the dustbin lids and milk crates with which policemen guarded themselves heralded the dawn of riot shields on the streets of London [at New Cross but used at the carnival the following year]. There were more than 200 reported cases of robbery, assault and theft, mostly committed by young blacks against respectable people of their own colour – two thirds of the victims were women and girls.[3]

The police suffered 400 casualties, civilians 200. Damage to cars and buildings came to £2m. A community worker, Cecil Gutzmore, blamed overpolicing for the response of those 'defend[ing] their rights'.[4] These rights, concluded one writer sympathetic to the police, included 'picking pockets and stabbing those victims who protested'.[5]

The Carnival was later claimed as the exemplar of multi-cultural Britain and a symbol for London's multi-ethnic mix. When Mayor

---

*It is the case, however, that in 1959, 4,500 black residents returned home, and that between 1960 and 1990 internal emigration from England to Scotland by black and Asian people rose markedly – 40 per cent of Scotland's black and Asian population in this period arrived this way. (See Richard Weight, *Patriots* (Macmillan, 2002), p. 438.)

Ken Livingstone set up the Notting Hill Carnival Review Group in 2000 it was clear that the event was to be treated as an official celebration authorized by the Greater London Authority and finally therefore legitimate. The Carnival's 're-structuring' accorded with a new wave of corporate sponsorship and white middle-class involvement. Nevertheless the deaths of Abdul Bhatti in 1999 and Greg Watson in 2000 during a Carnival time which saw 19 stabbings, 69 other casualties and 129 arrests created increased tension and concern, and in 2001 the Carnival Co-ordinating Committee and Kensington and Chelsea Council were locked in a violent debate following the committee's refusal to hand to the officials the names of the various organizers of individual parade participants for fear of their use for 'racist' purposes (the actual carnival went off without incident). Time had progressed for some, regressed for others.

The Notting Hill race riots of 1958 have to be placed in a context of growing demands by Conservative backbenchers and other activists to restrict immigration. In early 1958, prior to the riots, the Conservative Conference called for immigration controls and even before this backbenchers such as Cyril Osborne had tried to get legislation on the statute book. On the whole, however, Conservative grandees preferred to look to the example of the Roman Empire for a definition of citizenship. Lord Colyton had made such a case in the Lords during the 1950s: 'We still take pride in the fact that a man can say *Civis Britannicus Sum* whatever his colour may be and we take pride in the fact that he wants and can come to the Mother Country.'[6] Lord Butler, who as Home Secretary in 1962 helped to frame the legislation (the Commonwealth Immigrants Act) that began restricting entry, reiterated such 'tolerance' again in 1966: 'I think Britain, like Rome, should be *Civis Britannicus Sum* – I am a British citizen. I like to feel that the overseas people feel that they are British citizens.'[7] Classic (and benevolent) paternalism was central to the belief in Britain as the 'heart' of Empire (and Commonwealth) where all would be equal citizens under a British sun: 'It would be a tragedy to bring to an end the traditional right of unrestricted entry into the Mother Country of Her Majesty's subjects, and quite unthinkable to do so on grounds of colour.'[8] The classical model of the Roman Empire was the model that most appealed to Oxbridge-educated intellectuals and it was in the language of the Roman Empire that the greatest attack on immigration finally came.

Its author was already a contender for the next leader of the Conservative Party. Enoch Powell had a mission to renew Tory policy, to liberate the market from false governmental controls, to preserve the position of Britain and its 'Empire' and to limit immigration. Powell had not, however, been overly preoccupied with the last issue until the late 1960s and had encouraged black workers to enter the National Health Service even as restriction was being debated. Through his years in government and on the front bench of the Opposition he had said little, telling Cyril Osborne in the late 1950s that the time was not right for outright condemnation of immigration. Indeed, Powell seemed supremely uninterested in immigration throughout the 1960s, ignoring issues of ghettoization in favour of praising individual immigrant effort. At a meeting of AJEX (the Association of Jewish Ex-Servicemen) in 1960 he had praised the Jewish contribution to contemporary society, ignoring the complex question of prejudice touched upon by the other speaker, John Baird. A classical scholar and a linguist, Powell was also as much at home in his favourite Indian restaurant or amongst working-class Indian constituents chatting in Urdu as he was debating the finer points of Roman rhetoric with Oxford professors.

The issue of immigration continued to 'fester' in Conservative Party circles throughout the 1960s. In 1964 a group of Conservatives including MPs from Birmingham met to plan an anti-immigration campaign following the successful model of Peter Griffiths, who had called for a complete ban on immigration and who had been part of a local swing against Labour in Smethwick during council elections. A sticker proclaiming 'If you want a nigger neighbour, vote Labour' had elicited Griffiths' comment that such attitudes were 'a manifestation of popular feeling'.[9] Powell may have sensed the mood but he shunned it: 'I have set and always will set my face like flint against making any difference between one citizen of this country and another on grounds of his origin.'[10] Nevertheless by late 1964 he had begun to sing a different song with ominous regularity. 'The West Indian or Asian does not by being born in England become an Englishman. In law he becomes a United Kingdom citizen by birth; in fact, he is a West Indian or Asian still'.[11]

Powell's own perspective was straightforwardly patrician. His view was clear: that Britain was essentially a homogeneous nation with a long and evolved sense of community and communal rights and duties. Small amounts of immigrants could be accommodated provided they assimilated quickly. Powell's contention, which grew from 1967 onwards, was that immigrants were coming in uncontrollably large and unassimilable numbers. His calculations were that over 3,500,000 'coloured people' of recently arrived immigrant families (since the 1950s) would be resident in Britain by 1988 and that this would rise to 5m–7m by 2000, the majority being *born in Britain* and altering the communal landscape beyond recognition. Yet he thought that because immigrants settled in self-restricting areas (due to poverty, etc.) the wider white population was left indifferent to the fate of their 'own people' in urban areas 'blighted' by ghettoization. There was, to him,

Astonishment that this event, which altered the appearance and life of a town and had shattering effects on the lives of many families and persons, could take place with virtually no physical manifestations of antipathy . . .

Acts of an enemy, bombs from the sky, they could understand; but now, for reasons quite inexplicable, they might be driven from their homes and their property deprived of value by an invasion which the Government apparently approved and their fellow-citizens – elsewhere – viewed with complacency. Those were the years when a 'For Sale' notice going up in a street struck terror into all its inhabitants.[12]

Two events sparked the final conflagration and Powell was only too aware of their significance. The first was President Jomo Kenyatta's decision to 'Africanize' his newly independent Kenya. The result of this blatantly racist aggression was the expulsion of the entire Kenyan Asian population. Powell called for restrictions on entry to Britain but the truth was that the Asian community, left with little choice, had applied for and been granted British citizenship to protect them from becoming stateless. The fact that such legislation was intended to protect *white* African farmers was too bad. A 'flood' of applications by Asians in Africa for British passports continued as newly independent African states ethnically cleansed their countries and daily television newscasts showed turbaned refugees arriving at Heathrow. On his return from a visit to the United States, Powell was even more convinced that 'races' could not mix if put together in too great a number. To an audience in Walsall on 9 February 1968 Powell talked of the resentment in white communities in Wolverhampton, Birmingham and Walsall itself.

The second was the introduction of a stronger Race Relations Bill in April 1968. The Conservatives were pledged to oppose it on the grounds that it undermined freedom of speech and freedom of action. It also seemed to undermine certain unspoken rights and traditions that exemplified British fair play, which would now be forced into the straightjacket of bureaucratic regulation on behalf of resident 'aliens'. Edward Heath, leader of the Opposition, had been inclined to take a cautious, non-inflammatory approach towards the coming debate. Powell was a shadow cabinet spokesman.

On Saturday, 20 April 1968, the weekend before the debate on the Bill (which tightened regulations on housing and employment), Powell went to address a meeting at the Midland Hotel, Birmingham. He rose to speak at 2.30 p.m. not only to the eighty-five local party members who came along but also to television crews who had turned up, most unusually, for a local MP talking to his local party followers. Powell had also 'leaked' his speech to the national papers in what could hardly have been less than a pre-emptive strike against his party leader (a fact he disingenuously denied later).

Powell's case was clear.

> We must be mad, literally mad, as a nation to be permitting the annual inflow of some 50,000 dependants, who are for the most part the material of the future growth of the immigrant-descended population. It is like watching a nation building its own funeral pyre* . . . The discrimination and the deprivation, the sense of the alarm and of resentment, lies not with the immigrant population but with those among whom they have come and are still coming. This is why to enact legislation of the kind before parliament at this moment is to risk throwing a match on to gunpowder.

The speech continued with the notorious anecdote of the 'widow of Wolverhampton', who is

> afraid to go out. Windows are broken. She finds excreta pushed through her letterbox. When she goes to the shops, she is followed by children, charming, wide-grinning piccaninnies. They cannot speak English, but one word they know. 'Racialist,' they chant. When the new Race Relations Bill is passed, this woman is convinced she will go to prison. And is she so wrong? I begin to wonder.

The whole long catalogue of disaster ended with an apocalyptic prophecy:

> As I look ahead, I am filled with foreboding. Like the Roman, I seem to see the River Tiber 'foaming with much blood'.

Powell's speech galvanized opinion and destroyed consensus; he said he did not intend it; his speech achieved it. Heath, taken by surprise and in a flap, dismissed him from the Shadow Cabinet. He would never be able to return. Meanwhile, he found himself the most popular politician in Britain – a twentieth-century equivalent of Lord George Gordon. Tens of thousands of letters poured into Powell's home offering support and telling tales of discrimination against whites. A march was organized in support. Four thousand London and Tilbury Dockers

---

*There are variations in memories regarding exactly what Powell said here. Many sources quote an alternative and possibly more authoritative version: 'it is like watching a nation busily engaged in heaping up its own funeral pyre'.

stopped work and 800 of their number marched on Parliament, as did Smithfield meat porters in their bloody overalls.

The furore after the speech was a great boost for the far right. A. K. Chesterton (cousin of G. K. Chesterton), the founder of the National Front (NF), saw Powell's views as essentially NF policy. This, Chesterton felt, provided the entrée to legitimate politics that the NF had lacked. The Union Movement activist 'Big' Dan Harmston led the Smithfield porters and the dockers were also organized by fascist supporters. The consequences of Powell's speech were greater harassment and unpleasantness for blacks and Asians, whereas for British National Party (BNP) recruiting in the Midlands it meant a helpful increase in funds. John Tyndall, writing in *Spearhead* (the NF journal), put Powell in a tradition dating back to the Notting Hill disturbances.

> The time is 1958. Race problems have just started to make themselves felt in Britain. A few souls venture to reply that race problems are not the fault of racialists, but in fact the fault of those who are standing smugly by while a huge coloured population builds up in Britain. Those few predict that the answer is not 'integration', nor the throwing of abuse at race-conscious whites, but to stop the flood and redirect the immigrants home, in their own interests as much as in ours.
>
> Now, coming forward ten years to 1968, it is well to recall these days, and to remember who those few men were. Among the gentlemen in Parliament, the lone voice of warning was that of Sir Cyril Osborne, the member for Louth. Outside Parliament, those who spoke out were regarded as even lower.
>
> Who were they? One was John Bean, editor of *Combat*. Another was A. K. Chesterton, now leader of the National Front. And, let us be fair, two others, although we may disagree with the rest of their politics, were Sir Oswald Mosley and Colin Jordan . . .
>
> Nothing had yet been heard from Enoch Powell on the subject. That Mr Enoch Powell has now spoken out is to be welcomed. But let us not forget those who uttered the warning long, long, ago.[13]

Was Powell a racist? For the grand old man of British fascism, Sir Oswald Mosley, Powell was merely an opportunistic dilettante liable to weaken the revolutionary role of the far right by putting votes at the disposal of the far right of the *parliamentary* Conservative Party. For Margaret Thatcher, 'Enoch was no racist', but she was a convinced Powellite who would also talk of being 'swamped' by people with a different culture! Powell was 'shocked' by the reaction to his speech but he was no fool. It was Powell who had alerted the press and it was Powell who had said, 'I'm going to make a speech . . . and it's going to go up "fizz" like a rocket [and] this one is going to stay up'. It was also Powell who had put in his speech 'I can already hear the chorus of execration' and it was Powell who had used the unsubstantiated 'widow of Wolverhampton' anecdote. More to the point, Powell was an expert rhetorician who could hardly have failed to be aware of the impact of his words. Powell may not have been a racist but his speech was.

His words did, however, convey something more than just a warning over racial tension. They articulated the unspoken fears and concerns of a white working-class population that felt it had had its voice robbed by consensual liberals. Powell put flesh on working-class fears and desires, which had only existed as mute antagonism, diffidence and outbursts of emotional anger. Richard Crossman noted in his diary that Powell had

> Stirred up the nearest thing to a mass movement since the 1930s . . . Enoch is stimulating the real revolt of the masses . . . he has changed the whole shape of politics overnight . . . It has been the real Labour core, the illiterate industrial proletariat who have turned up in strength and revolted against the literate.[14]

Inherent racism was not a prerequisite of Tories alone. Powell's attitudes had long been mirrored in the Labour Party. Bob Mellish, MP for Bermondsey and a junior housing minister, told his party conference as early as September 1965 that our 'own people' would be given precedence over 'coloured people'. He was cheered. The Labour elites in local parties and local unions throughout London were also often deeply paranoid groups jealous of their old power and privileges as the aristocrats of labour. This meant a fear of all foreigners moving into the local borough, whether these were black, Asian or white middle-class 'gentrifiers'. Ian Mikardo, local MP for Poplar and on the receiving end of abuse after 'Rivers of Blood', found the entrenched local Labour Party attitudes utterly hardened to all newcomers. There was, he noted,

> a racism which ran wider and deeper than [he] had expected . . . I never saw a black face in any of the docks in my constituency or on any tug or barge or lighter. To the dockers, keeping out the 'foreigners' was a part of the operation of a closed shop which excluded everybody who wasn't of their ilk. . . . Poplar Labour Party was just another closed shop. Neither was Poplar alone. Anti-Indian feeling ran high in the Southall Labour Party for instance. The Southwark party was apparently ruled by four families who 'froze out newcomers, and indeed discouraged membership!'. And the new London Borough of Islington inherited much of its

pre-1965 metropolitan borough parochialism which had been 'exclusionary', feared local activists and had a council leadership made up exclusively of older members who had lived in the borough all their lives. In this climate, 'foreigner' could easily encompass the white middle classes as well as black newcomers.[15]

The routing of Labour in the following London borough elections meant that such attitudes were part of a whole way of thinking that was becoming outdated.

With the party flung into opposition it became easier for middle-class newcomers to make a mark. Well-educated, articulate, trained to argue, their self-confidence often honed by working in the media or in professions (like law or architecture) which brought special and useful knowledge to party discussions, the gentrifiers dedicated themselves to moving the party in new directions. For if the 'old guard' – a favourite phrase of the time – had been so effective why had they lost power in 1968? When they had held power, why had they done so little, most of all to improve housing conditions? And how could a 'socialist' council tolerate black people living in worse conditions than whites? . . . But the old guard did not give in easily. The 1970s were characterised in Labour Parties throughout London by factionalism, shifting alliances and internecine strife. There was a bitterness that had not been seen since the 1920s . . . in Hackney, for instance, Africans, West Indians, Asians (Muslim and non-Muslim), and the Orthodox Jews negotiated their separate allegiance to one or another faction on the basis less of ideology than of the practical benefits to be gained for their communities.[16]

By the 1970s the poorest sectors of London's population were largely composed of immigrant families whose presence amongst equally poor white groups meant that racism was directly generated from competition for employment and housing. What added to problems was that immigrant groups were seen as an *intrusion* into a *settled* community. The poorest boroughs, being the only ones available to poor immigrant families, found themselves the cockpit of the greatest racial conflicts. In Hackney, for instance, the 1971 census stated there were 14,000 Caribbean residents, 4,000 Cypriots, 3,000 Indians and Pakistanis and 3,000 Africans; only 11.5 per cent of the borough's population but enough to chase off those whites wealthy enough to leave (this was before the gentrification of the 1990s). This left only poor and resentful white families as well as some groups, such as the Chassidic Jews, who had made a conscious decision to live in the area. By 1981, 20 per cent of Hackney's population were born outside

Britain and 42 per cent of households had foreign-born heads; 27 per cent had heads of household from the New Commonwealth, the third highest percentage behind Brent and Haringey. Underfunded and understaffed social services were themselves crippled in dealing with problems by ideological conflicts, anti-government policies and corruption. During the 1970s, race hatred was common gossip and race violence a daily fact in areas such as Hoxton.

> They come here, they should live as we live. Look at those Ugandan Asians. They had all new houses given them when we couldn't get them ourselves.
>
> (Doris) 'Every shop you go in now you've got a Pakistan [sic] there. Every post office round here has got a Pakistan in. They'll talk to you as they want to, but you can't talk to them, as you want to. It reminds me of years ago, the Jews, when they come in here.
>
> (Ellie) 'This country has never been like this, everybody fighting one another. A lot of this violence what's coming up is a lot to do with the Race Relations Board. By law, a white man has to take on a coloured worker, but a coloured man don't have to take on a white, does he? There's a flat upstairs in this block, it's one lot of Nigerians out, another lot in. They're selling the key to each other. Now if that was a white person you'd get slung out.[17]

Racial harassment and race attacks in Hackney steadily increased with the volume of gossip and the level of intervention by right-wing groups. In 1974 the NF increased their vote by a third in wards in North Hackney and Shoreditch. In Shoreditch they gained 9.4 per cent of the vote – a small total, but for opponents a worrying trend. During the 1978 council elections the NF were able to gain more votes than the local Liberals in seven wards. Racial tensions steadily increased and led to murder.

> In December 1980, West Indian and Asian traders in Ridley Road market suffered a spate of burglaries and daubings of racist slogans and swastikas. The gravest attack – if race was the motive – occurred on Kingsland estate, near Dalston, in July 1982. Norma Cunningham, aged twenty-seven, and her nine-year old daughter, Samantha, were stabbed to death, and seven-year-old Syreeta Cunningham was drowned in the bath. The initials of the National Front party had been scrawled on the door of the flat.[18]

Firebombing, window smashing, name-calling, beatings and harassment were simply steps leading to murder, the victims Jews, Turks, West Indians and Pakistanis.

As many parts of Hackney continued to decline into inner-city deprivation it was unlikely that the dangerous tensions building up in other boroughs would leave the area unscathed. On Easter bank holiday, 20 April 1981, nine days after the Brixton riots and just over three months before Southall, Hackney had the first of its own series of riots, part of a sequence of violence and disorder which was to reach a zenith during the summer as street battles engulfed. 'Toxteth in Liverpool, Moss Side in Manchester . . . Bristol, Southampton, Leicester, Nottingham, Derby, Birmingham, Wolverhampton, Bradford, Halifax, Leeds, Huddersfield, Blackburn, Preston and Teeside', as well as London areas from Acton in the west to Haringey in the north, Clapham and Brixton (again) in the south and Walthamstow and Ilford in the east.

The problem had begun some time before, with the appearance of black gangs of teenagers roaming the Hackney and Finsbury areas. As the bank holiday fair held at Finsbury Park came to an end, large numbers of black teenagers began attacking the stalls and bank-holiday makers with homemade and improvised weapons. In May, just under two weeks later, black clubbers leaving Cubies Discotheque looted jewellers and police fought a hundred teenagers. During the night of 24 June, again after an evening at Cubies, youths attacked shops and fast-food outlets on Kingsland Road and also attacked and mugged some passers-by. London Transport bus crews were, by now, operating a no-go area around Cubie's, where they refused to stop. This, of course, left more revellers in one place for longer later at night.

By July, things had changed in character as juvenile delinquency became bolder and gangs started to attack police vehicles, usually by throwing stones or coins. Between 8 July and 10 July, the police patrolled the streets or spent their time in confrontation with black crowds. Fights on 10 July broke out around 5 p.m. near an Argos showroom and close to Johnson's Café, frequently used by black pickpockets and drug dealers and regularly targeted by police. Trouble was the result of opportunism as much as harassment. After another jeweller's was attacked, police moved in and closed the cafe. A crowd slowly began to gather. About 7.30 p.m. the sporadic activity around Kingsland Road and Sandringham Road escalated as two molotovs (milk bottles filled with petrol and stuffed with flaming rags) were thrown at the Argos store and at a policeman near the Stoke Newington social security office. The use of firebombing was a new and worrying escalation of disturbances in the 1980s.

The police, exhausted, frustrated at what could be seen to be only partly a genuine protest and unable to restore proper control, now began charging the crowds, who themselves were engaged in looting Argos. Things escalated at midnight when a young girl was beaten by police and hospitalized. By midnight the area was saturated by police haring after targeted individuals or groups as black and white teenagers looted a menswear shop and an off-licence which was assaulted by looters from the street and at the rear. In the end, and despite the injuries caused to over forty police and civilians, the events had little social significance compared to those in Brixton, Toxteth or Moss Side. Fearing further violence, shopkeepers boarded and grilled their shops the next day.

Despite the fact that much of the trouble had come from opportunism, young black people in the area were frustrated at the lack of jobs and social outlets and at the general attitude of local police (Stoke Newington police station being notorious for deaths in custody), at their own dull lives and at their no-hope prospects in Thatcher's Britain – 'She needs a knife through her heart,' one young woman suggested; 'Tonight,' said another, 'we have to *kill* one of them', but the police appeared, surrounded Johnson's Café, from which the 'evil' seemed to emanate, and cleared the street. The Brixton riots re-enacted in Hackney were not to be, even if resentment between young West Indians and the police, and young underprivileged blacks and the local Chassidic (ultra-orthodox Jewish) population, Turkish and Pakistani shopkeepers continued. One social investigator, attracted by the claims of the young black community, nevertheless concluded:

> I was almost convinced, when I arranged to spend several days with Hackney police, G District of the Met, that I was about to enter a lions' den. I cannot speak for earlier periods, but from what I saw and heard, I came to the conclusion that, while there are obviously far too many individual cases of misconduct, for the majority of the allegations there are more innocuous and more credible explanations than the charge of systematic racism and brutality among the police . . .
>
> It is an unfortunate fact of cultural diversity that many young Afro-Caribbeans, innocent or otherwise, behave in a way that makes those hairs stand up on white policemen's necks. They tend to hang around in the street more. More of them are out partying in the small hours. Many run away on principle when they see a police officer – which most police also take as a prima-facie sign of guilt, as they cannot understand why any law-abiding person could possibly wish to avoid meeting them. But this is not simply a matter of cultural misinterpretation. For while in many cases these signs are innocent, they are also, often, the places, the times and the patterns of behaviour that do, regardless of race, fit in with actual or imminent crime.[19]

More significantly, many in the minority population feared a more sinister side of arrest – death in custody. This was an area of such growing concern in London that during the 1980s black monitoring groups began a series of investigations into alleged police brutality and callousness.

From a relatively low figure of two to four per year from 1978 to 1982 the figures rose alarmingly in succeeding years. They included James Ruddock, arrested for drunkenness during February 1983 and left unconscious at Kensington police station where he died of sickle cell anaemia and Nenneh Jalloh, a petty shoplifter who 'fell' from a fourth-floor window at Marylebone police station in April 1987. There were many other Londoners whose deaths could not be properly accounted for: John Mikkelson from Feltham in 1985, Winston Rose from Leytonstone in 1981, Janice Stewart from Holloway in 1987; Roger Sylvester from Tottenham in 1999; and so on. The most significant death in all these cases in terms of its social consequences (prior to Stephen Lawrence) was Cynthia Jarrett in Tottenham in 1985.*

The most significant episode at Stoke Newington police station was the mysterious 'suicide' of Colin Roach in January 1983. He was a young pickpocket recently released from jail who was found with a fatal shotgun wound in the mouth in the empty foyer of the station. Believing the death to be murder, local and national anti-racist groups as well as trade unionists and the local Labour Party and Commission for Racial Equality became involved. Vigils and marches left eighty-four people arrested.

In this regard the death of Michael Ferreira at Stoke Newington police station should also be noted. He had gone to the station after being stabbed. Ignored for too long he finally died in an ambulance called to take him to hospital. Prior to that an even more disturbing incident had involved Aseta Simms: arrested for being drunk and disorderly in 1971, she died in her cell. The police medical report left much to be desired:

> It is arguable that some people might die with this level of alcohol in their blood stream; but we have people with much higher levels who are still alive today. The bruising was consistent with someone falling about or someone who had been beaten. There was very little evidence that she had inhaled vomit, but this was not the cause of her death. I cannot truly say what was the cause of her death.[20]

The cycle of self-fulfilling prophecy thus became a 'fact' of urban living – a set pattern of action and counteraction across the poorest of London's districts.

---

* For the story of Cynthia Jarrett and Stephen Lawrence see Chapter Twenty-Two.

20
Like Rorke's Drift
Hackney, Brick Lane and Lewisham

The problems in Hackney were a gift for-far right involvement, but for the most part this did not occur except in isolated wards, and skinheads and others marching with Union flags demanding the return of law must have seemed inappropriate to an area where black and white youngsters had sometimes acted in unison and where some of the white youngsters were themselves skinheads. Nevertheless, this did not stop ultra-racist anti-Semites distributing hate literature around the borough.

After the bank holiday disturbances in April 1981, a crudely typed, four-page propaganda leaflet was sent to a number of residents. It was produced by a 'group' calling itself White Active Resistance (WAR) from 'SW1' (possibly the Arnold Leese Information Service) and under the heading 'Blacks go on Rampage at Finsbury Park Bank Holiday Fair' it read:

> What was once an enjoyable day out for Londoners in North London has now become a Nightmare because of GANGS OF BLACKS . . . HARASSING, MUGGING, ROBBING, and SMASHING SHOP WINDOWS.
>
> Just what the Hell is this country coming to when we cannot go out to a Fairground, in our own country, with our children, to enjoy a day out, without being MUGGED, or pushed into the road by gangs of BLACKS?

The problem was not ultimately the black muggers on Britain's streets, however, for they too were caught up in a massive 'conspiracy to use BLACK TERRORISTS to subdue White Resistance'. The leaflet then went on to expose the world conspiracy as advocated by the 'communist spokesman, Israel Cohen'.

> We must realize that our . . . most powerful weapon is Racial Tension. By propounding into the consciousness of the Dark

Races that for centuries they have been oppressed by Whites, we can mould them into the programme of the Communist Party. We aim for subtle victory.

But it seemed the Communists were themselves the 'front' for a much older party whose aim was world domination, reformulated after the Second World War in a 'secret' meeting held in Budapest during 1952. Aiming to bring about 'the third World War [sic]', the chief spokesman for this secret cabal, 'Rabbi Rabbinovitch', set out the plan for Jewish world domination.

We will openly reveal our identity with the races of Asia and Africa. I can state with assurance that the last generation of white children is now being born. Our control commissions will in the interests of peace and wiping out inter-racial tensions FORBIDE THE WHITES TO MATE WITH WHITES. The white women must co-habit with members of the dark races, the white man with black women. Thus the WHITE RACE WILL DISAPPEAR . . . We shall embark upon an era of ten thousand years of peace and plenty, the Pax Judica [sic], and our race will rule undisputed over the world. Our superior intelligence will easily enable us to retain mastery over the world of dark people.

And so for the paranoid in their lonely war against black and Asian Londoners, Communist and Zionist world domination, Hackney became for a few brief months the latest battlefield in an 'apocalyptic' and conspiratorial cold war fought out between the white and black 'races'.

The immigrant community's fear of occasional racial harassment was much less of concern to poor families than earning a living. Wages and conditions were often notoriously low in the traditional sweatshops employing large numbers of women who had little English or education with which to defend themselves. It was not in the casual world of the sweatshop, however, that the contemporary economic hardships of immigrants was to come to light, but in the 'white-collar' work of photographic film processing carried on at a laboratory in Willesden, North-West London.

Grunwick Processing Laboratories was a business of approximately 500 people developing and printing holiday snaps for the growing number of tourists who went abroad each year. Of the main group of workers most were women and since 1974 they had increasingly been drawn from the displaced East African community. Most of them could speak English to a reasonable standard but few could read it or write it well, Gujarati being their first language. Wages were low in the processing plant, hours long and overtime compulsory

and the women were not allowed any form of collective representation. The 'factory' remained staunchly non-union. Nevertheless,
the firm provided much-needed work in a relatively poor suburb of
London.

The various issues that made a confrontation finally inevitable
between the immigrant women and the white male management
were never clear cut nor straightforward but they had a cumulative
effect which was devastating. The origin of the dispute lay in an
argument which occurred between a young Asian mail-order packer,
Devshi Bhudia, and his manager, Michael Alden. Bhudia had been
asked to supervise a group of casual workers made up of students,
but he was allowed no extra pay to do this job. When he went on
a 'go slow' he was sacked. A quite separate row involved one of the
women, Jayaben Desai, who had been asked to work late on a Friday
night. She refused and walked out. Although Desai had left spontaneously it was clear that Bhudia, who was younger than the students,
had thought about his actions before the incident.

During August 1976, Desai and Bhudia, having talked together,
began to rally support on their behalf for the creation of a union.
On the 23rd they marched with their supporters and broke windows
at one of the premises owned by the company, by which time the
management had called the police and a 'violent scene ensued'.[1] By
now 137 strikers were out and approaches were being made to the
Association of Professional, Executive, Clerical and Computer Staff –
the union APEX. APEX enrolled the strikers (who were soon dismissed
anyway) and began a futile negotiation with the management which
was over almost before it began.

By September things had got out of hand. Support for the strikers at Grunwick who APEX could not help alone was solicited from
the whole TUC and mass picketing and 'blacking' now followed.*
Secondary pickets barred the way to chemist shops dealing with
Grunwick and local post office sorters (at Cricklewood) refused to
handle Grunwick mail in the fight against 'a reactionary employer
taking advantage of race and employing workers on disgraceful terms
and conditions'.[2] Finally, after weeks of getting nowhere, the union
movement began mass picketing in 1977, bussing in demonstrators including miners led by Arthur Scargill (later President of the
National Union of Mineworkers, in 1982), who hoped to repeat the
success he had had with flying pickets in 1972, when they shut down
Saltley Gate coke works. All this created a state of virtual siege in

---

* 'Mass picketing – if I can use that misnomer – and violent street demonstrations are acts of terrorism without the bullet or bomb.' James Anderton, Chief
Constable of Manchester.

which police and union sympathizers battled it out for possession of Chapter Road, a small turning in Willesden. The publicity given to the case by the press and television brought further numbers, including many militant students out to fight racism and capitalism and little interested in the particulars of the actual problem. Indeed, of the 137 original strikers, 46 were casual student labour, happy to have a 'cause' before returning to their studies in the autumn. The genuineness of the women's position was, therefore, clouded by outside issues: the two independent polls by MORI and GALLUP of workers at the factory which showed 8 per cent did not care to unionize were dismissed by those determined to find prejudice as mere exercises in propaganda.

As the dispute continued throughout 1977, the government commissioned Lord Justice Scarman to hold an inquiry, which submitted its report on 13 June. The inquiry, whilst laying less blame than had been expected on the firm (which had always acted lawfully), did, however, conclude that

> Where the workforce consists largely of immigrants of the female sex, language difficulties, job insecurity, the spectre of unemployment, and a lack of knowledge of British industrial relations practice and organisation impose even greater responsibilities upon management. Such people are vulnerable: they are particularly at risk when they are employed in a fiercely competitive business where low prices and rapid service bring great rewards.[3]

Scarman also recorded that this was a case relating to 'fundamental human rights and basic freedom' which touched the very heart of English law and tradition.

> The English reconciliation of these rights and freedoms has been traditionally sought through the development of voluntary collective bargaining . . . in the context of the common law. [. . .]
>
> Industrial action is a form of organised self-help e.g. the lockout, the strike, 'blacking', and the picket. And there is always a risk that self-help, if not coupled with self-restraint, may end in violence. English law, if it is to work, requires of parties to an industrial dispute a modicum of self-restraint in the pursuit of their rights. Men must act reasonably within the law. The British tradition of compromise is implicit in the modern English law governing industrial relations.[4]

The case of less than a hundred striking Asian women had by now become symbolic of the struggle of the Tolpuddle Martyrs, fought over unionization 140 years previously.

*

The mixture of economic deprivation, uncertainty in a foreign land, overcrowding and 'ghettoization' proved a dangerous formula for racial tensions with local poor whites especially in the East End of London and the Borough of Tower Hamlets. This came to crisis point in 1978 with violence against Bangladeshis living around Brick Lane, violence which finally gave impetus to the growth of organized anti-racist groups and a widening of awareness of the threat of neo-nazism prior to the 1979 elections.

During the 1950s and early 1960s the large East End Jewish population had moved out to suburbs in the east, north and north-west of London. Pakistanis and Bangladeshis, although present from at least the late 1940s (371 in the 1951 census), only arrived in large numbers during the 1960s. In the census of 1961, 700 Pakistanis are recorded in the old Borough of Stepney. Most of these workers were single men; nevertheless the area was already being called a ghetto. This 'ghetto' comprised Middlesex Street (Petticoat Lane), Princelet Street, Old Montague Street and the spine of Brick Lane leading from Whitechapel to Hoxton. By 1964 the Register of Electors showed almost 20 per cent of names were Muslim and nearly 14 per cent Sikh. The once traditional 'coloured quarter' around Cable Street (during the 1940s) and the centre of life for black seamen now shifted to the Brick Lane area.

Although by 1965 racial tension was sufficiently high to alarm Pakistani community leaders it was in the early 1970s with the rise of skinhead 'culture' that really serious 'Paki-bashing' began, the term apparently originating in the media on 3 April (or 5 April) 1970 after an attack on Asian workers at the London Chest Hospital in Bethnal Green. By 7 April at least one local Asian, Tosir Ali, was dead. On 26 April, fifty rioters attacked Pakistanis in Brick Lane and the creation of anti-racist defence groups was actively discussed amongst the immigrant community, but the Anti-Racist Committee of Asians in East London (ARCAEL) did not appear until 1976. Tension rose with the murder of Gurdip Singh Chaggar in Southall and attacks on students at Queen Mary College, Mile End Road. National Party threats were crystallized by John Kingsley Read's infamous comment, 'One down – a million to go', on the news of Chaggar's death.* On the day of Read's comments ARCAEL held a mass meeting at the Naz

---

*John Kinglsey Read, who had had leadership roles in both the NF and the National Party, also belonged to a gun club and ran a paramilitary group called the Frontiersmen. He was prosecuted for incitement to racial hatred; tried but acquitted; the judge wished him 'good luck'.

Cinema in Brick Lane addressed by Darcus Howe of the Race Today Collective, Trevor Huddleston, Bishop of Stepney and Dan Jones of Stepney Trades Council. Three thousand protesters then marched to Leman Street police station.

By 1976, things had got worse not better for the Bangladeshi community living around Brick Lane, who were beginning to find themselves in a permanent state of siege. On 20 November the East London Conference Against Racism passed a resolution condemning the activities of the National Front (NF) in the area and its attempts to create a base in Bethnal Green. Nothing changed. By 1977 there were again calls for vigilante patrols and even *The Times* reported the increase of attacks (23 December 1977). By now the NF had a newspaper pitch in Brick Lane 'supported' by skinhead newspaper sellers who threatened and abused Asian passers-by. In June 1977 the High Commissioner for Bangladesh demanded an urgent update from the Metropolitan Police and later in the year anti-racists marched through Hoxton and Bethnal Green, led a multicultural fair and began erasing racist graffiti some of which was prominently displayed on the wall of Bethnal Green police station. Tension, however, rose.

At 7.40 p.m. on 4 May 1978, Altab Ali, a Bengali clothing worker, found himself attacked by white youths in Adler Street, Whitechapel. He died from the attack. It seemed that this might be the last straw for the Bengali community. Ten days later Bengalis held a protest march from Brick Lane to Downing Street behind Ali's coffin but this did nothing to prevent an orchestrated white riot in Brick Lane on Sunday 11 June (a market day), when a gang of 150 jean- and T-shirt clad skinheads smashed windows and damaged cars and property. The riot was a 'response' to the press suggestion that there had been a tacit acknowledgement by the Greater London Council (GLC) that Brick Lane was indeed a 'ghetto', a suggestion triggered by a GLC report, *Housing of Bengalis in the London Borough of Tower Hamlets*, produced by the Director of Housing, Leonard Bennett. The report suggested blocks of flats might have only Bengali tenants with white tenants asked to see if they would move. More anti-racist marches followed and so did more race attacks leading to the arrest of fifty anti-racists and ten NF supporters.

By now the violence in Brick Lane had made the national news, and it brought a visit from David Lane, the Chairman of the Commission for Racial Equality (CRE), as the Brick Lane Defence Committee and the Anti Nazi League (ANL) prepared an indictment of policy in the area. For some Asian commentators, 'Brick Lane '78 [was] becoming the focus of attention as did Cable Street in the 30s and Notting Hill in the 50s'. Occupation of the NF newspaper pitch followed 'advice' from Chief Superintendent John Wallis, whose officers then arrested those who did so. The situation was, however, not out of hand even though the Hackney and Tower Hamlets Defence Committee and the ANL had fallen out over an ANL mass rally in Brockwell Park, Brixton whilst failing to properly defend Brick Lane against an NF counter-march in the East End. Temporarily defeated in Brick Lane, the NF now set up its headquarters close by in Great Eastern Street, Shoreditch, half a mile away from their target area. It was, at least for the moment, business as usual.

On 24 September 1978, a paunchy Martin Webster, the National Activities Organizer for the NF, dressed in a striped short-sleeved shirt, and the rapidly balding John Tyndall, Chairman of the party, held a rally in front of their new headquarters. The podium was, as usual, draped with a Union flag, while others fluttered around held by numerous supporters. A photograph of the rally shows Webster looking contemptuously at the camera person, left hand on his hip, microphone in the right. Tyndall sits stony faced whilst Webster speaks, a nervous woman waves at the camera, some supporters grin, a leather-jacketed man near the camera threatens. A fascist 'rally' in a 'hostile' area is, despite its bravado, a nervous event for all.

With the new headquarters set up tension increased but the CRE refused to use the Race Relations Act to prosecute the NF and violent nationalist and racists groups continued to operate in the East End. In 1979, Martin Webster held two Sunday meetings before the general election outside a public house in Cheshire Street, Bethnal Green. This particular public house had been the meeting place on 29 May 1958 at which the London branch of the fascist National Labour Party had been formed. This group, led by John Bean, had merged with Colin Jordan's White Defence League to form the British National Party (BNP) in 1960. The site was therefore soaked in NF mythology. The BNP also held meetings outside the pub in the 1960s, selling their newspaper, *Combat*. By 1972 NF candidates could expect between 6 per cent and nearly 9.5 per cent of votes in Hackney South and Shoreditch, the highest in Britain. The British Movement (BM) was also active, campaigning against Jews, liberals and black and Asian East Enders. Its paper, *British Patriot*, advertised Nazi songs and the speeches of William Joyce as well as hard to find racist propaganda from America. Events came to a head during 1978, when one campaigner, the Reverend Kenneth Leech, a staunch anti-racist, found himself the subject of death-threat letters from the extreme terrorist group Column 88. The letters were written in blood.

The eruption of violent antipathy that threatened the Asian community of East London was paralleled in South-East London as campaigns and bombings threatened Afro-Caribbean immigrants and their British-born families.

Black people had a long association with South-East London, firstly because of the seafaring connections of Deptford and secondly because of the occasional needs of the court at Greenwich. Henry VII had employed a black herald, John Blanke, and black slaves and servants had lived and died in Deptford, as the grave to the 'blackamoor' Cornelius (d. 2 March 1593) attests. This did not stop Elizabeth I from banishing all black people from England in 1596.

> Her majestie understanding that there are late divers blackamoors brought to this realm, of which kinds of people there are already too manie, considering how God hath blessed this land with great increase of people of our own nation . . . those kinde of people should be sent forth of the land.

St Nicholas's Church in Deptford, burial place of Christopher Marlowe after his stabbing, was also the last resting place of black servants such as 'Affee', 'John Punch', 'Jane Williams' and 'Richard Murrey', and in 1737 John Cuffy, a possible relation of the Chartist leader William Cuffay. This long and generally unnoticed history of black South London was brought into general view only during the immigration that followed the docking of the *Empire Windrush* with its 492 Jamaican men in 1948.

From the late 1940s onwards the presence of black men and black clubs in Lewisham began to focus local white hostility and press attention. On 18 July 1949 there were race riots when approximately 800 whites and 50 police battled outside Carrington House in Brookmill Road, where a number of black men were besieged. Unsurprisingly the frightened occupants armed themselves with knives, for which act they *not* the rioters were arrested. The magistrate hearing the cases of attack by the black men against the police reprimanded the accused for failing to show proper gratitude to their saviours!

The arrests which followed continued harassment and nights of rioting, prompted not only the Communist Party to demand anti-racist laws but also the local Trades Council, Council of Christian Churches and the National Council of Civil Liberties to demand proper laws to protect 'the coloured men', British citizens in their own right, 'who were attacked for no other reasons than that their skins are coloured!'

Aggression, suspicion and occasional violence continued into the 1950s. In 1954, the Anglo-Caribbean Club in Greenwich was threatened with attack from Union Movement. Continued harassment during the 1950s led to a conference headed by the Mayor of Lambeth. Needless to say, passive resistance by white locals continued in both covert and overt fashion. Under the headline 'PUB PUTS BAN ON "COLOUREDS"', the *Kentish Mercury* reported in 1958,

Coloured folk in Deptford who want a drink had better not go to The Robin Hood and Little John publichouse in Deptford Church-Street. For, after asking his regular customers if they liked drinking with coloured people, publican Peter Sparkes is barring them.

The reason he is operating his 'no drinks for coloureds' rule is because he fears trouble from local hooligans who beat up coloured men in a recent racial flare-up in Tanners-hill.

'Don't get me wrong', said publican Sparkes. 'I have no private objection to coloured people. But my problem in this part of Deptford is a special one. I have to avert trouble before it starts, I am the joint licensee and I don't want any trouble with the police. When the bottles start flying I am the one who has to step in and stop it'.

Mr Sparkes took over the mock-Tudor style public house in September. 'I was told that it was a tough house when I took it over', he said. 'When I decided not to serve drinks to coloured people, I wrote to the brewery – Courages – and told them what I was doing. They told me that I was the licensee and that I was responsible for the way I ran the pub'.

Mrs Sparkes said, 'We found that when coloured people walked in to the bar everything went quiet. We asked our regular customers if they minded coloured people drinking in the pub. They preferred it without them.

'After all, our regular customers were here before the coloured people came. We have to consider them first'.[5]

The Anglo-Caribbean club was not the first to warrant the attention of racist thugs. The *Kentish Mercury* itself showed the peculiar ambivalence of the time when in June 1959 it demanded the closure of the Chicago After Midnight Club in Telfourd Road, Peckham after it had been attacked by *white men* throwing three petrol bombs.[6] In November 1977 the Moonshot Youth Club found itself with the unwelcome attention of the NF. On 18 December that year it was firebombed.

Clubs and cafes where black young people gathered were often the target of sporadic police raids throughout the 1950s to 1990s. Such clubs were places where petty criminals and drug dealers might gather and surveillance often suggested this was the case. For the armed police of SO19 (Force Firearms Unit), black criminals were 'Zulus' even into the 1990s, the language of police raids couched in the rhetoric of Queen Victoria's imperial wars (filtered through the imagery of films like *Zulu*).

Crasshh! Chris hit it again. On the third attempt the lock gave up the fight, sending the door smashing inwards . . . MP5 now drawn, Chris blanked out the dim light from within as he and his cover-man silhouetted the door, then I was in, adrenalin racing as I scanned the small, cramped interior . . . Fuck, Fuck, Fuck, my brain cried out as I took in the sea of black faces staring at me! There seemed to be hundreds. It was Rourke's [sic] fucking Drift.[7]

By the early 1970s tensions between the indigenous local black population and the indigenous white populace of South-East London, especially between young black people and white youths, were becoming intolerable.

In March 1968 Enoch Powell had called for statistics verifying the birth rate of 'immigrant children' in comparison to 'British children'. This was a cue to bring into public view the maternity rate of black women recently resident in areas such as Lewisham. Most of the women under scrutiny, those from the West Indies, were British and giving birth to British children. They had been legally British all their lives and their parents and generations of foreparents had always been British, as Enoch Powell was only too well aware. Thus, the distinction between the two categories, 'immigrant' and 'British', at least in the case of immigrant workers from the Caribbean, was largely a spurious one.[8]

The man required to draw up Lewisham's statistics was councillor Richard Wells, who although a member of the Lewisham Council for Community Relations (LCCR) believed the Race Relations Act 'odious' and supported repatriation. Wells's attitude was counteracted, however, by the appointment of a black professional, Asquith Gibbes, as Community Relations Officer for the area, an appointment which provided a much-needed boost to community liaison. Gibbes was especially concerned with black families and single people who could not find housing or get onto council lists, but when control of Lewisham Council passed to the Tories in 1971, Gibbes was under scrutiny for his alleged 'pro-communist activities'. Deteriorating relations between the council and black families were exacerbated by the lack of educational opportunities for black children and the fact that 40 per cent of Lewisham's black children were now classified as educationally subnormal, with West Indian children especially noted for their 'maladjustment'.

A more violent disturbance to community relations was the firebombing of a party in Sunderland Road, Forest Hill on 3 January 1971, by a group of white boys and girls. Twenty-two people were injured, some badly. Of the bombers only Pamela Holman and Derek Reynolds were sentenced. For the most part, the press ignored the incident. The Sunday following the attack, a group of teenagers (both black and white) visited the victims in hospital. Outside they were jostled by white youths, and police did little to help, finally arresting the black teenagers on their way home. Such callousness by the police brought a worried response from local black leaders.

> We are extremely disturbed by evidence of deterioration of relations between police in Lewisham generally and Ladywell in particular and the coloured community with whom they come in contact. We feel that action must be taken by the responsible authorities, particularly the police, to see that this trend is reversed if serious and damaging incidents and an atmosphere of mutual distrust and dislike is to be avoided. We have evidence from more than one source, which demonstrates the growing sense of injustice felt by the local coloured community against certain local policemen.[9]

Concern was hardly unjustified. The arrested hospital visitors had had seven of its party found guilty of 'threatening behaviour' and one, George Joseph, was given a three-year suspended sentence. The disturbances outside Lewisham Hospital had been reported on police messages as one involving 'coloured youths' using 'knives'. After a black teenager was beaten up at Peckham Fair in 1973, the subsequent fighting between blacks and stallholders only led to black arrests. A Borough report stated that 'Police/Immigrant relations in this Borough [leave] much to be desired'.[10] Whilst local police Chief Superintendent Morgan Thomas, based in Lewisham, denied any tension existed, Scotland Yard warned that they would not be threatened or 'provoked by West Indians'. Labour members of Lewisham Council immediately called for a public inquiry but this was rejected by both Conservative councillors and the Home Secretary, Robert Carr, who concluded that the police knew best. Nevertheless, a Police/Immigrant Sub-Committee was set up and local liaison officers put in place. Hopes for a resolution were, therefore, high.

Things might have continued to improve if statistics related to the rise in 'muggings', suggesting that almost all street crime was the action of black teenagers, had not been made public. The rise in anti-immigration (i.e. anti-black) propaganda during the early 1970s soon led to the NF putting up a candidate in Deptford during the 1974 general election. Winning only 1,731 votes, the appearance of an NF candidature was significant enough to suggest the need for an anti-racist group. The All Lewisham Campaign against Racism and Fascism (ALCARAF) was finally launched on Saturday 22 January 1977. Such action did not prevent the police filming suspects of street crime in April that year, which led to raids on sixty homes and the arrest of a large number of suspected petty thieves and pickpockets, all of whom were black. With little hard evidence, most of the accused were found guilty of 'conspiracy', a highly problematic legal area as no theft charges were brought against sixteen of the nineteen defendants, all being convicted on 'inference'. The use of such surveillance techniques was kept a secret by police but was known to community workers, who were now cast as quislings and collaborators.

Why were relations with the police so poor by this point? This was due partly to the complex turn to the right by government agencies determined to control public order and prevent the threat to government itself by those alien elements branded 'the enemy within', and partly to the use of saturation policing by semi-autonomous tactical units such as the Special Patrol Group (SPG). Both the strategic and tactical plans of Home Office approved initiatives and those of Chief Constables were always responses to the perceived collapse of law and order: the moral panics of authority. The formation of the Police Federation in 1975, for instance, was a conscious attempt to create a police lobby to pressure politicians into a position in favour of law and order on behalf of the 'silent majority'. The Federation aligned itself with the morality of Mary Whitehouse and her highly successful pressure group, the National Viewers and Listeners Association (NVALA), and the Christian moral majority group which had organized the Festival of Light,* but it also utilized the tactics of liberal lobby groups active in the 1960s.

The 1970s were plagued by what appeared to be a breakdown in law and order, especially in immigrant areas and during strikes, a direct assault on the government and its agencies by groups such as the Angry Brigade and Tartan Army and the sustained mainland bombing by the IRA. Equally concerning was the growing interconnection between terrorist groups and foreign 'rogue' nations who seemed to sponsor and direct terrorist cells within London, in undeclared wars against foreign diplomats and embassies. Inter-racial strife seemed symptomatic of a growing helplessness in the face of organized anarchy.

---

*This group held two evangelical rallies in Trafalgar Square in 1971 and 1972. These were organized by Peter Hall, a missionary recently returned from India who wished to combat the 'moral landslide' he found in the United Kingdom. Other groups included the Order of Christian Unity, founded in 1956 by Ernest Tapp, which was active in 1974 fighting on behalf of 'moral moderates' but dedicated to Christian fundamentalism and the end of liberal secularism.

21
Anarchy in the UK
Private Armies, Vigilantes and the New Cross Fire

In 1967 a machine-gun attack on the American Embassy in Grosvenor Square gave notice of future troubles, which continued into 1968 with the bombing of the Spanish Embassy and the American Officers' Club, located at Lancaster Gate. Five further bombs targeted Spanish diplomats and an Iberian jet at Heathrow. These attacks, by the Basque separatist group ETA, were supplemented by the planting of devices in 1970, outside the Metropolitan Police Commissioner's house in Putney in August and the Attorney General's in October. These bombs were planted by the First of May Group with connections to Spanish and Italian revolutionaries. On 18 September 1972, the Middle Eastern group Black September also began a bombing campaign, against Jewish and Israeli targets in London. In January 1973 they sent out forty-three letter bombs, all capable of killing the recipient; the first killed an Israeli diplomat but most were intercepted. By this time, however, a new police unit, the Anti-Terrorist Branch, had become operational, having been formed from the original Bomb Squad set up in 1971. By 1973 all Bomb Squad officers were armed. The Special Patrol Group (SPG) was also armed when necessary. There was also new and powerful weaponry.

The use of tear gas (referred to officially as 'tear-smoke' in the 1960s) has only once been used as a means of controlling crowds on the British mainland but it has always remained a potential deterrent, despite an early Assistant Commissioner disliking its American gangster film image. CS gas has been available since 1928 when two Americans – Carson and Stoughton – invented it. Its use had been restricted to disarming violent criminals under siege. Nevertheless tear-gas grenades were being stockpiled at Kensington Palace barracks during the 1950s and training with gas guns continued throughout the 1960s at Lippitts Hill training camp in Epping Forest near Woodford, Essex. The use of CS gas in Northern Ireland changed the intention of those who had advocated its use on the mainland from one of specific and targeted prevention of dangerous crime to one in which it would be adopted to the general and vaguely targeted need to prevent civil disturbance. The use of gas would be advocated for crowd control in London from the early 1980s to the riots in Bradford in July 2001.

Of even more concern within the debate over the increasing arsenal available to the police was the leaked report of a 'secret' Home Office investigation into the use of expanding bullets, usually known as 'dum-dums'. Outlawed for military use by the Hague Convention of 1907, the Home Office report had, nevertheless, recommended their adoption by civil police forces. Under media pressure, the proposal was dropped.

These new police, trained in paramilitary style and formed as an elite, were almost the only effective response the Home Office could come up with barring a fully militarized 'third' force outside civilian control. Such a force would be a true political police and this had to be avoided. Nevertheless, quasi-military units, with their own identity and esprit de corps, were felt necessary and throughout the 1980s such units were increased, strengthened and armed. They were there to cope with increased crime (of a violent nature), disorder and terrorism.

> Without much public debate *de facto* 'third forces' developed, specifically trained and readily mobilisable to cope with riots. The Metropolitan Police Special Patrol Group, originally formed in 1965 as a mobile reserve, clearly developed a paramilitary role in dealing with public order and terrorism. All forces now have similar units (under various names), specially trained in riot control, use of firearms and sometimes CS gas. Since 1974 all forces have also formed Police Support Units to help in controlling crowds, strikes and demonstrations . . . They are all specially trained for public order duties, including the use of shields, but they are normally engaged in ordinary policing at local level. However, they are readily mobilisable to deal with problems arising outside their own force under mutual aid arrangements.
>
> The PSUs are coordinated in a crisis by the National Reporting Centre, established in 1972 and located at Scotland Yard. When in operation it is controlled by the current President of the Association of Chief Police Officers (ACPO).[1]

All of these new units were the result of the debates following the incapacity of the police to re-open Saltley Gate Coke Depot when it was targeted by flying pickets led by Arthur Scargill during the miners' strike of 1972. A further refinement was the creation of the National Reporting Centre (NRC) under the control of ACPO and intended to create properly coordinated intelligence and liaison between forces working in alliance. Although not directly intended as a means to provide information on public disorder, it proved invaluable against the miners in 1984.

Thus the control of industrial action was directly related to the new public order anti-terrorist roles that the police were increasingly required to fulfil. Such chains of association linked militant strikers to angry black communities and thence to terrorist bombers. When the miners (now led by Scargill) went on strike again during 1984, Nigel Lawson recalled 'it was just like rearming to face the threat of Hitler in the late 1930s'. Margaret Thatcher in an address to the Carlton Club on 26 November was quite clear about the connective and causal links that threatened her: 'At one end of the spectrum are the terrorist gangs within our borders . . . At the other end are the hard left operating inside our system, conspiring . . . to break and subvert the law'. Britain was clearly under sustained attack not only by foreigners but also from the 'enemy within': striking miners, militant black communities, rogue local authorities (such as Liverpool and the Greater London Council) and the far left of the Labour Party. The deeply paranoid fears of Manchester's Chief Constable, Sir James Anderton, seemed only to confirm the 'panic' felt by police commissioners faced with new and unexpected threats to public order.

We are now witnessing the domination of the police service as a necessary prerequisite of the creation in this country of a society based on Marxist Communist principles. The current concern over policing being expressed by certain political factions has got precious little to do with better community participation in police affairs, or the improvement of democracy – rather it is the first conscious step manifesting itself towards the political control of the police, without which the dream of a totalitarian, one-party state in this country cannot be realised.[2]

Arab groups were still operating during 1978 when a car bomb killed two Syrian Embassy workers. The representative of the PLO in London was also killed in his office and both the former Prime Minister of Iraq and the Ambassador were attacked, the Prime Minister being shot dead outside his hotel. In the summer of 1978 an El Al coach was also machine-gunned and attacked with hand grenades in Mayfair. Four years later the Israeli Ambassador was attacked and shot in the head whilst standing outside the Dorchester Hotel, in Park Lane. His attacker, Hussein Said, a member of the Abu Nidhal terrorist group, was armed with a formidable Polish machine-pistol. Said himself was shot and wounded by the Ambassador's bodyguard, Detective Constable Simpson.

By 1984 the government was sufficiently concerned with security to decide to train Special Branch in the use of sub-machine guns in preparation for an economic summit in June that year. Questioned by the Labour front bench about the decision, Mrs Thatcher reminded them that such weapons had been approved for purchase as long ago as 1976, when Labour was in power. But such reminders could not allay fears that the security branch of the police was rapidly turning into another group of secret government enforcers.

The government did indeed have such a group of enforcers in the men of the Special Air Service Regiment (SAS), formed and commanded by Lieutenant Colonel David Stirling to fight behind enemy lines in the western desert in the Second World War. Deliberately unknown to the general public, the regiment came abruptly and spectacularly into view with its highly successful (and fully televised) attack on the Iranian Embassy in May 1980 when it liberated twenty-six embassy hostages (and British policeman Trevor Lock) from a terrorist kidnapping by six armed Arabs belonging to the Democratic Revolutionary Front for the Liberation of Arabistan. What television viewers saw were gas-masked commandos, dressed 'ninja' style in black and combat dull green, armed to the teeth and protected by flak jackets, scale and storm the embassy using smoke, stun grenades and automatic weapons. The rescue bid was entirely successful, killing or capturing all the terrorists and getting twenty-five hostages to safety (one was killed and another died of wounds later). Britain's secret regiment of real-life James Bonds abseiled into action at 7.24 p.m. and completed operations by 7.50. They immediately caught the imagination of the public and the regimental motto 'Who Dares Wins' became a national catchphrase.

The SAS had long planned for such an operation. After the dreadful catastrophe of the 1972 Munich Olympic massacre of the Israeli team, British and Federal German counter-terrorist training had created not only the German Grenzschutzgruppe Neun (GSG-9) but had also set up a Counter Revolutionary War Wing (CRW) at 22 SAS Headquarters in 1973. Although the CRW units were intended to fight abroad there was no doubt that they might one day be used in Britain (or more obviously in Northern Ireland).

Supplementing police units such as D11 police marksmen, armed SPG officers, C13 anti-terrorist officers and C7 technical support units at the Iranian Embassy, Princes Gate, there were now two SAS special projects teams under the command of Lieutenant Colonel Mike Rose. After consultation with MI5 (which had planted listening devices), MI6 and the Ministry of Defence in the Cabinet Office Briefing Room A (COBRA), the decision had been taken to 'send in the troops'. Sir David McNee, the Commissioner, then handed over control to Rose.

The spectacular theatricality of Princes Gate cheered a public hungry to be told Britain was still the best and still had a role to play in world events, but it also revealed a more sinister and authoritarian world of secret organizations acting outside any democratic control and engaged in a subterranean world of deception and political intrigue – a state within the state.

This secret 'state' had started to take shape in the late 1960s when rising student rebelliousness and union militancy had led a small number of influential right-wing politicians, newspapermen, military leaders and secret service officers to believe that only a 'third' force could save the country from chaos. Such chaos was not the product merely of social unrest and youthful exuberance but an orchestrated attempt to destabilize the country by Communist elements working through the Labour government and using Harold Wilson as their (willing) dupe.

Cecil King, owner of the *Daily Mirror*, wanted, it seemed, to set up a 'government of national unity' backed by the army. A meeting was arranged through an intermediary, Hugh Cudlipp, an executive at the paper, and on 5 May 1968 Solly Zuckerman (Wilson's scientific adviser), Cudlipp and King met Lord Mountbatten at his flat in London. 'King painted a picture of the breakdown of government, rioting in the streets and the need for Mountbatten to take over as leader of some kind of government of national salvation',[3] which even Mountbatten believed the Queen might back. Although Zuckerman left immediately, shouting that the thing was 'rank treachery', Mountbatten was not immediately appalled and, curiously attracted, did 'toy' with the idea.

King had already contacted MI5 and promised to leak any titbits they could offer him about Wilson's over-pally relationship with security 'risks' such as Rudy Sternberg* or cabinet ministers such as the Secretary to the Treasury John 'Jack' Diamond, who were meant to be in the clutches of the KGB. Equally worrying was the list drawn up by some intelligence officers in the army of who might be interned in camps on the Shetlands if a coup occurred. George Kennedy Young, a former vice-chief of MI6 (then a merchant banker and Chair of the Monday Club) and at the time organizing a neo-Nazi political group working with violent anti-Communists and anti-Semites such as Lady Birdwood, later drew up a list of the types to be sent to such camps.

---

*Rudy Sternberg was a German-born refugee from the Nazis. He was created Lord Plurenden of High Halden in 1975 and served as Chairman of the British Agricultural Export Council. It was on Lord Plurenden's farm that BSE (so-called 'mad cow disease') was first identified in the 1980s.

> Under threat of invasion . . . a security counter-action need cover no more than 5,000 persons, including some 40 MPs, not all of them Labour; several hundred journalists and media employees, plus their supporting academics and clerics; the full-time members and main activists of the CPGB and the Socialist Workers Party; and the directing elements of the 30 or 40 bodies affecting concern and compassion for youth, age, civil liberties, social research and minority grievances.[4]

It was quite clear to him that Wilson's cabinet contained 'five Ministers of the Crown whose membership of the Communist Party is not known to have been renounced, and overlapping with them, other Ministers whose ultimate allegiance is outside Britain.'[5]

Two groups would have to be 'dealt with' once such a coup had taken place. The first group would be Wilson's 'Jewish' friends, as Peter Wright concluded whilst at MI5.

> Other people who were associating with Harold Wilson right from before he became PM in 1964 were Sternberg and his East European friends and [Robert] Maxwell of Pergamon. We were very suspicious about these people and warned Wilson repeatedly about the risks . . . [Sidney] Bernstein [the founder of Granada Television] was a very suspicious character and had a file.[6]

The 'dirt' would be provided by Wright. Both he and Young referred to Jews as 'snipcocks' or 'snips' and both thought them disloyal and too fond of Israel (deeply disliked in MI5/MI6 circles). More difficult might be a 'solution' to the black community.

> One fundamental change since [internment in 1940] would be the presence of those 3.5 million non-Europeans whose loyalties centre round their own communities, and whose conduct would be unpredictable under threat of conquest. *National survival demands that this delicate factor be fully evaluated and taken into account.*[7]

By 1976 the fear of national collapse, Communist takeover and anarchy on the streets had even infected television programmes. On the immensely popular talent show *Opportunity Knocks*, the superpatriotic host, Hughie Green, not only offered a message of hope to his 10 million viewers but was followed by a massed band of air, sea and army cadets and a full choir singing his own patriotic anthem 'Stand Up and Be Counted'. He had previously finished a show with 'Land of Hope and Glory'. When his show was finally axed, the furious Green blamed the new 'lefty' Controller, Jeremy Isaacs.

The priority given to keeping public order in a period where 'anarchy' was perceived by many in authority to be on the rise put the police in direct and immediate conflict with those whose presence on the street was either overly visible or perceived as being a direct threat (by simply being there) to public order. The West Indian community and especially its young men were 'criminalized' by the use of police targeting methods at the same time as the allies of black Londoners were progressively being denied the road space to adequately protest at the injustice. The ownership of the geographical spaces of the urban landscape – streets, clubs, squares, houses, housing estates, public buildings – would be the single issue of policy and black community politics for over thirty years.

As the mid-1970s approached, the professional army and police were considered by many on the right of the Conservative Party to be inadequate to the task of controlling the crisis in public order. Geoffrey Rippon (Secretary of State at the Department of the Environment from 1972 to 1974) suggested they be augmented by a citizen's Volunteer Reserve similar to the Organisation for the Maintenance of Supplies used by the government as a pool of loyal workers during the General Strike of 1926.

> . . . at a time when the foundations of our society are being shaken by violence and extremism we must take steps to ensure the maintenance of order. A Conservative government must provide for an adequate level of reserves and for the strengthening of the Territorials, and strengthen the police and create a Citizens' Voluntary Reserve for home defence and duties in aid of the civil power.[8]

More extreme were MPs Jill Knight, Airey Neave and Norman Tebbit, who advocated a citizens' 'police' force on the lines of the Specials. Others such as Colonel David Stirling (later Sir David) began to organize a strike-breaking force called Great Britain 75 (GB-75), and both he and Sir Walter Walker endorsed the use of 'private' or governmentally sanctioned armies of volunteer civilians and patriotic idealists to fight the red menace. Sir Walter had retired by then from his role as Commander in Chief, Allied Forces Northern Europe and had turned his attention to plans for martial law.

By the mid-1970s the secret war in Ireland also seemed out of control with MI6 refusing to cooperate with MI5 when the latter handed over control in 1973. More worryingly, army intelligence had started using highly unorthodox methods to gain information, including the use of coercion and blackmail in order to get 'moles' inside the IRA. This was supplemented by the utilization of such groups as the Ulster Volunteer Force (UVF) and the Military Reaction or

Reconnaissance Group (MRF), which had recruits from both the army and Protestant terrorist organizations. Their tactics included random acts of Protestant killing and bombing in order to draw fire from the Provisionals.* These groups, with their far-right connections in Britain and Europe, were clearly not military in their activities, being closer to the 'Black and Tans' of the 1920s and to the terrorists they were fighting in their methods. In effect, the army now had a highly efficient black propaganda and assassination machine only partially controlled by Whitehall and of whose actions Whitehall was only dimly aware. One writer has suggested this was a 'state-sponsored murder' conspiracy.[9]

In 1979 Peregrine Worsthorne of the *Telegraph* mused in print:

> I could easily imagine myself being tempted into a treasonable dis-position under a Labour Government dominated by the Marxist Left . . . Suppose, in these circumstances, one were approached by an official of the C.I.A. who sought to enlist one's help in a project designed to 'destabilise' this far left government. Would it necessarily be right to refuse co-operation? . . . Coming from the representative of any other foreign power such a request would not be entertained by me for a moment. But the United States is not just any other foreign power. I am and always have been passionately pro-American, in all senses of believing that the United States has long been the protector of all the values which I hold most dear. To that extent my attitude to the United States has long been that of a potential fellow traveller.[10]

The crisis which terrified the centre-right and centre-left of British politics allowed those on the extreme left and extreme right who were dedicated to anti-parliamentary politics jubilation and hope. Thus an opening occurred where parties such as the Trotskyist Socialist Workers Party (SWP) might play a central role.

By 1977, the SWP had evolved from a small group led by Ygael Gluckstein (who wrote as Tony Cliff (d.2000)). The International Socialism Group (IS) were, according to Tariq Ali, 'refreshingly undogmatic' if eccentric in 'their view of world politics'. They were

---

*Secret loyalist assassination squads were allegedly organized by the army's Force Research Unit (FRU) under the command of Colonel Gordon Kerr (by 2002 he was a brigadier and the military attaché to Beijing). Investigated between 1989 to 1993 by the Stevens Inquiry under Sir John Stevens, the Commissioner for the Metropolitan Police, the FRU denied all knowledge of such activities. Witnesses claimed however that their lives were threatened by Special Branch operatives. (See the BBC's *Panorama*, 23 and 29 June 2002.)

certainly more open than their rivals the Socialist Labour League (SLL), led by the rather doctrinaire Gery Healy (d.1989). The SWP emerged from the pointless and insignificant rivalries of the SLL, IS and International Marxist Group (IMG) and its membership reflected the confused and not always well-informed arguments of the time – at one meeting at the London School of Economics an IS heckler told Ali that he should go back to his own country, Pakistan! The comment suggested not only confusion over what the heckler meant (go back to fight?) but also showed the problem of working with well-intentioned but not very bright white middle-class revolutionaries.

The SWP had long since occupied the revolutionary ground that they contended the CPGB had abandoned and they looked to increasingly militant union action between 1972 and 1974 to establish a foothold from which to bring about Denis Healey's nightmare vision of 'political and social strains . . . too violent for the fabric of . . . democratic society'. The lesson was quite clear and the historical parallels suggested revolution was just around the corner.

> 1972 was a magnificent year for the British working class. The class struggle rose to new heights in terms of the number of workers involved, in the size and duration of the strikes and, above all, in the quality of the struggle. There were many more large-scale and prolonged strikes in that year than in any of the previous ten. Even if we exclude the miners' strikes, only once in British history was the number of strike days greater – in 1919.*,11

In the fantastic imagination of SWP activists the return to 1919 was the return to true proletarian revolt in authentic Bolshevik style. The SWP leadership contended: 'Factory occupations are a political weapon, and must be led politically. They must be turned not only against the employer but against the government of the day, and against the capitalist system itself'. It was a lesson few militant trade unionists were willing to endorse.

Although warning for some time that confronting British neo-Nazi groups was a necessary but not central issue for SWP activists, it was clear that direct confrontation with the NF and other Nazi groups gave the SWP an obvious leadership role in any popular anti-Nazi federation from which (ironically) confrontation with the forces of authority (the police) *might* lead to a direct confrontation with

---

*Strike days lost in the UK in 1972, 23,909,000; lost (exc. mining), 13,109,000. Strike days lost in the UK in 1926, 162,233,000; lost (exc. mining), 15,777,000. (B. R. Mitchell, ed., *British Historical Statistics* (Cambridge: Cambridge University Press, 1988), pp. 145–6.) Thus much *lower* than Cliff claimed.

capitalism itself. It formed the Anti-Nazi League (ANL) in November 1977. The SWP would thus be linked to both the cause of liberal multicultural tolerance and the war against capital every time it took its propaganda, newspaper and people onto the streets, usually in 'support' of other people's causes.

Amidst the apparently rapidly approaching collapse of British culture the far right was itself reorganizing. It was far from a spent force even if Mosley was now merely a figure from history who only made the occasional statement. There was Colin Jordan,* an outright Hitlerist and racist who had run the White Defence League during the 1950s. He enjoyed dressing in SA uniforms (brown shirts) and wearing Nazi-style regalia which openly incorporated the swastika. Their hero was not Mosley but the rabid anti-Semite Arnold Leese, whose home would later become the centre of British Nazi activity.

Tyndall was (and remains) a hardliner, using the journal *Spearhead* as the voice of his paramilitary dreams. He was also a man happy to sport weaponry, and found himself arrested and imprisoned in 1966 for a firearms offence. (He was back in jail in 1986 for offences under the Race Relations Act.) The 'führer' of a number of Nazi groups, Tyndall fronted the Greater Britain Movement before joining the National Front in 1967, leaving thirteen years later to form the New National Front and then the British National Party (BNP) in 1982 (the fourth movement to bear the name). Before the appearance of Nick Griffin, Jordan and Tyndall supplied the intellectual weight of far-right groups.

The National Front (NF) was created during 1967 under the chairmanship of Mosley's old supporter A. K. Chesterton. It came about from the merger of the British National Party (the 1960s version), the League of Empire Loyalists and the Racial Preservation Society. With a 'softer' approach, which appealed to Conservative nationalists, the NF found a large anti-immigration base which gained them 100,000 votes during the 1974 elections. By 1977, despite an internal split, the NF had doubled its vote and recorded 100,000 local election voters in London alone. It was a success abruptly destroyed by the election of Margaret Thatcher, whose 'hardline' approach robbed the NF of its disenchanted Conservatives. The NF split as it declined into the New National Front, the Constitutional Movement and the British Democratic Party. Having robbed the NF of its rising success, Mrs Thatcher now became its deepest enemy, especially as she was clearly too fond of Asian businessmen and Jewish politicians, many of the latter being in her cabinet. She did appeal, however, to

---

*On 16 May 1975 Jordan was arrested for shoplifting. He had stolen three pairs of red women's knickers and a box of chocolates from Tesco.

right-wing lobby and vigilante authoritarians and their groups who now looked to her leadership for the salvation of the country.

A number of such organizations already existed, some with pedigrees going back to the General Strike and all dedicated to free enterprise, the defeat of trade unionism and Communist infiltration of the Labour Party and the reassertion of Christian values. The destruction of the Labour Party and its trades union base was often paramount in their agendas.

Most prominent of all of these organizations was the National Association for Freedom (NAFF) with a large membership, a well-organized publicity machine and an in-house newspaper. Other groups included Aims for Freedom and Enterprise, the British United Industrialists, the Economic League and the Institute for Economic Affairs. The Economic League was the oldest, formed by steel and coal magnates in 1919 to fight revolution; the British United Industrialists (formed in 1959) was the most secret. Other groups included the Society for Individual Freedom (formed in 1942) to curb big government. This, along with all the other organizations, could boast both overt and covert links with the Conservative Party, although right-wing Labour Party members (usually those on the Greater London Council) sometimes joined.

Ross McWhirter meanwhile had created the Current Affairs Press to 'stand up to the unions'. His organization's support of democracy was at best lukewarm – democracy meant Conservative governments. 'Parliamentary Sovereignty is acceptable, and only acceptable, so long as it is not manipulated [i.e. socialist]', his news-sheet, *Majority*, declared. By November 1975, McWhirter had been assassinated by the IRA and the organization he led, now called Self-Help, had fallen into the hands of Jane Birdwood, a virulent anti-immigration and anti-Semitic campaigner. Its most significant action during the 1970s was to challenge the legality of union actions during the Grunwick dispute.

In 1976 a number of these freedom associations were considering amalgamation. Thus in October Sir Walter Walker, leader of Civil Assistance (CA), a group with a strong private army and vigilante image, was negotiating with NAFF to form a libertarian bloc aimed at influencing and being at the right hand of Margaret Thatcher in any showdown with unions or Communists. In order to woo NAFF, Walker sent an open letter to NAFF's 'regional, country and area co-ordinators' in which he distanced himself from his 'gung-ho' image.

> I intend to confine my activities to supporting any properly organised and viable campaign whose aim would be firstly, to prevent a breakdown of law and order, and secondly, to restore the power of

judges and magistrates, including corporal punishment as a deterrent. Indeed, ever since CA started more than 2 years ago I have been highlighting our slide towards a lawless society . . .

I have never ceased to warn of the imminent threat from the 'Enemy Within' as well as the 'Enemy Without' . . .

From her strong pronouncements, it is perfectly clear that Mrs. Margaret Thatcher is fully alive to both these threats. It is now my firm belief that the salvation of this country, which has sunk to an all time low, lies in the early return of a Conservative Government to power.

Therefore, another of my activities will be to campaign vigorously for the return of Conservative Government, with such a strong working majority that the will of the people – and not that of a small but immensely powerful clique of extreme left-wingers – shall prevail.[12]

NAFF resented Walker's intrusiveness and broke off talks. In January 1979 it became the Freedom Association to avoid being confused with the NF.

Thatcher's occupation of the middle ground of 'commonsense' racism opened the way for the far right to become more overtly Nazi and more revolutionary in its stance. Yet the groups involved were hopelessly split on a range of ideas, including political tactics and who to recruit. It was clear that, at least in some quarters, it would be better to have a hard core of 'toughs' than a broad voter base (that might follow in troubled areas) and that there would be a need for a network of secret Nazi organizations that might coordinate activities or support a variety of clandestine activities. Such thinking informed leaders such as Martin Webster, who had joined John Tyndall's organization as a teenager (at fourteen) and now led the NF, which, at least on the surface, eschewed Nazi sentiments. Its membership, however, was intimately involved with a more secret world of Nazism centred on the clandestine League of St George. Through the League contacts existed with a pan-European network of Nazi sympathizers, the Ulster Volunteer Force, the American Ku Klux Klan, anti-Israeli Palestinian groups and Italian fascist terror organizations.

In the background were extreme racist militants who hoped to provoke a race war or bring about a military coup. One such was former Major Ian Souter Clarence, who ran a private army training camp in Poole, Dorset, had links with the Security Services and had been helped by them to set up Column 88, a Nazi group used nevertheless as a conduit and occasional trap for right-wing extremists. His Viking Commando was ostensibly a boy-scout style unit of his school pupils (he was a local teacher) but he was also closely linked with Belgian and German Nazis. He was also an associate of Tony Hancock, a racist

publisher and safe house activist from Brighton. From the earl
(if not before) Clarence drew on his SAS experience to train pa
tary terrorists and provide safe houses for fugitive German neo-N
some of whom were arrested at his house in 1983. Moreover he also
provided bodyguards for the BM and corresponded with and aided
right-wing militants who could contact him through the League of
St George's secret publication, *League Review*. Clarence's German connections also linked him to Palestinian training camps in Lebanon
and consequent attacks in West Germany which included the bombing of the 1980 Munich Oktoberfest. 'For European Nazis, Britain
had been regarded as the perfect safe haven: EEC laws gave them the
right freely to live and work here, while our particularly strict extradition rules made it extremely difficult to get them out.'[13]

Throughout the 1980s, Clarence and others (including people like
Tony Lecomber (also known as Tony East or Tony Wells, who was
imprisoned for bombing and assault and later became the head of
security for revisionist historian David Irving), were providing bolt
holes for European terror groups.

> Within the network of Europe's criminal nazi groups, the role
> of British nazis was seen as being to keep their heads down and
> make sure that safe housing, and whatever other help was neces-
> sary, was available to any continental comrades who had to flee
> from their own countries. They even had a name for it: the shelter
> network was called 'Brown Aid' after the brownshirt uniforms
> worn by Hitler's SA troops. While their comrades in France, Italy
> and Germany were causing mayhem in the early 1980s, Britain's
> nazis did nothing to draw unwarranted official attention to their
> vital role in the movement as a whole.[14]

In the 1930s and 1940s, people such as Arnold Leese represented
the most extreme form of Hitlerism and anti-Semitism. Leese's influence on extreme British Nazism from the 1950s onwards cannot be
underestimated, and rivals and eclipses Mosley's. Leese was a man
single-mindedly dedicated to his task, producing pamphlets, distributing books, collating anti-Jewish cartoons, offering his home for
meetings and producing a crudely reproduced news-sheet called *Jew-
Wise*. (All of these activities were coordinated by the Arnold Leese
Information Bureau (ALIB) or Arnold Leese Information Service
(ALIS), which continued to produce occasional documents after his
death.)

Leese was convinced that all Jews were out to kill 'Goys' and 'gain
control over the Gentile' using a communication system based on a
'secret Yiddish cypher'. As part of this takeover Leese (and his followers in the 1970s) believed the Jews had control of the media and were

manipulating it to create a new world war from which they would emerge the victors. Typical of such publications is a *Jew-Wise* issue of the late 1970s.

> The Jews using our media, which they control, have launched an all out smear campaign against the National Front. Isn't it then about time the National Front started to inform the British Public about the Jews. The 'Front' have no need to smear the Jews . . . simply tell the truth about them . . . This is something the Jews dread hence they are making plans to have all material censored by them before it is published (who do they think they are this Asiatic scum). The National Front has a duty to do so . . . before it is too late. There are so many Jews filling the newspapers (Red propaganda sheets) with hysterical rantings.[15]

> TO PREVENT EXPOSURE . . . the Jews in Britain have made it known that they intend censoring all publications prior to them being published. Well we have got news for them . . . they are not going to censor this one. We know they have their KGB (Special Branch) out looking for us in order they might put us in prison . . . but who do they think they are kidding when for the last 50 years we in our own country of Britain have experienced Jewish censorship (that is why the British have no knowledge about the Jewish Conspiracy against them). What is meant by their statement is that they are going to apply their Socialism (Jew control) a little more to bring us in line with Russia where the Jew will not allow the Russian to own a typewriter or duplicator without a licence.

After linking almost every prominent political leader to the Jewish conspiracy the pamphlet concludes with an attack on the Jewish 'evil'.

> KING EDWARD THE FIRST in 1290 kicked the Jews out of England. Apart from carrying on subversion they were carrying out RITUAL MURDER OF ENGLISH CHILDREN.
> *THE JEW IS VILE . . . THROUGH AND THROUGH*. This is not news to those who know what the Jews book of instruction . . . the 'Talmud' contains. Those who are 'Jew Wise' know also that Pornography is Jewish. Two Jews making a fortune out of luring children into having photographs taken in the nude and committing sexual acts appeared in the *London Evening News* (16 December, 1977). One of those poor persecuted Jews named 'JOSH' JOSHUA runs his filthy business from a small office above a chemists in Kensington High Street. In looks he has the appearance of an Indian . . . is of course a good example of the Asiatic Jew.

Even the Queen, in fear of her life, had become a pawn of Jewish conspirators.

Kenneth (Roderick) McKilliam worked from his home at 25 Morpeth Mansions SW1, the flat itself being used as the headquarters of the National Front during the 1974 elections. Here he produced a variety of legal and illegal scholarly and quasi-mystical histories of the Von Däniken/conspiracy theory type. His illegal writings used a background of Old Testament readings and occult knowledge to argue that the Khazer Jews were actually a pre-Adamic race of Mongol-Turks (not 'Jewish' at all) who were the servants of a Satanic conspiracy to pollute the White Adamic race. The Khazer 'Jews' were the creators of Communism and the controllers of world finance preparing world revolution in order to destroy the white (European) race. They had been converted to Judaism as part of a conspiracy that was cosmic in its dimensions and they could be distinguished from 'real' Jews by the shape of their skulls. These 'Khazar' Jews had set up Israel, created Soviet Russia, 'invaded' England during the 1880s and were hell-bent on the utter liquidation of Britain and the setting up of the 'satanic world government of Esau-Edom' which had 'stolen the name of Israel'. As such the Jews of McKilliam's fantasy were the agents of Antichrist. McKilliam, who belonged to the National Front, produced his own illegal pamphlets under cover of the ALIS, authorship given (if at all) under an occult nom de plume. At other times McKilliam's group organized vigilante patriots, looking for black 'muggers'.

McKilliam certainly represented the more bizarre end of Aryan conspiracy theory. His associates in the grandiose National Assembly of Voters included anti-Semites such as Birdwood, and ultra-royalists such as Mary Stanton (who was considered 'batty' even by associates) and Ralph Herbert, who ran the Free Society and believed the House of Commons had usurped the divine right of the monarch. All seemed to have interests in Templar and grail 'histories' that confirmed their own worldviews. Moreover, these ideas came from a long history of fascist occultism associated with people like Nesta Webster, whose book *Secret Societies and Subversive Movements* found popularity during the 1960s. By the 1970s 'ultra'-Nazism was strongly Odinist in attitude.

What of the old comrades of the prewar BUF and postwar Union Movement? Sidelined though they were from contemporary right-wing politics they continued to hold annual reunion dances in honour of 'the Leader' attended by Mosley himself and Lady Mosley. A roll of honour was also kept of those 18b detainees who had died over the years, and in March 1986 the group produced the first issue of a news-sheet called *Comrade* dedicated to 'godlike Mosley' and 'run by Mosley Men' in the 'ever-present undefeated spirit of Mosley'.

The 'old comrades' no doubt drank a toast to 'those strange disturbing men who rallied to his cause'.

Mosley himself had stood for Parliament in 1966 hoping to pick up East End votes but had polled only 1,600 at Shoreditch and had then 'retired' to run the Mosley Directorate. He died in November 1980, an old man with Parkinson's disease, his wife and his Bentley living on after him. His son Nicholas became a prize-winning novelist and his father's faithful biographer. Union Movement, its focus anti-black since the 1950s, stumbled along through the 1960s until, renamed the Action Party for Britain First, it finally collapsed after more electoral defeats in 1973.

The belief that public order was under real threat from criminals, trade unionists, socialist and anti-racist groups, and in a lesser form from the far right, mobilized the police to find solutions which they could not provide. The apparent 'protection' of legal marches by far-right groups merely seemed to confirm that the police were themselves racist, especially given the 'policy' on arrests at anti-racist meetings or marches. This led to the obvious spiral of mistrust and the self-fulfilling problem of police/black community relations. As one study put it in 1983,

> When black people protest against the type of policing they are being subjected to, they come into conflict with the very same structures of policing that led to their protest in the first place. Black demonstrations and events are also viewed by the police as a public order problem. Stemming as they often do from a protest against continuing police indifference to racist attack, or police brutality towards black people, these marches, in turn, are viewed by police as threatening to their authority, which must then be asserted promptly and forcibly on the streets. This, in turn, being viewed by the black community as criminalising of black people, leads to protests against such criminalisation and, in turn, leads to further 'criminalisation' and a further increase in intensive policing of black areas – in an upward spiral of pent-up violence.[16]

For Sir Kenneth Newman, Commissioner of the Metropolitan Police from 1983 to 1987, the young West Indian community were, in essence, a fifth column – another group to be identified with 'the enemy within'. In a 1983 press release, he declared 'war' in order to restore the public space of the inner city to proper authority.

> It is already apparent that the Metropolitan Police must guard against the deterioration in public confidence, and that there is a problem with young people, particularly young West Indians . . . In some areas, there is a brand of obstruction and hostility which

has led to deliberately engineering confrontations with the police. It is, therefore, a priority to restore order to such areas.[17]

Such extremes of opinion amongst those in authority, and at the very top of the Metropolitan Police, simply confirmed the growing distance between police and the black and Asian communities.

This complex melange of ideas was only partly formed during the 1970s but was sufficient to create an unbridgeable gulf between the police and the policed. Into this (on Saturday 13 August 1977) marched the NF in the figure of John Tyndall who, under a law and order, anti-mugging campaign, came to New Cross in order to deliver an attack on 'Black Muggers' and a defence of 'the native people of Lewisham'. The NF march through New Cross, Deptford and Lewisham was a 'territorial bid' designed to make a claim to an area similar to Brick Lane. The area was, of course, the home of many black people.

Against the NF march, one was organized 'for peace' and set out from Hilly Fields. A march on behalf of Church leaders was also organized, headed by the Bishop of Southwark, Mervyn Stockwood, and the Mayor of Lewisham, Roger Godsiff. Under the ALCARAF banner, churchmen, liberals, activists and trade unionists, as well as Communists and a variety of Trotskyist groups, took to the street. At the junction of Lewisham Way (now Loampit Vale) and Algernon Road the anti-racist marchers were rerouted away from the NF march. Nevertheless, members of the Socialist Workers Party (SWP) had escaped police attention and grouped around Clifton Rise in the hope of a direct confrontation with the NF coming that way. As the NF gathered its small march (and very many Union flags) in nearby Achilles Street, the police began operations to break up the crowd in Clifton Rise. At 2.30 p.m. casualties began to arrive at Lewisham Hospital. 'The police arrived and it was clear that they had been given orders to break up that meeting, disperse everybody. The situation changed very dramatically. The next 15 minutes were very chaotic . . . violence . . . arrests . . . confusion.'[18]

In a cynical attempt to align the police with NF policies, Martin Webster, who had accompanied Tyndall, thanked the police for a 'splendid job' and promised absolute support for police action to sort 'the Red mob out' when the NF 'get in power'.

As anti-racist protesters linked hands across Lewisham Way a police car sped round a corner stopping only 'inches' away from the protesters. A man hit the bonnet with a piece of wood causing the police driver to retreat at high speed some fifty yards along the road only to return moments later supported by SPG officers in full riot gear. Having cleared the road of protesters, the police allowed the NF marchers to move on, to board coaches or trains in order to get home. Violent though the police action was, it was, to a certain extent, justified in clearing the NF marchers out of the area. This did not prevent fighting breaking out around Lewisham clock tower between the SWP and police with riot shields. It was the first appearance of riot shields in mainland Britain.

What was even more worrying for black activists, and more especially for ordinary black people living in Lewisham (and London in general), was the way anti-NF action could be hijacked for other purposes, especially by 'socialist' elements looking for a fight with the police.

> The NF demo was embedded in the psyche of black people in the borough. It was the first major publicised confrontation. It was unsettling because we had thought it can't happen here and it was happening. We didn't feel better afterwards because, although people had stood up to them, it had ended up with looting and fighting. It got taken over by left wing agitators or whatever you want to call them, rent a mob, thieves and others. It wasn't in our control anymore.[19]

In January 1981, however, much more worrying and terrible events occurred in New Cross. Two friends, Yvonne Ruddock and Angela Jackson, held a joint birthday party at 439 New Cross Road. Through a series of circumstances that remain obscure a fire began which was either deliberately or accidentally started. It killed fourteen of the teenage partygoers and despite a large reward of £5,000 no one was ever caught for the alleged arson. The black community rightly had cause for deep anguish but also real frustration as police investigations failed to come up with concrete evidence. Meanwhile, the victims' families received hate mail. The *Daily Mirror*'s headline, 'ONE COOL COP CALMS A MOB', in reference to the deputation of the families involved, appeared particularly callous.

The Black People's Day of Action followed on Monday 2 March 1981, a march organized by Darcus Howe, editor of *Race Today*, and John La Rose, a Trinidad-born writer, publisher and film-maker, cofounder of the Caribbean Arts Movement (in 1966) and an activist for black rights. The intention was to demonstrate to the police and the government that black people in Britain had had enough. It was a march born of desperation at unemployment, discrimination and denied opportunities as much as to commiserate with the deaths at the party. The New Cross Massacre Action Committee (MAC) strongly believed that the New Cross fire was deliberately started, probably by an unidentified white man who drove off in an Austin car. The march was intended to give a clear indication that black people 'will not be killed, maimed or injured with impunity and that if the state would not protect its citizens then the black population and its allies in the country would'.[20]

Fifteen thousand black protesters joined the march from New Cross to Parliament, via Fleet Street. Unfortunately some groups started looting jewellers in Fleet Street. The action seemed to confirm police 'changing-room' attitudes.

> The Policy Studies Institute survey of Police in London released in 1983 contained damning and very rarely publicised evidence of how the fire 'had the effect of focusing racialist attitudes within the Met'. A series of racist jokes about the renaming of Deptford to 'Blackfriars' spread through the police force and officers were heard to describe the march as 'hundreds of rampaging niggers' who were considered 'animals' and 'should be shot'.[21]

For many in the black community of South-East London nothing had changed since they had called for the dismissal of the police community relations officer, Chief Inspector Douglas Merry, in July 1972, and a full investigation into the alleged corruption and violence perpetrated against black detainees at Ladywell police station. Little, perhaps, had happened to ease tension since 1962 when Joseph Finch, a head teacher and President of the Deptford and Greenwich Teachers' Association, had helped form a local anti-fascist group and had warned of the levels of 'anti-colour feeling among children . . . [of] 13 to 15'. By the end of the 1970s, the grim predictions and clear concerns of the early 1960s and 1970s were crystallized in the sudden (and to those outside the areas, unexpected) rioting of the 1980s.

22
Living on the Front Line
Brixton to Broadwater Farm; the Stephen Lawrence Case to the Soho Bomber

Soon after their activities in Notting Hill in 1958, racist elements targeted Brixton as a likely site for aggressive action, especially at election time. For the 1962 local council elections, the National Union of Fascists (NUF), a breakaway group of Union Movement, put up a candidate from Clapham Road. Keith Goodall, a founder of the NUF, polled enough to come last. This was hardly surprising as his supporters dressed in full Blackshirt uniform, and at least one, Alan Whereat, had been arrested and charged with wearing an illegal political uniform. After his appearance in court, where the case was dropped, he gave a Nazi salute and his supporters pinned a Union badge onto the black shirt he had worn for the hearing![1]

In the general election of 1970 leaflets circulated in Clapham which purported to come from the Conservative candidate. They read: 'If you desire a COLOURED for your neighbour VOTE LABOUR . . . If you are already burdened with one vote TORY'. The leaflet promised a new Conservative 'Ministry of Repatriation' to 'speed up the return of home-going and expelled immigrants'. The leaflet had been crudely produced with the misspelt 'burdoned' corrected in ink! The Conservatives hotly denied their involvement, as did the NF, who pointed out that their 34,000 leaflets distributed in Battersea had proudly displayed their beliefs and party emblem. Meanwhile the campaign of disinformation stopped Dr David Pitt becoming the first black MP* in a 10 per cent swing against Labour – over twice the swing of other inner London constituencies. The official campaign was, nevertheless, an unpleasant one with Labour accusing the Conservative candidate, William Shelton, of making racist speeches and remarks.[2]

On 24 November 1965 Lambeth Council issued a statement on 'Immigration from the Commonwealth', central to which was an

---

*There had, of course been Asian MPs earlier in the century.

alarming shortage of housing accommodation in the borough. The 'chronic housing situation' and the subsequent pressures on social services were themselves exacerbated by a council trying to deal in an even-handed way with immigrant families who were 'living in dreadful conditions'. Yet if the council took over slum property whose leases had expired and offered them as immigrant accommodation the council itself would become a 'slum landlord'. It was a dilemma without solution, tackled by neither the GLC at London level nor the government at country level. During 1965 discussion of the 'motorway' known as Ringway 1 had even led the Chair of the Greater London Housing Committee to remark casually that the new road would demolish much of Brixton and thus solve 'the overcrowding of houses by immigrants' once and for all. Trouble brewed for sixteen further years.

During the late 1970s, Brixton became the subject of intensive policing, patrolling SPG groups and much plainclothes surveillance, and (in 1981) become the specific target of Operation Swamp (Swamp 81). It would take very little to cause trouble under such pressure. The riots in Brixton started almost accidentally and in an unpremeditated way.

> There was no plan . . . the raw material of the explosion was the spirit of angry young men: the spark their anger at a piece of police action of no great consequence . . . The disorders were centred on Atlantic Road, Railton Road, Mayall Road and the surrounding streets . . . the width of the street where Atlantic Road divides into Mayall Road and Railton Road is known locally as 'the Triangle'. Railton Road, . . . is known as 'the Front Line'.[3]

The trouble began around six o'clock on a warm Friday evening, 10 April 1981. A police constable named Stephen Margiotta noticed a young black man running towards him chased by a crowd. The man fell on him and the policeman, now covered in blood, realized that the youth had been stabbed in the back (a wound that punctured a lung). Margiotta was joined by other policemen who got a minicab to take the boy to hospital but a hostile crowd of forty to fifty people dragged the boy from the cab as they thought the police were attacking him. 'Look, they are killing him,' and 'We will look after our own,' were being shouted as more people came along to see what the fuss was about. By now a large force of thirty to forty police were faced with a crowd of some hundred or so. A police van's windscreen was smashed by a missile. As the person was pursued and arrested, more missiles were thrown and police vehicles attacked.

The police armed themselves with shields and broke up the crowd. Four police vehicles were damaged, six policemen injured and six arrests made. Meetings that night with community leaders failed to sort out the problem especially, as Chief Superintendent Jeremy Plowman, in charge of Operation Swamp, decided he would continue the current intensive policing.

The next day two 'Swamp' officers decided to question a cab driver about drugs they (wrongly) believed were hidden in his car. PC Thornton and PC Cameron soon found themselves surrounded by a large crowd and when they made an arrest (of a bystander) they were in need of rescue. The police van was immediately mobbed and attacked, one of its doors flying open. Duty Inspector Scotchford, realizing danger and believing the incident to have been more violent, went to the scene where 'the air was electric'.

The surging crowd now not only began to throw missiles but set fire to a police van and police car. The police charged and cleared the road. The problem had not been contained, as the crowd in Atlantic Road was one of a number gathered in Leeson Road, Railton Road and elsewhere. Leeson Road was the scene of the first petrol bomb attack in the United Kingdom outside Northern Ireland.

> As Inspector Scotchford and his officers – about 20 in number – turned right into Leeson Road, they saw that the Road was packed with people and were met by a hail of bricks, bottles and other missiles including broken lengths of metal railing. Without protective shields, the officers took what shelter they could behind parked vehicles and in the angle of the Windsor Castle [pub] at the junction of Mayall and Leeson roads. Some officers commandeered dustbin lids. They subsequently made a number of attempts to advance into Leeson Road but each time the barrage of missiles forced them back. Police casualties were heavy. Inspector Scotchford called for urgent assistance and for protective shields. A privately owned vehicle was turned over and set on fire. It was here in Leeson Road, that, at about 5.45pm, the first petrol bombs were thrown at the police.[4]

Reinforcements did not stop the Windsor Castle being set alight, its occupants running for cover. Other pubs, shops and houses were also fired.

Meanwhile, the police had secured Atlantic Road to the Triangle and the crowd had control of all the other streets. A bus was now hijacked and driven at police lines but to little avail; the petrol bombing intensified, the burning liquid running over shields and setting police uniforms alight. Elsewhere, in Electric Avenue and Coldharbour Lane, mobs of black *and white* looters had taken to gutting shops in incidents quite separate from the main action and only peripherally related to it. Two more pubs, the George and the Hamilton Arms, were also attacked, and fires burned out of control as the fire brigade (and ambulances and paramedics) were subjected to attacks. Frustrated and fighting off a crowd that had broken police lines, Chief Inspector Robinson in Railton Road commandeered a fire hose and aimed it at his assailants. Although reprimanded by the fire officer, this first use of water cannon proved effective.

By ten that evening the area was under police control. Eighty-two people had been arrested, 279 police and nearly 50 civilians injured,* and 61 cars and 56 police vehicles burnt out; 145 buildings had been damaged of which 28 were fire-gutted shells. Next day it happened all over again, if to a lesser extent, with mounted police needed to protect Brixton police station: 122 police were injured on what was considered a quieter day. As a foretaste of events at Broadwater Farm, SPG officers were pelted and stoned from upper-storey balconies and walkways when they entered Stockwell Park Estate.

As the clear-up began one outstanding question remained: who was responsible for the petrol bombs?

> The evidence does suggest that a sinister contribution was made by strangers in making and distributing petrol bombs. Indeed, it is possible, though the evidence is not sufficient to warrant a finding that without the guidance and help of certain white people the young blacks, who were the great majority of the rioting crowds, would not have used the bomb.[5]

Who were these sinister white men? Brixton had been the subject of NF and neo-Nazi attention prior to the riots. Two of the police were accused of having NF badges during the Saturday arrests and during the night's rioting some people noticed that one police line was reinforced by 'plainclothes' officers who appeared from nowhere and who disappeared just as fast. If not just an urban rumour the suggestion remained that extreme right-wing groups were supplying help to both blacks and police without either side being aware in order to create the urban destabilization needed for the long-awaited 'race war'.

The riots in Brixton gave notice of continuing trouble between black and Asian communities (essentially the young men) and the police. Such riots plagued the years from 1981 to 1985, concentrated

---

*Unlike police or emergency service injuries, which are logged, civilian injuries are usually little more than estimates.

as they were in the deprived inner-city areas that were a legacy of the 1970s. Brixton was the first riot in which protesters and police saw themselves as opponents in a battle for the streets – the 'no-go areas' of London (Brixton and Tottenham), Manchester (Moss Side), Liverpool (Toxteth), Wolverhampton and Birmingham (Handsworth) – and for both sides this became 'all-out war' with sporadic and spontaneous rioting occurring whenever policing became too heavy-handed. The police remained 'Babylon beasts' whilst their 'coloured' opponents remained an unknown quantity.

Tension remained high despite a call for more sensitive 'community policing', and Brixton police station was the scene of a mass picket by Black History for Action in September 1990. The picket was intended to draw attention to the plight of wrongly accused black prisoners (see Broadwater Farm, below) and deaths under suspicious circumstances.

It is now 5 years since police shot and permanently disabled Cherry Groce an innocent Black woman, in her Brixton home. Days later 'the Bill' murdered grandmother Cynthia Jarrett in Tottenham. Both attacks were followed by an orgy of police violence, which was strongly resisted in local uprisings.

While hundreds of people, including the Tottenham 3 were framed up, none of the criminal police were ever brought to justice . . .

These attacks represent the state's brutal efforts to keep Black and oppressed people down and divided. They will not cease until we ORGANISE, UNITE and STRUGGLE against our oppressor – the British capitalist state.[6]

In 2001 rioting was only narrowly avoided in Brixton when a black man was surrounded and shot dead when he appeared to be wielding a gun. The man (it turned out) was brandishing a 'gun' lighter and was of diminished responsibility. The police, fearful of 'Yardie' gun crime, took no chances; the community saw it otherwise.

It was whilst Lord Scarman slowly and painstakingly heard evidence and prepared papers (his Report would not reach Parliament until November 1981) and the government organized its financial help for the inner cities that more violence occurred in Liverpool, Toxteth and Southall in West London in July. The Southall disturbances began when skinheads and Asian youths began fighting. The skinheads, attending a concert by the Nazi band Screwdriver at a public house in the Broadway, had arrived from the East End intent on causing a riot.

Southall had witnessed serious disturbances before. On 23 April 1979 there was a major clash between police and anti-fascist protesters, which led to the death of a schoolteacher, Blair Peach.* It started with a strike by local Asian workers who left their work or shut shops at lunchtime. After local negotiations and fearing possible violence (or, perhaps, wishing to make a clear statement about public order), the police responded by drafting in nearly 3,000 officers, the SPG, horses, helicopters and the full panoply of riot-precaution equipment. The town was sealed and the protesters hemmed in. Stewards who protested were themselves detained. What followed was described at the subsequent Inquiry.

> The police, according to eyewitnesses, went berserk and vans were driven straight at crowds of people, people were hit on the head with truncheons, mounted police charged and long batons were used. According to a *Daily Telegraph* reporter: 'Nearly every demonstrator we saw had blood flowing from some sort of injury; some were doubled up in pain. Women and men were crying'.
>
> Blair Peach, a schoolteacher, died after being chased down the road and hit on the head with a truncheon by unidentified members of the SPG. Members of the SPG went to the Peoples Unite Centre in 6 Park View Road, which was being used as a first-aid post. They kicked down the door of a room used by the medical unit and ordered everyone to get out. All those inside were forced down the stairs to run a gauntlet of police wielding truncheons. Virtually every item in the building was smashed to pieces, including PA equipment worth thousands of pounds. Clarence Baker, a member of Peoples Unite, was rushed with a fractured skull to intensive care, where he remained for several days fighting for his life.[7]

The extraordinary brutality of the police action seemed to confirm growing suspicions that there were elements in the Met acting as a paramilitary enforcement group. The National Council for Civil Liberties decided to hold their own independent inquiry, at which they heard that, 'searches of SPG officers' lockers . . . revealed a number of unauthorised weapons, including one metal truncheon encased in leather with a lead weight in the end, one sledge-hammer, one rhino whip, two crowbars, one knife with a long blade case and

---

*On 27 April, 2010 the *Evening Standard* revealed that a secret internal police report headed by Commander John Cass had accepted that Blair Peach's death was probably caused by police action which was later covered up by those involved. No charges or disciplinary action were ever taken even though the vehicle (U.11) from which the officer who struck the fatal blow was identified at the time.

a stave of wood three feet long'.[8] Calls for the disbandment of the highly controversial (but useful) SPG were not successful.

The revelations did, however, throw a retrospective light on the 'accidental' death of Kevin Gately, killed by a police baton at an anti-fascist rally at Red Lion Square on 15 June 1974.

> After the events in Southall on 23 April 1979, 342 people were eventually charged. The trials were held in Barnet, 25 miles away from Southall, which made it difficult for local people to show their support for those arrested. Most people were charged with assault or obstruction, or possession of offensive weapons. Charges were changed so that only a handful of defendants could opt for trial by jury. Police evidence was initially accepted as a matter of course, and the conviction rate, accordingly, ran in the first few weeks as high as 90% until a protest by lawyers focused media attention and forced a drop in the conviction rate.[9]

None of the critical civil rights reports that followed the death of Blair Peach seemed to come close to the reality of Southall as experienced by the police on duty. Indeed, these reports appeared not only biased but pernicious in trying to blame the police for his death and the many injured protesters when it was clearly they who had intended to attack the police all along, enemies not only of the NF but of all authority and especially the police. From the police point of view, there was a concerted and well-orchestrated attack by 3,000 demonstrators using concrete, smoke bombs and metal chairs, and Peach was directly involved, killed accidentally by a blow on his unusually thin skull by an 'unknown person'. Two policemen had been violently attacked and one stabbed and of 122 injured people, 97 were police officers. There was never any doubt that left-wing groups did target the police that day. This was also the attitude of authority to the riot in Red Lion Square in which Kevin Gately died.

> Police, playing in their usual position as piggy in the middle, were violently attacked by the International Marxist Group allegedly as the result of a prearranged signal to the mob. In the ensuing battle an unfortunate student fell among the crowd and, although dragged clear by some policemen, later died of his injuries.[10]

Sent to do a very unpleasant job the police had done it honourably and fairly, preventing disorder and mob rule. It was not they who had thrown down the gauntlet. Public order issues are rarely one sided and during the 1970s and 1980s both sides became increasingly embittered and accusatory as the situation deteriorated.

*

On Monday 6 July 1981, after the end of the weekend disturbances that occurred in Southall (on Friday and Saturday, 3 and 4 July 1981), William Whitelaw, the Home Secretary, read a prepared statement to the Commons.*

> The disturbance in Southall began when a group of white skinhead youths began smashing shop windows in the Broadway. Word of this soon passed within the local community, and a group of Asian youths gathered near a public house where skinheads were listening to a pop group. The pub was attacked, and the police, in their attempts to keep the two sides apart, were assaulted with petrol bombs, bricks and other missiles. As the police were increasingly reinforced they brought the disorders under control, but 105 officers, two firemen and three ambulance men were injured. Twenty-five members of the public were treated in hospital. There was damage to property, and 23 arrests were made. There were some further disturbances in Southall on Saturday, but the scale of the violence of the previous evening did not recur.[11]

As he spoke he talked also of Toxteth and the 'extraordinary ferocity' with which the police were attacked, including the use of petrol bombs, to which they had responded with CS (tear) gas. The Home Secretary's conclusion suggested a new stage had been reached in urban 'warfare'.

> In the light of the new intensity of the violence I have decided that better protective headgear and fire-resistant clothing must be available to the police, and steps will now be taken with police authorities to this end.

Roy Hattersley, replying for the Labour opposition, also condemned the 'arson, looting and mindless violence' but continued by suggesting that the root of the problem was social deprivation, to which even 'the skinheads who invaded Southall . . . [were] part'. Richard Crawsaw, the Independent Social Democrat (ex-Labour) MP for Toxteth, denied an overtly racial element to troubles in his constituency, preferring to highlight the gulf between the police and the community. Sydney Bidwell, the MP for Ealing, Southall then spoke.

> Does not the Home Secretary agree, as he seemed to suggest in his statement, that these events arose from provocative action by

---

*Local councils also held emergency debates, as did Camden on 27 July 1981 on 'Preventing Riots and Harassment'.

skinheads, some of them members of neo-Fascist racist organisations? Will he undertake to ensure that the Commissioner of
Police of the Metropolis carried out a thorough investigation into
those undoubtedly premeditated acts, which brought 300 to 400
skinheads from other parts of London to trigger off the disturbance in my constituency? . . . the people of Southall cannot take
this sort of action from outsiders who come in and smash up
Asian people's property.

But Bidwell's comments about self-defence played into the hands
of the conspiracy theorists. Anthony Steen, MP for Wavertree,
Liverpool, a Conservative constituency, was given a perfect opportunity to allude to the new agenda generated around the 'total
breakdown of law and order', the solution to 'discontent and anarchy' being an immediate declaration of a state of emergency. A few
further questions on the issue left the Honourable Members free to
discuss 'Flags of Convenience' – the next issue on the agenda.

The debate was now taken up in the Lords, where at 3.45 p.m.,
after discussions on 'hereditary peerages', 'oil depletion' and 'the
casualties caused by Nuclear War', Lord Belstead repeated William
Whitelaw's Commons statement. The crossbencher Lord Boston of
Faversham encapsulated the government's dilemma regarding what
to do in 'a serious breakdown of law and order' in which police faced
with 'criminal acts, violence, arson, looting and wanton destruction'
resort to CS gas. 'It must be said', Boston continued, 'that that brings
a new dimension to these outbreaks' in which police attempt to
open up 'no-go areas'. Lord Wigoder (a Liberal Democrat in 2001),
believed the disturbances to be a conspiracy of 'extremists' of 'the
Left and Right, and particularly from the Left'; Lord Boyd-Carpenter
(d. 1998; Conservative) called for 'water cannon'; Lord George-Brown
(a Labour peer who died in 1985) tried to add a homely touch.

May I ask the Minister to accept from a very large number of us
that there is no regret, no hesitancy, over the use of CS gas, or water
cannon, if these methods prove to be the best way of breaking up
these mobs? I do not weep any tears for those who would be on
the receiving end, and I ask the Minister whether he believes that
that is in fact the view of most of the people of Brixton? I know
Brixton, I know Southall. I do not know the 'scousers' in Toxteth
but I suspect that they, too, believe much the same.

He then attempted to drum up some trade.

My second point concerns the question of proper riot gear. The
Minister says that this matter is going forward with all speed.

By an accident I happen – I declare an interest – to represent a commercial organisation concerned with both the production of headgear which policemen can wear for any reasonable period of time and the invention of flame-resistant overalls (long coat and trousers) which they can put on when the time comes. Will the Minister please consider representations from me to the effect that we, private enterprise, are not receiving the encouragement that we need to proceed with this matter.

The nonagenarian Lord Barnby (d. 1982) then spoke in order to voice 'the very strong anxiety about the insufficiency of the reduction of the inflow of ethnic groups other than British'. He reminisced, 'I was brought up in the Victorian era, when the very presence of a policeman commanded respect and order and at a time when "patriotism" was a noble word'. The noble Lords were now losing patience and began barracking and calling 'Question'. Barnby nevertheless continued, 'These riots, which have taken place recently, do not contain people who have any respect for Britain, the police or the monarchy and what it stands for'. Overwhelmed, Barnby finally got in the phrase 'voluntary repatriation' before being roundly reprimanded by Lord Belstead, who reminded the noble fossil that 'most of the ethnic minority community in Liverpool came from families, which have lived in that city for some generations. They are British citizens by birth, and there can be no question of their repatriation'. The House then turned to educational matters.

In the Commons meanwhile, there had been one question, asked but not requiring an answer: a reply in itself to an ancient prophecy. The question had come from the Ulster Unionist Member for Down, South, in Northern Ireland and it was as simple as it was doomladen. It went, 'In which town or city does the right hon. gentleman expect the next pitched battle against the police to be fought?' The questioner had not expected an answer and he had not got one, but Enoch Powell already knew the answer he sought.

Now a Unionist, Powell was the maddest, baddest political figure in the Commons. He was an isolated and pathetic figure, not yet the fascinating and imaginative figure of the biographers, not yet the John the Baptist (alongside Keith Joseph) to Margaret Thatcher's free-market messiah, and yet no longer the powerful, dangerous, seductive voice that broke the liberal consensus in one mighty, terrible and violent speech in 1968.

*

Scarman's report was presented to Parliament in November 1981. For the most part it concentrated on the problems and policy of inner-city multi-ethnic areas. After 124 pages describing the context and the events in Brixton, he made a number of comments regarding the *context* of the disorders, to which 'Swamp 81' was, perhaps, an inappropriate response. 'The social conditions in Brixton do not provide an excuse for disorder. But the disorders cannot be fully understood unless they are seen in the context of complex political, social and economic factors, which together create a predisposition towards violent protest.'[12] He then gave his recommendations, which included an amendment to the Public Order Act regarding permission to hold specific marches.

Of relations with the police, Scarman concluded that there had been 'loss of confidence' because of 'hard' policy methods as well as 'unlawful and, in particular, racially prejudiced conduct by some police officers' resulting in 'racial harassment', 'racial prejudice', 'inflexible policy', 'over-reaction', 'delays' (in handling the riots), and failure to prevent 'looting'. These failings had left the police vulnerable to the accusations that they were no longer accountable or independent of political pressure and were no longer policing by consent. At the same time Scarman recognized the problem of dealing with rising street crime ('mugging') and he found, therefore, that 'neither the police nor the local leaders can escape responsibility for the breakdown of relationships between the police and the community in Brixton. Both must accept a share of the blame.'[13]

His conclusion, which caused extraordinary waves almost two decades later during the Stephen Lawrence Inquiry, was that 'the direction and policies of the Metropolitan Police [were] not racist'. 'Racial prejudice' was only a problem with a 'few officers', thus, 'while nothing can excuse the unlawful behaviour of the rioters, both the police and the community leaders must carry some responsibility for the outbreak of disorder. Broadly, however, the police response to the disorders, once they broke out, is to be commended, not criticised'.[14]

After a long and considered set of recommendations regarding black recruitment to the police and better training in race relations for all police recruits, Scarman again turned to the nature of public disorder and the need to equip the police to deal with such events.

> I recognise the importance and necessity . . . that such equipment as water cannon, CS gas, and plastic bullets should be available in reserve to police forces. I *recommend* that such equipment should not be used except in a grave emergency – that is, in circumstances in which there is a real apprehension of loss of life – and then only on the authority of the Chief Officer of Police himself.[15]

CS gas had been part of the police armoury when trouble broke out in Toxteth in Liverpool during July.

Finally, Scarman recognized the usefulness of the pragmatic nature of 'stop and search' whilst expressing amazement at 'the state of the law', which he felt was a 'mess' and which required urgent safeguards especially around the 'sus' laws.* As for public order, he felt it was not time for a new Riot Act but that 'it should be possible to ban "racist" marches in racially sensitive areas' under an amendment to the law.

Scarman's report suggested certain ways forward, but it also highlighted certain intractable problems of housing and employment, which might take years to cure. An uneasy ceasefire was declared by the media and the general public but a rumbling and bitter 'war' continued daily on the streets of London at such a frequency that it might be concluded that in Brixton and Southall the report had *heightened* the tension rather than dissipated it. Among numerous incidents, a year to the month after the Scarman Report reached Parliament, riot-clad District Support Units (DSUs) fresh from Greenwich riot training centre 'protected' council workers clearing derelict squatter premises in Railton Road in order for the council to rebuild the areas known as 'the Front Line' and 'the Triangle', where 'hard' policing had continued despite Scarman; on their return to Tottenham and seeing a group of thirty black youths near the police station, they jumped out of their vans and went into action to clear the area. Violence flared at an NF rally in Tottenham in 1983 in which riot-clad officers had arrested black protesters. During the same period, Hackney, just down the road, saw protracted demonstrations regarding the death at Stoke Newington police station of Colin Roach. Brixton was again the site of a massive police operation in January 1985 in which SPG officers were deployed in a targeting operation. Certain black leisure and recreation centres across London were also the target of long-term surveillance. One was the Olympian Pub opposite the Mangrove Restaurant in Notting Hill (the latter often visited by police and the scene of the arrest of black activist Darcus Howe). When two people fled they were promptly arrested, provoking a confrontation with a gathering crowd. Instant Response Units (IRUs) in full riot gear and unidentifiable flameproof overalls sealed the area and fought a running battle with locals. Sixty people were injured in this incident alone. The Mangrove had also been under surveillance by police searching for 'four petrol bombers'.

---

*The 'sus' law refers (in England) to section 4 of the Vagrancy Act 1824, 'under which people can be arrested on suspicion that an offence is likely to be committed' (OED). It was replaced in August 1981 by the Criminal Attempts Act.

The most disturbing aspect of all these accruing and escalating problems was the belief that the police were now a uniformed
vigilante force. Nowhere was this more evident than in the chase and
subsequent beating of five men (three white, two black) near Holloway
Road in North London in 1984. The police involved jumped out of
their van and attacked the boys with truncheons and fists and also
administered a kicking. It took three years to prove the guilt of the
assailants and then only after immunity had been granted to police
officers who gave evidence. The attackers, charged with assault and
conspiracy, were not finally jailed until July 1987.

One area of particular concern was the growing number of suspicious deaths amongst detainees held in police custody or in jail
(see p. 391). A monitor group called INQUEST had been set up as
early as 1980 to help 'friends and families of people who had died in
police custody'. In 1982 the group was part funded by the GLC, then
under the direct threat of abolition by Margaret Thatcher's government in its crusade against socialist councils. It was not long before
a catalogue of worrying cases, going back to the death of Stephen
McCarthy in 1970, revealed a variety of concerns, not the least of
which centred on the use of Coroner's Courts to 'hide' or 'obfuscate'
evidence. The Coroner's Inquiry into the death of Blair Peach at
Southall on 23 April 1979 (see above) seemed itself to be a clear case
of 'conspiracy'. For instance, the police internal inquiry report was
disallowed as evidence. The most crucial of all documents, the Cass
Report, was therefore not available to the jury. Witnesses too were
chosen at the coroner's discretion and the venue was changed (to
Barnet in North London) when it appeared that too many people
might want to attend. Worse still, lawyers for the family and Anti-
Nazi League (ANL) were not allowed access to police evidence or legal
aid. Costs of £20,000 were found through public donations.

It is against this background of 'unreformed' police and court activity, urban depravation and black criminalization that the tragedy of
Broadwater Farm must be set. The Broadwater Farm Estate (on an
area that was once farmland when Wood Green and Tottenham were
London hamlets) was built to provide a showcase for modern council comfort with a mixture of tower block accommodation placed
amidst older Edwardian streets and backed by schools and a medical centre. The estate was completed in February 1973 and consisted
of twelve blocks of flats in which there were 1,063 dwellings. Ten of
the blocks were 'low rise' and two were 'high rise' and consisted of
eighteen storeys each. All were joined by walkways. The centre block,
called 'Tangmere', was ziggurat shaped and enclosed flats and shops.
Surrounding these blocks there were a number of traditionally built
houses. Although used almost immediately to house poorer people,
single parents and problem families (almost all black), the estate was

not considered a 'sink' for the first few years. It was noted as early as 1976 that even though Broadwater Farm was 'racially harmonious',[16] efforts needed to be made to avoid turning it into a ghetto. Little was done and things did not improve.

Even by the mid-1970s dampness and vandalism had dramatically reduced the desirability of flats on the estate and violence was turning the area into a 'concrete jungle' 'like a prison'.[17] The sociologist Hugo Reading felt the area was in 'a state of complete social disorganisation' – a statement contemptuously denied by the *Weekly Herald*.[18] Five years later, in 1983, 300 residents signed a petition demanding that Broadwater Farm stop being referred to as a 'slum'. This was a week before PC Geoffrey Betts was stabbed during an arrest. Young black people felt they were the subject of constant police surveillance and harassment, an attitude compounded when the youth club (built to help ease tension in the 1970s) organized a trip to France, only to be turned back by French passport control, who did not believe a coach full of black kids could be anything other than an attempt at illegal entry! Despite heightening tensions, police believed there was no call for alarm.

Trouble at Broadwater Farm began away from the estate. On 5 October 1985 Floyd Jarrett, a black man, was taken to Tottenham police station by a white police officer on suspicion of handling a stolen vehicle (it was not). Whilst in custody Floyd was recognized by Detective Constable Michael Randall as a notorious handler of stolen goods (without any proof) and a decision was taken to search his mother Cynthia Jarrett's home even though he did not live there. During the search, carried out under improper circumstances, Mrs Jarrett was accidentally knocked over, and because of her size and poor health, she collapsed and died.

When Floyd heard the news he went to speak to the leaders of the Broadwater Youth Association. It was run by a middle-aged woman called 'Dolly' Kiffin, a remarkable figure who had brought up a large family and then turned to providing leisure and work facilities for black youngsters on the estate. She had helped gain large grants, and had organized a youth club in a disused fish and chip shop and set up a workshop, a launderette and a meals service for pensioners, so successfully that government agencies wanted to speak to her about urban regeneration. She was also instrumental in twinning her hometown in Jamaica with Haringey. Princess Diana had visited the estate and congratulated all on the progress she found, especially in the youth club.

> When we say youth, this is funny because most of them are not really youths in the conventional use of the term. They are actually young men, some of them well into adulthood, but because

they are not in employment, because they don't have total control of their future, they don't really see themselves as being men in the conventional use of the term. They allow themselves to be called youth because they believe they are in a kind of transitional period.[19]

Cynthia Jarrett's death came close on the heels of that of Cherry Groce, a Brixton woman, in September, and feelings against the police and their methods of search and arrest were running high. Floyd contacted Kiffin and Martha Osamor (another community leader) and alongside others went to meet police at Tottenham Station. Meanwhile a hostile crowd gathered outside. A meeting was arranged off the estate at the West Indian Centre but local leaders returned to the Youth Association to decide strategy and simply let off anger. There were demands to march again on the police station and Bernie Grant, the charismatic black leader of the Council, was shouted down for being too 'White minded'.

The police, anxious about developments and aware of rumours a month old that rioting was being planned for Wood Green or Broadwater, began deploying and calling in reserves. They were therefore in riot uniforms *before* they arrived at the estate. This was of great significance as locals believed the police intended to orchestrate a riot and had dressed in preparation. The appearance of white police vans, 'aggressive' policemen and a huge build-up of police vehicles entering the estate's roads frightened and angered residents who began shouting, pelting the police and setting cars on fire as a barricade.

The police in the vans [knew] that young people have been assembling on the estate. They [were] aware that their colleagues [had] been attacked twice during the afternoon. They react[ed] to the banging on the side of [one] van by immediately calling for assistance. The nature of the call [was] indicated by the claim . . . that 'they would have almost certainly have been killed'.[20]

The rioting that followed was dissimilar to that in Brixton in three respects. One was that the police were assaulted from above, from the flats and walkways. Secondly the police were not simply outnumbered but lost control in a very intense melee that needed the policing available only in Northern Ireland. Thirdly the rioters used offensive weapons, including 'machete' style knives, petrol bombs and firearms. The intensity of the violence was 'murderous' on both sides.

Many petrol bombs were thrown . . . Leonardo Leon, looking from the Rochford block over the Griffin Road area, saw: 'People with bottles, then some people syphoning off fuel from cars, three or four people laughing and putting cloth inside. There was a white cloth, a large piece, and they were tearing it apart and then putting it into the bottles, and throwing it. But of ten bottles they threw, one of them would actually light up and land in the road. All the others would just be nothing'.[21]

Surrounded by burning cars, and by a barrage of missiles from above and from all sides, the police were thrown on the defensive. Exhausted by the assaults against which they seemed powerless, the police began to beat their shields 'Zulu style' in defiance and hurl back missiles or shout racist abuse. Some were too worn out to respond and were stood down. The estate seemed to really become a 'no-go' area for a short while. Soon a building began to burn, maisonettes were evacuated and the local schools that backed on to the estate were looted. In the Tangmere block (the Ziggurat) all the shops and a flat were set alight. Many of the rioters were children but some were older and clearly intent on more sinister action. One witness, whose comments were corroborated by others, saw:

> Three or four people moving and giving signs to each other with their hands. They were people in bomber jackets with trainers and jeans. I cannot say absolutely for sure if they were White, but I think they were White. And they were moving like a group. You could see they were White by their hands.[22]

Police reports made much of the idea that basement car parks had been flooded with petrol to be set alight when the police entered. There was considerable petrol on the floor but by accident rather than intention. Intention was, however, behind the random shooting incidents when police and journalists were under fire from someone using a shotgun. The worst incident was the death of PC Keith Blakelock after he fell on a grass verge during a police retreat. Here he was set upon by a group of fifty rioters who kicked, stabbed, punched and hacked him to death.

The death of Keith Blakelock (the first policeman to be killed in a riot since Cold Bath Fields in 1833) darkened the circumstances surrounding the disturbances, which were now seen in terms of mere mob violence, the worst in the capital for over a century. A massive hunt was mounted to catch his killers, who by all accounts were indeed a mob, and bring to justice those who had made petrol bombs or committed arson or assault. Intensive police interrogation of juveniles and children produced a series of names of possible murder suspects but the investigation was plagued with almost total lack of evidence and the confessions of dubious (underage) witnesses who rarely told a consistent story. Nevertheless it was vital for the police to gain a conviction. Mark Braithwaite, Engin Raghip, Winston Silcott and three juveniles were duly sent for trial at the Old Bailey on 21 January 1987. The three adults, despite conflicting and problematic evidence, were all convicted, Silcott on little more than inferential presupposition. Silcott was sentenced to a thirty-year minimum stretch for murder, riot and affray, Braithwaite and Raghip each got life sentences (minimum eight years) for riot, affray and bomb-making. All three men were considered educationally subnormal.

Newspaper coverage of the rioting was inevitably split between those that took a condemnatory line, and those that were more sympathetic to the underlying problems. The *Telegraph* (7 October 1985) wrote of 'black mobs' and the orchestration of the violence by 'anarchists' but also recognized that there was a 'mob of white youths pelting police' and that the 'police advanced, batons pounding Zulu-style on their riot shields'. The *Express* (8 October) considered the affair a 'small war' whilst the *Mail* (8 October) wrote of the rioters 'out to kill' and the white residents terrified of the estate's black people. The *Star* (8 October) concluded that PC Blakelock's killers were 'death hyenas'. At least two newspaper reporters, Peter Woodman of the *Express* and Mark Souster of the *Mirror*, and his photographer Jim Bennett had been hit by shotgun pellets and a BBC sound recordist, Robin Green, had been shot in the head.

Most dailies were quick to round on the local black councillor, Bernie Grant, whose outspoken language about police practices had resulted in a speech outside Tottenham Town Hall in which he stated that 'the police were to blame . . . and what they got was a bloody good hiding'. The *Mirror* (9 October) named him the 'black "godfather" of hate' and Douglas Hurd (the Home Secretary), interviewed for the *Evening Standard* (10 October), said he and Ted Knight (at Lambeth Council) were the 'High Priests of Race Conflict'. The *Sun* (8 October) meanwhile called for 'the lot' (CS gas, water cannon, plastic bullets) to combat inner-city riots, referring to Cynthia Jarrett as 'grossly overweight' and therefore an accomplice in her own demise. On 13 October the *Observer* noted with some satisfaction that Grant had withdrawn his comment made outside the Town Hall and that he'd moved in with a blonde councillor, Sharon Lawrence. The *Caribbean Times* (11–17 October) nevertheless put its support behind Grant, as did the *Voice* (26 October) and the *Asian Times* (18–24 October), which reported the large protest meeting at the Town Hall and the comments of Asian youngsters that the police 'want war' and 'now we know how our brothers and sisters in South Africa must feel'.

What of the remarkable if rather shadowy Menzie 'Dolly' Kiffin? With Clasford Sterling, Vice-President of the Broadwater Farm Youth

Association she had certainly made an impact on the lives of those living on the estate: she had 'rescued' it from 'a nightmare', said *The Times* (8 October). When she had returned to Jamaica in summer 1985 she had been treated as a celebrity, and accompanying her were Bernie Grant (then Haringey Council Leader), Haringey Chief Executive Roy Limb and twenty-five members of the Broadwater Youth Association amongst others. It seemed she had found a political conscience and talked revolution whilst making comparisons with South Africa. Whether naively or not she seemed to model herself on Winnie Mandela and like Mandela she was open to the darkest accusations. The *Mail on Sunday* (27 October 1985) and the Tottenham Conservative Association pointed out that she seemed to own property in Jamaica above her means and that on the estate she had 'financial interests' in many small shops whilst her property and that of her friends was left undamaged during the riots. Significantly, she had orchestrated a break-in to secure the empty fish and chip shop, which was destined for a community police station. The Youth Association was later awarded a grant of £100,000, and more pointedly she was alleged to be the 'godmother' of the estate, sending 'laundered' grant money destined for the Youth Association back to Jamaica whilst being a little too knowledgeable about local crime.

At least Tottenham Conservative party has no doubt about who should shoulder some of the blame.

In its report to Mrs Thatcher it says: 'The root cause was the efforts made over the past three years by Dolly Kiffin, Bernie Grant and various far-Left activists which have brought about racial hatred and hatred of the police to an extent unknown in the civilised parts of this country.'[23]

The government was in little mood for an inquiry.* It wanted quick arrests, restoration of order, a return to normality and above all to make clear its intolerance of such violence (at least in mainland Britain). The Scarman Inquiry into the Brixton riots would be sufficient. A broad-left alliance therefore employed Lord Justice Gifford to produce a report, which he duly did in 1986, but despite the gravitas of the proceedings the report lacked any official status. A further report produced by the Broadwater Farm Defence Committee and written by

---

*'The Home Secretary is right to reject a public inquiry into the Tottenham riots. There is no time now for the delays, the distractions, or the sociology of such an investigation.

The senior London police officer, Sir Kenneth Newman, gave his response yesterday. The capacity of the police to contain and disperse rioters has to be strengthened; that means gas and bullets' (*The Times*, 8 October 1985).

Free Winston Silcott sticker

Judge Margaret Burnham and Professor Lennox Hinds (both from the United States) sought to highlight the miscarriage of justice regarding the conviction of 'The Broadwater Farm Three'.*,24 The language used in the report suggested that 'the government' had wanted instant (though unsafe) convictions, the confusion between government and state suggesting the case was one of political expediency.

Meanwhile Dolly Kiffin and Martha Osamor had organized 'the first Civil Rights Demonstration ever held in Britain' (on 3 October 1987) and produced a 'Manifesto' for 'Civil Rights and Justice' following 'the uprising'. In February 1988 Amnesty International concluded that the Broadwater Farm riot was a legitimate political action and that those arrested (for whatever reason) were 'political prisoners'.

Amnesty International maintains that detained suspects, including juveniles, were denied access to lawyers and family during lengthy periods of police interrogation. Some were allegedly tricked by the police into signing documents waiving their rights and some claimed they had signed statements under duress, sometimes not even having been allowed to read them first . . .

Amnesty International uses a broad interpretation of the term 'political prisoner' so as to cover all cases with a significant political

---

*Without witnesses much hung on Silcott's enigmatic answers to questions and thus the Court of Appeal accepted that the original conviction was 'unsafe'. This is not the same as agreeing the verdict was incorrect. Silcott was awarded £50,000 damages for false imprisonment and malicious prosecution by the Metropolitan Police but he remained in jail for the murder of a partygoer some months before the disturbances at Broadwater Farm. He was released in October 2003.

element. The offence itself may be of a clearly political nature such as belonging to a banned political party. In other cases, however, a person may be charged with an ordinary crime but the context in which it is said to have been committed is political. The events surrounding the Broadwater Farm disturbances took place in a highly charged and political atmosphere, bringing investigation of the cases within the framework of Amnesty International's work.[25]

Rioting also reoccurred in Brixton, destroying local shops. One resident recalled:

When dem burn down Harris [a furniture shop], me was near to tears. Bu'n it to the ground mahn. Shameful. A whole heapa black people used to buy them settees and dining-tables there. Give the mahn a little money every month. Then when you pay so much you can take away whatever you buying. It not there anymore.[26]

The belief that the years following Broadwater Farm were a period of reconciliation and reconstruction became a truism of general white British society, which had come to feel that racism was a thing of the past and that there was both peaceful integration and a new and much lauded British sense of multiculturalism. A pluralist society underpinned by tolerance seemed to make the question of racism a dead letter.

Such beliefs were destroyed on the morning of 22 April 1993, when schoolboy Stephen Lawrence and his friend Duwayne Brooks were attacked at a bus stop by a gang of white boys shouting, 'Nigger!' Lawrence, thrown to the ground, was stabbed twice and bled to death. The whole incident, vicious and unpleasant as it was, might have remained a local tragedy if police incompetence and judicial procedures had not led to an almost wilful bungling of the case, the suspects flaunting their apparent immunity. The murder inquiry seemed a fiasco from the very beginning, ignoring witnesses and contaminating the scene of the crime, and at least one police officer connected to the case seemed to have an overfamiliar relationship with one of the suspects' fathers, a known South London criminal.

What slowly emerged from the long drawn-out proceedings was that racism was still a force amongst disaffected young white (male) groups – a sign of 'tribal' machismo for many boys on the estate in Eltham where two of the suspects, Neil and Jamie Acourt, lived. This racism was aggressive and deadly. Stephen Lawrence's death followed other killings in the area, those of Rolan Adams, Orville Blair and Rohit Duggal, considered by many to have racial elements. The BNP had their offices in Welling, just down the road, and found receptive ears amongst the disenchanted in Greenwich, Woolwich and

Eltham. The police press conference called by Chief Superintendent John Philpott was quick to recognize the attack as racially motivated and to assure the public that all would be done to catch the criminals. The conference was as much an attempt to find witnesses as to avoid a retaliatory black riot against the police or the BNP (who were not involved in this particular incident).

The achingly slow and painfully useless investigation, which achieved nothing except opprobrium for the authorities, exposed a pattern of racism which many had believed long dead in British society but of which black and Asian people had complained (to little effect) for years. With the final failure of the private prosecution brought by Lawrence's parents and the refusal of the Conservative government to hold an inquiry things simmered until the election of Tony Blair in 1997. The Labour Party had pledged itself to right this wrong and to give justice back to the black community. They could not, however, re-prosecute the original suspects. In February 1999, Sir William MacPherson delivered his report to the Home Secretary, Jack Straw. The inquiry, which had sat at the Elephant and Castle and listened to evidence since March 1998, had itself been the scene of a sensational appearance by the suspects (who were spat at and threatened) and the unexpected appearance of a guard of honour for Stephen's parents provided by an utterly unwelcome Nation of Islam. It had also witnessed an emotional speech by the dead boy's now politically active mother, Doreen. Yet none of this prepared for the inquiry's greatest sensation. MacPherson concluded that at the very heart of the Metropolitan Police Force there was 'unwitting and collective racism' amounting to systemic or *institutional* racism, defined as:

> The collective failure of an organisation to provide an appropriate and professional service to people because of their colour, culture or ethnic origin. It can be seen or detected in processes, attitudes and behaviour which amount to discrimination through unwitting prejudice, ignorance, thoughtlessness and racist stereotyping which disadvantage minority ethnic people.[27]

This effectively reversed Lord Scarman's findings in 1981 after the Brixton riots. Sir Paul Condon, Commissioner of the Metropolitan Police, pledged to rooting out institutional racism since his appointment in 1993, did not resign, although clearly he had utterly failed. On the day of the report's publication white paint was thrown over the plaque to Stephen Lawrence put up in Well Hall Road whilst Duwayne Brooks, Neville Lawrence (Stephen's father) and even Bishop Sentamu (of the inquiry) found themselves subject to police surveillance and stop and search. Neville and Doreen, broken in spirit, drifted apart and finally divorced.*

The Stephen Lawrence Inquiry had 'corrected' Scarman's conclusions, finding the police to be prejudiced not only in its staffing but also in its procedures. The term institutional racism was now applied in its fullest and, many believed, its most condemnatory force. The Home Office and the new Commissioner of the Metropolitan Police immediately looked to necessary reforms. Such reforms however were to be prefaced by Home Office sponsored research especially into areas such as the controversial practice of stop and search.

In September 2000 the Home Office released a briefing note for the media summarizing the findings. The research was intended to consider the legality, legitimacy and effectiveness of stop and search procedures by looking at a number of areas across Britain. The research was also intended to scrutinize areas where community trust in the police was low either because of poor policing of incidents or because of antagonism in areas with high populations of black or Asian families.

After some time shadowing police on the beat and in police stations, as well as listening to people stopped or searched and community groups, the researchers came to a range of conclusions which suggested police procedures did not always lead to proper reports and that 'young officers' were often seen by ethnic groups as 'patronising' and 'arrogant'. Blacks and Asians felt that, as expected, they were overly singled out for police attention especially at night. All this seemed on the face of it to condemn police practice in regard to the black and Asian community; however, the methodological procedures used by the researchers, which divided 'available' populations (that is, on the street at any one time) from residential populations, were both complex and arcane. The result was not what might have been expected but rather one which suggested (from the statistical results) that there was '*no* [emphasis added] general pattern of bias against people from minority ethnic groups'; instead 'white people tended to be over-represented in stops and searches', whilst Asians were underrepresented and the representation of black people was merely variable.

Responding to the Home Office briefing paper, the Commission for Racial Equality (CRE), then making a case for the inclusion of

---

*There is a personal footnote to be added by the present author. Whilst preparing the research for this chapter I bought Brian Cathcart's excellent study *The Case of Stephen Lawrence*. My paperback copy was purchased in Electric Parade in Brixton during 2000. It was not until I got the book home that I realized someone had impressed over the picture of the victim on the cover, 'what he deserved . . . wanker'.

'indirect racism' in a revised Race Relations Bill, came to somewhat different conclusions. Their most serious objection to the Home Office research was that the statistical methods used by researchers were not only calculated on an erroneous basis but that the analysis was weighted by factors which were already prejudicial. These included using forms which distorted the ethnic group question on the 2001 Census Form (then being prepared), 'shadowing' officers on the beat and therefore creating an atmosphere in which some police acted in an artificial way and using a bizarre method to calculate results. Of those actions by police that require registration in official records 70 per cent went unrecorded, even as actual stops and searches dramatically increased during the 1990s. Worse still, researchers failed to provide clear and precise records of *where* stops or searches occurred, leaving between 14 per cent and 20 per cent of incidents without a proper location. Focusing on the belief that suspicion might fall on someone appearing out of place on the street or acting 'furtively', the CRE condemned such attitudes as generalizations whose basis appeared to be that blacks or Asians were conspicuous (i.e. suspicious) if in a predominately white area and that no account was taken of the unsociable hours of poor ethnic workers. Highlighted for particular concern (and some contempt) was the finding that 'being young is probably a reasonable basis to raise suspicion, given that offending is particularly common among young people'. The exoneration offered to the police by the Home Office and repeated by *The Times* and other papers seemed, perhaps, slightly premature.

In spring 2000 David Copeland, a 'National Socialist . . . Nazi' who believed in 'the master race', began a nail-bombing campaign aimed at killing blacks and Asians in Brixton and Brick Lane (Whitechapel) and members of the gay community at the Admiral Duncan public house in Soho. He succeeded in murdering Andrea Dykes, John Light and Nick Moore. Dykes was pregnant and about to get married. Conveniently labelled a lone 'nutter' by the tabloids, Copeland saw himself as a political soldier and was involved with a number of extreme Nazi groups.

The turn towards Nazi *direct* action was initiated by activists such as Joe Pearce, who had taken part in a 'whites only' invasion of Barking, East London, his home town. Pearce was the editor of *Bulldog*, an aggressive NF youth paper that advocated a greater level of direct action. He had been the organizer of Young NF since 1977 and advocated 'third position' political agitation. To take 'politics beyond the Party' it would be necessary to create a 'strategy of tension' in otherwise calm neighbourhoods into which NF 'political' soldiers could be placed. Such ideas had filtered into NF thinking via Italian terrorists who themselves had been influenced by early fascists such as Julius Evola and the Strasser brothers from their time in the Sturmabteilung (Brownshirts). Otto Strasser continued as a friend of both Mosley and A. K. Chesterton. The concept of the 'political soldier' came from Roberto Fiore of the Armed Revolutionary Nuclei. Ian Souter Clarence, Tony Lecomber, Tony Malski of the National Socialist Action Party and Joe Pearce all had connections with contemporary European fascist activists. In 1981 Tony Malski had gone as far as concocting a plan to bomb the Notting Hill carnival, with snipers to kill black revellers once the bombs had detonated. The magazine *Searchlight* and the *Daily Mirror* exposed the plot. He was also in possession of a hit list of left-wing activists.

By the 1990s, the NF was in decline and the BM was moribund. Central to the resurgence of extreme right-wing groups during the period was Combat 18 (C18) – the numbers standing for the position of Adolf Hitler's initials in the alphabet. This group of hardline working-class Nazis centred on the brothers Charlie and Steve Sargeant and a number of others including Will (the Beast) Browning.

Initially used as a bodyguard at BNP meetings, the group split from John Tyndall, then leader of the BNP, and set itself up as an Aryran supremacist terror group with links to Ulster loyalist gangs, whose income came not only from sales of magazines but also from control of much of the growing Nazi CD industry centred on Blood and Honour.

The group also had links with football hooligans such as the Chelsea Head-hunters, and Nazi networks in Scandinavia and Germany. In 1995 it formed itself into the core of a revolutionary cadre called the National Socialist Alliance (NSA) but C18 split when an internal war between the Sargeants and Browning saw the stabbing to death of Chris Castle in Harlow and the exposure of Steve Sargeant as a possible MI5 informer.

The ideology of the most extreme members of C18 was provided not only by American fascists but also by an eccentric but dedicated Nazi 'philosopher' named David Myatt, who had been a monk, was now a Satanist and had long contemplated a race war and a final showdown with the 'Zionist Occupation Government' (ZOG). In 1998, Myatt set up the National Socialist Movement (NSM). His 'revolution of the soul' needed 'uncompromising, fanatical individuals', one of whom turned out to be David Copeland, who had links with his group.[28]

On 28 August 2000 newspapers reported that a cache of bomb-making equipment had been found at a former police training college at Witney in Oxfordshire. The destination was said to be the Carnival. The use of so-called political soldiers would have importance during 2001 when riots occurred in Oldham and Bradford.

As the twenty-first century began racial tensions believed long since past seemed to resurface in ever more violent forms. The practice of noting suspected racially motivated murder increased the numbers of such crimes being recorded and suggested a society whose margins bred ever increasing numbers of alienated and violent thugs. There was the suspicious death of a black child called Damilola Taylor in Peckham in south London and the worrying case of an Asian man allegedly beaten by Leeds football players outside a nightclub.[29]

In April 2001, a wedding party for a white schoolteacher, Gareth Williams, and his Hindu bride, Jyoti Narbheram, held in a Bradford pub ended as a riot when white pub goers became abusive. Bradford had already been the scene of escalating violence. Using mobile phones, Asian youths organized a reprisal attack on the Coach House even though the wedding party was continuing inside and at the same time police were clearing the white gang (mainly football supporters of Bradford City) from the town centre. The unexpected consequence of the white gang's retreat was that the rioters who attacked the Coach House and destroyed cars and property were considered mostly Moslem by their Hindu victims. The intervention of white hooligans had dramatically increased intra-Asian feuding within the town.

Meanwhile, on Thursday 19 April, Robin Cook, the Foreign Secretary, had made a forceful speech in favour of a multicultural Britain, claiming (quite rightly) that chicken tikka masala was now *the* British national dish. His intervention had been caused by the need to answer William Hague's attack on Labour's soft policing on asylum seekers, especially those from the Balkans. Cook's speech, however, cleverly wrong-footed the Conservatives by forcing them to defend a position they did not hold. Thus it was hoped William Hague would emerge as a racist little Englander, as had Conservative backbenchers John Townend and Sir Richard Body who had both spoken against a multicultural Britain.

As the general election grew nearer riots broke out in Oldham near Manchester after prolonged harassment of Asian families, inter-racial gang rivalry and an assault by Asian youths on a white pensioner. During the weekend of 23–24 June, rioting occurred in the otherwise peaceful mixed-ethnic communities of Burnley in Lancashire. Trouble began when Asian youths, angered at an attack on a taxi driver by white youths, and frustrated at police vigilance, attacked the Duke of York public house, a meeting place for white gangs. Coming so close to the election the violence boosted openly racist groups who travelled north looking for a fight. At the election, Nick Griffin, who had taken over from Tyndall as BNP leader and was now candidate for the BNP at Oldham West and Royton, polled 6,552 votes or 16.4 per cent, whilst his colleague, Mick Treacy, was able to amass 5,091 votes or 11.2 per cent in Oldham East and Saddleworth. Griffin appeared at the count with tape over his mouth – 'gagged' for his patriotic views.

Fulminating in the *Daily Mail* (20 April 2001), Roger Scruton, the right-wing philosopher and self-elected eulogist for England, charged the Home Secretary with using accusations of racism to silence opponents in a growingly authoritarian Britain. The substance of his argument, the virtues of the British, their sense of community and fear of being swamped (this time by 'European' immigrants), sounded curiously reminiscent of the distinguished member for Ladywood, Birmingham, the echo of whose speech could not be silenced by the passage of over thirty years of political consensus. Thus would Scruton argue that

> Homes paid for by the taxpayer and set aside for those who cannot afford to rent or buy are no longer available to the ordinary British citizen, since asylum-seekers are having to be housed in them . . . [Britain] is an old and overcrowded country, which has succeeded in maintaining peace within its borders through centuries of European turmoil by virtue of the common culture, common language, common law and common loyalty of its people . . . Peaceful assimilation can benefit both the immigrants and the host community itself.
>
> But now we are being asked to absorb 100,000 or more every year, without effective border controls or any real proof of loyalty to, or even respect for, the institutions of our country. Is this not a matter worthy of the most open-minded debate?

Arch Conservative Norman Tebbit* mused in June, 'what . . . would Enoch Powell have made of this?'[30] Yet Powell's ghost belonged to another era from whence other currents of dissent would arise to disturb the last decades of the twentieth century.

---

*Norman Tebbit had been the reinventor of the 'bloody question'. In this case, proof of loyalty was reduced to the national cricket team one supported.

23
One, Two, Three, What Are We Fighting For?
Grosvenor Square to Moon at the Monarchy 2000

The anti-Vietnam War movement created a focus for the counter-culture. The Vietnam Solidarity Campaign (VSC) was created by Trotskyists Ken Coates and Pat Jordan who ran a magazine called *The Week* and who refused to ally themselves with Labour Party entryists (people using the party for their own ends). In that sense they were also independent of the British Campaign for Peace (a CP front) or the Peace Conferences (a Soviet front). Young activists such as Tariq Ali (of IMG) and established cultural figures such as Vanessa Redgrave (of the Revolutionary Workers Party) were attracted to their anti-war/anti-American stance. Their hero was Che Guevara, who had dedicated his revolutionary life to 'uniting [people] against the great enemy of mankind: the United States of America'.[1]

Ali, Redgrave, the International Socialists (IS) and others took their first protest march to the American Embassy in Grosvenor Square on 22 October 1967. A peaceful march of 10,000 found themselves remarkably close to the building, something not lost on organizers the following year. The next rally took place on 17 March 1968: leaflets and stickers declared 'All out on March 17. March to Grosvenor Square'. The call was answered by a crowd of 80–100,000: trade unionists, CND supporters, students, politicians, pacifists and good-timers, who gathered in Trafalgar Square to hear Ali and Redgrave proclaim the revolution. The previous night, twenty London theatres, including one showing the Black and White Minstrels, had been disrupted by protesters supporting North Vietnam's National Liberation Front (NLF). At his home in Crouch End, Ali had prepared for the following day but once in Trafalgar Square he realized that there might be a chance to attack the embassy. It was agreed in Trafalgar Square that 'a serious attempt should . . . be made to occupy the embassy'[2] if a chance arose. This would either allow them to hoist the NLF flag or force the marines inside to open fire – fantastic publicity in both cases.

From Oxford Street, the march filed into North Audley Street and thence into Grosvenor Square. There was a massive police presence, however, which precluded the concept of a 'rush'. Ali recalled:

> Then we saw the police horses. A cry went up that 'the Cossacks are coming', and an invisible tension united everyone. Arms were linked across the square as the mounted police charged through us to try and break our formation. A hippy who tried to offer a mounted policeman a bunch of flowers was truncheoned to the ground. Marbles were thrown at the horses and a few policemen fell to the ground, but none were surrounded and beaten up. The fighting continued for almost two hours. An attempt to arrest me was prevented by a few hundred people coming to my rescue and surrounding me so that no policeman could get very near.[3]

The fighting in the small park which filled the square and in the surrounding roads was violent and unpleasant. The police, without proper riot-protection overalls, were at some disadvantage but the protesters suffered most, jeered at by the more militant German student activists who had come along for the march but who considered the British ill prepared for battle. Mick Jagger, watching the events from the sidelines of pop music, conjured up a suitable epitaph, the anthem 'Street Fighting Man'.

The anti-Vietnam War movement of the 1960s was quite different from its predecessor and co-protest movement, the Campaign for Nuclear Disarmament (CND). This was well organized and bipartisan, and had come together in February 1958 to protest against nuclear proliferation. Its marches to Aldermaston (where they design the weapons) and its protests in Trafalgar Square were always orderly and respectable, headed by members of the clergy and leading politicians and cultural figures such as Bertrand Russell. Occasionally arrests might occur or might be sought. A co-organization, the Committee of 100, was determined to use passive civil disobedience to 'fill the jails' and although in September 1961 1,314 people were arrested in Trafalgar Square and a further 351 at Holy Loch (where American Poseidon nuclear-missile submarines were based) it was conducted peaceably and reasonably. From the late 1950s to the late 1960s 'Ban the Bomb' marches achieved very little apart from giving an enduring symbol to the counterculture.

> The symbol [was] a composite of the semaphore signal for the letters N and D. [The designer] Gerald Holtom also saw in the central motif an indication of a human being in despair; t3he circle represented the world, the black background eternity. Eric Austin, who made the first badge version of the symbol, subsequently found

that the 'gesture of despair' motif has historically represented the death of man, and the circle the unborn child. The symbol was first adopted for the use on the 1958 march by Pat Arrowsmith and Hugh Brock. Of course it has since been used to symbolise nuclear disarmament, peace and related causes all over the world.[4]

The protests against the war in Vietnam were different in kind. The war had focused a whole range of protests against racism, imperialism and capitalism and had forged alliances between students and radicals on issues such as sexual and racial equality. This loose collection of protest groups, who might well have distanced themselves from each other on issues that many would see as merely ideological and sectarian, were all united in their hatred of American imperial intervention in South-East Asia and the support given to the United States by a British Labour government. The movement, only vaguely tied to the left wing of the Labour Party or the mainstream of the CPGB, was of the extreme left, and its disillusion with Sovietism and the old politics of the CP led to a growing fascination with Trotskyism, Maoism and the symbolic iconography of Guevara, Castro and Ho Chi Minh. It also saw its goal as a new utopianism heralded by the young and the marginalized, a revolt at once as much ethical as political in which the 'lifestyle' of the older generation was decisively rejected.

The troubles which began at the London School of Economics (LSE) in the autumn of 1966 and which escalated in the spring of 1967 were initiated by a South African student union president and American students and lecturers. The initial cause of the demands for greater student democracy was the appointment of a Rhodesian to the post of director. Indeed, the major policy adoptions of the National Union of Students in early 1967 were centrally concerned with Vietnam and Rhodesia* *not* internal British political problems. The LSE had a significant level of foreign students, including many from the United States who considered issues in the light of American experience. The 'Radical Student Alliance' stood for more than its British context and the problems that year at the LSE could not really bear the might of questions of international importance. The specific question of student democracy was a translation into parochial terms of a wider *international* debate in which the American émigré New Left led the indigenous socialist New Left.

---

*Southern Rhodesia's Prime Minister, Ian Smith, announced the Declaration of Unilateral Independence (UDI) on 11 November 1965. In 1970 Rhodesia declared itself a White Republic, effectively barring blacks from taking power. Independence (as Zimbabwe) only came in 1980 after a long war.

The American New Left was formed around real and pressing issues (civil rights, the Vietnam War, state repression) uniting a broad spectrum of beliefs into a loosely knit but effective *mass* movement. In contrast, the British New Left was an *onlooker* to those issues; it was narrow in political focus (Marxist) and recruited from a narrow band of enthusiasts. The most successful elements of the British counterculture were those *outside* the New Left, through their embrace of anarchistic-individualist critiques, which were both personal and social. The New Left's cultural critique was therefore far more successful than its political critique, which in a period of high employment, rising wages and a successful Western state was utterly lacking in the domestic targets available in the United States. The British New Left would have remained the British Old Left if these American pressures had not existed.

Just as most of the pressing issues of the anti-war, antiimperialism coalition were generated from abroad in the new 'internationalist' consciousness of the left, so too were many of its leading ideologues: Germaine Greer and Richard Neville from Australia, Ralph Schoenman from the United States and Tariq Ali from Pakistan. Of all these Tariq Ali came to personify the British protest movement.

Ali was born in Pakistan, son of a wealthy family of a newspaper editor. After an education at Jesuit College (although he was a Muslim – in name at least) he fell foul of the Pakistani authorities once he had begun university. Already, Arab nationalists such as Gamal Abdel Nasser appealed to his innate dislike of all things American, an attitude that would lead to his support of 'neutralists' such as Tito in Yugoslavia and Nehru in India and his ultimate support for anti-imperialist struggles. In 1967 he was one of the few invited to tour Vietnam and Cambodia as part of the worldwide condemnation of American involvement. By 1968 he was under Special Branch surveillance.

Early in the 1960s, Ali's family visited Britain and Ali himself was soon deeply involved with the political debates and radical groups at Oxford University, where by the mid-1960s he had risen to become President of the Oxford Union, mixing with such diverse and significant figures as Bertrand Russell and Malcolm X. Throughout, however, Ali remained aloof from any one political group, enjoying the company (and ideas) of Trotskyists but preferring to work with a 'rainbow coalition' of anybody from the left both inside and outside the Labour Party, including activists such as Michael Foot and Tony Cliff.

The great tide of 1960s' anti-Americanism, anti-imperialism, anti-sexism, anti-capitalism and anti-'oldism' was driven by a new youthful and hopeful utopianism yet left a backwash of the disaffected and the disdaining. In the commune and squatter community that had grown up on the fringes of protest society which finally became the heart of the counterculture, a new and more aggressive 'hippiedom' born of disillusion and marginality had crystallized amongst hard-line radicals.

It was these hardliners who began a bombing and arson campaign as early as the mid-1960s. Formed as the First of May/International Revolutionary Solidarity Movement, they had close connections with the Spanish anarchists fighting Franco. Machine-gun attacks and bombings were directed at the American Embassy against 'Yankee Fascism' and against Spanish targets such as airline offices and banks. Amongst the revolutionaries was Stuart Christie, who had already spent three years in Spanish jails for attempting to assassinate Franco. There was also Ian Purdie, jailed for fire bombing the Ulster Office in Savile Row. Others soon to be hunted included Jim Greenfield, a small-time fraudster who had joined up with Anna Mendelson and Hilary Creek. All three were dropouts from Essex University and all lived in squats in Hackney, Stamford Hill, Notting Hill and Stoke Newington except Christie, who settled in Manchester. There was also John Barker, washed up in Notting Hill and living in the house Nicholas Roeg and Donald Cammell used for the film *Performance*, one of the seminal movies of the 1960s and notorious for its gender-bending and psychedelic approach.

The group (as the police continually tried to prove) were influenced by the theories of the situationists and student *enragés* which had been central to the Paris student movement of 1968. The Situationists were 'left' without being Marxist, seeing life as banal and capitalism as overwhelming, producing a life in thrall to the alienated unreality of the spectacle, in other words, total consumer society. To return to the real and authentic, 'situations' had to be created in which people saw their true potential and overthrew the system of illusion which was the basis of power. The campaigns in Britain were aimed at this end. Barker and Greenfield had met Christie at the offices of Freedom Press in Whitechapel in February 1970, and helped revive a group called the International Black Cross. In Germany the Red Army Faction was also getting under way.

By the start of the 1970s this loose alliance of squatter-activists, calling themselves 'libertarian socialists', had (in the retrospective view of the police) begun a bombing campaign in London with a bomb (which did not explode) at Paddington Station. Fire bomb-ings followed at the Brixton Conservative Association and Ulster Office, for which Purdie received his nine months in jail. He shared a cell with Jake Prescott, who joined the group. Prescott himself, like Christie, came from a 'rough' Scottish background: he was a her-oin addict, a delinquent and a man who had already waved a gun about in a police station! In August 1970 a bomb exploded at the home of Metropolitan Police Commissioner Sir John Waldron and the first Angry Brigade communiqué was sent to Scotland Yard, this one written in execrable English in the style of the Jack the Ripper correspondence.

> DEAR BOSS . . .
>> YOU HAVE BEEN SENTENCED
>> TO DEATH BY THE REVOUATIONARY [sic]
>> TRIBUNAL FOR CRIMES OF OPPRESSION
>> AGAINST MANY WHO ARE OPPOSED TO
>> THE CAPITALIST REGEIME [sic] WHICH YOU
>> KEEP IN POWER.
>>> THE EXECUTIONER HAS BEEN SEVEERLY [sic]
>> REPRIMANDED FOR FAILING. WE WILL
>> MAKE NO FURTHER MISTAKES
>>> BUTCH CASSIDY
>>>> THE SUNDANCE KID P.P THE TRIBUNAL

In October a booby-trap grenade bomb was discovered at the BOAC office at Victoria and another at the Attorney General's home, which exploded. At the same time bombs exploded at various Italian offices in London, Birmingham and Manchester as revenge for the police-custody death of anarchist Giuseppe Pinelli in Milan. Special Branch immediately targeted Stuart Christie. Meanwhile a flour bomb attack on the Miss World competition was also blamed on those now being identified as terrorists, although in this case the police were mistaken. The people they were hunting seemed amorphous, their motives difficult to understand and their modes of operation merely random. They were also petty criminals who had stolen cheque books (Greenfield was caught stealing turkeys at Christmas) from the University of Cambridge and Essex University and they lived by fraud. They also had a sly sense of humour: some of the 'group' in the heady days of 1968 belonged to the Kim Philby Dining Club, a wheeze thought up at Cambridge and taken to its extreme by Ian Purdie, who concluded:

> To me Philby is the real life Guy Fawkes – the guy who actually made it. It gives great satisfaction to me who's lived all his life in the UK to know that there was one guy who completely pissed on the upper echelons of the ruling class for years, devastating MI5 and MI6, and along with it the plans of imperial intrigue.[5]

On 12 January 1971 bombs exploded at the house of Robert Carr, Secretary of State for Employment, and the chief mover of the Industrial Relations Bill – an attempt to curb the unions. Carr lived in Barnet and letters postmarked 'Barnet' arrived next day at *The Times*, the *Guardian* and the *Mirror* with another Angry Brigade

A violent logo for the Angry Brigade

communiqué: 'Robert Carr got it tonight. We're getting closer.' It appeared Ted Heath was next, or so another communiqué hinted.

Put in charge of the case, Chief Superintendent Roy Habershon of S Division, a former Fraud Squad detective, was convinced of a 'large scale criminal conspiracy' centred on Christie.

> I formed the view at that early stage that there existed in Britain a group of people of anti-Franco persuasion prepared to do bombing who had close contact with persons of similar mind on the continent, who themselves had access to French explosives . . . Secondly that this group had either extended its aims to include demonstrations against such things as police and government and authority in this country, or had joined forces with a second group who had those aims, and thirdly that the series of bombings with these new aims [was] being carried out under the label of the Angry Brigade.[6]

Such instinctual conviction did not prove guilt and despite police surveillance and numerous arrests the suspects could be charged with little other than chequebook fraud. Christie, an employee at Harrow Gas Board, continued to plead his innocence and to complain about police harassment even as fire bombings continued in Glasgow and in a West End cinema. As Habershon searched for traces of bomb-making equipment the Angry Brigade issued another communiqué on 27 January. It read, 'we are no mercenaries. We attack property not people', and another communiqué said the Conservative Party would be next on the list (because of support for South Africa). Most of the original group of squatter activists, however, were now in jail or heading that way. In March, Purdie and Prescott were arrested along with twenty-three others, none of whom could be directly connected with either the bombing of Robert Carr in Barnet or with the Angry Brigade. As one Angry Brigade message ran, 'we were invincible . . . they could not jail us for we did not exist'. Politically, the situationists' position was clear – revolution was spontaneous and autonomous, no longer directed by union or CP directives.

Some sort of wider anarchist–terrorist network did seem to exist, however, for police surveillance on a Grosvenor Avenue squat near Canonbury station provided evidence that radical groups were starting to communicate with each other. A visitor arrested on arrival at the squat was found to have in her car a key to a locker at Euston in which there were stolen papers and cheque books belonging to a German activist called Wolf Seeberg, who foolishly telephoned the police from the home of IRA suspects Jerry and Rita O'Hare to reclaim his confiscated Volkswagen. Such skeins of connections became part of a network of mutual support and alliance amongst terrorist groups.

Even with many known suspects in jail, the bombing campaign continued with Ford's offices at Gants Hill in East London then further bombs at Leicester Square, the Whitechapel branch of Barclay's Bank, the home of a Conservative MP living near the University of Essex and *The Times*. The message became 'Revolution now' and as Purdie, Prescott and others awaited their trials another bomb went off at Biba's fashion boutique in Kensington and at the Metropolitan Police computer centre. Communiqué nine spelt out the threat: 'We are getting closer. We are slowly destroying the long tentacles of the oppressive State machine . . . The Angry Brigade is the man or women sitting next to you. They have guns in their pockets and hatred in their minds. We are getting closer . . .'

With the police searching for Greenfield and Mendelson, more bombs exploded at the Ford Dagenham plant and at the home of the Ford chairman, William Batty. The Commissioner, at his wits' end and under instructions from the Prime Minister, had concluded not only that the Angry Brigade must be 'found and smashed' but that Habershon must be replaced. His replacement was Commander Ernest Bond, then unknown to the general public and referred to enigmatically as 'Commander X'. As summer approached, Purdie and Prescott awaited trial, Barker, Creek, Greenfield and Mendelson were being hunted and Christie was, for the moment, left alone. By this time, Mendelson, Creek and Greenfield had taken a flat in an old house in Amhurst Road, Stoke Newington, disguising their identity by using stolen chequebooks. Another bomb now exploded at the home of the Secretary of State for Trade and Industry, John Davies, which proved deeply embarrassing for the authorities who had provided twenty-four-hour security.

In August, however, things seemed to be going the police's way at last. Creek had apparently been watched on a journey to Paris, where she allegedly collected thirty-three sticks of gelignite at the home of a lecturer, Garcia Calvo. This was sufficient to create real urgency to the police investigation and on 18 August the police stormed a number of squats including Amhurst Road. Here they found gelignite and detonators, nine machine-guns, a pistol, and the John Bull printing set used to create Angry Brigade communiqués. The police settled in Amhurst Road and arrested Christie and John Bott as they turned up. Both were allegedly beaten up. Uppermost in the mind of the authorities would, however, have been the struggle of the West German police with the Baader-Meinhof gang (the Red Army Faction, or RAF), and arrests and successful convictions (by any means) of the main Angry Brigade suspects would be absolutely vital to restore the confidence of those involved with the investigations.

The charges read out at Clerkenwell Magistrates' Court included conspiracy to cause explosions between 1 January 1968 and 21 August 1971, possession of explosives, a pistol, ammunition, two machine-guns and detonators, as well as attempting to cause an explosion (in Manchester) and receiving a stolen vehicle. A large group was now in jail, including Creek, Greenfield, Mendelson, Bott, Purdie, Prescott, Seeberg and Christie as well as a number of other squatters who had associations with them, including Martin Housden, Peter Truman, Christine Haisall and Rosemary Fiore. More bombings nevertheless occurred at both Ipswich Court and Dartmoor Prison. Angry Brigade communiqués suggested things were all rather fishy.

> Two weeks ago Commander X – known to his friends as Commander Ernest Bond of the Yard – master-minded operation gelly-party. This resulted in 5 raids on London flats (put out by ever-reliable Scotland Yard as 20 raids) – and finally bumping into some real live gelignite and ammunition, busting 6 brothers and sisters in the process. Scotland yard emphatically denies the suggestion that these explosives found at Amhurst Road, Stoke Newington, were planted. Surprise, surprise Stuart Christie, the 'mad bomber' of Spain – the man they were dying to get – was among those arrested, for just being in the same street.

In October, the viewing galley and restaurant of the Post Office Tower were also bombed to such effect that despite the restaurant reopening the entire revolving tower top was finally permanently closed to the public. In Birmingham the home of Christopher Bryant (of Bryant Homes) was also bombed during a strike as was a Glasgow army barracks in attacks that may or may not have been linked and by more and as yet unknown assailants. During

November, bombings began in Europe in support of the Stoke Newington defendants and in Germany the RAF began a spate of bank robberies and assassinations.

After further arrests the Stoke Newington defendants were brought to trial at the Old Bailey on 24 January 1972. Although the proceedings were the longest in a case of conspiracy ever heard (109 days) the results, informed by often flimsy and circumstantial evidence, were less than satisfactory for the prosecution, which was never able to conclusively prove the defendants' connections to the 109 potential bombings and 25 actual bombings the Angry Brigade were charged with causing. The judge's summing up was a masterpiece of equivocation, but there was no ambiguity about the severe sentences.

> As long as you know what the agreement is, then you are a conspirator. You needn't necessarily know your fellow conspirators, nor need you be always active in the conspiracy. All you need to know is the agreement. It can be affected by a wink or a nod, without a word being exchanged. It need have no particular time limit, no particular form, no boundaries.[7]

Despite this advice the jury fail to agree and finally brought in majority verdicts against Barker, Greenfield, Mendelson and Creek, each of whom was given ten years for conspiracy. Christie, Bott, Weir and others were acquitted but the Angry Brigade as a viable revolutionary movement was effectively crushed by the imprisonments and even the acquittals.

At the end it was all a muddle and no clear-cut evidence ever proved that there was either a conspiracy or an organization called the Angry Brigade. Mendelson and Creek, increasingly unwell in prison, were quietly released five years later. Christie continued to propagandize on behalf of the revolution from a remote croft in Orkney, and Greenfield and Barker, released after their full term in 1982, turned to drug smuggling.[8] Roy Habershon, meanwhile, after heading the police (internal) investigation into the death of Kevin Gately in Red Lion Square in 1974 was promoted as Head of the Bomb Squad and participated in the Balcombe Street siege in 1975.

The activities of the Angry Brigade and the subsequent trial of the Stoke Newington defendants seemed to sum up the rising tide of anarchy that threatened to engulf Britain. In choosing the name Angry Brigade the perpetrators of the bombings and arson attacks of the period found a perfect identity for all who felt left out or desperate. Anyone could join the Brigade by a deed in its spirit. In that sense the Angry Brigade was not an organization but a disorganization and an act of violence against the state made one a member and gave that person the right to claim the name.

As a background to the new 'anarchy in the UK' the outside world seemed to be ever threatening: the IRA had commenced a decade's worth of bombings, Black September and other terrorist groups were hijacking planes, killing Israelis at home and abroad, murdering athletes in Munich and machine-gunning tourists at Lod Airport, whilst ETA, the RAF, and Japanese and Italian terrorists were declaring war on capitalism, America, exploitation of every variety and on pure boredom and consumer banality.

In Britain the visible counterculture petered out in the trials of the *OZ* magazine defendants in 1971 and the Stoke Newington collective in 1972. Yet such groups now represented a new type of urban life – marginal, vagrant, diffuse, ignored and precarious, a breeding ground for disaffection and resentment.

> These intense, private groups, compacted around a core of symbolic objects and ideas are very serious symptoms of a metropolitan condition . . . Huddled, defensive, profoundly complacent in their indifference or hostility to the rest of the city, they are the foxholes [sic] for all those whom the city has isolated, for whom no larger reality is habitable.[9]

The British anarchist movement of the 1990s grew from these distinct roots and the remnants of the failure of the radical counterculture of the 1960s. This had led to the breakup of an organized popular front and the appearance of more isolated and sporadic terrorism exemplified by the appearance of the Angries, Tartan Army bombers in Scotland and the Welsh nationalist arsonists.

Important too was the loosening of control of the CP over the squatter movement of the 1970s as well as the growth of 'tribal' lifestyles based on squatting, travelling, festivals and general alternatives that grew from punk. The third influence was a growing environmentalism and New-Ageism that increased with the coming millennium and saw the concerted efforts of local and national (full-time) protesters who opposed major road-building plans, tree felling and what they saw as environmental vandalism by the motor car.

Such a background proved a rallying point for situationists, believers in class war, art freaks, activists and kids looking for kicks. Thus, Malcolm McLaren moved effortlessly from art school activist to owner of the boutique Sex in the King's Road to manager of the carefully cultivated 'Art' yob group The Sex Pistols, whose foul language on 'tea-time' television was the visual and verbal equivalent of an Angry Brigade bomb. 1970s anarchism looked to the future both of terrorism and New Age anti-globalism.

Thus was produced a loose alliance of New-Age pagans, vegetarian and vegan pacifists, eco-warriors, libertarians and a general gathering of those who wished to do something positive towards destroying capitalism and oppression but who saw the traditional 'extreme' opposition of the Communist Party of Great Britain or 'Militant' as authoritarian and the left ideology of the traditional Marxist groups as 'centrist', 'parliamentary', 'bureaucratic' and 'statist', all of which were opposed to anarchist tradition. Such attitudes would not easily fit into the mould of accepted political activity and so it was quite possible to detect elements of fascism in the politics of ecological groups, for instance, which sat uneasily with the elements culled from Christian communitarianism or multiculturalism. As with all extreme and relatively small republican political movements (and all anarchists are republican) such views were not just political but formed a raison d'être. Those to whom these elemental, *obvious* and non-political (in the traditional sense) views appealed most were middle class and white – the marginalized from suburbia who had turned politics into morality.

The modern anarchist movement is therefore not a political party or lobby group in the traditional sense, but an alliance of direct action groups (some pacifist, some not) whose beliefs roughly coincide on a number of issues. These include the need to oppose capitalism, ecological destruction and corporate exploitation, the symbols of such exploitation such as cars, roads, chain-stores, banks and government buildings being prime targets for contempt. Unlike traditional socialist revolutionary groups, and particularly unlike the traditional Marxist-Leninist model, anarchists are *totally opposed* to strong central governments and *centrally* directed workers' control. Equally, anarchism is not the politics of a lobby group, as all anarchists groups oppose parliamentary democracy as part of the capitalist conspiracy. Anarchists are not liberals or socialists in any mainstream sense; rather, for them, the 'political' realm is a matter of personal identity, action and ethics. Thus anarchism can embrace 'primitive' communists and absolute libertarians united only by issues they see as ignored by cynical politicians and officials. Much of anarchism is driven by emotion and 'rightness' rather than political theory and dogma, although there exists a very large body of anarchist thought from Bakunin to Chomsky and Kropotkin to Bookchin. Moreover, anarchists have an acute sense of the power of art and theatre which they have carefully integrated into their political philosophies and which have immediate appeal to the media. Anarchism uses elements of Dada, absurdism and situationism to further ethical positions that embrace tribalism, communalism, squatting, ecological protest, Gaia mysticism, New-Age paganism, 'tree-ism', polymorphousness, androgyny, mutation, cycling, play and liberation; many anarchists groups choose to call themselves (dis)organizations. The term anarchist (which anarchists avoid when in front of the media) is, therefore, an honourable and exact description.

One of the most extreme versions of anarchist libertarianism came in the form of Vincent Bethell's 'Right to be Naked in Public' campaign, which was part of the 'Freedom to be Yourself' campaign that he and some like-minded friends began in the 1990s. Bethell stripped naked to protest: up ornate lampposts near the Old Bailey in 1998 with bemused policemen as onlookers, at the Royal Courts of Justice in 1999 with only a placard reading 'NO CULTURE' and a backpack in front of press and television camera and at 'Legalise Yourself' naked press conferences. On 15 July 2000 he protested naked outside Scotland Yard. The previous year, he had lamented there were only six protesters, maybe this time there would be a few more – a 'ball-naked' march on Downing Street did not, however materialize. Bethell's protests had a charm and wit about them which even the Metropolitan Police Service Solicitors' Office could not resist; after all, they agreed, Bethell was a mild-mannered person, both non-violent and non-destructive, who hardly created a breach of the peace. His campaign to make people happy with their bodies and fight sexual stereotyping was, as he explained, 'about being happy and being human' and was usually greeted by onlookers with an amused and sympathetic smile.

Vincent Bethell's naked street theatre had its ancestors in the yippy 'happenings' of the 1960s. These events were themselves based upon the situationist antics of French and Dutch avant-garde artists of the 1950s. In essence situationism sought to unite dada-esque theatricality with political will by creating spontaneous 'events' that aimed to undermine the pomposity of state institutions by laughter.

Such was the case with the event organized by the 'Movement against the Monarchy' (MA'M), an anarchist group closely associated with Class War, held at Buckingham Palace on 3 June 2000. Called 'Moon at the Monarchy 2000', it was part of a number of anarchist activities organized to coincide with the millennium and which followed the Guerrilla Gardening event of 1 May. The aim was to get as many people as possible to drop their trousers and point their bottoms at the palace. Leaflets demanded

> 2000 BARE BUTTS TO MAKE THE YEAR 2000
> AN ANUS HORRIBILIS FOR THE WINDSORS.
> GET YOUR ARSE ALONG THERE!

The whole event was timed for 3 o'clock, allowing the changing of the guard to pass off peacefully. At the same time MA'M targeted the Queen Mother (soon to be a centenarian) with an intended demonstration for 4 August where she would be politely asked to 'Drop Dead' for the crimes of 'Knocking around Clarence house [sic] and district terrorising the good citizens with pitiless walkabouts and gumming of children.'

Moon at the Monarchy: an anarchic attempt to undermine the pomposity of state institutions by laughter

The entire affair was accompanied by a witty and barbed attack on police and journalists made through MA'M's Web page.

MA'M is deeply sympathetic to the problems faced by newspaper reporters. It's not easy having to stay sober enough to write 200 words about a subject you [know] nothing about, using only an alcohol stunted imagination as your guide. To this end, below is a composite news story you can just cut out and print out as an EXCLUSIVE without bothering either MA'M supporters or people who live at a similar sounding addresses [sic] in the early hours of the morning: . . .

Royal detectives/Tired and emotional newspaper editors/Auntie Doris and Uncle Jim were shocked/apoplectic/delighted to discover that Movement Against the Monarchy (MA'M) were planning a lighted-hearted demonstration/full-scale armed insurrection/ a re-enactment of the finale of *Carry On Up The Khyber* opposite Buckingham Palace on Saturday, June 3rd, 2000.

The shadowy/anarchist/Cuban-funded/sun-light avoidance committee MA'M was set up by punk rocker Ian Bone/ex-Eton public school boys/disillusioned members of the Partick Thistle Supporters Group (Kettering Branch) and is run out of a squalid council flat/ rather attractive council flat/Eton College for wealthy scum.

MA'M has forged links with Dutch Anarchists/with Partick Thistle Supporters Group (Northampton Branch)/out of iron to make a long chain.

New Metropolitan Police Commissioner Sir John Stevens was amazed to discover that anarchists were targeting the Royal family/that the Pope was a Catholic/what bears did in woods. And has promised to stamp out dissent wherever it appears/crush the last few remaining civil liberties/to become an ever greater laughing stock in the future.

On 3 June at the appointed time a mere thirty mooners surrounded by police and press found themselves arrested for causing a breach of the peace. They left peacefully just as two performance artists from Goldsmith's College, Jian Jun Xi and his partner, put on their own semi-naked 'Soy and Sauce' fight 'event', also to mark the millennium.

If the event was intended to create a comic situation in which Metropolitan Police Commissioner Sir John Stevens would be seen to be arresting mass mooners, a position little less than ludicrous and bound to make him look a fool, it was also intended as part of a wider agenda which was deadly serious.

MA'M is part of the growing combative anarchist BLACK BLOC which has mobilised in Seattle, Washington and elsewhere in the spirit of global resistance through J18 [the protest against the G8 summit in summer 1999] . . . in solidarity with the Black Bloc actions in Prague against the IMF. Now . . . we can build some combative class resistance across Europe.

The conjunction of politics and performance was nowhere more evident than in the 'Anarchy in the UK Festival' held in late October 1994 at various sites and venues across London after a series of demonstrations against the Criminal Justice Bill. Participants were promised

The biggest ever anarchist festival, slap bang in the middle of London, with over 500 meetings at a hundred venues. All currents of anarchist thought, practice, culture, history and lifestyle will be there.

From DURRUTTI to DADA, RAVACHOL to ROTTEN, McCLAREN to MALATESTA, SITUATIONISM to SYNDICALISM, PUNK to PAGANISM, STONEHENGE to SEX, ANIMAL LIBERATION to ANARCHA-FEMINISM, FOOTBALL to ANTI-FASCISM, DRUGS to DRUIDS, RIOTS to RAVES, EARTH FIRST to CLASS WAR . . . This one's got the lot! If you don't do anything else for the rest of the millennium don't miss out on this!

PLUS . . . Anarchist film and video season, live music from those anarchist bands day and night, comedy club, poetry, raves, dancing and the best ten days social life you're ever likely to experience!! PLUS . . . all night central political debate for ten days and those anarchist eye witnesses you always wanted to hear from Barcelona to Brixton.

PLUS worldwide participation and massive anarchist STREET MOBILISATION!!

The main organizer was Ian Bone, co-founder of *Class War*. 'As it turned out, the festival was remarkable for its diversity of ideological strands, including (in random order) Green, feminist, anti-fascist, animal liberation, syndicalist, libertarian, anti-roads, pagan, communist, and class war tendencies.'[10]

Whilst modern British anarchism has emerged as an alliance of apparently disparate beliefs and ways of living not catered for by mainstream politics or society it would not be true to say that the anarchist movement is *merely* a collection of like-minded people whose actions are spontaneous, determined only by a fluid response to local and particular needs. This may be the case with local or young activists, but not so for those who lead the movement and who trace their political life back into the 1970s and early 1980s. The three main groups that have emerged as the coordinating backbone of the anarchist movement are the Animal Liberation Front (ALF), Class War and Reclaim the Streets (RTS).

The Animal Liberation Front came into being in 1976 after a hunt saboteur called Ronnie Lee was released from Winchester Prison, having served a sentenced for an arson attack on Hoechst Pharmaceuticals in Milton Keynes. Lee had been part of a revolutionary animal rights group called the Band of Mercy which had formed in 1972 and took the cue for its actions from the success of the Angry Brigade and the resolve of the IRA. 'Being kind to animals, in the traditional, rather soppy English sense was irrelevant: this was a liberation movement, and it owed more to the struggles of women, gays and blacks than to the RSPCA. A new "ism" had been invented to stand alongside sex-ism and racism: the crime of "speciesism".[11]

The desire to liberate animals from experimental laboratories and fur and battery farms united sectors of society whose consciences were pricked or who used animal rights as a respectable way to attack ethnic minorities (Jews and Muslims) whose slaughter methods were disliked. Disappointed with traditional protest and the establish-ment nature of groups such as the Royal Society for the Prevention of Cruelty to Animals (RSPCA), Ronnie Lee and his friend Cliff Goodman had created a radical cell of the Hunt Saboteurs Association (HSA) in 1971 and then the Band of Mercy in 1972, a non-violent direct action group with Greenpeace credentials that, nevertheless, soon took to arson. Finally imprisoned, Lee emerged with a messianic (and practical) sense of the revolution.

> Ronnie's year in Winchester prison had given him plenty of time to think about tactics and organization. He was already an admirer of the IRA and its political wing Sinn Fein: he had also got involved in the pro-Republican 'Troops Out' movement as a sideline to his animal rights activities. What was admirable about the Provisionals was their structure, the series of cells connected by only the thinnest line of communication. Above all, after the fiasco that had led to his arrest, Lee was obsessed with the need for security. Combining this with his anarchist convictions, what he came up with was a system that allowed for minimal co-ordination and maximum freelance action by ALF units up and down the country. There was to be no central high command or 'army council' or in fact any precisely defined hierarchy.[12]

Animal Liberation would be the last great revolutionary strug-gle carried on as a form of clandestine warfare against the scientific research establishment, farming community and retail fur trade, all of which seemed legitimate targets for those who saw such activi-ties as the equivalent of creating 'animal Auschwitzes'. By the 1980s, local councils such as Ealing and Hackney had appointed animal rights officers, and public awareness had created debates over factory farming and virtually extinguished the retail fur trade.

The public front of the various animal rights movements of which ALF was the most famous created a highly successful propaganda cam-paign during the 1980s, which coincided with a new youth culture and a greater public sensitivity to ecological issues. Nevertheless, secret cells of animal activists began a campaign of bombings, arson and personal intimidation. A hoax poisoning campaign cost Mars £3 million, sci-entific establishments were attacked, individual scientists (considered unpleasant vivisectors) were bombed and threatened and a number of department stores in Sheffield, Luton, Plymouth and London's Oxford Street were burnt down by incendiaries or damaged by raids.

By 1985 things were considered sufficiently worrying for the government to take action. A specialist animal rights squad was formed by Scotland Yard in order to hunt down the Animal Rights Militia (ARM). This finally led to the arrest of Ronnie Lee and his lieutenant Vivian Smith for the attack on Rackhams department store in Sheffield in 1986. In 1987 Lee received a ten-year prison sentence. Things did not improve for authority, however. In the same year as Lee's arrest, 1986, ALF's young supporters group came into being and bombings continued into 1988 and 1989 when Bristol University Senate House was blown up with high explosives.

Animal Liberation actions and protests caught the imagination of a considerable section of a usually quiescent middle class over the cruel export of live calves (veal exports), and helped to blockade ports to Europe. The continuous campaign against animal experimentation focused during 2000 and 2001 on the work of Huntingdon Life Sciences in Cambridge. Through a direct campaign of intimidation against the laboratory and its financial backers in the City, ALF and other liberation groups gained media attention and a political platform (represented as moral reform), and found a powerful means of attacking the animal experimentation industry in Britain. Like the IRA, ALF is almost the only radical group that has been able to intimidate City financiers, forcing financial investors like NatWest and Charles Schwab (an American investment firm) to hastily withdraw from projects disapproved of by animal liberationists.

By the 1990s, ALF had merged into the general anarchist movement, its membership fluid and open enough to allow the old ideological barriers (such as fascist and Marxist antagonisms) to be avoided. ALF members might well participate in other activities on behalf of anarchist protest, but they soon began to imitate the look of the IRA: full-mask balaclavas and combat wear worn in public during marches or demos as a mark of solidarity and symbolic of the avenging dark angels that the young cadre believed themselves to be.

Taking its cue from the intellectual fervour, emotional grip and heady adventurism of ALF, Class War began publishing a newspaper (called *Class War*) in 1983. By the late 1990s, Class War was one of the main organizing forces behind the anarchist movement in Britain and like ALF it was dedicated to direct action by any means. Its general credo was little more than a poorly restated (and unacknowledged) nineteenth-century Bakuninist socialism lacking the sophistication of mainstream Marxism but retaining the excitement of anarchist spontaneous revolution. Symbolized by a grim red skull and cross bones on a black background and with its slogan of 'Class Unity, Class Pride', the Class War Federation claimed itself as an organization of groups and individuals who have come together to change the Society we live in, to improve the lot of working class people.

This society is divided into classes based on control of its institutions and wealth. The Ruling Class – those who 'own' the factories or natural resources – whether it's through shares or being chairman [sic] of the board etc., who are under normal circumstances supported by the Middle Class – those who gain their position in society by patronage of the Ruling Class – who carry out their dirty work of controlling and (dis)organising the working class who do all the necessary work. Such a society is the root cause of most of the problems experienced by Working Class people the World over. As the Ruling Class has every intention of keeping its privileged position it must be destroyed – this is Class War.

Direct action is necessary against the individuals and institutions who stand in the way . . . There is no alternative. Violence is a necessary part of the Class War – not as elitist terrorists but as an integrated part of the Class – they started it, we'll have to finish it! . . .

The Class must fight these divisions, on all fronts. Above all the CWF believes that politics cannot be separated from life – and life from politics. We reject the missionary/righteous so called 'revolutionary' Left. Our politics must be fulfilling and relevant to our every day lives.

Class War's co-founders, Martin Wright and Ian Bone, had a taste for street politics, public houses and antagonizing the police. Bone, the son of a butler from whom he supposedly learned his class hatred, also had a wicked and vulgar sense of occasion. It was Bone who set up MA'M and Bone who was the first to drop his trousers on the 'Moon at the Monarchy' event after giving a press conference.

Bone began his activities as an anarchist activist in London and Bristol, Wright had a history of teenage violence against black teachers and had been attracted by the politics of the National Front (NF). Both sought to harness the new organized violence of football 'firms' for political purposes. In organizations such as ALF and Class War the old political antagonisms became blurred; ALF, for instance, used agitators like Dave Nicholls, a tax inspector by day. 'Rucks' with the BM and other neo-Nazi organizations were the sort of forum in which anarchism could attach itself to the Anti-Nazi League (ANL) and also find its own voice.

Within the general pattern of political life during the early 1980s it now seems no surprise that direct action by anarchist groups coincided with the liberalism of entrepreneurial Thatcherism and Thatcher's own brand of direct action *conviction* politics, nor that more radical 'Strasserite' and paganist Nazi groups took on ecological issues as the BNP under Nick Griffin attempted to create a more acceptable mainstream agenda.

The third significant group, Reclaim the Streets (RTS), was formed in 1994/5 from the experiences gained at various road protests and especially the fight against the M11 Link Road. Labelling itself a 'disorganisation' in order to highlight its non-hierarchic sensibility and heterogeneity, RTS was formed from an alliance of groups to fight biological meltdown, and urban dysfunctionalism brought on by capitalism and its symptoms, motor cars and pollution. More acutely the RTS aimed, if only briefly, to reclaim areas which they considered *public* space from private exploitation.

Their first major coup was 'Street Party 1' held in Camden High Street on Sunday 14 May 1995. After a staged car crash, the two 'drivers' demolished their vehicles as a sign for a mass street carnival in which politics and theatre, play and activism were to be united. Demanding greater pedestrianization, one campaigner said, 'It is time the streets were free for people to walk along in safety. It is about highlighting the freedom from pollution, congestion, and danger which can be achieved by creating street-space from which cars are excluded.'[13] Surprisingly many motorists, although inconvenienced, agreed with the aims of the day.[14]

'Street Party 2' took place on Sunday 23 July 1995, in Upper Street, Islington where the street was blockaded by campaigners for another carnival protest. Yet 'Street Party 3' (Saturday 13 July 1996) was their greatest success, when 10,000 protesters invaded the M41 (now A40(M)) and held a giant picnic and rave, stringing banners across the motorway, which declared 'The Society that abolishes every adventure makers its own abolition the only possible adventure'.

By the late 1990s, RTS had caught many people's imagination with masses of Beijing-like bike-riding protesters who soon became a feature of alternative direct-action politics, and by 2001 they had many interactional links, coordinating its activities with Class War and others, especially for May Day demonstrations. With their usual wit and eye for a media coup they declared 1 April to 1 May 2001 'Operation Dessert Storm', intending personalities around the world to be targets for pie attacks! During the planned demonstrations for 1 May 2001, 'May Day Monopoly', they were organizing mass bike rides intended to cause gridlock in London.

RTS are, however, not just an organization dedicated to the wilful mishandling of custard pies. They have a darker and more pointedly aggressive side. During the 1997 general election one RTS rally marched down Whitehall intending to 'squat' the Department of the Environment. One demonstrator did succeed in getting into the Foreign Office by an open window, 'liberating' Foreign Office paperwork to the waiting crowds. This particular 'Festival of Resistance' ended when the final street party in Trafalgar Square turned into a riot.

More significantly RTS were also part of a major global protest against arms dealing, Third World debt, ecological destruction and corporate exploitation during the G8 summit held in Cologne in summer 1999. A carnival-style procession was organized to wind its way through the heart of the City of London. Drums and whistles attracted onlookers and amused participants from the offices around Liverpool Street and some City traders wittily responded to the atmosphere by photocopying £50 notes and sending them fluttering down on the heads of the anti-capitalist marchers!

For some of the protesters the march was rather more like a Trojan horse with which to get access to an unsuspecting City. By late in the afternoon an attempt was made by about a hundred hardliners to storm Liffe, the international futures exchange, a major target for anti-capitalists. Traders fought to keep their enemies at bay as security grilles sealed capitalists in and anarchists out. Protesters trashed and then smashed up the lobby and then moved on to attack the Rabobank building and other offices as well as destroying a Mercedes showroom and numerous expensive cars in the street. A motorist was attacked and arriving police vans only succeeded in hitting two protesters. Running battles and flying missiles, a burst water main and a toll of injuries and arrests that left the day's events comparable to the poll tax riots nine years earlier, nevertheless put Third World debt and other injustices firmly on the political agenda and into the public's mind. J18, as the day was called, became one of a series of international disturbances, of which Seattle (2000), Gothenburg and Genoa (2001) were to be the most notorious.

24

Back to the Future

Poll Tax Rebels and Tenant Strikers

In 1990 the nascent contemporary anarchist movement came to public attention when serious rioting broke out in Trafalgar Square after a poll tax demonstration.

The Conservatives, having privatized and liberalized the market during the early 1980s, now turned to a policy intended to make local government taxation more equitable. The community charge ('poll tax') would replace local rates and spread the cost of local taxation by charging a flat rate per head instead of by rateable value of property. The seeming fairness of the tax was hardly obvious when the rich and poor paid the same amount per person and protests soon occurred. The tax was experimentally introduced in Scotland in 1989 but protest began to grow and withholding the tax became a tactic. In England and Wales it was vigorously resisted but the government stuck to its policy (despite its own members' disquiet) until 1991. It was with the mounting protests during spring 1990, however, that the modern British anarchist movement had its birth, and, in the battle for Trafalgar Square, its baptism.

The confusion and confrontation that finally came to epitomize the poll tax riot stemmed partly from the split that occurred between the rally proper in Trafalgar Square where speakers from Militant Tendency and the Labour Party could be found, as well as control by Militant stewards, and the backup of protesters in Whitehall, especially opposite the Ministry of Defence. Two centres of protest resulted in a number of more aggressive agitators rallying to Class War banners whilst Militant attempted to keep control in Trafalgar Square. The antagonism between Militant, the SWP and anarchists as well as a clear hatred of police, long since seen as the enemy at earlier colliery battles and at the *Sun* dispute in Wapping, meant that tensions would not take long to come to crisis point. At first the crowd was peaceful. '[A] Saturday afternoon stroll in the park on a warm sunny day is a chance to put on summer shirt and shades. In Kennington Park we look up the anarchists, who are raggier than ever. The demonstration is leisurely with no heavy police or Militant (stewarding) presence'. Already, however, some elements of the crowd, like the police, were itching for a showdown.

> The cops have kept a low profile and the official line that this is a family protest of 'ordinary' people has so far held. Then the police throw a line across the end of Whitehall, diverting the back half of the demo down to the bridge and along the Embankment . . . There is no ammo in Whitehall. A flag off the Cenotaph is burned. Then the horses are bought out – a crude way to control a crowd, especially one with nowhere to go as they've blocked the other end of Whitehall too.

By the time the procession reached Whitehall, things had changed and the legendary nature of the day began to take shape in counter-cultural memories.

> The trouble is getting heavier and more people are either stopping or getting involved. The police bring in some riot cops – some mounted, others in little snatch squads. The next 20 minutes is pretty confusing. There's some hand to hand fighting and some missile throwing . . . for an hour or so it was class war . . . Stroll to Charing Cross road. Fuck . . . some serious looting is going on here. Loads of shops attacked . . . A few doors down, a flash car showroom BMWs the lot etc wrecked completely, may never have one but neither will anyone else! Proceed eastwards, Long Acre now, with such speed and fury does this mob attack Covent Garden that it's difficult to find your own window! Sprint up the road, but still lag behind those at the front . . . Full of clothes shops, a spontaneous fashion show occurs, old clothes swapped for new . . . Go to Cecil Gees, virtually cleared, clothes litter the street, cast aside. Into the mayhem strolls an unsuspecting special (part time cop), fuck off, piss off, physically he's pushed aside, boots fly in his direction but mostly miss . . . he's lucky to be alive. A sunglasses shop attacked, £150 Georgio Armani's lifted, rioters not only furious but now cool!! The Rock Garden goes, tables over, HP sauce flies through the windows. Into the covered area . . . every shop smashed, some rather becoming porcelain ducks lifted, discarded a moment later (through a window).[1]

The riot left much of London's West End sacked. Trafalgar Square had seen much of the worst with the scaffolding around South Africa House set on fire and left to burn. Fifty cars were attacked and overturned or set on fire, and 394 shops or offices in Long Acre, St Martin's Lane, Charing Cross Road, Oxford Street, Haymarket and

Regent Street looted; 1,900 criminal acts were reported and nearly 500 people arrested on the day and afterwards; over 500 policemen were injured, 60 ending up in hospital, with large numbers of protesters also injured or hospitalized; numerous police vans were vandalized and much police equipment was destroyed. As a damage limitation exercise by police and by Militant the day had proved an overwhelming failure – both had lost control and Militant had forfeited respect with its approval of a police campaign to catch rioters still at large. It was always concerned that the media images of the riot would alienate ordinary television viewers and newspaper readers sympathetic to the protest.

To many the working-class struggle had finally bypassed the guardians of the true revolutionary way – the SWP and Militant. Militant had already had a disastrous period of control of Liverpool Council during the 1980s and was finally expelled from the Labour Party (under Neil Kinnock). For the new 'anarchic' left, SWP orthodoxy and Militant entrism had been a blind and dangerously assimilationist game that replicated the very language of the 'boss' class. Thus the reformist Neil Kinnock condemned the protesters as 'enemies of freedom'[2] just as Tommy Sheridan of the Militant-organized All Britain Anti-Poll Tax Federation (ABAPTF) condemned them as 'individuals intent on causing trouble' when interviewed on the BBC programme *Newsnight*.[3] The whole episode suggested to anarchists that Militant had finally allowed its mask of respectability to slip in order to expose its real adherence to old CPGB authoritarianism.

> As the parliamentary wing of the movement they were able to seize control of the organising body, the All Britain AntiPoll Tax Federation, through a series of dirty tricks, dodgy deals and phony groups claiming voting rights. Once in control of the Central Committee the Militants were in control of the flow of information, they decided who was allowed to address rallies (occasionally threatening violence to impose this choice) and could rule motions calling for their recall 'out of order' completely autonomously. They also imposed their own programme and their own judgements of the morality of anyone else involved in the movement. Any dissent could result in a visit from the police as 'troublemakers' were to be 'weeded out' . . .
>
> The distaste felt for them through the rest of the anti-Poll Tax movement (in spite of their u-turn over the Trafalgar Square Defendants Campaign) was marked towards the end of the campaign by leading figures (Tommy Sheridan and Steven Nally) needing body guards when making public appearances. Their pedigree as descendants of the CPGB is all too clear.[4]

A series of police actions followed. The first was Operation Carnaby, which brought 491 people before the courts, most charged with riot or violent disorder under the new Public Order Act. The Trafalgar Square Defendants' Campaign came about when participants in the 3D Network ('Don't Implement, Don't Collect, Don't Pay') began to set up a defence organization *outside* the All Britain Federation, which had sided with the official view of the day. Courts were monitored, evidence gathered, video footage scrutinized and police statements carefully read. In July 1990, the Haldane Society of Socialist Lawyers offered the use of its offices. Police evidence, shaky at best in a number of cases, was often thrown out, the police themselves coming under suspicion during a period in which police morale and public image were both low. Court cases

came just a month after 39 miners were given £500,000 compensation for assault following the riot at Orgreave in 1985; the investigation into the West Midlands Serious Crimes Squad; police compensation for violent attacks at the 'Battle of the Beanfield' – Stonehenge; the release of the Birmingham Six and the Guildford Four; and serious doubts ab   out the Broadwater Farm murder conviction. It [all] supported growing historical evidence of police corruption.[5]

Whilst the TSDC was being set up and cases continued to come to court, ABAPTF decided to hold a march (based on the Jarrow Hunger marches of the 1930s) joining Scottish, English and Welsh protesters and ending in London. Of seventy-five marchers, seventy were Militant supporters. The protest became merely 'symbolic', the papers ignored it and the whole thing fizzled out.

Meanwhile the TSDC decided to hold a rally in Brockwell Park in Brixton on 20 October. A picket would be held at Horseferry Road Magistrates' Court which would then march to Brockwell Park for a rally, to be followed by a march on Brixton Prison, where a large number of poll tax prisoners were held. On the day 1,500 pickets marched to Brockwell for a 25,000 strong rally after which 3,500 demonstrators marched towards Brixton. Patrolling the march were 3,000 police (only 2,000 police had been initially available at Trafalgar Square).

It was clear that the march would be tense, as Deputy Assistant Commissioner Metcalf, in charge of policy, had suggested to the organizers. At about four o'clock a police officer was heard to shout, 'I'd like to start kicking some people's heads in.' Police Support Units (PSUs) had started to organize in riot gear in front of the prison and by 4.40 the police had split the marching column in two. Pushing and shoving started. Drinkers at the George V pub were warned away by police, one of whom was heard to say 'This is it.' Just before 5 p.m. riot police were deployed and moved into the marchers.

A very violent riot followed which resulted in 135 arrests and 40 police injured. As is usual, no civilian casualties were recorded. This was clearly 'revenge' for the police humiliation on 31 March.

The work of the TSDC now paid dividends with carefully prepared video footage, clearly recorded events, legal observers, liaison volunteers and witness statement scrutiny and cross-checking. Although by January 1991 the TSDC was still supporting twenty-seven long-term offenders, their organizational knowledge (including the use of thousands of 'bust' cards*) meant that protesters would begin to accumulate the necessary legal information to help their own defence. This was to be a lasting legacy in organized protest.

The poll tax agitation proved the moment at which local groups with unaligned political views found a forum, a cause and an identity. This was particularly true in the poorer boroughs of London and especially Haringey in North London, an area including Tottenham, Wood Green, and Edmonton. Here it was expected that the poll tax would be heaviest, as proved to be the case, although the local rate was capped by central government.

The anti-poll tax campaign had already begun in Scotland, as Edinburgh Community Resistance, but both the Labour Party and the TUC had an official policy of compliance due to the legality of the tax, and only proposed marches and petitions, modes of action which suggested simple official impotence. Haringey already had a number of groups that had participated in earlier protests.

> Several independent groups such as the Unwaged Centre in West Green Road, members of the anarcho-syndicalist group Direct Action Movement (now Solidarity Federation), an independent anti-nuclear group, and the remnants of the Seafarers Strike Support Group came together informally to discuss the impending Tax and the possibility of a non-payment campaign. There was also at that time still a core of left activists in the Labour Party.[6]

These groups came together in an alliance dedicated to non-compliance and passive (in practice active) resistance to the collection of the tax. By the summer of 1989, a number of groups had organized and begun pooling resources. These included anti-poll tax groups in Tottenham (TAPT), Hornsey and Wood Green (H&WGAPT), Green Lanes (GLAPT) and South Hornsey (SHAPT). Haringey Anti-Poll Tax Union (HAPTU) was formed as a delegated union.

The first major meeting, called by TAPT at the Polytechnic of Central London (now the University of Westminster), was held in September 1989 in order to set up local coordination and forge national links.

---

* 'Bust' cards were specially printed leaflets with legal information regarding protesters' rights once arrested.

It was Militant, however (then part of the Labour Party but soon to be expelled, thence forming the Socialist Party), who used their organization to create nationwide anti-poll tax unions (ABAPTF). Tensions between the anarchist opposition and Militant soon emerged even if to the general public they seemed similar in intent and action, which consisted in refusal of payment, mass pickets and disruption and protest marches.

> Haringey Council met to set the Poll Tax rate on Monday 5 March. A crowd of 1,000 gathered outside the Civic Centre to protest and over a hundred people got into the public gallery and disrupted the meeting for several hours. Eventually the police dragged people outside to where other protesters were blocking the road. As the numbers finally died away the police charged the crowd. In the resulting scuffles 11 people were arrested. The Poll Tax setting meeting had to be abandoned until the following Friday.[7]

Demonstrations and pickets were followed by the Trafalgar Square demonstration and riot on 31 March 1990 after which a new group calling itself the Trafalgar Square Defendants Campaign (TSDC) was set up by Haringey activists and others to put the legal case (and raise the finances) for those previously arrested. This careful and inspirational use of monitoring and information gathering was to become a model for all future demonstrations and has grown to become a sophisticated network. The group also stole Militant's thunder as the main oppositional body setting up the Legal Defence and Monitoring Group.

Local action continued apace and by July 1990 there were 97,000 non-payers in the borough. Bailiffs trying to collect the tax found an increasingly hostile response, as had inspectors before them – chased, doused in urine, verbally abused, attacked, pelted with eggs, confronted with dogs and, in one instance, finding themselves face to face with a naked man 'brandishing a knife'.[8]

Another mass rally was now called by the TSDC, who had gained an agreement to use Trafalgar Square. The police considered applying for a ban and the TSDC considered ignoring any such order. On 21 March 1991 John Major abolished the tax and his government replaced it with a more equitable and more traditional one (although no less expensive). The *Tottenham Journal* recorded the continued animosity against the collection of the outstanding tax even though the scheme had now been abolished.

> Anti-poll tax demonstrators stormed Tottenham Job Centre and Dole Office to protest against a deduction of the tax in income support payments.

Fifteen members of the Tottenham Anti-poll tax union and claimants union forced their way into the office. Some climbed on to the roof with banners while others leafleted the public . . . Staff . . . 'are fearing for their safety'.[9]

The intimidating nature of a visit from the bailiffs (in this case Madagens Ltd of Leytonstone) was reversed with graffiti sprayed across their shutters and superglue poured in their locks. Non-cooperation, non-attendance at court and angry crowds at collections meant that the council would have a long fight to collect its dues and punish non-payers.

In 1999, the anti-poll tax alliance in Haringey had used the lessons of that struggle to create the Haringey Solidarity Group (HSG), one of the most significant of the country's self-help, direct-action libertarian groups. 'In most places the anti-Poll Tax movement disappeared. But in Haringey the decision was taken to turn local anti-Poll Tax groups into Solidarity Groups to preserve the links and knowledge gained during the campaign and use them in other struggles.'[10]

The message, if optimistic, was also darkly threatening, for the poll tax action and its subsequent legacy had 'proved' to such groups that 'direct action can change things and bring down unpopular governments, without the need for an election'.[11]

The threat from non-payment organizations and the Trafalgar Square rioters might have been contained and dismissed if the tax had not also offended the heartlands of traditional suburban conservatism. The rebellious language of *Daily Mail* reading, middlebrow, middle-income old-age pensioners from 'safe' Tory strongholds such as Christchurch in Dorset proved more deadly than a riot – as did the wrath of Mrs Thatcher's alienated back-bench 'wets' and the challenge posed to her leadership by Michael Heseltine.

> The problem, in electoral terms, was not to any great extent the economy. Not only did all the polls consistently show that, despite all the difficulties, the public continued to believe that the Conservative Party was more competent at managing the economy than Labour, but more important no Tory Member was under the illusion that a change of leader would make any difference. By contrast, where there would be a difference was over the hated Poll Tax, the greatest single political blunder of the Thatcher years. It was clear that so long as Margaret remained, so would the Poll Tax.[12]

'Savaged' by 'the dead sheep' that was Geoffrey Howe in his resignation speech of 13 November 1990 and unable to secure a clear majority in the leadership ballot against Heseltine, Thatcher reluctantly (and bitterly) resigned on 22 November.

Throughout the 1990s and into the new millennium the anarchist movement remained a broad alliance, split between 'fluffys' (advocates of non-violent direct action) and 'spikeys' (advocates of confrontation by any means). Through the 1990s these two groups were still part of a broad 'front' which included elements of mainstream parties like the Liberal Democrats and Labour, organizations like Greenpeace, the SWP and Militant and radical elements in the trade unions.

These groups came together for a series of protest rallies against the Criminal Justice Bill, a piece of legislation described by civil rights barrister Michael Mansfield as 'fascist' and at the least draconian and authoritarian. It was certainly seen by many as a measure hastily drawn up to assuage fears about travellers and rave parties. The rally at Hyde Park in October 1994 was one of three that year (previous ones had been held in May and July). Speakers included Tony Benn, Bruce Kent, Jeremy Corbyn (MP for Islington North) and miners' leader Arthur Scargill, but there were others including speakers from Liberty, United Sound Systems, the National Association of Probation Officers, the SWP, the Society of Black Lawyers and anti-road campaigners.

The rally had gathered after a march from the Embankment but in the late afternoon a dispute between police and organizers over two sound systems that had entered the park threatened to get out of hand. At 6.30 p.m. as the rally ended 'boxed-in' protesters found themselves facing riot squads. After an alleged CS gas canister was lobbed at police, they charged to clear the park. Rioting continued into the night as did some looting. Yet for many it was clear who had begun the trouble – indeed they discerned a pattern.

> The pattern is alarmingly similar every time: near the end of a demonstration, the police change the plans (change the route of a march, close a sound system before time, lock the agreed exits), and seal off a portion of the dwindling crowd. Behind the normal uniformed officers, police in full riot gear seal off side streets and other exit routes. The crowd are hemmed in on three sides. Then the uniforms withdraw, leaving the advancing riot police to start a riot.[13]

The finding of Class War's leaflet 'Keep it Spikey' had been widely believed by police and press to be a sign of a coordinated and centralized 'anarchist' plot, and from now on 'anarchists' appeared in the popular press of the 1990s as the same target of opprobrium they had been for readers of the 1890s. Such vilification also signalled to mainstream groups that the 'popular front' approach was effectively dead.

The poll-tax protest groups soon began to claim their place as the heirs of the Peasants' Revolt of 1381, children of Wat Tyler and John Ball. The M11 protesters would see themselves as protectors of the green woods and inheritors of the anti-enclosure movements. Working-class activists certainly saw direct action resistance to the community charge as continuing in the tradition of the Peasant's Revolt. To align themselves with a labourers' revolt of the fourteenth century against pernicious 'head' taxes was ingenious but somewhat disingenuous. The peasants hoped to remove pernicious advisers from the presence of Richard II; the activists hoped to remove Margaret Thatcher from government altogether.

In truth the anti-tax and anti-road direct action of the 1990s had more in common with the destruction of turnpike gates and buildings in the eighteenth and nineteenth centuries and the rent strike and squatting movements of the twentieth. These were themselves related to the direct action used to remove enclosure fencing and the encroachment of common land which had a long history stretching back into the sixteenth century.

*

The attacks on turnpikes in the eighteenth century which led to sporadic riots in Somerset, Gloucester, Hereford and Leeds tumbled over into violence and disorder on London streets when toll gates were destroyed and officials roughed up in Old Street during 1753. By the 1830s and 1840s anti-turnpike groups of labourers who dressed in their wives' dresses to avoid detection (and as a symbol of the world turned upside down) had given such disturbances the name of the Rebecca Riots. Such direct action by local communities against developers, landlords or farmers (Captain Swing) upheld tradition and continuity against change and perceived exploitation. They embodied a communal sense of rightness and order which outsiders or unscrupulous landlords had attempted to disturb. Direct action was an immediate, often clandestine and very effective way of creating delay and unnecessary costs to developers. Such activity took unarticulated politics onto the streets and used the raw eruption of perceived injustice against 'the people' as a powerful weapon. These tactics had real emotional and propagandistic value with regard to the possibilities of resistance, and the immediate appeal of spontaneous action brought on by outrage would be a significant factor when anti-poll-tax groups began to form in the 1990s.

Equally the refusal of an entire community to cooperate with local or government officials was powerful if orchestrated effectively, and nowhere was refusal more effective (at least emotionally) than in the refusal to pay rents. The circumstances were analogous to the refusal to pay taxes (rents being considered a form of 'tax' by the rich landlord against the poor labourer). Rent strikes had a more recent history than anti-turnpike agitation, a history attached to the twentieth century and the organizing of the working class (rather than the mere lower orders or mob) by trades unions and the nascent Labour and Communist parties.

The appalling housing of navvies was made apparent in a report of 1907, whilst the extraordinary levels of poverty in many areas was brought home in the censuses of 1891 and 1911. Conferences on housing attended by socialist and trade union delegates were held in 1902, 1905, 1907 and 1909, and thus by the early years of the twentieth century a sense of working-class outrage at their living conditions had been sufficiently conveyed to the middle classes that they too began to be concerned to protect the poor from the injustices of landlords and rackrent freeholders. Attempts to raise rents in Wolverhampton in 1913 met with direct action resistance and refusal to pay. Tenants' Defence Leagues were formed around the country. In Leeds rent rises led to organized resistance coordinated by the Labour Party. The rent strike was not just a refusal to pay up to a local exploiter but was seen as part of organized working-class resistance to the very nature of capitalism itself. 'We want a strike that week by week will add to our income while it lasts . . . and at the same time cut at the very roots of the Capitalist System'.[14]

The London boroughs soon had their problems too. There were strikes against the London County Council, activity in Bethnal Green, Hammersmith, Camberwell and Woolwich. Elsewhere, Liverpool, Luton and Edinburgh had disturbances, as did Manchester, but the greatest strike of all was on Clydeside in Scotland. Activists in the squatting and anarchist movements, as well as Communists and Labour Party supporters, saw the legendary defence of workers' rights in Scotland as directly leading to the Rent Act (1915), which created a framework for rent controls. The myth of the tough Clydesider as hero of a working-class frontline crystallized here.

The most important post-war rent strike was the highly significant but half-forgotten action that occurred in 1960 in St Pancras, a large borough that embraced Highgate, King's Cross and Regent's Park. Its population was largely made up of working-class council tenants, but it was a prosperous borough with commercial and small industrial firms and a stable population that had been steadily rehoused as building programmes replaced the old housing stock demolished during the Second World War. Expanded public housing was central to Aneurin Bevan's post-war vision of an equitable society, which needed to avoid the 'grave civic damage' of 'colonies of low income people' and colonies of 'higher income', which through enforced segregation brought about by mistaken housing policy created a 'monstrous infliction upon . . . the biological one-ness of the community'.[15] Bevan pursued policies which gave local authorities power to subsidize housing and requisition empty property. This was of considerable importance in St Pancras.

In the mid-1950s the immediate crisis had subsided, and the new Conservative government began to revert to a more liberal market-led policy. The Rent and Repairs Act (1954) allowed private landlords to increase rents if essential repairs were needed and the Requisitioned Houses and Housing (Amendment) Act (1955) repealed Bevan's Act and required all such stock to be eliminated by 1960. Such property was, however, vital, to St Pancras and its loss would have to be made up. The following Housing Subsidies Act (1956) removed all local authority help except to the very needy and the 1957 Rent Act led to a free market for landlords and helped create the scandal of 'Rachmanism'. Meanwhile land values in St Pancras began a spectacular rise.

The Labour council which had been elected in 1956 was, however, in the mould of George Lansbury and in the tradition of the pre-war politics, known as 'Poplarism'. John Lawrence, the leader of the council, had a strict closed-shop policy for council workers and even sanctioned the flying of the red flag on May Day. The radicalism of such actions and the militant obduracy the council group showed at Labour conferences led to the local Labour group finding itself under review, and after rioting at the Town Hall in May 1958, when the red flag was again hoisted, Lawrence found that not only had he been expelled from the Labour Party National Executive Committee but also that he and thirty local activists had been expelled from the party altogether.

These disturbing activities, alongside growing council debts, led to the defeat of the local Labour Party at the next council elections. The Conservatives were mindful of the need for low rents (if possible) but also the need to clear council deficits. They proposed a two-tier rent scheme which would still subsidize the very poor. The problem was that it dramatically raised over 50 per cent of rents on other council homes. This was clearly a challenge to local tenants and an opportunity for local political activists.

On 14 August 1959, after a meeting at the Dolphin public house, next to the Town Hall, the United Tenants' Association (UTA) came into being to coordinate action against the council. A committee of committed local trade unionists was formed and centred on three members of the Communist Party, Don Cook, an Amalgamated Engineering Union shop steward at Handley Page, Charlie Taylor, a Fleet Street print chapel member, and Jim Swain also at Handley Page. The major eviction protests were to focus on Cook at Kennistoun House in Leighton Road and Arthur Rowe, also a Communist, at Silverdale House, Regent's Park Estate. Although the official Communist Party line was, in the final days of open conflict, to disavow the activities of the tenants' leaders as 'adventurism' and opportunism, the organizers' initial actions were to set up local tenants' soviets in the council blocks.

> The UTA organisation was thoroughgoing and effective. Committees were set up in every block and every week some 200 tenants would meet, representing all the associations in the borough. These meetings decided UTA policy and in this sense the tenants themselves were the real leadership. Masses of people were involved on a day-to-day basis in keeping the struggle going. At one stage the UTA were putting out leaflets three times a week. They could produce a leaflet within 24 hours so the gap between the elected leadership and the rank-and-file tenants could be kept to a minimum.[16]

As the tenants organized they also acted. A petition gathered 16,000 signatures to little effect, but organizing rent payment refusal was another matter, as was the organized harassment of councillors and council officials by a core of sixty women from the tenants' groups who continuously followed people home, banged on doors at night and made life uncomfortable.

Despite the growingly clear iniquities of council policy and the large number of people on rent strike the Labour Party insisted on lawful protest, which did little to help tenants threatened with eviction and of course led directly to some becoming more aggressive, using the occasion as a reminder of class war. The UTA now came up with a policy of highlighting individual eviction cases. Three were chosen, those of Don Cook, Arthur Rowe and Gladys Tower, although Tower (with no political battle to fight) soon dropped out. This left Rowe and Cook to fight it out as proletarian Davids against the council Goliath. Extensive defence preparations were already in hand.

> The extension of the eviction order, given by Bloomsbury Court, expired at midnight on 28 August. By that time well-constructed barricades had gone up, both at Kennistown House and Silverdale. Don Cook had 12 pianos in his flat barricading various doors, as well as other old furniture and doors put against windows, and barbed wire and an old bedstead on the roof to discourage bailiffs from entering that way. There were also plans for human barricades; tenants and trade unionists were to be involved in a 24-hour picket of both flats so that in an eviction attempt, defence and warning could be simultaneous. Preparations were made at

Kennistoun House for a bell to be rung and rockets fired if the bailiffs arrived on the scene. On hearing or seeing the warning, workers all over the borough were prepared to down tools and rush to the assistance of the two beleaguered tenants. An intercom system was set up between Don Cook's flat and the campaign headquarters in another flat in Kennistoun House.[17]

The violence of the bailiffs' methods was a foretaste of the M11 protests.

I heard the rockets. We all ran out in our pyjamas. Everywhere there were people running towards Kennistoun House. But when we turned into Leighton Road all we could see were police. There were hundreds of them. We could do nothing. We could not get near. The police are here to help the bailiffs if they are resisted but we never had a chance to resist.[18]

The first we knew about the raid was when about five bailiffs came in through a hole in the roof. They came down the stairs and forced open the sitting room. We retreated to the kitchen and rebarricaded . . . In the kitchen we made a cup of tea while the bailiffs were pushing and shoving to get in. The bailiffs used crowbars and hacksaws. Those who had come through the roof let more bailiffs in through the window. When they broke into the kitchen we offered them a cup of tea. They drank it . . . They were unable to get through the window because of the barbed wire so they ripped the slates off the roof and made a hole in the plaster with their axes.[19]

As fighting broke out, a protester called John Lawrence had made his way to the Shell Site on the South Bank and encouraged the builders there to down tools and march to St Pancras. They later joined a march from Kennistown House to the Town Hall that evening, when 14,000 protesters found themselves in running battles with police. Whilst the Council debated rents policy, police horses charged angry tenants. The *News Chronicle* righteously intoned: 'The hooliganism in St. Pancras must be sternly suppressed. It is an outrageous outburst of unjustified indignation which deserves no sympathy. No responsible politician will ally himself with the rioters.'[20]

Despite more cautious coverage in the *Mirror* and *Daily Herald*, the *News Chronicle* line prevailed, events quietened down and rents were paid or adjusted. Yet the idealism of the cause was to motivate a new generation of socialist activists and act as an inspiration for the squatting and tenant movements of the 1970s.

The St Pancras rent strike was soon forgotten amid the clamour of the counterculture that started to emerge a few years later but it remained a significant, if little-remembered, episode in working-class solidarity and its importance to housing agitation was not lost on the rent strikers of the early 1970s or on the later squatter movement. More significantly it had lessons for the poll tax protests of 1990, with its pattern of local opposition defined by Labour Party and union legalism and hesitancy, the appearance of spontaneous associations of local rate payers, growing militancy leading to rioting and disorder, initial involvement and then disavowal of 'adventurism' by extreme socialist groups and Communists and a final and slow corrosion when solid union support failed to materialize and the courts and bailiffs moved in. For many in 1960 the violence of the bailiffs and police seemed to reveal the new brutalism of the ruling elite whilst the spontaneous appearance of building workers from the South Bank suggested the hope of revolution from below as labour finally united against the bosses. The poll tax protests in many of their manifestations, especially in London's poorer boroughs like Haringey, repeated the processes and half-forgotten lessons of St Pancras along with the promises, hijackings and betrayals that marked inner London protest thirty years before.

25

The Free Republic of Wanstonia

The Fight for London's Green Spaces

Attracted to the seventeenth-century Digger movement they might have been, but modern anti-road protesters had much closer affiliations with more recent attempts to halt the encroachments of land speculation and house building. As long ago as the very early seventeenth century London's growth seemed both phenomenal and monstrous. On seeing his new capital James I had exclaimed that soon London would 'become all England!'. By the nineteenth century, land speculation and building had overwhelmed many of the villages near the city and had begun a relentless march into the last remaining green areas around Hampstead, Highgate and Epping. In 1829, George Cruickshank produced his famous cartoon 'London Going Out of Town', which showed a relentless array of bricks and mortar pounding the surrounding countryside into submission. As bricks spew out of a giant brick-firing cannon haystacks and farm animals run in horror, a tree forlornly declaring, 'I am mortally wounded.' It soon became vitally important to oppose this spread of London, both on aesthetic and on social grounds. What aggravated opposition was the private nature of most 'inclosure acts' which meant that local protesters might only know what was going on when actual fences or contractors moved in. It was over 250 years before public notices had to be posted on acquired land.

Things did not, however, go the developers' way in every case. Sir Thomas Maryon Wilson's attempt in the 1830s to overturn his father's will and develop most of Hampstead Heath was debated three times in Parliament and three times defeated. With local and national press opposition it was recognized that the social benefits of the Heath to the London poor and to other classes enjoying the Heath's natural beauty far outweighed housing needs. The Heath was saved.

The saving of over half of Hampstead Heath (240 acres) was a bloodless victory but it was certainly not a precedent as enclosures continued and as building ate up trees and open spaces. By 1836 an Act of Parliament began the long process of protecting land from development. The General Inclosure Act of 1845 and a further Act of 1852 required prior consultation and parliamentary sanction for new development. In 1866 Parliament passed the Metropolitan Commons Act (London) followed by a further Act in 1876 in order to regulate commons near the capital. Much of this work, was, however jeopardized nearly a hundred years later with the Commons Registration Act of 1965, which put a time limit on common land registration, land not registered forfeiting its commons status. Green belt legislation was also eroded by progressive exceptionalism and road building (especially motorway) schemes.

These dry though vital Acts of Parliament hide much of the human drama contained in attempting to protect open spaces and 'green' neighbourhoods. Nowhere was this more pertinent than in the numerous small-scale skirmishes between developers and local people whose frustration led to direct action. Hampstead Heath may have been saved by the late nineteenth century but odd corners like Fortune Green and West End Green in West Hampstead were still available. After negotiations with the local Manor Court, a property developer called John Culverhouse began to put up his hoardings.

Culverhouse was opposed by a local resident, Captain Notman, who soon came to represent local interests, but the brave captain, despite entreating his fellow residents to avoid acting like Fenians, was soon unable to control local anger. On 17 July 1882 groups of local men armed with crowbars and axes and carrying a two-gallon oil can descended on the open land, tore down hoardings and created a blaze which the fire brigade and the rain could not extinguish. A policeman (PC Splaine) then made some arrests before a squad from S Division arrived to dispense the 2,000 strong crowd. Clearly unimpressed by Mr Culverhouse's representations, the magistrates at Hampstead Police Court acquitted the eight men arrested.*

Direct action by locals was frequently used in tandem with 'constitutional' means and the actions at Fortune Green looked forward to similar activities on Wimbledon Common, where fences were set on fire by a large crowd at least one of whom blew a bugle before the

---

*The fight for London's green spaces was not always a battle with rapacious landowners. Typically, the groups that threatened recreational space as much as landlords were gypsies and Irish tinkers. Securing Fortune Green on the edge of Hampstead Heath in 1893 required the forcible eviction of a gypsy encampment. Such actions against travellers and gypsies continue unabated to the present day. (See Dick Weindling, 'The Fight for Fortune Green', *Camden History* 10, 1982, p. 15.)

walls fell down!* Eruptions of anger continued late into the nine-teenth century and were sometimes aimed at halting the new sub-urbanism which had gentrified South-West and South-East London and taken over much of the land which had belonged to large and recently demolished country houses and encroached on common grazing and pasture.

This was the case at Honor Oak, also called One Tree Hill, near Crystal Palace and Dulwich. The Hill itself had long been 'waste' with locals giving little thought to its actual ownership. Many thought it had no owner but was literally common land. It was also a legendary spot reputed to be the site of Boudicca's last battle with the Romans, the place itself allegedly named after Queen Elizabeth, having drunk herself stupid, knighted the oak tree there rather than a courtier. Much later, William Blake probably had his first great vision of angels look-ing towards the oak from Peckham Rye. Beyond all this the Hill was the favourite haunt of locals escaping the cares of the working week.

This was apparently set at naught when Alfred Stevens, one of a number of 'land-thieves', laid claim to the land and sold it on for development into a golf course. A large meeting held on Peckham Rye in the early summer of 1897 resulted in the creation of a defence committee headed by local dignitaries, but legal negotiations soon foundered, leaving many local people annoyed and disaffected. It was not long before riotous crowds began to organize and on Sunday 10 October a crowd of 15,000 attempted to destroy the enclosing fences. These plans being frustrated, the crowd attacked the ground-keeper's cottage and caused considerable damage. The following week a crowd of at least 50,000 gathered and set fire to the enclosure fenc-ing, after which fighting led to arrests. Even with this sort of pressure it was only the compulsory purchase of the land by Camberwell Council in 1905 that finally brought it back into public ownership as a park.

One aspect of the disturbances outside the golf course was the dif-fering tactics adopted by the various classes opposing development plans. The main committee was essentially committed to legal and procedural protest and was middle class in aspect. Aggravated at the slowness of the whole process, a breakaway group formed itself around skilled and semi-skilled workers who were willing to use direct action against the 'trespasses' of the wealthy (especially for their hob-bies) and the protection of that trespass by the police and courts. The group included men like Ben Ellis, a brush maker, Herbert Triggs,

---

*Sir Henry Peck (1825–93) saved not only Wimbledon Common from enclo-sure by Lord Spencer during the 1860s and 1870s but also Burnham Beeches. Wimbledon Green, detached from the Common, was lost to developers after a campaign by protesters from 1901–2.

a boot maker, Charles Hawken, a French polisher, and Henry Martin, a boot and shoe maker. Their leader was Frederick Polkinghorne, a man who conspicuously dressed in the 'style and habitude of an artisan . . . wearing a cloth cap and carrying a bit of blackthorn'.[1] Polkinghorne, a saddler by trade, was in his own words a 'social revolutionary', although he was also a pragmatist who was happy to curb direct action if it might lead to two months' hard labour.

Polkinghorne's views represent a new practical socialism that would more and more come to dominate land protests. The local Social Democratic Federation had long been active in Camberwell, Battersea and Lambeth and a guest speaker from the Land Nationalization Society had called for One Tree Hill to be 'nationalized' as early as 1898.

The protection of common land and especially its preservation for public use required vigilance, patience and deep pockets. Court cases were often very protracted and costly and those whose interests opposed commoners and the public were usually wealthy, obstinate and quite willing to erect fencing when no one was looking. Hampstead Heath passed into the hands of the Metropolitan Board of Works in 1869 but it had to take other action in 1889 to secure it, ending with the gift of Kenwood House in 1924 to the London County Council to crown the achievement. Blackheath was saved in 1871 and Clapham Common in 1877 but Wandsworth was greatly reduced, not least by the building of an asylum, workhouse and prison. Streatham Common was all but obliterated.

The epic struggle to save Epping Forest from enclosure was itself brought to a head in 1865–6 by the challenge of a family of labourers whose traditional livelihood had been threatened by the rector of the parish of Loughton enclosing (as Lord of the Manor) some 1,300 acres. Tom Willingdale and his two sons soon found themselves in trouble with the law for trespass and lopping trees illegally. All three were given two months' hard labour which broke the health of one son and led to his early death. Summonsed the next year and fined, the three refused to pay and were clapped into Ilford jail. Distaste for these aggressive punishments came to the notice of the Commons Preservation Society which had been formed in 1865 by a campaigning barrister, Charles Shaw-Lefevre (Viscount Eversley), Thomas Hughes, author of *Tom Brown's Schooldays*, Sir Thomas Foxwell Buxton and his brother Charles (sons of an anti-slave trade radical) and John Stuart Mill. Shaw-Lefevre was a tough opponent – he had sent a trainload of navvies to Berkhampstead to remove illegal fences – and the Society began a law case against illegal enclosures in Epping Forest.

Enquiries showed that the Corporation of London, having bought land for a cemetery in Ilford, had unwittingly become commoners. The Corporation's 200 acres would now be used to break the monopoly of manorial holdings. Indeed it was soon established that Epping was *one* 'waste' not a collection of manors and that, therefore, a ruling or veto in one area carried for *all*. Persuaded to clear the Forest of enclosures and preserve it for the public, the Corporation began a major lawsuit in July 1871. The Epping Forest Enclosures Act of 1878 made the Corporation the conservators of the Forest and its sole owner. Arriving at Chingford Station, Queen Victoria opened Epping for public use in 1882. Tom Willingdale died in 1870, one of the last in a line of commoners whose obstinacy and belief in traditional rights had long opposed the enclosing lords of the manor. It was this tradition of opposition to the enclosing of land around the capital that linked Tom Willingdale and his sons to the protests of those who opposed London ringroads and motorways.*

Protest against the notion of London 'link' roads and bypasses was certainly much older than the visible activities of those at Twyford, Newbury and Wanstead during the 1990s and certainly older than the gauntlet thrown down by Margaret Thatcher in her implacable support for a 'car economy' (of individual owners). This history, of which the attempt to halt the M11 link was the final stage, began in the 1940s and the need for strategic planning for transport and communication once the war ended and the debris of the Blitz had been cleared.

The desire for 'rational urban planning' had led the Labour government to pass the Town and Country Planning Act (1947), legislation that formed a basis for local planning and negotiation.[2] For Patrick Abercrombie, one of the leading thinkers in town planning, there emerged the possibility of a planned 'holistic' framework for urban life. This ideal would essentially be technocratic and modernistic, separating transport and living space, but planners of the 1940s had not taken into account the growth of the use of cars. By the very early 1960s, the 1947 legislation began to seem dated.

The next stage was the concept of 'structure planning'. It formed the core of the Greater London Development Plan (GLDP) of 1969, which was intended to create an equilibrium between the way people 'really' lived and worked and predictive needs, and would require massive road building schemes and house clearance, mainly through apparently poor areas.

The main, and easily most controversial part of the GLDP was its attitude to roads. The plan proposed three giant ring roads: an inner ring linking inner city areas both sides of the Thames (Ringway 1); another ring through the suburbs (Ringway 2); and a further motorway linking

---

*In 2005, Epping Council planned to mark the life of Tom Willingdale with a blue plaque in the graveyard of the Church of St John where he was buried in a pauper's grave.

the entirety of London and connecting all roads going into the centre, proposed by the Ministry of Transport (Ringway 3). The idea behind Ringway 3 eventually led to the construction of the notorious M25, Ringway 2 found only partial success and Ringway 1 was abandoned except for a north–south link intended to allow the A2 to join a proposed new motorway (the M11), creating a continuous system of transport from Dover through the Blackwall Tunnel, Bromley by Bow, Stratford, Wanstead, Leytonstone and finally on to Cambridge and Harwich. This would be the first proper north–south link across London. The abandonment of other schemes or their partial commission would still leave this as a pressing need in an area of notorious congestion.

With publication of the GLDP, the public inquiry received 30,000 objections and hundreds of representation groups were set up or reactivated to fight plans for what was considered a 'motorway plan, which makes transport the master'. This perception was not wholly mistaken, as the Greater London Council (GLC), which had been created in 1965 as a replacement for the old London County Council (LCC), had inherited a bias against housing and exaggerated concern for road building, the Council's Planning and Transportation Department being its most significant section. The GLDP itself had benefited from a three-volume traffic survey produced in 1962, whilst the equivalent survey for housing was not completed until 1968, too late to have any influence.

The 1969 London borough elections had, by contrast, produced 100,000 voters for a 'Homes Before Roads' party and had clearly indicated a miscalculation by the GLC, especially in the wake of a number of television programmes on homelessness and the press attention given to 'Rachmanism' (a form of rackrenting). The beliefs amongst officials that people would be irresistibly drawn to make journeys from 'Dagenham to Putney, Greenwich to Hampstead' or that ringway roads would, as Robert Vigars, Chair of the Highways Committee, put it, be 'social roads' seemed simply ridiculous and a gross misunderstanding of London's 'village' nature. Very large numbers of local groups believed that they lived in reasonably intimate areas tangentially attached to their surroundings, and many of these groups were made up of owner-occupiers and those who were buying up the older eighteenth- and nineteenth-century properties in the rundown areas that the GLC proposed bulldozing.

> The route plan of Ringway 1 amounts to a gazetteer of gentrificiaton, taking in Canonbury, Barnsbury, Hampstead, Highgate, riverside Greenwich, Blackheath, Battersea and other parts of the nineteenth-century urban rim, where middle-class colonists were renovating old but sturdy and attractive property. This was a phenomenon that the GLC consistently – almost wilfully – misunderstood.

It stressed the dereliction of much inner area property as a selling point for Ringway 5 . . .

'London is, you know, a number of villages', the Inquiry was told, 'each village with its group of suburbs which link together'. Not only nominal villages like Blackheath and Highgate, but Chiswick and Barnes, even Lewisham and the Isle of Dogs were depicted as villages by their defenders. Highgate was 'favoured by writers and thinkers to whom quietness is essential'; Chiswick was 'one of the few remaining village centres in London where they still play cricket on the Green on Saturdays in summer'. The Ratepayers' Association in Beddington, known to many as the site of the Croydon sewage farm, submitted a lengthy account of their village's history since the Conquest. What these 'villages' did was nurture 'community' which the Ringways would destroy.[3]

By 1973 there were already 700 community pressure groups, requiring the publication of a *London Community Planning Directory*. Such groups ranged from ratepayers' associations to antiquarian societies, from anti-motorway groups such as the London Motorway Action Group to the feminist group Women on the Move.

The professional planners, preferring design to the muddle of urban life, fought back. The GLC's Public Information Branch created continuous positive propaganda and held meetings to 'put the record straight'. Yet by 1970 public opinion had forced a public inquiry, and the Labour government appointed Sir Frank Layfield to provide a full scrutinizing process. Sitting for 235 days between 1970 and 1972, the Layfield Inquiry was the longest public inquiry to that date. Moreover, GLC civil servants were themselves undermining plans prepared by their bosses, carrying out 'bureaucratic guerrilla warfare' against capitalists, gentrification *and* road building and instead offering support and information for poorer inner-city groups. It remained the case, however, that what was to be termed NIMBYdom ('not in my back yard') *did* save important and substantial parts of London. More to the point, such protests were not just NIMBY whingery for they were, on the whole, aimed at stopping dead one or more of the Ringway schemes.

Things had been very different in the early 1960s. For a moment the motorway ideal had seemed modern, sexy and cool.

Unlikely as it may seem today, the M1 was part of 'swinging' Britain. Charles Forte's motorway snack bar at Newport Pagnell, forerunner to today's services, became quite trendy . . . This cosy man-made island called out to Britain's youth, the generation of teenager . . . From the steamed-up windows of the snack-bar you could watch the Bentleys and the Rolls-Royces streaming into the car park. Out of them stepped cult figures like singer Tom Jones, the Beatles, the Rolling Stones and the cast of Coronation Street, all heading for the up-market Grill and Griddle . . . Customers would queue for hours just to get a seat and the Grill waitresses were the envy of us all. We saw the first miniskirt here.[4]

It took a mere decade, however, to turn the vision into a nightmare and lead to a generation of activists dedicated to halting the motorway madness. One such protester was John Tyme, a former Sheffield Polytechnic lecturer whose full-time anti-road campaigns began at an inquiry into the M40's proposed route. Campaigns over the M42, M20, M56, M25, M16, and A55 used tactics pioneered in student occupations: 'From this moment, . . . this inquiry is occupied,' Tyme told the government inspector at the North London Archway Inquiry of 1977. Concepts of civil disobedience pioneered by Tyme accompanied most subsequent inquiries and building work.

Although the Motorway Box had been broken up other schemes still beckoned. In the early 1990s the Conservatives unveiled a vast new road-building scheme which included a road cutting through Twyford Down, one of the most significant parts of the landscape of the south of England. One writer has called it 'one of the most wanton acts of environmental vandalism ever perpetrated in Britain'.[5] It was even condemned by Carlo Ripa di Meana, the European Environmental Commissioner. John Major, then Prime Minister, dug his heels in despite growing pressure both from the establishment and Friends of the Earth.

Other groups were also attracted to the cause, such as 'Earth First', an American environmental '(dis)organization' dedicated to militant civil disobedience. A British group had been created by two University of Sussex students in 1991. Following the example of the Greenham Common (Women's) Peace Corps, set up to fight cruise missiles being based in Britain, Twyford was soon dotted with 'Dongas tribe people' who had called themselves after the oddly named deep tracks on the Downs. (The name was taken from the Xhosa word for drainage channel.) Threatened with sequestration of its assets (like the miners' unions earlier), Friends of the Earth withdrew from open and active participation but this meant 'Twyford now acquired a different class of protestor . . . "Twyford and later camps provided a magnet for New Age travellers and for individuals simply seeking to escape from authority, family commitment or urban unemployment."'[6]

Extreme levels of intimidation and violence followed. On 9 December 1998 Group Four personnel (employed as security guards) dressed in yellow identifying jackets 'attacked' the Dongas camps. After the attack many women protesters complained of sexual assaults and a number of the security guards, having no taste for the extremity of the action, resigned. The day became known as 'Yellow Wednesday' in road protest circles. The road was finally opened in 1999.

The fight for the Newbury bypass (1994–8) was even closer to a military campaign than previous operations at Twyford.

> The Dongas were well dug in. Along the path of the bypass there were nine different camps with names like Tree Pixie Village and Granny Ash. Other, more militant anti-roads campaigners were actually underneath the route, burrowing out a network of tunnels, some extending 150 feet into the clay, while high above ground they created a colony of 60 connected tree houses . . . the protesters were armed with a formidable array of high tech weapons: mobile telephones, pagers, CB radios and battery-powered laptop computers connected to the Internet.[7]

On the first day of work, a Dongas attack successfully blockaded Abbots Farm, where the security guards were billeted, but with the use of a private detective agency (used to identify known 'troublemakers') as well as huge numbers of security men, police, chainsaws, 'cherry pickers' (mobile cranes with platforms) etc. the work continued. The protesters, slowly winkled out and removed, turned to machine smashing and 'ecotage' but to little avail even though, in a last ditch action, on 12 February, 'a group of masked activists raided the Newbury offices of the construction company Tarmac Roadstone. Thirty employees watched helplessly as the protesters disabled computers, fax machines and telephones, rifled files and threw a fire extinguisher through a window.'[8]

Amongst the protesters were not merely people with odd single names that appeared to come straight out of *The Hobbit* but also Arthur Pendragon of the Council of British Druidic Orders. 'Arthur' had emerged some years previously from Camelot (actually a council house) and armed with Excalibur (confiscated by a magistrate but returned) had gone in quest of a lost England awaiting the return of Merlin. An image of a seemingly harmless but dotty New-Ageism, Arthur was a regular figure at environmental protest camps and frequently arrested. When Ken Kesey visited Britain with the (old) Merry Pranksters and a (new) Magic Bus, the *Big Issue* arranged for them to meet in the summer of 1999. Penniless and nomadic as this King Arthur may have been he also ran a Web site for 'political pagans', something that the *Big Issue* suggested already made 'Kesey's form of sixties protest "old hat"'.

> Let's face it, seeing a psychedelic bus isn't exactly unusual any more – only now they're more likely to be filled with contemporaries of Arthur rather than acolytes of Kesey. Radicalism these days isn't

just about rejecting conventional wisdoms, it's about living for a purpose or cause which is more likely to get you patronised than canonised. It'll be interesting to see whether Kesey realises this during his tour of the postcard haunts of Merlin.[9]

Arthur Pendragon was just one of a number of 'tribes' people to emerge for a brief moment of fame. Others included Swampy (Daniel Hooper), famous for his tunnelling at controversial building projects but soon a media star, commissioned by Fourth Estate to write *The Eco-Terrorist Handbook*, and General Survival (Matthew Morris-Steward), a dreadlocked eleven-year-old from a disruptive council estate family who was offered a £10,000 contract for his life story by *The News of the World*. London's Dongas war was just about to begin.

On Wednesday 6 October 1999, flanked by executives from many of Britain's leading construction companies, Lawrie Haynes, Chief Executive of the Highways Agency, posed for a final picture before cutting the ribbon officially opening the A12 Hackney to M11 Link Road.

> Following a brief ceremony, including the cutting of the tape, officials and guests were taken on a tour of the full length of the road, which goes from Redbridge roundabout through to the Eastway in Hackney. All agreed that the Link Road is a magnificent achievement for both civil engineering and all those involved in its design and construction. The eastbound carriageway of the tunnel was opened to traffic at 11.30am and the westbound carriageway some 30 minutes later.[10]

The eight executives (all male) smiled in the sunshine, possibly partially from relief, for this had been one of the hardest fought of all road projects, a fact attested to in an earlier newsletter relating to security.

> Questions are still being asked at both Wanstead and Leyton Link Road offices about the security guards working on the Link Road contracts. It is appreciated that some local people have reservations about the numbers involved and their high profile presence. However, while protesters continue to trespass and to squat properties, there will be a need for security staff to protect site works and equipment.
>
> The visible presence of security staff is likely to remain a feature of Link Road contracts for as long as disruptive activities continue. Two firms were employed. Reliance Security Services Limited provide the security for the Link Road contractors' construction sites. They wear boiler suits and hard hats, often augmented by yellow

reflective jackets. Each guard now wears an armband with an identity number. Essential Security Services Limited, whose guards wear more traditional security uniforms, are mainly employed to look after empty properties.[11]

The M11 Link Road scheme, as it came to be known, had existed as a dream as long ago as the 1920s, the original proposal being for a long arterial road creating links to the Kent and Essex coasts. The scheme which was finally built was in part a modification of the Ringway scheme of the 1960s and in part a result of the 1980s thinking of planners looking for fast European road links. The road cut through Wanstead and Leytonstone in East London to cross the Hackney marshes and join the Dover Road at Bow. Wanstead was still a relatively leafy suburb with ancient trees and pleasant roads; it had a green, and a village school set back against its High Street. It was a relatively wealthy area of home owners. Unfortunately, it was also one of the worst congestion spots in London, with dreadful pollution from terrible queues and hold-ups on roads leading to Leyton and Forest Gate. The M11 Link plan would, in its mildest form, require a huge tunnel to be built necessitating the destruction of some of George Green including an ancient sweet chestnut, the demolition of a number of old Victorian villas and *years* of extreme disruption by engineers.

If Wanstead still had the vestiges of a village suburb (Wanstead Park was originally the site of Wanstead House, one of the major stately homes of the eighteenth century), then the opposite had to be said for Leytonstone. On the other side of the park, it was a poorer and more rundown neighbourhood where house ownership was lower and property considerably cheaper. Yet this too was a community with many older residents having lived all their lives in an area they considered home. Unfortunately this area too had one of the worst records for traffic blight north of the Thames. To build a link road here would require hundreds of homes to be demolished at a time of acute housing shortages in London.

The official attitude was that 'community relations during the construction of this new trunk road were always considered of paramount importance' but such relations soon degenerated. On 13 September 1993, the day allotted for Phase 4 (Redbridge to Green Man Roundabout), protesters stopped work when they occupied houses on the A12/Eastern Avenue. For the awaiting media, the protesters were happy to explain who they were.

The jubilant occupiers represented local people and representatives from Alarm UK (The Alliance Against Road Building, Reclaim the Streets, the Waltham Forest Environmental Forum, Hackney

Green Party, FoE London Cycling Campaign etc). They also received help and support from some new blood recruits from the Twyford Down, Dragon, Earth First, Dongas and Flower Pot Tribes . . . They categorically refute the misrepresentations in the local press that they are new age travellers. 'Basically, the press have no idea what new age travellers are. We are a group of young environmentalists who are effectively reclaiming back land and houses for the people.'[12]

The protest groups soon congregated around two symbols: the chestnut tree on George Green and a road in Leytonstone that they had decided to defend. The chestnut tree was soon festooned with banners and 'occupied' by squatters who claimed the tree as a 'house': a letter had been received at 'the Chestnut Tree, George Green, Wanstead', and tree fellers had had to get an eviction order rather than simply felling it. Despite the tree receiving hundreds of letters, including many from local schoolchildren, an eviction order sent in tree fellers protected by police and security guards. The events of the next few hours were recorded in the protesters' *Newsletter* for December 1993.

In the rain and hail of the small hours of Tuesday 7 December the fight began and lasted all day. Campaigners were 'tipped off' – 200 people gathered in force to protect Wanstead's famous Old Sweet Chestnut – and the people living in it – on the George Green. Defenders chained themselves together – arm locked inside metal tubes – facing inwards about the trunk of the Chestnut with four or five rings of people protecting them. Within five minutes, two buses and 15 police vans had lined up . . . It was still dark, hundreds of police swarmed onto the George Green and formed themselves strategically into an outer cordon about the tree defenders. The crowds yelled 'no more roads', 'save our children, save our trees' and drummed and chanted earth songs to the rhythmical beat of the drums. The atmosphere was charged! It was quite frightening!

The police linked together like penguins in blue. They flung, pushed *and shoved people with* excessive force out of the cordon to other officers who dragged them away – often by their hair. Some people were punched in the face. Campaigners came back – not because they liked being hurt – but they just had to protect the tree. These Police (TSGs)* are not your regular 'evening all' bobbies. They are specials from across the capital – specifically trained to deal with rowdies and subversive aggression . . . Day dawned – the

---

*Members of the Territorial Support Group.

struggle went on for hours. There were horrendous scuffles, screaming and shouting. The Police eliminated people from the cordon and the Sheriff's men moved in . . . By early afternoon it was cold and grey. A 'cherry picker' advanced and was resisted.

The machine stuck in the mud . . . back and forth manoeuvrings to release it resulted in several people being hurt. Campaigners blocked a second cherry picker by the lying in its path [sic]. Police threw protesters away violently. The A12 was blocked with a sea of heaving people for half an hour . . .

A formal complaint has been made today against the Police. Two top solicitors groups are collecting evidence of excessive power and brute strength metered [sic] out by the TSG and Bailiffs – this includes throwing and punching children! Senior Officers would not intervene – not even to get an ambulance for an unconscious girl they had pulled across the fire.

Verbal confrontation ensued between police and people – it was the only way it seemed to release anger and frustration as the cherry picker moved in on the tree. The seven people up the tree locked onto branches but were dragged down. People witnessed one man being punched in the face by a bailiff. He escaped from the cherry picker basket and climbed up the arm of the machine and locked himself to it – despite the danger the operator defied health and safety rulings and kept it moving. The tree people were grappled down and their 'home' cut to bits and dragged down (including the bucket toilet – how else could you stay up there for 12 hours?!).

Campaigners kept stressing 'no violence' to the bailiffs. Campaigners tried to hug Police to get through the message – we are peaceful.

By mid afternoon the tree was unceremoniously smashed down by a digger.[13]

The tactics that turned a tree into a (temporary) *des. res.* could also be used to convert an area threatened with demolition into a Ruritanian fantasy. With an eye to the 1949 film *Passport to Pimlico*, protesters barricaded themselves in some houses due for the bull-dozer and declared themselves residents of the 'autonomous free area of Wanstonia' (2–12 Cambridge Park, the course of the A12). The Republic of 'Leytonstone' (187–189 Fillebrook Road, next to the course of the A102M) soon followed. Any move by police or bailiffs would, they hoped, be an attack on a foreign state! The media, as to be expected, loved the idea. Wanstonia fell in February 1994, wit-nessed by press photographers and journalists.

The bailiffs deliberately began the demolition while the protesters were still in the building, and it is a miracle that no-one was either struck by falling masonry or dropped from the 'cherry-picker' hydraulic platforms. I watched with horror as sledgehammers and crowbars were used to smash up the roof around people's heads, while the protestors scrambled on loose slates and dangled dangerously over 30-foot drops. Back on the ground, I complained vigorously to the police commander of the operation, chief superintendent Stuart Giblin, who sneered that this was just what he would expect someone from the National Council for Civil Liberties to say.[14]

Riot police skirmished with hundreds of protesters in East London yesterday as bulldozers demolished five Edwardian houses in the path of the M11 extension. Most of the demonstrators had arrived on coaches from all over Britain. Only a few came from Wanstead. The police included members of the Territorial Support Group in full riot gear. The officers went in at 7.30am in wave after wave. The early morning silence, punctuated by the flutes and drums of the protesters was shattered by the sound of breaking glass as the bailiffs, with sledgehammers and crowbars, crashed into the house.[15]

The police were also there to identify and arrest protesters known for criminal behaviour elsewhere.

Kevin Vaughan was a black anti-roads protester present in Wanstead on 16 February 1994. He was seized by five uniformed police officers, who dragged him inside a white police Transit van. He was told he was being arrested for riotous assembly at Welling. He was taken to Edmonton police station for six hours while police searched through video film of the demonstration at Welling [the anti-Nazi rally in 1993 following the death of Stephen Lawrence]. He was told his face looked like the face of an alleged rioter published in the *Evening Standard*. But this photograph of the alleged rioter bore no resemblance to Kevin Vaughan. He was eventually released without charge.[16]

The M11 Link Road protests did not stop the completion of a major London road, which cut a deep concrete and asphalt cavern through East London. It also cut ten minutes from London east–south travel. Despite every protestation to the contrary by the Labour government that followed, which cancelled some building projects but raised car taxes to inordinately high levels, the car remained unchallenged into the twenty-first century. The next road battle would be with the car users and long-distance hauliers, not the inhabitants of the long-lost 'Republic of Wanstonia'.

26
Never Underestimate a Minority
Guerrilla Gardeners and the Countryside Alliance

The poll tax riots and M11 protests highlighted the new marginal counterculture growing up around squatting and life on the street, in New Age traveller convoys and free festivals fuelled by drugs and mysticism. Panicked by the 'rave' scene and the appearance of travellers at Stonehenge and other prehistoric sites, the government formulated laws to control 'riotous' gatherings. Such laws were the descendants of the anti-union laws which had been passed in order to control secondary picketing. By the late 1990s, the anarchist movement had emerged not as a powerful counterforce to parliamentary government but as a major and uncontrollable *lobby* which could put unbearable pressure on the City and its investors and on government policy on environmental and scientific issues. Its amorphous nature and transient 'population' also made it difficult to penetrate by Special Branch and MI5.

May Day 2000 was not intended as a demonstration ('This is not a protest' said leaflets) but a celebration at which a mass 'Guerrilla Gardening' event would use non-violent direct action (NVDA) to reclaim the streets. Leaflets publicizing the event agreed that London was 'at the heart of Global Capitalism', 'dedicated to the reckless pursuit of profit . . . at the expense of people and ecosystems everywhere'.

> Imagine an ecological city, where communities are based on voluntary co-operation not competition, mutual aid not private profit, cultural diversity not globalised monoculture, permaculture not consumer culture.
>
> Where the land is everyone's, and allotments replace carparks, where we own our own time – liberated from the role of passive consumers alienated from each other and the world around us.
>
> A city for living in – London could be like this . . . Free the city . . .

With the slogan 'Resistance is fertile', participants in this piece of mass street theatre were asked to come

Armed with trowels, seeds, and imagination, the idea is to garden everywhere and anywhere. An urban adventure at the threshold of nature and culture, Guerrilla Gardening is about taking back our own time and space from capital.

Guerrilla Gardening is creative autonomous work, work that is about LIVING, not 'working' to 'make a living'.

The point was that

Direct action is about taking control of every aspect of our own lives, the homes we build, the food we eat, the way we travel, the culture we enjoy, the games we play – it's not just about the occasional protest but about taking power away from the politicians, businessmen and bureaucrats, and participating immediately and directly in radical social and ecological change.

The event would be prefaced by a two-day conference to be held at a secret location in the Holloway Road. In the event, this turned out to be the local community building (Holloway Resource Centre), which had once been a Jones' Brothers store. To find out about the activities planned for May bank holiday anyone interested had to either phone the number given on the stickers that littered London Underground station billboards for the previous month or look up the main anarchist Web sites. For reasons that are often paranoid but sometimes intelligent, anarchists are suspicious of giving out information on landline telephones (they much prefer mobile phones and the Internet).

Despite its underground and cultish publicity (or maybe because of it) the pre-event conference held on 29 and 30 April 2000 was well attended and lively. As with the anarchist book fairs held at Conway Hall in Red Lion Square every October, this event was also swamped under the weight of samizdat posters, stickers, leaflets and appeals. Most of these publicized events or were intended to focus concern on an international or ecological issue, and the newsletter of the Jewish Socialists' Group could be picked up alongside *Link Up*, the network newsletter for anarchist librarians. The approaching London mayoral elections saw publicity for the London Socialist Alliance (with supporting comments from John Pilger and Ken Loach), 'Ken 4 London' leaflets printed in mauve and a spoof copy of the *Evening Standard*'s free newspaper *Metro* now renamed *Maybe* and carrying articles attacking Ken Livingstone and supporting ecological and anti-capitalist action. Throughout the two days of the conference one could attend seminars and workshops as diverse as reports from the recent violence that had erupted around the World Trade Organisation (WTO) meeting in Seattle, fighting the Anti-Terrorism

Bill (which became law in 2001), 'first aid in demos and actions' and 'new revolutionary paganism'.

Participants at such meetings are, on the whole, quiet, respectful and engrossed, even if sometimes poorly informed or overenthusiastic for something different. At the paganism seminar, a middle-aged hippie (low-level) priestess announced that there would be a twenty-four-hour performance of *The Warp*, a theatre 'happening' presented by Ken Campbell in the Victorian vaults near London Bridge.

> The Warp is a cycle of plays following the hero Phil Masters through the Fifties, Sixties and Seventies on a mind blowing search for enlightenment, taking in hippie orgies, fallen angels, UFO's, Soho, intergalactic travel, Martians and naturally, acid.
>
> It follows the history of the Bohemian Movement, the stream of visionaries and rebels who can't or won't conform to the common norms and established truths forced on us by authority. Looking back over the occult – the Freemasons, the Illuminati, the witches, magician Aleister Crowley, once named 'the most evil man on earth', the plot offers a deep historical insight. Starting in 1457 Bavaria, where Phil, in a previous incarnation, meets his fate at the hands of the unscrupulous local baron, through to the first joint that was lit at the beginning of the Jazz Era, till LSD is discovered. The Warp follows the evolution of the global counterculture. It joyously melds elements of music hall, science fiction, story telling, sex and adventure into a unique theatrical experience.

The hippie priestess duly handed round her own leaflets. The conference finished with fancy dress and radical karaoke at a local pub in Finsbury Park.

May Day began sunny and warm, light and space emphasized as small knots of protesters emerged from the techno depths of Westminster Station. Groups had already begun to collect in Parliament Square, many brandishing gardening tools and carrying flowers: bedding plants, geraniums, sunflowers and seeds. The whole affair was light-hearted and had a carnival atmosphere. A tout sold party whistles and blowers and did a brisk trade, as did a vegan food seller. Legal observers in red jerkins patrolled and handed out yellow 'bust' cards. Everybody had mobile phones or video cameras.

Meanwhile there was the usual queue for Westminster Abbey and open-top tourist buses took uncomprehending tourists around the square as they clicked their cameras at the growing number of fancy dress costumes (a cheer when these arrived) and cyclists (another cheer). The crowd appeared friendly, organic, amorphous and fluid. Some of the fancy dress participants, including a man in a 'Scream' outfit and scythe and a man dressed as Pan, were photographed and interviewed by journalists and television reporters; the Green candidate for the London mayoral election stepped out to be interviewed. Someone was selling the good news about Jesus – but no one wanted it that day.

As the day progressed, the road began to fill up, clogging traffic. An unsuspecting driver found his car surrounded as protesters attempted to 'plant' flowers on his roof. After a few minutes' commotion (very scary for the driver), the police intervened and all returned to a party atmosphere. Later, the square's own turf would be 'replanted' in the road, whilst a maypole was erected and huge black and green banners hung from lampposts by acrobatic feminist climbers.

Things were not entirely to be taken at mere face value. Hidden discreetly but visibly behind every available corner were police and vans. True, however, these police were not dressed for a riot. Also in one corner, masked, black-clad and furtive, were a small group of teenage ALF supporters. The usual surveillance teams sat on the roofs of buildings and the angry buzz of a helicopter crossed the crowd of carnival musicians.

The day's celebrations were to be coordinated by flags: black for the anarchist movement, green for ecology, which meant 'converge', and red for socialism and 'action'. It was under the red flags that in the early afternoon about half the crowd blowing whistles and banging drums moved down Whitehall towards Downing Street. The attack on Downing Street was little more than ritualistic – flying beer cans and chanting. The gated road was protected by a barrier and riot police. McDonald's restaurant further up towards Trafalgar Square was an easier and more precise target as the food chain had long been the bête noir of anarchist ecologists and had been embroiled in a long-running libel case (McLibel 1994)* that it had recently only partially won. Protesters accused McDonald's of destroying rainforests to create pasture and then 'murdering millions of animals'. Locked about an hour previously but not shuttered, and defended by a half-dozen ordinary uniformed 'bobbies', the restaurant was a sitting target.

The attack began as the crowds gathered to watch a number of masked (and unmasked) protesters try to kick in the plate-glass windows and doors. These proved resistant until a burly rugger-playing type kicked in the door to enormous applause. Curiously this assailant appeared rather different from the rest – more like an office worker in dress and appearance. Later he appeared in no press photos and in no photos of the event and the question remains as to his role.

---

*Helen Steel and Dave Morris, the defendants, were both long-standing anarchist protesters.

(It is quite conceivable that he acted as an agent provocateur – but for whom?) The place was soon ransacked by ALF and others and the crowd moved towards Trafalgar Square, which had already been occupied by the Haringey Solidarity Group (HSG) and the activists with the red flags. As protesters moved into Trafalgar Square, twelve white police vans cut off the Whitehall/Parliament Square end of the demonstration. First police cordoned off Trafalgar Square at the St Martin's Lane end. Abuse followed from protesters with some attempts at a rush. It was all half-hearted, people got bored, drifted away and went home. Another riot was over.

The next day the Prime Minister, Tony Blair, spoke from the Cenotaph about a new dark age of 'disrespect'. The papers were full of pictures of destruction and 'rioting yobs'. But they were also full of pictures of Winston Churchill's statue, spray painted and topped by a large strip of grass-covered turf. This was perhaps anarchist aesthetics' greatest hour – Winston Churchill in a green Mohican, a punk Winston for the new millennium. This was spontaneous art of a high order, equivalent to Marcel Duchamp putting a moustache on the Mona Lisa. This beat Damien Hirst's 'shark' and Tracey Emin's 'bed'. This was anarchism's greatest photo-opportunity in Tony Blair's new swinging Britain.

Not surprisingly the papers next day were full of articles berating the mindless vandals who had attacked both Winston Churchill's statue and the Cenotaph. The *Mirror*, with stories on five pages, led with the headline 'THIS WAS THEIR VILEST HOUR' juxtaposed against a colour picture of 'hippy' protesters with balloons and cut-out cardboard flowers standing raising their fists and laughing defiantly on Churchill's plinth (2 May 2000). Tony Blair was quoted condemning 'the mindless thuggery' and the injuries to twelve police. 'It is only because of the bravery and courage of our war dead that these idiots can live in a free country at all,' the *Mirror* quoted him as saying. A double-page spread was devoted to 'nail[ing] the yobs' who destroyed McDonald's. Its reporter Barbara Davies (one of a *Mirror* team of ten covering the events), with a weather eye for the sensationalism needed of a tabloid, could not resist a tone of hysteria.

> One minute they were singing and laughing, strumming guitars and playing drums. Next they were hurling missiles at police – which landed indiscriminately.
>
> Alongside the militants I saw smartly dressed, middle-aged people handing out leaflets for more moderate causes and groups such as the Green Party and genetically modified foods.
>
> 'We are here to highlight the fact that we can't go on abusing our planet', said Teresa Arnold. 'We don't condone violence but people feel strongly'.

I watched sickened as Trafalgar Square, usually bustling with tourists, buses and taxis, became a forum for destruction, littered with beer cans, smashed bottles and paint and covered in graffiti.

Women squatted in the streets to relieve themselves while men turned doorways into urinals.

I had been in the riots last November and I knew what these people were capable of.

The violence of mob rule is unlike anything I have experienced.

While the young and the old, the skinheads, the smartly dressed and the students muttered about their beliefs, their causes seemed to disappear in the mood of hatred which descended across the crowd.

By the time the square had become embroiled in the ugliness of violence, the only thing they had in common was their determination to damage the great landmark and hurt the police.

Those of us caught between the mob and the riot squad were at the mercy of them both.

We were pushed back by the officers to find a similar solid black line behind us.

It was a terrifying experience.

The *Sun* (which had twelve reporters and photographers at the event) managed to find the occupants of the car mobbed in Trafalgar Square.

Driver Martin Eentan and his pregnant wife Marion endured a frightening half-hour ordeal as their Mercedes sports car was surrounded, kicked and vandalised.

Marion said, 'It was terrifying, I couldn't stop crying'. (2 May 2000)

Moreover they also had reporters stationed at McDonald's restaurant in Whitehall (almost certainly a journalistic fiction) whose description of the attack on the premises suggested the escape of diners via a back door accomplished in the nick of time as a swarm of anarchists broke down the front, the ALF happily distributing stolen (and meat-filled) burgers!

More than 20 terrified diners, including kids, were quickly ushered out through a back entrance.

Onlookers cheered as the thugs smashed furniture and fixtures with sledgehammers, tore down the restaurant's golden arches sign and sprayed graffiti.

They grabbed burgers and chips and distributed them outside.

It soon turned out that at least some of the 'mindless thugs' pictured in the *Mirror* and the *Sun* were also from the highly intelligent and wealthy upper middle classes. Three days after the riot the *Express* crowed 'ETON BOY ARRESTED AT RIOT' (4 May 2000) and smugly headlined the expulsion from Eton of seventeen-year-old animal liberationist Matthew MacDonald, son of a professor of mathematics at Brunel University and a King's Scholar, after it had become known that he had been detained by police (although not yet convicted of anything).

This was a small riot: twelve police injured, one restaurant destroyed, a new lawn needed for Parliament Square and an amusing arrest. Once the blame had been apportioned to yobs and upper-class rich kids the papers lost interest. But the situation was far more complicated and confused. We have already seen that the day was to be coordinated by various coloured flags – green, black and red – but it would only be the red flags (the traditional flag of socialist revolutionaries) that would prove of any significance.

These particular flags had arrived in Parliament Square around eleven o'clock in the morning, waved not by green protesters but by two Kurdish liberation groups, the Turkish Revolutionary Communist Party (TIBK) and the Turkish Communist Party/Marxist Leninist Group (TKP/ML). These groups were not New Agers but traditional Maoist revolutionaries whose flags had yellow hammer and sickle emblems (both crossed by a Kalashnikov). It was the raising of these banners that led the march past Downing Street and into Trafalgar Square and some of these groups helped in the attack on McDonald's. With their occupation of the plinth of Nelson's Column accompanied by the HSG who had helped accomplish the manoeuvre they effectively barred the way to 5,000 Rover Group trade unionists protesting against recent job loss announcements. Press photographs clearly showed Kurdish graffiti alongside or over anarchist slogans on the plinth to Churchill's statue (in red) and on the figure's coat (in pink). For the papers it was easier to blame 4,000 rioters in Trafalgar Square (there were probably between 5,000 and 8,000) than to look for complex and more traditional causes elsewhere. Effectively, a pacifist 'celebration' had been hijacked by elements which had joined the event later in the afternoon and by a foreign militant-dissident group. Months later it was still possible to read sprayed on the corner of Farringdon Lane and Clerkenwell Road the enigmatic slogan, 'TIKB Long Live May Day'.

If fascism was the bogeyman of the 1930s, Communism of the 1950s, Trotskyism of the 1960s and Militant of the 1980s then anarchism fulfilled that role for the 1990s. With the growingly similar policies of (New) Labour and the Conservatives and an obvious increase in bureaucratization both from government and from external agencies like the European Union it became increasingly obvious that extra-parliamentary action and direct action might be the only way to create changes which traditional lobbying had failed to bring about. Greenpeace had long led the way in this area, and at the end of the millennium was deeply involved with a well-publicized attack on a field of genetically modified (GM) crops carried out in white radiation-protection outfits. As with other protest groups, anarchists soon realized the significance of the media, which could be used to publicize large demonstrations and hype relatively minor events. Concerns about ecology, road building, capitalism and Third World debt could be used as a rallying point for those sympathetic middle classes who felt guilty over the destruction of calves or the countryside or who were attracted to organic food and who retained vestiges of an older liberalism. Indeed, linking global issues to local concerns seemed in some sense to re-awaken the spirit of the 1960s which had been cynically exploited by Labour in its successful bid for power in 1997. Labour's hijacking of the outward trappings of the 1960s without the underlying ethos seemed to expose the corruption both of government and of the very liberalism that had supported Tony Blair (as a boy) and which Margaret Thatcher had declared anathema: was it not the case that Tony Blair was an admirer of the Iron Lady? What was Labour's 'Cool Britannia' but a slogan in which the entire history of the counterculture could have been presented as leading to a Labour victory – Labour and its 'presidential' style parliamentary politics as nothing less than the correct focus for a caring alternative and multicultural society. The green movement had long since been co-opted by governments and turned into a mere lobby group (the Green Party candidate dropped out of the London mayoral contest).

The failure of 1960s mainstream radical protest still left a 'remnant' which survived in sufficient numbers to create *secret* protest movements based around festivals and travelling. These new, if disparate, movements, based upon Avalonian, druidic, hippie-punk and rave cultures took an alternative view of the organic community (ecological and folkloristic) which they put into *practical* effect *within* mass culture. This was popular culture (and revolt), within mass culture (and consensus), lived simultaneously.

> Throughout the 1970s and 1980s, fairs, free festivals and gatherings began to proliferate throughout southern and eastern England, some peaceful, some confrontational; some hippy, some punk; some legal, some illegal. For many organisers, the inspiration was as much California as 'merry old England', extending and adapting Monterey, Altamont or New York State's Woodstock cultures. The use of 'Albion' [moreover] illustrate[d] a desire for a truly alternative society, even an alternative history, a dub version of Britain.[1]

Such constructions of history, myth and self were, however, *self-aware*. These were conscious attempts to remake a social environment *of choice* based on a third, though 'organic', communal sense: nostalgic and contemporary.

By the late 1980s, such groups as made up the 'Albion Free State' had allied themselves with more conformist groups and individuals protesting against the poll tax, veal exports and unnecessary road developments. Dongas (road protesters), travellers and Tree People became the new 'enemy within', vilified in the popular media but ironically turned into eco-icons by many ordinary readers. The margin was now centre; had, finally, come home for a few brief radical moments when the critics weren't looking, put up its banners and maypole in Parliament Square, created a 'guerrilla garden' and had itself a riot.

It is dangerous to idealize the events of 1 May 2000. They illustrated the danger of loose networks and spontaneity whose core contained a complex and unclear melange of issues open to appropriation by violent, neo-fascist or uncontrollable elements who did little except divert attention from the issues at hand. Equally of concern were those anarchist-communitarian developments (so-called non-hierarchical determinants) that could easily lead not to liberation but to cantonment, retrogression, neo-feudalism, aimless nomadism and accumulative primitivism. Moreover, one cannot turn a blind eye to the fact that the often confusing mixture of elements that make up anarchist protest also make it prone to infiltration by fascist and Nazi ideologies – especially within class war and animal liberation. Nor can one ignore the fact that earlier syndicalist and anarchist spontaneity failed to unite the working classes before and after the First World War, a consequence of which was ironically the creation of the Communist Party of Great Britain.

Conservatives soon learned the lesson that direct action paid off. Media coverage of French farmers and hauliers showed that governments listened when ports and cities were blockaded by those in charge of transportation. Anarchist opposition to road building and government eco-taxation could be challenged by tax-paying motorists. Equally, the countryside began to gather as a powerful lobby under the immediate sting of the Labour government's adoption of anti-fox-hunting legislation and its incompetent handling of an epidemic of foot-and-mouth disease. Direct action by right-wing traditionalists and Conservative entrepreneurs could also be used as a powerful tool to *halt* legislative change that undermined established ways of life or threatened freedom of consumer choice. If the hauliers' lobby was only partially successful in its attempt to reduce petrol duty in line with Europe it was, by its adept use of the media, the clogging of motorways and Parliament Square and by the closing of petrol stations able to show how dangerous such direct action can become when orchestrated by a powerful *commercial* alliance. The Countryside Alliance, which emerged from this background and which contained members of the fuel lobby, was without doubt the most significant lobby group to have emerged in many years, as an ironic and unexpected result of British anarchist protest!

On Sunday 22 September 2002, the Alliance organized a vast protest march through Central London. The 'March for Liberty and Livelihood', which encompassed a range of issues from rural unemployment to fox-hunting, saw over 400,000 protesters converge on Westminster from starting points at Hyde Park Corner and the Embankment. The march was entirely peaceful, and was, until exceeded by the 'Not In My Name' anti-war march of Saturday 15 February 2003, the largest seen in London for over a hundred years [see Introduction to this edition for developments since 2002].

27

The Man in the Third Carriage

7/7 and its Consequences

T. S. Eliot called the Thames 'a strong brown god' and for two thousand years it has flowed through London an immutable and implacable force, indifferent to the human drama enacted daily on its banks. 'Almost forgotten' the river flows on as a 'reminder of what [we] choose to forget'.

For untold millennia, London's river flowed slower, wider, more shallow. This came to an end with the great Embankment Scheme of 1864 carried out by the Metropolitan Board of Works' Chief Engineer, Joseph Bazalgette (1819–91). The new Embankment smoothed and raised the banks of the Thames and added over thirty-seven acres of land to London, infill which became gardens and a main road as well as extending the Metropolitan and District's railway line and hiding London's new main sewer. For the first time London had a continuous waterfront that was not merely a series of wharves, docks, water stairs and muddy creeks. Bazalgette's great achievement not only beautified the city but it also put millions of tons of solid earth where thousands of years of London's history had been enacted. The old waterfront, on its gently sloping banks, now found itself high and dry some hundreds of yards from the water, the old medieval by-pass of Carter Lane finally replaced by a wide and majestic road built for cars, lorries, buses and trams. The little Walbrook stream had vanished under bricks and mortar as early as 1440 and by the sixteenth century had been all but forgotten. The Fleet had re-emerged briefly in the seventeenth century when it was emptied of filth and rebanked, but it too succumbed when Farringdon Street was built over it. Once it had had a splendid bridge decorated with pineapples; London's first daily paper, the *Daily Courant*, was published nearby, giving birth to a new industry. The Fleet had an even nobler past, flowing alongside Henry VIII's splendid Bridewell Palace where the Holy Roman Emperor Maximilian had feasted and danced. Yet Edward VI had given the palace to the City Corporation as a hospital and prison, which by 1862 had also finally closed its doors. On its site at 14 New Bridge Street (leading to Blackfriars Bridge) arose a hotel and a Victorian office block. The old gates and courtyard light remain to this day, forgotten and unmarked. Only the Lea still flows to the east, drained of its marshes and straightened in its course to take the malt barges from Hertfordshire to Bow (now the barges are gone).

The political life of London also flows through every street and thoroughfare of the city, organized by the urban geometry first imagined by the Romans and developed ever since by successive generations whose political aspirations take them on marches through concrete and asphalt landscapes towards the heart of power.

The core of Westminster's democratic system has long been confrontational, with parties sitting opposite each other in order to reinforce both a ritualized and sometimes actual combative relationship. Thus, the very nature of our system, developed in fits and starts, without plan or forethought, is not consensual but competitive division. Such division is itself a compromise brought about by a long and tedious guerrilla war fought against monarchs and aristocrats who themselves have, on occasion, rallied the people to their defence.

Since the 1980s it has been clear that the British democratic system, a system that has evolved as a fluid and complex compromise (the 'British Constitution'), has moved into yet another phase in its short history. London has been particularly susceptible to such change. The long consensual moratorium agreed on so many issues between Liberals, Conservatives and Labour created groups so marginalized that only by occupying the centre of the capital could they make their voice heard. Right-wing farmers, foxhunters, hippie travellers, anarchists, punks and old-age pensioners take to the streets, march, cycle and blockade until Westminster is forced to listen.

Meanwhile, under threat from IRA terrorists, 'Islamic' extremists and anarchist nomads, the very centre of British political life has become an armed camp. Surveillance cameras watch from every building, street corner, tunnel or station, recording every detail of life on the street for ordinary Londoners whose every move in shop, office or petrol station is also filmed, documented and filed. The ancient City itself is ringed with checkpoints and unmarked vehicles travel the streets filled with armed police. The ring of steel around London, more insidious because of our acquiescence, remains long after the IRA ceased fire, a deterrent to any and every foe who might break our laws or threaten our lives. The Thames is quiet now, few arrive or leave London by it, but Heathrow is full of gun-toting police and immigration and customs officials are armed with powers little scrutinized by the public. Few of us object, most of us feel safe and reassured.

The river remains a reminder of what we choose to forget: that the British have always made governments that balance on the fragile edge of the people's tolerance and that nowhere is that edge so sharp as in London, home to monarchs, the financial crucible of the City and the fulcrum of Parliament. Devolution and provincialism have hardly blunted London's centrality to the affairs of Britain and the world. It is still London that provides the enduring focus for political dissent and terrorist threat.

The bombing of the World Trade Center in New York in 1999 signalled that new terrorist threats might also come from extreme Islamic fundamentalists angry at American support for Israel and British support for America. The Gulf War heightened awareness of the complexities of the issues. On 17 October 2000 a man of 'Algerian' appearance attacked a Chasidic Jew named David Meyers with a hunting or large kitchen knife on a bus going from Aldgate to Euston. Luckily the incident was isolated but anti-Israeli propaganda began to increase as the election of 2001 came closer. MPs who supported the new Anti-Terrorism Act or who openly backed Israel were targeted in areas where a Muslim swing might oust them. The Association of Ilford Muslims (AIM) thus targeted Ilford South MP Mike Gapes with leaflets in Urdu, Gujerati and English that accused him of 'Islamophobia'. Gapes nevertheless still retains his seat.

A much more serious threat came from semi-secret organizations working with Islamic revolutionaries such as Osama bin Laden and with connections inside Pakistan, Kashmir and Afghanistan. Al-Muhajiroun was one such group, whose activists were becoming more aggressive in their actions. One member, Amer Mirza, petrol-bombed a West London army base in response to the organization's call for a jihad against the US and British governments. An unidentified bomber also attacked another army base in East London. Raucous demonstrations simultaneously occurred outside Downing Street. After a 'Jihad for Chechnya' meeting during December 1999, a Russian film crew was beaten up. Furthermore a growing network of extreme freedom fighters were being sent to fight in Yemen under the direction of Abu Hamza (Mohammed) al-Masri and 'Sheik' Omar Bakri Muhammed from a head office in Tottenham.

The Prevention of Terrorism Act 2000 replaced the Prevention of Terrorism (Temporary Provisions) Act 1974, which had been mainly directed at Irish nationalists. Through a complex chain of further legislation both permanent and temporary as well as a judicial review conducted by Lord Lloyd of Berwick a new anti-terrorism Bill which did not violate the Human Rights Act 2000 came into being.

It became quite clear, however, that the new law was partly intended as a defensive measure not only against known political terrorist groups but also against the growth of so-called fundamentalist Muslim organizations that were increasingly target-ing the United States, Britain, France and Israel. Al-Muhajiroun put out a press statement as the Bill was debated.

> Al-Muhajiroun, on behalf of Muslims in Britain, want to make it clear to the Blair government that they will not be deterred from supporting the Mujahideen in Kashmir, Chechnya, Palestine or indeed in Iraq since we do this as a divine obligation and this is not a matter of negotiation or compromise. It appears from the proposed Bill that Muslim activists who are working to overthrow the corrupted regimes in Muslim countries are now to be the tar-get of a witch-hunt by the British government in order to secure its economic, military and political interests in those countries, at the expense of the interests of Muslims.[1]

In parallel, civil liberty campaigners, environmentalists and ani-mal rights activists were alarmed at being seen as 'terrorists'.

The Bill nevertheless was designed to curb international 'hate' organizations and strengthen the power of the state, especially in stopping money-laundering and transfers amongst terrorists. 'Ultra'-Muslims saw the threat as directed against them alone as fourteen of the twenty-one proscribed groups were Islamic. In this they were justified.

> Al-Qa'ida,* Egyptian Islamic Jihad, al-Gama'at al-Islamiya, Armed Islamic Group (GIA), Salafist Group for Call and Combat (GSPC), Babbar Khalsa, International Sikh Youth Federation, Harakat Mujahideen, Jaish e Mohammed, Lashkar e Tayyaba, Liberation Tigers of Tamil Eelam (LTTE), Hezbollah External Security Organ-isation, Hamas – Izz al-Din al-Qassem Brigades, Palestinian Islamic Jihad (PIJ – Shaqaqi), Abu Nidal Organization, Islamic Army of Aden, Mujaheddin e Khalq (MKO), Kurdistan Workers' Party (PKK), Revolutionary People's Liberation Party – Front (DHKP-C), Basque Homeland and Liberty (ETA), 17 November Revolutionary Organisation.[2]

Despite Omar Bakri Mohammed's fatwa on the Bill it neverthe-less passed into law during July, apparently proof of Britain 'remain-ing subservient to the Zionist occupation' [of 'Palestine'] and of her 'subservience to the USA'. The cataclysmic events of 11 September 2001 and the loss of over 3,000 people in the Twin Towers in New York seemed merely to harden and confirm both sides in their beliefs,

---

*The government spelling is not used by most commentators. I have ren-dered it as al-Qaeda throughout.

with promises by David Blunkett, the Home Secretary, to strengthen the Act by quickening extradition procedures, hardening immigration laws and giving greater powers to the police. Sheik Omar awaited arrest by Special Branch and the world awaited the outcome of the Allies' attack on Kabul on 7 October 2001.

A year after '9/11' (the name given to the September 11 bombings) most of the world was holding sombre memorial ceremonies. Yet on Sunday 25 August, al-Muhajiroun held a small rally in Trafalgar Square in support of the action taken by al-Qaeda extremists the previous year. When chanting of Osama bin Laden's name was encouraged by one of the speakers, Sulayman Keeler, the stage was rushed by BNP and NF counter-demonstrators shouting, 'England, England, England'. On the first anniversary of the New York attack a number of supporters of bin Laden met at Finsbury Park Mosque to express their support for the attacks, which speakers called 'legitimate'. The main speaker was Abu Hamza. He was accompanied by Omar Bakri Mohammed and Dr Mohammed al-Mass'ari, who had previously run al-Qaeda's press office in London. The meeting threatened terrorist reprisals in the United Kingdom. The following week, on the night of 18/19 September, six men were arrested in London on terrorism charges after an operation by the Metropolitan Police Anti-Terrorist branch and MI5. The group did not include the speakers at Finsbury Park Mosque.

As I finished the first edition of *Violent London* the consequences of the death throes of the Taliban had yet to show in the streets of London; increasing numbers of supporters of both the Palestinians and Israelis occupied Hyde Park or Trafalgar Square as war continued to flare in the Middle East; anarchists made their hatred of global capitalism felt outside the Albert Hall as Henry Kissinger sweet-talked business leaders inside; Greenpeace supporters occupied the Cabinet Office in protest at the alleged use of rainforest wood for two civil service doors; May Day marchers let their anger show in wealthy Mayfair; the Countryside Alliance marched, swiftly followed by marches against Britain's involvement with America's plans to invade Iraq. The official end of the second Gulf War left continuing doubts over the reason for the conflict and the efficacy of the outcome: no weapons of mass destruction had been found, Saddam Hussein remained at large and more and more casualties were occurring among the forces of occupation. Many British people remained sceptical about George Bush's motives and were unhappy at Tony Blair's acquiescence in the situation. Thus the state visit of President Bush during November 2003 was bound to be controversial.

Unprecedented security meant that half the Metropolitan Police (reported in the press as 14,000 officers, but actually 14,000 officer shifts) would join 400 American agents (250 armed) in protecting

Bush during his stay at Buckingham Palace and meeting with Blair. Protection against terrorist attack and attempted assassination were uppermost in Deputy Assistant Commissioner Andy Trotter's mind when, on 17 November, Lindis Percy, a vicar's wife from Hull, breached the police cordon around the palace, climbed the gates and unfurled a protest banner declaring, 'Elizabeth Windsor, George Bush is not welcome here'. On 19 November, a day of 'civil unrest', there were demonstrations in the Mall and on the next day the official demonstration of the 'Stop the War' campaign, the biggest ever on a weekday, estimated at 130,000 by the organizers and 70,000 by the police, marched down Whitehall to a rally in Trafalgar Square. On the same day two massive car bombs were detonated in Istanbul killing, among others, the British Consul-General, Roger Short. London's political street life continued.

*

The borders of London have become porous. Once, invaders had to land on the south coast and fight their way inland, the hazards of fortifications and wild countryside slowing their progress. They might take the river route, slowly sailing up the Thames from its mouth in the North Sea. Either way, it would be a long trip with the ever present hazard of discovery as an enemy negotiated the seventy miles or so to the centre of the capital. Nevertheless, with the coming of air travel all that was to change, a fact that wasn't fully grasped until after 9/11. Heathrow, Stansted and Gatwick now form the 'virtual' borders of the capital and not the Port of London through which the threats to Victorian and Edwardian London flowed. Our airports now form the vulnerable and porous links which bind us to the dangerous world outside. The border is now a just a Piccadilly Line ticket away from Leicester Square. And this joins the whole underground system to our border structure and to the transport network that keeps the capital's human traffic flowing like an artery. An attack on either the airports or on the tube network is effectively an attack on the vital organs of movement.

Yet there is another way in which the old security of the border has effectively been breached. The Internet has flattened the world, allowing information flows and communications instantly between countries. It is, itself, a type of border and is now monitored by GCHQ and others as if it were a true border. Yet its power for instant response has meant that this border is even closer than an airport because it is already in your house, in the silent corner of a bedroom, perhaps. It is this dual space, where communication on the Internet may lead to attacks on the transport infrastructure, that terrorism has occupied before, during and after 9/11. This new threat, which uses the latest technology to radicalize Muslims in the name of an Islamic ideology that poses as more 'pure' and therefore more original than later interpretations, is the culmination of ideas that had been fermenting for almost four decades in Egypt and elsewhere, but which had now gained a supreme communicative tool to spread its hatred of Western values.

The roots of al-Qaeda lay with the ideas and actions of men such as Ayman al-Zawahiri, originally to oppose Egyptian foreign policy one of the men responsible for the assassination of president Anwar el-Sadat and the attempted assassination of Hosni Mubarak. The original revolutionary group was joined by the most famous revolutionary since Che Guevara, the Saudi Arabian Osama (or Usama) bin Laden who was born in 1957 into a wealthy engineering family. His conversion to jihad and the politics of Islam, meant that his money could fulfil much that was dreamt of by the original organization. Whilst living in Sudan, bin Laden combined Islamic revolutionary activity with hard-nosed capitalist construction projects. It was the Afghan war against the Russians that finally moved bin Laden and his millions to Afghanistan and Pakistan where in 1984, he set up a 'guesthouse' for Islamic freedom fighters. In creating a network of contacts through the guesthouse, al-Qaeda or 'the network' was essentially formed as it runs today. Westernization had to be fought by a new jihad against the West, and the United States and its allies who were now seen as the real enemy.

The organization was now large and growing, international in scope and provided for by front organizations and corporations. Bin Laden however came to realize the power of the Internet in terms of propaganda. His image was to become the image of the new world after the fall of communism, as ubiquitous and recognizable as any celebrity, and a celebrity he has become to millions of dissatisfied Muslims who cannot make their accommodation with the West. This situation was greatly increased by the ease with which video and other material can get on to the Web and then circulate freely in cyber space where it may be viewed or downloaded in the privacy of the home or (teenage) bedroom; even homes of which al-Qaeda knew nothing in West London, in East London, in Luton, Birmingham or Leeds might gather the seeds of jihad for another day.

Recruitment could go on through such informal exchange networks until the recipient was willing to take things to the next step of being trained in bomb construction, fighting techniques and martyrdom. Jihad material as a revolutionary tool is effective because it creates a generalized hatred of things in the decadent West, provides a sense of communal solidarity to young males (and sometimes females) and gives a set of violent solutions to what appears to be intractable problems – in short it empowers those who feel impotent. Books, videos and dvds of jihadi material and of sermons preaching hate, mobile phone networks, chat rooms, I-pods all circulate to create a fanatical atmosphere where imaginative dreaming of holy war may finally be turned to account. In October 1968, Sheik Muhammad Abu-Zahra, then operating from in Cairo, defined jihad.

> Jihad is not confined to the summoning of troops and the establishment of huge forces. It takes various forms . . . . [T]here should arise a group of people reinforced with faith, well equipped with means and methods; and then let them set about the usurpers . . . until their abode is one of everlasting torment . . . Jihad will never end [until] the Day of Judgement.[3]

It was a powerful message: the last day of judgement, a war to the end, fought by any means using any tactics, but containing one supreme weapon – fear. Al-Qaeda would become the supreme terrorist organization. These messages held great appeal for those who were second generation *British Muslim* boys whose searching for a grounding in their roots had found instead the world of al-Qaeda in which their own social alienation was finally revealed. Such a revelation came not to those who were necessarily poor and socially excluded but to those whose social background was comfortable, whose families were stable, whose education and sporting inclinations were British, but who held to a sense of 'intellectual' alienation and social injustice they felt only jihad in the name of Sharia answered. S. K. Malik, a Pakistani brigadier suggested the psychological component of terror in Islamic warfare in 1979. 'Terror', the brigadier suggested, 'is not only a means, it is the end in itself'. Indeed, 'once a condition of terror into the opponent's heart is obtained hardly anything is left to be achieved.' It was the 'means and the end'; it was the decisive 'decision'.[4]

Monitored by the security services of the United States, the mujahedeen had, during 1979 to 1984, originally been supported by the United States in its war with Russia, but since the assassination of Sadat this alliance had fractured. By 1986 the first training camp, Al Masadah, had been set up and in 1988 al-Qaeda itself had been formed. In the same year bin Laden set up the International Islamic Front for jihad against the Jews and Crusaders, thus revealing the next targets. As early as 1992, bin Laden targeted American forces in the Sudan and on 23 February 1993, the first attempt was made to blow up the World Trade Center. The numerous attacks that followed culminated in the successful and spectacular demolition of the Twin Towers, and the declaration by President George W. Bush of the 'war on terror'. The invasion of Iraq and the search for bin Laden in Afghanistan would prove a burning fuse.

The first ominous inkling of something not right in the capital and that the security forces were preparing for an attack of some sort was staged as a gas attack on the London Underground in September 2003 in order to test London's defences. The gas was meant to be sarin, the poison used in the Tokyo underground attacks on 20 March 1995. The exercise was a failure with gaps in communication and problems with applying the theory to the immediacy of the situation. In the four years of phoney war, it was all a bad joke. Abu Hamza al-Masri, a cleric with an eye patch and metal hook was Britain's favourite Islamic scare figure, stirring up hatred in Hackney and Finsbury Park whilst claiming benefits. He was Britain's favourite ranting lunatic in 2004, called 'Hooky' or 'Captain Hook' by the tabloids. A year earlier, security at Buckingham Palace had been breached when Aaron Barshak, had got into a party thrown for Prince William dressed as Osama bin Laden in a dress!

Things, however, were getting progressively more serious. On 30 June 2004, illegal Algerian immigrant Kamel Bourgass was sentenced for a plot to kill thousands with ricin. Bourgass was already under investigation whilst living in Islington, but was 'lost' to the security services and not discovered until he turned up at a Manchester bedsit. In his struggle to escape he had knifed to death a policeman, Stephen Oake. The alleged al-Qaeda cell of which he was a part intended to smear the poison along the Holloway Road in London and to attack the Underground with a cyanide spray. The plot had appeared very serious: an attack with biochemical weapons. Police had raided a flat in Wood Green, north London on 5 January 2003 and arrested six men on suspicion of the manufacture of ricin. On 12 January a further twelve people were arrested in Bournemouth, but on 14 January the raid in Manchester went wrong and detective constable Oake died trying to arrest Bourgass and three other men. Samples of bomb-making equipment sent to the Biological Weapon Identification Group at the Porton Down Defence Science and Technology Laboratory found no trace of ricin, a fact withheld from the public. The police and MI5 had known where Bourgass had been plotting and with whom, but had done nothing, but watch him. It was time to act decisively. So on 20 January a hundred armed police finally raided Finsbury Park Mosque which was suspected to be the centre of this and other conspiracies. It was the centre for much more besides.

Bourgass's conversion to Islamic fundamentalism was blamed on or exacerbated by his attending Finsbury Park Mosque (after 2005, renamed the North London Central Mosque) which was becoming known as a centre for radicalized ideology after Abu Hamza al-Masri had been installed as Iman in 1996 and had been preaching and promulgating more and more extreme views about Islam and the West. The mosque had started well. It is a large red brick building near Finsbury Park underground station and Arsenal football club's Emirates Stadium and it was opened by the Prince of Wales in 1994. The mosque soon got a reputation for revolution, however, gathering Algerian exiles and home-grown enthusiasts or converts. Richard Reid (the 'Shoe Bomber') was said to have attended the mosque, some of the 7/7 bombers attended sermons, men loyal to the Chechen warlord Shamil Basayev were known to go there and the ricin plotters also were said to have been. Jihadist sermons were preached as well as the death of non-believers and weapons training was said to go on secretly in the basement. It was also a central information centre for al-Qaeda and its operations.

At the core of these activities was Abu Hamsa, born Mustafa Kamel Mustafa in Alexandria in Egypt on 15 April 1958. On 16 May 1980 he married a Muslim convert called Valerie Traverso to gain a British passport and after three years of marriage became a British citizen despite the fact that the marriage was invalid because Traverso was not properly divorced. Hamsa later divorced and remarried producing a large family. His radicalization led him to Yemen and Bosnia where he fought in the extremist Arab Wahabbi mujahidin before going to Afghanistan to clear landmines left by the Russians and where he claimed he had lost an eye and his hand. Having got the position of Iman, his extremism led to his being suspended in 2002 and then dismissed from the mosque in 2003 by the Charity Commission. Needless to say, he carried on preaching in the road outside the mosque to much media publicity. He led 'Supporters of Sharia' who wished to impose Sharia law in Britain and he also addressed a rally held by al-Mujahiroun, open supporters of al-Qaeda. On 27 May 2004, he was finally detained by the police as the United States wanted to extradite him for allegedly helping to set up a terrorist training camp in Oregon.

Yet it was not this that finally settled the account. On 26 August 2004, the Iman was arrested under section 41 of the Terrorism Act 2000 which covers the propagation or instigation of terrorism. Inexplicably released and then re-arrested on 19 October. He was charged with sixteen crimes including encouraging race hatred and murder. The trial was to begin on 5 July 2005, two days before the fateful railway journeys of the 7/7 bombers, but had to be postponed until 9 January 2006 when he was eventually convicted and sentenced to 57 years and 11 months to run concurrently, 7 years after which he may be extradited to the United States.

Whilst Hamsa amused and irritated the public by turns a more sinister presence loomed behind him. Omar Bakri Muhammed (born in 1958 in Syria and named Omar Bakri Fostock) was brought up within a devout family and from an early age immersed in religious teachings. At the Sari'ah Institute at Damascus University he also became politicized and joined the Muslim Brotherhood but did not take part in their revolutionary activity. Having finished university in 1979, he left Syria for Egypt and then Saudi Arabia. Whilst in Lebanon he is thought to have joined Hizb-ut-Tahrir and organized its cells in Cairo and in Saudi, but after the organization was banned there, he formed another faction called al-Muhajiroun. He was twice arrested in Saudi, but was able to leave for Britain on 14 January 1986 also travelling to the United States. He moved to Tottenham with his wife and his six children and proceeded to live on welfare benefits. In Britain he worked with Hizb-ut-Tahrir, but fell out over policy and 'left'. For some time Bakri had made cause with international Islamist culture but not with jihad, an attitude that changed immediately after 9/11. Bakri was excited that al-Qaeda had struck and he openly praised the bombers and made quite clear his support for jihad against a 'hostile West'. The security forces waited and watched and may have actually facilitated some of Bakri's activities. Despite public outrage nothing was done. In November 2004, feeling immune from prosecution, Bakri began setting up his revolution (apparently despite 'warnings' from MI5 not to go too far) and made even more inflammatory statements some of which may have been a real influence on the London bombers who struck a few months later and who may have co-ordinated some of their plot through Bakri or his huge circle of terrorist associates. He was also linked to a number of prominent al-Qaeda operatives some of whom were based in London. It would be via a chat-room lecture during January 2005 that Bakri would stigmatize Britain as Dar al-Harb or a 'land of war' and thus open the way for the 7 July attacks.

Things were quietly going out of control. On 21 April, at the parliamentary hustings in Bethnal Green prior to the forthcoming election, and as MP Oona King and George Galloway argued about the Iraq war, thirty Islamic radicals broke in and tried to disrupt the meeting. And so slowly and by small degrees, jihad came to London, lightly prepared as it was against the threat and poorly monitored by ill-prepared security services. Home Office information warned of biological weapons and dirty, nuclear or chemical devices exploding in Trafalgar Square, but the porous nature of terror and its international reach would ultimately come down to four men with backpacks and a little chemistry who came from Yorkshire.

It must have seemed to the men as they calmly parked their car at Luton Station and paid their fare to London that the day of final reckoning had arrive. They appeared calm, perhaps not exactly relaxed, but not so nervous as to arouse suspicion. They were determined and knew what they had to do: attack London from the north, south, east and west and do it simultaneously. Mohammad Sidique Khan blew himself up on the 8.50 a.m. Circle Line train from Edgware Road.

He killed six people and injured one hundred and twenty. Sheehzad Tanweer blew himself up and killed seven others and wounded many more on the 8.50 a.m. Circle line train from Liverpool Street heading towards Aldgate. Germaine Lindsay known as Abdullah Shaheed Jamal, since his conversion, exploded his rucksack on the 8.50 a.m. Piccadilly Line train travelling south from King's Cross to Russell Square. Hasib Hussain, unable to get on a train at King's Cross, began to panic, He phoned the others to ask advice, wandered the streets and finally boarded a No. 30 bus. He sat upstairs fiddling with the detonation mechanism. It finally worked at 9.47 a.m., killing thirteen people.

London Transport first reported a 'power surge' which had paralysed the system, but the bus bomb gave the lie to the excuse. London was at war. Throughout the day live broadcasts brought harrowing pictures and much anxiety. The dead and wounded were a cross section of the multi-racial and multi-faceted London that had emerged over the last fifty years. Amongst the dead were Poles and Chinese, Nigerians and Vietnamese, Afghans, Bengalis and Iranians, Muslims, Hindus, Jews and Christians, students and office workers, white, black and brown skinned, male and female, young and old. The dead were a roll call of London's new diverse population.

Andy Hayman was back from the gym and sitting down to his breakfast at New Scotland Yard when he first heard about the crisis. Hayman had worked his way up from his early career in the Essex police. Now he was assistant commissioner, Special Operations in charge of Counter-Terrorism Command and Special Branch and the UK's national counter-terrorism co-ordinator as well. On 7 July he was preoccupied with security discussions for the 2012 Olympics to be held in London. At 8.52 a.m., Suzanna Becks, a senior colleague popped her head round the door to tell Hayman of 'a fire on the Underground'.[5] It was the first hint of the trouble to come. At that point, the City of London police would be dealing with the problem. A few moments later she reported other fires and two deaths from a 'power surge', but fearing this was not the cause Hayman alerted Special Branch.

At 9.07 a.m., Peter Clarke deputy assistant commissioner in charge of the anti-terrorist branch, SO13, reported that policemen were at three scenes with specialists standing by. So far reports from M15 and GCHQ 'revealed nothing'.[6] At 9.15 a.m. 'an emergency' was declared and evacuation began on the tube. London Underground was still co-ordinating the emergency and had set up headquarters at the London Underground Network Operations Centre just behind St James's Station. The crisis had not yet been reported to Sir Ian Blair, the new commissioner, nor to Chris Fox head of ACPO.

Hayman admitted to himself at least that 'we were in a fog'.[7] At 9.47 a.m., the last explosion went off (almost an hour after the others) on the No. 30 bus in Tavistock Square. It produced a frisson of fear. 'Now we had to push the terrorism button hard . . . why hadn't we had an inkling that this was imminent.'[8] All the intelligence agencies were scrambled and forensic teams dispatched and hospitals made ready for casualties. At 9.52 a.m. Hayman told Ian Blair the news that 'we're in the middle of a wave of terrorist attacks'. Blair would be left to deal with strategic questions and public fears. Ian Blair had to make a quick and accurate assessment. He had arrived at a momentous decision an hour later: 'by eleven o'clock he had declared London temporarily shut'.[9] In order to meet the mounting emergency a number of groups and agencies had to co-ordinate their response. They included the Fire Brigade, the Ambulance Service, London Transport, London Transport Police, the Home Office, COBR (Cabinet Office Briefing Room A) and the army. Communications between the services were poorly managed at first. Indeed the various communication systems were not even compatible.

Nevertheless, the Fire Brigade had managed to activate 240 fire fighters and over 50 appliances while there were 200 ambulances and 400 staff dealing with the injured and dead. Hospitals had freed one thousand beds for the wounded and despite shortfalls in communication all the injured had been evacuated in three hours. Meanwhile, at 9.50 a.m., Downing Street called to ask Hayman to meet COBR where he could fully explain the crisis. Hayman left Peter Clarke in charge of tactics whilst he briefed the committee. Chaos in the streets delayed his arrival and he considered simply running to the meeting; the mobile phone network was also paralysed. The Home Secretary, Charles Clarke was in charge of the meeting as Tony Blair was at Gleneagles for the G8 summit. Eliza Manningham-Buller, head of M15 attended as did John Scarlett, the head of the Secret Intelligence Service, MI6; Hayman represented the Metropolitan Police. The meeting, which should have been calm broke into a cantankerous row between Patricia Hewitt, Secretary of State for Health and Hayman with Hewitt insisting, from a position of apparent ignorance, that there had been between six or eight incidents rather than the four known about. This would be the first piece of obfuscation by politicians around the events of 7 July.

At 10.45 a.m., Hayman had returned to his desk. He authorized Suzanna Becks to officially inform the City of London financiers of the crisis under agreed arrangements known as 'Operation Griffin'. 'Griffin' had been developed after 9/11 to ensure financial security and continuity and to minimize any effect on the Stock Market. A quarter of an hour later, Ian Blair was on television reassuring the public that all was 'under control'. It was not. There was still no indication of who planted the 'bombs' nor why, nor if the bombers were still at large. By 11.30 a.m., it was clear that there had been mass casualties and at noon, Tony Blair broke off from the G8 summit to go on television. He confirmed for the first time that the attacks were terrorist in nature.

At 12.55 a.m., the Home Secretary announced the situation to the House of Commons. Whoever had perpetrated these attacks had slipped under the surveillance network. JTAC (the Joint Terrorist Analysis Centre) based at MI5 had downgraded the threat to London only three weeks before. Could there actually be a large and dangerous al-Qaeda cell operating clandestinely in Britain that the security services did not know about? If so might they strike again? Hayman and others thought so as did a nervous population. Tony Blair now had left Gleneagles and was on his way to Downing Street to chair COBR. At the meeting that followed, Hayman thought the prime minister, 'outstanding'. After the meeting, RAF Northholt was ordered to prepare to deploy its specialist biological, nuclear and chemical teams if needed.

At 10.19 in the evening, the first break in intelligence came when the family of Hasib Hussain reported him missing. An hour and a half later, officers found evidence (including gym membership cards) that put other names forward for the possible perpetrators. These were for 'Sidique Khan' and 'Mr S. Tanweer'.[10] Further investigations and corroborative CCTV footage and other forensic evidence finally put names to all the perpetrators. All appeared to have died, perhaps unsurprisingly; what was worrying was that all appeared to be British.

London was not so easily cowed and on 11 July, 250,000 people turned up in the Mall to celebrate the 60th anniversary of the end of World War II. It was a show of defiance and community spirit. The queen suggested 'that during the present difficult days for London, people turn to the example set by [the war] generation, of resilience, humour and sustained courage'.[11] Andy Trotter, deputy chief constable of British Transport Police made it clear that 'it was business as usual' expressed in that platitudinous language that is the equivalent of a good British cuppa. Despite this the names of the missing still filled papers, 56 finally being confirmed dead and seven hundred injured. The London Underground was, however, already running a normal service.

Anti-Islamic sentiment rose after 7 July and tempers were frayed. Two things happened to make Londoners fear that their bravado on 11 July was misplaced. The first was the attempted reprise bombings two weeks after 7 July and the subsequent temporary escape of the bombers. The second was the killing of Jean Charles de Menezes the day after the failed attack of 21 July during the hunt for the second terrorist cell.

De Menezes was in the wrong place at the wrong time. Born in Gonzaga, Brazil on 7 January 1978, he had arrived in Britain on a six month's visa granted on 13 March 2002 and a subsequent student visa granting an indefinite stay and although the actual stamp suggested a forgery, it was later confirmed as authentic by Jack Straw the Home Secretary. Immigration may therefore have been breached. Nevertheless, de Menezes had gone to Ireland on 23 April 2005 and then returned a complicated but apparently lawful action under the Common Travel Area system of the European Union.

On 22 July 2005, he was living at a flat in Scotia Road in Tulse Hill, South London, working as an electrician and about to go on a call to fix a broken alarm at Kilburn. His identity as a potential terrorist bomber had been misconstrued from jumbled evidence. In order not to go to Kilburn on the overground train, the Brazilian would walk a longer distance to Stockwell Underground Station. At 9.30 a.m., police watched the man exit the flat and activated their plans. The surveillance officer known as 'Frank' at the subsequent (first) inquiry gave evidence that he had wanted the CCTV footage checked, but went to the toilet and did not return in time to double check if the footage had got to Gold Command at the Metropolitan Police headquarters. 'Frank' was confirmed at the inquest as 'Tango Ten', an undercover soldier.

CO19 (now renamed SO19), the armed response unit of the police were also alerted and followed the suspect as he walked to a bus stop. Ironically, he got off the bus at Brixton which was closed because of a terrorist alert, but found another and got off at Stockwell having travelled about two miles, in which time the police had not realized that he did not look like their suspect (although he did look Mediterranean and therefore a possible Algerian, Algerians being high on terrorist wanted lists). Operational police contacted Gold Command and confirmed that he did fit the description of Hussain Osman, one of the second cell of bombers still on the run. Gold Command then handed operational command to CO19 who sent officers to Stockwell. The chain of command had already sent ambiguous orders, regarding shooting or detaining the suspect and had thereby fatally compromised the chain of command. Three surveillance officers, 'Hotel 1', 'Hotel 2' and 'Hotel 3' followed the suspect onto the platform at Stockwell. De Menezes boarded the train as 'Hotel 3' blocked the door and shouted 'He's here' at which point armed officers boarded the train and shot the Brazilian without warning and with hollow point bullets, considered illegal and banned in warfare, but used by police forces where it might be necessary to put 'down' an assailant with certainty. The body was identified the day after the shooting.

There was still a gang to capture. On 30 July the *Sun* headline screamed 'Got the Bastards' following the arrest of the second group of bombers. The attack had been planned for 21 July as a follow up to 7 July, but this time the attackers were abject failures, thwarted by their own apparent incompetence. Two of the bombers, stupefied and bewildered surrendered in their underwear as the media watched. Four men were to be held after raids by the SAS and heavily armed police. Muktar Mohammed-Said finally came onto the balcony of his flat near Notting Hill after CS gas was used and armed police had broken in. He expected to be shot, 'like the guy at Stockwell Station'.[12] Two women were also arrested at Liverpool Station. Hussain Osman had been previously arrested in Rome after an international hunt. The other bombers were Ramzi Mohammed of Notting Hill and Yasin Omar of Birmingham. Ramzi's brother was also held. Their intention was to replicate 7 July by attacks on Warren Street Station and Oval Station and attacks on the No. 26 bus and at Shepherd's Bush underground.

The second set of bombers' plans collapsed after their devices failed to explode, the underground and bus bombs merely fizzing after they were ignited, one bomber was caught by CCTV camera running from an underground station whilst another dumped his half exploded package near Little Wormwood Scrubs recreation ground. The police operation that followed to capture the men was spectacularly successful and went some way to restoring confidence after the bombings on 7 July and the killing of de Menezes on 22 July. Two women led the search, Eliza Maningham-Buller the head of MI5 and Jane William head of Special Branch. SO19 (the CO19), the specialist police unit who carried out the operation was kitted out in body armour of Kevlar helmets and vests, hi-tech assault boots, fireproof boiler suit, vest pockets stuffed with ammunition, night vision gas proof masks, Heckler and Koch machine guns and Glock leg holster pistols.

Despite the carnage of 7 July and the superb operation that caught the 21 July bombers, it was the killing of de Menezes that seemed to remain both unexplained and scandalous. Why was an obviously wrong suspect gunned down? As time went by it became evident that the police had killed the wrong man. They could be forgiven for making the mistake under such extreme circumstances, but not for covering it up. Panic manoeuvring followed. It was said that the police thought they were following Osman, the man arrested in Rome; de Menezes was supposedly carrying a heavy coat under which there appeared to be a large package, but CCTV showed him wearing a denim jacket; he was meant to have been running and vaulted the barrier, but he was walking and picked up a free newspaper; worst of all the smear that he was an illegal immigrant, but he was not. The operation had been faulty as one might have expected at a time of great uncertainty and apprehension and when another terror group was being hunted. This was not a hijack situation where the hostages were released by a group of SAS heroes as in the Iranian embassy siege of 1980, but what appeared to be a deliberate police assassination. Operations must have been stretched as the second terror group had struck only the day before. London was under siege. Yet the mistake was covered up from the beginning and although Sir Ian Blair, then the Commissioner had apologized, the apology seemed inadequate to the occasion in which an innocent man had been shot eleven times, seven times in the head, one in the shoulder and three which missed, all at point blank range.

On 27 July, the Independent Police Complaints Committee (IPPC) began an inconclusive investigation called 'Stockwell One'. On 12 October, the de Menezes family complained about the process and it was restarted in a second parallel inquiry known a 'Stockwell Two'. On 16 March 2006, reports started to circulate that an unnamed person in Sir Ian's office knew there had been a mistake by operational officers. That person was shown to be a secretary called Lana Vandenberghe who wished to expose the 'lie' that the Commissioner did not know the details of the circumstances of de Meneze's death. On 17 July, the Criminal Prosecution Service sought to bring health and safety charges and on 3 August Sir Ian was cross-examined. A year had passed and no one was as yet accountable nor was it clear what had happened, although it had long been clear through CCTV that the story of the dead man's last moments were not as originally suggested. On 11 May 2007, the police were accused of lying by the family after eleven officers were exonerated. On 2 August, Stockwell Two concluded that Sir Ian was uninformed during the crucial period. Meanwhile Stockwell One suggested there had been major errors of judgement. It all led to a cul de sac. On 21 December, the IPCC said that four officers including Cressida Dick (who was directly in charge of the operation) should not face any charges or disciplinary proceedings. On 30 June 2008, Sir Michael Wright granted forty-seven officers anonymity at the inquest.

The closing of ranks by the establishment over the issue and the immunities granted as well as the obfuscation that has so frustrated the family may have a more sinister undertone. The operation that killed the Brazilian may have been undertaken by a secret army intelligence squad that had its origins in the Irish conflict. The 14th Intelligence Company was set up to liaise with UDF assassins and undertake missions that could be disowned by the government. It was this secret army group that transformed into the Special Reconnaissance Regiment (SRR) formed from the remnants of the 14th and others. CO19 police who received training from the SAS and the SRR were present on 22 July. Regimental personnel may also have been already on the underground train. It was a surveillance unit of SRR that identified de Menezes as an 'IC1' or 'white northern European'.

The action itself fell under aegis of 'Operation Kratos' which had been set up after 9/11. The circumstances of Kratos and the rules under which the army and police might operate were such that they had never had been scrutinized by parliament. The Association of Chief Police Officers (ACPO) had produced guidelines for allowable homicide in February 2005, that stated that an officer might open fire if they felt so threatened they could take no other action to protect themselves or others around them. What the interpretation of those guidelines might be would have to be left to operational units. Nevertheless, the guidelines still violated the *actual* law where there are no special powers which allow a policeman to kill or injure other than those laws available to other civilians. An officer cannot authorize a killing. It makes them an accomplice.[13] The conclusion would be inevitable. There was a unit of military trained assassins who could operate outside the law and with the Home Secretary's approval, using guidelines never approved by parliament and with impunity as long as they acted in secret. The old days when first the SAS flashed onto our television screens as heroes were long gone. So far none of the actions of the security services on 22 July can be confirmed and they may never be able to be.

This was not quite the end. In July Cressida Dick was still in post and had been given a massive pay rise and new job. No one was yet held responsible for the death or the police disinformation that followed. Sir Ian Blair had been implicated not merely in his hesitation to release information over the shooting of de Menezes, but of delaying or 'tampering' with evidence too. Although cleared by the IPCC, the accusations stuck which accused Blair of trying to persuade a colleague, Deputy Assistant Commissioner Brian Paddick to 'doctor' his evidence. The mayor, Boris Johnson took the unprecedented step of actually forcing Blair to resign. In his defence, Blair suggested his fall was not because of his tarnished reputation, but was part of a 'turf war' within the Conservative party and his 'big' personality.

After the London bombings something like panic gripped the security services. Deputy Assistant Police Commissioner Peter Clarke, former head of the anti-terrorist branch told the inquest into the de Menezes shooting that there was 'a tangible air of tension and expectation' of further attacks. Anything at all suggestive of an attack brought an immediate reactive response. Thus parliament was 'locked down' for ninety minutes during July 2005 as police awaited another possible al-Qaeda attack.[14] Birmingham city centre was also evacuated on the night of 9 July 2005, after police got a tip-off that an attack was imminent. Controlled explosions were heard as twenty thousand people were moved from bars, pubs and clubs.

Were the security services really prepared for the attacks? One area seemed more suspect than most: the lack of relevant language training in the security services. This took a long time to recognize and to act upon. It was only in August 2009, that MI5 specifically undertook a recruiting campaign to find speakers of 'Arabic, Somali, Sylheti with Bengali, Sorani, Kurdi, Pashto, African languages, Russian or Chechen'. The languages were a de facto definition of the threat. As the security forces rushed to fill the language gap, police were criticized for stopping innocent people under Section 44 of the Terrorism Act, 2000. As many as 125,000 people were stopped and searched during 2007 to 2008, itself an increase of 42,000 on the previous year, but which had resulted in only 1 per cent being arrested. Watchdog Lord Carlile criticized the 'self-evidently unwarranted searches' which were 'almost certainly unlawful', but defended the number of black and Asian people stopped as a 'proportional consequence' of the fact that terrorist attacks were overwhelmingly from Islamic groups.[15]

Arrests and prosecutions continued. On 7 September 2009, Abdullah Ahmed Ali, Assad Sarwar and Tanvir Hussain were convicted at Woolwich Crown Court of a conspiracy to take home-made bombs, consisting of hydrogen peroxide hidden in Lucozade bottles, onto a number of aircraft in order to destroy some six or seven planes flying out of Heathrow and create the sort of havoc that would close airports and emulate the attacks of 9/11. Police considered the bombs 'viable' and 'sophisticated'. The gang was under surveillance during 2006 in one of the biggest Metropolitan Police operations. Operation 'Overt' carried out over one hundred searches, took 9,710 statements and seized 26,000 exhibits, the investigation itself moving from Japan to Pakistan, Mauritius, South Africa and Belgium. Group members were tracked from Pakistani training camps to their meeting with Iraqis and through their e-mail messages. The operation had been sparked by the arrest in Pakistan of Raschid Rauf an al-Qaeda operative from Birmingham who had contact with Hussain (who called himself '007'), a 28-year-old computer fan from Leyton, East London. It took investigators some time to piece together the relationship of Hussain to Rauf only to have Rauf slip the police who did not see the threat. It took eighteen months to finally arrest him. The leader, Abdullah Ali, also 28, from Walthamstow, East London, who was described by police as a 'bungler', said he was inspired by the attack of 7/7 and made a video in which he expected 'floods of martyr operations'.[16]

On 14 September the three were sentenced. Ali was jailed for a minimum of 40 years, Hussain for 32 years and Sarwar for 36 years. It was a triumph for the security services which had been in disarray after 7 July and heavily criticized. Mr Justice Henriques was 'satisfied that there [was] every likelihood that the plot would have succeeded but for the intervention of the security service'.[17] Ali read a prayer book during sentencing. A fourth man, Umar Islam of Plaistow who was a friend of the other three was convicted of conspiracy to murder, but not of the airline conspiracy. He received 22 years.

A further three men who aided the conspiracy were also jailed during December 2009. These were Adam Khatib, Nabeel Hussain and Mohammed Shamin Uddin. Khatib had helped bury the explosives in a wood in High Wycombe, Buckinghamshire, he had also been seen at the Walthamstow 'bomb factory'. Uddin had actually applied for a loan of £25,000 from the HSBC for shop improvements, but in truth to fund bomb making. The dangers of the old East End at the start of the twentieth century had by the twenty-first been transferred to East London, Walthamstow, Leyton, Upton Park and Forest Gate where a ninth suspect called Mohammed al Ghabra lived with his mother and sister. Despite being on American wanted lists, al Ghabra was cleared of charges of fraud and other crimes and freed from Belmarsh high security prison in Thameside after being held for nine months. His mother accused 'spies and police' of hounding him since his acquittal.[18]

The Iraq conflict and Britain's close relationship with American neo-conservatism was seen by many as the catalyst (or at least an accelerator) of Islamic attacks, Tony Blair was being named a war criminal by some and a 'liar' by many. The fight against al-Qaeda was now turning to distaste for the government itself. The question of culpability remains controversial. Al-Qaeda's war had, for the most part, been directed at the United States, but a series of explosions at Madrid's commuter stations on 11 March 2004 (inspired by al-Qaeda) had changed not only the Spanish government but also forced a Spanish withdrawal from Iraq. The Iraq war could therefore be directly affected by European interventions. The British government had to be mindful of the problem of directing foreign policy against a background of an internally hostile population, some of whom were dangerous and would act in concert and in secret.

The 7 July bombers were not the first Islamist fanatics who were British citizens. In December 2001, Richard Reid tried to blow up an American airline with a shoe bomb. Reid was a Londoner of mixed parentage who had converted to Islam whilst in jail. Two years followed in which two others trained for a deadly mission. In April 2003, Asif Mohammad Hanif and Omar Khan Sharif, both British, travelled to Israel as suicide bombers. Hanif's belt failed to detonate and he drowned himself, but Hanif's bomb killed three people and injured sixty. This was a long way from London and perhaps appeared as an aberration, but it was not. It was a warning that things had started to change within some sections of the British Muslim population.

Nevertheless, such radicalization was still aimed abroad and might be tolerated or ignored.

As early as 10 February 2003, the Joint Intelligence Committee had warned that the threat of attacks had been heightened by the invasion of Iraq. It was a rather obvious conclusion for a country embarking on a war in which the attacked country had so many sympathizers in Britain. The estimates of radicalized Islamists from Britain produced in a dossier by the Home Office and Foreign Office in May 2004 was alarming and, given the circumstances, appeared alarmist when reported on the BBC news. According to the dossier there was 'a thousand-strong groundswell of al-Qaeda sympathisers in the UK, actively involved in terrorist activity'.[19] These radicalized Muslims were a mixture of middle-class and university-educated men as well as 'under-achievers'. Lord Stevens, a former Metropolitan Police Commissioner added his belief that at least three thousand British-born Muslims had passed through bin Laden's training camps. He pointed out that most of these trainees would forever remain dormant and that less than 1 per cent of the British Muslim population were inclined to martyrdom, but he also pointed out the international links and the possibility of fanatical converts from the white and West Indian communities (for example, Richard Reid). Other estimates put the number of hard core recruits at around three hundred or at least as large as the IRA and less predictable in their aims and targets.

To many this information might have seemed as if the security services were exaggerating their adversary to justify their role after the end of the Cold War. And that was the trouble, this too seemed like the sort of disinformation that had taken the United Kingdom to war in the first place, especially as the government was telling the population that on the other hand they should try to be more sympathetic to Muslims and not to demonize communities. Indeed, immediately after the Madrid train bombings, 'Operation Conquest' was set up as a political move to defuse the 'anger', 'sense of helplessness' and 'frustration' of the Muslim community. The joint initiative by the Home Office and the Foreign Office was contained in the report *Young Muslims and Extremism*, the report concluding that anger seemed to 'have become more acute post 9/11'.[20] In mid-June 2005, just prior to the invasion itself the 'Joint Terrorism Analysis Centre' concluded that the Iraq war was 'continuing to act as a motivation and a focus of a range of terrorist-related activities in the UK', MI5 saw Iraq too as 'a dominant issue'.[21] This still leaves difficult questions of motivation on both sides, for a country cannot run a foreign policy driven by fear of either popular distaste or of reprisals by a small group of fanatics.

Did the war in Iraq radicalize the bombers or were they predisposed to carry out such an attack anyway? Would an attack have followed regardless as part of the 'war on the West' or did Iraq tip the conspirators into action? Was al-Qaeda an inspiration that would have remained dormant but for the invasion, a 'liberation' group embodying a set of unfulfilled wishes, but those wishes remaining only that until the war came and made the wish list a possible reality in the capital of the enemy?

Immediately after the attacks of 7 July and 21 July, the disbelief that the attacks were both from home-grown fanatics who seemed to reject the hospitality of the country of their birth and were in effect traitors required much soul searching and a media free-for-all in the search for the bombers' family backgrounds and motivations. Opponents of the Iraq war such as the then Mayor of London, Ken Livingstone were voicing doubts about British culpability. His apparently extremist views on this and other subjects (including an invitation to an extremist Islamic cleric for talks at the Mayor's office in the Greater London Assembly building) would cost him the election. And yet the idea of culpability did not quite go away, nor was it the merest paranoid fantasy of conspiracy geeks.

In the end there have been two official inquiries – both flawed: the House of Commons Intelligence and Security Committee's *Report into the London Terrorist Attacks on 7th July 2005* which was published in May 2006, but submitted to the prime minister in March and the Home Office *Report of the Official Account of the Bombings in London on 7 July 2005* and published in May 2006. Both reports were faulty, mainly through lack of definite answers and apparent factual errors but both reports were, perhaps, as honest as could be expected. Worryingly, many choose to believe the conspiracy canards of people like Nick Kollerstrom, a holocaust denier, and 'Muad Dib' whose nom de plume is derived from a science-fiction novel and whose Internet video 7/7 *Ripple Effect* has been widely accessed since 2005. The maker is actually John Hill, an Englishman living in Ireland and someone who believes himself to be the messiah. Following a BBC exposé he was arrested awaiting extradition in 2010.

The Security Committee's report commented on the details of what could be learned by the intelligence agencies from the investigation which 'continue[d] to change'.[22] It explained the threat, dealt with lessons and explained the strategy of the security services prior to 7 July. According to the report there was no collusion with the parallel Home Office investigation. The report did accept that there had been a terrorist threat prior to July but that targets were abroad, although there had been recognition of the possibility of an attack on the transport network from the beginning. Having identified the bombers, the committee concluded that they were 'home

grown' and used bombs that '[did] not require a great deal of expertise' and that the video that linked the bombers to al-Qaeda was 'not
assessed to be credible' although the report did not rule out outside
involvement.[23] Indeed although two of the bombers had travelled
to Pakistan and had been monitored by MI5 neither was considered
a terrorist threat. The conclusion was clear. These were home-grown
terrorists not linked to any international network, working alone
and with little more than simple ideas of chemistry. The security
services were unable to prevent the attack because they were unsus-
pected British citizens who had been radicalized more quickly than
thought possible. The report went on that 'lessons' had to be learned
about 'the potential diversity of those who can become radicalised
and the extent to which they can become radicalised'.[24] The policy
of preventing home-born terrorists (or 'Tier 3') was to be stepped up
under the government's anti-terrorist programme 'PREVENT'.

The comments regarding both the bombs themselves and the
connection to al-Qaeda still left questions unanswered. The Home
Office report attempted a close narrative of events and a detailed
social and psychological profile of the killers. It too concluded that
the bombs were simple affairs, that the group was self-financed, that
the motivation if not actual training came from al-Qaeda, that the
attack was not linked to the G8 Summit and that the bombers were
self-motivated men rather than mere dupes, although the possibility
could not be ruled out that people like Abu Hamza, Abu Qatada and
Omar Bakri Mohammmed were influential in their 'conversion' to
extremism.

Many people were not convinced by the government narrative and
were prepared to believe in a cover-up. A whole series of questions
seemed to remain unanswered. Nevertheless, of these questions most
are merely fiction or the wildest paranoid speculation. There remains
no evidence that the two government reports deliberately changed
facts or deceived. There is clear evidence to suggest that the bombers
were guilty, were not somewhere else or patsies, or airbrushed in, or
taking part in a training exercise nor that police or M15 had planted
the bombs, nor that the office of Mossad at the Israeli Embassy knew
of the attack in advance, nor that the security briefing of just such an
eventuality held by Peter Power (a former policeman) was not a terrible coincidence, nor that the mysterious men shot in Canary Wharf
that day were not the merest fiction of fevered brains nor that the
accounts given by officials of the day's events were not perfectly honest. What does remain disturbing is the collusion of terrorists and the
security services before the attacks and it is this possible collusion
that is at the heart of all the rest of the speculation.

In 2006, Nafeez Mosaddeq Ahmed published *The London Bombings:
An Independent Inquiry* that established links between the security

services, Omar Bakri, Abu Hamsa, the Finsbury Park Mosque and many others implicated in the attacks of 7 July and 21 July 2005. These links predated 9/11 and were not broken afterwards. Indeed, although the bombers were 'home-grown', they flourished through a set of complex connections both to al-Qaeda headquarters, bomb experts in Bosnia and propaganda and organization from Britain as well as influence from a radical bookshop in Yorkshire, grooming by Sidiqui and simple self-persuasion watching online films of perceived injustice. Even if the attacks by the 7/7 and 21/7 terrorists could not have been prevented it certainly appears that the security forces of Britain knew of and encouraged their activities in order to gain information. As such, at least some of the network at home and abroad may have been double agents.

Omar Bakri was singled out as Britain's most poisonous preacher in 2005. On 20 July 2005, the *Sun* demanded he be 'booted out of Britain'. Bakri who had come to Britain seeking asylum twenty years previously openly preached the end of the West and his hatred of Britain. He was protected from extradition by the Human Rights Act which the *Sun* wanted abolished as we were at war. Finally, he left for Lebanon on 6 August 2005, when he thought he would be arrested in Britain under terrorism legislation and was later refused re-entry to the United Kingdom by Home Secretary Charles Clarke. It remains the case that he is still at large and it remains a suspicion that he was allowed to leave and not return under an agreement with the security services who wished to buy his silence with their complicity in his 'escape'. All this still remains speculation. Abu Hamsa was not so lucky. He now languishes in Belmarsh (high security) Prison, one of his daughters is a stripper and three of his sons were jailed at Southwark Crown Court for fraud involving stolen cars.

Was there collusion between the security agencies and terrorists, that, perhaps, the victims and survivors are hoping to elicit from the inquest which is getting underway as this book goes to press. The inquest has been a long time coming and its remit will be closely watched. The coroner, Lady Justice Hallett will first hold a short hearing at the Royal Courts of Justice to update relatives and then decide whether the four suicide bombers will be included in the dead or separately and whether the survivors as 'interested persons' should be allowed representation. As there was no public inquiry, the inquest is expected to be more wide ranging than usual, but even so it will have to wait until the autumn of 2010 to begin.

The main culprits of the 7 July bombings are dead by their own hands. Those that groomed and handled them as well as those who may have supplied the weapons and training are similarly in prison or permanently abroad. Those who are still alive are keeping quiet in possible collusion with all those in the security forces whose culpability may never be proven, but whose machinations made terrorism the guarantee of their livelihoods and who, plotting their deadly plots, did not, but could have, envisioned the disaster that they were concocting. As for extremist views, these are still to be found. The government has still not proscribed Hizb ut-Tahrir even though its influence is growing on campuses, David Lammy, the New Labour Minister for Higher Education in February 2010, ruling out government intervention and favouring the self-policing of universities instead.

With the retirement of both Tony Blair and George Bush the term the 'war on terror' was quietly dropped by Gordon Brown when he took office on 27 June 2007, there was no longer to be an 'axis of evil', but a 'long war'. The 'long war' was not long in coming either. Two days after Brown had become prime minister, Bilal Abdullah and Kafeel (or Khalid) Ahmed parked as Mercedes outside the Tiger Tiger nightclub in Haymarket. The club was packed with revellers. Another car was parked in Cockspur Street. Both cars had explosives on board. The first car was reported as suspicious when an ambulance crew noticed strange fumes coming from it and the second was towed away after being ticketed for illegal parking. Nether car caused any damage, but the bombers were already heading for Scotland and the attack on Glasgow Airport. The attempt on the London nightclub caused official panic in London.

Police Commissioner Sir Paul Stephenson ordered an immediate increase in stop and search actions under Section 44 legislation. These searches were aimed at finding terrorists by disrupting activity on the street, but were highly unpopular and seen as divisive. Of the 256,000 searches during 2008 (which included stop and search of 755 ten-year-olds), for instance, only 191 led to arrests and even fewer convictions.[25] The amount of searches had actually doubled since 2007 and, despite being seen as necessary by government and police were viewed as draconian and ill-targeted by most Londoners.

Long after Blair's departure London remains a place of shadows. In February 2010, Umar Farouk Abdulmutalab, a student educated at University College in Gower Street and possibly radicalized there, attempted to destroy a plane going to Chicago. This led not only to outrage at lax security in the United States, but also accusations from the Nigerian Nobel Laureate Wole Soyinka that 'England [sic] is the breeding ground of fundamentalist Muslims'. According to Soyinka it was the British heritage of colonialism and 'tolerance' that was to blame.[26] Dirty, muddled and old London might be forgiven for that.

The Thames flows on indifferent.

28

Operation Glencoe

G20, Ian Tomlinson and the Future of Street Protest

A shadow hung over London the week of 1 April, 2009. According to Class War's web site it was the shadow of the guillotine dripping with the blood of Sir Fred Goodwin, the disgraced chairman of the Royal Bank of Scotland. Fred 'the Shred' Goodwin was the newly 'retired' chairman of the 'bankrupt' Royal Bank of Scotland and the unacceptable face of greedy banking, not quite a man of straw, for he was sufficiently implicated in the near collapse of world banking to deserve the invective, having accepted a hugely inflated cash bonus and pension whilst sinking his banking institution through speculation in poor investments. Public outrage demanded natural justice and saw none in the face of corporate arrogance and disdain. As Goodwin contemplated taking himself to South Africa and away from the public gaze, a group calling themselves 'Bank Bosses are Criminals' smashed the windows of his Edinburgh home and vandalized his car in attacks reminiscent of an eighteenth-century mob. The attackers even released a statement in which they put the point many were feeling, 'we are angry' they said, 'that rich people, like [Goodwin] are paying themselves a huge amount of money, and living in luxury, while ordinary people are made unemployed, destitute and homeless. This is a crime. Bank bosses should be jailed'.[1]

The collapse of world finance heralded an entirely unexpected crisis in capitalism. Would anti-capitalists be able to exploit people's grievances with an unfair system before the system itself mended its problems and revived? Would Marxist analysis have one last triumphant ride to glory and finally be vindicated? It might be, but the old infrastructure of protest had long since fallen away. No longer would there be the mass rallies of the trades union movement, nor the vocal presence of the Communist Party of Great Britain, Socialist Workers' Party, or even the bedrock of Labour Party regulars. What was left from nearly twenty years of attrition was a core of about 5,000 political activists of all persuasions who would effectively be needed to replace the protesters of the past. The crisis, which may have brought mass picketing and strikes, huge demonstrations and violence in the 1960s or 1970s was in jeopardy of fizzling out in abject failure for want of a practical mass base of those not already alienated by media talk of 'anarchists'.

Coincidentally, the twenty most powerful banking nations were coming to ExCel, the conference and exhibition space in Docklands, East London to discuss world finances and the recession in particular. A mixture of climate-change protesters and those infuriated by the banking system as well as political militants who now sniffed an opportunity for a revival of an alternative left politics threatened not only to string up effigies of bankers around the City of London and set fire to them, but also to hold camps at the European Climate Exchange in Bishopsgate, march on ExCel, the Bank of England and the American Embassy, as well as smashing up as much financial institution property as they could lay their hands on. The organization for the protests was being co-ordinated by a group headed by a militant anarchist anthropology professor, Chris Knight from the University of East London, under the banner 'G20 Meltdown'. Knight was provocative and intemperate in his language to the media, which gained huge interest, but which saw him suspended from his post. 'We are going to be hanging a lot of people like Fred the Shred from lamposts and I can only say let's hope they are just effigies. If he winds us up any more I'm afraid there will be real bankers hanging from lamposts'.[2]

 Later Knight made it clear that this was to be a good natured protest, but he knew that this was the sort of inflated rhetoric that the media would love and which would effectively scare the City into drastic action. Knight was later to take part in the demonstrations dressed as a bowler-hatted city gent, wielding a placard saying 'Storm the Banks' and with a banner hanging from his neck saying 'Eat the Bankers'. This was brilliant street theatre and fulfilled the carnivalesque sense of most protests since 2000, but it diminished the serious message and deflated the political value, reducing the protest into a series of violent or amusing tableaux which could more easily be digested by the media (see the question of sequentiality in the Introduction).

Whatever the potential threat of disruption and whilst financial institutions renewed their insurance policies and checked out the local glazier, the Home Office were sufficiently rattled to put out a 'spoiler' on 24 March, one week before the proposed demonstration which was picked up by the newspapers. Jackie Smith, the then New Labour Home Secretary (soon herself to be dismissed for her husband's overfamiliarity with pornography paid for out of parliamentary expenses), put out a piece of disinformation supplied by 'the security services' which suggested that a 'dirty bomb' was possibly going to be used in Britain and, given the timing, likely to be used by 'terrorists' under cover of the protests.* The report which reached Parliament on 24 March was, to say the least, vague. Terrorists could now obtain chemical, biological and nuclear material on the open market which might be targeted on 'crowded places'. Smith proposed that 60,000 shop workers and others should be trained to deal with terrorism as a 'workers army'. Was this the new vision of the worker, no longer unionized and protesting on the streets, but passive, trained and spying for the government? The timing of the release of the Home Office dossier called *Contest Two* was intended to create alarm and fear about the forthcoming events in London and actually said nothing that was not already in the public domain. What the statement unconsciously showed up was the real fear in government not only that anarchy might just erupt on the streets of Britain, but that, just as with the poll tax in 1992, general dissatisfaction amongst voters would create a much wider and systemic crisis in society that the government might not be able to stem. Would the G20 protests be the spark for much wider unrest? The government thought so and feared a repeat of the summer of 1981, the trade unions hoped so, warning the government of civil unrest if cuts to jobs were not halted.[3]

As April Fool's Day came nearer banks began the laborious job of putting shutters up at their windows and advising those going to work at places like Canary Wharf to abandon their suits and 'dress down'. Financiers were advised to work from home. Businesses near financial buildings also prepared for trouble. Security companies were, of course, doing brisk business, whilst 2,500 police would be drafted in, including the usual intelligence and riot units at a cost of £10 million. The proposed number of actual protesters in the City was estimated at 3,000 which effectively meant that there would be one policeman for every three protesters and in some places that might amount to a personal policeman assigned to each protester!

Apocalyptic headlines ran during the week up to 1 April. On the 30 March, some protest websites published *Squaring up to the Square Mile* which identified banks and other financial institutions on a map of London and which led to a flurry of last-minute speculation in newspapers that protesters would masquerade as peaceful and then turn violent in some co-ordinated, but hitherto secret, plan. Gordon Brown huffed 'that the police would take a zero-tolerance stance against threats to people and property', whilst an unnamed

---

* 'Sixty per cent of all Home Office press releases have misleading or incorrect and unsubstantiated information according to the sub-commitee of the Home Office Scientific Advisory Committee' (*Daily Mail* 30 March 2010).

minister added 'the police will act very quickly if there is any threat to people or property'.[4] Such statements go some way to explain the liberal use of force by the police on the day, its extremity concomitant with government panic, and its result the death of one man and the abuse or injury of many others. Such was the effect of the prime minister's message (and presumably the trickled down messages of senior Metropolitan and City Police organizers) that the actions of the police that day actually created a crisis of such proportion that Her Majesty's Inspector of Police was forced to act to quiet public fears that it was the police not the protesters who were the real 'anarchists'. The only violence to occur on the run up to the 'G20 Meltdown' was, rather ironically, the use of pepper spray to restrain Tory magazine owner, Ian Thomas when he became abusive after a House of Commons' reception. On the same day Barack Obama and 500 American officials flew into London for talks on financial regulation, fiscal stimulus, trade, the IMF, tax havens and the environment, whilst it was reported that the first arrests had been made in Plymouth where fireworks, 'imitation weapons' and 'anti-capitalist' literature were seized from protesters; fireworks being banned from political rallies.

April Fool's Day, Financial Fool's Day or 'G20 Meltdown' was to be a themed protest. The Four Horsemen of the Apocalypse (giant puppets on frames) were coming to town, but there would be no Death on a Pale Horse, only colour coding to lead the numerous marches: green for climate change; silver for the monetary crisis; black for no borders; and red for protest against involvement in the Iraq war. The G20 protesters wanted to get rid of the bankers, get rid of corrupt politicians, remove all national borders, stop climate change and abolish capitalism. The overt aims of the protesters were to 'participate in a carnival party at the Bank of England, support all events demonstrating against the G20 [and] overthrow capitalism'. The catchphrase was 'let's make this a very English Revolution!' in honour of the rather spurious 360th anniversary of the Diggers.[5] They even had a manifesto demanding the end of bankers, corrupt politicians and capitalism and extolling the virtues of sustainability, guaranteed jobs, removal of all border controls and government by the people (whatever the last meant). Perhaps a reasonable agenda for four days of planned protest, but a diffusion of aims and a confusion of purpose nevertheless.

The planned protests were to begin with a rally in Hyde Park on 28 March which went ahead without incident, to be followed by more contentious activity in the City which was to culminate at the Bank of England at 12 o'clock. On 2 April protests were to be held outside the G20 Summit at ExCel. Right from the beginning it should have been plain that the numbers of protesters needed to stop this appearing as just another protest by the 'unwashed' and lazy would not materialize. There was no mass base or mass support. Approximately 4,500 protesters marched on the Bank of England and targeted the Royal Bank of Scotland (RBS); roughly another 2,300 marched into Trafalgar Square and other followed people like Arthur Scargill on a small march against Israel. As promised the climate change camp began filling the road at Bishopsgate. The press, quite rightly, gathered at the Bank of England. They may have thought that ExCel would be a good bet for photographs the next day, but the police cordon and the lack of mass protesters made the whole event a desperate disappointment.

So on April Fool's Day, 2009, the press awaited the violent demise of capitalism. It was hardly likely, the forecast end of capitalist exploitation merely being the required tag line for any 'left wing' demonstration. Indeed, the very term itself which had sustained protest for a century and defined those whose stance was oppositional and progressive had evaporated in the very practicality so praised by contemporary protest groups, the real theoretical ignorance of their constituency and the vapid ranting of its 'moral' demands at the gates of the opposition. In the desire for 'carnival' Karl Marx had been replaced by Groucho Marx.

Demonstrations nowadays have to have at least two ingredients to be successful. On the one hand they have to be visually interesting and, amid the buzz of so much informational flow in the capital, they must be media friendly and especially televisual. In short, demonstrations that get noticed whether large or small have to be entertaining for those who have not attended. With 24-hour news coverage it is now possible to watch a demonstration develop from one's armchair, allowing the vicarious pleasure afforded by security and a panoptic view. Demonstrations are about seeing and being seen, about mobile phones clicking mug shots of police action, police camera crews and filmed interviews as things progress. A modern demonstration is, for both sides, about watching and doing things that will be watched. As little as possible needs to happen away from a camera, for not only are such moments lasting momentoes of the occasion, they are also potential evidence, and a captured visual-bite for the information-hungry media. There is no point in doing something that will not declare itself on screen or in print as 'an action' and so actions are now clearly 'staged' for the cameras of the world's riot paparazzi. For most of 1 April, the media had to be content with the usual almost generic pictures of confrontation and rather staged window breaking and ridiculous arson attempt (twelve minutes with a cigarette lighter trying to make something burn) by one masked protester, a Lithuanian called Mindaugas Lenartavicius who was later jailed for two years.

The police at first appeared even handed and reasonable but it very quickly emerged that there had been unreasonable force used by some officers whose aggression was caught on camera. The police tactic of 'kettling' or bottling up and holding protesters in a narrow area, used since 2000, was also debatable in its ferocity and necessity, one pregnant woman being held and refused exit from Bishopsgate was pushed back by a shield and thought she might miscarry. Complaints soon came in of brutal police behaviour and brutalized individual responses to incidents. Ninety complaints led Nick Hardwick, the head of the Independent Police Complaints Commission (IPCC) to suggest that there were questions to answer especially regarding the offensive use of shields, deliberate disguising of identification badges and the destruction of database evidence which might incriminate an officer.*

Rather thin fare, perhaps, but what started to emerge in the evening was a much larger story that elevated the event from media spectacle to tragedy. Ian Tomlinson, a 47-year-old newspaper vendor was dead on the street. This was not quite the same as incidents years before such as in Red Lion Square (1974) or at Southall (1979) and Tomlinson was not a Kevin Gately or Blair Peach for he was not only a bystander but the actual assault from police was caught on camera, the film of which was sent to the *Guardian* newspaper. Tomlinson, himself, wearing a blue t-shirt and hands in pockets had been making his way through the crowd, down King William Street and into Royal Exchange Passage. There at 7.20 p.m. he passed some police in riot gear and some dog handlers; his apparent insouciance at the police order to move on provoked anger in a member of the Territorial Support Group (TSG) who struck him on the leg with a baton and then lunged at him pushing him over. Tomlinson, with his back still to the officer and hands still in pockets, fell to the pavement. Dazed and sitting on the floor Tomlinson then remonstrated with the officers for a few seconds ; 'What the fuck are you doing', he

---

* This was especially acute as one officer had already been suspended following the death of Ian Tomlinson. Nicola Fisher had every reason to be wary of police tactics as she was assaulted by sergeant Delroy Smellie from the TSG who was filmed hitting her with a baton at the vigil for Tomlinson on 2 April. Fisher was severely bruised. Smellie was charged with assault. Police horses were also used to disperse a peaceful, if angry, crowd. Another march took place on 11 April. In March 2010, it was reported that the case against sergeant Smellie might have to be dropped as Fisher had decided not to give evidence, having apparently sold her story to the publicist, Max Clifford. It went ahead however with film evidence substituting for witness evidence. Smellie was acquitted and returned to active service on 31 March 2010.

appears to say. The police, hesitating, leave him there to be helped up by a demonstrator. Having got to his feet Tomlinson walks to Cornhill and falls down. People gather to help, one of whom Lucy Apps is a third year medical student. Tomlinson at first appears to be bemused and well, 'laughing' as Apps reported, yet he soon ceases to respond to questions and mysteriously and suddenly dies. At that moment the police who so far have failed to deal with the incident, move the crowd along. Two trained police medics were unable to save Tomlinson.

The incident appeared a tragic accident, an unfortunate effect of protest. A spokesman for the TSG was soon on television to refute rumours of police brutality. In the statement the officer made it quite clear that the police and ambulance response was delayed by a mob throwing missiles. The story, which could easily be tested against CCTV and television evidence was quite evidently untrue. Police also accused Tomlinson of being a vagrant to diminish public sympathy. Nevertheless, by now potentially damning evidence was starting to emerge on other mobile phone footage. To counter this, Tomlinson's family was told by a senior City of London policeman that their father may have died from a blow delivered by a protestor 'dressed in a policeman uniform'.[6] Such a statement following the camera evidence was patently absurd and the police and IPCC were accused by campaign group Inquest (who assist relatives when there are deaths in custody) not only of a cover-up but also of incompetence as forensic evidence was not collected immediately. Indeed, the IPCC, also claimed that there was no CCTV coverage to show what happened, which delayed the investigation. As with the de Menezes' incident during 2005, the death of Tomlinson suggested serious systemic problems with police reliability both in terms of information exchange and of accountability. Two post mortems followed which could not agree on cause of death; the first suggested a heart attack whilst the second suggested Tomlinson's injuries were consistent with an 'abdominal haemorrhage'.

Frustrated by the slowness of the police investigation, *Channel Four News* decided to forensically analyse the footage and especially the footage of one officer in particular, a man (or woman) who wielded a baton in the left hand, did not carry a riot shield, was ungloved, had their fluorescent jacket tucked into their trousers and had their balaclava-style top pulled up under the riot shield that showed only their eyes. The officer is watched on CCTV chasing and holding on to protestors, one of whom escapes. Finally, after several days of investigation the suspected officer (a sergeant) had still not been suspended. The outrageous and apparent deliberate incompetence by the police in their investigation suggested to many that there was no taste for tracking down the perpetrator, an apparently identifiable and known policeman. The officer's eventual suspension led to a third autopsy.*

Following the quite slight disturbances, but disastrous policing of the G20, it was clear that there was a real problem with the Metropolitan Police's capacity to keep law and order without the police themselves being seen to abrogate the laws they were meant to uphold. It was clear to all that the ordinary policeman required to deal with disturbances was poorly trained in riot control and had a rather loose grip of what was and was not lawful in situations of trespass, arrest and human rights legislation. In all, this was suggestive of a wider and deeper problem as the TSG had been accused of 159 assaults, some sexual, before G20, during the period up to April 2009. The G20 protests brought 282 more complaints, 90 from those either a victim of or witness to alleged police brutality and 60 examined by the Metropolitan Police's professional standards department. These included such actions as being hit with the edge of a riot shield, being deliberately stamped upon (and a worrying trend), women being dragged across tarmac by their hair.[7] Of the 730 men in the squad, there had been 547 allegations in 2009 and 289 officers investigated but not one conviction.[8]

At the IPCC Inquiry, Hardwick made it quite clear that the police needed greater supervision and that 'the police [were] here as public servants' and not as 'masters'.[9] The scandal was such that Sir Paul Stephenson, then Acting Commissioner had called for the disbandment of the group. Indeed, Stephenson, had been brought in to replace Sir Ian Blair, whose actions after the shooting of de Menezes, had effectively forfeited the confidence of the mayor, Boris Johnson, was now also worried about a 'Menezes moment'.[10] Intense scrutiny of the legality of the action of the police led in May to the High Court banning the routine storage of the photographs of protestors by police. The original investigation into the keeping of a comprehensive database of UK wide protestors had been instigated by the *Guardian* newspaper in March 2009. The judges ruled such actions breached the Human Rights Act. Lord Justice Dyson said that 'there were [sic] very serious human rights issues which arise when the state obtains and retains the images of persons who have committed no offence and are not suspected of having committed any offence'.[11] Lord Collins said such databases had a 'chilling effect' on lawful protestors.

The fact that a number of police were caught on camera acting in an unprofessional way by hiding or swopping their identification number or by using excessive force or brutal behaviour did not help. The confidence of the public was however, effectively destroyed when

---

*The policeman's identity was not revealed until 22 July 2010. He is Constable Simon Harwood of the TSG. No action was recommended against the officer because of lack of clarity in the autopsies.

the suspicious death of Ian Tomlinson was revealed on the film footage shown on national television. As the G20 protest was just one of a number that had recently occurred across Britain which had been dealt with using different methods and with various degrees of success, but following different policing practice, it was felt that an overarching policy document might clear up misunderstandings, clarify training procedures and reassure the public. The document called *Adapting to Protest – Nurturing the British Model of Policing* was published online by Her Majesty's Inspector of Police (HMIC) in 2009. On 25 March 2010, the Metropolitan Police Authority issued its own report on the G20 disorders. The report on Operation Glencoe, the police code name for the policing of the protest, was produced by its Civil Liberties panel and arrived at findings little different from those of the Inspectorate.

Although prompted by issues over the policing of the G20, the Inspectorate's report itself concentrated on a series of other diverse protest situations. These were the Camp for Climate Action held at Drax power station in 2008 during August to September; the Camp for Climate Action held at Kingsnorth in Kent during July to August; the Tamil protests in April to June; the BNP's 'private' rally and anti-fascist counter-demonstration in Derbyshire during August; the Camp for Climate Action held at Blackheath in London during August and September and two actions against the EDL, one the ban in Luton in August and the other the policing of the EDL (or Casuals United) riot in Birmingham. From these and other international scenarios the HMIC hoped to draw reasonable conclusions about British policing, create a greater sense of training and discipline, provide good practice guidelines, remind forces of their lawful commitments and above all restore confidence in the British 'bobby'. The difficult conclusion of the report with regard to present practice during 2009 was that,

> When thousands of protesters converge from around the world on a particular location that is hosting, for example, a G20 . . . the level of risk increases substantially, as does the possibility of significant levels of disorder. It is difficult in such circumstances to assess the intent of the thousands of protesters and it becomes more likely that restrictions or conditions may be imposed on protesters. The policing response to mass global protest in the majority of jurisdictions evaluated [in 2009] tended to be much more *militarised* in character [emphasis mine].[12]

The Inspectors found at least nine areas of concern, ranging from 'a disconnection between individual officer training and public order training' especially with regard to the use of batons; diversity in the levels at which officers understood current legislation; inconsistency in approach and tactics; inconsistent equipment; 'lack of public order command capability'; out of date training, both with regard to the police manual and especially with regard to human rights; 'inappropriate use of public order powers' such as stop and search at demonstrations; and a general vagueness as to methods of accountability.[13]

'The original (nineteenth-century) policing model' began the report, 'plac[ed] a high value on tolerance and winning the consent of the public', but the report concluded pressures were building from a number of 'highly charged events' which might lead to the 'British model being easily eroded by premature displays of formidable public order protective uniform and equipment'.[14] The report continued that 'there [were] likely to be more highly charged events in the future . . . as we move[d] towards the Olympics in 2012'.[15] The report then highlighted a number of 'failures' at all levels which would prove difficult to remedy without proper order and proper discipline seen to be working by the world's media, for the report acknowledged 'the world of protest has gone global . . . with images sent around the world'.[16] 'Like it or not, the media are the eyes and ears of the people.'[17] Indeed, 'it [was] no longer an option for the police not to include the media in briefings before, during and after large scale public order events'.[18] The key shift had to be 'a movement away from the system of "escalated force" . . . towards a system of 'negotiated management'''.[19] A 'dynamic crowd' had to be managed by 'dialogue' and 'communication'.[20]

What of radical protest in the future in a period when the old divisions of left and right have collapsed and when the word radical may as easily denote an environmental protester as an Islamic jihadist? What indeed might be the future in a world where 'progressives' seek to make alliances with 'reactionaries' in a show of solidarity 'against' the latest foreign policy of the United States or the next banking collapse which might prove the bankruptcy of neo-conservatism? The demands of multiculturalism, environmentalism and anti-corporatism are as emotional in their focus as they are political, but their heterodox nature has to function without the old certainties guaranteed by a solid working class, a strong trade union leadership and Marxist principles.

And such strange alliances between those who would naturally have little to say to each other potentially realign traditional political options but they also decrease the likelihood of clear and effective action except in very circumscribed and limited circumstances where the cause is temporary. No more evident confusion could be discerned than in the Stop the War coalition march against the Iraq war. The journalist Nick Cohen mused

> If I were to ask you to name the most prominent Left-wing politician in Britain, you would probably name Ken Livingstone.

Yet he has welcomed those who opposed feminism and democracy in the Arab world. The Stop the War coalition was no better. One of the largest demonstrations in British history, it was led by Trotskyites who proclaimed themselves to be Left wing, and then formed an alliance with ultra Right-wing Islamist groups rather than Muslims of liberal background. The protest's chief figure was George Galloway, who during a visit to Iraq in 1994 was reported to have commended the 'courage' of Saddam Hussein (BBC News, 22 April 2003). The Left did not mind that it was being led by a man who had apparently praised a genocidal dictator. Indeed Galloway was elected to Parliament at the last election as the first allegedly far Left-wing MP in 50 years (he was defeated however in the general election of 2010).[21]

These confusions of identity and purpose were exemplified by the formation and partial success of RESPECT which was created from an unlikely alliance opposing the Iraq war.

In the aftermath of the anti-war demonstrations in 2003, sections of the Marxist Left in Britain (led by the Socialist Workers Party) launched 'RESPECT – The Unity Coalition', an electoral front supported by the Muslim Association of Britain. Although this prompted criticism from many on the radical Left, who saw the coalition as opportunistic, 'communalist' and overly influenced by conservative community leaders, it nevertheless succeeded in attracting a layer of Muslims into Left-wing community activism.[22]

Such, however, is the apparent usefulness of such alliances between 'white' middle-class liberal revolutionaries and Islamic reactionaries that they are maintained whenever the cause is anti-America or the actions of its allies in the Middle East which was the case on 3 January 2009 when protesters of the British far left and the Islamic far right marched to the Israeli embassy in Kensington to protest against the Israeli incursion into Gaza. Both Tony Benn and Ken Livingstone had earlier addressed crowds, uniting those whose views on matters of participatory democracy could not have been more opposed and yet whose opposing voices might be momentarily stifled in hatred of Western decadence (whether capitalist or imperialist). Such confusions of political outlook have fatally weakened the sense of purpose amongst progressive social democrats who would not hesitate to label their old domestic enemy the far right as fascist, but who falter and retreat with Islamic reactionary views.

Perhaps the most revolutionary groups in London today are those from the Muslim community in the East End and whose 'headquarters' appears to be centred on the East London Mosque

(ELM) on Whitechapel Road. Such groups as the Islamic Forum for Europe (IFE) are apparently using tactics such as entrism to gain power in the council (Tower Hamlets) and local Labour Party (they may perhaps have abandoned George Galloway and RESPECT).* Such tactics, if proven, which attempt to form bloc interests on a one issue agenda (Sha'ria) are a partial return to the older politics of the Militant Tendency of the 1980s, but are also the more contemporary and subversive by the nature of their use of organization, new media and word of mouth in a tight-knit community. Fundamentalist Islamic philosophy may portray itself as a return to values lost to Muslims adrift in the West, but it is in fact a thoroughly contemporary movement based upon an ideological platform that can be spread by Western communication networks. Islamism as a political movement rose in exact proportion to the fall of communism and uses many of the latter's often secret revolutionary tactics to gain its universal strategic end. Unlike communism, its power base may ultimately remain the East End (whose MP in 1945 was the communist Phil Piratin; like Galloway voted in under special circumstances) until the affluence of the current community sees it decamp for the suburbs.

The other area considered to need urgent attention is green politics, it being usually opposed to corporatism and finance, both of which have fuelled the scientific and information revolutions of the last century. Science once led the way to the future. Now we no longer trust science and the future has been put on hold. We have long been told that there are finite resources and our relentless sacking of the planet has made us the problem. Was the idea of the 'future' and of progress simply an ideology like all the others, collapsing under the weight of the melting ice caps? The Green Party has never done as well as it might and has only now gained a single member of parliament (Caroline Lucas: Brighton Pavilion). Tamsin Omond stood against Glenda Jackson in the constituency of Kilburn and Hampstead in the 2010 elections. Whilst Jackson represents the old style Labour Party, Omond was hoping her brand of fiery rhetoric and action would galvanise younger voters. The founder of Green campaign group Climate Rush, Omond has taken part in stunts such as climbing the Houses of Parliament, stopping traffic on Westminster Bridge and gluing herself to a statue.** She had canvassers dressed as suffragettes and more importantly used social media networks to target her voters, using the latest media and the savvy of the young

---

*This at least was the accusation made by journalist Andrew Gilligan on the Channel 4 programme *Dispatches* on Monday 1 March 2010 (though vehemently denied by both the ELM and the IFE).

**Omond's tactics proved very media friendly.

who use such things everyday to bypass Jackson's traditional (and apparently tired and discredited) approach to politics. With all her flamboyant tactics Omond still polled only 123 votes! Omond's localism and community-based political platform peculiarly replicated some of the Conservatives own current rhetoric on community self help. She was nevertheless defeated.

Where will radicalism go now that traditional party politics has been smeared with corruption, laziness and moral laxity? The public appear keen on alternatives to those greedy politicians who seem always on the take and rarely seem to work for their constituents? Will people turn to 'alternative' political parties such as the United Kingdom Independence Party (UKIP) or the BNP, outraged by those in power who seem deaf to every complaint or will this be an opportunity for radical outsiders to capitalize on the moment? It is, perhaps, symptomatic of the fear mainstream politicians have of a disillusioned and frustrated electorate that the nearly inaugurated and much heralded 2010 electoral debates were held in front of a selected audience who were barred from showing their appreciation by clapping or their disapprobation by booing and heckling (but not in Scotland). Such sanitized electioneering, carried on only in the media demands its corollary on the streets, both emotional and visceral as its antidote. During the 2010 election campaign, open air political rallies were carefully staged managed and swiftly over. Nevertheless, that did not stop an egg being thrown at David Cameron in Saltash nor Gordon Brown's 'bigot' gaffe in Rochdale.

Progressives have for the last twenty years not merely made alliance with those opposing progress they too have become reactionaries themselves, opposing scientific progress, the expansion of transport networks, the greater consumption of resources, universalism and Western progressive enlightenment. What has remained is a feeling of moral rectitude and a sustained sense of grievance which as often as not lacks focus, definition or moral certainty. Such desperation to 'do the right thing' by those people recognized as minorities, the oppressed, the 'South' or the apparently repressed has meant that there has been little thought given to the old universal certainties that tied protest to a belief in advancing human rights and civilization generally. Identity politics which stresses origins, fluidity and pluralism and makes much of the intrinsic nature of self might be fine if it was still attached to the idea of becoming which has no use for the stultifying inertia of origination and selfhood, but instead talks of universalism, brotherhood and development – a politics of change using now as year zero: what I can become rather than what I am.

Appendix One

Shadow of a Warrior Queen

BOUDICCA AND THE DESTRUCTION OF LONDON: UNANSWERED QUESTIONS

We know very little about Boudicca and even less about her anonymous daughters, her husband the shadowy Prasutagus, their household and retainers, where they may have lived, fought, died or been buried. We have no strong grasp of who or how many were the Iceni, or what their daily conversation was or their immediate hopes and fears. Our words for Iceni society are already packed with duplicity: tribe, warrior, priest, native, barbarian, king. Many of these definitions come directly from Roman historians trying to make sense of a closely knit agricultural society based upon ties of kinship and allegiance. Even the 'tribal' names (which changed for unknown reasons between the Caesarian and Claudian invasions) tell us almost nothing and may be little more than dynastic titles for groups of people joined under a certain ruler. For a Roman, all non-Romans were essentially barbarians – fascinating, exotic, very dangerous and, at least on first contact, utterly alien and 'other' (hence the terror engendered in the legions every time they came into contact with an army of indigenous warriors). Tacitus remarks, 'remember we are dealing with barbarians' – who, however familiar by looks, were simply *unknowable*.

It is of course, a truism that the Romans were not racially biased.

> There is little evidence that the Romans had any general racial prejudice in the modern sense. Hence they assumed anyone, or almost anyone, could absorb Roman culture and manners, even as they themselves (despite the protests of moralists and conservatives) borrowed extensively from other cultures, especially in the fields of art and religion.[1]

Yet this disguises the fact that Romans demanded conformism. Absorption equalled assimilation into the civil, legal and religious structure of being governed as Roman. Refusal meant persecution or extermination (policies adopted towards both religious dissenters such as the early Christians and tribal opponents). For the rulers of an ethnically diverse, multilingual empire, the Romans were ever conservative and conformist. Otherness came from a wilful refusal to become Roman and learn Latin. The determining quality of Roman civilization was similarity in terms of recognition of the cultural rules. The Romans simply could not understand the stubbornness of other highly civilized metropolitan peoples (in the Middle East) or the supposed haphazardness of agrarian tribespeople.

The war of AD 60 itself is recorded in full by only two Roman historians, from whom the name Boudicca has come down through history. The evidence of destruction exists as a layer of blackened earth in Colchester, St Albans and London. The Roman texts are therefore supported only by the circumstantial evidence of city fires (a frequent occurrence in wooden towns). There is almost no *direct* evidence of violent destruction through deliberate human intervention, although skulls purportedly from the period were found in excavations around the Walbrook in London. The archaeology has therefore always been used to support the Roman texts (like biblical archaeology supporting the Gospels), for no independent voice records the narrative of events and no oral tradition remains. Indeed even the name Boudicca is complicated by the fact that it translates as 'Victory', a rather convenient name for a warrior queen and one she may have adopted or been given at a symbolic or ritual event. She may have been therefore Boudicca or another Celtic variant, Buddia, or neither to her followers. She does not name herself in Tacitus's narrative.

The first written record of the war occurs in the work of P. Cornelius Tacitus, a Roman administrator and historian who was the son-in-law of Britain's most famous governor, Agricola, a participant in the war himself. Born around AD 55, Tacitus had a personal interest in Britain through his marriage and was sufficiently close in time to be able to write from contemporary evidence, Roman records and the oral traditions of legionary families. He did not visit Britain, however, and was only too well aware of the generic requirements of history, the stylistic shape and tone needed for a retelling. Boudicca fascinated him, not merely as a person in her own right but because she represented a power against which Roman honour and virtue could be tested. For Tacitus it was Roman incompetence that allowed Boudicca to cause trouble but it was equally important that Boudicca and her followers were not represented as mindless savages, for then Roman virtue would have no worthy opponent. Read this way, Tacitus's account is determined by a Roman readership for whom history is a way of recalling a republican ideal in a world fallen into decadence and led by greed and political intrigue. The nobility of the Roman generals is contrasted with the barbarian warrior leaders. However noble, brave and honourable Boudicca's speeches, they are predicated upon a background of wanton terror and atrocity, which can never be forgotten. Natives always reverted to type. Roman generals, however, trusted their troops and the *discipline* of the legions; they were capable of following the path of virtue and many did so even when prosecuting a punitive campaign. Only when campaigners went too far, as with Paulinus's revenge ride into East Anglia, or legionaries got out of hand, does Tacitus condemn them, for discipline and virtue (truth to an unspoken Roman personal code of honour) had broken down and on these two alone Roman power allegedly rested. It was the ability of the legions to recover from disaster and disadvantage that marked their superiority over undisciplined natives and barbarian hordes.

Tacitus's account gives only glimpses of the political state of Britain during the war of AD 60. The independence that Prasutagus thought that he had won by making the emperor co-heir was cruelly stolen away when Roman troops arrived to protect Roman administrators and their slaves who were intent on occupying the Icenian territories just as they had occupied the area in Essex and Suffolk of their neighbours the Trinobantes. It is unclear what this 'occupation' meant for Boudicca (or her representatives) as they had obviously not expected an attack and had prepared no forces. The Romans may therefore have arrived uninvited from nearby Colchester or, more likely, marched from London on the orders of the imperial agent Catus Decianus. The Iceni may have believed this to be a diplomatic mission to renegotiate terms. Either way, it is clear that the Iceni felt themselves to be *outside* Roman rule and independent of Roman taxation or law. They were willing to pay tribute, the naming of the emperor as co-heir clearly a *symbolic* gesture verifying neighbours (British and Roman) in kinship. No one expected an occupying force nor one intent on such violence. The Romans clearly intended to cash in their cheque and turn Iceni lands into part of the military province.

Things then turn very ugly. Boudicca is seized and flogged. We do not know why, but this and the rape of her children is clearly a symptom rather than a cause of the war. The daughters may have been raped by Roman 'slaves', something that would have been deeply humiliating to the royal household. Yet these slaves were not mere menials but clearly the civil servants and administrators of the Roman authorities. Slaves such as Narcissus and Polyclitus could rise to become the most important men in the empire below the Emperor, so the term is very wide and impossible to interpret.

Why then were Icenian lands occupied, the royal household humiliated and the nobility deprived of its estates? Because the Romans *knew* they were plotting a war. It seems clear that the Iceni and Trinobantes were possibly conspiring *before* the occupation, which itself was a punitive raid to show once and for all who was in charge. Tacitus tells us that the Trinobantes were already plotting to regain *their* ancestral capital (Colchester) for 'they had secretly plotted together to become free again'. Insulted by the ex-legionaries who had made Camulodunum their home and expelled the aboriginal inhabitants, the Trinobantes were witness to the building of the largest structure yet seen in the British Isles, 'a blatant stronghold of alien rule'. This itself was an insult but even more insulting was the fact that the priests of the emperor cult were of Trinobantian origin and so the Romans were using Trinobantian administrators to tax their own 'tribe' for constant tribute for the temple. This was extortion in which the Trinobantes had become unwilling partners. Even more dreadful was the fact that the retired legionaries seemed to be under no legal or disciplinary restraints. For all intents and purposes the north-east corner of modern Essex and the southern part of Suffolk were under permanent martial law designed to uphold an arbitrary system of legalized banditry. Nevertheless, Tacitus tells us 'servitude had not broken them'. The bonds of household and kinship still held amongst these Britons as it did still with those non-provincial Britons north of the Thames and west of the Sussex Weald.

Some modern historians have suggested that 'the rebellion of Boudicca' was a consequence of the 'new' status of tribal life in Norfolk, hence 'By AD 60 we may expect a number of the British tribes to have been formally recognized as *civitates*, or non-citizen but regular local authorities on the Roman pattern, to whom various functions were delegated, and it is likely that the kingdoms of Prasutagus of the Iceni and of Cogidubnus and perhaps others were similarly regulated.'[2]

Not only is there scant evidence for such an assertion, but the 'status' that came from recognition as *civitates* for a Roman must surely in East Anglia have been a scandalous humiliation and degradation (although not perhaps on the south coast of the province of Britain proper). The Iceni had been forced to take on exorbitant loans that were the immediate cause of the Roman delegation's visit to Norfolk. Either way, what to the Romans were taxes (and therefore legitimate) were probably extortionate loan charges to a bitter Icenian nobility. Constant debt brought fiscal as well as moral obligations. It is possible that Prasutagus hoped to 'buy off' the Emperor in his (Roman style) will in order to alleviate the entrapment of debt. Such a 'payment' would make the Emperor a sleeping partner in the kingdom, an arrangement of symbolic honour to replace a situation of actual bankruptcy. The Emperor's men, acting as unruly bailiffs, understood debt quite differently. The war therefore was between contracted and equal partners – not a rebellion; for the Iceni at least a war of opposing 'nations' with equal but opposite diplomatic rights. The dispersed Trinobantes, still sensible of their independence, saw the war as a way of returning 'home' to ancestral lands.

The war may be seen as part of the entrepreneurial phase of the early Roman Empire, where the boundaries of the geographical limits of conquest also constantly shifted the power structures in Rome itself. Britain refused to remain peaceful for over a hundred years, the German borders remained in a state of continual flux and alert and within ten years the Middle Eastern provinces rose in a series of wars of 'independence' to which the Romans answered with extermination and dispersal. We may not be surprised to find that Suetonius Paulinus, ex-Governor, having quit Britain, is next seen as a central figure in the growing disturbances in the heart of the empire, nor that a former commander of legions in Britain, Vespasian, was in command in the Middle East.

The Icenian war is, in this context, a war caused by rapid imperial expansion on behalf of a Roman machine unable to comprehend the speed of its own conquests or absorb the diplomatic lessons of imperial rule. Druid, Jew and German tribesman were therefore united in a strange and prolonged period of major world disturbance in which the Romans were the *sole* aggressors. This was a world war of sorts carried out sporadically and across global dimensions. Such a situation was not lost on Tacitus, who suggests that the lesson was also not lost on the leaders of later British wars of independence who were aware of struggles on the German borders and the meaning of those struggles.

> You have mustered to a man, and all of you are free . . . We, the most distant dwellers upon earth, the last of the free . . . the Romans, . . . pillagers of the world . . . create a desolation and call it peace . . . can you seriously think that those Gauls and Germans – and, to our bitter shame, many Britons too – are bound to Rome by genuine loyalty or affection?[3]

The destruction of Camulodunum was perhaps being prepared before the final outrage committed by the Roman administrators. Rumour-mongers, fifth columnists and saboteurs roamed the environs of the city near the theatre and senate-house. A night raid by Trinobantian warriors toppled the statue of Victory – they had entered the town by stealth, knowing its layout and knowing that it was unprotected by any effective defence earthworks. Alternatively, it may have been the work of Trinobantian freemen or slaves whom the Romans trusted and who were already within the city. The east coast was filled with portents and wonders all the way to the Thames itself.

The confused and concerned Roman inhabitants began a partial evacuation (through Mersea Island in the Blackwater estuary or Fingringhoe, on the Colne estuary) but they also appealed to Catus Decianus, who in the absence of Paulinus was now district commander. He miscalculated and sent 200 men, probably auxiliaries. If such was the case, and given the preparation and marching time, the crisis now entered its final phase, some months after the first preparations for war by the Iceni and Trinobantes.

By a series of forced marches Paulinus got back to Londinium with a skeleton force, news already brought to his headquarters that part of the Ninth Legion had ceased to exist. In order to re-organize, he abandoned the town leaving women, old people and those who already had made it their permanent home. It is these people Boudicca slaughtered, although Tacitus leaves it quite unclear why escape by river, or by the bridge or with the regrouping Roman forces, would not have left a ghost town. The slaughter in London alone is meant to run into tens of thousands adding to the thousands slaughtered elsewhere, at Verulamium, Camulodunum and elsewhere in Suffolk, Essex and Hertfordshire. Tacitus puts the total deaths by Boudicca's forces alone at 70,000 Romans and 'provincials'. By provincials can he mean anything less than British 'collaborators' settled peaceably under Roman rule and following Roman gods and ways? This was a war against both the Romans and their British accomplices. Indeed the atrocities committed by Boudicca's forces (if not artistic licence) suggest a war to settle old scores, gain revenge against Roman and Briton alike with especial hatred reserved for quiescent tribes.

This was a war of annihilation fuelled by a deep and ancient anger and a desperate craving for satisfaction in blood. Its centre was in Icenian territory but its ideological centre was on besieged Mona – or at least that is how it appears on a first reading of Tacitus's account. It may be more likely that the Trinobantes and Iceni had already abandoned some of the traditional Celtic religious beliefs by the rising of AD 60. Trinobantian priests worked in the Temple of Claudius and as Tacitus tells us Paulinus's campaign in Wales was a strategic opportunity not to be missed. It may be that druidic 'agents' travelled amongst hostile tribes fomenting dissent. Tacitus suggests as much. This was a war to destroy the alien Romans and their collaborationist friends rather than an ideological war to defend the ancient groves of druiddom. There is no suggestion that activities on Mona would themselves had led eastern tribes to war. Druidic justification was only part of the political mix, which saw the destruction of Roman provincial life and Londinium in flames.

Why did Boudicca destroy Londinium with such extraordinary violence? Tacitus again gives us two tantalizing clues. The first relates to the role of Catus Decianus, the Roman bureaucrat and second in command to Paulinus. Either during or just before Paulinus's Welsh campaign the Iceni had been visited by Decianus' agents intent on their due. It is quite possible that the order to carry out the occupation was merely a routine procedure on orders of Decianus's office before Paulinus's departure but with Paulinus's cooperation (as it needed Roman 'offices').

Paulinus emerges as a violent and vindictive soldier bent on absolute revenge ('as if every injury was personal'). He had left for Wales without securing his rear, and believed he had lost a whole command (the Ninth Legion). The Ninth had been destroyed, Londinium and Camulodunum had been abandoned as undefendable, Mona had only been temporarily occupied and the commander of the legions called to Paulinus's aid had feared to leave barracks because of concern about an immediate local insurrection (he later committed suicide). Paulinus had now lost control and, worse, Boudicca had escaped his clutches by poisoning herself. An imperial inquiry suggested the immediate removal of this incompetent general whose 'failures [were] attributed to perversity – and his successes to luck'. To make things worse Decianus and Paulinus seemed to have nothing but dislike and contempt for each other. There were two Roman power centres in Britain in AD 60.

It is clear that the destruction of Londinium was not intended to draw Paulinus into a trap, as the destruction of the Ninth was quite sufficient. Clearly, in some ways, the destruction of Camulodunum may have been intended to draw the Ninth into a trap on the line of march (Paulinus blamed the commander's 'rashness' for the failure). Rather, Londinium may have been taken not for 'loot', as Tacitus puts it brutally, but because it represented the new overt collaboration that was emerging between Romans and Britons ('those attached to the place'). London was also the probable headquarters of Decianus, who was the epitome of the rapacious colonial administrator, the symbol of all the Iceni hated and the direct cause of their humiliation. It is ironic therefore that at the same time as Paulinus arrived in Londinium, Decianus was catching a boat to Gaul, quite possibly from Mersea near Colchester (if not London itself), 'horrified by the catastrophe, and by his unpopularity', for, Tacitus tells us explicitly, 'it was his rapacity which had driven the province to war'. Decianus escaped to continue his complaining about Paulinus but his town did not, nor those who wished to find an accommodation with Decianus and his Roman ways, taxes and tithes. Tacitus sees only obliquely the political significance of Londinium, a town fitted to traders, merchandise and travellers.

We know next to nothing about the Romanized population of London, a handful of names preserved through later monuments and inscriptions. No wonder this produces such diverse views as the following:

> The most abundant source for the nature of a Roman town's population is its inscriptions. The inscriptions of London are not numerous, the recorded names very few. But the few that are known are all Roman; there are no signs at all of freeborn persons with native names, who formed the overwhelming bulk of the population of all classes in the normal cities of Gaul and Britain in the early empire. Though the quantity of information is exceedingly small, what it says is clear; as far as the limited available evidence goes, the early population of London was of foreign, continental, Roman, not of British origin.[4]

and

> That Londinium was home to thousands of 'Britons' as well as 'Romans' would seem likely simply from the size of the population that was massacred.[5]

In the mind of a Roman historian London was not a *home* to the indigenous population but a magnet for booty-hungry and vandalizing barbarians come to prey on peaceful Roman citizenry and their provincial partners. Londinium becomes thereby a cockpit for the theatre of war, a dramatic and climactic scene for a barbarian success and *theatricality*, and a place to rehearse barbarian excess.

And this excessive theatrical violence (reported by Cassius Dio but not by Tacitus) is a further clue to the motives behind the Iceni advance, sack and occupation of London. Tacitus tells us that the Britons used 'crucifixation' in their repertoire of vengeance. If this is the case then they were using Roman means of punishment against Romans (we do not know whether crucifixions ever occurred in Britain). Perhaps, not knowing what they did, Tacitus merely invented a *Roman* scenario, which he then imparted to the tribes. Cassius Dio, however draws our attention to non-Roman torture-rituals, committed in the sacred grove of Andastre (possibly near the Walbrook Stream). One commentator suggests that the singularity of this deity (unique to Dio's writing and unknown from archaeological evidence) may be because, as a god of war and fertility (death and sex), Andastre had another more common name elsewhere. It may be that Andastre was an ancestor of Morrigan, Queen of Nightmares, but it is possible the name stands for 'victory' – Boudicca's own name. The *British* recovery of London may have had meanings lost to its Roman historians.

One final set of clues emerges for Boudicca's attack on London. The first rests in the suggestion that at the final battle the Britons were blocked by their heavy wagons and the second in the fact that the Iceni had neglected to sow their fields. These clues are both odd and intriguing. What are we to make of these wagons, which are clearly not the same as the chariots of the warriors? It is true that indigenous populations often moved with their families in wagons but why do so when the circuit of travel is so limited? London is only two days' march from Colchester, merely forty or so miles away along a straight road. Any attack could have been made by a war band or army marching on light rations and expecting a good store of food to be awaiting them once they arrived on the banks of the Thames. This is indeed what Tacitus tells us, but he also says that the Iceni neglected to sow crops. Why? Could this have been because war plans existed *prior* to early spring AD 60 and that a short campaign would ensure allowing time for sowing? This would require a war to begin at the worst time of year. The granaries of

London seem to be the target of Boudicca's forces as much as revenge. The granaries were certainly an outward sign of decadent and luxurious plenty but what if they were more? What if Iceni crops had begun to fail and that therefore the wagons were part of a greater movement – a migration eastward (possibly exacerbated by movement in the Brigantean population) which would therefore include the bulk of the population, some 80,000 migrants? (Ancient numbers are always suspect but one can conclude that this represented the bulk of the Iceni/Trinobantian army.) As far as Tacitus is concerned the Iceni had become little more than a booty-hungry horde by the time they reached London.

Such an explanation holds little water, despite the almost continuous butchery of the previous two or three weeks. The presence of wagons suggests connected movement which could have been avoided if an Iceni army had only needed to sally out of Norfolk for a series of raids and then build defences around their fen-protected homeland. The Iceni and their allies turned around at London either because they had reached their goal, or because they could not or would not fight the southern tribes or because they turned to face Paulinus. Their 'plunder' would have meant relief from a starving winter if the crops had failed.

And what then of the final catastrophic battle? Tacitus tells us only that it took place somewhere with a wood and a defile. Basing their evidence on this and Roman military displacements modern historians have put the Icenian army on the move north-west and north-east back towards Norfolk by circuitous routes. Archaeologists have long since dismissed Victorian romantics who saw Boudicca staging a last-ditch battle in Epping Forest or on the present site of platform 10 at King's Cross Station! The site, however, remains unknown.

Boudicca now controlled all of eastern Britain from the Wash to London, other tribes were restless, and only Paulinus opposed her. Given the above argument there is no reason to believe that Boudicca was *returning* to Norfolk. Instead she either turned to *defend the approaches to London*, which would now have become part of a greater Icenian kingdom, or she turned to protect her lines of communication. Boudicca would have calmly and optimistically waited for Paulinus to turn up. The romantic idea of a battle for London remains a real possibility despite lack of archaeological evidence (there is almost none elsewhere). Only *after* the disastrous defeat would the British remnant retreat homeward to their ancestral land. The Iceni empire had lasted perhaps less than a month.

Boudicca died and was buried away from Roman eyes and Roman revenge, yet, ironically, it was a Roman who caused her corpse to speak to us across the ages, of lost freedom and restored honour.

Appendix Two

The Huguenot and Italian Legacy

All aliens might be foreigners but not all foreigners are alien. Prominent amongst the foreigners in London were the Huguenots, Protestants from France who had arrived in England in ever increasing numbers. By the seventeenth century, between 200,000 and 250,000 Huguenots had left their homes and set out for Holland, England and America. Of these, 20,000 to 25,000 settled in London, by far the most important immigrant group after the Irish, taking root in Greenwich, Wandsworth, Spitalfields and Soho (not to mention an important colony in Colchester), and as far south as Wandsworth and Putney, bringing the skills of market gardening, paper making, dyeing and hatting to the semi-rural villages along the south-west bank of the Thames. The cry went up again that bloodsucking foreigners were swamping London. In 1593 the following verse was nailed to the Dutch Church in London:

> You strangers that inhabit this land!
> Note this same writing, do it understand;
> Conceive it well, for safety of your lives,
> Your goods, your children, and your dearest wives.

No one was caught, despite widespread concern within the Privy Council and City. Even in the eighteenth century, after long association with England and English ways, Huguenots and their descendants met abuse. One French visitor was horrified at the 'volley of abusive litanies' he faced 'at every street corner', 'the constant burthen of these litanies was, French dog, French b--------; to make any answer to them was accepting a challenge to fight; and my curiosity did not carry me so far'. In many instances, however, support for the *Protestant* Huguenots took second place to the abuse dolled out to the French generally, especially during the 'Popish Plot'.

There were riots in 1675, 1681 and 1683 as Irish and other weavers attacked the Huguenot workers living in Spitalfields whose superior cloth outsold their own. Charles II and his brother James (later James II), happy to have refugee Huguenots when it was convenient, had little intention of helping them towards naturalization despite the fact that in 1685, with the revocation of the Edict of Nantes (which had allowed freedom of belief), Protestantism was outlawed in France and its followers besieged. After all, the French were allies. London companies opposed Huguenot integration, and a new Huguenot church was opposed on grounds that it would create a permanent 'alien' body in London.

Relations with Huguenot families were ambivalent. People applauded their Calvinism and hated their economic power, complaining of foreign speech and strange ways – French food was anathematized for creating 'noisome' urine! In 1695 a Huguenot family were threatened by English dyers living in 'Wandsor' after the rejection in 1694 of a Bill to naturalize the refugees. 'Let us kick the Bill out of the House, then the foreigners out of the kingdom,' demanded one MP. Despite everything, the Huguenots quickly became 'English', readily accepting the rules and position of the Church of England, which welcomed their congregations. When Wandsworth became a borough in 1965 it included in its coat of arms the 'tears' of the Huguenot refugees.

By the eighteenth century Huguenots accounted for 20 per cent of the population and were sometimes resented for their industriousness and wealth. The industrial mills on the Wandle, which ran into the Thames, were also owned by these French immigrants. London could easily absorb them, its population so large by the 1750s that no group could make any real demographic crisis occur. Indeed, the population had risen from just under 200,000 in 1600 to 500,000 by 1700 and 675,000 by 1750; by 1700 it was already twenty times the size of the next largest city, with 9.5 per cent of the population within its increasing boundaries. Huguenots brought skills that fitted in to the new consumer culture, which required food, drink, clothing, wig makers and textile workers, not to mention doctors and ministers.

The Italian presence in London has roots deep in the Middle Ages; the majority of those who came from the many city states of Italy were aristocrats, ambassadors, doctors and craftsmen. The growing stereotype of the 'machiavel' in English drama created Italian villains with twirling moustaches, insatiable libidos and cloaked stiletto knives who would live on to haunt the pages of Georgian Gothic, but Italians, though considered subtle and crafty, were rarely personally victimized after their reputation during the Middle Ages as bankers and merchants faded from memory. During the nineteenth century small groups of artisans from northern Italy began settling in Manchester and in Clerkenwell, then the traditional destination of foreign skilled immigrants. Poor settlers arrived in the 1820s and 1830s, walking their way across Europe to catch the ferry for Britain. New arrivals (usually beholden to a 'padrone') dealt in semi-skilled work such as knife grinding, ice-cream vending, statuette making or food production. Others were the highly skilled terrazzo craftsmen much in demand during the 1880s. Ice-cream manufacture alone was so successful it tripled the Italian immigrant population.

By the 1880s, the London Italians could boast a school, a large Catholic church and a hospital. They also formed political clubs such as the Mazzini Garibaldi Club. With the success of Mussolini in Italy after the First World War, London Italians flocked to the newly formed fascist clubs. It is often forgotten that British Italians played a part in the rise of British fascist consciousness. The community was especially proud of its war heroes, whose military honours and ceremonial uniforms were paraded on Armistice Day. *Ex-combattenti*, as the veterans were called, soon became black-clad *fasciti*, and led by their commander, Captain Gelmetti, could be found giving the fascist salute at the tomb of the Unknown Warrior at Westminster Abbey. With its great portrait of Il Duce, the Club Co-operativo in Greek Street became the centre for activities during the early 1930s, followed by new premises in Charing Cross Road later in the decade.

The fascist clubs organized outside Italy were intended as social centres and centres of education. An Italian school was based at the London fascist headquarters for young Italians whose language skills needed to be improved. Joining such clubs was not merely patriotic (many London Italians still felt *alien* in Britain) but was a good way to find husbands and wives with a suitable background.

British neighbours tended to ignore these Italian clubs and their activities until things came to a head as war approached. Then the Italian community metamorphosed into the 'enemy', leading to rioting in Scotland and window-breaking amongst the delicatessens and restaurants of Soho. One Soho grocer's carried notices telling customers that it was 'entirely British' and the Spaghetti House renamed itself the British Food Shop.

On 10 June 1940 all Italians between sixteen and seventy with less than twenty years' residence were interned, to the outrage of many who considered themselves British and now were behind wire with real enemies. Roundups could be random. The restaurateur P. Leoni, well-known owner of the famous Quo Vadis in Soho, was arrested even though he had been in Britain since 1907 and was obviously no threat. Tragically 400 internees (sent abroad as security risks) were drowned when the *Arandora Star* was torpedoed. Hatred was short-lived: the war over, Italians returned to the affectionate position they had always enjoyed in London life and continue to enjoy today.

Appendix Three

Assassination Attempts on the Royal Family

In 1842, two men, John Francis and John Bean, shot at Queen Victoria in front of Buckingham Palace. It all seemed utterly futile. Sir Robert Peel simply thought these 'shabby' men had expressions of mere 'idiocy' rather than malice and let it go at that.[1] Francis was tried for high treason and sentenced to death, but this was commuted to transportation for life on 2 July. He went to Van Diemen's Land and entered an unsuccessful petition for mercy. In September 1855 he vanished. John Bean, convicted of a misdemeanour, served eighteen months.

In 1849, William Hamilton unsuccessfully tried to kill Victoria, as did Robert Pate in 1850 – he attacked her with his stick. Sent for seven years to Van Diemen's Land, he too was refused mercy. Another attack in February 1872 was again put down to imbecility rather than political compunction. This time the failed assassin was Arthur O'Connor, whose 'weak minded[ness]' had left him 'long the victim of delusion'.[2] With corroded pistols incapable of firing and unloaded anyway, his defence was that he only intended to scare the Queen. Either way, to avoid a state trial for treason, which would lend gravitas to the case, he was quietly tried and forgotten.

In 1881 royal correspondence was full of concern over Irish assassination squads. The scare had been caused by intelligence information that had contained a press clipping of the New York Irish paper, the *Irish World*, which had darkly hinted that the Queen's days were numbered. In March 1882 these fears seemed realized: Roderick MacLean (or McLean) jumped out at her when she arrived at Windsor Station and fired one of two cartridges from a revolver. A letter from Sir Henry Ponsonby, the Queen's private secretary, on 2 March despairs at this 'insane fellow of 26'. For Sir Henry and his class to be a regicide was proof of being 'insane'.

It should not be forgotten that for Victoria such 'insane' attacks were the result of another mania that she feared more than assassins: 'democratic' government. Echoing Her Majesty's feeling on the matter, Ponsonby wrote to Gladstone, the Prime Minister, on 23 April 1882:

> It is satisfactory to the Queen to observe that you consider it doubtful whether justice is properly vindicated under the present form of acquittal on the ground of insanity in cases of attempting to take away life, by eccentric individuals.
>
> In the trial of Maclean, the charge of the Lord Chief Justice certainly left no choice to the Jury and if this was the necessary effect

of the Law, Her Majesty thinks it worth consideration whether this Law should not be amended.

In Macnaghten's trial (1843) the feeling was so strong against the acquittal for insanity that the opinion of the Judges was asked, and they appear to have thought that such a verdict was scarcely a proper one.

Punishment deters not only sane men but also eccentric men, whose supposed involuntary acts are really produced by a diseased brain capable of being acted upon by external influences.

Acknowledging that they would be protected by an acquittal on the grounds of insanity will encourage these men to commit desperate acts, while on the other hand a certainty that they will not escape punishment will terrify them into a peaceful attitude toward others.[3]

Such memories were not quite accurate. McNaghten had attempted to shoot Sir Robert Peel, had failed and hit his private secretary Drummond instead.[4] He was declared 'not guilty on account of insanity' by all three judges. On 4 March, the Sunday of the verdict, Peel sent a letter to Victoria declaring his amazement at the decision when McNaghten had clearly *planned* his attack. Victoria replied in equally flabbergasted terms on 12 March, '*Not Guilty* on account of *Insanity* . . . everybody is convinced [he] was perfectly conscious and aware of what [he] did!' The Queen was not amused.

The strangest of all would-be assassins was George Andrew McMahon who, on 16 July 1936, threw a gun at Edward VIII as the King was riding up Constitution Hill having presented the King's colours to the Brigade of Guards. For this McMahon was sentenced to twelve months' hard labour, the King insisting privately on the full sentence. McMahon's story, however, only begins to unfold at this point.

McMahon's real name was Jerome Bennington. He was an Irishman living in London under an assumed name, the reason for which has never been discovered but nevertheless relates to an earlier imprisonment and a rich fantasy life. He first came to police attention after libelling two police sergeants in 1933 for which he was jailed in 1934. From then on, feeling the injured party, he continuously petitioned the Home Office for compensation.

In 1935 McMahon again approached the Home Office in order to offer his services as an informer against the Irish Free State and illegal gun-running. No guns were ever found. By now he was both a nuisance and a cause for concern. In April 1936 he was back offering information on a Communist plot to assassinate the King. Even a Communist-obsessed secret service could not find any evidence. McMahon's next move was to throw his gun at the King.

Despite being clearly 'unbalanced', McMahon went to Brixton and served his sentence. It was at that point that his last and most extraordinary tale emerged. The story revolved around his enrolment in German intelligence, which he said had supplied the gun. During the trial there was much made by the defendant of a mysterious 'foreign power'.[5] The story he told was that the Germans, believing Communists, British agents or both were plotting to kill Hitler, had devised a plan to destabilize Britain by killing its monarch. 'Do it for Ireland,' McMahon had been told by his spy master in the German Embassy, a man only known as 'the Baron'. The turmoil caused by Edward's death would, McMahon believed, have allowed power to slip into the hands of an enemy agent.

Throwing the gun at the King was an act of desperation by a self-declared loyal subject who had played the enemy along until the last minute and who had hoped that such an action would publicize to the general public (and the King in particular) that warnings to MI5 were not personal fantasy but the truth. Released from prison, McMahon continued to petition and, from his home at 215 Gloucester Terrace in Bayswater, issued loyal appeals direct to the Royal Family. In September 1938 he issued the following:

APPEAL

As you are known as a humanitarian and a lover of justice, I appeal to you to mete out to this plea for justice your humane consideration.

I am George Andrew McMahon, the unhappy person who was arrested two years ago for that regrettable affair known as the 'Revolver Incident,' which occurred at Constitution Hill when His Majesty King Edward VIII was riding past at the head of his troops . . .

I had, through a vile misfortune, become entangled with alien agents and assisted them with certain missions. When, however, they began to suggest that I should undertake work which I realised was prejudicial to my country, I at once reported the matter to the Home Secretary, who placed it before the War Office. I then continued to act under the instruction of M.I.5.

In this way I learned of the dastardly plot to harm His Majesty. As previously stated, it was admitted at my trial that this was correct and, though I was advised not to speak about these matters at my trial, I did so – as I then thought that even at that late hour His Majesty King Edward might still be in danger. Because I dared to mention these facts I was – against all evidence – sent to prison . . .

I fully realise that I cannot expect a speedy justice from a group who betrayed their King and used a disgraceful subterfuge to hound him from his Throne and Empire, but right will prevail and I know that some day a kindly providence will decree that Britain will give a belated vindication to those who tried to provide their loyalty to EDWARD, GREAT KING, GREAT GENTLEMAN, and GREAT HUMANITARIAN.

The appeal was headed by two photographs, one showing McMahon suited and bespectacled and his wife Rose smartly dressed in hat and fur stole. Opposite was represented a portrait of Edward as Duke of Windsor. The appeal was filed and left unanswered. On 24 April 1956 a CID letter from R. L. Jackson to J. W. Wheeler Bennett again referred to McMahon but the trail was already cold and McMahon had vanished long since.

The most serious attack on a member of the Royal Family, however, was probably the attempted kidnap of Princess Anne on Wednesday 20 March 1974 as she travelled along the Mall in her Rolls-Royce. Just before 8 a.m., a white Ford Escort driven by an unemployed drifter called Ian Ball pulled across the path of the royal car as it passed the junction with Marlborough Road. Ball jumped out and raced across towards the Rolls-Royce. Inside were Anne, her (then) husband Captain Mark Phillips, a security officer, Inspector Beaton, the Lady-in-Waiting, Miss Brassey, and the chauffeur, Alexander Callender. Trying to avoid an altercation with a disgruntled driver, Beaton left the Rolls, had a word with Bell but found himself confronted with a .38 revolver. Bell fired at Beaton and Beaton, drawing his Walther, fired back only to miss and then find his gun had jammed on the second attempt. Beaton, however, had been hit in the right shoulder. Bell was now free to wrestle with the door of the Rolls as Anne and Mark Phillips struggled to keep it closed. Miss Brassey ducked out on the offside and ran for cover.

By this time the fuss had attracted attention and John McConnell, a freelance journalist passing in a taxi, went to help. Unfortunately Ball had another gun, a .22 Astra that he levelled at Connell. He fired, Connell was hit in the chest and fell back, but the pause allowed the Princess to pull the car door closed and Beaton (now without his gun) to put himself in front of the door where she was sitting. Again Ball fired, hitting Beaton a second time, in the hand. At this point PC Hills arrived from St James's Palace only to be shot in the stomach by Ball, whose situation was growing desperate. He then shot Beaton again in the stomach and did the same to the chauffeur.

The brawl now intensified as another chauffeur, Glenmore Martin, and a taxi passenger, Ronald Russell, joined in – Martin, threatened with being shot, took cover, but Russell attacked Ball as Ball dragged Anne out of the car. Ball fired and missed. By now PC Hills's emergency call to Cannon Street police station, made as he arrived on the scene, paid off. Police began to come in numbers and Ball was finally captured. His kidnap plans, without motive except ransom, had failed. He was tried and found to be psychologically disturbed. Inspector Beaton, Ronald Russell and PC Hills received the George Cross and Alexander Callender and John McConnell were presented with the Queen's Gallantry Medal.

Notes

PREFACE TO THE PALGRAVE EDITION

1. *Evening Standard*, 26 May 2010.
2. Ibid., 20 April 2010.
3. *Serious Organised Crime and Police Act*, 2005, (London: The Stationery Office, 2005) p. 94.
4. Ibid., p. 101.
5. Ibid., p. 97.
6. *Metro*, 8 December 2005.
7. *London Paper*, 7 April 2009.
8. Ibid.
9. *Adapting to Protest – Nurturing the British Model of Policing*, http://www.statewatch.org/news/2009/nov/uk-hmic-adapting-to-protest.pdf p. 51.
10. *Intelligence and Security Committee Report 2007–8* (London: The Stationery Office, 2008) pp. 17–18.
11. Ibid., p. 7.
12. Ibid.
13. Ibid., p. 37.
14. Ibid., p. 33.
15. Ibid., p. 37.
16. Keith Laidler, *Surveillance Unlimited* (Thriplow, Cambridgeshire: Icon Books, 2008) p. 44.
17. Ibid., pp. 63 and 65.
18. *Evening Standard*, 9 February 2010.
19. *Daily Mail*, 30 March 2010.
20. *Evening Standard*, 26 August 2010.
21. Ibid., 2 February 2010.

1. A DESOLATION THEY CALLED PEACE

1. *Julius Caesar, The Conquest of Gaul*, tr. S. A. Handford (Harmondsworth: Penguin, 1953), p. 122.
2. John Morris, *Londinium: London in the Roman Empire* (London: Weidenfeld and Nicolson, 1982), pp. 102–3.
3. The poet Lucan, quoted in Barry Cunliffe, *Iron Age Britain* (London: Batsford/English Heritage, 1995), p. 111.
4. Cornelius Tacitus, *The Annals of Imperial Rome*, tr. Michael Grant (Harmondsworth: Penguin, 1996). All quotations from this edition.
5. Graham Webster, *Boudicca: the British Revolt against Rome AD60* (London: Routledge, [1978] 1999), p. 1.

6. G. H. Pittock Murray, *Celtic Identity and the British Image* (Manchester: Manchester University Press, 1999), p. 13.
7. Web page: www.druidorder.demon.co.uk.
8. In J. M. Scott, *Boadicea* (London: Constable, 1975), Chapter 1.
9. *The Times*, July 1871.

2. 'OFFENCE – A LONDONER'

1. Bede, *Ecclesiastical History of the English People*, tr. Leo Shirley-Price and R.e. Latham (Harmondsworth: Penguin, 1990) p. 112.
2. Ibid., p. 114.
3. Glyn Williams, *Medieval London: From Commune to Capital* (London: Athlone Press, 1963), p. 234.
4. Matthew Giancarlo, *Parliament and Literature in Later Medieval England* (Cambridge: Cambridge University Press, 2007) p. 30.
5. Rodney Hilton, *Bond Men Made Free: Medieval Peasant Movements and the English Rising of 1381* (London: Methuen, 1973), p. 179.
6. Ibid., p. 192.
7. Ibid., p. 193.
8. Martin J. R. Holmes, 'Evil May-Day 1517: The Story of a Riot', *History Today* XV (1965), p. 644.
9. Ibid., p. 648.

3. 'WE'LL NO NEED THE PAPISTS NOO!'

1. D.M. Loades, *Two Tudor Conspiracies* (Cambridge: Cambridge University Press, 1965) p. 56.
2. Ibid., p. 52.
3. Ibid., p. 55.
4. Pauline Gregg, *Free-Born John* (London: Phoenix [1961] 2000), p. 37.
5. Ibid., p. 38.
6. Reverend Ian Paisley, *Protestant Telegraph*, 9 January 1982.
7. Charles Nicholl, *The Reckoning: the Murder of Christopher Marlowe* (London: Picador, 1992), p. 97.
8. Ibid., p. 96.
9. Ibid., p. 97.
10. Lady Essex to Robert Cecil in Henry Ellis, *Original Letters of English History*, vol. III (London: Harding, Triphook and Lephard, 1824) p. 88.
11. Ibid., p. 108.
12. Ibid., p. 112.
13. Ibid., p. 111.
14. Antonia Fraser, *The Gunpowder Plot: Terror and Faith in 1605* (London: Arrow, 1999), p. 88.
15. Ibid., p. 98.
16. Ibid., p. 150.
17. Ibid., p. 283.

4.   FREE-BORN JOHN

1. John Adair, *Puritans: Religion and Politics in Seventeenth Century England and America* (Stroud, Gloucestershire: Sutton, 1998), p. 79.
2. Ibid., p. 92.
3. H. N. Brailsford, *The Levellers and the English Revolution* (Nottingham: Spokesman [1961] 1971), p. 45.
4. Pauline Gregg, *Free-Born John* (London: Phoenix [1961] 2000), pp. 35–6.
5. Ibid., p. 39.
6. Ibid., p. 63.
7. In Godfrey Davies, *The Early Stuarts* (Oxford: Clarendon Press, 1937), p. 32.
8. Ibid., p. 87.
9. Quoted in Patricia Higgins, 'The Reactions of Women, with Special Relevance to Women Petitioners', in Brian Manning (ed.), *Politics, Religion and the Civil War* (London: Edward Arnold, 1973), p. 190.
10. John Milton, *Areopagitica* (1644).
11. In Norman Cohn, *The Pursuit of the Millennium* (London: Pimlico [1957] 1993), p. 320.
12. Ibid., p. 321.
13. Ibid., p. 323.
14. Ibid., p. 323.
15. D. O. Pam, 'The Rude Multitude', Edmonton Hundred Historical Society (Occasional Paper) No. 33 (1977), pp. 13–14.
16. Anon., 'Bloudy Newes from Enfield Chase', nd.

5.   MURDEROUS FANTASIES

1. Neil Hanson, *The Dreadful Judgement: The True Story of the Great Fire of London* (London: Doubleday, 2001), pp. 168–9.
2. For entries to the entire period of the Fire see E. S. Beer, ed., *The Diary of John Evelyn* (Oxford: Clarendon Press, 1955). See also Robert Latham and William Matthews, eds, *The Diary of Samuel Pepys*, vol. VII, 1666 (London: G. Bell and Sons, 1972), pp. 267–81.
3. John Bedford, *London's Burning* (London: Abelard-Schuman, 1966), p. 152.
4. Ibid., pp. 154–5.
5. Ibid., p. 165.
6. Ibid., p. 172.
7. Gamini Salgado, *The Elizabethan Underworld* (London: Alan Sutton, 1995), pp. 144–5.
8. Alan Davidson, 'A Further Note on Bedlam' in *The London Recusant* 4–7 (1974–77), p. 65.
9. John Kenyon, *The Popish Plot* (London: Phoenix [1972] 2000), p. 177.
10. Ibid., p. 248.
11. Ibid., p. 177.
12. Ibid., p. 264.
13. Ibid., p. 255.

14. Ibid., p. 236.
15. Ibid., p. 289.
16. Ibid., p. 293.
17. B.S. Capp, *The Fifth Monarchy Men* (London: Faber and Faber, 1972) p. 222.
18. David C. Hanrahan, *Colonel Blood* (Stroud, Gloucestershire: Sutton Press, 2003) p. 66.
19. Ibid., p. 69.
20. Ibid., p. 73.
21. Iris Morley, *A Thousand Lives: An Account of the English Revolutionary Movement of 1660–1685* (London: Andre Deutsch, 1954) p. 57.
22. Ibid., p. 90.
23. Ibid., p. 147.
24. U. G. O'Leary, 'A Small Riot in 1688', *London Recusant* 4–7 (1974–77), p. 67.
25. Robert Beddard, 'Anti-Popery and the London Mob, 1688', *History Today* VIII (1988), p. 36.
26. Stephen Knight, *The Killing of Justice Godfrey* (London: Grafton [1984], 1986).
27. Alan Marshall, *The Strange Death of Edmund Godfrey: Plots and Politics in Restoration London* (Gloucestershire: Alan Sutton Press, 1999).

6.   GEORGE'S WAR

1. Nicholas Rogers, 'Popular Disaffection in London during the Forty-five', *London Journal* (1975), p. 5.
2. *General Evening Post*, July 1746.
3. Christopher Hibbert, *King Mob: the London Riots of 1780* (New York: Dorset Press, 1958), p. 8.
4. Ibid., p. 21.
5. Ibid., p. 30.
6. John Paul de Castro, *The Gordon Riots* (Oxford: Oxford University Press, 1926), pp. 33–4.
7. Ibid., p. 41.
8. Ibid., p. 62.
9. Ibid., p. 66.
10. Ibid., pp. 66–7.
11. Ibid., p. 72.
12. Ibid., p. 76.
13. Ibid., p. 77.
14. Ibid., pp 89–90.
15. Ibid., pp. 90–91.
16. Ibid., pp. 131–2.
17. Ibid., p. 136.
18. Ibid., pp. 162–3.
19. Hibbert, op. cit., p. 103.
20. Ibid., p. 123.
21. Paul Edwards and Polly Rewt, eds, *Letters of Ignatius Sanchez* (Edinburgh: University of Edinburgh Press, 1994), pp. 230–31.

22. Ibid., p. 232.
23. Ibid., p. 233.
24. Ibid., p. 15.

7. THE APE-LIKE IRISH

1. George Rude, 'Some Financial and Military Aspects of the Gordon Riots', *Guildhall Miscellany* Vols. 52–59, p. 37.
2. Thomas Paine, *Common Sense* (1776).
3. See Tony Hayter, *The Army and the Crowd in Mid-Georgian England* (Basingstoke: Macmillan, 1978), p. 128.

8. 'WILKES AND LIBERTY'

1. *The Review*, January 1710.
2. The description is in Ian Gilmour's *Riot, Rising and Revolution* (London: Pimlico, 1995), p. 45.
3. Ibid., pp. 47–8.
4. See Tony Hayter, *The Army and the Crowd in Mid-Georgian England* (Basingstoke: Macmillan, 1978), p. 128.
5. Ibid., p. 130.
6. Gilmour, op. cit., p. 307.
7. *Annual Register*, 1768.
8. Gilmour, op. cit., p. 340.
9. I. G. Mitchell, *Charles James Fox* (Harmondsworth: Penguin, 1997), p. 25.
10. Ibid., p. 53.
11. Anthony Shaw, 'The Mayor of Garratt' (Wandsworth: Wandsworth Borough Council, 1980), Cameos No. 1.
12. Ibid., pp. 6–7.
13. Anthony Babington, *Military Intervention in Britain: From the Gordon Riots to the Gibraltar Incident* (London: Routledge, 1991), p. 11.
14. Hayter, op. cit., p. 10.
15. *Gentleman's Magazine*, August 1802.

9. THE UNITED STATES OF ENGLAND

1. In C. Desmond Greaves, *Theobald Wolfe Tone and the Irish Nation* (London: Connolly Publications [1963] 1989), p. 37.
2. Philip J. Haythornthwaite, *The Armies of Wellington* (London: Brockhampton Press, 1996), p. 191.
3. Roger Wells, *Insurrection: The British Experience 1795–1803* (Gloucester: Alan Sutton Publishing, 1986), p. 738.
4. Ibid., p. 238.
5. Ibid., p. 43.

6. David Johnson, *Regency Revolution: the Case of Arthur Thistlewood* (London: Compton Russell, 1974), p. 5.
7. *Morning Chronicle*, Thursday, 24 February 1820.

10. MONSTER RALLIES

1. Rodney Mace, *Trafalgar Square: Emblem of Empire* (London: Lawrence and Wishart, 1976), p. 149.
2. *The Atlas*, 19 August 1832.
3. *Poor Man's Guardian*, 11 October 1830.
4. Robert W. Gould and Michael J. Waldren, *London's Armed Police* (London: Arms and Armour Press, 1988), p. 14.
5. Robert Reiner, *The Politics of the Police* (Hassocks, Sussex: Harvester, 1992), pp. 1–2.
6. *Gentleman's Magazine*, 4 April 1766.
7. Ibid., 19 August 1763.
8. Mace, op. cit., p. 149.
9. Lewisham Library Archive, File: Woolwich General 1826–1839.
10. *The Times*, 5 June 1848.
11. Ibid.
12. Ibid.
13. Mace, op. cit., p. 152.
14. *Illustrated London News*, 3 September 1848.
15. Carol Lansbury, *The Old Brown Dog: Women, Workers and Vivisection in Edwardian England* (Madison: University of Wisconsin Press, 1985), p. 10.
16. Philip Thurmond Smith, *Policing Victorian London* (Westport, Connecticut: Greenwood Press, 1985), p. 145.
17. Ibid., p. 145.
18. *Kentish Mercury*, 5 February 1867.
19. In Stephen Humphries, *Hooligans or Rebels? An Oral History of Working-Class Childhood and Youth 1889–1939* (Oxford: Basil Blackwell, 1981), p. 104.

11. PERSECUTING PIGEONS

1. Rodney Mace, *Trafalgar Square: Emblem of Empire* (London: Lawrence and Wishart, 1976), p. 52.
2. Ibid., p. 54.
3. Ibid., p. 16.
4. *The Times*, 6 March 1848.
5. Stefan Petrow, *Policy Morals: the Metropolitan Police and the Home Office 1870–1914* (Oxford, Clarendon, 1994), p. 32.
6. Frederick Harrison in Philip Thurmond Smith, *Policing Victorian London* (Westport, Connecticut: Greenwood Press, 1985), pp. 123–4.
7. Karl Beckson, *London in the 1890s: a Cultural History* (New York: W. W. Norton, 1992), p. 12.
8. Ibid., p. 8.

12. 'GOOD OLD DYNAMITE'

1. John Quail, *The Slow Burning Fuse: The Lost History of the British Anarchists* (London: Grafton, 1978), p. 7.
2. Ibid., pp. 21–2.
3. Ibid., p. 37.
4. Ibid., p. 61.
5. David Nicoll, *The Walsall Anarchists* (London: Hurricane, nd), p. 13.
6. Ibid., pp. 9–10.
7. Quail, op. cit., p. 112.
8. Ibid., p. 152.
9. Joseph Conrad, *The Secret Agent* (1906), Chapter Twelve.
10. Quoted in Richard Parry, *The Bonnot Gang* (London: Rebel Press, 1987), p. 35.
11. Martin Dillon, *25 Years of Terror: the IRA's War against the British* (London: Bantam [1994] 1999), p. 14.
12. *News of the World*, 5 February 1939.
13. Dillon, op. cit., p. 117.
14. Quoted in Robert Kee, *Trial and Error* (Harmondsworth: Penguin, 1986), npn.

13. WOMEN BEHAVING BADLY

1. Antonia Raeburn, *Militant Suffragettes* (London: New English Library, 1973), p. 28.
2. Ibid., p. 30.
3. Ibid., p. 34.
4. Ibid., p. 64.
5. Ibid., p. 120.
6. Ibid., p. 133.
7. Ibid., p. 170.
8. Ibid., pp. 170–71.
9. Ibid., p. 204.
10. Iris Dove, *Yours in the Cause; Suffragettes in Lewisham, Greenwich and Woolwich* (London: Lewisham Library Services and Greenwich Library, 1988), p. 5.
11. *Women's Bulletin*, 11 September 1953.
12. Ibid., p. 8.
13. Ibid., p. 9.
14. Carol Lansbury, *The Old Brown Dog: Women, Workers and Vivisection in Edwardian England* (Madison: University of Wisconsin Press, 1985), p. 7.
15. Ibid., p. 15.
16. Ibid., p. 18.

14. HUNS AND HASHISH

1. Sax Rohmer, *The Return of Dr Fu-Manchu* (1913), Chapter One.
2. *East Ham Echo*, 9 October 1914.

3. Ibid., 30 October 1914.
4. Ibid., 14 May 1915.
5. Ibid.
6. *Kentish Independent*, 14 May 1915.
7. *Kentish Mail*, 14 May 1915.
8. Sidney Robinson, *Sid's Family Robinson: the Story of an Early Twentieth Century Enfield Working-Class Boy* (London: Middlesex Polytechnic, 1991), p. 17.
9. See *Enfield Observer* (14 May 1915) and *Tottenham and Edmonton Weekly Herald* (14 May 1915).
10. Colonel W. T. Reay, *The Specials: How they served London: the Story of the Metropolitan Special Constabulary* (London: William Heinemann, 1920), pp. 3–4.
11. Ibid., p. 157.
12. Ibid., p. 158.
13. Ibid., pp. 164–5.

15.   COMRADES ALL

1. Francis Beckett, *Enemy Within: the Rise and Fall of the British Communist Party* (London: Merlin Press, 1995), p. 13.
2. Ibid., p. 18.
3. Rupert Allason, *The Branch: A History of the Metropolitan Police Special Branch 1883–1983* (London: Secker and Warburg, 1983), p. 78.
4. Ibid., p. 85.
5. Bob Darke, *The Communist Technique in Britain* (Harmondsworth: Penguin, 1952), p. 88.
6. Brian Pearce and Michael Woodhouse, *A History of Communism in Britain* (London: Bookmarks, [1969] 1999), p. 6.
7. Ibid., p. 37.
8. Bob Jones, *Left Wing Communism in Britain 1917–21: An Infantile Disorder?* (Sheffield: Pirate Press, 1991) npn.
9. Asa Briggs, *Victorian Cities* (Harmondsworth: Pelican [1963] 1982), pp. 333–4.
10. Ibid., p. 333.
11. Jerry White, 'Governing the Ungovernable' (unpublished paper), p. 5. This information is now available in Jerry White, *London in the Twentieth Century* (Harmondsworth: Penguin, 2002), chapter 9.
12. Ibid., p. 12.

16.   BRAVE BOYS OF THE BUF

1. In *Labour History Review* (Vol. 57, No. 3 Winter 92), p. 74.
2. Ibid., p. 75.
3. Francis Selwyn, *Hitler's Englishman: The Crime of Lord Haw Haw* (London: Routledge and Kegan Paul, 1987), p. 29.
4. Ibid., p. 37.
5. Robert Skidelsky, *Mosley* (London: Papermac, 1990), pp. 368–9.

6. Ibid., p. 374.
7. Ibid., p. 372.
8. Ibid., p. 377.
9. Police Record Office (PRO) HO45/25883, p. 407.
10. Ibid., Special Branch Report (10 September 1934), p. 602.
11. Ibid., p. 9.
12. Ibid., p. 619.
13. Ibid.
14. Collin Brooks, *Daily Mail*, 6 June 1936.
15. Imperial War Museum (IWM) Sound Archive 9308/5.
16. IWM Acc 10210/10/5, pp. 27–8.
17. Ibid., p. 63.
18. In Cable Street Group, eds, *The Battle of Cable Street* (London: np, nd), npn.
19. IWM, Acc10210/10/5, p. 69.
20. Phil Piratin in Cable Street Group, op. cit.
21. Jim Wolveridge, ibid.
22. Joyce Goodman and Mr Ginsbury, ibid.
23. National Sound Archive, 728018.
24. Board of Deputies of British Jews, 'The Nordic League' (report), p. 8.
25. Richard Griffiths, *Patriotism Perverted: Captain Ramsay, The Right Club and British Anti-Semitism 1939–40* (London: Constable, 1998), p. 184.
26. Ibid., pp. 255–6.
27. Ibid., p. 265.
28. Nicholas Mosley, *Rules of the Game/Beyond the Pale* (London: Pimlico, 1994), p. 428.
29. Ibid., p. 360.
30. *Comrade*, November/December 1999.

17. NOT QUITE KOSHER

1. *The Times*, 23 November 1917.
2. J. H. Clarke, quoted in Sharman Kadish, *Bolsheviks and British Jews* (London: Frank Cass, 1998), p. 10.
3. Ibid., p. 14.
4. Ibid., pp. 31–2.
5. Ibid., p. 58.
6. Tony Kushner, 'The Impact of British Anti-Semitism 1918–1945', in David Cesarini, ed., *The Making of Modern Anglo-Jewry* (Oxford: Basil Blackwell, 1990), p. 203.
7. Anon, 'Report on Hamm' (Board of Deputies of British Jews).
8. Maurice Beckman, *The 43 Group* (London: Frank Cass, 1993), p. 58.
9. Anon, 'Police – Public Meetings June 1947' (Board of Deputies).
10. Richard Thurlow, *Fascism in Britain: From Oswald Mosley's Blackshirts to the National Front* (London: I. B. Tauris, 1998), p. xii.
11. Nicholas Mosley, *Rules of the Game/Beyond the Pale* (London: Pimlico, 1998), p. 30.

12. Richard Griffiths, *Patriotism Perverted: Captain Ramsay, the Right Club and British Anti-Semitism 1939–1940* (London: Constable, 1998), p. 68.
13. Ibid., p. 137.

18.   ALIEN NATION

1. In Rosina Visram, *Ayars, Lascars and Princes, Indians in Britain 1700–1947* (London: Pluto, 1983), p. 83.
2. Ibid., p. 85.
3. In Anon., *For Soviet Britain* (London: Communist Action Group, 1995), p. 4.
4. *Sunday Telegraph*, 3 October 1999.
5. *London Chronicle*, 13–16 March 1773.
6. In Nigel Rile and Chris Power, *Black Settlers in Britain 1555–1948* (London: Heinemann, 1981), p. 25.
7. *Public Advertiser*, 27 June 1772.
8. Prince Hoare, *Memoirs of Granville Sharp*, vol. 2 (London: Henry Colburn, 1828), pp. 176–7.
9. *Morning Post*, 3 December 1786.
10. Peter Fryer, *Aspects of Black British History* (London: Index, 1993), p. 28.
11. Ibid., pp. 46–7.
12. Ibid., pp. 48–9.

19.   THE TIBER FLOWING WITH MUCH BLOOD

1. Arthur Moyse, 'From the Step of a Bus', *Anarchy* 44 (Vol. A No. 10), October 1964, p. 291.
2. Gene Martin, *Sorry No Vacancies: Life Stories of Senior Citizens from the Caribbean* (London: Notting Hill Urban Studies Centre, n.d.), pp. 4–5.
3. Robert W. Gould and Michael J. Waldren, *London's Armed Police: 1829 to the Present* (London: Arms and Armour Press, 1986), p. 167.
4. *Daily Mirror*, 31 August 1976.
5. Ibid.
6. Paul Foot, *The Rise of Enoch Powell* (Harmondsworth: Penguin, 1969), p. 31.
7. *Listener*, 28 July 1966.
8. *Manchester Guardian*, 10 October 1958.
9. *The Times*, 13 October 1964.
10. *Wolverhampton Express and Star*, 10 October 1964.
11. Speech at Eastbourne, 16 November 1968.
12. Robert Shepherd, *Enoch Powell: A Biography* (London: Pimlico, 1996), p. 326.
13. Foot, op. cit., p. 127.
14. In Simon Heffer, *Like the Roman: the Life of Enoch Powell* (London: Weidenfeld and Nicolson, 1998), p. 166.
15. Ian Mikardo quoted in Jerry White, 'Governing the Ungovernable' (unpublished paper), p. 8.
16. Ibid., pp. 7 and 9.
17. Paul Harrison, *Inside the Inner City: Life Under the Cutting Edge* (Harmondsworth: Penguin, 1985).

18. Ibid., p. 377.
19. Ibid., p. 359.
20. In Darcus Howe, *Black Deaths in Custody* (London: Institute of Race Relations, 1991), p. 71.

20.   LIKE RORKE'S DRIFT

1. Lord Scarman, *Report of a Court of Inquiry under the Rt Hon Lord Justice Scarman, OBE, into a Dispute between Grunwick Processing Laboratories Limited and Members of the Association of Professional, Executive, Clerical and Computer Staff* (HMSO: Cmnd 6922, 1977), p. 7.
2. Ibid., p. 10.
3. Ibid., p. 15.
4. Ibid., p. 20.
5. *Kentish Mercury*, 11 July 1958.
6. Ibid., 19 June 1959.
7. Steve Collins, *The Glory Boys* (London: Arrow, 1999), p. 55.
8. Joan Anim-Addo, *Longest Journey* (London: Deptford Forum Publishing, 1995), p. 21.
9. *South East London Mercury*, 21 January 1971.
10. LCCR Report, 8 June 1972.

21.   ANARCHY IN THE UK

1. Robert Reiner, *The Politics of the Police* (Brighton: Harvester/Wheatsheaf, 1992), pp. 95–6.
2. *The Times*, 18 March 1982.
3. David Leigh, *The Wilson Plot* (London: Heinemann, 1988), p. 158.
4. Ibid., pp. 158–9.
5. Ibid., p. 158.
6. Ibid., p. 160.
7. Ibid., p. 159.
8. *Observer*, 8 September 1974.
9. Martin Dillon, *25 Years of Terror: The IRA's War Against the British* (London: Bantam, 1999), p. 101.
10. *Sunday Telegraph*, 4 November 1979.
11. Tony Cliff, *The Crisis: Social Contract or Socialism* (London: Pluto, 1975), p. 114.
12. Correspondence: Board of Deputies of British Jews. See also Roger King and Neill Nugent, *Respectable Rebels: Middle Class Campaigns in Britain in the 1970s* (London: Hodder and Stoughton, 1979), pp. 76ff.
13. Ray Hill with Andrew Bell, *The Other Face of Terror: Inside Europe's Neo-Nazi Network* (London: Grafton, 1988), p. 200.
14. Ibid., pp. 200–201.
15. *Jew-Wise*, 3.
16. Anon, *Policing Against Black People* (London: Institute of Race Relations, 1983), p. 72.

17. New Scotland Yard press release, 24 January 1983.
18. Joan Anim-Addo, *Longest Journey* (London: Deptford Forum Publishing, 1995), p. 134.
19. Ibid., p. 139.
20. John La Rose in ibid., p. 138.
21. Ibid., p. 139.

22. LIVING ON THE FRONT LINE

1. *South London Press*, 1 June 1962.
2. Ibid., 26 June 1970.
3. Lord Scarman, *The Brixton Disorders 10–12 April 1981* (London: HMSO [1981] 1991), p. 17.
4. Ibid., p. 28.
5. Ibid., p. 48.
6. Picket leaflet.
7. Anon, *Policing Against Black People* (London: Institute of Race Relations, nd), p. 77.
8. Ibid., p. 3.
9. *Searchlight*, no. 53, November 1979.
10. Robert W. Gould and Michael J. Waldren, *London's Armed Police: 1829 to the Present* (London: Arms and Armour Press, 1986), p. 120.
11. Hansard, 6 July 1981.
12. Scarman, op. cit., p. 125.
13. Ibid., p. 127.
14. Ibid., p. 128.
15. Ibid., p. 131.
16 *Hornsey Journal*, 22 October 1976.
17. *Weekly Herald*, 5 August 1977.
18. 12 October 1978.
19. Lord Gifford, *The Broadwater Farm Inquiry* (London: Karia Press, 1986), p. 24.
20. Ibid., p. 103.
21. Ibid., p. 186.
22. Ibid., p. 108.
23. *Mail on Sunday*, 27 October 1985.
24. Margaret Burnham and Lennox Hinds, *The Burnham Report* (London: Broadwater Farm Defence Campaign, 1987).
25. Anon, 'Alleged Forced Admissions during Incommunicado Detention' (London: Amnesty International, [February] 1988), Bruce Grove Museum Archive PA89/24, p. 1.
26. In Ferdinand Dennis, *Behind the Frontlines: Journeys into Afro-Britain* (London: Gollancz, 1988), p. 193.
27. In Brian Cathcart, *The Case of Stephen Lawrence* (Harmondsworth: Penguin, 1999), p. 409.
28. See Nick Lowles, *White Riot: the Violent Story of Combat 18* (Bury: Milo Books, 2001), p. 131.

29. *The Times*, 8 May 2001.
30. *The Mail on Sunday*, 17 June 2001.

23. ONE, TWO, THREE, WHAT ARE WE FIGHTING FOR?

1. Tariq Ali, *Street Fighting Years: An Autobiography of the Sixties* (London: Collins, 1987), p. 143.
2. Ibid., p. 177.
3. Ibid., p. 180.
4. John Minnion and Philip Bobover, eds, *The CND Story* (London: Allison and Busby, 1983), p. 16.
5. Tom Vague, *Anarchy in the UK: The Angry Brigade* (London: AK Press, 1997), p. 35.
6. Ibid., p. 40.
7. Ibid., p. 106.
8. Ibid., p. 119.
9. Jude Davies, 'Anarchy in the UK? Anarchism and Popular Culture in 1990s Britain', in Jon Purkis and James Bower (eds), *Twenty-First Century Anarchism* (London: Cassell, 1997), p. 64.
10. David Henshaw, *Animal Warfare: The Story of the Animal Liberation Front* (London: Fontana, 1989), p. 4.
11. Ibid., p. 9.
12. Ibid., p. 50.
13. *Guardian*, 15 May 1995.
14. See *New Camden Journal*, 18 May 1995.

24. BACK TO THE FUTURE

1. Anon, *Poll Tax Riot* (London, Acab Press, 1990), pp. 15; 9; 21; 13; 30; 31.
2. *Guardian*, 2 April 1990.
3. 31 March 1990.
4. Bob Jones, *Left-Wing Communism in Britain 1917–21: An Infantile Disorder?* (Sheffield: Pirate Press, 1991), npn.
5. Danny Burns, *Rent Strikes: St Pancras, 1960* (London: Pluto, 1972), pp. 115–16.
6. Haringey Solidarity Group, *The Poll Tax Rebellion in Haringey* (London: Haringey Solidarity Group, 1999), p. 5.
7. Ibid., p. 7.
8. *Evening Standard*, 5 April 1990.
9. *Tottenham Journal*, 25 July 1991.
10. Ibid., p. 7.
11. Haringey Solidarity Group, p. 5.
12. Nigel Lawson, *The View from No. 11: Memoirs of a Tory Radical* (London: Corgi, 1993), p. 100.
13. 'Merrick', *There's a Riot Goin' On?* (Leeds: Goodhaven/UK, nd), p. 3.
14. Burns, op. cit., p. 19.

15. Ibid., p. 20.
16. Ibid., p. 8.
17. Ibid., p. 15.
18. *North London Press*, 23 September 1960.
19. *Star*, 22 September 1960.
20. 23 September 1960.

25. THE FREE REPUBLIC OF WANSTONIA

1. Sonia Richmond, 'An Examination of the One Tree Hill Anti-Enclosure Movement in South London' (unpublished paper, 1994), pp. 18–19. See also John Nisbet, *The Story of One Tree Hill Agitation with a Short-Sketch of Honor Oak Hill* (reprinted 1997, no publisher).
2. John Davis, Unpublished paper, pp. 12–13.
3. Ibid., p. 10.
4. Chris Mosey, *Car Wars: Battles on the Road to Nowhere* (London: Vision, 2000), pp. 60–61.
5. Ibid., p. 109.
6. Ibid., pp. 125–6.
7. Ibid., p. 134.
8. See also Ellis Stamp, *To Wanstonia* (London: Zalus Press, 1996).
9. *Big Issue*, 16–22 August 1999.
10. Contractors Newsletter, October 1999.
11. Contractors Newsletter, August 1994.
12. *The Roadbreaker*, No. 14, October 1993.
13. *Newsletter*, December 1993.
14. Conor Foley, *New Statesman*, 25 February 1994.
15. *The Times*, 17 February 1994.
16. Paul Foot, *Guardian*, 28 February 1994.

26. NEVER UNDERESTIMATE A MINORITY

1. George McKay, *Senseless Acts of Beauty: Cultures of Resistance since the Sixties* (London: Verso, 1996), pp. 37–8.

27. THE MAN IN THE THIRD CARRIAGE – 7/7 AND ITS CONSEQUENCES

1. Michael Whine, 'Britain's New Terrorism Act' (Press Release of the Board of Deputies of British Jews), 1 March 2001, p. 2.
2. Ibid., p. 4.
3. Yossef Bodansky, *Bin Laden: The Man who Declared War on America* (New York: Random House, 1999), p. xiii.
4. Ibid., p. xv.
5. Andy Hayman, *The Terrorist Hunters* (London: Bantam, 2009), p. 9.

6. Ibid., p. 12.
7. Ibid., p. 16.
8. Ibid.
9. Ibid., p. 21.
10. Ibid., p. 43.
11. *Metro*, 11 July 2005.
12. *Sun*, 30 July 2005.
13. Nafeez Mosadaq Ahmed, *The London Bombings: An Independent Inquiry* (London: Duckworth, 2006) p. 118.
14. *London Lite*, 29 September 2008.
15. *Metro*, 18 July 2009.
16. Ibid., 8 September 2009.
17. *Evening Standard*, 14 September 2009.
18. *London Lite*, 8 September 2009.
19. Ibid., p. 121
20. Milan Rai, *7/7: The London Bombings, Islam and the Iraq War* (London; Pluto, 2006) p. 18.
21. Ibid., p. 19.
22. *Intelligence and Security Committee: Report into the London Terrorist Attacks on 7 July 2005* (London: The Stationery Office, 2007 [Cm 6785]) p. 3.
23. Ibid., p. 25; 11–12.
24. ibid., pp. 30.
25. *Metro*, 27 November 2009.
26. *Evening Standard*, 1 February 2010.

28.   OPERATION GLENCOE – G20, IAN TOMLINSON AND THE FUTURE OF STREET PROTEST

1. *London Lite*, 26 March 2009.
2. *The Times*, 26 March 2009.
3. *Metro*, 14 September 2009.
4. *London Lite*, 31 March 2009.
5. www.g-20meltdown.org/node/31
6. *London Lite*, July 2010.
7. *Sunday Times*, 19 April 2009.
8. *Evening Standard*, 13 May 2009.
9. *Metro*, 20 April 2009.
10. *Sunday Times*, 19 April 2009.
11. *Guardian*, 22 June 2009.
12. *Adapting to Protest – Nurturing the British Model of Policing*, http://www.statewatch.org/news/2009/nov/uk-hmic-adapting-to-protest.pdf p. 43.
13. Ibid., pp. 6–7.
14. Ibid., p. 5.
15. Ibid.
16. Ibid., pp. 7 and 27.

17. Ibid., p. 31.
18. Ibid.
19. Ibid., p. 40.
20. Ibid., p. 32.
21. Nick Cohen, 'New Left and Old Far Right: Tolerating the Intolerable' in Jonathan Pugh ed., *What is Radical Politics Today?* (Basingstoke: Palgrave, 2009) p. 164.
22. Ibid., p. 175.

APPENDIX ONE: SHADOW OF A WARRIOR QUEEN

1. Peter Salway, *Roman Britain* (Oxford: Oxford University Press [1981], 1998), p. 505.
2. Ibid., p. 111.
3. Cornelius Tacitus, *The Agricola and the Germania*, tr. H. Mattingly and S. A. Handford (Harmondsworth: Penguin [1948] 1970). All quotes this edition.
4. John Morris, *Londinium: London in the Roman Empire* (London: Weidenfeld and Nicolson, 1982), p. 104.
5. Francis Grew, 'Representing Londinium: the Influence of Colonial and Post-Colonial Discourses' (unpublished paper), p. 6.

APPENDIX THREE: ASSASSINATION ATTEMPTS ON THE ROYAL FAMILY

1. Royal Archive: VIC/L13/II2.
2. RA/VIC/L13/112.
3. RA/VIC/L14/141.
4. See letter of Sir Robert Peel, 23 January 1843.
5. *The Times*, 15 September 1936.

Index

Page references in **bold** refer to illustrations.